W9-AGD-354

Health and Medicine

1993

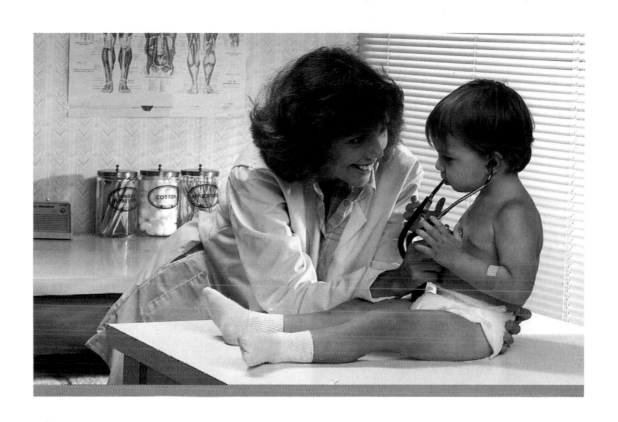

Health and Medicine

1993

The *Health and Medicine Annual* should not be used in lieu of professional
medical advice. The editors urge all readers to consult a physician
on a regular basis as part of their normal health-care routine and
to seek medical attention should symptoms arise that require
professional diagnosis or treatment.

PUBLISHED BY THE SOUTHWESTERN COMPANY 1993

Contributors

NATALIE ANGIER, Correspondent, *The New York Times*
WHY SO MANY RIDICULE THE OVERWEIGHT

DOUGLAS S. BARASCH, Free-lance writer specializing in medical issues
THE MAINSTREAMING OF ALTERNATIVE MEDICINE

PAUL BARASH, M.D., Chairman and Chief, Department of Anesthesiology, Yale University School of Medicine, New Haven, CT
ANESTHESIOLOGY

LEWIS A. BARNESS, M.D., Professor of Pediatrics, University of South Florida College of Medicine, Tampa, FL
PEDIATRICS

EDWARD J. BENZ, JR., M.D., Jack D. Myers Professor of Internal Medicine, University of Pittsburgh School of Medicine, Pittsburgh, PA
BLOOD AND LYMPHATIC SYSTEM

SUE BERKMAN, Free-lance writer specializing in medicine
WEE PAWS FOR HEALTH — PETS ARE GOOD FOR YOU

JAMES A. BLACKMAN, M.D., M.P.H., Professor of Pediatrics, University of Virginia; Director of Research, Kluge Children's Rehabilitation Center, Charlottesville, VA
IMMUNOLOGY

EDWARD E. BONDI, M.D., Professor of Dermatology, Hospital of the University of Pennsylvania, Philadelphia, PA
SKIN

CHRISTIANE N. BROWN, Assistant Editor, *Good Housekeeping* magazine
FINAL DECISIONS

LINDA J. BROWN, Free-lance writer specializing in health, fitness, and environmental issues
ENVIRONMENT AND HEALTH
ORIENTEERING: MAPS, MAGNETISM, AND MIND GAMES
SNEAKERS

MICHAEL COATES, M.D., Professor, Department of Family Medicine, University of Virginia, Charlottesville, VA
HOUSECALLS: PRACTICAL NEWS TO USE

STEPHEN V. COREY, D.P.M., Assistant Professor, Department of Surgery, Pennsylvania College of Podiatric Medicine, Philadelphia, PA
PODIATRY

GODE DAVIS, Free-lance writer based in Salt Lake City, UT
DIGESTIVE SYSTEM
THE RESURGENCE OF RABIES
SEXUALLY TRANSMITTED DISEASES

JOSEPH C. DeVITO, Free-lance writer
WORN IN THE USA: THE PSYCHOLOGICAL FABRIC OF UNIFORMS

HERBERT S. DIAMOND, M.D., Chairman, Department of Medicine, Western Pennsylvania Hospital, Pittsburgh, PA
ARTHRITIS AND RHEUMATISM

DIXIE FARLEY, Staff Writer, *FDA Consumer* magazine
VARYING VIEWS ON VEGETARIAN DIETS

BRIAN FEINBERG, Life-Sciences Editor, *Encyclopedia Americana*
THE FUTURE OF MALE CONTRACEPTION

STEVEN FINCH, Contributor, *Health* magazine
BEYOND BREAST IMPLANTS

ALBERT J. FINESTONE, M.D., Professor of Medicine and Director, Institute on Aging, Temple University School of Medicine, Philadelphia, PA
AGING

BRENDAN M. FOX, M.D., Clinical Associate Professor, Department of Urology, University of Connecticut, Farmington, CT
UROLOGY

SUE GEBO, M.P.H., R.D., Consulting nutritionist in private practice; author, *What's Left to Eat?* (McGraw-Hill, 1992)
FIGURING OUT THE NEW FOOD LABELS

JEFF GOLDBERG, Free-lance writer specializing in science and medicine
HEART SURGERY'S HIDDEN HEARTBREAK
WHO'S READING YOUR MEDICAL RECORDS?

MARIA GUGLIELMINO, M.S., R.D., Registered dietitian and exercise physiologist
NUTRITION AND DIET
PASTABILITIES

GREG GUTFELD, Fitness Editor, *Prevention* magazine
A BEGINNER'S GUIDE TO WEIGHT TRAINING

MARY HAGER, Correspondent, *Newsweek* magazine
HEALTH-CARE COSTS

LINDA HUGHEY HOLT, M.D., Chairman, Department of Obstetrics and Gynecology, Rush North Shore Hospital, Chicago, IL
OBSTETRICS AND GYNECOLOGY

ERIN HYNES, Free-lance writer based in Austin, TX
THE EDIBLE BOUQUET

IRA M. JACOBSON, M.D., Division of Digestive Diseases, The New York Hospital — Cornell Medical Center, New York, NY
LIVER

JAMES F. JEKEL, M.D., M.P.H., Professor of Epidemiology and Public Health, Yale University School of Medicine, New Haven, CT
AIDS
PUBLIC HEALTH

KENNETH L. KALKWARF, D.D.S., M.S., Dean, The University of Texas Health Science Center at San Antonio Dental School, San Antonio, TX
TEETH AND GUMS

PAUL KEFALIDES, Medical student, University of Pennsylvania School of Medicine, Philadelphia, PA
ANESTHESIOLOGY: MORE THAN JUST GAS

JENNIFER KENNEDY, M.S., Account professional, Johnson and Johnson Health Management, Inc., Washington, DC
HOUSECALLS: FITNESS AND HEALTH

CHRISTOPHER KING, Research analyst, Institute for Scientific Information, Philadelphia, PA
NOBEL PRIZE: PHYSIOLOGY OR MEDICINE
THE PSYCHOLOGY OF DISASTER: REPAIRING THE INVISIBLE DAMAGE

ROBERT L. KNOBLER, M.D., Ph.D., Professor of Neurology; Associate Director, Division of Neuroimmunology, Jefferson Medical College, Philadelphia, PA
BRAIN AND NERVOUS SYSTEM

GINA KOLATA, Correspondent, *The New York Times*
KIDS AND SPORTS
THE BURDEN OF OBESITY

LOUIS LING, M.D., Associate Medical Director, Academic Affairs, Hennepin County Medical Center, Minneapolis, MN
EMERGENCY MEDICINE

REX L. MAHNENSMITH, M.D., Clinical Director of Nephrology, Yale University School of Medicine, New Haven, CT
KIDNEYS

ANDREA MALLOZZI, Free-lance writer specializing in consumer affairs
DANCING FOR HEALTH

THOMAS H. MAUGH II, Science writer, *The Los Angeles Times*
GENETICS AND GENETIC ENGINEERING

ELIZABETH McGOWAN, Free-lance writer based in New York, NY
SQUARE PEGS

WENDY J. MEYEROFF, Free-lance medical writer based in New York, NY
PREGNANCY IN LATER YEARS

ALFRED E. MITCHELL, M.D., New Milford Orthopedic Associates, New Milford, CT
BONES, MUSCLES, AND JOINTS

ALISON A. MOY, M.D., Postgraduate Fellow in Endocrinology and Metabolism, Yale University School of Medicine, New Haven, CT
ENDOCRINOLOGY

RICHARD L. MUELLER, M.D., Cardiovascular Associate, Division of Cardiology, The New York Hospital — Cornell Medical Center, New York, NY
HEART AND CIRCULATORY SYSTEM

WILLIBALD NAGLER, M.D., Chairman, Rehabilitation Medicine, The New York Hospital — Cornell Medical Center, New York, NY
REHABILITATION MEDICINE

ALICE NAUDE, Free-lance writer based in New York, NY
NOT ALL PROCEEDS GO TO CHARITY

SUSAN NIELSEN, Free-lance writer specializing in consumer advocacy and health issues
GETTING THERE SAFELY

MARCY O'KOON, Free-lance writer based in Atlanta, GA
REFLECTIONS OF TORMENT

MARIA LUISA PADILLA, M.D., Associate Professor of Medicine, Pulmonary Division, Mount Sinai School of Medicine, New York, NY
RESPIRATORY SYSTEM

DAVID A. PENDLEBURY, Editor, *Science Watch;* Research Analyst, Institute for Scientific Information, Philadelphia, PA
WHY DOES AMERICA'S HEALTH CARE COST SO MUCH?

CATHY PERLMUTTER, Senior Editor, *Prevention* magazine
ARRESTING YOUR APPETITE

DEVERA PINE, Free-lance writer based in New York, NY
HIV AND HEALTH-CARE WORKERS
MEDICAL SPIN-OFFS FROM SPACE

ABIGAIL W. POLEK, Free-lance writer/editor
MEDICAL TECHNOLOGY
PANIC ATTACK: WHEN ANXIETY BECOMES DISABLING

EDMUND A. PRIBITKIN, M.D., Assistant Professor, Department of Otolaryngology — Head and Neck Surgery, Thomas Jefferson University Medical Center, Philadelphia, PA
EAR, NOSE, AND THROAT

DIANA REESE, Free-lance writer specializing in dentistry and health issues
CROWNS AND BRIDGES
NUTRITION IN THE EARLY YEARS

MICHAEL X. REPKA, M.D., Wilmer Ophthalmological Institute, Johns Hopkins University School of Medicine, Baltimore, MD
EYES AND VISION

CYNTHIA PORTER RICKERT, Ph.D., Assistant Professor of Pediatrics, University of Arkansas for Medical Sciences, Little Rock, AR
CHILD DEVELOPMENT AND PSYCHOLOGY

MACE L. ROTHENBERG, M.D., Assistant Professor of Medicine, University of Texas Health Science Center at San Antonio, TX
CANCER

JAMES A. ROTHERHAM, Ph.D., Senior Associate, Chambers Associates, Inc., Washington, DC
GOVERNMENT POLICIES AND PROGRAMS

KAREN M. SANDRICK, Free-lance medical writer
HEALTH PERSONNEL AND FACILITIES

NEIL SPRINGER, Free-lance writer covering the energy and chemical industry, as well as health and science matters
OCCUPATIONAL HEALTH

CHERYL A. STOUKIDES, Pharm. D., Director, University of Rhode Island Drug Information Center, Providence, RI
MEDICATIONS AND DRUGS

MONA SUTNICK, Ed.D., R.D., Spokesperson, American Dietetic Association; Consultant in nutrition communication and education
HOUSECALLS: NUTRITION

ROBERT M. SWIFT, M.D., Ph.D., Associate Professor, Department of Psychiatry, Brown University Medical School, Providence, RI
SUBSTANCE ABUSE

JANET C. TATE, Associate Editor, Special Reports Network, Whittle Communications, Knoxville, TN
PELVIC INFLAMMATORY DISEASE
THE PERILS OF OVERTRAINING

AUBIN TYLER, Free-lance writer specializing in health and medicine in the New York, NY area
THE EYE EXAMINATION: PEERING THROUGH THE BODY'S WINDOW

STEPHEN G. UNDERWOOD, M.D., Associate faculty member in psychiatry, University of Pennsylvania School of Medicine, Philadelphia, PA; Consulting psychiatrist, Bryn Mawr College Child Study Institute, Bryn Mawr, PA
HOUSECALLS: PSYCHOLOGY
MENTAL HEALTH

GEORGE VALKO, M.D., Instructor, Department of Family Medicine, Jefferson Medical College; staff member, Thomas Jefferson University Hospital and the Jefferson Family Medicine Office, Philadelphia, PA
HOUSECALLS: MEDICINE AND THE HUMAN BODY

BARBARA ALDEN WILSON, Free-lance writer specializing in health and medicine in Seattle, WA
CONQUERING INCONTINENCE

CONNIE ZUCKERMAN, J.D., Adjunct Assistant Professor of Medicine, Department of Medicine, State University of New York Health Science Center, Brooklyn, NY
MEDICAL ETHICS

Contents

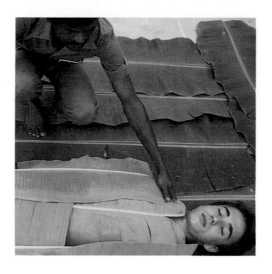

Review '93

New advances in medicine, coupled with innovative thinking about ways to broaden access to quality health care, are improving people's chances of enjoying long and healthy lives. Some of the most exciting developments are occurring in the area of genetics and gene therapy. Scientists are identifying the genes that comprise human DNA—the blueprints of heredity. Many of these genes are suspected of causing hereditary illnesses. Other genes are believed to increase susceptibility to certain conditions. For example, it was reported in 1992 that scientists had discovered genetic variations that predispose people toward hypertension, which is a major factor in cardiovascular disease.

Gene therapy involves introducing healthy genes into the cells of people who lack those genes. In late 1992, two groups of researchers received government approval to use gene therapy to treat cystic fibrosis patients. Cystic fibrosis is a lethal hereditary disease in which the lungs and other organs become clogged with thick mucus. Victims lack a gene for a protein that controls salt flow within the body. Using genetic-engineering techniques, the researchers will insert the missing gene into harmless viruses. The viruses will then be sprayed into the patients' respiratory passages. The researchers hope that the viruses will enter some of the respiratory cells, installing the gene, which will then produce the needed protein.

Intensive research is being conducted on the use of gene therapy in attacking virtually all human diseases, including cancer, heart disease, hemophilia, sickle-cell anemia, and muscular dystrophy. Already researchers have received permission to use gene therapy for treating a fatal type of lung cancer called non–small cell carcinoma, and for helping patients with AIDS fight the disease.

At the same time that people are coming to accept such advanced technologies as gene therapy, they also are showing growing interest in some ancient practices. So-called alternative medicine is being taken seriously, not only by lay people, but by increasing numbers of physicians. This acceptance has been fueled in part by research showing that many nontraditional methods do indeed work.

There also is a growing appreciation of the effects of environmental pollutants on human health. Even low levels of some pollutants can cause medical havoc. A study by epidemiologists Alice Stewart and George W. Kneale of the health records of 35,000 workers at the U.S. government's Hanford nuclear facility in Richland, Washington, concluded that 200 of the workers have died or will die from radiation-induced cancer.

As part of his program to "curtail the monster of spiraling health-care costs," President Bill Clinton named his wife Hillary to head a special task force on health-care reform.

Pollutants may also be responsible for the growing incidence and severity of asthma. The U.S. death rate from asthma climbed 46 percent during the 1980s, with women and blacks the hardest hit. The illness also is on the rise among children.

Another resurging illness is tuberculosis. A decade ago, U.S. physicians expected to see progressively fewer cases of tuberculosis, a bacterial disease that is spread through the air and typically infects the lungs. Instead, tuberculosis once again is a serious health problem in the country. Active cases are most common among the urban poor, the homeless, migrant farm workers, drug abusers, and people with weak immune systems, such as the elderly and people infected with the virus that causes AIDS. Exacerbating the problem are dangerous, drug-resistant strains of the bacteria.

Tuberculosis is curable. AIDS is not, and experts agree that it is unlikely that there will soon be any pharmaceutical solution to this problem. Meanwhile, signs indicate that the AIDS pandemic is accelerating. Worldwide, an estimated 2 million people have the disease, with an additional 10 million infected with HIV, the virus that causes AIDS.

In many countries, poverty is a prime cause of disease and death. The world's richest countries are not immune to this problem. Recent research estimated that some 30 million Americans suffer from some degree of hunger. Because these people do not consume enough nutrients, they experience more illness and, particularly among the young, learning difficulties.

Poverty also limits people's access to medical care. More than 35 million Americans are believed to be without health insurance—a figure that has grown with a decline in employment-based insurance coverage, partly as a result of increased unemployment and rampaging health-insurance costs. A study directed by Helen R. Burstin of Harvard University Medical School found that uninsured hospital patients receive treatment inferior to that received by insured patients.

Lack of insurance coverage is only one aspect of the health-care crisis in the United States. Spiraling costs are at the base of the problem: U.S. health-care expenditures are the highest in the world. In recent years, noted a 1992 report from the U.S. General Accounting Office, "States have taken a leadership role in devising strategies to expand access to health insurance and contain the growth of health costs. . . . Most states have adopted measures to make it easier for people with high-cost health conditions and small-business owners and employees to obtain affordable health insurance in the private market. Almost half the states have created high-risk pools to make insurance available to the medically uninsurable—people who cannot obtain conventional insurance because of their medical conditions—and to spread the risk of covering them among all insurers in the state."

Even before he took office, President Bill Clinton indicated that health-care reform would be a major goal of his administration. "We can't do anything else on the deficit if we fail to curtail the monster of spiraling health-care costs," he told attendees at a two-day economic conference he held in late 1992.

Clinton, who strongly believes that every American should be covered by health insurance, is an advocate of managed competition, an approach that proponents say combines the best aspects of government-run and free-market health-care systems. Consumers would be enrolled in large cooperatives that, because of their size, would theoretically be able to negotiate favorable prices with insurers, doctors, and hospitals.

Even longtime opponents of health-care reform have begun to change their views; both the Health Insurance Association of America and the American Medical Association (AMA) have endorsed some principles of managed competition. Industry support, coupled with demands for action by consumers and strong leadership from the administration, may well lead to major improvements in America's health-care system.

The Editors

Health and Medicine: Features '93

Medicine and the Human Body

See also:
Individual articles in the second half of this book, arranged in alphabetical order, for additional information.

The human body is the most complex organism on earth. When its cells, tissues, and organs work in harmony, the body functions smoothly and efficiently. But diseases and injuries damage and interrupt body processes. Some of these problems are easily treated. Others are intractable and deadly.

Through the ages, as we have learned more about the human body, we have also greatly increased our ability to fight illness. Today researchers continue to expand the frontiers of medical knowledge, offering hope to patients whose illnesses have long been untreatable.

Diseases of the heart and blood vessels are the number one killers in the United States, taking one American life every 34 seconds. But the encouraging news is that death rates from these diseases are declining rapidly, thanks to better medical treatment and healthier lifestyles.

Better treatment does not necessarily translate into higher costs. The main cause of admissions to hospital coronary-care units is angina, a painful condition that often results from a blood clot that partially blocks a heart artery, preventing the heart muscles from receiving enough blood. A major study published in 1992, conducted at Oxford University in England, evaluated the three drugs used to dissolve blood clots: streptokinase, eminase, and tissue plasminogen activator (t-PA). Researchers found that the drugs were equally effective in saving lives, but streptokinase—the oldest and by far the cheapest of the three—was found to be the safest.

This is not meant to imply that new drugs and procedures are not needed or lack value. A vaccine introduced several years ago has sharply cut the leading cause of meningitis in children. The vaccine, approved for infants age two months or older, prevents hemophilus meningitis, a sometimes-fatal brain infection that often results in blindness, deafness, and mental retardation. During the mid-1980s there were 12,000 to 20,000 cases of hemophilus meningitis annually. In 1991 there were only 1,900 cases. Data gathered by the Centers for Disease Control and Prevention (CDC) suggested that almost no cases of the disease occurred in children who had been fully vaccinated.

Still-experimental vaccines offer exciting promise in preventing hepatitis A and B, sometimes-fatal liver infections, and in eliminating Lyme disease. Three new studies reported that injections of brain tissue from aborted fetuses caused dramatic improvement in patients suffering from Parkinson's disease.

Scientists have found that Alzheimer's patients have elevated levels of a protein called glutamine synthetase in their spinal fluid; the discovery may enable physicians to definitively diagnose the disease. Another potentially definitive test for Alzheimer's measures spinal-fluid levels of amyloid precursor protein (APP); researchers have found a link between low levels of APP in spinal fluid and the brain plaques that distinguish Alzheimer's from other brain diseases.

Proscar, a new drug to treat benign enlarged prostate, was approved by the Food and Drug Administration (FDA) in 1992, as was Recombinate, the first genetically engineered drug for the treat-

ment of hemophilia A. The FDA also approved deoxycytidine (DDC) for use in combination with azidothymidine (AZT) in the treatment of adult AIDS patients. And it approved a new blood test to detect HIV infections. The test, developed by Murex Corporation, can be processed in a physician's office in 10 minutes, yielding results with 99 percent accuracy.

In the past the FDA was frequently criticized for the slow pace of its drug-approval process. This is expected to change as a result of the Prescription Drug User Fee Act of 1992, which requires companies to help cover the FDA's cost of reviewing drug safety. In return for collecting an estimated $300 million over the next five years, the FDA agreed to hire 600 new specialists.

A technology that offers a range of benefits is telemedicine—a two-way interactive system that allows physicians to examine patients at other locations. The procedure enables rural patients to go to small nearby hospitals for consultations with big-hospital specialists rather than having to travel to distant cities.

The frontiers of medicine have expanded, giving hope to patients whose illnesses have long been untreatable.

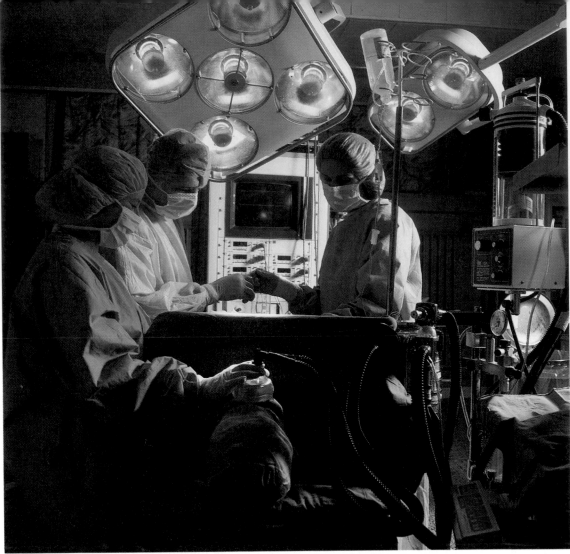

The anesthesiologist (left foreground) is an essential member of the surgical team. Throughout the operation, the anesthesiologist continuously monitors the patient's vital signs.

Surgical Anesthesiology: More Than Just Gas

by Paul Kefalides

Nancy Lewis is shaking with apprehension. As she sits, dangling her legs over the edge of the operating-room table at the Hospital of the University of Pennsylvania (HUP) in Philadelphia, an anesthesiologist inserts an epidural catheter—a long, thin tube—into the space outside Nancy's spinal cord. Nancy will be undergoing abdominal surgery, which the HUP doctors classify as a mild to moderately stressful procedure. They have prescribed sedation, general anesthesia, and postoperative analgesia (pain relief) via the catheter in the hopes of making Nancy's stay as pain-free an experience as possible.

A Crucial Medical Specialty

Roderic Eckenhoff, M.D., assistant professor of anesthesiology at the University of Pennsylvania Medical School, sums up the field's advancements and the public's misunderstanding of it in four simple words: "more than just gas." Indeed, not so long ago, physicians specializing in anesthesiology were concerned solely with putting people to sleep for surgery. Today the anesthesiologist's armamentarium contains a range of techniques: local anesthesia, similar to that used in a dental office; regional anesthesia, like epidurals, which numb entire sections of the body by blocking sensations at the spinal cord or other large nerves; and general anesthetics —a veritable cocktail of gases and drugs that can put a patient to sleep for days.

Anesthesiologists now strive to use more focused procedures, numbing only the part of the body being operated on. Regional anesthetics may allow surgeons to operate on sicker patients who otherwise would not be able to tolerate the complete medical surrender of general anesthesia. Some anesthesiologists cater to *all* patients who suffer pain, either during hospitalization or in everyday life.

Nancy's epidural anesthetic is a technique traditionally used to numb patients below the waist. The catheter will serve as the "plumbing" to deliver analgesic drugs for several days following Nancy's surgery. To quell her anxiety for the forthcoming operation, an intravenous (I.V.) line inserted in her hand carries short-acting sedatives and narcotics.

To prepare for unconsciousness, a mask is placed over Nancy's mouth and nose to fill her lungs with pure oxygen. An injection of sodium pentothal produces "sleep" temporarily, and she is then paralyzed with vecuronium, a muscle relaxant. Because the relaxant temporarily paralyzes breathing muscles, the anesthesiologist must work quickly to slide a tube into Nancy's airway and use a ventilator to breathe for her before she uses all the oxygen in her lungs. Through the tube, she inhales oxygen laced with various anesthetic gases to keep her asleep for the three-hour operation.

Eckenhoff likens the practice of anesthesiology to piloting an airliner—the hardest parts are takeoffs, landings, and any surprises that may arise in flight. Once Nancy is "asleep," the tempo of the operating room changes. It is as if this jumbo jet of an operation is now in a level cruise. But the anesthesiologist's work is not over—the doctor must keep Nancy in this precarious state by titrating (adjusting the concentration of) the anesthetic gas and other drugs so that she has stable vital signs, and no pain or memory of the trauma inflicted on her belly.

Checklist

Like an airline pilot, an anesthesiologist has a long list of checks to consider before the patient is put under. To begin with, the doctor must consider the type of operation and the part of the body that will be worked on before recommending local, regional, or general anesthesia. The patient's mood is also taken into account. Anxious patients often receive general rather than a regional anesthetic, as do patients undergoing lengthy surgery in the upper abdomen or chest. Pre-existing medical problems may also dictate the type of anesthesia used. For instance, asthmatics are often given a regional anesthetic, as the airway manipulation of general anesthesia can trigger an asthmatic attack.

Anesthesiology is one of the most important—and perhaps the most misunderstood— specialties in modern medicine.

How much gas or other drugs to give is also an issue of debate and is part of the "art" of anesthesiology. A patient's requirement for anesthetics will increase once a surgeon starts cutting. If too little anesthetic is given, the patient may be partially aware of the operation. Some patients even claim they remember events and dialogue from their operations while under general anesthesia. Eckenhoff stresses, however, that "there is a difference between being able to react to stimulus and being aware." Anesthesiologists constantly look for signs of light anesthetic, such as coughing or movement, to tell if a patient might be aware. Not to worry, however: it is very unlikely that a patient will suddenly awaken.

How Anesthetics Work

Anesthetics work medical wonders by acting on the nerve-cell membrane to disrupt the transmission of signals. Interestingly, no one is precisely sure *how* anesthetics cause this disruption. Issaku Ueda, M.D., Ph.D., a professor at the University of Utah in Salt Lake City, notes that "there are three theories fighting each other these days. First there is the fat theory—that anesthesia binds the fat in the membrane and expands it, compressing the ion channels." The squeezed pores cannot conduct ions into the nerve cell, so nerve transmission ceases. Other researchers believe that anesthetic drugs bind directly to proteins lodged in the nerve cell's fatty membrane, inactivating the pores and channels necessary for signal transmission.

Ueda offers a third theory, his own version of how the drugs exert their powerful effect.

He proposes that the anesthetics dehydrate the nerve-cell membrane, rendering it disorganized and dysfunctional. "A protein-lipid membrane cannot be made without water," he says. "If you take away water, everything goes haywire."

Potential Problems

General anesthesia may cause more side effects than regional anesthesia. After the surgery, patients who have inhaled the gases occasionally experience nausea, fatigue, and possibly difficulty with breathing. Regional anesthetics may have fewer complications, but occasionally they cause backaches, headaches, or itchiness, and may make it difficult

---

Techniques For General Surgery

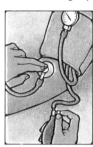

1 Before surgery, an anesthesiologist arranges to meet with patients to answer their questions and examine them to assess their fitness for the rigors of anesthesia and surgery.

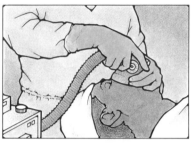

4 In some cases, anesthesia may be induced or maintained with gases delivered by mask. If no muscle relaxant is used, the patient may be able to continue breathing naturally.

5 In other cases, a breathing tube is inserted for delivery of anesthetic gases. If a muscle relaxant is used, artificial ventilation is necessary.

2 Premedication may be given prior to surgery, including drugs that relieve pain and anxiety, or prevent excessive salivation.

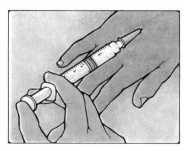

3 A cannula, a thin, hollow tube, is inserted into a vein and is used throughout surgery to administer drugs to the patient.

6 During surgery, the patient's vital signs, such as heart rate, breathing, blood pressure, temperature, blood oxygenation, and exhaled carbon dioxide, are continuously monitored.

to walk or urinate for a few hours. During the operation, anesthetic gases can disturb the body's temperature regulation. "Patients become 'cold-blooded' in the operating room," says Eckenhoff, "and afterwards, shivering, cold patients have increased oxygen demands."

One rare reaction to general anesthesia is malignant hyperthermia, a genetic disorder that occurs in about one of every 50,000 patients. This syndrome may not be detectable until a patient is in the operating room and receiving anesthesia. In such patients, some of the drugs may trigger a sustained elevation of calcium in the skeletal muscle cells, which make the muscles hyperactive and contracted—often leading to death. Fortunately, mortality with this disorder is now reduced due to the availability of specific drugs, like dantrolene (Dantrium).

To avoid complications, "vigilance is the key," says Eckenhoff. An anesthesiologist spends most of the time during an operation adjusting the anesthetic to the surgical procedure and keeping an eye on the patient's blood loss and vital functions. He or she has drugs on hand to produce a wide variety of effects on the cardiovascular system. Half a dozen electronic devices help the doctor monitor all of the patient's bodily functions.

Blood pressure and heart and respiration rates are continuously monitored and displayed on a CRT monitor. An electrocardiograph gives a readout of the heart's electrical efforts, an electrode checks the level of paralysis in the muscles, and separate probes for oxygen, carbon dioxide, anesthetic gas, and temperature transmit messages from inside the trachea and esophagus.

Nancy's anesthesiologist is particularly reassured by the pulse oximeter on her middle finger. This instrument monitors the concentration of hemoglobin carrying a full load of oxygen. Oxygenated blood is brighter red than deoxygenated blood. "Pulse oximetry has made a big difference in decreasing morbidity and mortality in the operating room," says Eckenhoff. Prior to the availability of pulse oximetry, the first sign that the patient lacked sufficient oxygen was when the surgeon noticed that the patient's blood appeared dark. That could be too late.

Anesthesiologists use an instrument called a pulse oximeter to monitor the level of oxygen in the patient's blood during surgery. The oximeter is placed on the patient's middle finger (above).

Know Thy Patient

Nancy is fine. Her blood hemoglobin is 100 percent saturated with oxygen. She is a relatively easy case—only 40 years old, with no serious medical conditions. She smokes, but the anesthesiologist has taken this into consideration when designing her anesthetic plan. (Smokers may have a higher risk for respiratory complications during and following surgery.)

Anesthesiologists grade their patients on a scale of one to five according to the severity of their initial medical condition. Class one means no pre-existing medical problems; five means death is imminent with or without surgery. Eckenhoff says Nancy's good physical status puts her into class one.

Knowing a patient's medical history is crucial for an anesthesiologist. Ideally, a patient is seen in an outpatient clinic about one week before elective surgery. There, an anesthesiologist will perform a physical, take a history, and may request blood tests or X rays. Key questions are repeated again the day before the operation in the preoperative interview. Anesthesiologists must know if a person is taking any medications, if the patient has any known allergies, how many times he or she has been hospitalized, how many times anesthesia has been given, and any reactions that occurred in the patient or the patient's blood relatives. Patients are told several times not to eat or drink anything for at least eight hours prior to their operation. Such fasting guards against the stomach contents entering the lungs, a potentially fatal complication of general anesthesia.

"The two basic principles of a pre-op interview," explains Eckenhoff, "are to get information about pre-existing medical conditions and to provide information to the patient about what they're going to undergo. A good interview the day before surgery reduces patient anxiety just as effectively as giving sedatives the day of surgery."

Eckenhoff laments that the abbreviated hospital stays and morning-admission policies of many health-care institutes and third-party payors now make the preoperative interview on the day before surgery virtually impossible. It must often be made by telephoning the patient at home or else by speaking to the often anxious patient the morning of the operation.

Know Thy Doctor

Despite these problems, the safety record for modern anesthesia *is* remarkable. Of the over 30 million anesthetics provided each year, the estimated death rate is as low as 1 per 200,000. But patient-advocacy groups are concerned that an anesthesiologist has a rather unconventional doctor-patient relationship that could contribute to mistakes.

According to Miami attorney Barry Meadow, "The anesthesiologist is the one you know the least about and the one who can do the most harm. I would want to know as much about the anesthesia as I know about the surgical procedure, because the knee operation is not going to kill me. If there is some negligence in the anesthesia, the injury is usually severe—you're dealing with either death or coma. The problem is, very few people select an anesthesiologist."

Laura Wittkin, executive director of the National Center for Patients' Rights, advises that "patients meet with the anesthesiologist a week before [surgery]—not the day of surgery, not even the day before."

Eckenhoff suggests that patients check that their anesthesiologist is certified by the American Board of Anesthesiology. In addition, the patient should verify that the anesthesiologist regularly conducts the type of anesthetic that the patient will receive. Eckenhoff predicts that the recertification tests, which are now optional, will become mandatory for all anesthesiologists in the future.

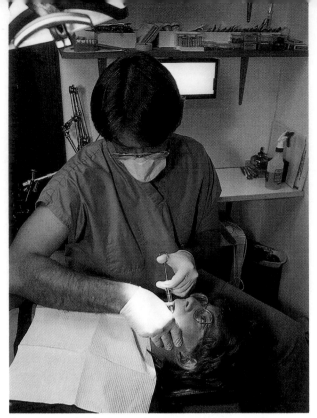

Local anesthesia is used to numb only a small part of the body. Dentists inject local anesthesia to eliminate the pain associated with drilling and other dental procedures.

Meadow also worries about the safety of outpatient surgical centers and surgical suites, where much cosmetic or dermatologic surgery is performed today. "You can run into the same problems in a doctor's office that you can in the O.R. of a major metropolitan hospital," warns Meadow. "The monitoring equipment is not as extensive as in a hospital."

Eckenhoff advises patients to make sure that the surgical center they choose is properly staffed and licensed. As for receiving anesthesia in your doctor's office, however, Eckenhoff is wary. "In many office procedures when a significant amount of sedation is used, things can get out of control quickly. Patients should inquire about the use of sedative and hypnotic drugs," he says. "I would want a local anesthetic, but not a hypnotic."

Wittkin issues the strongest warnings to anyone considering having an operation outside a hospital. "Just as bad doctors hide out in these offices, so do the anesthesiologists," she says. "We have seen cases where anesthesiologists who cannot get privileges to work in hospitals are working in these private clinics." These anesthesiologists are not likely to be board-certified.

Drugs Used in General Anesthesia

Type	Action	Examples
Drugs given as premedication	Reduce anxiety, discomfort; reduce saliva and mucus production	Diazepam, morphine, atropine
Induction agents	Induce unconsciousness	Thiopental sodium
Anesthetic gases and volatile agents	Induce and/or maintain unconsciousness	Nitrous oxide, halothane, enflurane, isoflurane, desflurane
Analgesics	Eliminate pain	Morphine, fentanyl, and derivatives
Muscle relaxants	Relax muscles	Pancuronium, vecuronium, atracurium, curare
Relaxant reversal agents	Reverse muscle relaxation	Neostigmine, Edrophonium

The Reversal Process

Once the surgeons begin to close Nancy's wound, the anesthesiologist begins the gradual process of reversal, or waking her up—sort of the approach to landing. The doctor may change her anesthetic gas from a long- to a short-acting agent, such as nitrous oxide.

Nancy's paralysis has been timed to wear off, but is also reversed with other drugs. The anesthesiologist then turns off the assisted-breathing function of the ventilator, allowing her to breathe on her own.

About an hour before the end of surgery, the anesthesiologists injected Nancy's epidural catheter with a dose of painkiller that should last 12 to 18 hours. Once the anesthesiologist is confident that Nancy is awake enough to protect her own airway, the endotracheal tube is removed and oxygen is given by mask or through her nose. Nancy is awake, but very groggy.

Postsurgery Pain Treatment

Reducing Nancy's surgical pain and improving her comfort will be the responsibility of HUP's newly minted "pain team." Led by Francis Riegler, M.D., a group of three anesthesia residents follows Nancy and the other postoperative patients in the recovery room and throughout their stay in the hospital.

As the hours following surgery march by, Nancy becomes more lucid. In the afternoon, she is complaining of severe nausea, especially when she sits up in bed. Riegler prescribes a skin patch to alleviate the nausea, and tells her he is pleased with her recovery. Riegler and his residents question the patients in the recovery room and throughout their stay in the hospital for any side effects to the anesthesia, and ask them to grade their pain on a scale of 1 to 10.

"We don't give any awards for pain in the hospital," Riegler tells one elderly lady, while reassuring her that she will not become addicted to any of the painkillers prescribed.

Riegler notes that certain patients with chronic conditions tend to demand more pain-killing medicine after an operation than do others. He also cites a study that suggests that patients who carry a higher level of endorphins (the body's naturally occurring painkillers) in their cerebrospinal fluid demand less postoperative analgesia.

Nancy Lewis had a smooth flight through surgery, and her recovery following anesthesia went well. She was released from the hospital after a couple of days.

"Anesthesia is one of the medical specialties in which we can almost always accomplish what we set out to do," says Eckenhoff proudly. "It can be very satisfying. For a patient to undergo a complicated invasive procedure and do it without memory or pain is amazing." ◇

A Resurgence of Rabies

by Gode Davis

On June 18, 1992, Francis Lueder, 82, and his wife Marian, 80, experienced a raccoon encounter of the closest, most dreaded kind. "This raccoon was actually in our house, scuffling with our Persian cat on the kitchen floor," said Marian Lueder. As Marian jumped into the fray, trying to get the raccoon away from the cat, Francis grabbed a hammer and beat the furious beast to death, but not before the animal had scratched both his wife and himself. The Lueders were both contaminated with the raccoon's saliva, and therefore required to get prompt postexposure rabies injections.

Getting the shots saved the couple's lives. Soon after the incident, postmortem tests confirmed that the house-invading raccoon had indeed been rabid.

In Tompkins County in upstate New York, where the Lueders reside, dozens of similar encounters between humans and rabies-infected raccoons have occurred since the first was recorded there in 1989.

In fact, as many as one in every six raccoons currently found in the eastern United States may be infected with rabies—part of a resurging epizootic (epidemic among animals). The epizootic began in Florida during the 1950s, saturated the mid-Atlantic states by the mid-1980s, and has continued encroaching at an ever more alarming rate (now up to 50 miles per year) into the Northeast—most recently entering the New England state of New Hampshire.

How alarming? According to national statistics kept by the Centers for Disease Control and Prevention (CDC) in Atlanta (the government agency to which all state health agencies must report any instances of rabies found in animals or humans), 3,079 reports of raccoon rabies were received in 1991 alone —the highest annual toll ever recorded in this country for a particular animal species. Primarily because of this epizootic among raccoons (a milder epizootic is simultaneously raging among midwestern skunks), U.S. incidences of animal rabies have now reached unprecedented proportions, rising to 6,975 cases, an increase of 43 percent over the previous year. Because raccoons often live in densely populated human areas, concern is mounting over when the first raccoon-to-human rabies transmission will occur. If it happens, the event would be catastrophic: once a rabies strain is allowed to incubate inside the human nervous system, the victim almost invariably dies. (In the three known cases of humans who survived actual rabies, all were left with permanent and devastating nervous-system damage.)

Perhaps because of serendipity, but more likely because of refined tissue-culture rabies vaccines (which are promptly administered and widely available in the United States), not a single person has yet been infected with rabies by a raccoon—despite innumerable exposures to rabid raccoons. (The improved vaccines are virtually foolproof and compared with cruder animal-brain-tissue remedies, relatively painless.) In fact, actual human rabies continues to be rare in America, the disease causing only 16 recorded deaths in this country since 1980.

Rabid raccoons have infected only relatively few cats and dogs during this ongoing outbreak. If an epizootic of raccoonlike pro-portions were to suddenly develop in the pet population, some sporadic human cases would then seem inevitable. Such a "pet" epizootic probably won't happen in the United States, however, because most American-owned dogs and cats are routinely given preexposure rabies shots. In fact, the most promising solution to the current raccoon menace might also involve vaccination—but by bait instead of injection.

Rabies: A Closer Look

The rabies virus belongs to the family Rhabdoviridae. As seen under an electron microscope, it has a coiled RNA core surrounded by a bullet-shaped envelope from which numerous surface projections, or spikes, jut. Rabies affects primarily mammals. Carried in saliva, the virus is usually transmitted through a bite or other contact (as through a wound or scratch) with the saliva of an infected creature. Human beings have also been known to contract rabies in more obscure ways: by breathing the air in caves inhabited by rabid bats or after receiving implants of eye corneas from human donors

Despite the alarming number of rabid raccoons in the U.S., few Americans have actually died from rabies. Outside North America and Europe, however, rabies represents a much greater threat.

A wild animal that brazenly approaches humans or a nocturnal animal that is overly active during the day may have rabies. Animal-control officials are trained to deal with such creatures in a safe manner.

who had undiagnosed rabies. Although it has never been documented, human-to-human transmission through contact with an infected *person's* saliva also remains a theoretical possibility.

Once it has entered the newly infected host body through the skin, the virus multiplies in muscle cells and neural pathways; as an encephalitis, it has an affinity for cells of the brain and central nervous system. Among domestic animals, disease vectors (sources) are most often cats, dogs, and cattle. Wild animals native to the United States most likely to be rabid have more recently been raccoons, although skunks, foxes, bats, rats, mice, and mongooses (only in Puerto Rico) have been proven to harbor (unlike raccoons) rabies strains virulent enough to cause human deaths.

Dreaded Symptoms
Precisely which symptoms occur in rabies-infected humans and other mammals depend upon the specific areas of the brain, central nervous system, or muscles that are affected. For instance, because the virus concentrates in the salivary glands of the infected mammal, the muscles involved in drinking and swallowing are often damaged, causing victims to suffer the most excruciating pain when swallowing liquids, and leading to hydrophobia, or terror at the sight of water.

The Lueders' raccoon invader was probably showing the "furious" form of rabies. Such rabid creatures often become extra-aggressive, fierce, and highly sensitive to touch and other forms of stimulation. They sometimes ignore usual behavior patterns: for example, nocturnal animals become active during the day.

A second form of animal rabies, paralytic (or "dumb") rabies, appears to attack the victim's central nervous system and musculature more than its brain. In such cases the animal becomes extremely lethargic, weak in the limbs, and unable to raise its head or utter any sounds because its throat and neck muscles are paralyzed. In "furious" rabies, it may be up to a month or longer before the animal succumbs; paralytic rabies causes an animal's death from heart or respiratory failure within a few days.

In mammals other than humans, symptoms usually develop within 10 days of exposure, but can take much longer. Animals may even carry a strain of the rabies virus without showing any symptoms, though this is exceptionally rare. (In Africa and Asia, however, healthy dogs have been observed to excrete the virus intermittently in their saliva for up to three years.)

If left untreated, a rabies-infected human experiences a symptom-free incubation period that ranges from 10 days to a year or longer (the average is about a month). Once this "grace" period ends, indeterminate "flu-like" symptoms appear. At this stage, patients may become anxious, and complain of insomnia, depression, or difficulty in swallowing. Two to 16 days later, signs of brain and nervous-system damage are observed: hyperactivity, hypersensitivity (including penile hypersensitivity with continuous erections and recurrent, involuntary ejaculations in males), and disorientation. These symptoms lead, with few exceptions, to seizures or paralysis, coma, and eventual death. For full-blown rabies-infected patients, death usually occurs within two to three weeks after the initial onset of symptoms.

Prevention Is the Next Best Thing

While no cure for rabies exists, untreated patients are "worst-case" scenarios. Because the rabies virus takes time to incubate, human patients can usually be successfully treated—and progression of the disease can usually be halted—before the dreaded symptoms begin appearing.

Once rabies is suspected, the patient should receive immediate medical attention. Any animal wounds or scratches, if present, should be thoroughly cleaned with soap and water. Rabies-vaccine treatment should be started as soon as possible after exposure, even in previously immunized (or vaccinated) persons.

In the United States, human diploid cell vaccine (HDCV) is in widespread use. The vaccine, essentially an inactive rabies virus produced in cultures of human cells, is almost 100 percent effective in making the patient's immune system produce antibodies to neutralize the invading virus before it causes disease. Counting the first day of vaccine treatment as day 0, single injections of HDCV are administered into the deltoid muscles of the patient's arms on days 0, 3, 7, 14, and 28. Besides the primary vaccine, patients who have not previously been vaccinated for rabies also receive an injection of rabies immune globulin (RIG) on the day they first get the primary vaccine (day 0). The

If You're Bitten. . . .

Before you do anything else—clean the site of the wound or saliva exposure thoroughly with soap and water. Then consider the following:

• Persons who are bitten, scratched, or who otherwise come into contact with the saliva of a suspect rabid animal should seek medical attention as soon as possible.

• In the United States, the standard course of treatment for suspected rabies consists of a precautionary tetanus booster shot (as with any animal or human bite, puncture, or treated scratch), followed by a series of five rabies vaccine injections of the active serum HDCV (human diploid cell vaccine) administered in the deltoid muscle of the patient's arm on days 0 (the day the patient first gets the vaccine), 3, 7, 14, and 28.

• Patients who have not previously been vaccinated for rabies also receive an injection of RIG (rabies immune globulin) on the day they first get the vaccine (day 0). This is to confer "passive" immunity during the period (usually several days) before the active rabies vaccine begins working within the patient's body.

RIG injection is to confer what's called "passive immunity"—protecting patients in the meanwhile before the "active" vaccine begins stimulating rabies-antibody production.

Outside the United States and other developed nations, such effective treatment (at $150 per vaccine course) is cost-prohibitive, and thus seldom available for rabies-infected persons. Throughout most of the Third World, the most widely used vaccine is the much cheaper ($5 per course) rabies neuro-tissue vaccine (NTV), made from the infected brain tissue of adult rabbits, sheep, and goats. NTV as a treatment leaves much to be desired, however. After a painful course of up to 24 daily injections, a host of excruciating local reactions, and possible neuroparalytic complications—which, like rabies, can also be fatal—several thousand of those persons so treated each year still die.

Countries that can't afford safe, potent rabies vaccines for their human populations also can't afford them for their pets. Though a successful rabies vaccine for dogs has been available since the 1920s, dogs remain the leading vector of animal rabies worldwide. In countries like the United States and Canada and in most of Europe, where little or no canine rabies exists because dogs are routinely vaccinated, human rabies is extremely rare. In many developing nations where animal vaccinations are the exception, canine rabies is often epizootic. The consequence is millions of human exposures to rabid dogs—a powerful factor contributing to up to 50,000 human deaths from rabies occurring worldwide each year.

Stopping Rabid Raccoons

In this latest American outbreak, rabid raccoons have already infected an estimated 1,000 to 2,000 dogs and cats. Considering how many dogs and cats exist in the United States and how long the epizootic has been raging, that figure represents a very small number.

Sporadic cases of raccoon rabies began appearing in central Florida in 1953. By 1955 there appeared to be a minor epizootic of raccoon rabies along the Atlantic coast of Florida. During the next few years, the disease kept spreading, and by 1962 had crossed into Georgia.

In 1977 a single rabid raccoon was reported in West Virginia. Two years later West Virginia reported eight, and Virginia four, rabid raccoons. It was later learned that hunting clubs in several mid-Atlantic states had unintentionally exacerbated the epizootic by importing raccoons into the area for sporting purposes; some of them were rabid. Suzanne Jenkins, D.V.M., a veterinarian with the CDC in Atlanta, documented a clear epizootic in 1982. By that year a total of 837 rabid raccoons had been reported in four states of the mid-Atlantic region and in the District of Columbia; in 1983 the numbers were still growing, with 1,608 rabid raccoons, six rabid dogs, and 32 cats. During the mid-1980s, reports of raccoon rabies kept increasing, and more domestic dogs and cats were becoming involved. Though raccoon rabies appeared to ebb, with "only" 1,465 cases reported to the CDC in 1988, it was a misleading phenomenon, since it now appears that the epizootic was then spreading northward at the alarming rate of some 50 miles per year. Since then, rabid raccoons have been infiltrating animal populations with alarming regularity; over 8,000 cases have been reported in the states of New York, New Jersey, and Connecticut alone!

Despite almost a decade of rising fears of contamination from raccoons, not a single raccoon-to-human transmission has oc-

---

Red Flags for Rabies

Two forms of animal rabies exist—the "furious" or "mad dog" variety and the equally dangerous paralytic or "dumb" form. While no animal can be positively identified as being rabid until after it is dead (the animal's brain tissue must be autopsied to be sure), here are some rabies "red flags" to watch out for in wild and domestic animals.

Furious or Paralytic Symptom
• Animal suffers excruciating pain when drinking or swallowing liquids and may even become hydrophobic—terrified at the sight of water.

Furious Symptoms
• Animal may become extraordinarily vicious, aggressive, or combative.
• Beware of excessive drooling or foaming at the mouth.

Paralytic Symptoms
• The animal appears to be lethargic.
• The creature is weak in one or more of its limbs.
• Because its throat and neck muscles are paralyzed, the creature is unable to raise its head or make sounds.

Household pets are much more likely to contract rabies from a wild animal than are humans. For this reason, many towns and cities have set up free or low-cost "rabies clinics," where people can have their pets vaccinated against the disease.

curred. In fact, in two of three human-rabies cases reported in the entire United States in 1991, the probable vectors were unvaccinated dogs—testimony to the combined effectiveness of routinely vaccinating pets and promptly administering refined vaccines to exposed persons.

Still, the raccoon epizootic continues. Is there an effective way to stop it, or even slow it down? The immediate response is to wipe out the raccoon population (raccoonicide), which is inhumane and impractical, if not impossible. Selective culling of raccoons by trapping and removing them from areas is a two-edged sword: although population density is reduced, thereby lessening the chances of transmission, new, younger animals that are especially susceptible to rabies may enter the areas precisely because of the lower density.

A better solution may be vaccinating the wild raccoons by using vaccine-loaded bait. Until recently, such a mass vaccination of raccoons wouldn't have worked. Traditional rabies vaccines made from weakened viruses were ineffective in the raccoon and, in any case, couldn't be used without risking an epizootic in other species, such as rodents and skunks.

A person with untreated rabies will die, but only after weeks of dreadful symptoms.

Fortunately, a "smart" rabies vaccine now exists. Genetically engineered in the laboratory several years ago at the University of Liège in Belgium, it's made from vaccinia—the cowpox virus that gave vaccination its name. The vaccinia is altered so that its surface is covered with proteins from the rabies virus. The target animal's immune system learns from the vaccine how to protect itself against invaders that look like rabies, without any potentially dangerous virus being released.

Already proven effective on experimental animals including raccoons, it remained for the product to be field-tested by scientists in the wild. Such a trial was conducted from November 1989 until the same month a year later. Using helicopters, an 850-square-mile area of the Ardennes Forest in southern Belgium was sown with vaccine-doped bait targeted for red foxes, the leading European vector of animal rabies. The helicopters made three sorties at six-month intervals. (The antibiotic tetracycline was used as a marker to tell investigators which animals had eaten the bait.)

At the study's onset, two-thirds of foxes found dead or shot by hunters were rabid. Once the second wave had gone in, only one of the 165 foxes examined had rabies (it had not eaten the bait), and the incidence of rabies among livestock in Belgium (a reliable indicator) had dropped to zero. ◇

THE MAINSTREAMING OF ALTERNATIVE MEDICINE

by Douglas S. Barasch

There was little more that doctors could do for Catherine Bettez. Afflicted for nearly 10 years with lymphocytic hypophysitis, a rare, incurable disease of the endocrine system that depresses immunity, the 43-year-old woman had become increasingly debilitated by pain and depression, conditions that persisted despite medication. Acknowledging their limitations, her endocrinologist and her psychiatrist referred her to another kind of healer—a practitioner whose treatments were meditation and yoga.

"It seemed off-the-wall," says Bettez, a former proofreader in Westminster, Massachusetts. "I'm going to sit around and meditate, and that's going to make me feel better?"

Because the healer her physicians recommended was not some robed mystic, but a professor of medicine, she decided to enroll in his program last spring. Since completing it, Bettez reports, she has been able to cut down on Naprosyn, an anti-inflammatory medication that helps alleviate her pain, and stop taking Ativan for her depression.

In recent years, unconventional therapies such as meditation, acupuncture, and homeopathy have begun to gain a foothold in American medicine. Catherine Bettez is one of millions of patients who have been treated with such methods, and her physicians are among the thousands of doctors who either refer patients to practitioners of alternative medicine or use elements of it themselves.

Biopsychosocial Approaches

This year the National Institutes of Health (NIH) established an Office for the Study of Unconventional Medical Practices to investigate a wide range of treatments, including herbal medicine and massage therapy. Next year, Harvard Medical School plans to offer a course on unorthodox medicine. Similar courses and lectures are already available to medical students at Georgetown University, the University of Louisville, the University of Arizona, and the University of Massachusetts in Worcester. David M. Eisenberg, M.D., an instructor of medicine who, after having studied acupuncture in China persuaded Harvard to offer the course, says his purpose was not only to introduce students to the theory and practice of alternative treatments, but also "to train students to think rigorously about them."

Acupuncture, a mainstay of Chinese medicine for thousands of years, came to Westerners' attention about 20 years ago, when China opened its doors to the modern world. American doctors were intrigued by the use of acupuncture as a surgical anesthetic, and researchers found that it works by inducing nerve cells to produce endorphins, the body's natural painkillers. Scientists have also found evidence to support the view, held by many cultures, that illness can not only be brought on by external forces, like viruses, but by one's state of mind. Stress seems to weaken the immune system, and happiness to strengthen it. Personality traits such as impatience increase the risk of heart disease. Studies show that meditation and other "mind-body" therapies confer various healthful benefits, including reduced pain and, for infertile women, a higher conception rate.

Many physicians now speak of a transition from the narrow biomedical model of Western medicine to a "biopsychosocial" one. With this approach, doctors would continue to marshal the tools of Western medicine to do what it does best: save the life of a patient who is acutely ill or in critical condition, by pumping him full of antibiotics when he has pneumonia, for example, or mending his skull after it has been

Unconventional therapies have begun to gain a real foothold in the American medical establishment.

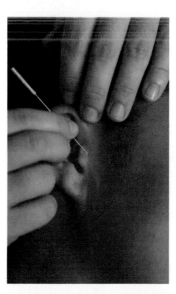

The roots of herbal medicine lie in the folk remedies of years ago. Many patients find relief from pain and discomfort from the balms and other preparations created by professional herbalists.

shattered in a car accident. Doctors would also draw on holistic techniques to help prevent killer illnesses such as heart disease, diabetes, and cancer, and to treat chronic conditions such as pain, hypertension, and anxiety—problems that often do not yield to high-tech medicine. Patients would then have the healer's touch and, if necessary, the magnetic resonance imaging (MRI).

Under the direction of Jon Kabat-Zinn, M.D., professor of medicine, the Stress Reduction Clinic at the University of Massachusetts Medical Center in Worcester has taught Buddhist meditation and yoga to thousands of patients, most of whom have been referred by physicians. At one recent class, there were 30 patients, whose ailments included AIDS, muscular dystrophy, hypertension, chronic back pain, anxiety disorder, coronary-artery disease, and cancer.

Outcomes studies show that most patients who go through Kabat-Zinn's eight-week program feel much better than they did before, regardless of their illness. "They're taking people that the system is not helping. They're taking the toughest patients and having significant outcomes," says John K. Zawacki, M.D., a gastroenterologist at the University of Massachusetts Medical Center.

The Relaxation Response

About 40 miles east, at Deaconess Hospital in Boston, is the Harvard-affiliated Mind/Body Medical Institute, founded in 1988 by Herbert Benson, M.D., a cardiologist at Harvard Medical School. The institute uses meditation, repetitive exercise, and yoga to achieve what Dr. Benson calls the "relaxa-

Alternative-Medicine Lexicon

Acupuncture—An ancient Chinese practice that involves inserting thin needles into the body at various points and manipulating them to relieve pain or treat illness.

Biofeedback—A technique for teaching people to become aware of their heart rate, blood pressure, temperature, and other involuntary body functions in order to control them by a conscious mental effort.

Guided imagery—The use of mental imagery to facilitate the healing process.

Herbal medicine—The use of balms and medications prepared from flowers, leaves, and other parts of plants.

Homeopathy—A medical system based on the idea of treating disease by using minute, highly diluted doses of the very substances that, in large doses, can cause it.

Hypnotherapy—A method of inducing a trancelike state characterized by extreme suggestibility in order to help patients relax, control pain, and overcome addictions such as smoking.

Naturopathy—An approach to treating illness with diet, exercise, and other "natural" means, rather than drugs or surgery.

tion response," a physiological state characterized by lowered blood pressure, heart rate, respiration, and metabolism that was the subject of his best-selling book of the same name.

The institute offers programs for cardiac-risk reduction and rehabilitation, infertility, insomnia, chronic pain, AIDS, and cancer. Cures are not promised at the institute. Patients can, however, hope for a reduction in symptoms, or at least a greater ability to cope with serious medical conditions, as well as with treatments (such as chemotherapy) that can be debilitating.

Dr. Benson has demonstrated the success of his methods in several clinical studies. One published last year in the journal *Fertility and Sterility* showed that women receiving medical treatment for infertility who also went through his infertility program had about a 35 percent conception rate, compared with a roughly 17 percent rate among women who got only medical treatment. A study last year in *The Clinical Journal of Pain* found that after going through Dr. Benson's chronic-pain program, people didn't feel the need to go to the doctor as often—the number of visits was reduced by an average of 38 percent. And a study published in the *Journal of Cardiopulmonary Rehabilitation* found that patients who had completed Dr. Benson's hypertension program showed reductions in blood pressure, anxiety, and depression.

Relaxation techniques as well as other alternative therapies such as biofeedback are now routinely taught to patients at medical centers and doctors' offices around the country. More than 2,000 physicians use acupuncture in conjunction with conventional medicine, according to the American Academy of Medical Acupuncture, and 5,000 use hypnotherapy, according to the American Society of Clinical Hypnosis. Dana Ullman, a board member of the National Center for Homeopathy, estimates that more than 1,000 doctors practice homeopathy.

Costs and Coverage

Alternative therapies have a reputation for being less expensive than conventional medicine, since practitioners prescribe fewer drugs and recommend fewer diagnostic tests and other costly interventions, and because they typically spend more time with patients

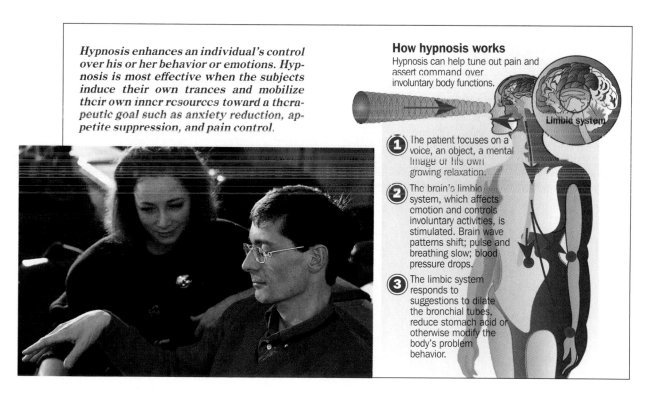

Hypnosis enhances an individual's control over his or her behavior or emotions. Hypnosis is most effective when the subjects induce their own trances and mobilize their own inner resources toward a therapeutic goal such as anxiety reduction, appetite suppression, and pain control.

How hypnosis works
Hypnosis can help tune out pain and assert command over involuntary body functions.

Limbic system

1. The patient focuses on a voice, an object, a mental image or his own growing relaxation.

2. The brain's limbic system, which affects emotion and controls involuntary activities, is stimulated. Brain wave patterns shift; pulse and breathing slow; blood pressure drops.

3. The limbic system responds to suggestions to dilate the bronchial tubes, reduce stomach acid or otherwise modify the body's problem behavior.

than regular doctors do. But the fees charged by practitioners of unconventional medicine can be high. An initial consultation with a physician, a nurse, or some other certified practitioner of homeopathy costs $60 to $300, depending on the location, although the visit lasts about an hour and a half, says William Shevin, president of the National Center for Homeopathy. Subsequent half-hour visits range from $45 to $80. Acupuncturists charge $50 to $100, says Joseph M. Helms, M.D., president of the American Academy of Medical Acupuncture. Jon Kabat-Zinn's stress-reduction program runs $565 for nine sessions, and Dr. Benson's programs cost an average of $1,000 for 10 classes.

Insurance reimbursement for unconventional medicine varies by the policy, the therapy, the practitioner, and the geographical region. Catherine Bettez's insurance policy covered most of the fee for Kabat-Zinn's relaxation program, and another patient, Ken Hokanson, says his policy covered all of it. Six states—California, Florida, Montana, Nevada, New Mexico, and Oregon—require insurers to reimburse patients who see licensed acupuncturists for pain relief. And in Alaska the services of licensed naturopaths, practitioners who treat disease with nonmedical approaches such as diet and exercise rather than drugs and surgery, must be covered.

Some insurance companies impose their own standards. The American Western Life Insurance Company in California, a $60 million insurer with 300,000 clients, recently launched a "wellness and preventative care health plan," which reimburses patients for alternative therapies such as homeopathy, herbal medicine, shiatsu massage, acupressure, acupuncture, guided imagery, hypnotherapy, and biofeedback.

But American Western is clearly the exception. Many major companies, including the Prudential Insurance Company of America and the John Hancock Mutual Life Insurance Company, two multibillion-dollar insurers, cover alternative therapies only if a medical doctor or a licensed practitioner performs them. A therapy must also be deemed medically necessary by the insurance company's own doctors. "It has to be documented to be an effective and safe intervention, not just prescribed by a doctor

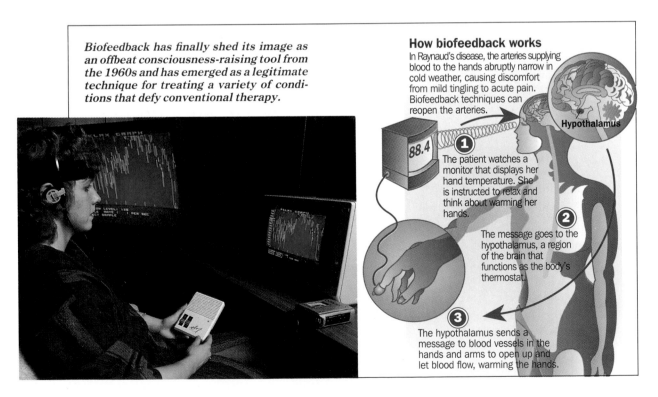

Biofeedback has finally shed its image as an offbeat consciousness-raising tool from the 1960s and has emerged as a legitimate technique for treating a variety of conditions that defy conventional therapy.

How biofeedback works

In Raynaud's disease, the arteries supplying blood to the hands abruptly narrow in cold weather, causing discomfort from mild tingling to acute pain. Biofeedback techniques can reopen the arteries.

Hypothalamus

1 The patient watches a monitor that displays her hand temperature. She is instructed to relax and think about warming her hands.

2 The message goes to the hypothalamus, a region of the brain that functions as the body's thermostat.

3 The hypothalamus sends a message to blood vessels in the hands and arms to open up and let blood flow, warming the hands.

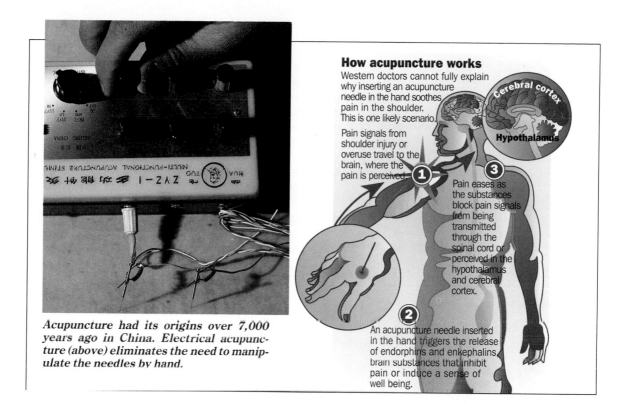

How acupuncture works

Western doctors cannot fully explain why inserting an acupuncture needle in the hand soothes pain in the shoulder. This is one likely scenario.

Pain signals from shoulder injury or overuse travel to the brain, where the pain is perceived.

①

③ Pain eases as the substances block pain signals from being transmitted through the spinal cord or perceived in the hypothalamus and cerebral cortex.

Cerebral cortex

Hypothalamus

② An acupuncture needle inserted in the hand triggers the release of endorphins and enkephalins, brain substances that inhibit pain or induce a sense of well being.

Acupuncture had its origins over 7,000 years ago in China. Electrical acupuncture (above) eliminates the need to manipulate the needles by hand.

or provided by a physician," says I. Steven Udvarhelyi, M.D., vice president of medical services at Prudential, which covers meditation, biofeedback, acupuncture, and shiatsu massage, but not hypnotherapy. "We base our coverage decisions on a careful and extensive review of the medical literature. We also consider the consensus opinion within the medical community."

Supporting Studies

The medical community's willingness to accept some alternative therapies has been strengthened by a few ground-breaking studies. In 1990 Dean Ornish, M.D., director of the Preventive Medicine Research Institute in Sausalito, California, published a study in *The Lancet* showing that techniques such as yoga and meditation, when used in conjunction with a low-fat diet, can reverse coronary heart disease, actually reducing the amount of plaque in the arteries. A year earlier, also in *The Lancet*, David Spiegel, M.D., a psychiatrist at Stanford University School of Medicine in California, demonstrated that women diagnosed with metastatic breast cancer who got medical care as well as "psychosocial treatment"—including support

groups and self-hypnosis—survived twice as long as patients who received only medical care. These studies "added significantly to the cumulative evidence that emotions and behaviors can influence physical health," says Halsted R. Holman, M.D., a professor of medicine at Stanford.

Scores of other studies have also suggested a link between emotions or attitudes and physical health. For example, a report last year in *The New England Journal of Medicine* found that stress increases a person's chances of catching a cold. Other research has shown that particular alternative therapies are effective against certain ailments. Homeopathic remedies can relieve headaches, colds, flu, and allergies, according to several European studies. And a recent article published in *The Lancet* concluded that a traditional Chinese herbal therapy reduces the symptoms of dermatitis.

As the scientific evidence supporting various unconventional treatments accumulates, some physicians predict nothing less than the transformation of American medicine from a biomedical model to a biopsychosocial one. Joel Elkes, M.D., professor emeritus of psychiatry at the University of

Louisville in Kentucky, believes that within 25 years, mind-body techniques will permeate medical practice, from primary care to the treatment of such illnesses as cancer and heart disease. The integration of approaches such as meditation, yoga, acupuncture, and biofeedback with drugs and surgery, he says, "will be as important to medicine as the discovery of antibiotics."

"I think that's possible," says Arnold S. Relman, M.D., former editor of *The New England Journal of Medicine* who now teaches at Harvard Medical School and is

Naturopathic physicians prescribe "natural" means to treat illness. At a naturopathy center in India (above), patients seem to benefit from being wrapped in oversized leaves.

writing a book on the health-care system. "But it all depends on whether we can get more scientific evidence."

Skeptics Abound

Like Dr. Relman, other gatekeepers of American medicine remain skeptical about much of the research on alternative treatments. Marcia Angell, M.D., executive editor of *The New England Journal of Medicine*, thinks many of the studies have been poorly designed and "characterized by exuberant interpretation."

Some scientists studying the interaction between the mind and the body are themselves skeptics, who say their work is often erroneously used by practitioners—including many physicians—as justification for alternative therapies.

"I resent being cited as the scientific basis for protocols and approaches that have never been tested scientifically," says Dr. David L. Felten, a leading researcher in the new field of psychoneuroimmunology, the study of the connection between the mind and the body's susceptibility to disease. Dr. Felten, a professor of neurobiology and anatomy at the University of Rochester School of Medicine and Dentistry in New York, who received a MacArthur fellowship in 1983, has been working out the "hard wiring" of mind-body communication. His research has helped uncover a fascinating network of communication pathways between the body's endocrine, immune, and nervous systems—a sort of physiological Rosetta stone. This network reveals that neurotransmitters, immune cells, and hormones act as messengers between our thoughts and emotions and our immune defenses.

What everyone really wants to know is which alternative therapies actually work. Many medical practices that are widely accepted today met stiff opposition from the medical establishment when they were first introduced. For example, doctors initially doubted the need to wash their hands before performing surgery to prevent infection, as well as the benefits of anesthesia. More recently the value of acupuncture in medicine has been questioned. "People thought acupuncture was way out, spooky, flimflam, a few generations ago," Dr. Relman says. "But there appears to be convincing evidence that it can relieve or prevent pain, and now it's more respected."

Some of the resistance to alternative therapies is giving way as more scientists study them. "The champions of alternative medicine shouldn't expect to be believed unless they meet rigorous standards," Relman adds. "But on the other side, the traditional biomedical establishment ought not to prejudge. All biases and prejudices ought to fall before the evidence." ◇

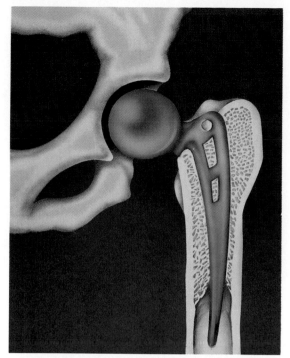

Implanted medical devices, such as this hip bone and socket replacement, improve a patient's quality of life. But for many implants, the long-term risks are still unknown.

BEYOND BREAST IMPLANTS

by Steven Finch

More than 11 million Americans have a medical device surgically implanted in their body. While most implants improve or save lives, no one really knows the long-term hazards of wedding silicone to skin or marrying metal to bone—not even the Food and Drug Administration (FDA), the agency responsible for reviewing them.

This ignorance means that silicone artificial breasts were used about 30 years before their dangers were recognized. And the Bjork-Shiley heart valve, never reviewed by the FDA, has killed 240 people. Worse, there's no way to find and warn the 11,000 or so North Americans who don't know their heart valve is a Bjork-Shiley.

Breast Implant Update

The Food and Drug Administration (FDA) has had the unenviable task of sorting out the pros and cons of silicone gel implants. Initially, the FDA recommended a voluntary moratorium on the use of silicone-gel implants until an advisory panel could make recommendations. The panel found, among other things, that all implants leak some silicone, but that the resulting health effects are unknown. On April 16, 1992, the FDA announced that silicone implants could continue to be used, but under very strict restrictions. Women who want silicone implants for reconstructive purposes, such as after a mastectomy, can still receive them under a special research program, in which they will be enrolled in a registry so that any new information can be made available to them. Women who want the silicone implants for cosmetic purposes must be part of a clinical trial.

Susan Randel

When the FDA became responsible for medical devices in 1976, there were more than 130 types of high-risk machines or implants and 830 medium-risk ones being put into or used on people's bodies. The woefully overtaxed agency set standards for proving the safety and efficacy of new devices, but those already on the market were "grandfathered in," or assumed safe. Their manufacturers were—and are—exempt from proving anything until the FDA sees fit to make them. Just eight grandfathered devices have been investigated since 1976.

In 1990 a new law gave the agency power to spot problems sooner and yank devices from the market faster. In March 1992, the FDA proposed that makers of certain devices be required to track patients receiving them.

The devices in this chart are among the most familiar on the long, dusty list of grandfathered gadgets. They may well be safe—but no one's ever had to prove it.

Status of Medical Implants

Device	What are they?	How many?
SALINE-FILLED BREAST IMPLANTS	These are elastic silicone shells filled with a salt solution and implanted to enlarge or reconstruct a woman's breast.	More than 6,000 were used in 1990 alone.
EAR-VENT TUBES	There are two major types: Endolymphatic shunts are plastic or silicone tubes put in the inner ear to relieve vertigo; some have a valve to control pressure. Plastic or silicone tympanostomy tubes ventilate or drain the middle ear and prevent fluids from entering the middle-ear cavity; about half are used to treat infection in children age 5 and younger. Some tubes have semipermeable membranes.	In 1988 one out of every 250 people in the U.S., or almost 1 million, had an ear-vent tube.
ENDOSSEOUS DENTAL IMPLANTS	Endosseous devices are metal anchors for artificial teeth that are surgically placed in the jawbone. Among the most common are "root forms," shaped like tooth roots. Less common are "blade" implants, which fit channels cut lengthwise into the bone.	As of 1988 Americans had 275,000 dental implants of all types.
ORTHOPEDIC HIP AND KNEE JOINTS	Artificial hip joints and knee joints, made of metal (cobalt-chromium or titanium) and plastic, replace severely arthritic (48%) or injured (28%) natural joints.	By 1988 about 816,000 artificial hips and roughly 521,000 artificial knees were implanted, 68% in people age 65 and older.
PENILE IMPLANTS	There are two common types of penile implants, both designed to treat impotence. A semirigid implant consists of a silicone rod or pair of rods surgically placed in the penis, providing constant rigidity. An inflatable device consists of two cylinders in the penis, connected to a bag of fluid in the abdomen and a manual pump in the scrotum.	An average of 27,000 penile implants are sold each year.
TESTICULAR IMPLANTS	Testicular implants are solid or gel-filled silicone balls that replace testicles removed for medical reasons, usually cancer.	An average of 3,000 testicular implants are sold each year.
VASCULAR GRAFTS LESS THAN 6 MILLIMETERS (¼") IN DIAMETER	These artificial blood vessels replace natural vessels, most often those blocked or damaged by atherosclerosis. They are made of woven or knitted polyethylene or Gore-Tex-like materials.	As many as 8,000 were in use by 1992.

Silicone-gel implants were introduced in 1962, followed by saline-filled in 1969. In 1992, the FDA proposed that manufacturers keep track of women with any type of breast implant. The agency will review the safety of saline-filled implants in early 1993.

Like all breast implants, saline-filled ones can hide small tumors normally found by mammograms. Scar tissue and calcium deposits can harden, causing pain or changing breast appearance. Between 1% and 3% of saline-filled implants will deflate and have to be replaced.

Surgery to relieve vertigo became common in the late 1960s. In 1989 the FDA put shunts with valves on a priority list of 31 devices it intended to review. Despite petitions filed with the FDA claiming these devices didn't need review, manufacturers were told in May 1990 that they would have to provide proof of safety and efficacy. The FDA has yet to require such proof from makers of tympanostomy tubes with membranes.

Endolymphatic shunts may, in fact, be useless: doctors report a roughly 70% success rate for surgery to relieve vertigo, whether or not the shunt is used. Also, the FDA believes that the valves could clog, causing fluid to build up in the inner ear. The tympanostomy tube carries a risk of perforating the inner ear, and the FDA also believes that semipermeable membranes could become blocked and result in hearing loss. As of 1988, 31% of all ear-vent tubes needed to be replaced.

Endosseous-type implants have been widely used by dentists only in the past decade. In 1989 the FDA put them on a list of 31 devices it intended to review, and recently notified manufacturers they will have to produce evidence of safety and efficacy. Meanwhile, manufacturers have petitioned the FDA to withdraw this requirement.

Gums may not heal properly, or there may not be enough bone in the jaw to bond with the implant, which then loosens. Implants can also cause bone loss or damage adjacent teeth. The biggest hazard, however, may be the dentist; some are inadequately trained. Possibly because of this, and depending on the type of implant used, the five-year success rate ranges from 50% to more than 90%.

The first cobalt-chromium joint was implanted in 1939, but joint replacement didn't become accepted until the early 1960s. About half of the 23 types of artificial hips and knees are approved. The other half may carry higher risk and have yet to be looked at.

Some types of artificial joints tend to loosen. About 30% of all joint-replacement patients complain of one or more problems—usually pain—and about 8% of their devices need to be reimplanted. The metal will corrode, and may migrate to other parts of the body; this has been linked to about 25 cases of cancer at the joint, and may slightly increase the risk of leukemia and lymphoma.

Semirigid silicone rods were developed in the 1960s, the first fully implantable inflatable device in the early 1970s. Inflatable penile implants are among five types of devices the FDA plans to begin collecting data on in 1993.

In a 1988 assessment, the American Medical Association found 95% of penile implants to be safe and effective regardless of type. Semirigid devices have complication rates up to 10%; problems include pain, infection, urinary retention, skin erosion, and even perforation of the penis. Inflatable implants have complication rates between 4% and 8%, due primarily to infection and mechanical failure.

These devices were first used more than 30 years ago. They are among five types of devices the FDA will collect data on in 1993, and the agency wants to require makers to keep track of men who receive them.

The FDA suggests that, as with breast implants, silicone from testicular implants may migrate in the body, possibly causing cancer or autoimmune diseases.

The first practical artificial blood vessels were used in the late 1940s. In 1992, the FDA proposed regulations that would make manufacturers track people who get these grafts.

Blood clots frequently form in artificial vessels narrower than ¼ inch, requiring further surgery. This is why most surgeons prefer to use one of the patient's own veins if possible.

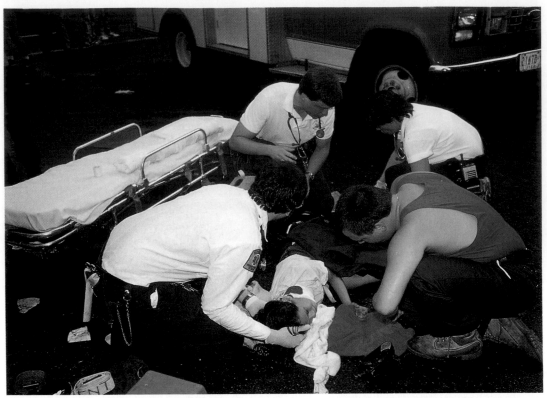

The risk of contracting HIV from a health-care worker is virtually nil. In fact, health-care workers run a higher risk of contracting the virus from a patient, especially in emergency situations.

HIV and Health-Care Workers

by Devera Pine

It's every patient's nightmare: you undergo a routine medical procedure—stitches or a tooth extraction, say—and months later you begin experiencing mysterious health problems. You visit your doctor, only to find to your horrified amazement that you are HIV-positive—you have been infected with the virus that causes AIDS. You do not use intravenous drugs, you are in a monogamous relationship, your partner is HIV-negative—in fact, you can think of only one episode that could have exposed you to the disease: that routine medical procedure.

This is not a fantasy: it happened to 22-year-old Kimberly Bergalis, who died of AIDS in December 1991. It also happened to four other patients of the same Florida dentist, David Acer. Could it happen to you?

Almost universally, experts say no. "An HIV-infected health-care worker can theo-retically transmit the virus to a patient," says M. Roy Schwarz, M.D., senior vice president for medical education and science for the American Medical Association (AMA) and chair of the AMA AIDS task force. "But with the exception of the five cases in Florida, there has not been another case." In fact, notes Dr. Schwarz, the Centers for Disease Control and Prevention (CDC) looked back at the medical histories of 18,000 patients who were treated by HIV-positive physicians —including more than 300 patients of a family physician in Minneapolis who was delivering babies "with gloves up to his wrist, in shirt sleeves, and with lesions on his arms that were draining." Of those 18,000 patients, only 84 turned out to be HIV-positive. "But," says Schwarz, "the CDC does not think a single one came from a physician. There isn't even one case that they're suspicious of."

The medical record for dentists is equally impressive: "Since 1981, there have been at least 2 billion dental appointments," says Richard Price, D.M.D., consumer adviser for the American Dental Association (ADA). "Yet there has only been one cluster of patients who contracted AIDS from a health-care worker," he says, referring to the Florida cases.

If the risk is so minimal, how did one dentist in Florida transmit the virus to five people? The exact mode of transmission is not known, says Kent Taylor, a CDC press spokesperson. "We feel it most likely was blood to blood. For instance, the dentist may have pricked himself and bled directly into the mouths of patients. We'll never know for certain the exact route of transmission."

Nevertheless, says Taylor, the risk of transmission in a health-care setting is practically nil for most medical procedures. For riskier procedures, there is a small chance of transmission: theoretically, a riskier procedure is one in which a practitioner cannot see as well or one in which there is lots of blood "boiling around," says Schwarz. "I say 'theoretically' because we haven't found any cases." Furthermore, even that theoretical risk drops dramatically if the doctor, dentist, or health-care worker follows the CDC's "universal precautions."

Universal Precautions

"Universal precautions" refer to the infection-control guidelines recommended by the CDC. Since even a thorough medical history and exam cannot *always* identify a person infected with HIV, the CDC recommends that health-care practitioners follow protective measures with *all* patients. Many of the precautions are simply common sense: for instance, the guidelines advise doctors and health-care workers to wear gloves, masks, protective eyewear, and face shields to prevent them from coming in contact with their patients' bodily fluids. Furthermore, practitioners should wash their hands before and after treating patients, and should change gloves after each patient. For dentists, the CDC advises gloves, protective masks, and eyewear; the guidelines also call for them to sterilize their equipment between patients.

These procedures may sound simple enough, but how can you be sure your doctor, dentist, or health-care worker is following them? "You can get a pretty good idea when you walk into the office," says Dr. Schwarz. Look around, he suggests: Is the office clean, orderly, and neat? Is the examining room clean and neat? Are medical instruments kept in sterilized packs? Is there a labeled disposal container outfitted with a plastic bag for medical waste? Does the health-care practitioner wear gloves? Wash his or her hands? Drape you if it's appropriate to the medical procedure?

In every office, notes Dr. Price, there should be someone in charge of sterilization. There are several methods to sterilize instruments—chemical, heat under pressure (an autoclave), and chemicals under pressure (a chemclave).

Anything that cannot go in the autoclave—fiber-optic instruments, for instance—are

Many dentists now rely on cassette autoclaves (above) to sterilize their instruments. Instruments should be sterilized between patients.

sterilized with chemicals. Even the prophyangle—the device that holds the rubber cup that the dentist uses to clean your teeth—is either sterilized between patients or disposed of. Recently there was also some concern that debris inside dental handpieces could transmit disease. Though no studies have shown that these pieces actually have debris in them—or that they transmit disease—the ADA modified its guidelines for sterilization of handpieces, calling for dentists to heat-sterilize them between patients. (This cuts down on the life span of the equipment, notes Dr. Price. However, the first disposable handpieces are now being introduced.)

Finally, Price also ensures that any surfaces that practitioners might touch with their hands—the handle on the light fixture over the dental chair, for instance—have a disposable covering on them. "I know that I won't transmit HIV to my patients because I know I won't transmit hepatitis B to them: Hepatitis B is a toughie [to kill off], so if my sterilization kills it, I'm not going to transmit AIDS," he says.

"I think dentistry is leading the sterilization techniques because the cluster [of HIV infections] happened in a dental office," he says. "If any one good thing came out of it, it's the

The risk of contracting AIDS from a physician during surgery is miniscule (as little as 1 in 420,000) compared to that of dying while undergoing general anesthesia (1 in 10,000).

focus of attention on infection control. It's better than it's ever been." However, he stresses, if you have *any* questions about the procedures your dentist, doctor, or health-care worker follows, don't be afraid to ask. Price has even taken patients on a tour of the infection-control procedures he uses.

To Ask or Not to Ask

This, of course, brings up a tricky question: Should you ask your health-care provider if he or she is HIV-positive? Neither the AMA nor the ADA require practitioners to disclose their HIV status unless they pose a significant risk to patients. This does not mean you cannot ask your practitioner their HIV status; it means only that they are not required to answer you. "I don't have to volunteer information, but I've had patients ask me," says Price. Sometimes, he says, patients try to ascertain his HIV status in a roundabout manner: "I've had patients call to ask if I'm married. They figure: if he's married he's straight; and if he's straight, he's O.K."

Again, however, an HIV-positive practitioner does not automatically pose a threat. In addition, both the AMA and the ADA have systems via which HIV-positive practitioners are monitored. The AMA's policy, for example, is for HIV-positive doctors to inform the infection-control committee in their hospital or community. This committee meets with the doctor, looks at his or her track record, and considers whether there should be restrictions on the doctor's practice. If the doctor starts to slip or his or her medical judgment deteriorates, the committee can remove the doctor from practice. "We don't know if all [HIV-positive] doctors are doing this, but we take comfort in the fact that there haven't been any transmitted cases," says Schwarz. In fact, he notes, some HIV-positive doctors instituted this sort of monitoring system on their own even before the AMA developed its policy.

The ADA has a similar system: ADA policy is that HIV-positive dentists should practice only if they are monitored by their physician and by an expert review panel established by their state.

What should you do if you think that your health-care practitioner exposed you to HIV? Turn to local or state authorities. If you think that individual did not adhere to universal precautions, file a complaint at your hospital, local medical society, or state medical court, says Schwarz. "I would urge [people] to do it at a local level for the quickest response," he says. "At the state level, it will take awhile and may not be as meaningful." ◇

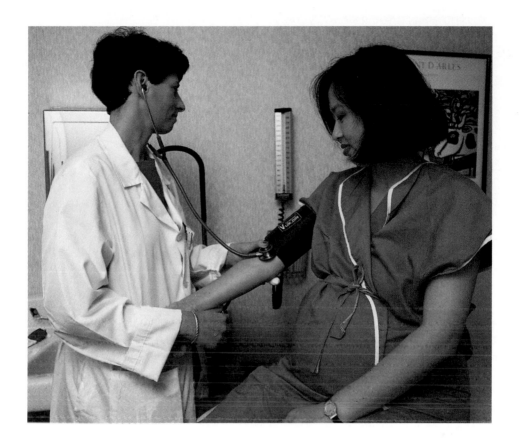

PREGNANCY IN LATER YEARS

by Wendy J. Meyeroff

A woman writes to an advice columnist saying she has finally "found love late." She'd like to have a child, but wonders if it would be fair to her youngster to have "a menopausal mother who looks more like a grandmother than a mother at PTA meetings."

It's a question that more and more "older" women are facing. Statistics for 1989 (the latest data available) indicate that, in comparison to 1988, the rate of first births increased by 9 percent for women 35 to 39, and by 13 percent for women aged 40 to 44.

And those numbers reflect only women having their *first* child. Faith Frieden, M.D., a perinatologist (a doctor who specializes in high-risk pregnancies) at New York City's Beth Israel Medical Center, points out that many of today's older mothers are having their second or even third child. She explains: "More and more, we're seeing the 'biological clock' being pushed back. Whereas 10 or 15 years ago, a mother would have her first child in her mid- or late twenties, and a second child in her early thirties, today we see the first-time mother is in her early thirties, and, if she chooses to expand her family, she's getting pregnant in her late thirties—and even beyond that."

What is causing this shift? One of the prime reasons experts cite is the fact that, beginning in the late 1960s, an unprecedented

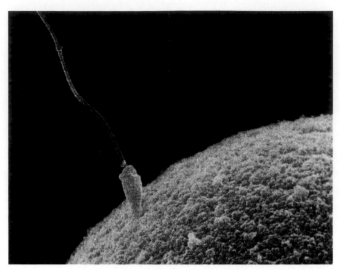

As a woman ages, she has fewer and fewer eggs left. Those eggs that are available are less apt to be fertilized (above), and those that are fertilized are less likely to be healthy.

number of young women entered the work force as serious career seekers, postponing both marriage and childbirth to fulfill their professional goals.

Obstacles to Fertility

With more and more women postponing childbearing, it becomes crucial to understand the factors that can affect a late-life pregnancy. The first key is that unlike men, who constantly replenish their supply of sperm, a woman is born with all the eggs she'll ever produce—approximately 2 million. Natural degeneration reduces that number to about 400,000 by the time she reaches puberty. That may sound like a lot, until one considers that each month, about 1,000 eggs wither and die, with only one being released from the *follicle* (the fluid-filled sac in the ovary that nurtures the ripening egg) to journey through the fallopian tube and hopefully become fertilized. Finally, of an initial supply of about 400,000 eggs, the average women will have only about 400 to 500 eggs available for actual fertilization in her lifetime. Of course the older a woman is, the fewer eggs she has left—and those that remain, being older, tend to be less optimal for fertilization.

Even when an egg *is* fertilized, it's less likely to be healthy. Notes Geoffrey Sher, M.D., executive medical director of the Pacific Fertility Medical Center in California:

"Whereas in women 35 or less, every egg ovulated has a four-out-of-five chance of being healthy, the odds after 45 is that four out of five eggs will have some sort of chromosomal damage."

Also, the longer a woman lives, the likelier it is that she'll have suffered some sort of damage to her reproductive system, due to factors ranging from sexually transmitted diseases to an overactive athletic regimen. Some fertility blockers like *endometriosis,* a disease in which the endometrium (lining of the uterus) grows outside the uterus, may not even offer any sign that problems exist—until a woman tries to become pregnant. In general, women over 40 have a 15 to 20 percent chance of problems with their reproductive system, which of course further reduces the already slim 4- to 5-percent chance that a *healthy* woman over 40 has of becoming pregnant each month (compared to a 20 percent chance for younger women).

However, not all the obstacles are of the *woman's* making. Resolve, a nationwide consumer organization serving the needs of infertile couples, always stresses that while "infertility is caused by a female factor in 40 percent of cases, it is a *male* problem in [another] 40 percent." (Another 5 to 10 percent of cases have no determining factor, while the remainder are generally due to problems in *both* partners.) Scientists are still not sure how a man's age affects fertility, nor have they determined how other factors, such as drug abuse, environmental and occupational hazards, or even medications, may play a role. However, it *has* been determined that even in apparently healthy men with no history of inheritable disease, 8 to 10 percent of sperm is abnormal.

The "biological clock" is being pushed back. More older women than ever before are having babies.

Technobirths

It might seem that the odds of conceiving and then carrying the embryo to full term are almost impossible for the older woman. Fortunately, a number of medical advances over the past 10 to 15 years continue to improve the chances.

Probably the most important of these advances is a group of procedures known as Assisted Reproductive Technologies (ART). The first such procedure, *in vitro fertilization and embryo transfer* (IVF-ET, or, more commonly, IVF), was successfully performed in England in 1978, when Louise Brown, nicknamed the world's first "test-tube baby," was born. That description was used because the baby was essentially developed in a laboratory dish. In simple terms, eggs from the female donor are combined in a laboratory dish with sperm from the male donor. Once fertilized (usually within two days), the new *embryo* is transferred back into the woman's

uterus, where—hopefully—it is carried to term.

In 1984 a variation of this procedure was developed. Known as Gamete Intra-Fallopian Transfer (GIFT), the main difference between this technique and IVF is that fertilization occurs, not in a laboratory dish, but *in vivo,* in the woman's body. Eggs and sperm samples are injected into the fallopian tubes, where it is hoped they will come together naturally, fertilize, and eventually move down into the uterus.

However, Ricardo H. Asch, M.D., who developed the GIFT technique, and Richard P. Marrs, M.D., one of the country's leading IVF practitioners, point out that in GIFT, there is no way to guarantee that the egg and

ADVANCES ON THE FERTILIZATION FRONT

GIFT Gamete Intra-Fallopian Transfer

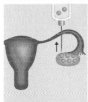

Eggs are collected from the mother-to-be

Ripe eggs, followed by the sperm, are loaded into catheter. An air bubble separates them.

Loading catheter
Air

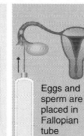

Eggs and sperm are placed in Fallopian tube

ZIFT Zygote Intra-Fallopian Transfer

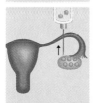

Eggs are collected from the mother-to-be

Ripe eggs are combined with sperm

Fertilization occurs

After 1 day, the zygote (still a single cell) is formed

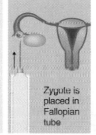

Zygote is placed in Fallopian tube

PREGNANCY AFTER MENOPAUSE

Using In-Vitro Fertilization

Ripe eggs are combined with sperm

Fertilization occurs

After 2 days, multi-celled embryo is removed

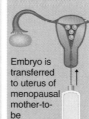

Embryo is transferred to uterus of menopausal mother-to-be

Eggs are collected from a younger woman

OPENING A BLOCKED FALLOPIAN TUBE

A balloon catheter is inflated to clear a passageway for the egg

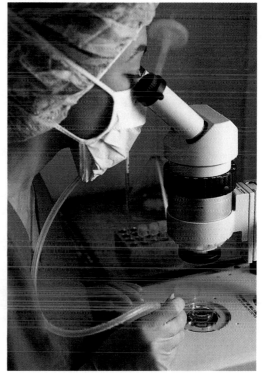

Medical technology has made available a wide range of means (left) for couples who have difficulty conceiving a child to still have a baby. In in vitro fertilization, the embryo (above, being examined) is transferred into the mother within two days of fertilization.

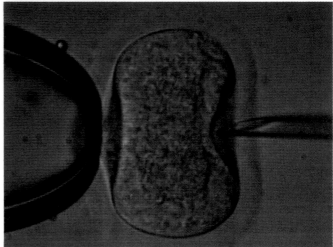

After an egg is extracted from the female donor, it is examined (left) to ascertain its suitability for fertilization. Using exacting microscopic technique, the surface of the egg can be scratched (below) to facilitate sperm entry.

sperm *will* come together. This is a major obstacle in cases where male fertility is the problem, since sperm that are not healthy and viable have less chance of reaching their goal.

A more experimental technique, known as Zygote Intra-Fallopian Transfer (ZIFT), combines the best aspects of IVF and GIFT. As in IVF, the embryo is fertilized outside the body in the laboratory. However, rather than being transferred directly to the uterus, the embryo is transferred to the fallopian tubes, as in the GIFT procedure. The use of the IVF technique, say Drs. Asch and Marrs, allows doctors to confirm that fertilization has actually occurred *before* implantation proceeds, while the GIFT method of transferring the embryo to the fallopian tube rather than to the uterus provides a more natural environment for early embryo development, and gives the uterus time to become more receptive to implantation.

Traditionally, in these *in vitro* fertility cases, the donated egg is from the woman trying to conceive. However, a team of researchers at the University of Southern California (USC) in Los Angeles has found that when women over 40 received eggs donated by younger women, the pregnancy rate was significantly higher than when older women used their own eggs. In fact, the researchers believe that by using the eggs of younger women, the success rate of IVF procedures in the over-40 female can be improved to

match the rate in younger patients. Thus, the theory is that the age of the egg, rather than of the recipient, is the key to ART success.

Low-tech Alternatives

There are still other advances contributing to successful conception and pregnancy among older women, including the crucial ability to pinpoint when a woman is ovulating (and is therefore most fertile). This is particularly critical for older women, whose menstrual cycles tend to be more irregular than those of their younger counterparts. Dr. Frieden points out that it is generally accepted that a woman's cycle is more likely to be irregular after age 44, running perhaps every six to eight weeks instead of the "normal" 28 days.

However, Frieden admits that 44 is an arbitrary cut-off: "Some women's cycles start changing when they're 40, while a 50-year-old may still be quite regular."

One of the oldest methods for tracking ovulation is the Basal Body Temperature chart, in which a woman notes her body temperature every morning. When the charts show that her temperature has gone up several days in a row, it can be assumed she has ovulated (barring any outside reasons for temperature variation, such as colds, insomnia, or indigestion). Newer methods of ovulation detection range from an *endometrial biopsy,* in which a small amount of endometrium is extracted from the uterine cavity and is examined for changes that signal the occurrence of ovulation, to at-home ovulation-prediction kits. The latter are designed to detect luteinizing hormone (LH) in the urine, since there tends to be an LH surge 12 to 44 hours before ovulation.

There are also an almost dizzying number of drugs available to help the older woman conceive. Of the so-called "fertility drugs," perhaps the most widely used is clomiphene citrate (one of the more common brand names is Clomid). It tricks the body into believing there is a shortage of estrogen, thus triggering an increase in both LH and follicle-stimulating hormone (FSH), and spurring the development of the follicle and its egg. Another drug is human menopausal gonadotropin, or hMG (Pergonal), which contains equal amounts of FSH and LH derived from the urine of postmenopausal women. It is designed to stimulate the ovaries to produce several eggs in one cycle.

A drug called FSH contains 75 units of follicle stimulating hormone (also derived from women's urine) and almost negligible amounts of LH. It is designed to stimulate egg production just like clomiphene citrate, but not for fertilization inside the body. Rather, its purpose is to develop eggs that can be used in IVF or other ART procedures. In late 1992 the first successful birth was achieved with a new, artificial version of FSH known as recombinant human follicle-stimulating hormone (r-hFSH). Although Gonal-F (the drug's trade name) is still in clinical trials, the fact that it is genetically engineered seems to offer major advantages in that it can be produced in much purer form and in almost unlimited quantities than if it were naturally occurring.

Gonadotropin-releasing hormone (GnRH) is a hormone that is released every hour or so and that stimulates the pituitary gland to secrete LH and FSH. Several GnRH drugs and GnRH analogs (synthetic hormones similar to GnRH) are currently available. Among the latter is Synarel, which has been approved to manage the pain and other problems of endometriosis.

Pinpointing the Problem

Unfortunately, none of these drugs will work if used improperly. That may sound obvious, but experts agree that many women find themselves being treated in ways that do not address their real problem. If a woman is ovulating normally, for example, there is no point in giving her a drug designed to regulate ovulation. Similarly, since FSH contains so little luteinizing hormone, it will work only in women who naturally produce adequate amounts of LH.

Fortunately, several medical developments are allowing doctors to better determine and treat potential barriers to pregnancy. *Laparoscopy* is a noninvasive technique that allows doctors to check the pelvic organs for problems by simply making an incision below the navel and inserting a long, narrow scope.

Transcervical balloon tuboplasty (TBT) is a new technique being performed by doctors at Chicago's Mt. Sinai Medical Center to clear blocked fallopian tubes. Blocked tubes are the principal cause of 25 to 35 percent of female fertility problems, and, until TBT, the only solution to the problem was either major surgery (an abdominal operation to open the tubes) or IVF. In this new 20-minute procedure, a tiny balloon is inserted into the fallopian tubes; when the balloon is inflated, the tube is cleared.

A variety of medical developments are allowing doctors to better determine and treat barriers to pregnancy.

Strange as it may sound, advances in contraception may also increase the older woman's chances for a successful pregnancy. David A. Grimes, M.D., chief of ambulatory-care services at Women's Hospital in Los Angeles, points out that today's birth-control pills, and even the new copper IUD (known as ParaGard T380A), allow an almost immediate return to fertility, unlike older methods, with which women sometimes waited anywhere up to a year before their ovulatory cycle returned to normal.

Prenatal Screening

Another area that has seen major advances is in the screening processes that can detect possible birth defects. Whatever one thinks of the process of abortion, the fact remains that for some parents, it is too heartbreaking to carry a baby to term and then see it die within a relatively short period of time. And if the pregnancy is to be terminated, it is generally acknowledged that there are fewer risks to the mother if it is done within the first trimester. However, the test most people have heard of, *amniocentesis,* does not allow that option. An "amnio" involves drawing a small amount of fluid from the amniotic sac and testing for signs of Down syndrome and other genetic diseases —but this procedure can't be done until the 13th or even 16th week of pregnancy. Results take another two to three weeks to develop. Thus, if the fetus does carry a birth defect, one that might encourage the parents to terminate the pregnancy, that step cannot be taken until a woman is well into her second trimester.

The health of today's would-be older moms plays a major role in their successful pregnancies.

Today women can check on the health of their babies much earlier, thanks to *chorionic villus sampling* (CVS). This test can be done when a woman is only 9½ to 10 weeks pregnant. Results usually take no more than a week, so decisions can be made in the first trimester. CVS also allows the woman who chooses to carry a child with a health problem to term to find the special care she and her baby will need much earlier in her pregnancy.

A still newer procedure called *embryo biopsy* seems to spare high-risk couples the heartbreaking task of choosing between termination and giving birth to a child who would probably have a circumscribed life span. The technique was pioneered in the United States by doctors at New York Hospital–Cornell Medical Center in Manhattan, including Jamie Grifo, M.D., Ph.D., assistant professor of obstetrics and gynecology. Dr. Grifo explains that this technique allows experts to check embryos fertilized in the laboratory (as part of IVF procedures) for a specific genetic defect, like cystic fibrosis or hemophilia, *before* reimplantation into the mother's womb. Thus, any embryos showing the defect are simply not chosen for reimplantation in the mother. Using this method has reduced the chance of high-risk couples passing along a specific problem to their child from 25 percent to about 1 percent.

Beyond all the drugs, tests, and other hi-tech paraphernalia, improvements in health and attitude among today's would-be older moms continue to play a major role in their successful pregnancies. Julie Tupler, R.N., director of Maternal Fitness, which develops specialized exercise programs for women at different stages of pregnancy, notes that not only is she seeing more women in the 35- and 40-plus age range in her exercise classes, "these women are generally more fit coming into our classes than women used to be. I had a woman in her 40s who did 100 sit-ups a week before she delivered!"

Finally, psychiatrist Magda Polenz, M.D., notes one of the most important advantages older women have on their side: "They tend to want their children." These pregnancies, says Dr. Polenz, have been planned very carefully; these women have generally arranged some sort of support system to help relieve the stresses of motherhood, and they're usually more ready financially to support a child.

"Why not spend your middle years raising a child?" Dr. Polenz asks. "If a baby is wanted, that tends to make you a better parent." Besides, she concludes, men have long become fathers even in their fifties and sixties. Why shouldn't women have the opportunity for late-life parenthood, too? ◇

THE EYE EXAMINATION:
Peering Through The Body's Window

by Aubin Tyler

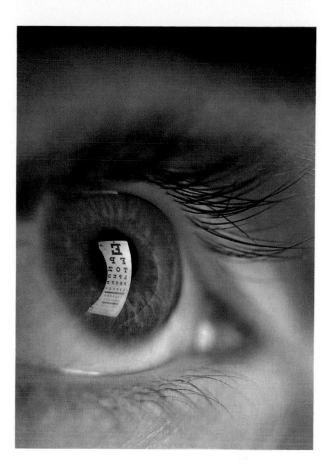

Jane, a 26-year-old computer programmer, hadn't been to an eye doctor in three or four years. But lately she seems to be having trouble reading the highway signs on her way to work. She scheduled an appointment for an eye examination. Jane suspected that her nearsightedness had grown worse since her last checkup, and she probably needed a new prescription.

As in Jane's case, most people visit the eye doctor because they think they need new eyeglasses. They might be surprised to learn that an eye examination does far more than determine the needed strength of eyeglasses or contact lenses. Because the eye is connected to the brain and blood-vessel system, the eye exam may provide the first clues to a problem that threatens not only vision, but the patient's life itself. Such disorders as diabetes, high blood pressure, arteriosclerosis, brain tumor, multiple sclerosis, kidney disease, blood disease, and even infections such as AIDS are often first diagnosed in what seems like a routine eye exam.

The Eye Exam

The History. Jane's ophthalmologist (a physician specializing in the eye) starts with a complete medical history to establish her current complaint—worsening distance vision—as well as the state of her overall health. Is she a diabetic? Is there any family history of high blood pressure? What about

allergy or past history of eye surgery or eye disease? Is she taking any medications?

The External Eye. The actual exam begins with an inspection of the outside of the eyes, the eyelids, and surrounding skin. Changes in those areas can indicate thyroid disease, strokes, or tumors of the brain or eye socket. But more characteristic are minor problems, such as the inflammation, crusting, and dandruff of *blepharitis,* an infection of the eyelids treatable with drops or ointments. A *sty* is a small pimple or boil on the eyelid caused by infection of the eyelash follicle or oil gland. Warm compresses applied for 10 minutes, three or four times a day, or an antibiotic ointment usually help symptoms subside.

The Cornea and Conjunctiva. A device called a *slit lamp* illuminates and magnifies the eye. It is used to examine the thin membrane covering the eye and lids, the *conjunctiva,* as well as the *cornea,* the transparent "window" of the eye directly in front of the colored portion, the *iris.* The pigmented iris controls the amount of light that enters the eye. Its opening, called the *pupil,* is controlled by involuntary muscles. The *lens,* behind the iris, expands and contracts to focus light rays from outside objects onto the *retina,* which transmits the image to the *optic nerve* and onto the brain. The *sclera* makes up the tough white part of the eye.

Conjunctivitis, or "pinkeye," is caused by allergy or infection (either bacterial or viral) affecting the conjunctiva. Characterized by a red, irritated eye, it is common in children and spreads easily through schools and daycare centers. It can even be spread by using old or borrowed eye makeup. Antibiotic eye drops clear most infections within a week.

Corneal infection and ulcers may be caused by bacteria or viruses. Compared to viral infections, bacterial infections tend to produce more outward symptoms, such as pus. If infection leads to an ulcer, it resembles a whitish abrasion on the eye. In either case, the cornea is painful, the eye is pink or red, and vision behind the area of the ulcer is blurred. Branch-shaped ulcers caused by the *herpes simplex* virus are sometimes visible only after coating the eye with fluorescein, a yellow dye that highlights abrasions or ulcers as green

areas when light is focused on the eye. Prompt treatment with antibacterial or antiviral drops prevents corneal scarring.

The glands inside the upper lids secrete tears every few seconds, which moisten and clean the eye with every blink. Dry, irritated eyes are caused by low tear production, which occurs with age, especially after menopause, and as a frequent side effect of certain medications, particularly antidepressants and diuretics. Extreme dryness can damage eyes, but "artificial tears" eye drops are an effective solution.

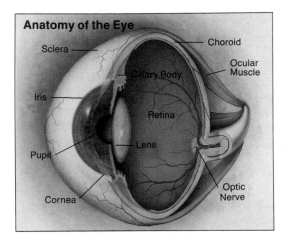

Anatomy of the Eye

Sclera

Choroid

Ocular Muscle

Ciliary Body

Iris

Retina

Lens

Pupil

Optic Nerve

Cornea

During a typical eye examination, the ophthalmologist uses an instrument called a slit lamp (below) to magnify and illuminate various parts of the eye (artwork at right).

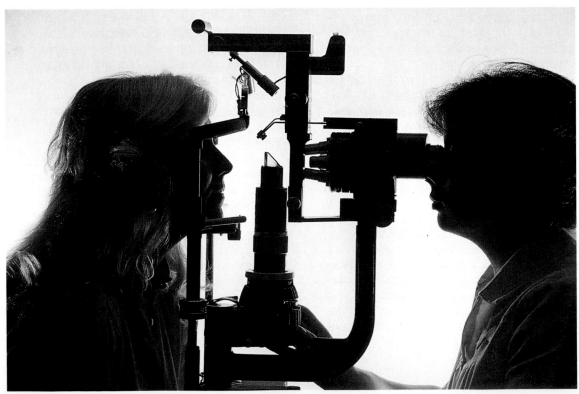

*The great
Roman orator
Cicero once said:
"The keenest of
all our senses is
the sense of
sight."*

The Lens. To fully examine the lens of the eye, the pupil must be widely dilated with drops, such as tropicamide or phenylephrine. Because the drops keep the pupil from constricting, light can be uncomfortable until this effect wears off. A common lens problem, particularly in patients over age 65, is a *cataract,* a clouding of the normally clear crystalline lens, that interferes with vision. While cataracts occur most commonly with age, they can also occur in young people, either at birth, after an eye injury, from exposure to ultraviolet light, or from medications, particularly cortisone. A recent study found that people who worked outdoors or spent much leisure time in the sun heightened their odds of developing cataracts by 50 to 75 percent compared to those who minimized their exposure to the sun; an eightfold risk was associated with topical or oral cortisone.

Forty years ago, cataracts were treated by removing the cloudy lens. The patient then had to rely on extremely thick cataract glasses to see. Experiments using an artificial-lens implant to replace the cloudy lens in cataract patients began in 1949. The late 1970s saw the forerunner of the modern implanted lens, called the *intraocular lens,* which today replaces virtually every cataract removed.

"The results are wonderful today—98 percent successful," says Manus C. Kraff, M.D., professor of clinical ophthalmology at Northwestern University Medical School in Chicago. New procedures like phakoemulsification—breaking up the cataract and suctioning it out of the eye—require only a tiny incision to remove the cataract. Today half or more of all cataracts are removed this way. Since 1986 a hard-silicone lens has been used that can be folded and slipped through an eighth-of-an-inch incision, where it unfolds in the eye. In some cases the incision is so small that stitches are not even required.

Eye Alignment. Normal eye movement depends on six external muscles of each eye.

The doctor tests Jane's eye movements, first moving a pen toward her and away, up and down, and then side to side. He looks to see if the uncovered eye aligns itself, if it follows the pen easily, and if both eyes focus on the moving object.

Strabismus refers to crossed eyes, where one eye is directed too far inward, or walleye, where one eye is directed outward.

Adult strabismus is rare, and usually results from persistent childhood strabismus. Misalignment of the eyes unrelated to a childhood problem can be caused by medical or

Using a complex device that resembles an eyeglass frame, an eye doctor determines the optical correction necessary to bring a patient's vision as close to 20/20 as possible.

neurological conditions, including diabetes, thyroid disease, myasthenia gravis, brain tumors, or strokes. The most common symptom of strabismus is double vision. Others include eyestrain, discomfort while reading, headaches, head tilting, or squinting. Depending on the cause, treatments include eye-muscle exercises, glasses, special lenses called prisms, drugs that paralyze the eye muscle, or eye-muscle surgery.

Refractive Errors. The clear cornea provides about two-thirds of the focusing power of the eye, while the crystalline lens behind the iris provides about one-third. For good

Germs introduced into the eye can cause serious infections, pain, and, in extreme cases, loss of vision. Easily contaminated items like eye makeup and applicators should never be shared.

vision the eye must focus, or "refract," light onto the retina in back of the eye, to send the correct image to the brain. Refractive errors, or errors of focus, are usually caused by differences in the length or shape of the eye.

Myopia, or nearsightedness, occurs because the eye is somewhat elongated, more oval than round, making it difficult for the lens to focus light from distant objects. Vision problems usually show up between the ages of 8 and 12, often when a child can't see the blackboard at school. Eyeglasses or contact lenses easily correct the problem. A new laser-surgery technique to permanently correct nearsightedness, called photorefractive keratectomy (see sidebar, page 51), is now showing promising results for myopic patients in experimental studies.

In *hyperopia,* or farsightedness, the eye is shorter than normal, making it difficult for the lens to focus on close objects. Young children tend to be farsighted, but their lenses are flexible enough to compensate. Crossed eyes in children may be associated with hyperopia, since the eye muscles must contract tightly to see up close. Headaches or lack of interest in reading may be clues that a child

is farsighted. Eyeglasses or contact lenses correct the problem.

In people with *astigmatism,* the front of the eye is warped, resembling a football instead of a basketball. The effect is to distort or blur objects at a distance. Eyeglasses or contact lenses, usually rigid gas-permeable or hard lenses, can correct small amounts of astigmatism. Large amounts can be difficult to correct because the lens tends to wobble on the uneven surface of the cornea. A *toric* lens, specially made for greater stability on an astigmatic eye, sometimes does the trick.

Presbyopia, an inability to shift focus from near to far, literally means "aging eye," and begins in middle age, when the eye's lens loses its near-vision focusing ability. Glasses usually correct the problem.

In Jane's case the problem was worsening myopia. After checking the power in the glasses she had been wearing, her doctor checks Jane's *visual acuity,* or central vision, by having her read the familiar wall chart, or Snellen chart, composed of letters that get smaller and smaller in size. Central vision is determined by the smallest line read at 20 feet. A finding of 20/20 is perfect; 20/40 would mean the last line Jane read at 20 feet could be seen at 40 feet by someone with perfect vision.

Jane's eye doctor fine-tunes the extent of her nearsightedness with a device called a Phoroptor. Resembling a metal "mask," it is used to store trial lenses, which are dialed into position as needed.

The doctor then checks Jane's color vision by having her read a series of cards composed of colored dots. He also tests her depth perception by having Jane wear special three-dimensional glasses to look at a series of letters and images. In people with normal vision, the images "pop out" from the card.

Retinal Disorders. Behind the lens is the vitreous chamber, which is filled with a clear, gel-like material called the *vitreous humor,* or vitreous body. Lining the back of the vitreous chamber is the *retina,* the light-sensitive tissue composed of the *rod* and *cone* cells that perceive light and color. Rod and cone cells in the retina convert light to electrical impulses, which are then carried to the brain by the *optic nerve.* The retina is nourished by the *choroid,* a layer of blood vessels underneath it.

To make sure that Jane's optic nerve and her retina and its blood vessels and nerves are healthy, the doctor uses a hand-held device with a bright light called an *ophthalmoscope* to look directly inside her eye. Diseases such as high blood pressure or diabetes, both of which cause bleeding or leaking blood vessels, can show up first in the eye.

In middle age and beyond, shrinkage of the vitreous body causes a tugging on the attached retina, creating small retinal holes or tears. Once torn, fluid leaks behind the retina, peeling it away from its moorings, a condition known as *retinal detachment.* Occasionally a blow to the eye can also cause the retina to detach. Retinal detachment occurs in one out of every 10,000 people in the United States. The sudden appearance of spots or flashes of light may signal vitreous shrinkage and retinal tears (under less ominous circumstances, harmless bits of vitreous, or *floaters,* can also drift across the field of vision). Some retinal detachments manifest themselves by producing a wavy or watery quality to the vision, or a dark shadow in the side vision. If the retina is torn but not yet detached, lasering or freezing the area can often seal the tear. In the case of detachment, the sooner the retina is reattached, the better the chance to regain vision. Excellent vision is regained in only about 40 percent of successfully reattached retinas. If the retina cannot be reattached, vision in that eye is lost.

Another disease of the retina, *diabetic retinopathy,* blinds 8,000 diabetics every year. It damages the retina's blood vessels, causing them to leak, bleed, and scar, which distorts or obscures vision. About 80 percent of people with a 15-year history of diabetes have some blood-vessel damage in their retina. Serious retinopathy can be present without symptoms, underscoring the importance of regular eye exams. *Fluorescein angiography* uses dye to produce detailed pictures of the retinal vessels.

Laser surgery can prevent or retard vision loss from diabetic retinopathy by sealing leaking vessels. And a recently reported 12-

Laser Sculpting: A Cure For Nearsightedness?

Almost anyone who's ever worn contact lenses or eyeglasses dreams of one day being able to throw them away. Technology is cashing in on that dream with a new laser technique that reshapes the cornea, inducing perfect or near-perfect vision. Called photorefractive keratectomy (PRK), the computer-guided procedure uses a 30-second blast from an excimer laser to sand off tiny amounts of tissue on the front of the eye, flattening the cornea and eliminating nearsightedness.

Although only a few thousand eyes have been treated with PRK in experimental trials in the United States, 85 percent display 20/40 vision or better at six months—good enough to drive without glasses. The results show that PRK is at least as good as its surgical cousin, radial keratotomy, which flattens the cornea with a series of cuts in the eye resembling the spokes of a wheel. But those cuts may weaken the eye, making it vulnerable to rupture.

Although the technique is being tried in cases of astigmatism, "there are still bugs to be worked out," says Peter McDonnell, M.D., associate professor or ophthalmology at the University of Southern California (USC) in Los Angeles. He has performed the procedure in several hundred patients enrolled in an experimental trial. Some complain of a temporary haze after the procedure. Ophthalmologists can't guarantee 20/20 vision, and no one knows for sure what the long-term aftereffects will be. Manhattan ophthalmologist Barry Belgorod, M.D., who has patented his own laser-sculpting device that uses a dome-shaped beam to reshape the eye, believes current techniques don't offer sufficient precision. He says: "If its promise is fulfilled, it's a brave new world, but I don't think we're there yet."

year study of early-onset diabetes suggests that insulin-dependent youngsters who maintain near-normal blood-sugar levels had a decreased likelihood of developing diabetic eye disease as adults.

High blood pressure can also cause hemorrhages and scarring in the retina, mirroring more-serious changes elsewhere, typically in the heart and kidneys. Lowering the blood pressure often corrects visual problems.

The macula is a small area of the retina responsible for fine details of central vision. Aging of blood vessels in the macula reduces blood flow, producing macular degeneration in which a painless blur develops in the center of one or both eyes. Colors appear faded, and objects look distorted in size and shape; peripheral or side vision is unaffected.

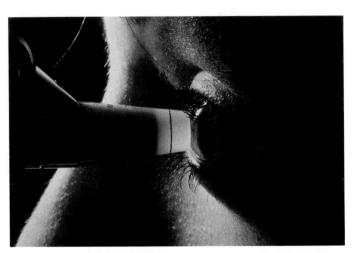

The pressure inside the eyes should be measured regularly to permit early detection of glaucoma. An instrument called a tonometer (above) is used in this essential part of the eye exam.

Light-eyed individuals are more often afflicted, as are smokers and those with high blood pressure or coronary-artery disease. For the most common type of macular degeneration, known as the "dry" form, the cause is unknown, and there is no treatment. The wet type—associated with the growth of abnormal new blood vessels—is rarer and potentially more serious, but, like diabetic retinopathy, it is often amenable to laser surgery. Recent research suggests that removing certain scar-damaged retinal cells may

allow new growth and restore vision, but those results are still preliminary.

Glaucoma. Behind the cornea is the anterior chamber, containing the aqueous humor, a clear liquid that cushions impact to the eye. If the tiny ducts that deliver the aqueous humor are blocked, the buildup of pressure damages the optic nerve and impairs peripheral vision, resulting in glaucoma, and ultimately, blindness, if the problem is not discovered and treated early. A *glaucoma test* is done with a device called a *tonometer,* attached to the slit-lamp microscope, which measures pressure in the eye.

"Glaucoma is a disease of attrition, as the part of the eye that regulates pressure fails to work with age," notes Dirk Dijkstal, M.D., associate clinical professor of ophthalmology, University of Wyoming in Cheyenne. "It hardly ever hits before age 40, but then shows a doubling every 10 years." African-Americans have a higher incidence of glaucoma, and it's harder to control pressure in eyes that are darkly pigmented.

Glaucoma is the leading cause of blindness in the U.S., estimated to affect between 2 million and 3 million Americans. It is responsible for 15 percent of blindness in adults. The most common type of glaucoma, *chronic open-angle glaucoma,* occurs in both eyes. "Symptoms are rare," says Dr. Dijkstal. "It just eats away at the periphery of vision." *Acute narrow-angle glaucoma* accounts for 10 percent or less of cases, but symptoms are impossible to ignore: the eye becomes hard, red, and so painful that nausea and vomiting may occur. Medication and eye drops can prevent further loss of vision.

Fortunately for Jane, she passed her eye examination with flying colors. She did need somewhat stronger glasses, however, to read all those highway signs perfectly. The ophthalmologist also reassured Jane that she showed no signs of glaucoma, cataracts, or diabetes, and that her depth and color perception were perfect. Jane was decidedly upbeat when she left the doctor's office. She wasn't exactly sure why, but, more than ever before, Jane felt a keen awareness of that miracle we call vision.   ◇

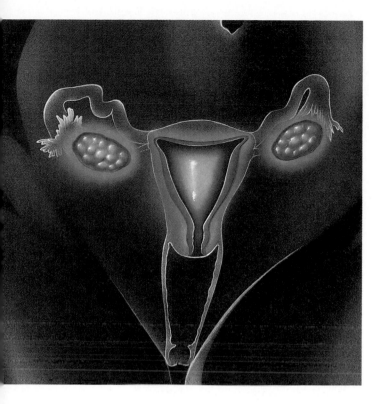

Pelvic Inflammatory Disease

by Janet C. Tate

L aura, age 25, had been dating Stephen for three years. She knew Stephen had briefly seen an old girlfriend during that time. Later, when Laura began to run a fever and to experience pelvic pain and symptoms of a bladder infection, including painful urination, she had no idea that the two occurrences could be related. Then came her gynecologist's diagnosis: pelvic inflammatory disease (PID). Like many women who find themselves in this predicament, Laura was horrified—and surprised—to learn that her condition was sexually related.

She's not alone in her confusion. Indeed, pelvic inflammatory disease can be puzzling even for doctors to pinpoint. Yet symptoms

related to PID bring more than 1 million women a year to the doctor for diagnosis and treatment. Some experts put the number of American women who will suffer from PID during their childbearing years at 1 in 10.

But Laura was lucky in several respects: she experienced some of PID's telltale symptoms early on—many women who have PID are asymptomatic. And Laura's gynecologist was well aware of the often-elusive signs of the disease. After her doctor performed a bacterial culture, he prescribed a cephalosporin shot followed by a one-week, twice-a-day round of the antibiotic doxycycline, after which Laura had no recurring physical symptoms or problems from the infection. Unfortunately, many cases of PID go undetected in the early stages, and it's the often-devastating consequences of such infections that tell the real story of PID.

What is PID?

Pelvic inflammatory disease is a sexually transmitted disease that infects the fallopian tubes, the endometrium (the lining of the uterus), and the uterus. It can also involve the ovaries and the perineum (the intra-abdominal cavity). It is a rather broad term that is used to define the various degrees and levels of infection in those organs, one-half to two-thirds of which involve the bacterial organisms *Chlamydia trachomatis* and *Neisseria gonorrhoeae*. "Women who have gonorrhea or chlamydia infections are going to have higher rates of PID," observes Jorge D. Blanco, M.D., professor and vice-chairman of the department of obstetrics, gynecology, and reproductive sciences at the University of Texas Medical School in Houston.

"It takes awhile for those organisms to grow, multiply, and then ascend from the cervix—which is usually the first site of infection—into the endometrium and to the fallopian tubes. That's why it not only affects different organs, but also presents itself in different stages or different ways, depending on how far it has been allowed to progress."

Pelvic inflammatory disease—or PID—often goes undetected in its early stages.

Understanding PID

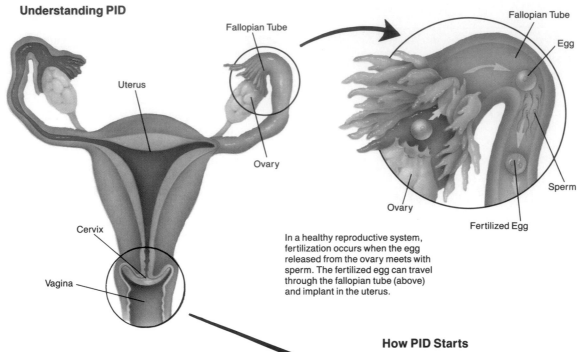

Uterus

Fallopian Tube

Ovary

Cervix

Vagina

Fallopian Tube

Egg

Sperm

Ovary

Fertilized Egg

In a healthy reproductive system, fertilization occurs when the egg released from the ovary meets with sperm. The fertilized egg can travel through the fallopian tube (above) and implant in the uterus.

How PID Starts

Disease-causing bacteria, such as chlamydia and gonorrhea, enter the vagina during sexual intercourse and attach to the cervix. The bacteria eventually pass through the cervix and spread into the uterus, fallopian tubes, or ovaries, causing scarring, abscesses, or a blocked fallopian tube.

PID occurs when bacteria move beyond the cervix opening

Bacteria adhere to the cervix

Bacteria enter the vagina

Symptoms and Diagnosis

In the 1960s and 1970s, a definitive diagnosis of PID was relatively difficult to make. "We were all tuned in to patients who were severely ill—they had to have high fevers, a lot of pain, and be very sick before we would recognize the disease and treat it," Blanco observes. "We now understand that some women may have fairly mild pain, perhaps no fever at all, and yet have a lot of damage done to their pelvic organs."

Indeed, the symptoms of PID lead many physicians to initially suspect a urinary-tract infection or even appendicitis: abdominal pain, specific-site tenderness, fever, or pain when using the bathroom. Upon examination, all a doctor sees might be signs of infection in the cervix and the urethra. There is no simple, unmistakable test, such as a blood or urine analysis, to precisely diagnose the disease before it advances to its more destructive stages.

PID's elusive nature leads many physicians to diagnose the disease by means of laparoscopy, a procedure in which a thin, lighted tube is inserted into the abdomen through a small incision to closely examine the pelvic organs. Although highly revealing, laparoscopy cannot be done during a routine office visit—it is a procedure that requires

hospitalization and anesthesia. And it is not foolproof—even with laparoscopy, a young woman's reproductive organs may appear normal, and gonorrhea or chlamydia infections may not be diagnosed until bacterial cultures are performed. Laparoscopy is also expensive, and, as with any surgical procedure, there could be complications arising from the procedure itself. In 1983 diagnostic guidelines were adopted by the Infectious Disease Society of Obstetricians and Gynecologists to help physicians make a specific diagnosis of PID without having to resort to laparoscopic techniques.

One new diagnostic tool more doctors are using is an endometrial biopsy. In this procedure a small tube is inserted through the cervix during a pelvic exam to remove a sample of the endometrial lining. Signs of infection that are apparent from the sample have been found to be consistent with findings of PID obtained through laparoscopy.

Results of the Disease

A severe episode of PID can be life-threatening. The pelvis may develop pockets of pus, known as tubo-ovarian abscesses, which usually heal once treated. But in a small percentage of cases, these abscesses can rupture, releasing pus into the abdominal cavity. Such an episode can be fatal if not treated immediately. On rare occasions, when an abscess ruptures, surgery will be required to drain and remove the abscess or perhaps even remove all the pelvic organs.

Left unchecked, PID can eventually cause inflammation in the fallopian tubes and uterus, and it is considered a leading cause of ectopic pregnancies in which the infection-scarred fallopian tube retains the fertilized egg instead of releasing it to enter the uterus. Eventually the fallopian tube could rupture and create massive bleeding that would require surgery to correct. "There are still some women who die from ectopic pregnancy," says Blanco. It is estimated that women who have had PID have six times the rate of ectopic pregnancy as women who haven't. Also, scarring from prior infection can lead to chronic pelvic pain.

But perhaps the most prevalent complication of PID is infertility, which can result when PID damages the lining of the fallopian tubes enough to prevent the egg and the sperm from uniting because of occlusion (or "closing up") of the tubes.

Who Gets It

Women get PID from infected partners—the bacteria pass from an infected male through the woman's cervix and into her reproductive organs. Seventy percent of women who ac-

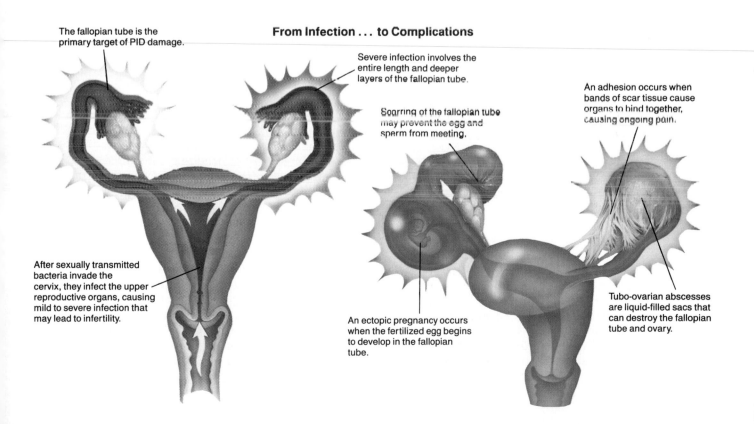

From Infection . . . to Complications

The fallopian tube is the primary target of PID damage.

Severe infection involves the entire length and deeper layers of the fallopian tube.

An adhesion occurs when bands of scar tissue cause organs to bind together, causing ongoing pain.

Scarring of the fallopian tube may prevent the egg and sperm from meeting.

After sexually transmitted bacteria invade the cervix, they infect the upper reproductive organs, causing mild to severe infection that may lead to infertility.

An ectopic pregnancy occurs when the fertilized egg begins to develop in the fallopian tube.

Tubo-ovarian abscesses are liquid-filled sacs that can destroy the fallopian tube and ovary.

quire pelvic inflammatory disease are under age 25. Most have had multiple sex partners and started having sex at an early age. Some studies suggest that women who douche frequently are at higher risk for PID.

How It Is Treated

Usually a dose of cephalosporin followed by a 10-day to two-week round of antibiotics will clear up PID in its early stages. Doxycycline, which Laura's doctor prescribed, is one of the more common antibiotics used to combat chlamydia, but some newer, one-dose-only antibiotics are being used successfully. "If we recognize the disease and catch it early enough, we can treat the acute episode with antibiotics and make the woman better. The main problem with PID is its aftermath. After you've had the acute illness, you are predisposed to having certain complications," notes Blanco. One of the most prevalent and serious of those is infertility, and the more episodes of PID you have, the greater your chances of becoming infertile.

It is also essential that a PID sufferer's male sex partners be treated with antibiotics to stop the spread of the infection. In 1989 the Centers for Disease Control and Prevention (CDC) issued recommendations for the treatment of PID, but some studies suggest that these guidelines aren't followed thoroughly enough, and that the infection is misdiagnosed or missed altogether in as many as 50 percent of all cases seen by physicians.

Some experimental treatments for PID are examining new approaches to deal with the disease's repercussions. Some researchers note that the bacteria that cause PID are only partially responsible for the resulting damage; that, in fact, our own immune defenses, in trying to kill the bacteria, inflict damage of their own to the reproductive organs. These researchers are investigating whether agents that prevent or modulate the immune response might also help reduce the disease's damaging effects.

The Role of Contraceptives

At least one recent study found that women had a lowered risk of acquiring PID when they used oral contraceptives. Another form of PID, known as pelvic actinomycosis, caused by the normally harmless oral bacteria *Actinomyces,* can grow on IUDs and cause infection. (In at least one case, such an IUD user subsequently had to have a hysterectomy.) Other studies report that IUD wearers stand a higher risk of acquiring PID during the first three weeks after the device has been inserted. It is recommended that women who have already had pelvic inflammatory disease not use IUDs, since those who have already had one episode are at higher risk to have another. ◇

Up to one-quarter of the women in the photo above have had at least one episode of incontinence; so have 10 percent of the men. Fortunately, treatments are available to remedy this problem.

CONQUERING INCONTINENCE

by Barbara Alden Wilson

Just about anyone watching television advertisements these days might assume that urinary incontinence is just simply one more unavoidable condition of aging—especially for women. And, with understandable trepidation, many younger women expect some incontinence as a natural result of childbirth. But wearing a form of clothing protection—such as adult diapers—and trying to live with incontinence is *not* the way to handle this often embarrassing problem.

Defining the Problem

"There's no medical definition of when you should start to worry about urinary-leakage problems," says Tamara Bavendam, M.D., assistant professor of urology at the University of Washington School of Medicine in Seattle. But there should be no reason to delay a visit to a physician for help. Bavendam stresses, "Even if the incontinence can't be cured, it can be helped if the patient is motivated."

Women vs. Men, Stress vs. Urge

That's good news for the more than 10 million Americans, most of them elderly, who must deal with an incontinence problem. Women are more prone to incontinence than men are, mainly because the continence mechanism—the sphincter muscle that controls the urethra, the tube through which urine flows to leave the body—is held in more delicate balance with the internal organs than in men. This balance can be disrupted during childbirth, when a great deal of pressure is exerted on the bladder and the sphincter muscle. In men an internal sphincter muscle provides an additional mechanism to keep men from urinating at an inappropriate time. These anatomical facts help explain why more than 25 percent of women between the ages of 30 and 59 have had at least one episode of incontinence, according to the U.S. Public Health Service. Fewer than 10 percent of men in the same age group report such incidents. Often, isolated or in-

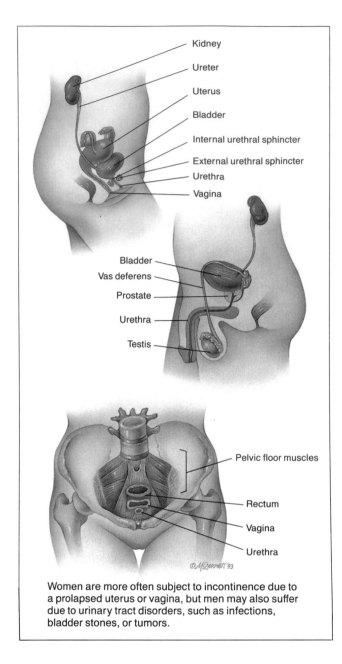

Kidney

Ureter

Uterus

Bladder

Internal urethral sphincter

External urethral sphincter

Urethra

Vagina

Bladder

Vas deferens

Prostate

Urethra

Testis

Pelvic floor muscles

Rectum

Vagina

Urethra

Women are more often subject to incontinence due to a prolapsed uterus or vagina, but men may also suffer due to urinary tract disorders, such as infections, bladder stones, or tumors.

Stress incontinence occurs when the urethral muscles can't close tightly enough to hold back urine when pressure is applied to the bladder. Ordinary events such as laughing, sneezing, and the like may all trigger urinary leakage as the abdomen presses on the bladder. Urge incontinence, named for the afflicted person's desperate physical urge to urinate, occurs when the person cannot hold the urine back long enough to reach the privacy of a bathroom. This type of incontinence is believed to come from the bladder having a spasm when it should be relaxed. Stress, urge, or the two combined (often referred to as "mixed incontinence") are responsible for about 85 percent of incontinence problems.

What Causes Incontinence?

The stress of pregnancy and childbirth on the bladder and urethra is not the only reason for urinary incontinence in women. With age the skeletal muscles of a woman's pelvic floor lose elasticity, regardless of whether she has ever given birth, simply because she does not use the pelvic muscles regularly. Because these muscles help hold back urine, it's no wonder that older women are more likely than younger women to develop leakage problems. Slack pelvic muscles let the urethra sag while the bladder also drops. The bladder, instead of filling and expanding upward, fills sideways and downward. The bladder's unnatural position and the incorrect angle of the urethra make stress incontinence all but inevitable.

Another cause of female incontinence is the urethra's sensitivity to hormones. During pregnancy, menopause, or before menstruation, the stretchy tissue of the urethra may soften. At these times the urethra may be unable to tighten enough to stop urine flow.

In some rare cases, male incontinence is an unwelcome result of prostate surgery. Experts vary in opinion about how likely a man is to experience postoperative incontinence: estimates range from less than 1 percent to 10 percent of all men who undergo such surgery. Usually, pelvic-muscle exercise and other nonsurgical treatment lessens the problem considerably, if it doesn't clear up on its own, Bavendam says.

termittent episodes of leakage occur during exercise, coughing, sneezing, or other events that cause the abdomen to press down on the bladder.

If such an episode happens when the bladder is very full, it's usually not a cause for concern. But if urine leaks almost every time a person does something to make the abdomen press on the bladder—even when the bladder is not full—a doctor should perform an exam for the possible culprit, usually either *stress incontinence* or *urge incontinence.*

In both women and men, various types of irritation or inflammation cause incontinence. The organs that may be affected include: the bladder, with a condition called cystitis; the urethra, with urethritis; in women, the vagina, with vaginitis; and in men, the prostate, with prostatitis. A number of other factors may also be the culprits: a urinary-tract infection; certain drugs, such as sedatives and sleeping pills, diuretics (water pills), decongestants, and antidepressants; an endocrine imbalance such as hyperglycemia; a bladder stretched from repeated "holding back" of urine; fecal impaction; depression; or a neuromuscular disorder caused by such illnesses as Parkinson's disease or multiple sclerosis.

To find the cause of accidental urine leakage, it's best to see one's doctor first for an initial evaluation. "The majority of people who have episodes of incontinence don't ever tell their doctors or a health-care professional," says Kathryn L. Burgio, Ph.D., associate professor of urology and director of the continence program at the University of Alabama in Birmingham. "They need to realize that incontinence is not normal and help is available." If the family doctor feels a specialist's training is necessary to get to the root of the problem, he or she can recommend a urologist, gynecologist (for women), or geriatrician—a physician who specializes in the treatment of older adults.

The Doctor Visit

The physician first will take a medical history that includes a description of all symptoms, how often they have occurred, and what medications are being taken. He or she will then perform a physical exam. The abdomen will be examined by pressing on it to look for enlargement of the bladder or a mass in this area.

For women, the doctor will perform a vaginal exam to check for a variety of physical problems, including the possibility that the bladder is pressing against the vaginal wall, the urethra is situated at an incorrect angle, or the pelvic muscles are weak. Both women and men must be examined rectally to test the tone of the anal sphincter muscle and its strength. The physician will also feel for any tumorous masses or a fecal impaction—a mass of stool that stays packed in the lower bowel and won't pass normally, irritating or completely blocking the urethra. In men the doctor will check the size and firmness of the prostate gland.

Part of the exam may include the patient being asked to cough, bounce on his or her heels, walk, or bend over while the physician checks for urine leakage due to stress incontinence. The doctor will also test the patient's reflexes to see if a neurological disorder is to blame. The patient's urine will be analyzed to show whether an infection is present. Blood may also be sampled to test for sugar, calcium, and how well the kidneys are working.

Even after all of this, further testing may be necessary for the doctor to diagnose the problem and recommend treatment. Whatever the type of incontinence, there is more than one treatment method.

Uncommon Causes of Incontinence

While stress, urge, or "mixed" incontinence account for most cases of urinary leakage, 15 percent of cases are due to the very rare cases of overflow incontinence, total incontinence, or functional incontinence. Overflow incontinence occurs when the bladder cannot empty properly, either because the bladder is unable to contract strongly enough or because the urethra is blocked. Total incontinence means all control of urination is lost, and urine leaks almost all of the time. This condition is usually caused by a bladder fistula (a hole in the wall of the bladder that allows urine to flow out continuously), an injury to the urethra, or an ectopic ureter (a ureter entering the bladder too close to the urethra or into the vagina in women). Functional incontinence stems from impaired mobility, depression, or severe dementia, which produces an inability or unwillingness to use the toilet appropriately.

Bed-wetting: A Problem Some People Never Outgrow

With children, bed-wetting is often chalked up to immaturity; most kids outgrow it by age 6. But there are mature adults—fully functional members of society—who are still plagued by this embarrassing problem. Experts estimate that about 1 percent of the adult population deals with the condition, also called nocturnal enuresis, on a regular basis. Adult bed-wetting seems to run in families and is more common in men. But the cause of the problem varies. Some cases can be traced to bladder, prostate, or undiagnosed neurological problems, all of which are treatable. An "irritable bladder" may also be to blame. This condition makes the bladder seem full even when it holds only a small amount of urine, causing a feeling of intense pressure to release the urine. Bed-wetters may want to avoid carbonated beverages, alcohol, caffeine, chocolate, and any foods or beverages that are acidic or spicy, all of which can aggravate an irritable bladder.

Kegel exercises to strengthen the pelvic muscles may be of some help. And some therapists recommend conditioning or behavioral therapy, such as alarms that wake up the patient when sensors detect the first sign of moisture on the bed.

An antidiuretic hormone called desmopressin acetate, or DDAVP, reduces urine production and has been used successfully by many adult bed-wetters over the past five years. Experts caution that it doesn't work for everyone, however, and should be considered a treatment but not a cure.

For more information about adult bed-wetting, contact The National Enuresis Society, P.O. Box 6351, Parsippany, NJ 07054.

Treatment Options

The major options for treating urinary incontinence are exercise, behavioral training, medication, and surgery. Of course, it is up to the doctor and patient to discuss the benefits and possible risks, if any, involved with each method before deciding which would be best. These are the options:

Exercise. For mild to moderate stress incontinence, exercises to strengthen the pelvic muscles can be very effective. Kegel exercises, named for A. H. Kegel, M.D., the gynecologist who developed them in 1948, can be helpful to both women and men—especially men who have post–prostate surgery problems, according to Bavendam—if they are done correctly. The key is to locate the correct muscles to exercise and to keep exercising them regularly, even after the incontinence problem is under control. "Too often, patients stop doing the exercises once they don't have any more leakage problems because they think they're cured," Bavendam says. "But the pelvic muscles are just like any other muscles that become stronger with exercise: Once you stop exercising them, they slacken again."

Specialists can teach various techniques for finding the correct muscles to use to perform the Kegel exercises properly. Another option for women is to use Kegel-exercise training weights. These tampon-shaped graduated weights—about 2 inches long—are inserted into the vagina to give the woman something to squeeze, ensuring that she is working and strengthening the correct muscles. These weights—marketed under the name Femina—may be available through the physician's office, or a patient may contact the Dacomed Corporation (1701 East 79th Street, Minneapolis, MN 55425) for price and ordering information.

Behavioral Training and Biofeedback. When incontinence is caused by inappropriate habits rather than a physical problem, behavioral training will be more effective than exercising alone. Behavioral training involves learning to lengthen the time between urinations and to ease bladder spasms. Another type of tactic, called habit training, deals with scheduling the times to void at shorter intervals than those when accidents had previously happened. In some cases, biofeedback is an effective tool for improving bladder function. In this case, visual or auditory feedback is used in conjunction with urination to teach better control.

Medication. With urge incontinence the bladder contracts when it shouldn't. Several available drugs improve bladder control by keeping the bladder relaxed, reducing the feeling of urgency and the likelihood of urine loss. Among these drugs are dicyclomine, flavoxate, imipramine, oxybutynin, and propantheline, all sold under several brand names. Women with urge incontinence that occurs following menopause or after a hysterectomy may also benefit from estrogen.

For stress incontinence, certain drugs may help strengthen the sphincter muscle by causing the pelvic muscles to contract. Such drugs include imipramine, phenylpropanolamine, and pseudoephedrine, all marketed under various brand names. Estrogen may be prescribed in conjunction with one of these medications for postmenopausal women with stress incontinence, since some experts believe estrogen helps keep the pelvic muscles strong.

Surgery. Surgery may be the most effective option when stress incontinence becomes severe. In men, stress incontinence following a prostatectomy (removal of all or part of the prostate) is usually caused by injury to the sphincter, making it unable to close tightly enough to prevent urine leakage. The surgical placement of an inflatable artificial sphincter can stop stress incontinence in 70 to 90 percent of men, according to Burgio, R. Lynette Pearce, R.N., C.R.N.P., and Angelo Lucco, M.D., in their book *Staying Dry: A Practical Guide to Bladder Control* (The Johns Hopkins University Press, 1989). This procedure is also an option for women with stress incontinence due to similar sphincter problems.

Women seeking surgery to correct stress incontinence caused by muscles too slack to support the bladder usually undergo one of three operations: the Kelly procedure, where an incision is made in the vagina to perform the surgery; the Marshall-Marchetti-Krantz procedure, performed through an incision in the abdomen; or the Stamey procedure, in which small incisions are made in the abdomen and in the vagina. All three types of surgery restore the bladder and urethra to a normal anatomical position.

Laparoscopic surgery offers a viable alternative for many incontinent women. In such a procedure, two needles, inserted at the pubic hairline, are used to wind stitches around the vaginal wall, pulling it up higher. The vaginal wall thus reinforces the muscles surrounding the bladder and urethra, providing the bladder the extra support it needs during physical exertion to prevent urinary leakage. The surgery uses local anesthesia, lasts only 30 to 60 minutes, requires only a two-day hospitalization in most cases (compared to possibly seven days for the other surgical options), and a shortened recovery time—10 days versus 12 weeks. Bavendam cautions, however, "This surgery may not be applicable for many women. And the clinical experience in women is still limited and thus far may not be widely available."

New Findings About an Old Treatment

Another procedure for stress incontinence, periurethral injection, was in use for more than 20 years until problems with it surfaced. The procedure involves injecting Teflon into the tissues surrounding the urethra to help it close. Recently, however, Teflon particles have been found in the lungs of some recipients of the injections. Long-term effects of Teflon in the body are not yet known, and the procedure has been put on hold until further studies are performed. Studies substituting collagen for the Teflon are still being conducted. Researchers are also considering human body fat as a possible substitute for the Teflon. Patients who have already had periurethral injections should consult their physicians about any health concerns.   ◇

For more information contact:

HIP (Help for Incontinent People)
P.O. Box 544
Union, SC 29379
1-800-252-3337

The Simon Foundation for Continence
P.O. Box 835
Wilmette, IL 60091
1-800-237-4666

Housecalls

by George Valko, M.D.

Q *I've heard about the technology called PET scanning that can actually take pictures of the brain performing certain activities. What is PET used for?*

A PET stands for *Positron Emission Tomography.* In order to image a particular site of the body, the patient is injected with an isotope of nuclear material attached to some other substance designed to coalesce at the desired location. The nuclear material emits gamma rays. An array of receivers on the imaging machine detects these rays, and a high-speed computer puts the information together to form an image. Specialists in nuclear medicine are already performing these scans to help patients, although many nuclear-medicine applications are still investigational.

PET can detect processes in motion, such as flow of blood and tissue activity. PET scanning is well suited for analyzing physiological and biochemical events as they are happening. It can, for example, create images of areas of the brain functioning. Nuclear-medicine specialists can stimulate an individual's eyes or ears, and then watch as the message transmits throughout the brain. They can also mea-

PET scans create images that can help medical specialists examine blood flow, discover tumors, or even watch as messages are transmitted throughout the brain.

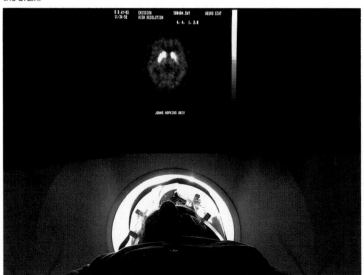

sure changes in blood flow and oxygen levels in the brains of patients who have had a stroke, or see various tumors as a result of the way these masses are able to metabolize sugars.

The technology accomplishes all this by split-second measurement of the gamma particles as they move throughout the cells or system in question. PET scanning may soon find application for evaluating the heart and musculoskeletal areas as well.

Q *My friend has to take antibiotics for a "heart valve" problem every time she goes to the dentist. Why is that?*

A The heart is a specialized muscle consisting of four chambers. Between each set of chambers and between the large chambers and the pulmonary and aortic arteries are one-way valves that help direct the flow of blood. If the valves are damaged by congenital abnormalities or by disease, then bacteria stick to the damaged areas more easily.

During procedures such as dental work, a large number of bacteria can enter the bloodstream, infect the valves, and cause a dangerous illness called bacterial endocarditis. Antibiotics taken before and after the dental procedure lessen the likelihood that this infection will occur.

Q *Do strokes ever strike young people? Why? And are there different kinds of strokes?*

A *Stroke* is a general term for the acute failure of a blood vessel in or near the brain, and for the symptoms that result from it. In one type of stroke, a blood vessel near the brain may narrow over many years. Eventually the vessel becomes blocked, allowing no blood to get through to the brain. In another type of stroke, an artery ruptures and causes significant bleeding into the brain. Whether by pressure or lack of blood, the brain is damaged in both cases.

Older people have the greatest incidence of strokes, which often occur after years of injury to the vascular system from risk factors such as diabetes, hypertension, high cholesterol, or smoking. But strokes do happen to young people, too. Usually these strokes come from congenital weaknesses of the arteries called *aneurysms*, which may occur in certain parts of the brain. Eventually aneurysms can bulge and then rupture. Other strokes can be due to injury or spasm of a blood vessel resulting from use of drugs such as cocaine. Still another form of stroke in young people stems from a clot formed someplace else in the body, for example in the heart, which then travels via the blood to the arterial system of the brain and ultimately blocks an artery.

In approximately 9 of 10 cases, doctors are unable to establish a cause for restless-leg syndrome.

Q *If AIDS is usually transmitted from a man via semen, how is it transmitted by a woman?*

A A woman may pass the HIV virus via vaginal secretions, especially if there is a skin injury or other opening or source of bleeding in her or on her partner. A woman can also transmit the virus to her baby during the birth process.

Q *I have been told that I suffer from restless-leg syndrome. What causes it? Is there an effective treatment?*

A People who have restless-leg syndrome say that their legs are irritated deep inside and twitchy or jumpy. The sensation begins when the person lies down at night to go to sleep, but resolves when the person gets up and walks around —or moves the legs around in bed, thus the syndrome's name.

Even more common are two related syndromes: *nocturnal myoclonus*, in which patients have regular leg movements during sleep, of which they are unaware but that wake them, resulting in complaints of insomnia; and a medication-related syndrome of leg cramping during the night.

Certain factors are associated with restless-leg syndrome in particular, such as anemias, including those due to vitamin B_{12}, folic acid, and iron deficiency; pregnancy; spinal peripheral vascular disease; diabetes; use of certain medications, such as water pills; spinal-disk disease, and other conditions; however, no single basis for the problem has ever been pinpointed.

Specialized clinics focusing on sleep disorders are where you will find the most informed diagnoses and treatments. Medications that help patients to sleep and that serve as muscle relaxants are most often prescribed for restless-leg syndrome. These include clonazepan, L-dopamine, and codeinelike substances. Physicians have prescribed various other treatments, such as a warm bath before retiring, or vitamin E.

Q *Why is it that I get an excruciating headache when I eat cold foods like ice cream?*

A A spasm of brain arteries above the roof of the mouth, in response to a very cold stimulus, apparently causes the so-called "ice-cream" headache. This unpleasant sensation is usually harmless and passes quickly. In very rare cases, it may continue for much longer, requiring medical attention.

Cold, among other sensations, can also trigger a migraine headache in persons prone to such problems. This type of headache shares some characteristics with the more typical ice-cream headache, but it is a much more debilitating problem.

Do you have a medical question?
Send it to Editor, Health and Medicine Annual, P.O. Box 90, Hawleyville, CT 06440-9990.

Nutrition

See also:
Individual articles in the
second half of this book,
arranged in alphabetical
order, for additional
information.

One of the most important things that people can do to improve their health and reduce their chance of disease is to choose a proper diet. People eager to "eat healthy" received encouraging news in late 1992, when a sweeping overhaul of U.S. food-labeling regulations received final approval. By mid-1994 virtually every packaged food will have to carry a standardized label detailing its nutritional values. Being able to compare the nutrients in various foods will help people make healthy dietary decisions.

The U.S. government also unveiled a new food pyramid that describes the ideal American diet. At the pyramid's base are bread, pasta, and other grain foods; these should comprise the main portion of a person's diet. Fruits and vegetables form the next level. Then come meats, dairy products, dry beans, and nuts. At the pyramid's tip are fats, oils, and sweets, which should be used sparingly.

High among people's reasons for good nutritional practices is a desire to maintain weight at healthy levels. Excessive weight is associated with such life-threatening diseases as colon cancer, diabetes, and atherosclerosis. The importance of preventing obesity in children, rather than trying to reverse it later on, was stressed by Aviva Must, an epidemiologist at Tufts University in Massachusetts. Must found that people who are overweight during their teens are at high risk of suffering from serious health problems as adults, even if they later lose the excess weight. Men who were overweight as teenagers had death rates almost twice those of men who had maintained normal weight in their youth.

New medical studies raised concerns about some of our favorite foods, such as beef and other red meats, which are rich sources of iron. A Finnish study suggested that excessive iron in the body increases the risk of heart disease. The researchers found that men with high concentrations of iron in their blood were more than twice as likely to suffer a heart attack as men with lower iron values. The study was interpreted by some to explain why premenopausal women are largely protected from heart disease: they lose

iron every month during menstruation. After menopause, stored iron builds up rapidly in a woman's body, increasing her risk for heart disease.

Not all nutritional studies add to the list of dietary "no-no's." Researchers reported exciting new evidence that vitamins help fight cancer and cardiovascular diseases. Of particular interest are vitamins A, C, and E, which act as antioxidants. They apparently prevent the oxidation of low-density lipoprotein (LDL)—the "bad" form of cholesterol—which clogs the heart's arteries when it becomes oxidized. For example, two major studies concluded that daily doses of vitamin E cut the risk of heart disease by one-third to one-half. The benefit occurred only in people who took at least 100 international units of vitamin E per day. This confirmed other studies that indicated that while a well-rounded diet prevents vitamin deficiencies, vitamin supplements are probably necessary to prevent LDL oxidation.

Foods soon may be fortified with folic acid, one of the vitamins that make up the B complex. Growing evidence indicates that women who consume sufficient amounts of folic acid decrease their risk of giving birth to infants with neural-tube defect. In this devastating birth defect, babies are born with either an open spine, a condition called spina bifida, or part of their brain missing, a condition called anencephaly.

A study conducted in France found that people who drank three to four glasses of wine a day substantially reduced their cholesterol levels and coronary blockages that lead to heart attack and stroke. Red wine contains resveratrol, a natural pesticide produced by plants to ward off disease. Earlier studies indicated that resveratrol reduces the risk of heart disease in laboratory rats. Cornell University professor Leroy Creasy found that grape juice also contains high concentrations of resveratrol. However, grape juice may be less effective than red wine because it lacks alcohol, which other studies have indicated fights heart disease.

A powerful anticancer compound, sulforaphane, was detected in broccoli by researchers at Johns Hopkins University. This may explain why people whose diets are rich in broccoli—and related vegetables such as cabbage and brussels sprouts—appear to have a significantly lower risk of cancer than people who avoid these foods.

New evidence suggests that vitamins help fight cancer and cardiovascular diseases.

Pastabilities

by Maria Guglielmino

It is virtually impossible to become bored with a food as versatile as pasta. With myriad shapes to choose from and only the limits of the chef's imagination in creating sauces, pasta can be served in an endless variety of delicious recipes. Not limited to main courses, this all-around grain product is also a perfect medium for appetizers, salads, and soups. These days pasta is more popular than ever, especially now that Americans have discovered its many virtues. Still inexpensive and generally easy to prepare, pasta fits into the busy life-styles of the nutritionally minded.

Yes, Americans have become big *mangiamaccheroni*. No insult intended here (the term means "macaroni eaters")—we're just eating a lot of pasta these days. The National Pasta Association cites per-capita consumption at 19 pounds per year, 8 pounds higher than in 1975. While that sounds like a lot of pasta, we don't even come close to Italy's per-person consumption of 60 pounds per year!

Pasta's Roots

The exact origin of pasta (meaning "dough" or "paste" in Italian), is unclear, although historians seem to agree that a primitive form of this food was being made by many different wheat-growing cultures, including the Romans, Chinese, Japanese, Greeks, Ethiopians, and Arabs. How pasta was introduced into Italy is not known for sure, but the myth that Marco Polo brought pasta back to Italy from China in 1295 has been disproved by city archives in Genoa. The will of Ponzio Bastone, dated 1279, contained the record of a *bariscella plena de macaronis* (a basket full of macaroni) as one item in his estate. Pasta was obviously a commodity of great value well before Polo's return from China.

According to Theodora Fitzgibbon, author of *The Food of the Western World,* pasta was brought to Italy by the Ostrogoths, a Teutonic tribe that invaded Italy in about A.D. 405. This theory is supported by the English word "noodle," which is derived from the Germanic word *nudel.* Evidence suggests that the Etruscans, a pre-Roman people who inhabited parts of Italy as far back as 700 B.C., were making a form of fresh pasta. A bas-relief in an Etruscan tomb in the town of Cerveteri 30 miles north of Rome illustrates all the tools for making fresh pasta, including a jug for water, knives, a rolling pin, a large pastry board, and a fluted-edge pastry wheel for cutting, says Julia della Croce, author of *Pasta Classica.* Under Roman rule, pasta making continued and included wide, flat, ribbonlike noodles known as *laganum,* possibly the forerunner of lasagna, and gnocchi, a dumpling type of pasta.

Dried pasta *(pasta secca)* appears to have been a staple food of nomadic tribes from Arabia, Persia, and Asia, presumably developed to preserve wheat for the long excursions through deserts. Historians believe that the Arabs introduced *pasta secca* to Italy when they conquered the island of Sicily. An Arab geographer in the 12th century recorded that Sicilians were making a pasta called *itriyah,* an Arab word for "string," according to Anna Del Conte, author of *Portrait of Pasta.* Today in Sicily and parts of southern Italy, a type of pasta called *trii* is still eaten, and Arab influence is still seen in classic Sicilian pasta dishes, such as pasta with sardines, raisins, and wild fennel.

How pasta was introduced to the United States still remains obscure. Thomas Jefferson purchased a pasta machine after his visit to a Naples pasta manufacturer, and he is often credited for its American importation. Based on information gleaned from letters and shipping documents, however, it is more probable that affluent Englishmen brought pasta with them when traveling to the New World. In fact, pasta became such a trendy food in certain elite English crowds during the 18th and 19th centuries that a Macaroni Club was formed.

Thoughts of pasta usually conjure certain tastes and aromas of a savory nature. Indeed, if asked to choose a topping for macaroni, the average American would probably choose the perennial favorite—tomato sauce. But imagine capping your meal with a dish of pasta for dessert. While the idea may seem odd to us, Renaissance cooks prepared pasta with sugar and spices. According to *Pasta Classica,* one Renaissance dessert recipe combines layers of fresh noodles with chocolate, sweetened poached oranges, pears, and other fruits. In fact, tomatoes were not used for pasta dishes until the late 17th century, when it was finally established that they were not poisonous.

Pasta's past is not without its share of irony. While the Italian people always had a deep respect for pasta and believed it even had magical qualities, a contrasting view was held by powerful men in academia, the religious sector, and in government. Girolamo Savonarola, a Florentine monk in the 15th century, felt that the Italians' frequent indulgence in pasta was an addiction that would prevent them from attaining salvation. Despite his intense preaching, the masses remained faithful to pasta, and Savonarola was eventually hanged and burned at the stake. In the 1930s Benito Mussolini, F. T. Marinetti, and the entire futurist movement attempted to prohibit the consumption of pasta. Propaganda denouncing pasta promoted the notion that pasta eaters were slow, passive, and too weak for a country on the verge of war. It was felt that overconsumption of macaroni would lead to slovenliness, pessimism, and loss of intellectual functioning. Fortunately, the Italian people protested the anti-pasta propaganda, ardent pasta supporters from the United States sent telegrams to Italy, and pasta consumption continued unabated.

If you're looking for a meal that's cheap, chic, and healthy, the answer is pasta!

1.

2.

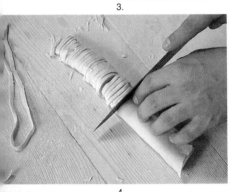

3.

4.

5.

To satisfy the gourmet tastes of their clients, some restaurants still insist on making pasta by hand. Pasta dough (1) is created from scratch using durum wheat flour, whole eggs, and oil. The dough is hand-kneaded (2), rolled into a narrow tube (3), and sliced (4). The sliced dough is then separated by hand to create spaghetti strands (5), before it is whipped into a delicious meal (right).

Pasta Manufacturing

Pasta manufacturing has come a long way from the old days when it was kneaded by foot, hand-cut, and dried in the sun. Mass production of pasta began in 1919, when a clever device was developed in Naples, Italy, to dry pasta by blowing hot air on it. Prior to that time, even factory-made pasta was sun-dried. Today most pasta plants are completely automated, and in some state-of-the-art factories, such as the American Italian Pasta Company in Excelsior Springs, Missouri, the control system is computerized.

Pasta manufacturing begins with the milling of wheat. Durum wheat is considered the finest for the manufacturing of pasta. "The raw ingredient is most important," explains Victor Bridgeman, director of quality control at the American Italian Pasta Company. "A high-quality durum wheat normally has a high gluten content and a high protein content, and it gives a golden, opaque appearance in the finished product." He adds that a higher gluten and protein content yields a stronger pasta that is more resistant to overcooking. If manufactured properly, pasta from durum

wheat does not absorb too much water or come apart during cooking. Although, by Italian law, pasta must be made only with durum-wheat flour, some American companies use a mixture of durum-wheat flour plus either farina or a refined flour that has been fortified with vitamins.

During milling, the wheat is gravity-fed through a series of cleaners, grinders, and sifters to filter out the semolina flour, one of the coarser grinds. The semolina then moves by a pneumatic-transfer system into mixing bins where water is added and the resulting dough is kneaded.

The fun part begins with the extrusion process, which creates all those wonderful shapes. The dough is pushed through cylinders and forced through dies (perforated plates) to make the finished product. Dies with small holes of varying diameters make the long, stringlike types of pasta, such as spaghetti or vermicelli. Ziti and other types of tubular pasta are formed by dies that have perforations containing steel pins. Ribbonlike noodles such as lasagna are made by forcing the pasta through dies with thin slits. An assortment of fancy shapes is formed by either accelerating or reducing the flow, while rotary knives snip off the dough as it passes through the die.

Once cut into shape, the pasta is then put through the critical drying process. Each variety moves into an automatic drying machine where a fast, hot flash of heat seals the pasta's exterior. Next comes a period of slower heating and then finally a cooling phase. As the pasta passes through several chambers of varying humidities and temperatures, its moisture content drops from about 31 percent to between 12 and 13 percent. If dried too slowly, the pasta may spoil due to mold, bacterial growth, or infestation; if drying is hurried, the pasta will crack and break easily. If kept free of moisture, dried pasta can be safely stored for up to two years without flavor loss.

Colored pastas are produced by adding vegetable juice—spinach to make green pasta; beet or tomato juice to make red types. A charcoal-gray or black-colored pasta can even be made by adding squid ink. Commercial pasta that requires refrigeration is made with eggs and refined white flour or durum flour. It is kneaded in the same way as dried pasta, then pressed through rollers to yield thin sheets of pasta. This type of pasta is packaged in airtight containers and must be refrigerated to retain its tasty freshness. When refrigerated, pasta has a shelf life of four days; it can be frozen for up to a month.

At a pasta manufacturing plant, durum wheat is fed through a battery of cleaners, grinders, and sifters to extract the purest semolina wheat from any gritty, coarse particles. The semolina is added to water and then moves on to the extrusion process (right), where the dough is shaped into spaghetti strings. The yellow strings are looped over moving rods and moved on to the critical drying process (below).

A Sampling of Pasta Architecture

One of the most versatile foods, dried pasta is said to come in 500 different shapes in Italy. Although seemingly named with whimsy, these shapes all have a purpose that the Italians take quite seriously. Some types of pasta, due to their size and density, are better suited to certain sauces. In fact, the thicknesses of the various pastas have a surprising effect on their taste. This chart highlights 14 of the most common pasta varieties with some recommended sauces.

Pasta Type	Description/translation	Best suited for:
Capelli d'angelo	Angel hair	Broths
Stelline	Little stars	Broths
Farfalline	Little butterflies	Broths
Orzo	Barley	Broths
Spaghetti	A length of cord	Oil-based sauces, pesto, tomato sauces, vegetable sauces, fish sauces
Linguine	Little tongues	White clam sauce, pesto, oil-based sauces
Fettuccine	Little ribbons	Cream sauces
Ziti	Bridegrooms	Meat sauces, vegetable or bean sauces, baked timballo (a casserole with a crust)
Penne	Quills	Chunky tomato sauces, meat sauces, vegetable or bean sauces, cream or cheese sauces
Lasagna	Wide ribbons	Layered casseroles containing cheeses, tomato sauces with or without meat and vegetables
Lumaconi	Large snails	Stuffing with cheeses or seafood
Fusilli	Short twists	Cheese sauces, such as ricotta sauces, meat sauces, cold pasta salads
Farfalle	Butterflies	Thick cream or cheese sauces, oil-based sauces, tomato sauces
Gnocchi	Large dumplings	Tomato sauces, meat sauces, vegetable sauces (the vegetables should be cut fine enough to eat cradled in the gnocchi)

A Nutritious Food

Pasta is a delicious and substantial food, enjoyed by people of all ages and ethnic groups. Kids love pasta and choose it second only to peanut-butter-and-jelly sandwiches. But can such tasty fare actually be good for us?

Pasta contains several important nutrients. For starters, it is an excellent source of complex carbohydrates, which are made from chains of simple sugars. These starches supply the body with energy for growth and activity and should provide 50 to 60 percent of our total calories. Nutritionists and other health educators advocate a diet that is high in complex carbohydrates and low in fat to lower the risk of heart disease, cancer, and obesity. Just a 2-ounce dry (5 ounces cooked) serving of pasta packs a whopping 42 grams of carbohydrate. By including pasta at one meal and eating plenty of other grains, fruits, vegetables, and low-fat dairy products over the course of the day, it's easy to consume enough carbohydrates.

Marathoners and other endurance athletes have long valued pasta as a great source of energy. In fact, it is the all-time favorite meal served at precompetition dinners. Carbohydrates, the most efficient fuel for muscles during vigorous exercise, are the mainstay of the endurance athlete's diet. Many competitors "carbo-load," tapering their exercise and increasing their carbohydrate intake to 70 percent of their calories three days before a big race, thus superloading the muscles with glycogen (the storage form of carbohydrate). Pasta is a perfect food for "carbo-loading." It is easy to digest and quite tasty, making it possible for athletes to eat the large amounts necessary to meet their carbohydrate needs. An athlete would need to consume approximately six medium potatoes to equal the carbohydrates in 8 ounces (dry weight) of pasta served with marinara sauce!

Pasta's protein content provides six of the eight essential amino acids. Plain pasta is approximately 14 percent protein. Simply by adding a sauce that contains a little meat, fish, or legumes, or by sprinkling on grated cheese, the pasta meal will provide complete

Penne with Puttanesca Sauce

2 cans (28 oz.) plum tomatoes
2 tablespoons olive oil
3-4 large garlic cloves, minced
½ cup chopped fresh Italian parsley
1 teaspoon fresh oregano or
    ½ teaspoon dried oregano

4 anchovy fillets, cut up
4 tablespoons black olives, chopped
    (about 10 olives – preferably Nicoise or Kalamata)
2 tablespoons capers
¼ teaspoon red pepper flakes
1 lb. penne or pennette

Separate tomatoes from their juice. Chop tomatoes. Strain juice to remove seeds. Set both aside. In a medium saucepan or skillet, sauté garlic, anchovies, and herbs until garlic is softened. Add chopped tomatoes and juice, capers, olives and red pepper flakes. Simmer for about 21 minutes, or until tomato juice evaporates and the sauce thickens. Cook the penne in water for about 8 minutes until al dente. Drain pasta and mix with sauce in a large serving bowl. Serve immediately.
Serves 4-6 people.

Nutrition information based on 4 servings; each serving has approximately 525 calories, 17 g protein, 90 g carbohydrate, 12 g total fat, 1 g saturated fat, zero cholesterol, and 78 mg sodium. Only 21 percent of the calories are from fat.

Adapted from *The Silver Palate Cookbook* by Julee Rosso and Sheila Lukins.

protein. There are infinite meatless recipes for saucing pasta—a boon for vegetarians trying to balance their diets. A pasta meal with 10 ounces of cooked macaroni (4 ounces dry), marinara sauce, and 2 tablespoons grated Parmesan cheese will provide about 18 grams of protein—39 percent of a woman's and 32 percent of a man's daily protein requirements.

Depending on the type of pasta and how it is sauced, pasta can be healthy for your heart. Dried pasta alone is virtually fat-free (only 1 gram of fat in a 2-ounce portion) and doesn't contain a speck of cholesterol. In contrast, fresh pasta, rich in eggs, contains some saturated fat and an ample amount of cholesterol. A 3-ounce serving of one popular brand of fresh pasta contains 2 grams of saturated fat and a hefty 55 milligrams of cholesterol. Individuals following a low-cholesterol diet would be wise to eat fresh pasta with meatless sauces to avoid adding further cholesterol and saturated fat to the meal.

Pasta is also sodium-free, unless salt is added to the cooking water. It is the sauces and grated cheese that add the extra sodium. Commercial spaghetti sauces are particularly high in sodium, averaging about 540 milligrams in a 4-ounce serving. Every tablespoon of grated Parmesan cheese sprinkled on pasta adds 93 milligrams of sodium. Individuals limiting their sodium intake for health reasons should use one of the commercial low-sodium spaghetti sauces or prepare their own without added salt. They should also limit other high-sodium foods such as cheeses, olives, capers, and cured Italian meats or fish—all common ingredients in pasta sauces.

What about calories? For years, pasta was given a bum rap. Along with bread, potatoes, and other starchy foods, pasta was considered "fattening." Fortunately, that myth has been dispelled, especially now that carbohydrates have gained recognition as a healthy food. Carbohydrates have 4 calories per gram, less than half the calories in the

Spaghettini with Scallops and Crabmeat

½ lb. sea scallops
½ lb. precooked lump crabmeat, flaked
2 tablespoons olive oil
3 medium garlic cloves, finely minced
1 large shallot, finely chopped
1 small red bell pepper, cut into very fine strips
2½ cups chopped canned plum tomatoes
   (with ½ cup of their juices)

½ cup dry white wine or dry vermouth
½ cup fresh basil leaves, chopped
½ tablespoon fresh thyme, chopped, or
   1 teaspoon dried
¼ teaspoon salt, or to taste
¼ teaspoon fresh ground pepper
1 lb. spaghettini or other thin pasta

Wash and thoroughly dry scallops. Slice each into 2-3 pieces and set aside. In a large skillet or saucepan, sauté garlic, shallots, and red pepper in olive oil for about 2 minutes, or until they soften. Add chopped tomatoes without juices, and sauté gently for 4-5 minutes. Add tomato juice and wine and let liquid evaporate down over medium heat for about 4 minutes. Add salt, pepper, scallops, and crabmeat, and sauté over low heat for 4-5 minutes, uncovered. Meanwhile, boil pasta for about 7 minutes, depending on which pasta you use. Drain pasta and toss with sauce. Serve immediately. Serves 4-6 people.

Nutrition information based on 4 servings: each serving has approximately 598 calories, 35 g protein, 88 g carbohydrate, 10 g total fat, 1 g saturated fat, 63 mg cholesterol, and 68 mg sodium. Only 15 percent of the calories are from fat.

Adapted from *The Pasta Book* by Julia della Croce.

Farfalle with Ricotta & Spinach

¼ lb. fresh spinach
12 oz. (1½ cups) part skim ricotta
¼ cup grated Parmesan cheese
¼ teaspoon nutmeg

¼ teaspoon salt
freshly milled black pepper to taste
1 lb. farfalle or other fancy shape

This is a classical Italian recipe usually made with whole milk ricotta. Steam spinach, then drain and squeeze dry. Cool and chop fine. Mix 1 tablespoon warm water with ricotta. Add grated cheese, nutmeg, salt and pepper. Stir mixture until creamy, then mix with cooled chopped spinach. Cook pasta in water until al dente. Drain pasta and combine with ricotta sauce. Do not overdrain pasta, as the moisture from the cooked pasta makes the sauce smooth and creamy. Serve immediately with more grated cheese if desired. Serves 4-6 people.

Nutrition information based on 4 servings: each serving has approximately 544 calories, 27 g protein, 85 g carbohydrate, 10.4 g total fat, 5.6 g saturated fat, 32.5 mg cholesterol, and 209 mg sodium. Only 17 percent of the calories are from fat.

Adapted from *The Pasta Book* by Julia della Croce.

same quantity of fat. High in carbohydrates, but naturally low in fat, pasta is a relatively low-calorie food. Two ounces of dried pasta contain only 210 calories (cooked al dente, this 1-cup portion provides 192 calories). Although 2 ounces is the quantity that manufacturers consider a serving size, most people would consider that a skimpy portion as a main course. Doubling that amount provides a very satisfying meal, and the calories remain low in comparison to many other meals. Topping 2 cups of cooked pasta (4 ounces dried) with 1 cup of low-fat marinara sauce and 1 tablespoon of grated Parmesan cheese brings the calorie scoreboard up to only 500. This pasta dish combined with a salad and low-fat dressing provides a mere one-quarter of an average adult woman's and about one-fifth of an average adult man's daily energy needs (2,000 and 2,700 calories per day, respectively). In contrast, an 8-ounce broiled rib-eye steak (a small portion for most Americans), a medium baked potato with sour cream, and a salad with French dressing contains approximately 950 calories and a frightening amount of saturated fat and cholesterol! Even if you are trying to lose weight by reducing your calorie intake by about 500

per day, our low-fat pasta meal fits in easily, providing between one-third (for women) or one-quarter (for men) of the day's calories.

Unfortunately, not all pasta sauces are low-calorie counterparts to pasta dishes. Many add lots of fat, and with that come extra calories. Sauces rich with butter, oil, cream, or cheeses are brimming with calories. A traditional fettuccine Alfredo recipe contains butter, heavy cream, and grated cheese. A 2-cup portion contains nearly 900 calories.

Almost any pasta sauce can be modified to reduce the fat and calories, and the availability of nonfat dairy products such as fat-free ricotta and mozzarella cheeses makes this task easier. Oil-based sauces such as linguine with clam sauce often call for as much as 5 to 6 tablespoons of olive oil (the oil alone adds 600 to 700 calories!). The oil can easily be reduced to 1 to 2 tablespoons, saving as much as 500 to 600 calories per recipe. By adding clam broth and a little extra white wine and herbs, the flavor is not spared. Those leery of experimenting with recipes can investigate the many cookbooks that contain low-fat pasta recipes.

The pasta recipes throughout these pages, low in fat and calories, are simple to prepare. Each meal can be on the dinner table in about 30 minutes. *Buòno appetito!* ◇

Although all vegetarians eschew red meat, individuals approach their diets in different ways. A "semi-vegetarian" takes a comparatively liberal approach, with a diet that includes dairy foods, eggs, poultry, and fish. A "pesco-vegetarian" avoids poultry as well.

Varying Views on Vegetarian Diets

by Dixie Farley

Many people are attracted to vegetarian diets. It's no wonder. Health experts for years have been telling us to eat more plant foods and less fat, especially saturated fat, which is found in larger amounts in animal foods than in plant foods.

C. Everett Koop, M.D., former surgeon general of the Public Health Service, in his 1988 *Report on Nutrition and Health*, expressed major concern about Americans' "disproportionate consumption of foods high in fats, often at the expense of foods high in complex carbohydrates and fiber—that may be more conducive to health."

And, while guidelines from the U.S. Departments of Agriculture and Health and Human Services advise 2 to 3 daily servings of milk—and the same of foods such as dried peas and beans, eggs, meat, poultry, and fish —they recommend 3 to 5 servings of vegetables, 2 to 4 servings of fruits, and 6 to 11 servings of bread, cereal, rice, and pasta— in other words, 11 to 20 plant foods, but only 4 to 6 animal foods.

It's wise to take precautions, however, when adopting diets that entirely exclude animal flesh or dairy products. "The more you restrict your diet, the more difficult it is to get all the nutrients you need," says Marilyn Stephenson, R.D., of the Food and Drug Administration's (FDA's) Center for Food Safety and Applied Nutrition. "To be healthful, vegetarian diets require very careful, proper planning. Nutrition counseling can help you get started on a diet that is nutritionally adequate."

Certain people, such as Seventh-Day Adventists, choose a vegetarian diet because of religious beliefs. Others give up meat because they feel that eating animals is unkind. Some people believe it's a better use of the Earth's resources to eat low on the food chain; the North American Vegetarian Society notes that 1.3 billion people could be fed with the grain and soybeans eaten by U.S. livestock. On the practical side, many people eat plant foods because animal foods are more expensive.

"I'm a vegetarian because I just plain enjoy the taste of vegetables and pasta," says Judy Folkenberg of Bethesda, Maryland. Reared on a vegetarian diet that included eggs and dairy products, Folkenberg added fish to her diet five years ago. "I love crab cakes and shrimp," she says.

Just as vegetarians differ in their motivation, their diets differ as well. In light of these variations, it's not surprising that the exact number of vegetarians is unknown. In a National Restaurant Association Gallup Survey in June 1991, 5 percent of respondents said they were vegetarians, yet 2 percent said they never ate milk or cheese products, 3 percent never ate red meat, and 10 percent never ate eggs.

Risks

Vegetarians who abstain from dairy products or animal flesh face the greatest nutritional risks because some nutrients naturally occur mainly or almost exclusively in animal foods.

Vegans, who eat no animal foods (and, rarely, vegetarians who eat no animal flesh, but do eat eggs or dairy products), risk vitamin B_{12} deficiency, which can result in irreversible nerve deterioration. The need for vitamin B_{12} increases during pregnancy, breast-feeding, and periods of growth, according to Johanna Dwyer, D.Sc., R.D., of Tufts University Medical School and the New England Medical Center Hospital in Boston, Massachusetts. Writing in 1988 in the *American Journal of Clinical Nutrition*, Dwyer reviewed studies of the previous five years and concluded that elderly people also should be especially cautious about adopting vegetarian diets because their bodies may absorb vitamin B_{12} poorly.

Ovo-vegetarians, who eat eggs but no dairy foods or animal flesh, and vegans may have inadequate vitamin D and calcium. Inadequate vitamin D may cause rickets in children, while inadequate calcium can contribute to the risk of osteoporosis in later years. These vegetarians are susceptible to iron-deficiency anemia because they are not only missing the more readily absorbed iron from animal flesh, they are also likely to be eating many foods with constituents that inhibit iron absorption—soy protein, bran, and

Replacing Animal Sources of Nutrients

Vegetarians who eat no meat, fish, poultry, or dairy foods face the greatest risk of nutritional deficiency. Nutrients most likely to be lacking, and some non-animal sources, are:
• *vitamin B_{12}*—fortified soy milk and cereals;
• *vitamin D*—sunshine and fortified margarine;
• *calcium*—tofu, broccoli, seeds, nuts, spinach, kale, bok choy, legumes (peas and beans), greens, and calcium-enriched gram products;
• *iron*—legumes, tofu, bean sprouts, green leafy vegetables such as spinach, dried fruit, enriched white rice, whole grains, and iron-fortified cereals and breads, especially whole wheat (absorption is improved by vitamin C, found in citrus fruits and juices, tomatoes, strawberries, broccoli, peppers, dark-green leafy vegetables, and potatoes with skins);
• *zinc*—whole grains (especially the germ and bran), whole-wheat bread, legumes, nuts, popcorn, applesauce, mangos, and tofu.

As all plant foods—including fruit—contain some protein, by eating a variety of fruits, vegetables, and grains every day, even vegans probably can get enough of this nutrient. To improve the quality of protein and ensure getting enough:

Combine

legumes such as black-eyed peas, chick-peas, peas, peanuts, lentils, sprouts, and black, broad, kidney, lima, mung, navy, and pea beans.

with

grains such as rice, wheat, corn, rye, oats, millet, barley, and buckwheat.

There are also foods made of products like soy that are made to look like meats (protein analogues) such as hot dogs, sausage, and bacon.

fiber, for instance. Vegans must guard against inadequate calorie intake, which during pregnancy can lead to low birth weight, and against protein deficiency, which in children can impair growth and in adults can cause loss of hair and muscle mass and abnormal accumulation of fluid.

According to the Institute of Food Technologists and the American Dietetic Association, vegan diets, if appropriately planned, can provide adequate nutrition even for children. Some experts disagree.

Gretchen Hill, Ph.D., associate professor of food science and human nutrition at the University of Missouri, Columbia, believes it's unhealthy for children to eat no red meat. "My bet is those kids will have health problems when they reach 40, 50, or 60 years of age," she says, "mostly because of imbalances with micronutrients [nutrients required only in small amounts], particularly iron, zinc, and copper." While meat is well known as an important source of iron, Hill says it may be even more valuable for copper and zinc. Copper not only helps build the body's immunity, it builds red blood cells and strengthens blood vessels. "A lot of Americans are marginal in this micronutrient," she says, "and, as a result, are more susceptible to diseases. Children can't meet their zinc needs without eating meat."

Also, vegetarian women of childbearing age have an increased chance of menstrual irregularities, Ann Pedersen and others reported last year in the *American Journal of Clinical Nutrition*. Nine of the study's 34 vegetarians (who ate eggs or dairy foods) missed menstrual periods, but only 2 of the 41 nonvegetarians did. The groups were indistinguishable when it came to factors such as height, weight, and age at the beginning of menstruation.

Can Veggies Prevent Cancer?

The National Cancer Institute (NCI) states in its booklet *Diet, Nutrition & Cancer Prevention: The Good News* that a third of cancer deaths may be related to diet. The booklet's "Good News" is: vegetables from the cabbage family (cruciferous vegetables) may reduce cancer risk, diets low in fat and high in fiber-rich foods may reduce the risk of cancers of the colon and rectum, and diets rich in foods containing vitamin A, vitamin C, and beta-carotene may reduce the risk of certain cancers.

Part of the FDA's proposed food-labeling regulations, published in the November 27, 1991 *Federal Register*, states: "The scientific evidence shows that diets high in whole grains, fruits, and vegetables, which are low in fat and rich sources of fiber and certain other nutrients, are associated with a reduced risk of some types of cancer. The available evidence does not, however, demonstrate that it is total fiber, or a specific fiber

A "lacto-ovo-vegetarian" can eat dairy food and eggs, but avoids consuming any fish, poultry, or red meat. Most people who consider themselves vegetarians fall into this category.

A "lacto-vegetarian" can eat dairy products, but avoids eggs, fish, poultry, and red meat. Nutritionists suggest that such a person choose low-fat varieties of milk products.

component, that is related to the reduction of risk of cancer."

As for increasing fiber in the diet, Joanne Slavin, Ph.D., R.D., of the University of Minnesota, in 1990 in *Nutrition Today* gives this advice: "Animal studies show that soluble fibers are associated with the highest levels of cell proliferation, a precancerous event. The current interest in dietary fiber has allowed recommendations for fiber supplementation to outdistance the scientific research base. Until we have a better understanding of how fiber works its magic, we should recommend to American consumers only a gradual increase in dietary fiber from a variety of sources."

The FDA acknowledges that high intakes of fruits and vegetables rich in beta-carotene or in vitamin C have been associated with reduced cancer risk. But the agency believes the data are not sufficiently convincing that either nutrient by itself is responsible for this association.

Pointing out that plant foods' low fat content also confers health benefits, the FDA states in its proposed rule that diets low in fat have been shown to give protection against coronary heart disease, and that it has tentatively determined, "Diets low in fat are associated with the reduced risk of cancer." The FDA notes that diets high in saturated fats and cholesterol increase levels of both total and LDL (low-density lipoprotein) cho-

lesterol, and thus also increase the risk for coronary heart disease, and that high-fat foods contribute to obesity, a further risk factor for heart disease. (The National Cholesterol Education Program recommends a diet with no more than 30 percent fat, of which no more than 10 percent comes from saturated fat.)

For those reasons the agency would allow some foods to be labeled with health claims relating diets low in saturated fat and cholesterol to decreased risk of coronary heart disease, and relating diets low in fat to reduced risk of breast, colon, and prostate cancer. "Examples of foods qualifying for a health claim include most fruits and vegetables; skim-milk products; sherbets; most flours, grains, meals, and pastas (except for egg pastas); and many breakfast cereals," the proposed rule states.

Dwyer, in her article, summarizes these plant-food benefits.

"Data are strong that vegetarians are at lesser risk for obesity, platonic [reduced muscle tone] constipation, lung cancer, and alcoholism. Evidence is good that risks for hypertension, coronary artery disease, type II diabetes, and gallstones are lower. Data are only fair to poor that risks of breast cancer, diverticular disease of the colon, colonic cancer, calcium kidney stones, osteoporosis, dental erosion, and dental caries are lower among vegetarians."

Death rates for vegetarians are similar to or lower than rates for nonvegetarians, Dwyer reports, but are influenced in Western countries by vegetarians' "adoption of many healthy lifestyle habits in addition to diet, such as not smoking, abstinence or moderation in the use of alcohol, being physically active, resting adequately, seeking ongoing health surveillance, and seeking . . . guidance when health problems arise."

Slow Switching

It's generally agreed that to avoid intestinal discomfort from increased bulk, a person shouldn't switch to foods with large amounts of fiber all at once. A sensible approach to vegetarian diets is to first cut down on the fattiest meats, replacing them with cereals, fruits, and vegetables, recommends Jack Zeev Yetiv, M.D., Ph.D., in his book *Popular Nutritional Practices: A Scientific Appraisal.* "Some may choose to eliminate red meat but continue to eat fish and poultry occasionally, and such a diet is also to be encouraged."

Changing to the vegetarian kitchen slowly also may increase the chances of success. "If you suddenly cut out all animal entrées from your diet, it's easy to get discouraged and think there's nothing to eat," says lifelong veggie-eater Folkenberg. "I build my meals around a starchy carbohydrate such as pasta or potatoes. Even when I occasionally cook seafood, I center on the carbohydrate, making that the larger portion. Shifting the emphasis from animal to plant foods is easier after you've found recipes you really enjoy."

Because vegans and ovo-vegetarians face the greatest potential nutritional risk, the Institute of Food Technologists recommends careful diet planning to include enough calcium, riboflavin, iron, and vitamin D, perhaps with a vitamin D supplement if sunlight exposure is low. (Sunlight activates a substance in the skin and converts it into vitamin D.)

For these two vegetarian groups, the institute recommends calcium supplements during pregnancy, infancy, childhood, and breast-feeding. Vegans need to take a vitamin B_{12} supplement because that vitamin is found only in animal-food sources. Unless advised otherwise by a doctor, those taking supplements should limit the dose to 100 percent of the National Academy of Sciences' (NAS's) Recommended Dietary Allowances (RDAs). Vegans, and especially children, also must be sure to consume adequate calories and protein. For other vegetarians, it is not difficult to get adequate protein, although care is needed in small children's diets.

Nearly every animal food, including egg whites and milk, provides all eight of the essential amino acids in the balance needed by humans, and therefore constitutes "complete" protein. Plant foods contain fewer of these amino acids than do animal foods.

An "ovo-vegetarian" can eat eggs, but avoids all dairy foods and all forms of animal flesh. A person following such a diet should be certain to obtain adequate calcium and vitamin D.

In avoiding all animal products, a "vegan" represents the most extreme type of vegetarian. Vegans must monitor their nutritional intake carefully to avoid vitamin deficiency.

The American Dietetic Association's (ADA's) position paper on vegetarian diets, published in its journal in 1988 and co-authored by Dwyer and Suzanne Havala, R.D., states that a plant-based diet provides adequate amounts of amino acids when a varied diet is eaten on a daily basis. The mixture of proteins included in foods like grains, legumes, seeds, and vegetables provides a complement of amino acids so that deficits in one food are made up by another. Not all types of plant foods need to be eaten at the same meal, since the amino acids are combined in the body's protein pool.

Frances Lappe, in *Diet for a Small Planet*, writes that it is best to consume complementary proteins within three to four hours of each other. High amounts of complete proteins can be gained by combining legumes with grains, seeds, or nuts.

Also available are protein analogues. These substitute "meats"—usually made from soybeans—are formed to look like meat foods such as hot dogs, ground beef, or bacon. Many are fortified with vitamin B_{12}.

The chart on page 75 lists sources of the nutrients of greatest concern for vegetarians who don't eat animal foods. As with any diet, it's important for the vegetarian diet to include many different foods, since no one food contains all the nutrients required for good health. "The wider the variety, the greater the chance of getting the nutrients you need," says the FDA's Stephenson.

The American Dietetic Association recommends:
• minimizing intake of less nutritious foods such as sweets and fatty foods;
• choosing whole- or unrefined-grain products instead of refined products;
• choosing a variety of nuts, seeds, legumes, fruits, and vegetables, including good sources of vitamin C to improve iron absorption;
• choosing low-fat varieties of milk products, if they are included in the diet;
• avoiding excessive cholesterol intake by limiting eggs to two or three yolks a week;
• for vegans, using properly fortified food sources of the very crucial vitamin B_{12}, such as fortified soy milks or cereals, or taking a supplement;
• for infants, children, and teenagers, ensuring adequate intakes of calories and iron and vitamin D, taking supplements if needed;
• consulting a registered dietitian or other qualified nutrition professional, especially during periods of growth, breast-feeding, pregnancy, or recovery from illness;
• if exclusively breast-feeding premature infants or babies beyond four to six months of age, giving vitamin D and iron supplements to the child from birth or at least by four to six months, as your doctor suggests;
• usually, taking iron and folate (folic acid) supplements during pregnancy.

With the array of fruits, vegetables, grains, and herbs available in U.S. grocery stores and the availability of vegetarian cookbooks, it's easy to devise tasty vegetarian dishes. People who like their entrées on the hoof also can benefit from adding more plant foods to their diets. You don't have to be a vegetarian to enjoy the wide variety of tasty dishes from a vegetarian menu. ◇

FIGURING OUT THE
NEW FOOD LABELS

by Sue Gebo, M.P.H., R.D.

Americans want to know what they're eating. In fact, studying food labels could well be called a national obsession. Store aisles are regularly clogged with consumers intently examining food labels.

The zeal to understand just what's in all those food packages has spawned growing concern over whether food labels are even intelligible to the average shopper. The words "lite," "light," "cholesterol-free," and "fat-free" have all but screamed from the shelves to grab a buyer. But bring the product home, turn it over, and just try to decipher the meaning of all those numbers on the nutrition label.

As of mid-May 1993, new food-labeling guidelines, designed to be more user-friendly, are expected to begin to dot supermarket shelves. By May 1994, virtually all

foods are due to bear these new labels. How helpful will these labels be? Will consumers, finally, really know what they are buying?

The Old Label

Food-labeling guidelines had last been revised in 1973. However, with growing consumer concern about nutrition, this old label design had become, in the minds of many consumer advocates, obsolete—and in many cases misleading.

One concern: Manufacturers could choose their own serving sizes for the label. For example, while one brand of margarine might have based its nutrition-label information on a serving size of 1 tablespoon, another might have chosen a serving size of 1 teaspoon. Consumers, comparing one margarine to another, could be confused. Similarly, companies could choose an absurdly small portion size—such as ½ cup of ice cream—to improve the product's nutrition profile. And then there is the package that might have been considered a single-serving container —a can of soda, for instance—that was divided into more than one serving for nutrition-information purposes. Again, consumers, thinking that the nutrition information was for the entire contents of the container, were likely to be misled.

Another concern: Nutrition labeling was not *required* on *all* foods. Unless a food product fell into a certain category—for example, unless it bore a claim such as "diet"—it was not required to list nutrition information.

Perhaps the most urgent issue dealt with the *front* of the label. With consumer focus on heart disease and cancer prevention, food manufacturers began emblazoning descriptive words such as "cholesterol-free" and "low-fat" on thousands of products. While these terms may have *seemed* helpful, no clear guidelines existed to ensure that these products actually *deserved* such descriptors and that consumers were not being misled.

An additional problem is that certain pieces of potentially useful information, such as *calories from fat* and *dietary fiber*, were not required on nutrition labels. Conversely, some pieces of less useful information, such as percent of the U.S. Recommended Daily Allowance (USRDA) of thiamine, were still required, even though thiamine deficiency is no longer a common U.S. problem.

Furthermore, the US-RDAs, on which part of the nutrition label was based, had been developed in 1968, despite the fact that several revisions of the Recommended Dietary Allowances (RDAs—on which the USRDAs were based) had been issued since 1968.

It seemed clear that some new information, removal of some old information, and control over the use of terms such as "light" and "cholesterol-free," would make the labels more effective.

> *New food labels will help consumers make wise decisions about the food they buy.*

Turning the Tide

In 1989, the Food and Drug Administration (FDA) joined with the Food Safety and Inspection Service (FSIS), a branch of the U.S. Department of Agriculture (USDA), to begin the process of food-label reform. In 1990, after a series of public hearings where both consumer and industry groups aired their views, the FDA began publishing proposals for the new, "improved" regulations.

While the FDA and the USDA had started the wheels turning, consumer groups and others concerned about an increasingly confused public propelled Congress to pass a food-labeling law in November 1990. Called the Nutrition Labeling and Education Act (NLEA), this law was intended to speed up the cumbersome process of creating and enforcing new regulations. It set up a shorter timetable than that of the FDA and the USDA for issuing final label regulations and for requiring manufacturers to comply, and it provided a solid legal basis for food-label reform. In effect, the law sent a message both to the food industry and to federal regulators: the current system *must* be changed.

The new law required that food-labeling proposals be issued by November 1991; that regulations be finalized by November 8, 1992; and that the food industry comply with the new rules by May 8, 1993.

Problems Arise

In November 1991, in accordance with the NLEA, the FDA issued additional proposals for food- and nutrition-labeling regulations. In early 1992 the FDA held public hearings to gather feedback from consumers, health professionals, and food manufacturers.

During these public hearings, a wide divergence of opinions was aired regarding the types of information that should be required on the label, and the timetable for implementation. Industry groups lobbied for a longer time period before implementation, citing burdensome costs for additional nutrition analysis of product lines and for the retooling of labels. Consumer groups countered that this was merely a delaying tactic to allow manufacturers to squeeze more sales from their misleading claims.

A series of label "format" proposals, culled from ideas set forth at the public hearings and from research with consumers, paraded through the ranks of federal regulators. In July 1992, the FDA released several proposed label formats and solicited public comment. It was the format issue that created the hottest controversy. Locked in a fierce debate were the FDA, which controls labeling of most food products, and the USDA, which controls labeling of products that contain meat and poultry. If these two groups could not agree, consumers would be faced with different label formats for foods containing meat and poultry than for other foods.

The FDA favored a label that included not only *numbers* of grams or milligrams of various nutrients, but also a *percent* listing for *all* listed nutrients to indicate how these numbers related to the consumer's diet. The USDA favored a label that simply listed *numbers* of grams or milligrams of nutrients without providing an indicator of how this related to the total diet. For example, if a product contained 23 grams of fat per serving, the FDA format would list the number of grams and then translate that number into a percent of a daily value; the USDA proposal would simply list the 23 grams.

What does 23 grams of fat mean in a total day's intake? That depends on how many calories one needs each day—and that was part of the controversy. Do consumers need to know? The FDA felt that they did; the USDA expressed concern that the "percent of daily value" would confuse people.

The New Label

Finally, on December 2, 1992, the FDA and the USDA announced that the stalemate had ended. Reports stated that then-President George Bush had helped break the impasse largely by siding with the FDA and its consumer concerns. One major casualty of the final negotiations was the compliance deadline for new labels. May 1994 was the new deadline for manufacturer compliance, but some products were expected to begin displaying the new label by May 1993.

New regulations cover such previously nebulous areas as:

Serving size: Most product categories now have designated standard serving sizes on which nutrition information must be based.

Single-serving containers: Products sold in single-serving containers can no longer be broken into multiple servings for nutrition-labeling purposes.

Required labeling: All processed foods, except those prepared and served in restaurants, are now required to bear nutrition labeling, unless the company is too small to

---

The New Food Label

The new food labels will provide an up-to-date, easier-to-use nutrition-information guide that should clear up the confusion that has prevailed for years and perhaps offer an incentive to food manufacturers to improve the nutritional qualities of their products.

Nutrition Facts

Serving Size ½ cup (114g)
Servings Per Container 4

Amount Per Serving

Calories 90	Calories from Fat 30

	% Daily Value*
Total Fat 3g	5%
Saturated Fat 0g	0%
Cholesterol 0mg	0%
Sodium 300mg	13%
Total Carbohydrate 13g	4%
Dietary Fiber 3g	12%
Sugars 3g	
Protein 3g	

Vitamin A	80%	•	Vitamin C	60%
Calcium	4%	•	Iron	4%

* Percent Daily Values are based on a 2,000 calorie diet. Your daily values may be higher or lower depending on your calorie needs:

	Calories	2,000	2,500
Total Fat	Less than	65g	80g
Sat Fat	Less than	20g	25g
Cholesterol	Less than	300mg	300mg
Sodium	Less than	2,400mg	2,400mg
Total Carbohydrate		300g	375g
Fiber		25g	30g

Calories per gram:

Fat 9 • Carbohydrates 4 • Protein 4

Source: Food and Drug Administration 1992

afford the costs of nutrition analysis and label redesign, or the food package is too small to bear the required nutrition information.

Nutrition data: Newly required data include saturated fat, cholesterol, complex carbohydrates, sugars, dietary fiber, and number of calories from fat, along with the previously required total fat, total carbohydrate, and protein. Required vitamin and mineral data are now limited to vitamins A and C, calcium, iron, and sodium.

New standards: To replace the 1968 USRDAs, the FDA has created two new sets of nutrient guidelines. One set, called Daily Reference Values (DRVs), provides standards for such items as total fat, saturated fat, unsaturated fat, cholesterol, carbohydrate, fiber, and sodium. Information on some of these reference values will be provided for 2,000 and 2,500 calories, and will be referred to as "Daily Values." The second new set of standards, called Reference Daily Intakes (RDIs), updates the old USRDAs for vitamins and minerals to show the adequacy of foods as sources of these nutrients.

Descriptors: Words such as "light," "reduced," "low," "free," and others now have uniform definitions. The term "cholesterol-free" cannot appear on foods with more than 2 milligrams of cholesterol per serving nor with more than 2 grams of saturated fat per serving. If a food contains more than 11.5 grams of total fat per serving or per 100 grams, the label must state those levels immediately after any cholesterol claim.

Health claims: Only seven specific connections between food and health are legal: calcium and osteoporosis; sodium and hypertension; fat and cardiovascular disease; fat and cancer; fiber and cardiovascular disease; fiber and cancer; and antioxidant-rich foods (vitamins A, E, and C) and cancer. To bear these claims, foods must meet certain nutrient-content requirements.

Ingredient labeling: Prior to these new regulations, ingredient labeling was required on *almost* all processed foods, except if the product had a federally regulated "standard of identity." Products such as mayonnaise, white bread, and ice cream were in this category. With new regulations, *all* processed foods are now required to list ingredients.

Color additives: In a move to protect consumers who suffer reactions to specific food additives, labels on foods containing certified color additives must now state the specific coloring agents used.

Juice labeling: In another consumer-protection move, juices purporting to contain specific fruit or vegetable juices must now declare on the label the actual percentage of such juices in the product.

Raw produce, fish, raw meat, and poultry: Before these new labeling regulations, consumers could find out more about a serving of instant potatoes than they could about an apple or an orange. With the new regulations, the FDA identified 20 of each of the most commonly consumed fruits, vegetables, and fish—all purchased in raw form—and created guidelines for point-of-purchase nutrition-information displays for these foods in grocery stores. Currently, these regulations are voluntary, but they may become mandatory in the near future. The USDA was working on similar guidelines for point-of-purchase displays for raw meat and poultry.

Dietary supplements: The Dietary Supplement Act of 1992, newly signed into law on October 30, 1992, exempted dietary supplements—vitamins, minerals, herbs, and other similar substances—from the requirements of the new food-labeling law until at least December 1993. The new RDIs and DRVs could not be used on labels for these products until at least December 1994; USRDAs would continue to be used. The Dietary Supplement Act of 1992 gave the FDA legal authority to approve health claims for dietary-supplement products, and it called for further study of issues surrounding the regulation of dietary supplements.

Those responsible for the new label are optimistic that it will help guide consumers through the morass of competing products on supermarket shelves. On the day the final regulations were announced, then-Health and Human Services Secretary Louis Sullivan, M.D. exulted: "The Tower of Babel in food labels has come down, and American consumers are the winners." Consumer-advocacy groups and health professionals generally agree: these new labels are a coup for the consumer.　　　　　◇

Parents should closely monitor the nutritional intake of their preschoolers. By the time school age rolls around (above), it may be too late to control a child's eating habits.

Nutrition in the Early Years

by Diana Reese

"You are what you eat," goes the old adage, and it still holds true.

What children eat—from the time they are born—may greatly affect their health later in life. The baby who was breast-fed may have a reduced risk for diabetes mellitus; the little girl who drank plenty of calcium-rich milk may be less likely to suffer from osteoporosis after menopause; and the child who followed a low-fat diet with lots of fiber and fruits and vegetables may have a reduced risk for heart disease and cancer.

What you eat can be pretty important when you consider that diet is linked to 5 of the 10 leading causes of death in the United States: coronary heart disease, some types of cancer, stroke, non–insulin-dependent diabetes mellitus, and atherosclerosis.

Although researchers are not in complete agreement about how much childhood diet always affects adult health, they do concur on such commonsense strategies as breast-feeding and low-fat diets.

Breast-feeding Still the Best

"Mother's milk is the ideal food for babies," wrote U.S. Surgeon General Antonia Novello, M.D., in a 1990 article for *Parade* magazine. She supports the American Academy of Pediatrics' recommendation that children be breast-fed until age 1. "It's the lucky baby, I feel, who continues to nurse until [age] 2," she wrote.

Researchers continue to find reasons why mother's milk is the best food for a baby. "Breast milk is a dynamic substance," explains Vicky Newman, M.S., R.D., a perinatal nutritionist with Wellstart International, an educational program funded by the National Institutes of Health (NIH).

"It's not a product: it's a living tissue, and it changes composition to meet the needs of the child," she explains. For instance, colostrum, the milk produced by a mother during the first five days after delivering her child, is very high in vitamin A, appropriate for the newborn whose stores of vitamin A are typically low at birth.

Researchers have found that although breast milk does not contain high amounts of iron, the iron that is there is very well absorbed by the baby. In fact, about 50 percent of the iron is utilized by the baby, compared to 7 percent of the iron in fortified formula and 4 percent in infant cereals.

Breast milk contains immunoglobulins and perhaps other substances that help protect the infant against infection. Breast-fed babies usually get fewer ear infections and urinary-tract infections than their formula-fed counterparts.

The role of mother's milk in fighting infections, although well documented, may be of minimal importance in a well-developed country like the United States. Nonetheless, although the incidence of gastrointestinal infections "may not be as important in affluent areas, it's still a real problem in the inner city," according to Alvin M. Mauer, M.D., professor of medicine and pediatrics at the University of Tennessee-Memphis and former chair of the Committee on Nutrition for the American Academy of Pediatrics.

Breast-feeding has been found to prevent or delay all sorts of conditions, including celiac disease, diabetes, inflammatory bowel disease, allergies, and certain types of childhood cancers. And the latest studies have shown that breast milk contains long-chain fatty acids (also known as omega-3s or fish oils) that are important to the baby's developing neurological system. One British study even found that premature babies fed mother's milk reported higher IQs at age 7½ to 8.

Oddly enough, even the mother benefits. The woman who breastfeeds is less likely to develop osteoporosis or breast cancer. Even so, just 54 percent of mothers breast-feed their babies when they leave the hospital, and only 21 percent are still nursing when the child is five to six months old. One of the goals of *Health People 2000*, a public health policy statement, is to increase those numbers to 50 or, better yet, 75 percent.

Older women who are well educated and relatively affluent, as well as those who live in the western United States, appear to be the most likely mothers to breast-feed. Least likely are mothers who are low-income, black, and under age 20, and those who live in the southeastern United States.

"As a society, we don't make it easy to breast-feed," Mauer points out. "Women don't have the support of their mothers [because they didn't breast-feed], and they may not have any friends [who have breast-fed]."

"It's a learned art that requires teachers," says Mary Grace Lanese, B.S.N., I.B.C.L.C., R.N., the U.S. delegate of the International Lactation Consultant Association. She's part of a growing number of "lactation consultants," who help new mothers in the hospital with nursing problems.

The American Academy of Pediatrics has said that 96 percent of new mothers can breast-feed successfully, "given adequate instruction, emotional support, and favorable circumstances."

TV Raises Cholesterol?

What kids eat may not be the only factor that influences their cholesterol. Television may also play a role.

Although the experts have decided that only children with a family history of high cholesterol or heart disease need a cholesterol check, some researchers have found that television watching may be a better indicator of high cholesterol in kids.

Children who watched two to four hours of TV per day were twice as likely as kids who watched less than two hours to have a cholesterol level of 200 or higher, according to a study in the July 1992 issue of *Pediatrics*. Children who sat in front of the television set more than four hours were four times as likely to have high cholesterol readings. The researchers found that those kids were less likely to eat lean meat or to be physically active.

Fight Cholesterol Early

The link between diet and heart disease has convinced some parents to start young with their kids when it comes to cutting down on fat in the diet. Too young, in some cases.

Reducing saturated fat and feeding low-fat or skim milk to children under the age of 2 can be a very unhealthy practice. "It's potentially hazardous," says Terry F. Hatch, M.D., associate professor of pediatrics at the University of Illinois College of Medicine in Urbana-Champaign and a member of the American Academy of Pediatrics Committee on Nutrition.

If low-fat diets are started too early, "kids don't grow," adds Mauer. "They can't take a lot of volume so they need calorie-dense food, and fat is calorie dense." Their fast rate of growth during the first two years also raises their requirement for calories. Breast milk, for example, derives half its calories from fat.

Teenagers should be careful, too, not to overrestrict fat and calories. The academy reports "growth failure" among adolescents who have gone overboard in cutting out fats.

Around age 2 to 3, however, most experts now agree that following a low-fat diet gets children started on healthy eating habits that will pay off later in life.

In September 1992, the American Academy of Pediatrics joined the growing list of low-fat advocates and revised its dietary and cholesterol guidelines, announcing that children over age 2 should get approximately 30 percent of their total calories from fat, less than 10 percent from saturated fat, and less than 300 milligrams of cholesterol a day. The academy had previously recommended that between 30 and 40 percent of total calories come from fat.

"The consumption of lower-fat dairy products and lean meats—critical sources of protein, iron, and calcium—should be encouraged throughout childhood and adolescence," says a policy statement from the academy. "A varied diet including foods from each of the major food groups provides the best assurance of nutritional adequacy."

The guidelines follow those issued by the National Cholesterol Education Program, part of the National Heart, Lung and Blood Institute. A report issued by a panel convened to study cholesterol levels in children and adolescents concluded that coronary heart disease, the leading cause of death in the United States, begins early in life. The panel also states that both eating habits and genetics affect blood-cholesterol levels and the risk for heart disease, and that lowering cholesterol levels in children and teens will be beneficial.

Just how much of a change do these recommendations represent in the normal kid's diet? According to food-consumption surveys, today's kids get about 35 percent of their calories from fat, 14 to 15 percent from saturated fats, and less than 300 milligrams of cholesterol a day—not all that far off from the academy's guidelines.

Both the academy and the Cholesterol Program recommend selective cholesterol screening of children whose family history puts them at a higher risk for coronary heart disease. In other words, children whose parents or grandparents have a history of heart disease before age 55 or whose parents have a cholesterol level above 240 should have their cholesterol checked.

Mauer disagrees with the concern over fat and cholesterol in childhood: "There are no studies in children showing this [low-fat] diet is safe or necessary."

He worries, too, that restricting what children eat sends them a "negative message" about food, and that it reduces the focus on other risk factors for heart disease, such as smoking, obesity, and lack of exercise.

He is not alone in his concern. Research studies have been published on both sides of the issue; the *Journal of the American Medical Association* ran one article on the case against childhood cholesterol screening, and then later ran another article on the case for childhood cholesterol screening.

Do You Know What Your Kids Are Eating?

Does the stereotypical child really subsist on a diet of potato chips and soda pop with an occasional chocolate-chip cookie thrown in for good measure?

First, the good news.

A *New England Journal of Medicine* study confirmed earlier research that, despite the erratic eating habits of kids age 2 to 5, children take in a constant number of calories each day. In fact, the researchers suggested providing children with a variety of healthy foods and leaving them alone, instead of resorting to threats, bribes, or punishment.

Mauer concurs: "You have to look at the diet not one day, but the trends over a couple of weeks or even, for adolescents, over a couple of months."

"From a nutritional point of view, we have the healthiest kids ever," says Hatch.

He hesitates to call any food "empty calories." Children need a high number of calories a day. "If you start with the basics and get the nutrients you need, those extra calories may be junk food, but you burn them up," he says.

More good news. Children are "reasonably knowledgeable" about nutrition, according to a study by the American Dietetic Association. Hatch points out, though, that "just because they know it doesn't mean they will do it."

And now for the bad news: information collected by the U.S. Department of Agriculture's Food Consumption Survey backs up Hatch's statement. Nine out of 10 teenagers did not eat any dark-green or deep-yellow vegetables on the day of the survey. Only half had any fruit. Two out of 10 teenage boys and 4 out of 10 teenage girls failed to drink any milk that day. Yet the average teenage boy drank 12 ounces of soft drinks, while girls consumed 9 ounces.

Those eating habits may have a lot to do with why the average intake of calcium falls below the Recommended Dietary Allowance (RDA).

Nutrients for boys that were below the RDAs also included vitamin E, magnesium, and zinc, while the average girl's diet was also lacking in vitamin B_6, iron, zinc, and phosphorus.

Children's diets have changed between the surveys done in 1977 and 1987: kids drink less whole milk and more low-fat or skim milk and more carbonated soft drinks. They eat less beef served alone but more meat mixtures, and about the same amount of fruits.

Kids have a remarkable taste for the wrong foods, according to a study of children

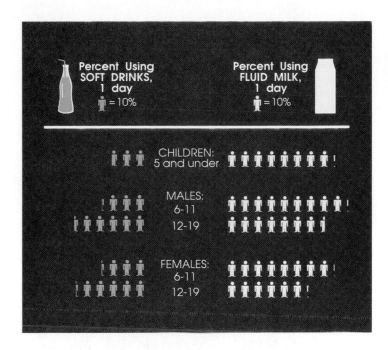

4 to 7 years old. When allowed to choose freely from a large variety of foods, they picked 25 percent of their calories from foods with added sugar. When told that their parents would monitor the meal they selected, the kids changed their minds and ended up with fewer selections and fewer foods high in sugar. The researchers concluded that young children, "when left alone to choose a meal, make poor nutritional choices," and "are likely to prefer foods high in sugar, saturated fatty acids, and sodium."

That yen for the wrong foods, coupled with a lack of physical activity, has led to a perceived increase in obesity among children. The issue of overweight children is a "reasonable concern," says Hatch, although no one agrees on the number of heavy kids out there. One survey by the National Center for Health Statistics indicates that up to 27 percent of children age 6 to 11, and 22 percent of those 12 to 17, are overweight.

Ironically, there is also a preoccupation with weight among children. As many as 70 percent of teenagers and young adults perceive themselves as overweight, and more than one-third of them are dieting. Those attitudes start young; a survey of Cincinnati children in grades three to six found that 45 percent wanted to be thinner, and 37 percent had already tried to lose weight. ◇

The Edible Bouquet

by Erin Hynes

Eating flowers isn't new. For centuries, pioneers and immigrants ate flowers as matter-of-factly as we eat vegetables today. After all, flowers are edible, and hungry people tend to develop great resourcefulness when it comes to their next meal. Still, somewhere along the line, flowers fell out of favor as a food of choice. Garden designer Liz Druitt laments this turn of events, pointing out that "it's a shame to waste the potential of a garden."

Druitt has even done something about increasing the popularity of flower fare. At the Peaceable Kingdom School, a nonprofit organic-gardening center in Washington, Texas, Druitt teaches a class on edible flowers. Her quest to move flowers out of the garden and into the kitchen has received a substantial boost from the coincidental upsurge in popularity of new ethnic and nouvelle cuisines, whose recipes often call for flowers to add color and flavor.

Sweet and Savory

That flowers add color is no surprise to anyone who's ever been outdoors. But how can they help food? According to Lucinda Hutson, author of *The Herb Garden Cookbook*, flowers are "beautiful in salads, or floated in soups, or frozen into ice cubes and added to the punch bowl." And, to top it off, they add flavor. When working flowers into the menu, says Hutson, it helps to think of them in two flavor groups. Savory flowers, like savory herbs, are suited to dishes such as meats, grains, vegetables, and salads. This category includes peppery nasturtium and the flowers of some savory herbs, including cilantro and rosemary. Flowers that are less pungent but still savory include borage, calendula, elderflower, dandelion, redbud, begonia, and sweet alyssum.

Newly popular ethnic and nouvelle recipes have helped flowers out of the garden and into the kitchen.

The second group consists of flowers with a sweet or floral flavor. These flowers are best used in desserts and sweetened drinks. Clove pink, daylily, lilac, rose, honeysuckle, violet, and orange blossom are the most aromatic. Milder sweet flowers include petunia, crape myrtle, Johnny-jump-up, pansy, tulip, and summer squash blossom.

According to Hutson, flowers are rarely eaten for their nutritional value. It's not that they lack nutrients —roses, for example, are loaded with vitamins A and C. Rather, the small quantities of flowers likely to be consumed have very little impact on the diet.

Flower Users Beware

Anyone trying flowers as food should heed a few precautions. First, never make substitutions, and don't experiment. Some flowers are inedible at best and poisonous at worst. Use only those you know to be edible.

Second, check to see whether you're allergic to any flower you intend to eat. Rub a blossom on your inner arm and wait a day to see if any redness develops. If it does, scratch the flower from the menu.

Third, eat only flowers that have never been sprayed with pesticides. That most likely means you'll need to grow your own or get them from a garden you trust. Although Druitt jokes that, as an English major terrified of starvation, she learned to eat whatever grew by the roadside, these wild plants are off-limits; most highway departments spray roadsides. Cookbook author Hutson cautions that flowers from florists are also unsafe, since commercial greenhouses routinely use pesticides. You may be able to find edible flowers in specialty grocery stores, although, Hutson notes, perishability guarantees you'll pay a high price for the flowers.

Culinary Applications

Flowers have many culinary uses. They can be candied and jellied. They can flavor butters and vinegars. They can be fried as fritters and baked into breads, fermented into wines, and brewed into tea. Peaceable Kingdom's Druitt prefers her blooms fresh and unadulterated, in salads or as garnishes. She suggests that the wary try the most popular

Flowers subjected to pesticide treatment are off-limits for culinary applications. Fanciers of floral fare should only use flowers from their own garden or from a reliable market.

BORAGE
(Borago officinalis)

Star-shaped, five-petaled flower starts out pink, turns blue when ripe. Contributes a nutty flavor to salads, candy, drinks, and wine. Leaf adds a cucumber flavor to cold drinks, salads, and sandwiches.

CLOVE PINK
(Dianthus caryophyllus)

Single or double, white, pink, or purple flowers with sweet clove-like perfume are used to flavor syrups, yogurts, sugar, jams, vinegars, and wines.

CALENDULA
(Calendula officinalis)

Also called pot marigold, the brilliant, yellow-orange petals are sometimes fluted. The crisp petals provide a tangy flavor in salads, quiche, butters, rice dishes, and soups.

DAYLILY
(Hemerocallis spp.)

Funnel-shaped orange-yellow flowers. Not all are tasty — take a small bite to test. Daylilies flavor pickles, salads, and soups. Dried daylilies are "golden needles" in oriental cooking.

CHIVE
(Allium schoenoprasum)

Globular mauve flowers produced in midsummer can be used whole in salads or broken apart and used in grain and egg dishes. The cylindrical leaves are used as oniony garnishes with sandwiches and soups.

ELDERFLOWER
(Sambucus canadensis)

Flowers of the American elderberry bush impart an added sweetness to fritters, teas, crepes, and wines. The berries are rich in vitamin C and are used to make wines and jellies.

CHRYSANTHEMUM
(Chrysanthemum x morifolium)

This florists' chrysanthemum has flowerheads of many forms, including single, double, and pompom florets. Used in teas and as a garnish for oriental dishes and salads.

HOLLYHOCK
(Alcea spp.)

Large showy flowers of various colors with a subtle fragrance, these petals can be used in fritters, teas, and as a garnish. The leaves can be boiled and eaten as a vegetable.

flowers first: violets, nasturtiums, daylilies, carnations, and borages.

Here are a bunch of flower foods to try. For all recipes except those requiring buds, pick healthy blooms that have just opened. If you're not going to use them immediately, store them in cool water.

Breads. Knead in between 1 tablespoon and ½ cup of flowers per loaf before baking. The quantity depends on how flavorful the flower is and how intense a flavor you like in your loaf.

Crystallized flowers like the violets at left add a decorative and delicious touch to cakes, pies, and other desserts.

Butters. Mash petals with softened, unsalted butter, then chill to harden. Try lilacs, pansies, roses, or calendulas.

Candies. Crystallize sweet flower petals with sugar to make lovely edible decorations for cakes, puddings, ice cream, and other desserts. To crystallize petals, clean well-shaped, newly opened blossoms by rinsing with a gentle mist of water. Whip an egg white until it's white but not foamy, and dip the blossoms or petals into the white until they're thoroughly coated (you can also paint the egg white on with a fine paintbrush). Then dip them in superfine sugar. Lay the sugary blossoms on a single sheet of waxed paper resting on a wire rack. Cover with another sheet of waxed paper to keep dust from settling on the goodies. If you're candying

HONEYSUCKLE
(Lonicera spp.)

The perfume of these tubular flowers with diverging lips is synonymous with summer days. These petals add a strong, sweet floral taste to syrups, puddings, and ice cream.

NASTURTIUM
(Tropaeolum majus)

The red, orange, or white trumpet-like flowers have a cress-like flavor that adds bite to salads and sandwiches. The young seeds can be chopped and substituted for horseradish in sauce tartare.

LAVENDER
(Lavendula angustifolia)

The pale pink flower is used to flavor jams and to make lavender vinegar. Mixed with savory herbs, it creates fragrant stews.

PANSY
(Viola x Wittrockiana)

These flowers with face-like markings and bold colors that range from purple, blue, and maroon, to red, yellow, or orange, are a colorful addition to salads, desserts, and butters.

LILAC
(Syringa vulgaris)

The strong, rich scent of these fragrant, densely clustered purple flowers add a sweet pungency to fritters, butter, candy, salads, soups, and desserts.

ROSE
(Rosa spp.)

Roses were considered the "gift of angels" by the ancients. Rose petals have been historically valued for jams, vinegars, pies, and as a garnish. Rosewater flavors desserts and drinks.

DWARF MARIGOLD
(Tagetes tenuifolia)

The bright yellow or orange flowers add a beautiful garnish to jellies, salads, and omelets, while the strongly scented leaves adds orange pungency to teas.

TULIP
(Tulipa spp.)

These bell- or saucer-shaped flowers make a beautiful and creative encasement for cold fillings, such as tuna salad or herbed ricotta. Hybrids in the Darwin, Fosteriana, Triumph, or Cottage groups are best.

blossoms, you can use a toothpick to separate the petals as they dry. Let the candied flowers air-dry in a warm room, or dry them on a cookie sheet in a warm (150°–200° F) oven with the door ajar. Air drying takes about a day; oven drying takes about two hours. When dry and brittle, store flowers between sheets of waxed paper in an airtight container.

Good flowers for candying are violets, rose petals, marigold petals, lilacs, borages, orange blossoms, bergamots, and lavenders.

Fritters. Dip flowers in batter and fry. Try borage, elderflowers, or lilacs.

Backyard gardens yield more than vegetables. Squash flowers (right) and other blooms from vegetable plants can be used in many recipes.

Jellies. You can make both savory and sweet flowers into jellies and jams, either as the main or secondary flavoring. You can also use rose hips; the hips are the fruit left after the petals fall.

For an aesthetically pleasing presentation, some gourmets use edible flowers to color-coordinate their food with the table settings (above). Salad lovers find that certain flowers give a flavorful tang to vinegar (right).

Vinegars. Because vinegar can make some metals rust, be sure all equipment you use—pans, sealable containers, bottles, and bottle caps—are stainless steel, enamel, or another nonrusting material.

To make the flower vinegar, place a cup of petals into a sealable container. Add any herbs or spices you want for flavor, such as cloves, dill, or peppercorns. Heat 4 cups of high-quality wine or cider vinegar until lukewarm. Pour the vinegar over the petals and seal the container. After about three weeks, strain the vinegar through a cheesecloth to remove the petals. Squeezing the petals will

remove the last drops of flavored vinegar. Pour the vinegar into a glass bottle and cover. Use on salads and vegetables.

Recommended flowers include clove pinks flavored with cloves, elderflowers with allspice and a little sugar, and nasturtiums with dill and peppercorns.

Wines. You can make wine out of almost any flower. Besides the classic dandelions, try elderberries, carnations, or roses. You can also steep flowers in wine to add flavor.

Whether you decide to try these dishes or stick with using flowers fresh from the garden, the idea is to have fun while jazzing up your meals. As Druitt says, "People shouldn't think of their gardens as objects. They should think of them as toys."　◇

Pickles. You can pickle the unopened buds of daylilies, squash blossoms, roses, and, says Druitt, "anything firm enough and large enough not to fall apart." That includes the unripe fruit of nasturtium, to make a caperlike delicacy. Pickle the buds or fruit as you would cucumbers, in cider vinegar seasoned with salt, dill, and garlic.

Sugars. Use sweet flower petals to flavor sugar to use in iced tea, cake frosting, and baked desserts. Use ¼ cup of clean petals to 1 cup of fine sugar. Alternate the sugar and petals in layers in a sealable container. Leave the container sealed for about three weeks before using the sugar.

Syrups. Make an infusion by steeping about 1 tablespoon of whole small flowers or petals of large flowers in 1 cup of hot water just shy of boiling. Steep for about half an hour, then add sugar and stir to dissolve. Try violets, rose petals, honeysuckles, or clove pinks. Pour flower syrups over puddings and ices.

Arresting Your Appetite

by Cathy Perlmutter

Like an unruly child, your appetite sometimes throws a tantrum and demands more food. Against all reason, the cravings may even hit right after a large steak dinner. Or right out of nowhere. Is there any rhyme or reason to these cravings? Scientists say yes. They've discovered that our appetites do indeed follow some underlying rules. Appetite, they say, is turned on both by what's happening outside of us—like whether someone's just offered us a doughnut—and what's happening inside our bodies —the biochemical signals between mouth, stomach, nervous system, and brain. In one of the hottest new areas of research, scientists are discovering that certain foods may even trigger the desire to eat more, while other foods tend to suppress that desire.

New research points to at least 10 different ways you can control the urge to eat, whenever or wherever it strikes you:

1. Drown your appetite.

"Drinking generous amounts of water is overwhelmingly the number one way to reduce appetite," says *Prevention* adviser George Blackburn, M.D., Ph.D., associate professor at Harvard Medical School. Reason: a lot of water takes up a lot of room in the stomach. The stomach feels full, reducing the desire to eat.

Water can quell the appetite in other ways. "Many people think they're having a food craving, when in fact they're thirsty," says Dr. Blackburn. So next time you get the urge to eat, try a cup of water instead.

Aim to swallow 64 ounces of fluids daily. Don't gulp down an entire glass at a time, as if it were medicine, or you'll never continue. Instead, sip 3 to 4 ounces at a time, throughout the day.

2. Graze sensibly.

Mom always warned us not to snack before mealtime, to avoid ruining our appetite. But nowadays, scientists are rethinking Mom's advice.

Grazing means nibbling small amounts of food frequently, instead of eating just one to three large meals a day. Scientists who en-

dorse it say grazing can keep your appetite down all day long and prevent binging.

James Kenney, Ph.D., R.D., nutrition-research specialist at the Pritikin Longevity Center in Santa Monica, California, believes that grazing quashes the appetite because it keeps insulin levels steadier—and lower— than eating a few large meals.

A large meal, especially one that's sugary and high in fat content, stimulates the body to produce lots of insulin. Its job: to remove all of those excess sugars and block the release of fats into the bloodstream.

Smaller, more frequent meals, on the other hand, keep insulin and blood-sugar levels more stable, so the brain doesn't signal an urgent need for more fuel.

But for grazing to be effective, Dr. Kenney warns, you have to munch the right kinds of foods. "You cannot graze on M & M's, potato chips, and Haagen Dazs. Your insulin levels and appetite increase. But if you graze on low-fat, high-fiber foods that aren't packed with calories—like carrots, peaches, oranges, red peppers, pasta, potatoes, oatmeal —you keep your appetite down."

If grazing feels like too much freedom to eat, it may be helpful to schedule your grazing in advance. Plan to eat every two hours or so. Bring your healthy goodies to work with you, so you aren't tempted by fattening fare.

3. Soup it up.
A lot of research over the years suggests that soup has the ability to turn off the appetite with far fewer calories than many other foods.

In a study at Johns Hopkins University in Baltimore, Maryland, researchers compared soup with other appetizers to see which most effectively dimmed the desire to eat. They invited 12 men to lunch for two weeks. On different days the men received different appetizers of tomato soup, Muenster cheese on crackers, or fresh fruit. Calories in each appetizer portion were equal. Then the men were given a main course to eat.

Results: tomato soup was the most satisfying appetizer. It beat out all the others in reducing the number of calories of the entrée that were consumed. The least satisfying appetizer: cheese and crackers. Soup reduced later calorie intake by 25 percent compared with cheese and crackers.

The researchers aren't sure just why soup is so satiating. In other tests, they found it wasn't the warmth of soup or the salt that made a difference; cold, less-salty soup reduced appetite about as well. The key may be the large volume of space that soup takes up in the stomach. Also, most of soup's calories come from carbohydrates rather than fat, and carbohydrates are more satisfying to the brain.

There may be a psychological factor as well, notes Dr. Kenney: "Hot soup is very relaxing if you have a nervous, gnawing appetite."

4. Eat more complex carbohydrates.
A few years ago, potatoes and pasta were forbidden foods among dieters. We were encouraged to dine on a hamburger (without the roll), with a side order of cottage cheese (nestled on a lettuce leaf).

Since then, high-protein, low-carbohydrate schemes have been debunked as unhealthy, ineffective in the long run, and even potentially dangerous. Foods like rice, potatoes, corn, and pasta that are high in complex carbohydrates and low in fat have made a big comeback. Among their many virtues for weight watchers is their powerful ability to satisfy the appetite with fewer calories.

Scientists offer a variety of fascinating theories to explain the appetite-quenching effect of high-carbohydrate, low-fat foods.

One hypothesis has to do with our body's primary fuel source, glycogen, a form of carbohydrate stored mostly in the liver and muscles. The body can store only a couple of thousand calories of glycogen at a time, com-

Food Cravings: Ride the Wave

You're sitting at your desk, concentrating hard on your work, when suddenly an image seizes control of your brain. Carrot cake! You can taste it; you can smell it; you have to have it!

Sound familiar? Whether the yearning is for carrot cake, kosher pickles, or chocolate-covered cherries, everyone has experienced a food craving at some time. "Food cravings are a normal part of living in a food-oriented society," says Linda Crawford, M.S., an eating-behavior specialist at Green Mountain at Fox Run, a residential weight- and health-management center for women, in Ludlow, Vermont.

The problem, notes Crawford, is that many people interpret food cravings as commands. "People believe that cravings keep getting stronger until they finally have to give in."

But, in fact, research by G. Alan Marlatt, Ph.D., of the University of Washington in Seattle, shows that cravings follow more of a wave pattern. The craving starts and escalates, but then it peaks and subsides. "People need to know that it will decline," says Crawford, "When a food craving strikes, they might imagine themselves like a surfer. They have to ride that wave till it finally vanishes."

It's much easier to ride the wave if you distract yourself, Crawford says. "Ideally, you should do something incompatible with eating, like taking a walk." Give yourself 20 minutes to wait it out, she advises. "In 20 minutes, reevaluate the situation. The craving has probably diminished. Now what are you going to do about it? You can more rationally decide what, if anything, you're going to eat and how much of it you'll eat." As in surfing, practice makes perfect, adds Crawford. "The more you practice riding a wave, the easier it becomes."

pared with over 100,000 calories that can be stored as fat.

High-fat foods don't switch off the "eat" message as effectively as foods that are high in carbohydrates, says Dr. Kenney. That's because dietary fat cannot be converted into glycogen, and glycogen (particularly that stored in the liver) appears to trigger the hunger signal to turn off. Carbohydrates, on the other hand, are quickly converted to glycogen, so they shut the hunger signal off more quickly. For example, take 1 ounce of potato chips versus a whole baked potato. Each has 160 calories, but which is more likely to fill you up? Obviously, you end up eating a lot more calories from potato chips, loaded with fat, than from a baked spud (whose calories come primarily from carbohydrates) before you feel satisfied.

Additionally, if those carbohydrates are derived from whole grains, fruits, vegetables, and beans instead of overprocessed sugars and starches, they refuel glycogen levels without overstimulating insulin levels.

What's more, Dr. Kenney adds, carbohydrates are digested and stored less efficiently than fat. "That means the metabolic rate goes up more when the body is metabolizing carbohydrates than when it's metabolizing fat. A higher metabolic rate produces more body heat, which is associated with reduced appetite. And according to my theory, whatever heats you up, slims you down."

There's yet another theory about why carbohydrates dim the appetite. It has to do with the connection between carbohydrates and the brain chemical serotonin.

Serotonin is a mood enhancer, and a lack of serotonin is linked with depression. The fact that many depressed people are also overweight has led some scientists to investigate the possibility that lack of serotonin stimulates food cravings, while boosting serotonin levels reduces appetite. They've discovered that carbohydrates seem to increase brain levels of serotonin—and reduce appetite. But this research is still in the early stages, says Thomas Wadden, Ph.D., director of the Center for Health Behavior at Syracuse University in New York. Whatever the reason for carbohydrate's satisfying effects, it is effective. Nutritionists recommend 6 to

11 daily servings of grains like bread, cereal, and pasta. It may take about 20 minutes from the time you eat a complex carbohydrate until the hypothalamus turns off your appetite. So if you're going out to dinner and concerned that you may overeat, try a high-carbohydrate, low-fat "preload" about 20 minutes before the rest of the meal. Order whole-wheat bread (without the butter) or soup with noodles or rice. You'll wind up eating less food at dinnertime.

Learn how to beat those highly caloric cravings that tend to sabotage weight loss.

5. Say *si!* to spicy foods.
Have you ever binged on a huge plate of spicy food—like Mexican, Thai, Szechuan, or Indian fare? You've probably found that it's nearly impossible. Those foods seem to quiet the appetite better than blander fare. One possible reason may be that "the flavor is so intense that we don't need as much," suggests Maria Simonson, Ph.D., Sc.D., director of the health, weight, and stress clinic at Johns Hopkins Medical Institutions in Baltimore, Maryland.

Spicy foods also speed the metabolism, says Dr. Kenney. "When people eat hot chili, they often sweat, a sure sign of increased metabolic rate. And the faster the metabolic

Appetite Turn-Ons

Want to gain a lot of weight in the unhealthiest way possible? Of course not. Yet millions of Americans regularly do the very things that turn their appetites on full throttle. Here are three big don'ts:

1. Don't diet or skip meals.
You only had to watch Oprah's exciting and rapid weight loss—followed by her depressingly rapid weight gain—to get the message: restrictive, ultralow-calorie diets don't work.

Few things can increase your appetite like a prolonged restrictive diet, says Maria Simonson, Ph.D., Sc.D., director of the health, weight, and stress clinic at Johns Hopkins Medical Institutions in Baltimore, Maryland.

Psychologically, we overeat after starving "because we feel like we've been punishing ourselves. We want a reward," says Dr. Simonson.

Physiologically, our body is doing what it can to fight starvation. It knows it's low on fuel. So our appetite eventually shoots up, either during the diet or, like Oprah, when we try to return to normal eating.

Even skipping meals can lead to a ravenous appetite, notes Wayne Callaway, M.D., obesity specialist and clinical professor at George Washington University in Washington, D.C. "People who skip breakfast or lunch then tend to binge after dinner in the evening, instead of eating moderately. It's a common problem among chronic dieters."

The problem with skipping meals is that the blood sugar and glycogen that the body uses as fuel drop to very low levels, signaling the body to demand more food and making you hungry.

Most responsible weight-loss experts these days are recommending that people worry less about cutting calories and focus instead on eating low-fat, high-carbohydrate, high-fiber foods. Those foods are less likely to be stored as fat, and they tend to reduce appetite and increase metabolic rate after meals so the body naturally limits the amount it takes in.

2. Don't Hang Out with the Notorious Gang of Two.
"Fats and sweets are a deadly combination," says Thomas Wadden, Ph.D., director of the Center for Health Behavior at Syracuse University in New York. Each, by itself, heightens appetite. But the combination is by far the best way to shift the appetite into overdrive.

It probably has a lot to do with our body's insulin response. "Eating sweets rate, the more heat produced by the body. Remember, whatever warms you up, in turn slims you down."

So it makes sense to learn to use hot peppers, horseradish, and chili powder, especially in place of salt. "Salt does make some people eat more, perhaps by upping insulin levels," says Dr. Kenney. "But the best reason to avoid salt is because its use often leads to high blood pressure."

6. Feast on fiber.
How does fiber satisfy? In many ways. Satisfaction begins in the mouth, and fibrous

Those foods that accelerate your metabolism will, in turn, slim you down faster and more easily.

foods provide robust mouthfuls that must be chewed thoroughly. It's a natural way to slow down eating, and eating slower means eating less—the extra time lets the body know it's received fuel and doesn't need much more.

Next, fiber takes up a lot of room in the stomach, and increased stomach volume translates into a reduced appetite. So the stomach feels fuller for longer.

Soluble fiber, best known for its cholesterol-cutting abilities, also dampens insulin response. Normally, after a meal, insulin levels rise to help metabolize sugar and fat. But

can lead to a big increase in the amount of sugar in the blood," explains Nori Geary, Ph.D., associate research professor at the Cornell University Medical Center in White Plains, New York. "That causes insulin levels to soar. Insulin stimulates the metabolism of sugars—not just the sugar you ate, but all sugars in the blood that the brain uses for fuel. In some people the result is a lower blood-sugar level than they started with. And that can turn up the appetite."

When fat is combined with carbohydrate, insulin levels are pushed up much more than with carbohydrate alone, says James Kenney, Ph.D., R.D., nutrition-research specialist at the Pritikin Longevity Center in Santa Monica, California. And the combination pushes insulin far above what either of them can do alone.

"That's why it's better to avoid high-fat, high-sugar foods entirely. Very few people can get away with 'just a bite,' " Dr. Kenney says.

If you do have an overwhelming sweet craving, go for a hard candy or mint. "You just can't eat that many hard candies," says Dr. Kenney. "It's when sugar is combined with fat, like in a chocolate bar, or when it's in liquid form, like in a soft drink, that you can get a lot of sugar down very fast and overstimulate insulin production."

3. Don't swim alone.
Many scientists have searched for reasons to explain why swimming, an excellent cardiovascular and muscle workout, doesn't seem to trim off body fat as effectively as walking or other exercises. Some say the body tries to retain fat for buoyancy. But Dr. Kenney thinks it has more to do with the fact that swimming, unlike other forms of exercise, does not raise the core body temperature. "And if it doesn't warm you up, it doesn't slim you down.

"Swimmers stay cool when they swim because the high heat capacity of water compared with air drains heat from the body," says Dr. Kenney. "So afterward, they're not only hungry from glycogen depletion, but also because their bodies don't heat up. That may be why people tend to climb out of the pool ravenous, but finish a fast walk hot but not hungry." Most research suggests that swimmers, unlike walkers, runners, and bicyclists, do not lose weight spontaneously.

Swimmers should be aware of the possibility of increased appetite and to counter it by being extra careful to eat only low-fat, high-fiber foods. If you really need to lose a lot of weight, don't rely on swimming alone; combine swimming with other, less appetite-enhancing forms of exercise, such as walking or bicycling.

soluble fiber keeps insulin levels lower after a meal, says Dr. Kenney. Richest sources of soluble fiber include barley, oat products, beans, apples, citrus fruits, and root vegetables like beets, carrots, and potatoes.

Finally, foods that are high in fiber tend to have fewer calories in every bite, which means fewer calories consumed overall. Research at the University of Alabama shows that people eat many fewer calories on a low-calorie-density diet than a high one, says Dr. Kenney.

Americans consume only about 12 to 15 grams of fiber daily, while 25 grams or more is recommended. Get fiber through food and not through fiber supplements; some of these products are fraudulent, and others, if abused, can lead to severe constipation.

7. Eat simply.
Your daughter-in-law has invited you to dinner, and she's eager to please. There's freshly baked bread, a shrimp appetizer, a roast beef entrée, a potato side dish, rice pilaf, noodles, fresh broccoli, and raspberry pie, chocolate truffles, and frozen yogurt.

If you're like most mortals, you'll want to try a little of everything. Unfortunately, by the end of the meal, that may translate into a lot of food.

Now imagine this: instead of the multi-course feast, she serves a simple dish of salad, a one-pot chicken-and-rice casserole, with raspberry pie. How likely is it that you'll overeat? Much less. "Serving a wide variety of foods at one meal can cause you to eat much more," says Dr. Wadden. "That's be-

cause each different food has its own satiety level." So after you've had as much shrimp as you want, you might still crave the roast beef. After the bread, you'll still want to try the potatoes, noodles, and rice. And of course, it's nearly impossible to resist "just a taste" of every dessert.

So limit entrées and side dishes to one each at every meal. And look for some one-pot meals that your family can enjoy.

8. Outbike your appetite.
Got the munchies? If you've already tried a glass of water or a high-carbohydrate, high-fiber snack, but they didn't do the trick, take a walk, ride an exercise bike, or do some other activity. Regular exercise reduces the appetite, in part by modifying the insulin response, which reduces the upward spike that has been associated with increased appetite. Exercise helps control blood sugar, leading to a steady state associated with fullness. Aerobic exercise reduces the appetite in the short run, says Dr. Kenney, perhaps because it heats the body. Not many people can eat a lot after exercise.

A regular exercise program does increase appetite somewhat. That's because you burn up your glycogen stores more quickly. This partially offsets the appetite-dimming effects of the temperature rise. But when you step up exercise, you usually don't eat quite enough calories to make up for the amount of fat you've burned off. Provided you're on a high-carbohydrate diet, you can replenish your glycogen stores without replacing the fat you burned off exercising.

Here's an example. Say you eat 1,600 calories a day, but burn only 1,500. Over the long run, those hundred extra calories a day turn into extra pounds. But then you begin a daily exercise program. It burns off 400 additional calories, so you're burning a total of 1,900 calories a day. Your appetite does increase—but probably not by much, says Dr. Kenney. It might grow by 200 calories, to about 1,800 calories of food consumed daily. Compared with 1,900 calories burned, that makes for a negative calorie balance of 100 calories a day, which leads to weight loss. So exercise away—it really can balance the appetite to a healthy level. (But beware: there is one kind of exercise that doesn't warm you up and may not slim you down or aid weight loss. See the sidebar on "Appetite Turn-ons" on pages 96–97.)

9. Ask yourself "why?"

Before you eat, ask yourself why you want to eat. It may help you realize that it has nothing to do with hunger.

Emotions are a major reason people eat. "Eighty-five percent of my patients have psychological reasons for overeating," says Dr. Simonson. "And one of the major reasons is stress. Stress makes you eat more quickly than anything else.

"Some people who are stressed out go for soft, creamy, comfort foods, like mashed potatoes with plenty of butter. Or they want baked foods, like a milk-and-cookies snack:

it's the 'nothing-says-loving-like-something-from-the-oven' syndrome." If you are turning to food in response to bad feelings, it's important to develop a strategy to feel better, says Dr. Simonson. "Before you eat, ask yourself, 'How am I feeling about myself right now? What's happened this week to upset me? Am I eating this because I'm hungry or because I'm upset?' "

Antistress measures, from counseling to yoga, can help you feel better and eat less. Above all, says Dr. Simonson, don't start a weight-loss program during a time of severe stress. "Always work on your emotional problems before you change your diet."

10. Know your own triggers.

The sound and smell of sizzling sausage. The crunchy texture of popcorn. The smell, sight, sound, and even texture of foods are the most powerful triggers we have to eat—and to overeat.

"I recently had a craving for a kosher hot dog," Dr. Simonson recalls, "not because I was hungry, but because I was thinking about the tight skin and how it goes 'pop' when you bite into it." Sometimes we eat things because they look good, even when they aren't. "Haven't we all eaten mediocre cookies, just because they looked delicious?" she asks.

And sometimes we eat them just because they're around. So eliminate the temptation by banishing fattening foods from the house. "Our eating is so dependent on external cues that just seeing foods makes us want to eat," says Dr. Simonson. If someone else in the family has to have sweets or high-fat foods, ask him or her to hide them somewhere that you can't find them.

Dr. Simonson's team has even found that slow, soft music makes people eat more slowly, take smaller bites, and even enjoy the food more. It tastes better, says Dr. Simonson, because when you eat slowly, you really smell the food—and odor enhances flavor.

Keeping a food record can help you identify these kinds of cues. For a couple of days, write down everything you eat, and try to recall what made you start thinking about food—whether it was an advertisement or an emotion or an aroma. That helps you outthink craving the next time it happens.   ◇

Housecalls

by Mona Sutnick, Ed.D., R.D.

Q *What are these natural brain cocktails that I hear are being served at parties and boutiques? Can they really enhance your brainpower?*

A There's not much evidence that anything you eat or drink makes you smarter (i.e., raises your I.Q.). Diet, in general, is important to a person's performance—and critical to a child's development—and poor nutrition is certainly detrimental to it. But remain wary of claims made for "smart drinks," "smart foods," or "smart drugs."

These products contain carbohydrates, amino acids, or both. Amino acids are the building blocks of proteins and neurotransmitters that allow your brain to work, but research has not shown that supplements of amino acids in a normal diet have any significant effects on the brain.

The drinks served at a handful of "smart bars" around the country usually have fruit juice as a base, which will give a passing energy lift from the sugars (fructoses) they naturally contain. They may also contain various amino acids, which at best will pro-

vide you some long-term nutrition, and at worst can be dangerous when not taken under medical supervision. In addition, smart pills often consist of prescription drugs with no proven "smart" effects.

The placebo effect with smart cocktails is probably strong. Their biggest benefit may be as an alternative to alcohol. In the long run, eating healthfully, exercising, and getting enough rest are the best ways to reach your greatest mental potential.

Q *My friend claims that a "nonfat" food can still be high in calories. Could this possibly be true?*

A Your friend is right. It's important to understand the definitions of the words "fat" and "calorie." A fat is a type of food; a calorie is not.

A calorie is a unit that measures energy given off when a food is metabolized. All foods have calories, and fats are the highest in calories. But a "nonfat" food can have significant amounts of carbohydrates and other nutrients that supply calories. New food labeling may soon give you help in remembering these distinctions. (See the feature on food labeling on page 80.)

Q *What is the definition of red meat? Does it include pork or "wild" meats such as venison or rabbit?*

A "Red meat" refers not just to the color of the meat when raw or cooked, but also to the type of animal it comes from and the relative amounts of fat, cholesterol, and protein.

Normally, "red meat" denotes conventional, farm-raised mammals, and thus includes beef, pork, lamb, and veal. Like poultry, meats from animals that are traditionally wild, such as deer and rabbits, have a reputation for being leaner and less rich than more common red meats, and this generally proves true in nutritional analyses. Partly for this reason, farm-raised venison, buffalo, and other meats have gained in popularity.

Whatever kind of meat you choose, buy lean cuts and eat it in moderation. Enjoy it, but consider getting some of your protein from other sources as well.

The placebo effect from "smart drinks" is greater than any enhancement to intelligence brought about by such preparations.

Q *I've heard that some foods have a kind of healthy cholesterol in them. But then I also hear that some "no-cholesterol" foods can give you high cholesterol. I'm confused.*

A Cholesterol is found in, and plays an important function in, every cell in the bodies of animals. In food, cholesterol comes in only one basic form. What you hear about "good" and "bad" cholesterol refers only to the different forms in which cholesterol circulates in the body. The body takes dietary fat and cholesterol and converts them to the different types of blood fat by combining them with proteins to form substances called lipoproteins.

The two major forms of cholesterol in your blood are high-density lipoproteins (HDLs, or "good cholesterol") and low-density lipoproteins (LDLs, or "bad cholesterol"). Both are essential for the function of the body, but must be kept in the proper ratio for optimal health.

Because cholesterol is found only in animals, foods from plant sources are cholesterol-free. However, they may still have a high fat content, which will affect cholesterol levels in your body.

Q *Is fasting a healthy thing to do? What effect does it have on the body? Is fasting a good way to diet?*

A At present, we know of no health benefits from fasting. As nutrients derived from the intake of food clear from the blood during a fast, a complex chain of reactions causes the body to begin using its stores of energy (carbohydrates, fats, and proteins). A popular idea that fasting might have a "cleansing" effect on the body remains purely speculative.

Most adults are not harmed by a day without food, but children and older people may not do well under such circumstances.

Fasting is not particularly effective as a form of dieting. People tend to gain back lost calories and broken-down tissues.

In one form or another, fasting is a component of almost every traditional religion. The reasons for this are many, but total fasting does affect blood-sugar levels. Thus, when combined with a day of special contemplation or quietness, fasting can contribute to a sensation of light-headedness, spirituality—or at least a more mellow mood. When combined with a day of normal activities, though, fasting may cause a person to feel tired, irritable, and just plain hungry!

Q *I was taught that it's important to obtain protein at every meal. Now I see everywhere that complex carbohydrates are the way to go. Which is true? And what makes a carbohydrate "complex" rather than just junk food?*

A The body cannot store protein, so it needs a fresh supply every day. People must have protein in their diet to survive, but most don't realize that almost everything we eat contains some protein. Most Americans get half again to twice as much protein as they need. In addition, many of our protein sources—meat, cheese, and other dairy products—are also fat sources, prompting the need for moderation.

Complex carbohydrates such as starch and fiber are made up of long chains of sugar molecules. These complex carbohydrates provide a more slowly metabolized supply of calories. The main sources are foods such as fruits, vegetables, grains, or legumes —which provide other nutrients besides the carbohydrates.

Flours are complex carbohydrates. Flour-based foods will vary in healthiness depending on whether the flour is whole-grained and if sugars, fats, and other ingredients are added.

As a complex carbohydrate, flour is considered a healthy food. But when flour is combined with sugar, butter, and eggs to make a cake, its nutritional value is somewhat negated by the other ingredients.

Potatoes are an excellent source of complex carbohydrates, but potato chips are not. Eating eight ounces of potato chips is like adding as much as 12 to 20 teaspoons of fat-saturated vegetable oil to an eight-ounce potato.

Do you have a nutrition question?
Send it to Editor, Health and Medicine Annual, P.O. Box 90, Hawleyville, CT 06440-9990.

Fitness
and Health

See also:
Individual articles in the second half of this book, arranged in alphabetical order, for additional information.

Regular physical exercise increases bone mass, maintains muscle tone, brightens one's mental outlook, and helps prevent a host of ailments and debilities. There's also a strong association between physical exercise and healthy aging. People who exercise vigorously at least one-half hour three times a week have smoother skin, a younger body shape, and delay the time when they suffer a mid-life crisis or feel "over-the-hill."

Gentler, less strenuous exercise also offers important fitness benefits. Yoga and T'ai Chi Ch'uan, a 300-year-old yogalike Chinese discipline, have become increasingly popular among people of all ages. Many physicians believe these practices may be especially useful for people age 75 and older. Statistics indicate that 40 percent of the Americans in

this age group cannot walk two blocks; 32 percent cannot climb 10 stairs; and 22 percent cannot lift 10 pounds.

An estimated 37 million Americans suffer from some form of arthritis. The most common form is osteoarthritis, which is characterized by a breakdown of the cartilage that cushions the surface of joints, resulting in pain and loss of movement. A study by Judith C. Bautch, associate professor of nursing at the University of Wisconsin in Madison, found that proper exercise in older people does not lead to greater cartilage breakdown in knees, and may in fact significantly decrease joint pain. "Exercise nourishes the cartilage and is important to a joint," she said.

Another common and painful form of arthritis is rheumatoid arthritis, which involves a reaction by the body's immune system that results in inflammation and thickening of the membrane that lines joints. The inflamed lining invades and damages bone and cartilage. A Swedish study indicated that aerobic exercise such as walking, bicycling, swimming, and skiing does not worsen disease progression in people with rheumatoid arthritis. The findings contradict standard medical advice in both the United States and Sweden.

While the benefits of exercise are numerous, too much exercise can injure the body. Orthopedists and pediatricians re-

ported a sharp increase in sports-related injuries among children, whose immature bones put them at increased risk of injury. Problems arise mainly because of improper training, poor quality equipment, and overly rigorous workouts. The most commonly seen sports-related injuries among young people include inflammation of tendons and stress fractures.

Sports-related injuries also can abruptly end a professional athlete's career. This sobering fact was brought home to football fans when Dennis Byrd of the New York Jets suffered a severe spinal-cord injury during a game, leaving him partially paralyzed from the chest down. Fortunately, thanks to excellent accident-site treatment and advances in drug therapy, Byrd was walking with crutches in less than three months.

The desire to be physically fit has led many people to avoid or give up cigarette smoking. Smoking in the United States has reached its lowest level since the Centers for Disease Control and Prevention (CDC) began monitoring smoking in 1955. Still, 25.5 percent of adult Americans (45.8 million people) smoke. Smoking causes or contributes to cancer, emphysema, heart disease, eye cataracts, premature aging, infertility, and other problems; it causes about 435,000 deaths annually, making it the single most preventable cause of death in our society.

In mid-1992 the American Heart Association (AHA) urged that smoking be banned in workplaces and public places as an environmental poison. People who breathe in smoke from other people's cigarettes are at increased risk of heart and lung disease. Indeed, so-called secondhand, or passive, smoking kills more than 50,000 nonsmokers a year in the United States, 3,700 from lung cancer, 37,000 from heart disease, and 12,000 from other cancers. Also, a report issued by the U.S. Environmental Protection Agency (EPA) said that each year, secondhand smoke causes at least 150,000 serious respiratory ailments in young children, especially infants.

Smoking is easy, but kicking the habit is hard, particularly for teenagers. The U.S. National Center for Health Statistics estimated that some 3.7 million teenagers smoke. While 92 percent of those surveyed said they did not plan to be smoking in another year, only about 1.5 percent of them actually quit. Teenagers greatly underestimate the addictiveness of tobacco and greatly overestimate their ability to control it.

A strong association exists between physical exercise and healthy aging.

DANCING FOR HEALTH

by Andrea Mallozzi

If you were turned off to the joys of dancing by those mandatory boy-girl dance classes in elementary school ("Let's do the hokey-pokey, everyone!"), then it's time to take another look. The truth is that dancing—from square dancing to tango to Jazzercise—is a great way for people of all ages to stay fit and healthy. Best of all, you don't need the talent or the experience of, say, John Travolta in *Saturday Night Fever* to join a dance program. Instructors agree that if you can walk, you can learn to dance. While fitness activities such as jogging, swimming, or cycling are more solitary, dancing is often done with partners or in a group, which adds an uplifting social aspect to getting in better shape. From a health perspective, people who dance are at a low risk for injury, and they benefit from increased self-esteem, overall muscle toning, improved flexibility, and aerobic conditioning.

For many, dancing is the best form of exercise: it's easy, it's sociable, and best of all, it's a fun way to get into shape!

Square Dancing

If square dancing conjures images of barns and pioneers, think again. Square dancing is a popular recreation nationwide. Over 6 million participants—from teenagers to senior citizens—enjoy the physical and mental challenge of do-si-do-ing with a partner. In addition to standard country-and-western music, modern versions of this traditional folk dance are now performed to pop music, golden oldies, and even Broadway hits.

Square dancing is traditionally a couples activity, with four couples dancing together in a square. If you don't have a willing partner of your own, square-dance clubs generally have nonpartnered members. A designated caller leads the group by calling out different steps, such as bowing to or swinging your partner, in patterns that eventually make up a dance. According to square dancers themselves, these patterns are easy to learn and master. Most people start square dancing by taking one or two lessons to learn the basic steps, then join a square-dance club that holds weekly dances. Dancers traditionally wear colorful Western-type clothing, such as blue jeans for men and long, full skirts for women, but any clothing that's comfortable is acceptable.

As an exercise, square dancing works the muscles of the entire body. Because the dances keep you constantly on the go, square dancing is a great way to improve aerobic fitness. According to Gordon Goss, editor of *The National Square Dance Directory,* several hours of square dancing generally provides the same amount of exercise benefits as 5 miles of walking. The dance movements are smooth and rhythmic—easier on the joints and the body than other well-known forms of exercise. In addition, square dancing is mentally stimulating—you have to react quickly to the caller's commands. Furthermore, square dancing is fun: participants say the upbeat, partylike atmosphere of a square dance makes them feel happy and energetic, and provides a perfect antidote to stress.

Ballroom Dancing

Many dances fall under this category: foxtrot, waltz, tango, samba, cha-cha, and swing, among countless others. As with square dancing, ballroom dancing is performed in pairs. "Most people enjoy ballroom dancing because it is romantic, intimate, and, once you have the skills, they can be used at weddings, nightclubs, or anywhere you happen to be," says Ken Richards, marketing director at Arthur Murray International, Coral Gables, Florida. According to Richards, ballroom dances are typically thought of as "touch" dances because partners move together and are usually holding or touching one another. In ballroom dancing, the man always leads the woman into the various steps. Dances are divided into two categories: smooth and rhythm. Dances like the elegant waltz, comprised of slow, graceful steps across the floor, are considered smooth, while the lively samba and swing involve more body movement and are considered more rhythmic. Like other types of recreational dancing, there's no true right or wrong way to ballroom-dance. Once you know the basic steps, you and your partner can flow with the music in your own style.

When performed often or for an extended period of time, this combination of slow and

Ballroom dancing provides a low-impact aerobic workout that tones muscles, and improves posture, and flexibility.

Not so many years ago, well-polished ballroom-dancing skills were a sure sign of good breeding. The intimate, romantic nature of ballroom dancing still attracts many people.

fast dancing offers a gentle, low-impact aerobic workout. Ballroom dancing also tones muscles and improves posture, coordination, balance, and flexibility. Women, in particular, benefit from toned muscles in the back of their legs from the many backward movements of their steps as they follow the lead of their partners.

Keeping your body active and healthy isn't the only reason to take up ballroom dancing. "Knowing how to dance increases confidence, particularly in social settings where a person is apt to feel self-conscious and uncomfortable," explains Richards.

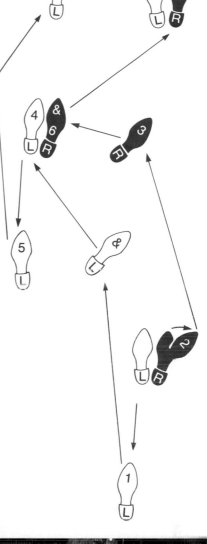

Nearly every city has studios in which people can learn the latest dance steps (above). Ballroom-dancing competitions are held all around the U.S. and abroad (right).

For Women Only—Belly Dancing

Career women do it. Housewives do it. Even 67-year-old women do it. For millions of women all over America, belly dancing is an exciting new dance form that can tone and limber the body, while offering relaxation and a chance to expand the imagination. You'll move your belly—and every other part of your body—with this ancient Middle Eastern dance form. Belly dancing is a uniquely feminine dance form and is historically an artistic and spiritual expression. The dance consists of isolated muscle movements, such as shoulder and hip shimmies, combined with arm, neck, and head movements. "Belly dancing is very gentle on the body," says Karen Kuzsel, belly-dance instructor and editor and publisher of *Middle Eastern Dance Magazine*, Casselberry, Florida. She adds, "Although the dance is sensuous, it's by no means intended to be sexual."

Many people enjoy belly dancing for its wonderfully theatrical nature. Dancers often wear glamorous costumes of lace veils, bustiers, and long flowing skirts adorned with beads and coins. Some even play metal finger cymbals.

Many women who are attracted to belly dancing are also intimidated. They often ask if you have to be extremely coordinated and flexible to move like a belly dancer. "Absolutely not," says Kuzsel. "A lot of this dance is expressive. You can interpret the moves and individualize them."

The ancient art of belly dancing has been embraced by many modern women as much for its theatrical nature as for the cardiovascular workout it provides.

Lauretta Caron of West Haven, Connecticut, who is 67, agrees that you don't need special talent to belly dance. Without any prior dance experience, she started belly dancing on a lark 17 years ago as a means of improving the circulation in her feet. Now she travels across the nation and around the world giving public performances, and is also an instructor. "It keeps me young," she insists.

In addition to some obvious benefits, like weight loss and body contouring, belly dancing on a regular basis promotes proper body alignment and flexibility, and tones muscles. It can also enhance poise, stamina, and balance, as well as develop cardiovascular fitness. Belly-dance enthusiasts also mention that the opportunity to create imaginative movements that expand their creativity and improve self-expression enables them to feel more attractive, feminine, and emotionally grounded.

To get started, look in your yellow pages for schools or individuals that offer instruction. Private lessons usually meet once a week for an hour to an hour and a half and can cost anywhere from $5 to $25. There are also group lessons and belly-dance seminars available. "Some instructors are strict technicians, while others are more interpretive," says Kuzsel. "So you may want to try out several until you find a teacher you're comfortable with."

Any kind of dancing on a regular basis promotes health. It's doubtful, however, whether the patrons of the country-western bar at left derive the same benefits from their slow dancing as the participants of an aerobics class do from their footwork (below).

Mastering a dance routine or technique gives many people a sense of pride and accomplishment. And nothing has the power of body communication like gliding and sliding through a series of perfectly attuned, synchronized steps. The physical exercise, combined with the graceful movements and the accompanying romantic music, appeals to all the senses.

Arthur Murray and other professional dance studios offer sessions of lessons that blend private instruction with group dancing. They even sponsor events where students can perform publicly. You can also often find ballroom-dance instruction at your local YMCA or community center.

Jazzercise workouts are challenging, but do not push a person to or beyond his or her physical limits.

Jazzercise

For a more individual and challenging approach to fitness that still gets you dancing, try Jazzercise. This activity incorporates jazz-dance-based aerobic movements with calisthenic and stretch exercises. But don't mistake Jazzercise for a standard aerobic-exercise class. "Our movements are loose and fluid and less repetitive than steps done in an aerobics class," says Lauren Spangler, M.A., exercise physiologist at Jazzercise, Inc. For example, a typical aerobic class may have you jog or do jumping jacks to pump up your circulation, while a Jazzercise class will involve pliés and relevés along with other dance-based movements, which are specifically choreographed to fit the music. "Yet anyone can take these classes," she stresses. "You don't have to have any prior jazz-dance experience."

Jazzercise, founded in 1969 by Judi Shepherd Misset, rapidly became a very popular

Dance for Rehabilitation

For many people with chronic pain or diseases such as arthritis, multiple sclerosis, cancer, and other diseases, dancing can be an aid to alleviating physical or mental discomfort, and it sometimes can help speed recovery. "Low-impact dancing such as the waltz, square dancing, and others can be therapeutic," says Jeanne E. Hicks, M.D., deputy chief of rehabilitative medicine at the National Institutes of Health in Bethesda, Maryland. "These dances help people stay flexible, toned, and can offer some aerobic conditioning, too." Dancing

Dancing can act as a form of physical therapy. By helping to maintain flexibility, dancing can help alleviate pain and discomfort while offering aerobic conditioning. The social aspects of dancing also have a positive impact on the disposition of many participants.

can also have a positive effect on the mental state of someone who is, or has been, ill, because it helps them feel more confident and more functional.

Lauretta Caron believes so strongly in the therapeutic abilities of dance that she teaches a free belly-dance class once a week for people with ailments. "I worked as a sewing-machine operator in a factory for 30 years, and the job left me with little circulation in my feet," relates Caron. "My feet were so numb my children would rub them every night." After trying modern dance and aerobics, which proved to be too strenuous for her, she stumbled into belly dancing, and her foot circulation problems immediately improved. Over the years, she's experienced other ailments—arthritis in her hands, a fractured hip, even compressed vertebrae—but daily belly dancing keeps her from being debilitated by these recurring problems. "Dancing takes people's minds off their health worries," adds Caron.

While dancing offers myriad benefits, people with cardiac or pulmonary problems or who suffer from acute musculoskeletal pain should avoid high-impact dances, and obtain a doctor's permission before taking a class, advises Hicks.

franchised business. The over 4,500 Jazzercise instructors around the world follow Misset's standards for excellence. In general, classes run for one hour and consist of a warm-up period, 30 minutes of Jazzercise dance, stretching, calisthenics, and a cooldown period. Jazzercise teachers are all trained in cardiopulmonary resuscitation (CPR), and have been tested in anatomy, dance, and teaching techniques in order to earn certification as an instructor.

On average a person will burn between 300 and 400 calories during a Jazzercise class, and will strengthen leg muscles, the upper torso, and abdominals. The stretching exercises help increase flexibility. This activity is especially good for aerobic conditioning. "Jazzercise routines are designed to get the heart pumping to 60 to 90 percent of a person's maximal heart rate—the rate recognized as necessary for enhancing cardiovascular fitness," says Spangler. But while the workout is challenging, it is not designed to push a person to his or her limits. Jazzercize instructors stress that students have control over the intensity of their workouts. There are even Jazzercise Lite classes for people who want to start off more gradually or who are physically restricted.

The only requirement of Jazzercise is a good pair of aerobic sneakers. To locate an instructor near you, call 1–800-FIT-IS-IT. ◇

Many parents encourage their children to participate in organized sports at a young age. Unfortunately, children not physically or psychologically prepared for such activities rapidly grow disenchanted with team sports altogether.

Kids and Sports

by Gina Kolata

For Jennifer and John Walsh of Princeton, New Jersey, physical activity is largely a matter of team practices, games, and meets. There's swimming almost every day for Jennifer, 14. In the fall, she also plays field hockey, and in the spring, she plays lacrosse. John, 11, practices with his soccer team twice a week; he has a game every Sunday and often a scrimmage on Saturday. He also plays ice hockey and baseball. Somehow he finds the time to swim as well.

Gradually, with little fanfare, organized sports have virtually replaced neighborhood pickup games and the informal groups of kids who used to play outside after school. In a majority of families with young children, both parents now work, and they are likely to send the children to after-school programs rather than turn them loose to roam the neighborhood. And then there's always peer pressure. If it is an honor to be picked for the soccer team, children will vie to join it and, once selected, will spend countless hours practicing and playing formal games.

Organized sports for children have exploded in popularity. The number of children playing on United States Soccer Federation youth division teams, for example, grew from slightly more than 100,000 in 1975 to more than 1.5 million in 1989. The number of girls on softball teams more than doubled from 1980 to 1990, surging from about 306,000 to over 638,000.

"These are really remarkable increases," says Vern Seefeldt, the director of the Institute for the Study of Youth Sports at Michigan State University in East Lansing. "There are fewer seven- and eight-year-olds today than in 1980, yet the actual number in organized sports has increased."

But there is a downside to this burgeoning of organized sports. Most children start with a burst of enthusiasm, but most also quit, discouraged and disheartened. They often develop "such a distaste for the sport that they never want to hear about it again," Seefeldt says. "They are the lost generation of sports participants."

Parents who wish to help their children stay active in sports need a good sense of what they are physically capable of doing at different ages. Children who try a variety of activities are more apt to find the ones that suit them best. And parents should encourage children to play for the fun of it, whether or not they become champion athletes.

The most important of these guidelines, experts say, is to make sure that the sport a

For many children, baseball represents their first taste of team sports. Often, by the age of seven or eight, boys are involved in formal leagues.

child has chosen is appropriate for his or her stage of development. Many parents try to push their children too far too fast.

Too Young to Play?

Barry Goldberg, M.D., director of sports medicine at Yale University Health Services and a member of the American Academy of Pediatrics sports medicine and fitness committee, says, "One of the problems we have is that coaches get the children before they're ready for a sport, and then label them as not capable. We see that across the board, in every sport— kids trying before they are ready."

Different sports require different skills, of course, and children develop at wildly varying rates. So there are no hard-and-fast rules about when to let a child plunge into orga-

Not until the age of seven has the vision of most children matured well enough for them to track a ball. Older children project much pressure upon themselves when performing athletically before parents and friends.

The Developmental Sequence of Kicking

The drawings below show the four stages in the development of mature kicking form, as identified through research conducted by Vern Seefeldt and John Haubenstricker, professors of physical education at Michigan State University in East Lansing. Boys tend to reach the final stage about a year before girls. Not all children attain the same stage at the same age. But the age at which a majority—60 percent —of children reach each developmental milestone has been identified.

Stage 1. With no leg windup, the child pushes the ball with his foot from a stationary position. He or she usually steps back afterward to regain balance. Most boys and girls reach this stage at about age 2.

Stage 2. The child again begins from a stationary position, but in preparing to kick, there is both leg windup to the rear as well as some opposition of the arms and legs. Balance is recovered by stepping backward or to the side. Most boys reach this stage by age 3½; most girls reach it by age 4.

Stage 3. The child takes one or more steps to approach the ball. The kicking foot stays close to the ground until the moment of contact. After the kick the child steps forward or to the side to regain balance. Most boys achieve this stage by age 4½, compared with age 6 for most girls.

Stage 4. The child approaches the ball with several rapid steps, leaps before the kick, and usually hops on the support leg afterward. The body generally inclines backward during the windup. Most boys reach this stage by age 7, most girls by age 8.

Young children have neither the hand-eye coordination needed to hit a tennis ball nor the strength necessary to cover a full-size tennis court. "Child-sized" courts are few and far between.

nized sports. Many pediatricians and other sports experts believe that children should not play regulation games on full-size fields until they are at least 9 or 10. Until that time, they should be learning basic skills, such as kicking a soccer ball or hitting a tethered T-ball. Or they should play modified games that allow everyone on a team, regardless of ability, to have adequate playing time.

> *Children should be allowed to find their own sport and progress at their own pace.*

"As soon as you get children involved in an adult model of a game, skill development falls to practically zero," Seefeldt says. "Children need to be in situations where their participation and ability to learn skills are maximized. In an adult game, you try to throw the ball so the batter can't hit it, or kick the ball where it can't be retrieved. With kids, you need to do just the opposite."

The problem is, the recommendations of the experts often don't correspond to reality. Seven-year-olds play tackle football in full gear, just like children on high school teams, and they have to run 100 yards to score a touchdown. Ten-year-olds play full-court basketball with 10-foot-high nets. Seefeldt urges parents to take the initiative and lobby their school districts and local teams to institute modified rules for children. Until kids' leagues come around to this view, however, here are some general guidelines based on milestones in child development.

Pediatricians have found that children do not have the physical ability to learn the skills needed for organized sports until they are about five years old. And it does not help to coach them when they are too young. Infants and toddlers are often enrolled in swimming classes, although, according to Seefeldt, it is "almost impossible to teach the basic competitive strokes to children who are younger than age 5." Toddlers who have practiced throwing a ball turn out to be no better at it when they get older than those who never practiced. In fact, warns the American Academy of Pediatrics, parents who insist on trying to teach athletic skills to children under age 5 often take all the fun out of the activity and discourage them from taking it up later.

While five-year-olds can generally learn to catch a gently tossed ball and ride a bike, they are far from ready for actual games, experts say. Many children do join soccer teams around this age, but Seefeldt describes what goes on at a typical game as "beehive soccer. Everybody is gathered around the ball, and there is very little concept of team play." Five-year-olds have particular trouble with sports like baseball, which require not only hand-eye coordination, but also an ability to follow a moving ball with their eyes and predict where it will land.

One reason children have such difficulty with these sports is that their eyes are not fully developed. Children tend to be far-sighted, and cannot easily follow moving objects. It is not until age 6 or 7 that most children's eyes have matured enough to track a ball.

Another problem is that young children are often clumsy and uncoordinated. Most six- and seven-year-olds are not coordinated enough to hit a pitched ball with a bat, for example. Children of this age can learn many basic gymnastics skills, however, like balancing, running, and jumping, Dr. Goldberg says. But he is skeptical of gymnastics centers that hoist children on harnesses so they can perform movements that they would otherwise be physically incapable of. "There is some enjoyment for children in flying through the air," he says. "But a lot of times, it is a more positive experience for the parent, watching the kid go through the motions, than it is for the kid."

Children around the age of 9 and 10 may be able to hit a baseball or shoot a basketball through a hoop, but they often do not have the attention span to concentrate during long practices in large groups. For this reason, Michael A. Nelson, M.D., chairman of the committee on sports medicine and fitness of the American Academy of Pediatrics, recommends that these lessons last no longer than 30 minutes.

Some organized sports for children carry a high risk for injury. Ice hockey, now played as much indoors as outdoors (above right), is increasingly popular. Football has the highest incidence of injury of all sports. In Pop Warner Leagues (right), seven-year-olds play tackle football in full gear.

Young gymnasts like Shannon Miller (left) have the agility to win Olympic medals, but often at the cost of bone and muscle problems later on in life.

The Perils of Overtraining

Going for Olympic gold—or even just the Little League trophy—is a tantalizing goal for many budding young athletes. But some health experts question whether the competitive emphasis in many youth sports programs is resulting in overtraining that can have lifelong consequences. Christine L. Wells, Ph.D., professor of exercise science and physical education at Arizona State University in Tempe, Arizona, points to factors that can contribute to what is known as "energy drain": How much exercise you've had, how much rest and recovery you get, and nutrition. "If you're exercising and burning tremendous numbers of calories, and you're not eating sufficiently, that's going to contribute to overtraining," says Wells.

It's easy for a young athlete to fall into such a pattern. Coaches, and in some instances the media, place a lot of emphasis on being very lean and fairly muscular. In certain sports—like diving, figure skating, and gymnastics, where it's not the clock, but the judge that counts—there is pressure to achieve a certain look. This can lead to erratic eating patterns or even an eating disorder, such as bulimia. A 1991 National Collegiate Athletic Association (NCAA) study reported at least one athlete with an eating disorder in 64 percent of the schools surveyed. Among bulimia's more serious immediate side effects: hypothalamic disturbances, which affect the thyroid and growth hormones; electrolyte imbalances from loss of body fluids; dehydration; and malnutrition. And, if eating disorders aren't dealt with during the critical adolescent phase of growth, skeletal growth may be irretrievably impaired.

For girls, the combination of eating too little and exercising too much can result in other problems as well. "If you're eating strangely, you're probably going to have late onset of your menstrual period, and one study shows that scoliosis is very high in girls who have late menarche [first menstruation]," says Wells. "If you've got late menarche, you've got low estrogen. How long is it normal to have low estrogen when your bones are developing? We don't know, but there seems to be a high incidence of injuries in those kids, and they don't recover."

The potential problems don't end there. Overuse injuries occur most often during developmental periods when children's bones are softer and their ligaments, tendons, and muscles are relatively tight. "You're almost 100 percent certain of developing osteoarthritis in a joint that gets injured, and many kids are having repeated injuries in the same joint," says Wells. "So if you have a little hip problem one year, you're likely to have a second or more severe hip problem the next year, and you're going to have osteoarthritis in that hip. There isn't any doubt about it."

Then there's psychological stress, often in the not-very-subtle form of pressure applied by coaches and parents. "I think we're putting too much emphasis on winning and excellence at too early an age; most kids are not fully conditioned and developed for some of this high stress," Wells observes.

Janet C. Tate

According to Vern Seefeldt, even age 10 is too young for any real proficiency at tennis, and he suggests postponing lessons until at least that time. The game requires considerable hand-eye coordination, beyond the developmental capabilities of most young children. In addition, children are usually expected to play on the same size court as adults, with the same height net. Obviously, it is extremely difficult for small children to range over the entire court and hit the ball high enough to clear the net.

While it is true that some children excel at tennis at an early age, experts say this is no reason for parents to push their kids to take lessons too soon. "When we say there are exceptions like Jennifer Capriati, we need to look at the thousands of players who fell by the wayside to produce one player like her," Seefeldt says. "We tend to lose sight of the children who never want to play tennis again because they were forced to play before they were ready."

Sports Injuries

It is not until adolescence and the onset of puberty that most children really come into their own as athletes. Their bodies are ready, and they have the motivation and drive to practice and succeed in sports they love. But since children enter puberty at different ages, there are great disparities in abilities among 11- to 15-year-olds. The best swimmers at this age, for example, are usually taller boys with muscular shoulders and lean bodies. Small boys who have not yet matured tend to be slower swimmers.

One sport where boys who mature late are at a particular disadvantage is football. "In football," says Dr. Goldberg, "where strength is a priority, differentials in size and weight and muscle strength are significant variables." To protect smaller boys, some leagues divide players according to their physical maturity. The idea is that young but physically mature boys can play with older teenagers, while teenagers who

With an eye on the Olympics, some children find themselves involved in intense training regimens at a very early age. Unfortunately, only a handful will ever even come close to qualifying.

are physically immature can play with younger boys. But according to Dr. Goldberg, older boys rarely agree to play with the younger kids. "You could count on one hand the number of boys who move down," he says.

Football has the highest incidence of injury of all sports in elementary and junior high school, but injuries are increasing even in sports generally regarded as "safe," such as swimming. As children try ever harder to compete, they can end up overtraining (see sidebar on facing page). Injuries caused by repeated trauma to the body—known as overuse injuries—were unheard of in children only a decade ago. Now they are a major concern among sports-medicine specialists. Studies of children's sports injuries suggest many could have been avoided if coaches, who often are untrained parent volunteers, knew more about technique, and if children were not pushed to train too hard.

Other than learning not to expect too much of children before puberty, parents also have to learn to let children find their own sports at their own pace. "Every kid has his own

Athletes are better than ever before, but, ironically, fewer kids are in sports for the long run.

medium," says W. George Scarlett, a developmental psychologist at Tufts University in Boston. "Sports is not sports is not sports. Swimming and biking are worlds apart." Children can usually find their sport if they have a chance to try different ones. Many communities have recreation programs that enable children to experiment with a variety of sports without having to make a major commitment of time.

Athletic Dropouts

Lyle J. Micheli, M.D., a pediatric orthopedist at Harvard Medical School who is a former president of the American College of Sports Medicine, says parents should not push children into sports they do not enjoy. Some children love team sports, for example, while others thrive when they can develop their own skills and essentially compete against themselves. "You'll know pretty quickly whether a kid enjoys a given sport, whether a little girl really enjoys going to gymnastics or whether she keeps finding excuses not to go," Dr. Micheli says.

Parents should emphasize the sheer joy of exercise rather than the drive for perfection and success.

What about the child who likes sports but feels hopelessly inadequate? Extra help and coaching from parents or even other children can help. It is not enough to tell a child to ignore his or her ineptness and play anyway, Seefeldt says: "If a child is not skilled, he will be embarrassed in a high-stress situation such as a game." He suggests asking the child's coach or physical-education teacher to recommend skills to practice. Often the extra help that makes a difference is as simple as playing catch in the backyard or throwing balls to the child to hit.

Children should be encouraged to drop a sport, at least temporarily, if they are truly miserable trying to learn it. Dr. Goldberg of Yale says that "it is not unreasonable for a parent to say, 'It looks to me like you're not having a good time. Would you like to try something else?' " Parents should never try to coerce a child to stay with a sport because they have spent so much time ferrying him or her to practices and games, or because so much money has been invested in lessons.

In one of the largest and most comprehensive studies of children and sports, involving a national sample of 26,000 boys and girls from the ages of 10 to 18, Seefeldt and his colleagues at Michigan State found that by age 15, 75 percent of children who had been involved in organized sports had dropped out. And, he says, "the earlier they began, the earlier they dropped out."

When the children who remained on teams were asked why they continued to play, one-third of the 10- to 14-year-olds said their parents wanted them to. Most of the children who had dropped out told the researchers that all the fun had gone out of playing. They complained that their coaches played favorites or yelled at them or did not allow them to play as much as they wanted to. Many also said they were required to practice too many hours a week, leaving them no time for other activities.

"There are a lot of practices that are two hours or longer a day," Seefeldt says. "Many of the kids had practices four days a week and had two games a week. Many were not willing to give up that much time."

Even children who don't mind devoting hours each day to practices, lessons, or meets sometimes get involved in so many sports that eventually they have to choose among them. John Walsh used to swim four or five times a week. But in recent months, he has frequently missed practice in order to have enough time for soccer, hockey, and baseball. Candice Walsh, John and Jennifer's mother, says she won't mind if the children drop most of their teams as long as they continue to exercise and play the sports for fun.

We may never return to the days when children ran outside for a neighborhood softball game before dinner. But if parents encourage their children to progress in sports at their own speed, if they emphasize the sheer joy of rigorous exercise rather than a single-minded drive for perfection and success, they will help their children develop a love of sports and set them up for a lifetime of physical activity. ◇

ORIENTEERING:
Maps, Magnetism, and Mind Games

by Linda J. Brown

Stick most people in the middle of the woods with a map and compass, and they'd be lost. Befuddled. Confused. Unless, of course, they were orienteers, practitioners of a lesser-known sport whose motto is, "Give me a map, and I'm magic." These folks thrive on tooling around the forest with ease, solving tough navigational challenges in the process.

By definition, orienteering—or "O," as enthusiasts refer to it—is a cross-country sport in which participants run or walk from point to point (called controls or checkpoints). A compass, topographic map, and smarts are the only tools used to find each location, or control. At each control, which is marked by a three-sided orange-and-white flag, there's a hole punch with its own distinc-

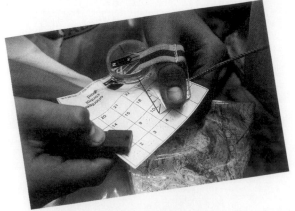

Orienteering participants must "check in" at specific points called controls along the course. At each control, the participants punch a hole in their card to prove that they've been there.

tive pattern. Participants punch their cards when they arrive at the control to prove they've been there. The one who locates all the controls in the least time wins. You can also just orienteer for pure recreation and pay no attention to the clock.

Sound tough? It's no piece of cake, but fortunately, orienteering maps are much more elaborate than your typical road map. They show very detailed topographic features in much larger scale than most maps. They also indicate the elevation and shape of the land along with many other features. An orienteering map is full of lines, symbols, and, most of all, colors. Black indicates rocks and such human-made features as roads, trails, buildings, or fences. Bodies of water are blue, normal forest is white, clearings and fields are yellow, and thick brush is green.

One of the most intellectually demanding parts of orienteering is interpreting the map. Participants are permitted a specific amount of time to study the map before the race begins.

Contour lines showing hills, valleys, ridges, and ditches are brown.

Besides a map, a compass, and comfortable clothing, orienteers need little else. "People wear all kinds of odds and ends," says Robin Shannonhouse, executive director of the U.S. Orienteering Federation. "It's mostly your brain that you need to bring."

It's a brainy bunch that gets into this sport. All but 4 percent have completed college, and more than half have earned graduate degrees. "Most of the people involved are technically educated problem solvers: computer people, engineers, lawyers, doctors, teachers," says Larry Berman, who, along with his wife, Sara Mae, publishes the magazine *Orienteering North America*. These professionals make good money—60 percent earn over $50,000 a year. Discretionary income comes in handy for orienteers because travel is a must: orienteering events with new courses keep it interesting. Most orienteers are over 35 and heavily weighted in the 40- to 50-year-old age groups. Men outnumber women by nearly 2 to 1.

All told, the number of people who partake in this thinking-person's activity is quite small compared to the majority of athletic endeavors. It's estimated that about 15,000 people orienteer at least once a year. Of those, approximately 7,000 belong to the 65 clubs sponsored by the U.S. Orienteering Federation. While this represents only a tiny slice of the general population, keep in mind that orienteering is still a rather young sport in the United States, having just made its way into this country about 50 years ago.

The Swedish Connection

Orienteering's roots lie in Sweden, where it originated as a military exercise in the early 1900s. One man, probably more than any other, is responsible for introducing the sport into the United States. Bjorn Kjellstrom, now in his early 80s, was a champion ski orienteer in Sweden in the 1930s. At that time, Bjorn, his brother, Alvar, and another Swede, Gunnar Tillander, developed the Silva (from the Latin for "forest") compass. This compass incorporates a plastic baseplate that can be set directly on the map. Orienteers had previously found their way

Controls are usually marked with flags or some other telltale sign. The orienteer concerned with strategy tries to approach the control as quietly as possible, so as not to give away its location to other participants.

using a compass in a wooden box, and a protractor—a cumbersome and somewhat inaccurate combination. Bjorn brought his Silva compass to America, introducing it along with orienteering. He later wrote a book called *Be Expert with Map & Compass,* now the orienteer's classic handbook. He currently lives in New York State, and continues to be involved in the sport to this day. (His

"O" Talk

Orienteers have a language of their own. Here's some shoptalk, "O" style.
• *Handrail:* A linear feature such as a stream, road, telephone line, or fence that you can use to help lead you toward a control.
• *The Postmortem:* Discussion after the race with other orienteers to commiscrate about the routes chosen.
• *Catching Feature:* A long feature (power line, river, highway) that intersects your route. These help put you back on track if you overshoot or get off your course.
• *Attack Point:* An easy-to-find landscape feature from which you can approach the usually harder-to-locate control.
• *Control:* A checkpoint along the "O" route marked by a flag.

business card reads, "Magnetism has shaped my life.")

At first, orienteering grew quite slowly in the U.S., though by 1971 it had gained enough of a toehold for the U.S. Orienteering Federation to form. The sport's incremental growth has continued steadily since then, although it recently reached a plateau.

The situation is quite different in Eastern Europe and Scandinavia, where orienteering has been embraced by the masses and is quite popular. Major competitions are televised and attract hundreds of onlookers. The Swedish O-Ringen, for instance, is a five-day event with over 20,000 contestants.

Mind Games

Perhaps "cunning running," as the sport is sometimes nicknamed, owes its popularity to the fact that it engages both mind and body. "The mental challenge is very appealing," says Shannonhouse. "Running up and down the road is good for your body, but it doesn't do a lot for your mind. This gives you something to do with your head while your legs are going." "O" attracts what she calls "puzzle freaks." "An orienteering course, in a way, is a puzzle. You have to figure out where you're going, and you have to get there."

"O" Racing

Orienteering events are geared for various ability levels, from beginners to seasoned competitors. Events typically have staggered start times, and maps have route-difficulty levels that are color-coded, each with their own set of controls. There are seven levels (although every event may not have them all):

• *White* is the beginner level. The course is all on trails under 1.8 miles (3 kilometers) long. Compasses are not necessary for participants at this level.

• *Yellow* courses are for advanced beginners. Teenagers and adults with any previous map-reading experience can usually enter their first orienteering event at this level. The course is 1.8 to 2.5 miles (3 to 4 kilometers) long. Most of the time, it follows trails or easy-to-spot features (streams, fences) called handrails.

• *Orange* is intermediate, with part of the course on trails, and the rest through easily navigable woods. The focus is on large features such as the northwest corner of a building, the top of a big hill, or a stream junction. Orange and the next level, Green, are the most popular courses in an orienteering event.

• *Green* courses run 2.4 to 3.7 miles (4 to 6 kilometers) as the crow flies—much like the orange courses as far as distance is concerned, but with considerably more-advanced navigation and a focus on such minor terrain features as the end of a ditch or a specific boulder.

• *Red* courses are just as hard as Green ones, but they run about 0.6 mile (1 kilometer) longer.

• *Blue* courses are the same difficulty as Red and Green courses. They usually range in length from 5.5 to 7.5 miles (9 to 12 kilometers) on moderate terrain measured as the crow flies. Distance traveled can be much longer, of course, since most people don't run as the crow flies; they choose to go around swamps and hills rather than through them. The winner usually finishes in 70 to 80 minutes; most of the other Blue-course finishers are out 90 minutes to two hours.

• *Brown* is a new level being tried in some orienteering events. It's as difficult navigationally as the Green, Red, or Blue courses, but only as long as the Yellow. "It's geared for older folks who can't quite make the longer distances anymore," says Shannonhouse, although participants of all ages seem to enjoy it.

Meeting success on the mental plane can produce a great sense of satisfaction. Regardless of whether you compete, Larry Berman says, "There's a reward from planning a route and executing it. When you come over the top of that knoll, there's the flag right where it's supposed to be."

On the physical side, "O" events can certainly be rigorous, with lots of high-stepping over obstacles and clambering up hills. The federation tells course planners to strive for an equal balance between mental and physical difficulty. In the end the brainwork tends to win out. Case in point: Shannonhouse sometimes walks courses and, in doing so, has outwalked runners. She notes wryly, "It doesn't matter how far or fast you run if you're running in the wrong direction."

Bumps and Bruises

Even though orienteering involves running through the woods over rocks, logs, and all kinds of other impediments, serious injuries are few and far between. "We do bash ourselves up, but nothing major," says Shannonhouse. "You come home with a scratch on your cheek, maybe a bruise on your elbow, and muddy, dirty, and sweaty." Bruce Wolfe, a highly competitive orienteer from Piedmont, California, says people will sometimes land on something wrong and wrench an ankle. Fortunately, as orienteers run more courses, their ankles and lower legs get stronger and thus less prone to injury. There's also an advantage to running on the softer forest floor compared to hard road surfaces—fewer overuse injuries. "It's a very safe and gentle sport," Shannonhouse says, "if you don't mind running through the rosebushes once in a while."

> *Orienteering is often referred to as the "thinking person's sport."*

Events and Variations

Clubs hold 400 to 500 events per year, with most occurring in the spring and fall. There are also regional, national, and international competitions. The United States has a national team of 25 men and 20 women. The top five men and five women represent their country at the World Championships every two years and, in alternating years, at the World Cup events.

For serious competitors like Bruce Wolfe, the top American finisher at the World Championships in Czechoslovakia in 1991, making even a small navigational error could drop him back many places. Among the skills he works on is map reading while running, to take in as much as possible at a glance without breaking stride. He even practices punching his card on a course he sets up himself to make sure he's fast and fluid. "You want to spend as little time as possible at the control marker. If you're standing right next to it, you act as a beacon to other competitors who are trying to find it."

Many orienteers aren't worried about such fine points, especially those who follow the "String-O" course. This short course for young kids is marked by continuous, simple-to-follow ribbon or yarn. Kids on the String-O and White (beginner) levels can join the Little Troll program and advance through its four levels of String, Chipmunk, Rabbit, and Roadrunner. Increasingly, orienteering is becoming a family activity, as it accommo-

Orienteering has undergone a great popularity spurt in the last few years. With some modifications, many orienteering competitions are now open to wheelchair-bound participants.

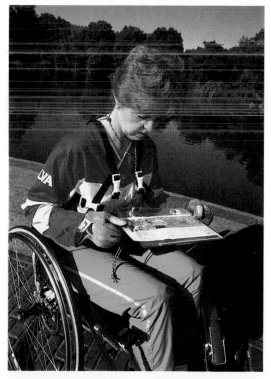

dates all ability ranges. Many children may first hear of orienteering through the Girl or Boy Scouts, who both award badges for the activity.

The String-O is just one variation of basic orienteering. There are "O" events held for the disabled. There's also Night-O, with heavy emphasis on flashlights and compasses; Street-O, which makes use of city street maps; and Mini-O, which takes place indoors. Orienteers compete in canoes and on bicycles. ROGAINE (Rugged Outdoor Group Activity Involving Navigation and Endurance), an Australian offshoot of "O," teams two pairs of participants who work together over large areas—perhaps 11.5 to 15.5 square miles (30 to 40 square kilometers)—during 12- or 24-hour periods.

The future of orienteering in the United States is all but assured, thanks to the number of youngsters who have embraced the sport in recent years.

Ski-O

Ski-O combines cross-country skiing and orienteering. The navigation is challenging, but a bit different than on foot, simply because much of the terrain is blanketed by snow. But it's easy to miss handrails, overlook attack points, whip by controls, and make other mistakes when skiing at high speeds.

So far, not many warm-weather orienteers have given Ski-O a try. Only about 300 people Ski-O, and, of those, perhaps 100 to 150 do it regularly. During the winter, 20 to 25 events are held, with two-thirds to three-quarters of them held in the New England states. The United States fields a national team that goes to the Ski-O World Championships.

As with most outdoor winter sports, if there's no snow, there's no Ski-O. "You can make the best plans in the world, and then if you have a warm winter or a sudden thaw, you can lose everything," says Sara Mae Berman. If the weather doesn't cooperate, race organizers sometimes just make the best of the situation and hold the competition on foot.

Reading, Writing, and Orienteering

Orienteering has even started to find its way into schools around the country. Through orienteering, students can learn skills in many different subject areas while working on problem solving, decision making, and their self-esteem. Ed Hicks, a longtime orienteer and retired schoolteacher with 32 years of teaching experience, heads up Orienteering Unlimited in Somers, New York. His aim is to bring orienteering into the classroom as "a way to integrate all subject areas: math, science, physical education, art—the whole nine yards." SCIGO Corporation in Colorado Springs, Colorado, also stresses a multidisciplinary approach. This young company currently has a pilot learning program in five New York schools and in nine junior high schools in Colorado Springs.

The bottom line: orienteering is a sport for young, old, and everyone in between. So if you like the outdoors and have a curiosity about map reading, give it a try. What have you got to lose? After all, orienteers never get lost, only mislocated. ◇

Many nonpractitioners perceive yoga as a series of strange physical postures performed to keep the body lean and flexible. To the true devotee, however, yoga is a way of life.

by Susan Randel

What do Dixie Carter, Raquel Welch, Kareem Abdul-Jabbar, and renowned cardiologist Dean Ornish, M.D., have in common? Yoga! Actresses Dixie Carter and Raquel Welch have each released fitness videos based on yoga, former professional basketball star Kareem Abdul-Jabbar demonstrates yoga poses for athletes in the February 1992 issue of *Men's Health*, and Dr. Ornish recommends yoga as a way to reduce stress in patients with heart disease in his book *Dr. Dean Ornish's Program for Reversing Heart Disease*. Medical experts and celebrities all tout yoga as a way to reduce stress, help an aching back, and, in general, shape up. There's no question about it: Yoga, long considered the "hippie" exercise of the 1960s, has gone mainstream in the 1990s.

Across the country, yoga classes are being offered in YMCAs, health clubs, and even as part of corporate fitness programs, as well as in special yoga studios. But not all yoga classes are the same. Some yoga programs are primarily a form of exercise—there are even classes that combine yoga and aerobics —while other classes emphasize the spiritual roots of the discipline.

What Is Yoga?

Yoga is an ancient discipline that is believed to have developed between 3000 and 2500 B.C. in the Indus Valley region of what is now India, where it is still practiced. Technically, there are at least five different types of yoga, including meditation, spiritual devotions, intellectual study, and service. The fifth type —the type most Westerners think of as yoga —is *hatha*, which combines a series of postures, or *asanas*, and coordinated breathing techniques.

Janaki Pierson, director of the Woodbury Yoga Center in Woodbury, Connecticut, explains that the postures and breathing techniques utilize all the muscles in the body, increase circulation, and stretch and align the spinal column to keep it healthy and flexible. Each posture has three steps—coming into the pose, holding it, and coming out of it. The postures balance each other: for every forward bend, there is a backward bend; for every twist to the right, there is a twist to

When practiced daily, yoga helps relieve stress on three levels: physical, mental, and spiritual.

the left. The idea behind the yoga poses is to develop muscles that are like a rubber band, says yoga teacher Jane Bastian-Barrett: "Stretchy, with strength."

A typical class at the Woodbury Yoga Center starts with a guided relaxation led by the teacher while students lie on their backs with their eyes closed. The class then goes through an hour of poses alternating with relaxation, and then a longer relaxation at the end. Some classes will also include breathing and meditation sessions. The beginner classes focus more on warm-ups, and assume each posture three times; more advanced classes will do a pose once, but hold it for a longer time. Pierson adds that "how you go in and out of the pose is as important as the pose itself."

Yoga Stands Apart

Yoga differs from other exercise classes in a number of ways. Pierson explains that yoga encourages a person to listen to and respond to his or her body, rather than "going for the burn" or stretching as far as possible. The alternation of stretches and relaxation helps a person feel more energized, rather than drained, after a yoga session. Coordinating the breathing with the movements brings a healthy supply of oxygen to the body during the session.

The Woodbury Yoga Center teaches a general *hatha* yoga, in which different asanas are performed according to a sequence so that each posture augments or counterbalances the one before. Different schools of *hatha* yoga have been brought to the United States from India by different gurus, such as Iyengar, Kripalu, Sidda, or Ashtanga, who studied and practiced the discipline in India. The styles developed by individual gurus each focus on different aspects of the poses. For example, Iyengar yoga emphasizes body alignment, muscular balance, and spinal extension, explains Bastian-Barrett, a teacher of Iyengar-style yoga. "The postures are the same, but we spend a lot of time on precision." Iyengar yoga may use props to help get into the proper pose. Iyengar yoga is a bit more dynamic than the classical *hatha* yoga, "but each class is geared to the students' needs and capabilities," according to Bastian-Barrett.

The form of yoga familiar to most Americans combines a series of postures with various breathing techniques.

In yoga, the lotus position (left) is considered ideal for meditation. After practicing yoga for just a short time, many older people find that they have more energy and a better outlook.

With their greatly enhanced sense of balance and astonishing degree of flexibility, longtime practitioners of yoga can maintain various hand- and headstand positions for extended periods.

Once learned, yoga is easy to practice at home, as long as a person has the self-discipline and willingness to keep with it. A daily routine of about 45 minutes to one hour is best, but Pierson acknowledges that it is preferable for a person to do yoga in whatever time he or she has available. Yoga is easier to do on an empty stomach, particularly if the routine includes inverted postures such as the headstand. Although it can be done at any time of day, the body tends to be stiffer in the morning, making it a little harder to get into some of the yoga poses.

Some people teach themselves to do yoga through the many books and videos on the subject. While supportive of this method of learning yoga, most teachers feel that people who learn yoga from books need to take a class to fine-tune the poses to make sure they are being done properly. In addition, people may be inclined to avoid some of the harder poses, or take on poses that they may not be ready to do.

Spirituality

Although yoga classes focus primarily on the physical side of the discipline, descriptions of the benefits of yoga invariably include the spiritual benefits. The underlying purpose of yoga is to reunite the individual self (jiva) with the pure consciousness (Brahman)—in fact, the word yoga means literally "joining." One of the first things most teachers mention is how a regular yoga practice forces people to take time for themselves, gain a better knowledge of their bodies, and learn to listen to what their bodies are saying. Jane Bastian-Barrett points out that yoga lets a person focus on his or her body, permitting outside distractions to melt away temporarily. Many teachers do tend to promote the physical aspects of yoga, however, in part to stay away from the negative stereotypes surrounding yoga that sprouted in the "hippie" era of the 1960s.

Even the medical community has begun to warm up to yoga. Dean Ornish, M.D., a San

Meditation

"What most people think of as yoga is the postures," explains Janaki Pierson, director of the Woodbury Yoga Center in Woodbury, Connecticut. "But meditation is an important part of yoga, too." Meditation, or *raja* yoga, reached the popular consciousness in the West during the 1960s, when the Beatles and other celebrities became involved in transcendental meditation. Interest in meditation cooled somewhat after 1970, but as Americans have acknowledged more stress in their lives—and the ways that stress affects health—interest in meditation as a means to relieve stress has increased once again.

Meditation, like sleep, cannot be taught—it comes by itself, in its own time. To speed progress, experts recommend establishing a specific time and place for meditation. Pierson includes meditation at the end of her yoga classes, not a typical practice among most yoga classes. She also offers separate meditation classes.

Among the benefits of regular meditation is its ability to reduce anxiety and stress, which in turn can stabilize blood pressure. With more published literature documenting the benefits of Eastern medicine, meditation has been slowly gaining acceptance in the medical community. The work of Dean Ornish, M.D., with cardiac patients—therapies that included both meditation and yoga as part of a unique rehabilitation program—helped guide these disciplines into the mainstream. Jonathan Alexander, M.D., chief of Danbury Hospital's cardiac-rehabilitation program, includes meditation as a significant part of the cardiac-rehabilitation process, with great success. Newtown, Connecticut, internist Jeff Friedman, M.D., has recommended meditation to some of his patients: "Not in place of Western medicine, but as an important adjunct."

Francisco–based cardiologist, devised a program to make patients with heart disease healthier. His program includes a vegetarian diet, aerobic exercise, and yoga and meditation to reduce stress. Ornish's program has been clinically successful, and studies with similar findings have been published in the British medical journal *The Lancet*.

John Rowley, M.S., director of the cardiac-rehabilitation program at Danbury Hospital in Connecticut, credits Ornish's book as one of the major influences on the hospital's program, which includes yoga and meditation. The response from both physicians and patients has been positive, although Rowley admits, "yoga and meditation is a little radical for some of the patients." Jonathan Alexander, M.D., medical director of the cardiac-rehabilitation program and a cardiologist at Danbury Hospital, feels that "yoga is the missing link that we were looking for."

Jeff Friedman, M.D., an internist in Newtown, Connecticut, has been practicing yoga for about three years. Although skeptical about yoga at first, he has found that it helps him manage and reduce stress. He points out that studies have found that the breathing techniques of yoga are helpful for people with asthma or high blood pressure. Friedman has even recommended yoga to some of his patients, although he says he is very selective in recommending it.

> For information about yoga classes around the country, try the local YMCA and health clubs, or call *Yoga Journal* at (510) 841-9200, for its annual directory of yoga teachers.

Mary Schatz, M.D., a Nashville, Tennessee, pathologist and an Iyengar yoga teacher, recommends modified yoga poses for patients with back and neck pain. She has made her program available to everyone in a new book called *Back Care Basics,* which helps a person evaluate his or her own back situation and develop a program to help keep it in shape.

All in all, yoga is a great way to keep the muscles healthy and flexible, without placing pressure on the joints as do more jolting exercises. And a yoga practice does not conflict with other types of exercise, says Jane Bastian-Barrett; rather, it complements and may even benefit other athletic activities. ◇

BETTER WALKING WORKOUTS

Of all fitness activities, walking is the easiest, safest, and cheapest (you need no equipment except comfortable shoes). It's also easy on your knees, ankles, and back. Briskly walking one mile at 3.5 to 4 miles per hour burns nearly as many calories as running the same distance at a moderate pace, and confers similar fitness benefits. A long-term program of walking can help you stay healthy and live longer. Indeed, the American Heart Association now classifies physical inactivity as a risk factor for cardiovascular disease on a par with smoking and high blood pressure.

A walking program is the easiest way to become active again if you have foregone regular exercising habits in recent years. As an adjunct to a low-fat diet, walking is a good way to lose weight. It also aids in strengthening bones, and thus may help prevent or minimize osteoporosis. Even strolling or slow walking (about 2 miles per hour) may confer some health benefits. And perhaps most importantly, walking is pleasurable, alone or with a companion. Few devotees ever get tired of it and quit. And while walking is not completely injury-proof, the injury rate is very low.

Here are some easy ways to vary your walking routine—for fun and for greater fitness benefits.

1. Walk Up and Down Hills

Combine hill walking with your regular flat-terrain walking as a form of interval training. You can vary the intensity of your workouts by walking briskly on level ground, then taking to the hills, and finishing again on the flats. When walking uphill, try leaning forward slightly—it is easier on your leg muscles. Walking downhill, contrary to what you might think, can be harder on your body than walk-

Walking is an easy way for a physically inactive person to become active again. A long-term walking program can strengthen bones, increase stamina, and help control weight.

ing uphill, because the downhill road can jar your joints, especially the knees, and cause muscle soreness. It may be tempting to speed downhill, but in fact it is a good idea to slow your pace slightly and take shorter steps. That way, you're less likely to end up with sore knees. Walking uphill, by the way, burns more calories. If you weigh 150 pounds, walking at 3.5 miles an hour on flat terrain burns about 300 calories per hour. At the same pace on a gentle incline (a 4 percent grade), you burn almost 400 calories per hour. On a slightly steeper incline (an 8 percent grade), you burn nearly 500. If you're walking on a treadmill, you can elevate the grade mechanically. Whenever you intensify your workout, do so gradually.

2. Let Your Elbows Do Some Walking

By swinging your arms, you'll burn 5 to 10 percent more calories and get an upper-body

Walking on grass or gravel burns more calories than walking on a track. Walking on soft sand boosts calorie expenditure by nearly 50 percent, provided one's normal pace is maintained.

workout as well. Move your arms in opposition to your legs—swing your right arm forward as you step forward with your left leg. This arm movement helps counterbalance the motion of your legs. As you increase your pace, switch to pumping your arms: bend your elbows at a 90-degree angle and pump from the shoulder instead of the elbow joint. (This is similar to the arm position in racewalking—see page 132.) Keep your wrists straight. To reduce fatigue, keep your hands unclenched. Swing your arms in a small arc: your elbow should come to about the middle of your chest and as far back as your buttock.

3. Try Striding
Lengthen your stride, swing your extended arms freely with increasing vigor, and aim for a faster pace (about 4.5 miles per hour)—this is called striding. As your pace increases, your feet will land closer to an imaginary centerline stretching in front of you.

4. Do Some Retro Walking
Like running in reverse, walking backward has a lot to offer. Besides providing a change of pace, retro walking helps strengthen the abdominal and back muscles, the quadriceps (the muscles in front of the thigh), and the hamstrings (at the back of the thigh). In addition, if you're recovering from a leg or ankle injury, retro walking is less stressful than forward motion. But you must take some precautions, too. Don't walk backward where there is automobile traffic or where you might run into a tree or another pedestrian. A partner who walks forward is useful as a guide, and then you can switch off. Start slowly to keep your calves from getting sore. Don't walk more than a quarter of a mile backward the first week. And use the technique only for variety: it doesn't provide as good a workout as brisk forward walking.

5. Take Up Waterwalking
Waterwalking started as rehabilitative therapy for people with injuries, and soon was recognized as a boon for everybody. You can waterwalk anywhere—along a lakeshore or beach or in a pool—without getting your hair wet or even knowing how to swim. If you walk at a steady pace, you can burn 300 to 500 calories per hour. Deep water provides more resistance, but you may do better in waist-high water since you won't tire so easily. Shallow water is O.K., too—just walk faster and longer. Because of the water's resistance, you don't have to walk as fast in water as you would on land to burn the same number of calories. Walking 2 miles per hour in thigh-high water is the equivalent of walking 3 miles per hour on land. With a friend, waterwalking can be a sociable activity.

6. Try Pole Walking
To enhance your upper-body workout while walking, use lightweight, rubber-tipped walking poles, sold in many sporting-goods stores. Think of this form of walking as cross-country skiing without the skis. When you step forward with the left foot, the right arm with the pole comes forward and is planted on the ground, about even with the heel of the left foot. This novelty, which is fun when you get used to it, works the muscles of your chest and arms as well as some abdominals. Find the right size poles—you should be able to grip the pole and keep your forearm about level as you walk.

A daily walking regimen can be enhanced by opting for stairs instead of an escalator whenever possible. Many doctors caution against the use of hand weights while walking (below right).

7. Skip Elevators and Escalators

Take the stairs. Walking up several flights of stairs every day is great exercise, since your legs lift the entire weight of your body at every step. It burns extra calories and provides an extra workout for your leg muscles. If you work or live on a high floor, get off a few floors below and walk up the last flights. Or you can, of course, also use stair-climbing machines, which are now found in most health clubs.

8. Use Hand Weights—with Care

Holding hand weights while you walk can boost your heart rate and caloric expenditure, but their use remains controversial. They may alter your arm swing, and thus lead to muscle soreness or even injury. They're generally not recommended for people with high blood pressure or heart disease. If you want to use them, start with one-pound weights and increase them gradually. The weights shouldn't add up to more than 10 percent of your body weight. Ankle weights are not recommended, as they increase the chance of injury.

Walking Speed Conversion Table

To estimate your walking speed, count how many steps you take per minute and compare the results with this table.

Steps per Minute	Minutes per Mile	Miles per Hour
70	30	2.0
90	24	2.5
105	20	3.0
120	17	3.5
140	15	4.0
160	13	4.5
175	12	5.0
190	11	5.5
210+	<10	<6.0

This table is based on an average stride (2.5 feet long). If your stride is closer to 3 feet long, here's an easy way to estimate your speed: count how many steps you take per minute and divide by 30. Thus, if you are taking about 105 steps per minute, you are covering about 3.5 miles per hour.

9. Step Up the Pace with Racewalking

Racewalking, a great calorie burner, turns walking into a sport. The object of racewalking is to move your body ahead as quickly as possible without running, and to avoid the up/down motions of regular walking. You accomplish this with a forward-thrusting hip swivel, which is meant to propel you more efficiently than the normal side-to-side swing of the hips. Here's how to start:

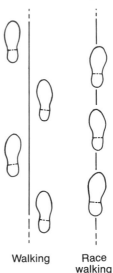

Racewalking rule of thumb: as one arm pumps backward, the opposite hip should swivel outward.

- Think of racewalking as walking a tightrope. In normal walking your feet make parallel tracks, but in racewalking, you put one foot down in front of the other, almost in a straight line. Because of anatomical differences, this may not be achievable for everyone. Come as close to it as you can.
- Swing your hip forward as you step forward—it's the hips and legs that act as the propulsive force.
- Your feet should stay close to the ground, with no wasted motion. Each foot should strike the ground solidly on the back of the heel with the toes slightly pointed up. Two rules of competitive racewalking are that one foot must always be on the ground, and your legs must be straight at one point in the cycle.

Walking vs. Other Activities

Calories burned by a 150-pound person per hour

Racewalking	600
Uphill walking, 10% incline (3 mph)	500
Walking with 15-pound backpack (4 mph)	410
Brisk walking (4 mph)	350
Slow running (5.5 mph)	550
Recreational tennis, singles	430
Swimming, slow crawl	400

- Use long strides. Your motion should be fluid, efficient, and smooth.
- Bend your arms at a 90-degree angle, and keep your wrists straight. With the motion coming from the shoulder, not the elbow, pump your arms rhythmically with your leg motion. When you pump back, your hand should come about 6 inches behind the hip, while on the swing forward the wrist should

Novice racewalkers often practice the sport by imagining that they are walking a tightrope. Rather than having their feet make parallel tracks as in regular walking (near right), racewalkers strive to put one foot down in front of the other, almost in a straight line (far right). In racewalking competitions, one foot must always be on the ground.

Walking   Race walking

be near the center of your chest. Keep your hands above your hips. The vigorous arm pumping counterbalances your leg/hip motion, allows for a quick pace, and provides a good workout for your upper body.

- Keep your torso, shoulders, and neck relaxed. Don't bend from the waist—this can lead to back strain. Some racewalkers angle their whole bodies forward slightly.

Since technique is important, you will need practice. If there's an experienced racewalker around who can give you pointers, so much the better. Start with the leg movement first, build up some speed, and then incorporate the arm motion. See what a difference it makes to have your arms bent 90 degrees instead of hanging at your sides. Your pace should quicken automatically as you learn to use your arms. Start slowly and increase your pace gradually. Try interval walking—that is, racewalk for a few minutes, then do normal brisk walking. Pause occasionally to check your heart rate. ◇

A BEGINNER'S GUIDE
TO WEIGHT TRAINING

by Greg Gutfeld

The thought of lifting weights used to seem pretty senseless to me. Pick something up and put it back down. Pick something up and put it back down. People get paid for this—they're called garbagemen. Lifting heavy objects for free struck me as absurd. Then I tried it . . . and before I knew it, I was hooked. It began as a casual experiment. A little beefing up, I thought, might boost my skills at my other sports. Stuck at my altitude (5 foot 6 on tiptoes), I figured a little more strength wouldn't hurt, either.

I began with a half-hour workout, three times a week. Within five weeks, my body had already started to improve: my chest had expanded, my biceps and triceps had started to take some shape, and when I flexed my abdominal muscles, you could see the faint beginnings of a ripple. Encouraged, even excited, I started working out longer and more often.

Funny part about it, not only was I getting stronger, I was actually beginning to relish the workouts themselves. There was the pleasant burn of muscles straining to their limit and the knowledge that this simple activity was delivering results. Results I could see. Quickly. All I had to do was lift something. When that became easy, I'd lift something heavier. How often in life do you find something so straightforward?

Actually, there's a lot more to pumping iron than bulging biceps and extension-cord veins. Experts used to think that only huff-and-puff exercises like running, swimming, or cycling did the body any real good. Now researchers are increasingly turning up valuable health benefits from strength training.

In fact, pick any area of preventive health care, and pumping iron is likely to offer something. A regular weight-lifting program can:

Help keep you slim. Strength training powers up your metabolism, the body's weight-loss engine, so you can eat more while fending off body fat.

Fight cholesterol. In one study, men who worked out on Nautilus machines three to four times a week for 16 weeks experienced an 8 percent drop in LDL cholesterol (the bad kind) and a healthy rise in HDL cholesterol (the good kind).

Keep blood-sugar levels down. Building muscle seems to help the body burn off excess sugar in the bloodstream. In studies, borderline diabetics who jogged and did weight training saw their blood-sugar levels return to normal.

Help control blood pressure. Previously, experts labeled weight training off-limits for people with high blood pressure, because their levels can go ballistic during the tough parts of the exercises. Now studies of mild to moderate hypertensives suggest this fear may be unwarranted, that blood pressure falls quickly and harmlessly back to earth after the exercise. Even better, a regular program of weight training may be a factor in helping keep mild hypertension in line.

If you're like me, all these good-for-you reasons to lift weights are nice, but not enough to get you into the gym. Let's face it: the immediate appeal is the transformation that takes place in the mirror—watching your stomach flatten out, your chest and arms get wider, your shoulders get broader. You get all that from weight training, and you

Crunch

get all the health stuff as well. You even get the intangibles that Charles Atlas used to brag about: the knowledge that nobody's going to kick sand in your face.

Your first step in beginning a strength-training program should be through the doors of a sporting-goods store. There you can pick up a basic weight set consisting of one 45-pound Olympic bar and about 110 pounds of weights. This standard bar is 7 feet long and 2 inches in diameter—sturdy enough to handle all the weight you can pile on it. Figure on spending at least $200 for the set. You may also want to pick up a curling bar to do arm curls, and a pull-up bar to wedge into a doorway for chin-ups. Tack on another $50 for each of those.

Next, you need a decent free-weight bench ($100 to $150) with a rack that can support your weights. Don't spend less than $100, or you risk having the whole unit collapse under you in the middle of a bench press.

As you get stronger, you'll need more weights. You can buy these one plate at a

Squat

Bench Press

time at prices ranging anywhere from 89¢ to $1.15 a pound.

As for workout gear, all you really need is a pair of leather-and-nylon gloves ($15 to $20) to fend off calluses, and a strength-training belt ($25 to $45), which adds stability around your trunk and reduces the risk of back injury.

While you can't beat the convenience of a home weight setup, public gyms offer a much wider variety of equipment than most of us can afford to buy for ourselves. When I joined my first gym, it wasn't a decision fueled by intense thought. I had simply surpassed the limits of my at-home weight supply, and I was

tired of my dog sniffing my ear while I did stomach crunches.

Where to join? I signed up at the place where all my friends worked out. A few years later, I moved away from home and had to find a new gym in an unfamiliar town where I knew no one. That time, it was harder. I learned that you've got to ask lots of questions and keep a critical eye.

There are several factors to consider. Money, to begin with. Yearly rates range from a couple hundred dollars (or even less) to thousands. Your basic low-rent House of Iron is just a big room crammed with equipment and machines from wall to wall: no showers, no lockers, no attractive receptionist in a leotard to banter with at the door. At the high end, you'll find lushly carpeted entryways, less crowding, and comfortable locker rooms—maybe even a pool. Then

Leg Extension

Military Press

there's everything in between. Here are some tips for picking the right club:

• Make certain there are competent personnel on the premises. A certified strength and conditioning specialist should be available to answer your questions. If the gym is run by a bored high-school kid making minimum wage, don't expect a lot of useful guidance.

• Avoid photocopied programs. The club's in-house trainers should address your needs directly, not simply hand you the same workout that's been given to everyone else.

• Beware of the muscleheads. Steer clear of gyms populated by overly sculpted employees who are too busy staring at their own reflections in the mirror to help you find your way around.

• Make sure the gym has everything you need. A workout that nails all the muscle groups calls for using both free weights (barbells and dumbbells) and resistance machines such as Universal and Nautilus. The gym you choose should have plenty of both. Also take note of the number and type of aerobic machines they have—StairMasters, stationary

bikes, treadmills, and so on. Nothing beats 10 minutes on an aerobic machine to get you warmed up for your lifting session. A good way to tell if there's enough equipment is to check the place out at 5:30 P.M., when traffic is heaviest.

• Look for a gym that will let you have a few free trial workouts before you sign on. I was actually able to go for a whole month bouncing from one gym to the next, before I had to make up my mind.

I eventually settled on a place that attracted young professional types—people a lot like me. That made it easier to find a training partner. Working out with a partner is a big plus. Just making a commitment to someone else that you'll show up can help you stick to your program. One morning, after a particularly harrowing party, I dragged myself out of bed and trudged to the gym in the rain because I knew my training partner was going to be there, expecting us to lift together.

The Beginner's Weight-lifting Program
You'll probably soon want to adjust this plan to suit your particular needs. That's fine. But it's important to hit all the major muscle groups of the body for balance and body symmetry. (You don't want to end up with a barrel chest supported on spindly legs.) In your workouts, target the larger muscle groups first: the shoulders, back, abdominals, chest, quadriceps (upper leg muscles), and calves. Follow these with exercises for smaller muscle groups like the triceps and biceps.

A little trick: Do the exercises you dislike most first. Once you get the worst ones over with, you'll be able to look forward to the rest

Let's Get Ripped: The Line on Lifting Lingo

How to talk like a muscleman even if you aren't one . . . yet

You might have heard some of these terms before and wondered if they were part of some coded lingo used only by men with tree-trunk necks and strategically ripped tank tops. Let's clear up some of the mystery.

Buffed: Unquestionably, the ultimate goal of many lifters. When you're "buffed," you have large, shapely muscles that are well defined.

Bulking Up: Trying to gain body weight by lifting very heavy weights and consuming massive amounts of food. Think of "bulking up" as amassing clay before starting a sculpture.

Burn: The burning sensation caused by exercising until the lactic acid builds up in your muscles. Imagine the feeling you get when your thighs get pumped after an uphill bike climb. Transfer that feeling to your arms and chest—see why strength training is so much fun?

Circuit Training: Doing your repetitions rapidly and moving from one weight-lifting station to the next weight-lifting station with only very short breaks between sets. Circuit training adds aerobic conditioning to your strength-training program.

Cutting Up: Reducing body fat and water retention to make your muscles better defined. Cutting up is considered a regular ritual among competition bodybuilders.

Easy Set: An exercise that isn't close to your maximum effort. It might be used as part of a warm-up routine before doing heavier weights.

Hypertrophy: Boosting the size of muscle fibers using resistance training. Essentially it's an expensive word meaning your muscles are getting bigger.

Lift-Off: The assistance rendered by a spotter in getting a weight to its proper starting position.

Max: The most—or maximum—amount of weight you can lift for one repetition of a particular exercise.

Plateau: A period when you apparently level out and new physical gains seem extraordinarily hard to come by.

Pumped: Describes muscles temporarily made bigger when you boost blood supply to them through various strength-training exercises. Usually bodybuilders "pump up" before a competition by doing push-ups, curls, or anything else that might get the blood flowing.

Repping Out: Doing as many repetitions as you can until you can't do even one more.

Ripped: Having extreme muscularity and definition. The kind of over-the-top development you'd glimpse at a bodybuilding competition: rippling muscles and bulging, three-dimensional veins.

Leg Curl

Lat Pulldown

of the workout, instead of dreading that approaching set.

The exercises described below and pictured beginning on page 134 are planned around a combination of free weights and machines. In general, machines are good for beginners because they guide you through the movements. Free weights give you more freedom.

Concentrate on form. For example, don't cheat the weight up by arching your back for more leverage during a bench press. Often, cheating puts extra stress on the muscles, which can result in injury—especially for beginners. It's better to work with less weight and keep the part of your body that's not lifting still. Work slowly, focusing on the muscle that's supposed to be doing the work. You don't get points for speed.

Crunch (builds the abdominal muscles). Lie on your back, knees bent, with your fingers lightly touching your ears. Slowly curl your upper torso until your shoulders leave the floor. Hold a few seconds, then return to the mat. Repeat.

Squat (hits the thighs and buttocks). In a standing position, grip a barbell and place it across your shoulders, behind your head. Still holding the bar, squat slowly until upper thighs are parallel to the floor. Return to original position, then repeat.

Bench press (strengthens chest muscles). Lie on your back on an exercise bench with your knees bent so your feet are flat on the floor. Grasp the barbell from the rack (or have a partner hand it to you) with your hands

Biceps Curl

slightly more than shoulder width apart. Slowly lower it to your chest. Press the barbell up until arms are fully extended, elbows locked. Repeat.

Leg extension (targets the thighs). Sit in the leg-extension exercise machine with your feet under the footpad. Raise the weight stack until your legs are parallel to the floor. Return and repeat.

Military press (builds the deltoids, or shoulder muscles). Grasp the barbell and sit at the end of a bench, with your feet firmly on the floor. Lift the weight over your head and rest it on the back of your shoulders. Push the bar up to arm's length, then lower it to the starting position and repeat.

Leg curl (bolsters the hamstrings and counterbalances leg extension). Lie facedown on the leg-curl machine, placing your heels under the footpad. To get support, hold on to the front of the machine. Curl your legs until the calves touch the upper part of your thighs. Return to down position and then repeat the exercise.

Lat pulldown (strengthens the latissimi dorsi, or V-shaped back muscles). Grasp the bar at the lat-pulldown station of a weight machine with your hands about 36 inches apart. Then sit down, allowing your arms to extend overhead. Pull the bar down slowly until it touches the back of the neck right above the shoulders. Then return to starting position and repeat.

Biceps curl (builds biceps muscle). Stand and hold the barbell with an underhand grip, allowing it to rest against your thighs. Slowly bring the bar up to your chest, bending your elbows, but keeping your upper arms motionless against your sides. Hold the bar against your chest for a beat, and then slowly lower it to the starting position. Repeat.

How many repetitions of each exercise should you do? Research suggests that you'll get the most out of your program if you repeat each exercise 8 to 12 times, working with 75 percent of your maximum weight. Your maximum is simply the most weight you are capable of lifting for a single repetition of a given exercise. For example, if the most you can bench-press in one shot is 100 pounds, one set at the bench press is 8 to 12 repetitions of the exercise with 75 pounds on the bar. Anytime you can complete 12 repetitions without straining too much, bump up the weight by about 5 percent. To stay motivated, it's good to set a tangible goal, such as increasing the weight 20 pounds in six months. That usually works better than a vague goal, such as "getting stronger."

For each exercise, you may want to start off with one set, and then, as you progress, work up to two, three, even four, allowing a minute or two of rest between sets. When you reach the point where you like how you look and feel, you can maintain your size without getting bigger by doing no more than one to two sets.

Be sure to sandwich a rest day between your workouts; your muscles need time to recover. A Monday/Wednesday/Friday or Tuesday/Thursday/Saturday workout schedule is best for starters. Later, if you become a true musclehead, you can exercise as often as six days a week by targeting, say, the upper body one day and the lower body the next. Even if you eat iron for breakfast, you should always take at least one full day off each week.

Lifting weights isn't an art; the required skill level isn't up there with golf or baseball. That's great news for beginners, because it means you can get good—and see results quickly. So what are you waiting for, someone to pay you? ◇

Housecalls

by Jennifer Kennedy, M.S.

Q *Which is better to apply to an athletic injury, heat or cold? Should the heat or cold be applied continuously?*

A Cold comes first, to treat the acute stage of injury; heat comes later, during the healing phase. Apply ice for the first 48 to 72 hours. Keep a towel or cloth between you and the ice, so that you don't damage skin or nerves in the area.

The cold not only relieves pain, but will reduce inflammation and swelling. Cold helps to limit the injury as it speeds recovery time. You may want to apply cold for as long as 10 or 20 minutes every hour.

After a few days, when the immediate reaction and pain of the injury have subsided, heat can then help in speeding healing time. Heat helps increase blood flow to the area. It will also reduce soreness and stiffness. You can use a heating pad or a compress with a low to medium amount of heat. You should warm your injury for 20 to 30 minutes, two to three times per day.

If you reaggravate the injury through activity, you may need to return to applying cold until the inflammation recedes again. You may also want to consult a physician, especially if the injury becomes chronic.

Q *If done over many years, can running have negative health effects, such as wearing down bones and joints, or causing varicose veins? Are certain of these effects specific to women?*

A Running can wear down bones and joints and aggravate varicose veins in women *or* men. Orthopedic wear tends to occur with high-mileage training regimens. In contrast, running sometimes exacerbates, but does not *cause*, varicose veins, a condition to which people may inherit a tendency.

Some orthopedists give an average of 20 miles or more per week as the level of running at which people may risk bone or joint damage. With very-high-mileage training, runners sometimes tear down tissue faster than they allow it to recover, which can lead to structural changes. Taking advantage of good running shoes, and cross-training with other sports, can help lessen risk.

Women who run long distances or otherwise exercise at very high levels may experience loss of menstruation. This effect, as well as the low-body-fat status shared by many serious athletes, causes a drop in estrogen levels that could, over time, contribute to osteoporosis.

Q *I enjoy exercising outdoors all through the winter. Do I need to worry about frostbite during a cold-weather workout?*

A You can safely exercise in cold weather if you don't overexpose yourself and if you dress carefully. Be aware of the signs of frostbite and hypothermia, though.

Frostbite usually affects the extremities —the fingers, toes, ears, face, and penis. Severe windchill is the main culprit. For example, at windchills far below 0° F, just a few minutes of full exposure of skin can begin the frostbite process. Many times the victim is unaware of the problem, be-

cause the coldness blocks sensory signals. Frostbite occurs in three categories of severity:

• Frost nip—The body area will grow numb and white. Apply warmth directly and gently. Frost nip may produce an uncomfortable tingling, but no lasting damage.

• Superficial frostbite—The skin may become white, waxy, and hard, and should be touched only carefully. Get yourself out of the cold, and immerse the area in warm water. You should seek medical attention for this type of frostbite.

• Deep frostbite—The area affected will look blotchy or blue. It will feel hard to the touch, with no underlying resilience. This condition requires immediate medical attention. Don't try to thaw the area yourself. Wrap it in a blanket to prevent bruising, and keep it elevated until you can get to medical care. Areas with very severe, deep frostbite sometimes require amputation.

For any of these conditions, avoid rubbing or massaging the affected area.

Q Are the kind of body-building pills that you can buy off the shelf in drugstores or health-food stores the same as the drugs athletes abuse, and do they have the same effects?

A The products you refer to qualify more accurately as dietary supplements than as drugs. Despite labels that make them look powerful, they are not the same as the drugs that athletes abuse.

The word "anabolic" in their labeling may confuse many people. We more often see this term in the phrase "anabolic steroids," which are the drugs of greatest abuse by athletes. "Anabolic" simply refers to any substance that increases muscle mass, weight, growth, and bone maturation. Anabolic steroids, which usually consist of testosterone and its derivatives, have a variety of unhealthful effects, and are available only by prescription or through illegal sources.

In contrast, the over-the-counter pills and powders consist primarily of amino acids, and thus may be anabolic in the sense of helping to build protein mass in the body through a more gradual process than with steroids. There are few scientific data about their effects.

Q I'm interested in joining a health club. What should I look for before I sign up?

A Some people want access to a particular type of exercise or instruction, some are interested in the social aspects of the club, and some just want a convenient nearby location and affordability. Many want all of the above.

Seek out a club with a certified, professional staff. Check the credentials of the instructors at the establishment before you sign up, so you'll know that the people who teach you about weight lifting, nutrition, or aerobics know what they are talking about. Also, you'll want to look for cleanliness; equipment that is safe, in terms of its condition and layout; and a staff that is CPR-certified.

The American College of Sports Medicine publishes a Health/Fitness Facility Consumer Selection Guide to help you better choose a health club. (For a copy of the guide, send a self-addressed, stamped envelope to the American College of Sports Medicine, P.O. Box 1440, Indianapolis, IN, 46206–1440.)

Do you have a fitness question?
Send it to Editor, Health and Medicine Annual, P.O. Box 90, Hawleyville, CT 06440-9990.

Psychology

See also:
Individual articles in the second half of this book, arranged in alphabetical order, for additional information.

Long, rich lives depend on a combination of mental and physical wellness. An increasing body of evidence indicates that, in the words of a well-known song, "you can't have one without the other."

A study conducted by scientists at Stanford University found that people with coronary-artery disease suffered a temporary decline in the heart's pumping efficiency when they became angry. The decrease in efficiency was potentially sufficient to trigger blood clots or arrhythmia. Gail Ironson, M.D., the psychiatrist who led the study, says that cardiac patients need to handle and resolve hostility in ways that minimize damaging effects to the heart.

A six-year study led by Jeffrey H. Burack, M.D., a physician at San Francisco General Hospital, found that depression led to early death among men infected with HIV, the virus that causes AIDS. Men who suffered depression during the first three years after diagnosis died at twice the rate of men who were not depressed. Although all the men tested positive for HIV at the time they began the study, none had signs of AIDS. But during the next few years, levels of CD4 cells—special immune-system cells that are used to chart progression of HIV infection—dropped 38 percent faster in the depressed men, resulting in more rapid onset of signs of AIDS.

The National Research Council, the research arm of the National Academy of Sciences (NAS), issued a massive report, *Understanding and Preventing Violence,* which indicated that biological and genetic factors such as hyperactivity and low IQ are among the risk factors associated with violence. The report noted that the average amount of prison time served for violent crimes tripled between 1975 and 1989. However, the increased severity of punishment had no measurable effect on deterring crime. The report's recommendations included early intervention in the development of potentially violent children. The authors based this recommendation on widespread evidence that young children who exhibit aggressive behavior are more likely to exhibit criminal or violent behavior as teenagers and adults.

Yale University psychologist Alan E. Kazdin reported a promising new treatment for conduct disorder. This mental-health problem affects millions of children. It frequently persists into adulthood and on to the next generation. Kazdin found that the antisocial behavior could be curbed by therapy that teaches better ways to interact with teachers and peers; the therapy was particularly effective when parents also received training.

Genetic factors may play a role in divorce. Psychologists David T. Lykken and Matt McGue of the University of Minnesota in Minneapolis studied 1,516 pairs of same-sex twins. They found that divorce was significantly more common among both identical twins than among both fraternal twins. The risk of divorce increased if a subject's parents or his or her spouse's parents had divorced. If both sets of parents had divorced, the risk of divorce was twice that when one set had divorced. An inherited personality characteristic, such as a tendency toward impulsiveness, might be an influencing factor in such behavior.

Divorce also was the subject of a study by John Mordechai Gottman and other psychologists at the University of Wash-

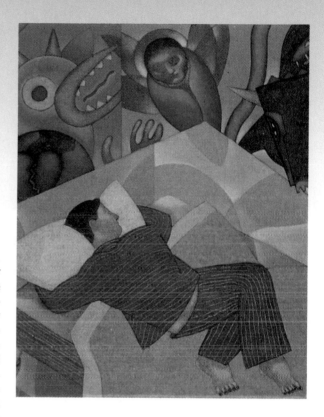

ington in Seattle. Depending largely on a questionnaire used during an interview with ostensibly happy young married couples, the researchers predicted with 94 percent accuracy which marriages would end in divorce within four years. Among the most important predictors of divorce were marital disappointment and tendency of one or both partners to see themselves as separate individuals rather than as part of a team.

Judging the behavior of others is something most of us do. But we do not do it evenhandedly, according to John Condry, professor of human development and family studies at Cornell University. He found that people are far less critical of the immoral behavior of someone they know and like than of someone they do not know or like.

The perception of lying also is affected by behavior. Charles F. Bond, Jr., a psychologist at Texas Christian University, found that people who accompany truthful descriptions with unexpected mannerisms are likely to be viewed as liars. Bond's conclusions were based on a series of videotape-viewing experiments.

Researchers continue to find new connections between mental well-being and physical health.

Americans of all ages derive great happiness from their pets. In a medical setting, animals can provide a similar uplifting effect.

WEE PAWS FOR HEALTH
—pets are good for you

by Sue Berkman

It could be a screenplay for a made-for-television movie: 65 young boys in a special school for difficult children. All have been labeled with attention deficit hyperactivity disorder (ADHD), all have been rejected from normal classrooms, and all exhibit behaviors that range from restless to ruthless. Each and every attempt at calming their destructive actions fails. Enter a psychiatrist who fills a huge room with hamsters, gerbils, doves, and lizards. Twice a week the boys visit the animals and learn to tenderly care for them. The boys begin to count the hours until the next "animal day." Their behavior becomes noticeably calmer. Their schoolwork begins to improve. Soon they grow so proficient at their work, so proud of their accomplishments, so bonded to the animals, that they are assigned to go out with the small creatures as teams to nursing homes, institutions—and schools much like the ones where they were once unwelcome.

While this could be just a fairy tale, it is, in fact, a real-life drama that took place at the Devereux School in Pennsylvania under the guidance of Aaron Katcher, M.D., from the University of Pennsylvania Schools of Medicine and Dental Medicine in Philadelphia. Dr. Katcher compared his subjects with boys of similar ages who were involved in other types of ADHD programs. In every way, the animal caretakers showed the greatest improvement. "Animals have the property to focus the attention of children with ADHD and motivate them to learn. Furthermore, I can foresee a time when animal therapy may actually reduce the need for medication generally used to treat such children," says Dr. Katcher.

In the United States alone, 51 million people own dogs, 56 million own cats, 45 million people are bird owners, and 75 million people keep small mammals and reptiles around the house. Do they share a common benefit?

"We can assume that there is at least a perceived benefit for those households, since it is unlikely that pet ownership is driven merely by altruistic urges," says Andrew Rowan, Ph.D., of the School of Veterinary Medicine at Tufts University in North Grafton, Massachusetts, and editor of *Anthrozoos,* a journal published by the Delta Society, an international nonprofit organization whose members include pet owners, volunteers, therapists, educators, health professionals, and veterinarians.

Actually, the healing benefits of animals were recognized as far back as 1792, when animals were used at the York Retreat in England to reduce the use of harsh drugs and shackles on mental patients. Now, 200 years later, the wisdom of that concept can be applied in many areas of medical research.

Peaceable Kingdom—Reducing Stress

As anyone who figures into the above statistics knows, a pet helps its owner establish a regular routine. It's hard to sleep in until 9:00 A.M. in the presence of a dog who is used to being walked at 7:00 A.M. Because it must be cared for, a pet makes its owner feel needed. Pets often act very silly and encourage us to act silly in return. A pet won't argue with you, castigate your work, or reject you for someone else. A pet can take your mind off your problems, and, indeed, act almost like a tranquilizer—with no bad side effects.

Children raised with pets appear to have better social skills than do their petless peers. Walking, feeding, and bathing a pet help children develop a strong sense of responsibility.

Karen Allen, Ph.D., an associate professor in the School of Medicine at the State University of New York, Buffalo, took the "dog tranquilizer" theory a step further. Dr. Allen conducted a study of 45 women. Each subject performed a stressful lesson in mental arithmetic, first in a laboratory with only a researcher, then again, two weeks later, at home in the presence of her pet dog, then in the presence of a best female friend, and finally with neither present. With pets standing nearby, the women's physical responses remained close to normal. With a human friend in the room, however, stress soared. The dogs also fostered diligence: in their presence, the women kept on with the task. With human friends the women tended to stop, hesitate, or make excuses.

The presence of a pet can considerably ease one of life's most stressful events—losing a spouse. In interviews with 89 women who had recently lost their husbands, Sharon E. Bolin, Ed.D., dean of West Suburban College of Nursing, Oak Park, Illinois, found that those who did not own a pet reported declining health once they were widowed. Pet owners were better able to pick up the pieces and move on.

Lowered stress yields its own rewards. In a yearlong study of 938 Medicare patients, Judith M. Siegel, Ph.D., professor of public health at the University of California in Los Angeles, asked questions pertaining to health, social support, pet ownership, visits to physicians, and stressful life events, such as loss of a job or death of a spouse or close family member. Among the patients who experienced the greatest amount of stress during the study, those without pets reported 16 percent more visits to doctors than did pet owners in general, and 20 percent more than dog owners in particular. One theory suggests that people who have a dog's ear have less need for the doctor's.

Heartfelt Healing

Ninety-two heart-disease patients from the University of Maryland Hospital in Baltimore were asked by Erika Friedmann, Ph.D., a clinical psychologist at Brooklyn College of the City University of New York, if they had a pet waiting at home. Of the 39 patients who

Many organizations arrange for animals to spend time with people confined in hospitals and nursing homes. Medical studies attest to the therapeutic value of such visits.

did not have an animal around the house, 11 died within a year of hospitalization. Of 53 patients who did have a pet to go home to, only three died in the same period. And it's not just the regular exercise of walking a dog that improves the survival rate, either; even physically undemanding pets like cats, birds, and lizards appeared to foster survival.

Then Dr. Friedmann decided to find out if pets could have a benefit on the hearts of healthy adults considered at high risk because they had competitive Type A personalities. In a group of 193 college students, the presence of a pet dog significantly reduced speeded-up heart rates, for the short term, at least. "These small effects, when repeated frequently, can have a real impact on the quality of life and in moderating the stressful effects of daily irritations," explains Dr. Friedmann.

The largest study on the cardiovascular benefits of the human-animal bond was completed at the Baker Institute for Medical Research at Monash University in Melbourne, Australia. Psychologist Warwick Anderson asked a variety of questions of people visiting the institute for preventive heart checkups about diet, exercise, alcohol intake, and pet ownership. At the end of three years, more than 5,500 people had been interviewed. Women older than 40—and men of all ages —who owned pets had lower blood pressure and 20 percent lower blood-triglyceride levels than did nonowners. Male pet owners between the ages of 30 and 60 had lower cholesterol levels than those who had no

pets. These differences weren't due to exercise, body mass, or eating habits: all these factors were pretty similar in the subjects questioned. Dr. Anderson points out that the study concluded only that the risk factors for heart disease were lower in pet owners, not the actual heart-disease rates. But, he adds, the results were certainly on par with what you might expect from other preventive therapies, such as a drug commonly used to lower blood pressure or cholesterol.

The need for pain relievers may also be reduced with help from the animal kingdom. In a study at the University of Pennsylvania, Dr. Katcher observed a group of patients about to undergo dental surgery. Some were hypnotized, others were told to gaze at an aquarium full of fish, and the rest sat quietly for 20 minutes. The first two groups experienced the least discomfort during surgery— watching fish was as effective as being hypnotized. Dr. Katcher speculates that stroking animals and talking to them stimulates the production of endorphins—the brain's own pleasure chemicals.

A Child's Best Friend

A number of researchers have confirmed the developmental benefits of pets for young children. There is general agreement that children who are raised with pets score higher on tests of self-reliance, social skills, sociability, and tolerance than do petless children. Further, children who have a close relation-

A visit by the family pet can sometimes be just enough to lift the spirits of a hospitalized child. Studies show that pet owners tend to be healthier than their counterparts who do not have pets.

Bringing Hope to the Hospital

Hope—a lovable 14-pound, dachshund-beagle mix—is in training to be a social dog. When she completes her training, she (and I, as her handler) will be qualified to visit lonely elderly people in nursing homes, hospitalized children, and others in need of a brief encounter with the outside world.

Our training classes take place at the American Society for Prevention of Cruelty to Animals (ASPCA) in New York City, under the direction of Mickey Niego, director of Companion Animal Services. The Pet Partners Program, as it is called, is a service of the Delta Society. To qualify as a Delta Dog in the Pet Partners Program, a dog must first pass certain parts of the Canine Good Citizen test, which is awarded to dogs who have been through basic obedience training. Then Delta Dogs must pass a further temperament test and health check by a veterinarian. At that point, Delta Dogs and their partners start a training program on how to participate in an animal-visitation or therapy program.

A huge difference exists between a "social" or "therapy" dog and a "service" dog. The latter animals are trained to obey 89 different commands. Their repertoire of deeds includes turning lights on and off, mailing letters, picking up dropped objects, pressing elevator buttons, giving money to cashiers, opening refrigerator doors, picking up the phone, and chauffeuring a wheelchair anywhere the user wants to go. The training for social and therapy dogs includes learning up to 35 commands. Social dogs visit institutions with their owners, while therapy dogs work with patients under the direction of a health-care professional. As a social dog, Hope must learn to maneuver through confined areas busy with wheelchairs, walkers, and canes being used by people who may have uncontrolled movements. She must allow contact from a person who may intend to stroke or pet, but who may hit or pinch instead. She has to refrain from begging for or grabbing food, and she absolutely must keep her nose to herself. Meanwhile, I will learn how to make the proper approaches to wheelchair-bound or bedridden patients, how to place Hope in a patient's lap, and, most of all, how to recognize any signs of stress that tell me to remove the dog from the situation.

Once the volunteer training is complete, Pet Partners apply to the Delta Society for registration. The pet accepted for registration receives a special tag that is renewable every two years; a special identification card is issued to the human partner as well.

The Pet Partners program has decided benefits, even for pet owners who visit patients in hospitals and nursing homes on their own. For one thing, Pet Partners qualify for personal-liability insurance and will benefit from networking opportunities, national recognition, and a complimentary subscription to the *Pet Partners Newsletter*, published six times a year, which contains tips and success stories about working partners.

In some states, Hope is granted the same privileges as a guide, service, or hearing dog. Traveling by bus or subway and strolling through a department store is, in fact, part of her training. She is always outfitted in a red harness with a highly visible red, white, and green badge that says "ASPCA Dog In Training." During such forays, I am frequently asked about the program. Recently one man observed, "This dog is a born healer; she'll be a terrific companion wherever she goes." That's my hope.   *S. B.*

ship with a pet show greater responsibility, nurturing, and compassion than do their pet-less peers.

Animals can sometimes touch a child in ways that humans are unable to do. In November 1991, 11-year-old Donny Tomei was hit by a car near his home in West Haven, Connecticut. For 10 days he lay in a coma at Yale-New Haven Hospital, despite the heroic efforts of doctors, family, and friends. One day, Donny's parents noticed that when they talked to Donny about his pet dog Rusty, he seemed to show a reaction by moving his arm and leg. Almost afraid to hope, they asked for permission to bring Rusty to the hospital for a visit. When the dog was placed on the patient's bed, Donny immediately reached out and hugged him, and laughed when Rusty licked his face. Thanks to Rusty's wake-up call, Donny's recovery is slowly progressing with physical therapy.

Senior Companion

Studies of pet-visiting programs for nursing-home and health-center residents suggest that the psychosocial benefits for at least some older persons in such settings are worthwhile. In general the presence of animals in institutional settings seems to lead to a happier, more talkative resident population. Perhaps more important, animals appear to enhance the alertness and attention span of residents. From a medical stand-point, such residents enjoy a greater sense of well-being and fewer symptoms of depression. In nearly every way, pet-visiting programs generate better psychosocial benefits in comparison to alternative therapies such as arts-and-crafts programs and conventional psychotherapy (see sidebar, page 147).

Mickey Niego, director of Companion Animal Services at the American Society for Prevention of Cruelty to Animals (ASPCA) in New York City has firsthand experience. Niego's therapy dog, Jake, an enormous bull mastiff, started his career with an 80-year-old woman named Rose, a resident of a Brooklyn nursing home. Rose was a cantankerous, uncooperative, and bitter woman given to throwing food at nurses and refusing to speak for weeks on end. Then Rose was introduced to Jake. From the moment of their first encounter, a mutual admiration was established. Rose began to tell the nurses that she lived only for Jake's visits, and Jake soon made it clear that he preferred Rose's company to that of anyone else in the home. "For the first year, Rose didn't say a word to me," Niego recalls. "She would tell Jake how she hated being in the home, how bad the food was, and throughout the conversation, she fed him cookies that she had saved from her meal trays. One day she looked at me and said, 'Do you want a cookie?' Now she talks to me about her life and about all the dogs she has owned."

In the nursing-home setting, pet-visitation programs seem to generate better psychosocial benefits than do the more traditional activities like arts and crafts. Sometimes, the animal visitors verge on the exotic (left).

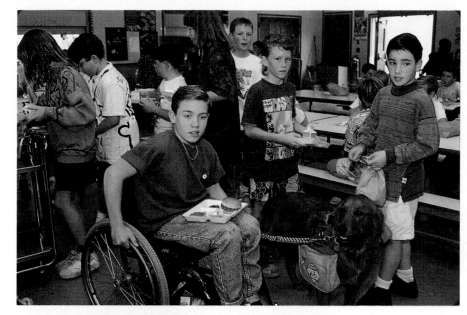

Service dogs improve the quality of life for people with disabilities. For a wheelchair-bound boy (left), a service dog also helps to open up avenues of communication with awkward classmates. Service dogs provide their owners with greatly enhanced independence by performing a variety of everyday tasks (below left).

Helping Hands

Guide dogs are so common that hardly anyone turns to stare anymore. But few people are aware of the variety of situations in which animals serve as a lifeline. Hearing dogs can alert their deaf and hard-of-hearing owners to ringing doorbells and telephones. For paralyzed people or those with movement disorders, a horse can help improve posture, balance, mobility, and function. Service dogs and other animals can act as arms and legs for people with multiple sclerosis, cerebral palsy, muscular dystrophy, and other neurological and orthopedic problems. In every role, animals serve to increase the quantity and quality of attention directed toward the disabled person by creating a "magnet" effect that breaks down social barriers.

The human-animal bond in all its facets offers unlimited opportunities. For instance, researchers in New York City are studying

dogs with the natural ability to alert their owners to an impending epileptic seizure. California researchers have launched the first comprehensive study of the psychological benefits versus the health risks of pet ownership for people who have tested positive for the AIDS virus. In Florida, studies continue to evaluate the value of animal-assisted therapy to the 100,000 crack-exposed babies born each year.

While it's tempting to think of animals as good for everyone, they are not. Some people have severe allergies to the dander on dogs and cats. Pets can also be a source of diseases as diverse as strep infection, pneumonia, and arthritis. Furthermore, veterinary care can be costly, and the responsibility for home care of pets can create family conflict. Then there is the risk of a mismatch: animals have likes and dislikes, just as humans do, and a case of "bad chemistry" can be disappointing for the person and stressful for the animal.

Will animals ever be a routine part of medical treatment? "Animals cannot be considered a panacea," says Dr. Friedmann. "They will not cure cancer, hypertension, or incontinence. But unless a person has an allergy to, or an extreme dislike of, animals, a physician prescribing a pet would not be violating an essential clause of the Hippocratic oath, 'First do no harm.' "   ◇

For Further Information
To learn about the human-animal bond, guide dogs, hearing dogs, service dogs, social dogs, pets in prisons, hospitals, and workplaces, contact: The Delta Society, P.O. Box 1080, Renton, WA 98057-1080.

REFLECTIONS OF TORMENT

by Marcy O'Koon

To people with body dysmorphic disorder (BDD), ugliness is not in the eye of the beholder: the ugliness they see is their own. To everyone else the victims of BDD look quite normal; some are even attractive. But when they look at themselves in the mirror, they recoil at the reflection of someone horrible and disfigured. They often wonder if life is worth living at all.

This psychiatric disorder, known colloquially as "imagined ugliness," usually begins its torment in adolescence or early adulthood. Somehow the mind plays a cruel trick on its owner and creates the belief that one physical feature, say the nose, is so hideous or so distorted in shape that no amount of makeup or reassurance from others, no number of nose jobs or disguises, no time spent staring in a mirror, and no beauty elsewhere on the body can make that nose any less monstrous or any more bearable. The mind's cruelty is so complete that its victim actually *sees* the ghastly flaw every time he or she catches his or her reflection.

Doug, a 36-year-old court clerk, has been diagnosed with BDD. His mind focuses its cruel eye on his face. "Every time I looked in the mirror, I got freaked out. I'd say, 'Oh, I feel something, oh my God, there's a bump there,' " Doug explains. "I'd be rushing up to the mirror and say, 'Oh, this is ugly. People are going to notice it.' "

With BDD sufferers, the mind may conjure up a flaw or may distort an insignificant problem, like Doug's facial bump, until the person feels a disproportionate sense of disgust and doom. Doug says that after spotting a bump, he would cry. "I've spent whole weekends in bed over a blemish. If I would go to work, I would have to go look close up in a mirror, and, of course, the mirror would magnify it. I would freak out and want to hide."

BDD patients are most often tormented by a facial or head-related feature. People with BDD have been found to focus their dread on imagined or minimal facial spots, scars, pale complexion, red complexion, swelling, wrinkles, thinning hair, facial hair, or on the shape or size of the nose, eyes and eyelids, eyebrows, ears, lips, teeth, jaw, chin, cheeks, and the head. Some patients have named features not on their face or head, such as their feet, hands, legs, shoulders, genitals, or breasts.

This fixation on a perceived defect causes severe distress. In many cases the distress can lead to problems with making a living or having a social life. People with BDD tend to make numerous visits to dermatologists, and they may have repeated plastic surgery or cosmetic dentistry in attempts to correct the defect (although they are usually not satisfied with the results). And, tragically, some sufferers are in such great agony that they may attempt—or succeed at—suicide.

One BDD patient, who wants to be known only as "Kathy," says, "I was totally debilitated. I thought of nothing but suicide. I knew I couldn't live looking the way I looked." Kathy has suffered with her imagined ugliness for 20 years. For one six-year period, she hardly left her house. "I felt like a monster and that everyone was looking at me. Cars would begin to crash if they saw me because they'd be too busy looking at how ugly I was. When I looked in my mirror, my heart would sink, and I'd know I couldn't live. I'd be heartbroken," she says.

Problems with Diagnosis

This disorder has been severely underrecognized by doctors, in part because of the ex-

cessive shame and embarrassment felt by the victim. People with BDD often keep their preoccupation a secret from their families, friends, doctors, and even their therapist. Patricia, a 32-year-old sign painter, works in seclusion in her basement studio. "I would cry there because no one could see me. I would cry and cry. I couldn't think of how to explain it to anybody. I didn't know where to start," she says. During one particularly alarming episode, she took a razor blade and scraped it along her face. She can't explain what it was, exactly, that she was trying to do. She says only that, "I couldn't stand the way my face looked. I'd feel so desperate, totally desperate, like I'd rather be dead. I was ashamed."

"Imagined ugliness" has been historically underrecognized in the world of psychiatry. Now one doctor has been working to change that: Katharine Phillips, M.D., a research fellow in psychiatry at McLean Hospital in Belmont, Massachusetts, and an instructor in psychiatry at Harvard Medical School. She initiated the recent surge of interest in BDD when she published a pioneering article on the disorder in the *American Journal of Psychiatry* in late 1991. She recognized BDD in several of her patients, but found little information on the topic. The *Diagnosis and Statistics Manual* (Third Edition-Revised), or *DSM-III-R*, the "bible" of psychiatric diagnosis, mentioned BDD, but, says Phillips, "most patients and doctors alike had never heard of it."

In her ground-breaking article, Phillips presented information she had gathered from around the world. She brought together facts, case studies, and theories from Japan and various European countries and former Soviet republics, places where the disorder, usually under the term *dysmorphophobia*, has been widely discussed and diagnosed for over 100 years. (The term derives from the Greek word *dysmorfia*, meaning ugliness, especially of the face, the area most likely to be the focus of BDD patients.)

In severe cases, victims of BDD are so tormented by an imagined flaw that often only suicide looks attractive.

The disorder can strike as early as age 7, producing such an overwhelming sense of shame that, before long, the afflicted can barely function.

Although Phillips was able to glean some helpful information about this disorder, there is still much to learn about it. Neither she nor her colleagues can answer many questions with certainty, including: What causes BDD? How many people have it? Is it a hereditary illness? Phillips, along with Eric Hollander, M.D., associate professor of psychiatry at Columbia University College of Physicians and Surgeons in New York City, have been working on the answer to another important question: How do you know who has the disorder and who doesn't? Based on the small pool of BDD knowledge, they have improved the diagnostic criteria for the upcoming fourth edition of the *Diagnostics and Statistics Manual* (*DSM-IV*) scheduled for publication in 1994. Accurate diagnostic criteria will give researchers and practitioners a common tool with which to work—even if that tool is only a working definition that will likely be further refined as more studies are completed.

One change in the upcoming BDD entry will be that the preoccupation must cause marked distress or significant impairment in the person's occupational or social functioning. The current *DSM-III-R* manual does not specify the severity necessary to be considered pathological. As a consequence of the new, stricter diagnostic criteria for *DSM-IV*, Phillips expects that fewer people with "normal concerns" will be labeled as having BDD.

"Nonetheless," says Phillips, "questions remain about how to define marked distress or significant impairment." Referring to one colleague, she says, "He is probably looking at a somewhat different group than I am. He doesn't require as much distress or impairment as I do [to diagnose someone with BDD]. He's finding more women than men, and I am finding an equal ratio of men to women. He's finding body weight to be a primary concern. And I'm not finding much concern with body weight. My view is that he's calling excessive normal concern BDD. From his point of view, I'm probably underdiagnosing it."

Another question is defining the relationship of BDD to other disorders, such as anorexia nervosa. Although both disorders involve disturbed body images, Phillips believes they are distinct. "Unlike patients with anorexia nervosa, BDD patients usually do not have a disturbance of the body image as a whole," she says. In addition, a diagnosis of anorexia nervosa requires that a person's body weight is 15 percent below that expected; by contrast, people with BDD look normal weight-wise and otherwise. Hopefully, further studies will provide the evidence needed to settle these questions.

Psychiatrists are just beginning to explore the causes and consequences of imagined ugliness.

Potential Treatment

Hollander and Phillips are having some success treating their BDD patients with antidepressant drugs known as serotonin-reuptake inhibitors. "We still can't claim to have the definitive treatment yet," says Phillips, "but our findings are encouraging." The two drugs now in use are fluoxetine (Prozac) and clomipramine (Anafranil). These medications have earlier been found to work well for patients with obsessive-compulsive disorder (OCD), a psychiatric condition in which the sufferer has repetitive thoughts or feels compelled to repeat a certain act over and over, such as hand-washing.

Hollander specializes in patients with obsessive-compulsive disorder and believes that, in time, the relation between OCD and BDD will be proven. Hollander recently did a study of 500 obsessive-compulsive patients

For many people with body dysmorphic disorder, no amount of makeup, plastic surgery, or cosmetic dentistry will reduce the stress of their imagined ugliness.

Ongoing research also suggests that certain cognitive-behavioral techniques, for example, techniques that help patients avoid excessive mirror-checking, may also be useful. It appears that a combination of medication and cognitive-behavioral therapy may be the most effective treatment for BDD, although this needs confirmation by research findings.

Doug says Prozac "takes the edge off" his illness. He is now able to shop in a depart-

and found that 37 percent met the diagnostic criteria for BDD, which suggests to him that the two disorders frequently occur together and may be related.

In both OCD and BDD, "there is something out of whack with the serotonin system," says Hollander. Serotonin's role in the brain involves anxiety, the sense of harm, or the sense that something doesn't look or feel right, he says. Serotonin works as a chemical messenger, or neurotransmitter, relaying information from one nerve ending to another. The serotonin-reuptake inhibitors block the reuptake of serotonin by a second nerve terminal after it has left the first nerve terminal. Although no one knows with certainty whether this action ultimately affects serotonin functioning, it does somehow manage to correct a disorder-causing "chemical imbalance" in the brain.

ment store that's filled with mirrors. "I'm aware there's a mirror there," he says, "but I'm not going to go zooming into it." When he finds a sweater he likes, he tries it on and stands about 20 feet away from the mirror to see how it looks. "If I go close, I look with my head down [to avoid seeing my face]. Why go look in the mirror and make my imagination go haywire?"

When Doug confronts his reflection, he still becomes nervous and shaky. Fortunately, Prozac gives him the ability to cope better; it is easier to look in the mirror when trying on a sweater and use an electric razor to shave without looking in the mirror. "Prozac has saved my life. Prozac, my support group, and my family. Those are the three things that have saved me. If it weren't for those, I don't know where I'd be. I might be dead, for all I know," he says. ◇

Some children simply do not fit in. Such "square pegs" may retreat into isolation or be picked on by other kids. Fortunately, these children usually grow into well-adjusted adults.

SQUARE PEGS

by Elizabeth McGowan

Paul is happily married and the proud father of a three-year-old son. His life, as he describes it, is "pretty normal." And no one is more surprised about that than Paul. "When I was a kid, I was sure I'd grow up to be a hermit living in a cave somewhere," he explains. "I didn't share the same interests as other kids . . . Not only did I feel out of place in my family, in school, and in my neighborhood, I felt out of place in the whole planetary system."

Kathleen's memories of her childhood, while not as extreme as Paul's, carry equal sting. Today she works as a nurse, a job that requires strong people skills. But Kathleen says that as a child, she was extremely shy and had trouble making friends. "I'd blush at the drop of a hat," she recalls. "The thought of going into a roomful of people would make me sick to my stomach. I always felt like I was outside looking in. I did well in school,

but mostly what I remember about being a child is being very lonely."

Though Kathleen admits, she's "still not too great at cocktail parties," both she and Paul have matured into socially competent, socially accepted adults. Many others who spent their childhoods sitting on the sidelines are not so fortunate. Lonely children, those children who have trouble fitting in with their peers, constitute a group that psychologists, psychiatrists, and educators increasingly view as children at risk. Peer relationships have earned equal billing with the Freudian emphasis on family relationships as determinants of healthy development and predictors of adult success.

The importance of childhood friendships was first championed in the 1940s by psychoanalyst Harry Stack Sullivan, who argued that a "chum," a peer with whom a child could share confidences, giggle about the mysteries of the opposite sex, learn about give-and-take and the importance of considering others, is an essential component of normal childhood development. A chum in childhood, he maintained, opens the door to the capacity for adult love and mature relationships.

"Irritant" Children

Research now supports Sullivan's contention that early rejection by peers can bode ill for later success, leading to problems ranging from substance abuse to dropping out of school to landing in jail. "For friendless children, the potential for maladjustment is huge," affirms Robert L. Selman, author of *Making a Friend in Youth,* and associate professor of education and psychiatry at Harvard University. "They don't usually end up doing well in our society."

Part of the reason, says Margaret Anderson, Ph.D., director of programming and diagnostics for the Manzano Day School in Albuquerque, New Mexico, may be the emphasis that our society places on conformity. She explains, "To have social connections, you have to give up some of your individuality. The square pegs are the kids who can't or won't give up their individuality. The other kids don't like them because they are irritants."

Psychologists divide these "irritant" children into two groups: rejected and neglected. Rejected kids are those whom other children actively dislike and avoid, usually because they are aggressive, insulting, divisive, or perceived as threatening. Neglected children are those that the other kids simply ignore—they aren't sought out, but they're not shunned either. This group tends to be shy and withdrawn, with some difficulty in asserting themselves.

Taking the Path to Loneliness

There are many reasons that a particular child may find him- or herself shunted into either a rejected or neglected category. Most adults, for example, can recall childhood classmates who were tormented by the other kids simply because they were, by schoolyard standards, too heavy, too short, dressed funny, or had big ears. Children who are new to America are often pushed to the sidelines because their born-in-the-U.S.A. peers (as well as their born-in-the-U.S.A. teachers) don't understand their cultural customs. Other kids, particularly boys, are left out because they lack the athletic prowess that is so highly prized in our culture—who wants the clumsy kid on their team?

Some kids, for a variety of developmental, social, or neurological reasons, respond to frustration with violence, and are avoided by other children, who, understandably, don't want to end up with a black eye. Still other children, with either a low IQ or with learning disabilities, are labeled early on as the class dummy. Conversely, children with above-average intelligence have trouble negotiating common ground with average kids, and thus get targeted as nerds or eggheads.

Indeed, kids who are "too smart" are sometimes the social victims of their own intelligence. Children who are truly brilliant are often recognized at an early age and placed in a gifted program offering the learning stimulus they crave. Unfortunately, explains Elizabeth Shaw, M.S., of the New York State Education Department, Office of Special Education Services, "there's a real disservice done to kids who are on the low end of the

Shy, withdrawn children often have trouble asserting themselves. Such kids may lack the courage to approach other children or to participate in simple playground games.

high-IQ spectrum. If you're in a class of 25 to 30 kids of varying abilities, and you're one of the kids who does well on your own, the teacher is often just relieved that she doesn't have to worry about you. No effort is made to offer greater intellectual challenge."

Unfortunately, however, high marks don't necessarily correlate with high popularity scores. Very intelligent children are sometimes excluded by their peers because they see the world differently than other kids do. As family sociologist Tanya F. Johnson writes in an issue of *Gifted Child Today,* "Most children are not interested in how fast your hair can grow in an hour or how hot the sun is, but, for the gifted child, this information may be fascinating." Sharing such "fascinating" facts with classmates, however, can quickly label the high-IQ child as weird.

Dyssemia

Another group stigmatized as weird by their peers are children with dyssemia, a term coined by clinical psychologists Stephen Nowicki, Jr., and Marshall P. Duke, authors of *Helping the Child Who Doesn't Fit In.* Children with this dysfunction can exhibit any number of inappropriate behaviors, from standing too close to other people, to not making proper eye contact, to smiling when they are trying to communicate sorrow, to injecting into a conversation a statement that has nothing at all to do with what everyone else is talking about.

Dyssemics also have problems interpreting what other people are trying to communicate to them. For example, children who fail to understand that a frown combined with a harsh tone of voice signals anger may miss the point when their teacher scolds them, and thus be labeled as defiant. Because dyssemic behavior is often so odd, normal kids are frightened by it and respond by giving these troubled children a wide berth. The problem is compounded by the fact that because dyssemic children can't pick up the nonverbal cues that are so automatic to normal children, they often have no idea that they are different or why they are being excluded by their peers.

A Parent's Role

Whatever the reason for a child's exclusion by peers, experts agree that early intervention can ensure that loneliness does not be-

Intellectually gifted children (left) are often considered weird and are therefore shunned by their less cerebral classmates. A supportive home environment (above) can help reduce a child's sense of rejection.

come a lifelong pattern. As Dr. Anderson puts it, "Experiences of rejection can leave marks on people clear into adulthood. Exclusion can become a vicious cycle."

How can a parent figure out if their child is having serious social problems, going through a normal phase, or just dealing with the social scrapes and cuts all kids must weather on the road to maturity? First, remember that more behavior falls into the normal range than does not. A quick consultation of one of the many readily available Dr. Spock–like books on childhood development will reassure most parents that they shouldn't be worried if Sally doesn't share her toys at 2 or is inept with boys at 12. A good pediatrician can also help allay fears about what behavior is O.K. and what behavior should be worried about. Keep in mind that children cannot and should not be sheltered from all of life's problems. Stress, including the stress of occasional rejection, prepares children to cope with adulthood.

Parents should not force their expectations upon their children. A girl who'd rather be playing baseball than piano may well be better adjusted than the most popular girl in the class.

How To Help Your Lonely Child

Specialized books can help your child confront and articulate fears and concerns. Available from some libraries and a handful of mail-order companies, these books are written for children with everything from hyperactivity to aggressive behavior. Catalogues are available from:
• Woodbine House (The Special Needs Collection)
5615 Fishers Lane
Rockville, MD 20852
301-468-8800
800-843-7323
• The Special Needs Project
1482 East Valley Road, #A121
Santa Barbara, CA 93108
805-565-1914
• Kapable Kids
P.O. Box 250
Bohemia, NY 11716
800-356-1564

In fact, in some cases, the parents feel much greater stress about their child's social situation than their child does. Although they are rare, some friendless kids are very comfortable with their solitude and don't feel lonely. Dr. Anderson says it is the child who *wants* to fit in but can't who has a problem.

Parents, Anderson suggests, should consider whether their own expectations for their child's future are in the best interests of their child—you want your son to join the soccer team; he doesn't like athletics and would rather stay home and read a book.

Nor should parents expect their children to win a popularity contest. Quantity of friends does not necessarily ensure quality. Many well-adjusted kids are perfectly content to have only one or two friends. Parental emphasis on popularity "can undermine much else that is of value in children's lives, including individual skills, tastes, ideals, and commitments," writes social psychologist Zick Rubin in *Children's Friendships.*

If, ultimately, parents determine that, in fact, their child is lonely and having social problems, they should remain calm. "The crazier the parent gets, the crazier the kid gets," cautions Elizabeth Shaw.

Observing Behavior

Signs that your child may be in trouble include recurrent physical symptoms like headaches and stomachaches, a change in eating patterns, a shortened attention span for activities usually enjoyed, depression, a lack of interest in interaction with siblings, distraction, and general irritability.

"Also take note if your child doesn't talk about kids in class, the work he's done, how his or her day was. If there are no revelations about school, there might be a problem there," advises Elizabeth Voluz, M.S., S.S., of the Bio/Educational Engineering Project for United Cerebral Palsy of New York City.

Encourage your child to talk about classroom encounters. Who are his or her friends? What do they like to do together? Look for consistency. Every child experiences rejection—today Johnny comes home from school crying that no one will play with him; tomorrow he's invited to three birthday parties.

In cases where the crying or the stomachaches persist, however, the next step is to make an appointment with the child's teacher. If the teacher agrees that the child seems to be having peer problems, elicit his or her suggestions. But keep in mind that the problem may, in some cases, stem from the teacher. "There can be a personality difference between student and instructor that will cause the child to revert in or act out," explains Elizabeth Shaw. "If the child were just taught in a different manner, the problem would disappear."

To eliminate the possibility of a conflict pattern with a particular teacher, investigate whether the child is having social problems in other school settings. Talk to the gym teacher and the cafeteria monitor. Also ask to see your child's previous year's school records, and talk to his or her teachers from earlier grades to ascertain whether this unpopularity is something new.

And don't look just at school to assess your child's behavior. Observe your child's interactions at the mall, at the playground. Does Sally relate to the other kids well? Does she wait her turn? Does she share? Does she seem to understand what the other children are trying to say to her? Does Johnny, in every situation, stand off by himself? Does he get into more fights than the other kids? Do other kids seem to shun him?

Getting Help

If your suspicions are confirmed that your child is having serious trouble fitting in, it's time to get professional help. Your child's school may recommend referral to a special-education committee that will administer tests designed to uncover everything from learning disabilities to attention deficits to dyssemia. After your child's areas of strength and weakness are determined, formal intervention may be advised.

A parent whose child seems particularly out of step with classmates can often benefit by meeting the child's teacher. Often, the teacher can offer valuable insight into the cause of the problem.

A best friend can often help a youngster emerge from his or her apparent withdrawal. Studies have shown that children learn much about the normal give-and-take of life through their relationships with childhood chums.

In most situations the child's problems can be addressed by supplementing mainstream classroom work with specialized sessions within the school. What type of intervention is recommended depends, of course, on the underlying causes of the child's interpersonal problems. Children who are withdrawn due to an emotional trauma, say a death in the family, may benefit from sessions with a guidance counselor or a psychologist. Speech therapy may do the trick for a child with a stutter. A child with a learning disability may require remedial classes in reading or math. Concentrated lessons on understanding facial cues may be part of the curriculum for a child with dyssemia. Some children may require a combination of therapies.

"Most kids, including those with neurological problems, can be taught strategies to cope—memory strategies, social strategies, strategies to deal with anger and not be impulsive," says Dr. Anderson.

As greater attention is focused on social-outcast children, techniques to address their problems are becoming increasingly innovative. Some psychologists, for example, are using hand puppets to teach proper playground etiquette to excluded preschoolers. Sensory-specific toys are proving effective for dyssemic children. And Harvard's Dr. Robert Selman has had success in Boston schools with a program called peer therapy, in which lonely aggressive children are paired with lonely withdrawn children.

In this program the two children meet in a supervised setting for one hour a week during which they are encouraged to negotiate conflicts and share experiences. Peer therapy works to eliminate a developmental Catch-22: Children are often excluded because they lack social skills, but because they are excluded, they never get the chance to gain the social skills they lack. The peer program requires that the two children agree to meet for at least a year. This way they are ensured, often for the first time ever, a consistent social relationship with a member of their own peer group.

Contrary to what you might expect—that the aggressive child would make the withdrawn child even more reticent, and vice versa—Selman reports that the interaction between the two personality types actually encourages more functional behavior in each.

Whatever the reason for a child's exclusion by peers, and whatever intervention is decided upon, parents can play a vital role in helping their child feel less lonely. You may not be able to protect your child from the outside world, but you can create a safe sanctuary of love and acceptance in your home.

Perhaps the best advice comes from one who's lived through the pain of childhood loneliness. As Paul, introduced earlier, puts it, "If my son had the same social problems I had as a child, I would make sure there was nothing lacking in our relationship. I would find ways every day to show him how much my wife and I love him and enjoy his company, his talents and abilities. I would make sure he knew that he can bring pleasure to other people." ◇

People dressed in uniforms can develop a strong sense of shared purpose among themselves, sometimes to the point that the goal of the group precludes the aspirations of the individual.

WORN IN THE USA:
The Psychological Fabric of Uniforms

by Joseph DeVito

Although Americans pride themselves on their fierce individuality, clothing made for the masses surrounds us. Uniforms are worn in the cafeterias and restaurants in which wc cat, and at the sporting events we attend. They are worn by the police who protect us, the soldiers who defend us, and the nurses and doctors who heal us.

More than 23 million Americans wear some kind of uniform. Forget about looking like a million—the National Association of Uniform Manufacturers and Distributors projects an annual dollar value of more than $2 billion by the end of the decade.

We design uniforms for a variety of purposes. They can be constructed for utility, identification with a certain group or service, or sometimes simply for a neat, clean appearance. What is woven into uniforms that can create impressions of security, efficiency, or anxiety? What is the psychological impact on people who wear uniforms, and on others around them? Is there more to the clothing than first meets the eye?

School Ties vs. Looks That Kill

In the late 1960s, American culture was in rebellion against uniformity and uniforms themselves. The war in Vietnam had inspired strong feelings about the men and women of the armed forces and what their garb represented. On the home front, the steady dissolution of school dress codes represented a freeing of young people from a society that frowned on individuality and suppressed personal expression.

The gradual integration of "hippie" fashions and attitudes into mainstream America made the school uniform a holdover reserved for stuffy private and parochial schools. If you weren't "doing your own thing," even as a child, you were a square and truly out of step. A quarter of a century later, that same freedom of choice has created tensions and pressures that would shock the bearded and the beaded.

Throughout the United States, and primarily in urban centers, the attention to appearance has become distracting and even dangerous. The school day is a vicious fashion show, a vain parade in which social standing is determined by $100 sneakers and leather bomber jackets. Children from financially strapped families suffer humiliation and low self-esteem if they are unable to participate in the daily runway walk.

In addition, styles particular to street gangs, known as "colors," have become popular as a means of declaring membership. Children and teenagers are more than simply envious; incredibly, students are robbed, beaten, and sometimes even killed for their status clothing. Others find themselves under attack by gang members simply because of the shade of their clothes.

The high value youngsters place on stylish appearance has translated into looks that kill. Shocking, violent acts have been committed for petty rewards. A student in Detroit was shot for his $135 jacket; another was killed for $100 Nike sneakers. A six-year-old Los Angeles girl was even beaten to death with a rock because her sweater was red, a local gang color.

In Baltimore, educators and parents witnessed this terrifying trend playing out in their own public schools. When a student from suburban Baltimore was shot in a fight over a $90 pair of shoes, they decided to take action. The Cherry Hill Elementary School was the first to begin a dress-code policy. Five years later, Principal Geraldine Smallwood claims the program has definitely improved the learning environment.

"The initial requests came from parents who were concerned about discipline," says Smallwood. "The children were constantly fighting over who had the most expensive clothes and the designer labels. Since we instituted the program, we have had none of these incidents."

The uniforms for the 387 students are simple: navy or light-blue slacks and ties for the boys, blue skirts and jumpers for the girls. Because Cherry Hill is a public school, administrators cannot make the dress code mandatory. But the parents who requested the

Uniforms can add a distinctly festive touch to just about any celebration. The ornate uniforms and flamboyant plumes worn by members of a marching band help produce the air of excitement felt by people watching a parade.

change have remained involved, voting on the policy as well as the uniform style.

"Although our dress code is by choice," Smallwood adds, "we have a participation rate nearing 98 percent." And uniforms are also much cheaper, relieving the financial burden of buying a new wardrobe each year.

As with school uniforms, the wearing of a scouting outfit (top) seems to have a positive influence on a child's behavior. Gang regalia (above) generates a markedly less-positive effect.

The students at Cherry Hill still have one day a week as a "dress-up" day when they can wear what they choose. Smallwood maintains that the impact of the uniform program goes far beyond just the clothes themselves. "It creates a positive image that the more self-conscious children lack," she says. "Instead of fighting over sneakers, we often find the boys looking out for each other when one misplaces his clip-on tie. Preparing their clothing this way has made them more responsible, and has given them a greater sense of respect." The program at Cherry Hill is considered such a success that most Baltimore public elementary schools have followed suit.

Public schools from Detroit to New York City have also tried uniforms on for size. Pro-ponents say the benefits are obvious. Uniforms are democratic because everyone looks the same, removing the class stigma of not having the right sneakers or jeans. They can end violence by eliminating crimes motivated by expensive shoes and jackets. Fashion-conscious children become less distracted, allowing them to focus on their schoolwork.

Uniforms can foster a sense of common respect and give a feeling of belonging, something studies show is especially important for minority children. The emphasis on appearance builds habits that can make a difference when entering the job market.

Irwin Hyman, Ph.D., of the National Center for the Study of Corporal Punishment in Philadelphia, disagrees. "It's an authoritarian concept," says Dr. Hyman. "Just because people look good doesn't necessarily mean that good behavior will follow." An expert on children's disciplinary issues, Dr. Hyman believes that "no real research on the topic exists," and the results of the programs can be traced to other factors.

His theory does find support. Although school officials across the country believe that requiring uniforms does enforce discipline, a recent Gallup survey showed that 85 percent of public school parents do not see discipline as a general problem. The initial burst of improvement may be due to the so-called Hawthorne effect, which claims that the extra attention paid to experimental schools will give the children and staff a much-needed sense of pride and self-awareness, and they will all try harder to succeed.

"We emphasize individuality to such an extent that mandating appearance runs counter to our culture," says Dr. Hyman. "I'm against the attempts to regiment children's lives. Parents in a public school situation have a constitutional right to dress their children as they see fit."

A dress-code program under consideration in Connecticut was shot down on similar grounds. A decision requiring uniforms at the Helene Grant Elementary School in New Haven was reversed under pressure from the Connecticut Civil Liberties Union.

Although wearing uniforms will not make a difference at all schools, the ones that need the extra attention will most likely benefit. Dr. Hyman acknowledges the potential good. "If the sense of pride in the school, its administrators, and the students themselves is already strong," he admits, "uniforms may play a positive role."

Smallwood concurs. "It's true that the children enjoyed the initial media attention when we were the first. There was a certain amount of momentum to be sure, but the continued success of the program speaks for itself."

The Scoop on Workplace Uniforms

Regardless of the type of business, a uniform creates an image of efficiency and tidiness. Customers can feel secure with a company where the service persons are validated by their clothing. A recognizable and familiar image provides continuity and reduces consumer anxiety, especially when familiar company colors or logo are featured. While we expect some type of uniform at the local grocery store or diner, the same transfer of credibility occurs when real estate agents and other professionals display their company's image on a blazer.

Uniforms play an important role in establishing the roles of both employees and customers. The effects of corporate dress codes are also felt on the other side of the counter. Because people often believe the well dressed are more intelligent, hardworking, and socially responsible, a sharp uniform can instill confidence in its wearer. It can be a tangible reward for achievement that the customers can appreciate, or a sign of belonging and acceptance within the organization itself.

In situations where customer relations require extensive interaction, it is not uncommon for salespeople to identify with the needs of the client instead of the company. A uniform reestablishes the claim of the collective interest and helps restore the sales focus.

Some workers, especially young persons, are unimpressed by their uniforms. Craig Colorusso, a college student who scoops ice cream at a Connecticut mall, agrees. "I was always getting yelled at for wearing my

Uniforms can serve a strictly utilitarian purpose. Restaurants often seek to produce an image of cleanliness through the clothing they require of their workers (above). Besides helping to create a sense of camaraderie, the uniforms worn by fire fighters (left) help enhance safety and comfort by being flame-retardant and waterproof.

hat backward because that just wasn't allowed," Colorusso said. "One customer even commented how comfortable and relaxed it looked. I told him it was a shame because it was against the rules."

Although it is required by health laws, Colorusso finds more insidious reasons for his job's dress code. "They make you wear a hat to depower the individual so people are getting ice cream from a machine and not a person," he adds. "My individuality reflects who I am, how I feel about people, and how well I can do my job."

The Issues of Government Issue

Nowhere are the conflicting aspects of the uniform more apparent than in the armed forces. Like religious orders and other closed organizations, the military strips away elements of personality upon induction. By enforcing common haircuts, clothing, or posture, these closed societies eliminate the differences and thereby remove individuality. New recruits must then depend upon the group to provide them with a new identity as a replacement.

Military uniforms produce a strong sense of conformity among soldiers. In the Persian Gulf War, the uniforms provided camouflage and otherwise met the needs of desert warfare.

Pryce Brodeur, a former Marine, found both good and bad in his experiences. "My first impression was that I was a part of something because I was surrounded by so many others who looked the same," he says. "A uniform makes you feel 'uniform,' as if you all were cut from a common cloth."

Brodeur is quick to make the distinction between the two types of uniform issued: the functional B.D.U. (Basic Daily Uniform) for work or combat, and the ornate dress uniform for ceremonial and formal occasions. "In your B.D.U., you're part of the machine instead of a person. My own B.D.U. was bulky and uncomfortable and never really fit like it was mine. But in full dress, I felt pride and dignity in being a part of a greater whole."

Do we really love a man in uniform? Brodeur agrees that the attraction is there. "People outside the military had immediate respect for the uniform and the person," he adds. "The commitment that went with it and what it represented was usually perceived positively."

Good News for the Boys in Blue

Television and film abound with slick detectives in designer suits and grubby undercover agents in dirty raincoats. Most people, however, prefer the men in blue to stay that way. Stanford University psychologist Robert Mauro conducted interviews in shopping centers to rate the assessment of police dress. The participants were shown photos depicting policemen in traditional khaki and blue uniforms, as well as in gray and blue suits.

Although there were no noticeable differences in the pictures, the respondents considered officers in traditional police uniforms to be more competent, helpful, and honest than those in civilian clothes. They considered all three to be friendly and kind, but something in the standard issue gave an aura of security and confidence.

Good Guys Don't Wear Black

Lyle Alzado. Howie Long. Jack "the Assassin" Tatum. The roster of Los Angeles Raiders greats reads like a rogues' gallery of professional football. Few fans can forget the sight of Tatum bellowing over New England

Patriot Darryl Stingley, who lay paralyzed by a punishing hit. From the evil eye-patched glare of their pirate logo to years of supremacy in the NFL playoffs, the Raiders have always been a breed apart. They rage like animals. They hit hard. They show no remorse.

And in recent years, they haven't won too many games. Although their dominance on the field has waned, the silver-and-black attack has produced merchandise that outsells nearly all other NFL teams combined. Raiders football means tough, hard-hitting football where attitude is an important part of the game. Raiders caps and jackets have been adopted by rap artists as representative of the music's outlaw status, helping to spur sales. Because of the influence of musical groups like N.W.A. and Public Enemy, the rebel Raiders have become black America's team.

According to a study by the American Psychological Association, a large part of the "bad boy" rep may be due in part to the uniforms. Ominously titled *The Dark Side of Self and Social Perception: Black Uniforms and Aggression in Professional Sports,* the study reviewed the role colors play in how athletes behave. The conclusion? In sports where intimidation and aggression are important, black uniforms substantially affect the way the game is played.

Case in point: in noncontact sports, where aggression is secondary, there is a noticeable absence of black-clad players. In the National Basketball Association, only two teams, the Portland Trail Blazers and San Antonio Spurs, wear predominantly black; in major-league baseball, only the Pittsburgh Pirates and San Francisco Giants.

In other sports power can be measured in fear. Nearly 20 percent of NFL teams—the Raiders, Pittsburgh Steelers, Cincinnati Bengals, New Orleans Saints, Chicago Bears, and, most recently, the Atlanta Falcons—wear black. In the National Hockey League, the percentage grows to roughly one-third of the teams.

For teams that adopt black uniforms, the difference can be measured more in attitude than performance. When the NHL's Vancouver Canucks changed their uniforms, they

The black uniforms worn by the Los Angeles Raiders may in part account for the team's "bad boy" image. To their opponents, black-clad players project intimidation and aggression.

did not win more games, but they did increase their penalty minutes. The study also reported a similar change for the Pittsburgh Penguins. Their black uniforms accompanied a move from number 14 (out of 17) to first in penalties. In the NHL, most penalties are for aggressive acts.

Darrin Lucas, captain of a New England collegiate club hockey team, recently organized an effort to replace the team's existing uniforms. The school colors, blue and white, were considered part of the team's lackluster play. So far, the change appears to have worked.

"We changed the colors to black and teal because it showed a more aggressive, stronger approach," says Lucas. "Our new coach is very big on physical hockey, and we felt black as a dominant color would represent our aggressive style. There definitely is a difference in our play."

While the new attitude and coaching of the rebuilding program must be given their due, there is a definite difference indeed. In 1991, the team won only one of 20 games. Halfway through the 1992 season, they remain undefeated.   ◇

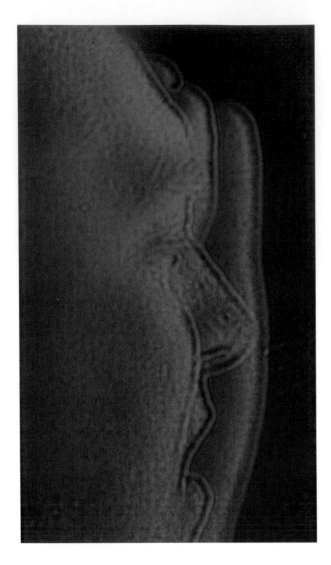

PANIC ATTACK:

When Anxiety Becomes Disabling

by Abigail W. Polek

Mary couldn't figure out what was happening. She had started to perspire profusely. Her heart beat wildly—so wildly, in fact, that Mary thought that death was imminent. Suddenly, like a tidal wave, a paralyzing sense of terror swept over her.

She could neither speak nor move—except for the involuntary trembling of her hands.

Mary was having a panic attack. The triggering event for the episode was so utterly insignificant that she never made the correlation. Although only in her twenties, Mary had her blood pressure taken once a month as a means of monitoring any possibility of developing hypertension, the disease that had killed her father. On the day of her attack, the nurse assigned to take her blood pressure was someone new. As soon as the nurse sat down, Mary's symptoms began.

After her panic attack, Mary stopped having her monthly blood-pressure checks. She also stopped going to the mall and to the movies. In fact, Mary stopped doing many things she enjoyed, simply out of fear of having another attack. And despite all these precautions, Mary kept having panic episodes, invariably while doing something entirely benign—like standing in line at a grocery store or sitting in a restaurant. It was not until Mary had become a virtual recluse that her friends and family convinced her to seek medical attention.

Anxiety versus Panic

In most people, anxiety, a feeling of apprehension that builds in response to threats, both physical and imaginary, is a typical reaction to day-to-day stress or actual danger. Anxiety makes people breathe faster than normal while their hearts race and their palms perspire, symptoms similar to a panic attack. In addition, they feel nervous and irritable. These anxiety reactions are considered perfectly normal as the body prepares for "fight or flight."

When anxiety turns to panic, victims become more fearful than nervous. They are paralyzed with terror and feel helpless to escape whatever is triggering it. They grow short of breath, experience dizziness, feel chest pain, or manifest at least four of the classic symptoms attributed to a panic attack: heavy perspiration; uncontrollable trembling; numbness or tingling, especially in the hands; or disorientation and a loss of reality. These symptoms usually last for only 2 to 15 minutes, but the terror they inspire may persist for an hour or more. Often the situation that triggers victims to panic is not one that most people would consider stressful; the example frequently given is that of simply standing in line at a department store. Or, if the situation *is* stressful, such as the thought of impending surgery, public speaking, or, as in Mary's case, meeting someone new, panic-attack sufferers react to it more severely than is normal.

Defining the Panic Disorder

Despite the utter despair that just one of these bouts with terror may inspire, one panic attack does not mean that a person has panic disorder. Many people who experience panic attacks never develop the full panic disorder as it is currently defined by the American Psychiatric Association. According to the association's *Diagnostic and Statistical Manual of Mental Disorders,* a person has panic disorder if he or she experiences at least four attacks within four weeks, or one or more attacks followed by a month of persistent fear of having another attack. Some of these attacks must occur suddenly, without provocation.

When panic strikes, victims become fearful and, ultimately, paralyzed with terror.

Panic attacks are one of several types of anxiety disorders recognized by the National Institute of Mental Health (NIMH) in Bethesda, Maryland. Others include general anxiety disorder, in which patients worry excessively about life; post-traumatic stress syndrome, which occurs in reaction to a previous traumatic event, such as battle experiences; and agoraphobia, a fear of open places that often develops concurrently in people, particularly women, suffering from panic disorder. Panic disorder is differentiated from these other types by the unexpected nature of the episodes and the lack of symptoms between attacks.

Experts estimate that over 3 million Americans will suffer from panic attacks at some point in their lives. But fewer than 2 percent of the cases will actually be diagnosed. In fact, over 95 percent of the people who suffer from panic attacks consult with 10 or more physicians before they are accurately diag-

nosed. This is not surprising, since the symptoms associated with panic disorder can also be caused by medical conditions as varied as Cushing's syndrome, a disorder caused by a high level of corticosteroid hormones; hypoglycemia; menopause; asthma; heart attacks; epilepsy; and ulcers—all of which excite the central nervous system in some way. A 1988 study by Wayne Katon, M.D., professor of psychiatry at the University of Washington Medical School in Seattle, found that nearly 43 percent of a group of patients tested for heart problems didn't have heart disease but rather suffered from undiagnosed panic disorder.

Proper diagnosis is also complicated by the fact that many panic patients believe that they are physically sick; therefore, they report only the physical symptoms of attacks to their doctors, rather than the situations that triggered them. In addition, panic attacks have been recognized as a disorder only since 1980, so many physicians have never been taught how to diagnose these episodes. Another complicating factor is the prevalence of other psychiatric disorders in people who suffer from panic attacks. According to the NIMH, over 70 percent of panic patients also suffer from other mental illnesses.

PET scans of the brains of panic-disorder patients indicate abnormalities in the section of the right hemisphere associated with emotion.

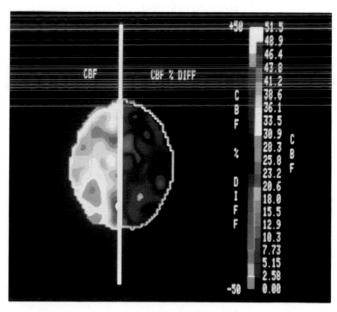

Cause for Panic

Typically, panic attacks occur most often in men or women in their early twenties. But recent studies indicate that the roots of this disorder may actually be present as early as childhood. A 1992 study of 754 sixth- and seventh-grade girls, published in the *American Journal of Psychiatry,* found that 5 percent of the girls had experienced at least one panic attack. A 1988 study performed by researchers at Harvard University found that extremely shy two-year-old children demonstrated some of the same physical signs of stress displayed during a panic attack.

Panic attacks tend to occur more often in women. But whether gender actually plays a role in determining who will experience panic attacks is unclear. Men may be diagnosed less often because they are reluctant to admit to emotional problems. Many men who suffer from panic attacks mask the symptoms with alcohol, and are more apt to be diagnosed with alcoholism than with panic disorder. Women may be influenced early in their lives to ignore their own feelings over those of others, which may lead to feelings of insecurity. These feelings may then predispose them to panic attacks later in their lives.

Panic attacks may also stem from purely physiological origins. Michael R. Liebowitz, M.D., of the Anxiety Disorders Clinic at the New York State Psychiatric Institute, says that a minute portion of the brain identified as the source of the "fight-or-flight" response may produce neurochemicals at inappropriate times, causing the body to panic for no reason. In studies that use electron-imaging techniques, the brains of people who experience panic attacks have been shown to have abnormalities in at least one of the areas that control emotion.

Other studies suggest a link between hyperventilation and panic attacks. Although excessive and rapid breathing has long been considered a symptom rather than a cause of panic disorder, some researchers now believe that stress can cause people predisposed to panic attacks to hyperventilate.

A combination of drugs and behavioral therapy may be the best way to treat panic disorder.

This hyperventilation deprives the brain of nourishing oxygen, which results in poor concentration and a sense of detachment or unreality and suffocation. From that point the experience blooms into a full-fledged panic attack. In a number of laboratory experiments, many patients intentionally encouraged to hyperventilate ended up having panic attacks. In a survey conducted by Ronald Ley, Ph.D., professor of psychology and a hyperventilation researcher at the State University of New York (SUNY) at Albany, 80 percent of the panic victims he questioned said that the irrational fear associated with a panic attack did not develop until after they had begun to breathe rapidly. According to psychologist David H. Barlow, Ph.D., director of the Center for Stress and Anxiety Disorders at SUNY Albany, "Half of all panic-disorder victims have episodes of rapid, shallow breathing, which creates an excess of oxygen in the blood and can cause dizziness, tingling, and other symptoms of a panic attack."

A genetic link has not been ruled out, either. Relatives of people with panic disorder are more likely to develop the problem than are members of panic-free families. In a study led by psychiatrist Jerrold Rosenbaum, M.D., chief of the Clinical Psychopharmacology Unit at Massachusetts General Hospital in Boston, the children of patients with panic disorder were also found to be more inhibited than other children in new situations. Furthermore, some of these children were more afraid of typical stressful events, such as a visit to the family doctor or a ride on an elevator.

Soothing the Panic

Unfortunately, only one in four sufferers receives appropriate treatment for the disorder. This treatment can take two forms: drug therapy and cognitive-behavioral therapy. Antidepressants and tranquilizers make up the front line of drugs used to treat panic attacks. Currently, only the benzodiazepine tranquilizer alprazolam (Xanax) is approved specifically by the Food and Drug Adminis-

People who suffer from debilitating panic attacks are advised to seek professional help. Many psychologists feel that panic attacks occur when the victim misinterprets normal physical signs of anxiety.

tration (FDA) for the treatment of panic disorder. This drug, while effective, can cause serious physical dependency since it must often be used in high doses for long periods of time to be effective. Many physicians prefer to use two other types of antidepressants: tricyclics such as imipramine (Tofranil), which does not cause physical dependence, and monoamine oxidase inhibitors (MAOIs) such as phenelzine (Nardil). These two types of drugs work by increasing the levels of norepinephrine and serotonin in the brain, to lessen the sensation of panic.

Cognitive-behavioral therapy seeks to treat patients by teaching them to recognize and change their destructive thoughts. Aaron T. Beck, M.D., a psychiatrist at the University of Pennsylvania, Philadelphia, pioneered this treatment, which today takes several forms. For example, in panic-control treatment (PCT), patients recreate the feelings of a panic attack and then learn how to deal with those feelings. According to Barlow, "Rather than futilely trying to avoid these situations, [patients] can learn to raise the threshold of what is tolerable and keep the attacks at bay." In relaxation-response therapy, developed by Herbert Benson, M.D., associate professor of medicine at Harvard Medical School, patients learn how to meditate to lower their blood pressure and slow their breathing—so they can reverse the effects of panic on the body. Jerilyn Ross, a clinical social worker and director of the Ross Center for Anxiety and Related Disorders, Washington, D.C., favors exposure or desensitization therapy, which slowly reintroduces sufferers to the situations that cause their attacks. Patients confront their feelings of fear and learn that these feelings are not dangerous.

Psychiatrists seem to favor drug therapy —many believe panic attacks are related to a chemical imbalance in the brain—while psychologists insist on cognitive-behavioral therapy, believing that panic attacks are caused when sufferers misinterpret the normal physical signs of anxiety. Many experts have found that a combination of both approaches is usually the most effective treatment, since the drugs relieve the physical symptoms, and the therapy helps patients change behaviors that may trigger the attacks. In addition, since the drugs are usually administered for 6 to 12 months and then stopped, it is crucial that a patient learn how to cope with, and even prevent, attacks once he or she is no longer on medication. According to Thomas W. Uhde, M.D., chief of the Section on Anxiety and Affective Disorders at NIMH, "Approximately 60 percent of patients will require drug treatment again within two years after . . . medication [is] stopped." Conversely, in a study at SUNY involving PCT, 80 percent of the patients who took part were still symptom-free after two years. Psychiatrist Layton McCurdy, M.D., from the Medical University of South Carolina, Charleston, notes that "a return of symptoms apparently occurs much less often after cognitive-behavioral therapy, compared with drug treatment."　◇

The damage from Hurricane Andrew (above) and other natural disasters happens quickly. Unfortunately, the psychological repercussions can extend for months or even years.

The Psychology of Disaster:
Repairing the Invisible Damage

by Christopher King

In the early morning hours of August 24, 1992, Hurricane Andrew, the first Force 5 hurricane to strike the United States since 1969, raked across the southern tip of Florida. Thousands of people, warned of the storm's approach, chose to flee north out of the hurricane's path. Many of those who elected to stay suffered through a night of interminable terror, huddling in bathrooms, closets, and automobiles as the winds tore apart their homes. The next day, people emerged from hiding to survey the devastation wrought by what was quickly acknowledged as the most costly natural disaster in U.S. history. Thousands of homes and businesses were destroyed. Damage was calculated in billions of dollars, and more than 50 lives were lost.

Local and state emergency-management agencies—the American Red Cross, the Federal Emergency Management Association (FEMA), and elements of the National Guard and U.S. Army—all went into action to provide food and shelter for the thousands left homeless. Almost immediately the effort was underway to repair the damage.

And not just the physical damage. Some of the professionals responding to Andrew's devastation were concerned primarily with addressing the storm's *psychological* effects upon its victims.

The presence of mental-health professionals at disaster sites is a relatively recent phenomenon. It is clear, however, that attending to the psychological consequences of disaster is a growing priority in emergency-response efforts. Researchers are learning more about how people respond psychologically to disaster, about the long-term effects of disaster trauma, and about the benefits of immediate professional care at the scene.

"Relatively brief intervention by mental-health professionals can make a tremendous difference in people's ability to cope with the disaster they've experienced," says Gerard Jacobs, a professor of psychology at the University of South Dakota, Vermillion, and an expert in disaster psychology. "I expect to see disaster mental health become a new specialty area—a new division of psychology —perhaps within a year or two."

No Shortage of Disasters

"In general," write psychiatrists Robert J. Ursano, M.D., and Carol S. Fullerton, M.D., discussing the nature of disasters, "such events are dangerous, overwhelming, and sudden, and are marked by extreme or sudden force from an external agent, typically causing fear, anxiety, withdrawal, and avoidance." Disasters, obviously, can fall into several classifications. In his book *Disasters and Disaster Stress*, Anthony J. W. Taylor offers three main categories: natural disasters, such as hurricanes, earthquakes, and floods; industrial disasters, including explosions, fires, and radioactive pollution; and human disasters, such as road, rail, and air accidents.

Disasters have affected a large proportion of the United States. Between 1965 and 1985, for example, 31 states suffered five or more catastrophes that were serious enough to be officially declared disasters by the president. During that time, relief money sent by FEMA to these sites totaled some $6 billion. It is a grim but unavoidable certainty that disasters will continue to occur. In the year 2000, according to some estimates, major disasters in the United States will account for property damages totaling more than $17 billion, and over 1,700 deaths. Disaster preparedness, of course, is crucial. And for mental-health professionals who respond to disaster, part of being prepared is knowing how disaster affects the human psyche.

The Experience of Disaster

Experts in psychology and psychiatry have developed various terms to describe the stages that victims typically go through. The first stage, during or shortly after the disaster, is often termed the *impact* phase. Fear, as might be expected, is the dominant reaction during this phase, along with an intense desire on the part of victims to preserve themselves and their loved ones. Some victims may feel helpless, stunned, or disoriented. The popular image of victims succumbing to blind panic, however, is more myth than reality. Indeed, many researchers refer to the initial stages of disaster as the *heroic* phase. "Everybody pulls together," says Jane Morgan, associate for Disaster

Survivors are not the only ones to suffer post-disaster trauma. Some rescue workers are still psychologically stressed years after the 1989 San Francisco earthquake.

Mental Health Services at the American Red Cross. "A person's house might have been flooded and all their stuff ruined, but they're next door helping their neighbor sandbag to try and save their belongings. People forget that they don't like the person down the street and just help out."

Soon after a disaster, victims revel in simply being alive and in the survival of their loved ones (below right). This euphoria diminishes once the impact of the disaster begins to sink in.

This spirit of altruism and cooperation continues into the next phase, often referred to as the *honeymoon* period. At this stage, people are happy to have survived the disaster, and are grateful for all the outside assistance they are receiving. As time passes, however, the honeymoon gives way to a period of *disillusionment*. "In this stage," says Gerard Jacobs, "people begin to realize the extent of their losses, and the impact of what they have been through starts to hit them. At this point, they begin to become discouraged." Dealing with relief agencies and insurance companies can cause frustration and anger. Family relationships may be strained by relocation to temporary shelters. Gradually, however, people work into the final stage of *recovery* or *reconstruction*.

Helping victims to reach this recovery stage is the aim of mental-health professionals. Jacobs puts the challenge this way: "Our goal is really to serve ordinary people in extraordinary circumstances."

The services provided can take many forms. One priority is to simply furnish information about the range of emotional reactions that victims might expect to go through. "You just let them know that it's normal to be angry, normal to start crying for no apparent reason, or even to start laughing," says Jane Morgan. "A lot of times, people feel that if they need to talk to a mental-health person, they must be crazy. And you have to let them know that they're not. They're just normal people reacting to an abnormal situation."

For people dealing with the enormity of a lost home or lost job, or perhaps even a death in the family, the circumstances can be overwhelming. "Sometimes the mental-health worker needs to sit down with them and break it up into manageable pieces—to say, 'What's the priority today?' " says Morgan. "It's important to help people take small steps so that they can begin doing things themselves." Arranging for shelter might be one such task. If necessary, other tasks might include assisting with funeral arrangements for the deceased, or helping to inform children of the death of loved ones.

Sometimes the intervention may involve simply letting people voice their fears and frustrations—a process referred to as "ventilating." In the aftermath of Hurricane Andrew, for example, many residents were forced to wait in long lines for interviews with

relief workers. Mental-health professionals worked the lines, listening patiently while people let off steam. Another tactic, often employed when disaster has befallen a single group, a neighborhood, or a community, is group therapy. In loosely structured community meetings that may last several hours, everyone involved in the disaster has the opportunity to tell his or her story, to listen, and to offer support.

Families Under Stress

Another challenge for mental-health professionals is relieving the great strains that disaster places on families. Often disaster destroys more than a home. The sense of familiarity, security, continuity, and the balance of relationships can suffer enormously when families are forced to relocate to shelters. Researchers studying the aftermath of a catastrophic flood caused by a dam break in Buffalo Creek, West Virginia, in 1972 noted this problem. The mass relocation of survivors, and the resulting social disorganization and family stress, were seen to constitute a "second disaster."

In Florida in the wake of Hurricane Andrew, the effects of lost homes and relocation began to tell in another way: reports of increases in family violence and child abuse. As *Psychology Today* reported, parents found themselves forced to spend an inordinate amount of time with their children in unfamiliar living conditions, often in close quarters, surrounded by strangers. In some cases, parents took out their anger and frustration on their kids. By helping parents anticipate such negative reactions, and by helping them find ways to regain a sense of control over their lives, counselors worked to head off the problem.

"Mental-health workers in the shelters were trying to provide opportunities for the parents to ventilate, and were also helping with activities for the kids," recalls Jane Morgan. "There were a lot of puppet shows, toys, and a lot of pictures drawn to allow the children the chance to express their feelings." One imaginative psychologist employed a mean-faced puppet named "Andrew." Children relished the opportunity to punch, kick, and generally release their frustrations on this effigy of the hurricane.

The tendency to consider natural disasters in terms of human attributes—to "anthropomorphize" them—is not uncommon. Mental-health workers in Jamaica noted that after Hurricane Gilbert caused heavy damage and killed 45 people on the island in 1988, local songs, newspapers, and conversations began to refer to "Gilbert" as the "bad man." This device seemed to provide a humorous outlet by which people could release anxiety. In Florida, children who were encouraged to draw pictures of Hurricane Andrew usually produced illustrations that resembled, as one

Makeshift kitchens and other forms of relief, while providing for the basic needs of survivors, do little to remedy the sense of dislocation suffered by those rendered homeless by a disaster.

counselor told *Psychology Today*, "a cross between the *Wizard of Oz* tornado and an image of Dennis the Menace."

Children are particularly susceptible to stress following a disaster. As Australian psychiatrist Beverly Rafael, M.D. writes in *When Disaster Strikes*, any physical reminder of a child's experiences may trigger fear. After a hurricane, the child might fear rain, lightning, or the sound of strong winds—even the rattle of a windowpane might trigger a reaction. Children can also exhibit heightened *separation anxiety*, becoming fearful when away from their parents even for short periods. Disturbed patterns of sleep, even nightmares, are also common. A child may have trouble concentrating, and may consequently exhibit learning problems in school. The feeling of disorganization, of being unable to focus, seems common to adults as well as children after a disaster.

"People tend to have recurring thoughts or nightmares about the event," says Richard Tanenbaum, a psychologist in Chevy Chase, Maryland. "There's a general sense of feeling tense and being hypervigilant—you're very alert. At the same time, there's a kind of depressive overlay. People may have difficulty making decisions, may feel short-tempered and irritable. There might be a sense of withdrawal, of what we call 'emotional numbing.' Feeling despair or hopelessness."

Victims may also feel guilt. "Why did this person die and not me?" might be a common reaction. Or, "If I hadn't moved my family down here, none of this would have happened." In such cases, notes Tanenbaum, the aim is to help people combat such negative, distorted thoughts and reorient them toward reality. Again, simply arming people with a knowledge of what they may go through seems to go a long way.

"It's important to let people know that it is going to take some time to heal," says Tanenbaum, "and that they need to give themselves time to do that. And also to let them know that if they continue to feel poorly and seem unable to get things going for themselves, they should seek professional help at some point."

The countless hours spent standing in lines, filling out forms, and dealing with insurance adjustors exacerbates the anger and frustration felt by many disaster survivors.

Post-traumatic Stress Disorder

More severe and protracted reactions to a stressful event generally fall into the category of Post-traumatic Stress Disorder (PTSD). The clinical recognition of this syndrome is a fairly recent development, having emerged largely from studies on veterans of the Vietnam War. Symptoms include recurrent and intrusive recollections of the trau-

matic event, feelings of depression or reduced involvement with the external world, and avoidance of activities that arouse recollections of the event.

Development of PTSD seems to be related to an individual's experiences during the stressful event. For example, a study of more than 5,000 schoolchildren in South Carolina, where Hurricane Hugo hit in 1989, examined levels of stress and anxiety three months after the storm. The children exhibiting the strongest indications of PTSD were the ones who had experienced the most severe exposure to the hurricane.

It also appears that people with preexisting psychological conditions, such as depression or drug and alcohol abuse, are at higher risk for long-term emotional disturbance after a disaster. One study examined college students who had been affected by the Loma Prieta earthquake, which struck the San Francisco Bay area in the fall of 1989. By chance the students had undergone tests to evaluate their emotional health just 14 days before the quake. This gave researchers a measure against which to compare the students' reactions in the subsequent days and weeks. Results showed that students who had indicated high levels of depression and stress symptoms before the quake showed even higher levels of these symptoms afterward.

Treating PTSD can be a long and difficult process. Victims are often withdrawn, angry, and unwilling or unable to talk about their traumatic experiences. By being encouraged to share their feelings in a supportive environment, whether with a single therapist or in a group setting, victims of PTSD are assisted in gradually confronting their fears and seeing them in a more realistic light. If necessary, therapy might be supplemented with drugs to control anxiety and depression.

Tanenbaum recalls treating a man who had been seriously injured in a rail accident in which several passengers had been killed. Unable to face riding the train, the man left his job. He continually experienced flashbacks and dreams of the accident. Soon his anxieties became so generalized that he feared any precarious situation, such as

Disaster psychology came into its own following the deadly fire at Boston's Cocoanut Grove in 1942. Hundreds of people died, many of them crushed or suffocated to death in the stampede to escape the fire.

standing on a chair to change a light bulb. In therapy, Tanenbaum helped the man talk about his experiences and fears. He also used a technique known as "systematic desensitization." The man was asked to construct a list of anxiety-provoking events related to the train. He was then taught a series of techniques to relax himself as he imagined experiencing each event on his list. Gradually a more relaxed response replaced the anxious responses that had been conditioned by the accident. Subsequently the man was able to return to riding the train and gradually re-involve himself in his life.

Fortunately, most victims do not exhibit long-term symptoms of PTSD. In the wake of Hurricane Andrew, mental-health professionals in Florida estimated that while as many as 80 percent of victims could experience some PTSD symptoms for a year or so, only 5 to 10 percent might be expected to develop longer-lasting disorders.

Victims are not the only ones who suffer the stresses of a disaster. Relief workers also share the hardships and hazards, often being forced to make do without electricity, telephones, or sanitation facilities. With so many people in need of assistance, the hours can be very long. In disasters involving large numbers of fatalities, the stresses on relief workers can be particularly great. For example, after the crash of a DC-10 jumbo jet on Mount Erebus, Antarctica, in 1979, workers were called in for the grim task of re-covering the bodies of the more than 250 passengers and crew. Even though many members of the recovery team were trained and experienced in handling human remains, more than a quarter of them showed significant symptoms of stress 20 months later.

In view of such potential sources of stress, disaster psychologists emphasize the need for relief workers—including mental-health professionals—to make sure that they take care of their own needs and, if necessary, avail themselves of the help of psychologists and counselors at the scene.

Much More to Learn

Disaster psychology is a relatively young discipline. Most experts point to 1942 as the beginning of the field—the year of the infamous Cocoanut Grove nightclub fire in Boston that killed nearly 500 people. This was one of the first disasters to be studied in terms of its psychological consequences. Other intensely studied disasters include the floods in Buffalo Creek, West Virginia, and Wilkes-Barre, Pennsylvania, in 1972; the Beverly Hills Supper Club fire in Kentucky in 1977; and the Three Mile Island nuclear accident in Pennsylvania in 1979. Researchers are learning more about how disaster affects people in the short and long term. But there is much more to know. "We're just beginning," says Gerard Jacobs. "The research is still relatively scattered. The biggest challenges we face right now are to find ways of performing research on disaster mental health, to find the most effective ways to intervene and support the victims, and to conduct that research while still protecting the rights and the quality of life of the victims."

By all accounts, 1989 was a critical year in disaster mental health. Three highly publicized disasters happened to occur that year: the crash of United Flight 232 in Sioux City, Iowa, in July; Hurricane Hugo in South Carolina in September, and the Loma Prieta earthquake in the San Francisco–Oakland area in October. These events focused attention on the value of mental-health intervention as a vital component in disaster relief. They also underscored the need for a more organized mental-health response.

Since then, much progress has been made. The Red Cross now has a formal training course and guidelines to prepare psychiatrists, psychologists, and counselors—all of

Psychologists have begun to focus increasingly on the impact of disasters on children. Entertainment and other activities help amuse and distract even the youngest disaster survivors.

whom are volunteers—to go into disaster areas and work with other relief agencies. Similarly, in August of 1992, the American Psychological Association launched its national Disaster Response Network. Under this new system, more than 1,000 psychologists have made themselves available for volunteer services in response to disaster.

"We mental-health workers are definitely the new kids on the block as far as disaster relief goes," says Deborah De Wolfe, a Seattle psychologist who helped to design and organize the Red Cross's mental-health component. "We're learning a lot about ways in which we can work more effectively in terms of organization and supervision. We still need to learn more about the other players in the disaster-response effort so that we can cooperate and liaison more effectively with them."

Thus far the response from volunteer professionals has been overwhelmingly positive. "Recently I had a debriefing session at my house with some mental-health professionals in my area who had gone off to work Hurricane Andrew in Florida and Louisiana and Hurricane Iniki in Hawaii," says De-Wolfe. "They all expressed the feeling that, despite the hardships, the work was very important and very rewarding."

The rewards, however, may come at a price. Jane Morgan of the Red Cross—who has assisted in earthquakes, hurricanes, and even war zones—remembers in particular a flash flood on the Guadalupe River near the town of Comfort, Texas, in 1987. Attempting to flee their stalled vehicles in the rising waters, a group of young campers had been swept into the churning river. Some were rescued by helicopter, but 10 drowned. Morgan came in and set up a shelter at a local school, living closely with the families and friends of the campers as they went out each day to search for the bodies of the missing. "That's still the event that I have the most difficulty with," she says. "Anytime things happen with kids, it affects you much more. The feeling of the kids, the support they provided for each other—that was something you don't see very often."

Why, then, do Morgan and her colleagues venture unhesitatingly into disaster areas where they are certain to confront scenes of devastation and even death? "Some people think we're kind of weird," she says with a laugh, "and I guess maybe we are. For one thing, you get to meet a lot of people and get close very quickly. You form relationships that last forever. It's the caring that you see. We care for people, and they care back." ◇

THE BURDEN OF OBESITY

by Gina Kolata

One day, schoolmates started throwing food at Aleta Walker as she sat at a table at lunch. Plates of spaghetti splashed onto her face, and the long, greasy strands dripped onto her clothes. "Everyone was laughing and pointing. They were making pig noises. I just sat there," she says.

Walker is fat. And, like most fat people, she has been dogged by ridicule and abuse throughout her life. She has felt discrimination on the job. She is constantly subjected to rude remarks and ugly noises, like pig grunts or moos, when she goes out, and she has had a hard time making friends.

Despite the consistent findings that most people actually have little control over their body weight, researchers find, and fat people confirm, that society continues to deride fat people for their condition.

Fat people are less likely to be admitted to elite colleges, are less likely to be hired for a job, make less money when they are hired, and are less likely to be promoted. One study found that businessmen sacrifice $1,000 in salary for every pound they are overweight. Fat people tell researchers that total strangers admonish them to lose weight. Often their own children are ashamed of them. Studies have shown that even many doctors find fat people disgusting.

They'd Rather Be Blind

In a recent study of formerly fat people who had lost weight after intestinal bypass surgery, researchers reported that virtually all said they would rather be blind or deaf or have a leg amputated than be fat again.

"Overweight people have a condition that is unacceptable in our society," says Kelly Brownell, Ph.D., an obesity researcher at Yale University School of Medicine. And, he adds, unlike the blind or the deaf, fat people are told that they could be thin if they really wanted to. "It's kind of a double punishment," Dr. Brownell says.

Albert Stunkard, M.D., an obesity researcher at the University of Pennsylvania in Philadelphia, agrees. "There's that implicit assumption that you really could lose weight if you stopped being such a fat slob."

Fat people are the last group that it is acceptable to discriminate against blatantly, says Esther Rothblum, Ph.D., a psychologist who studies the social consequences of obesity. Sally E. Smith, executive director of the National Association to Advance Fat Acceptance, an advocacy group in Sacramento, California, says Michigan is the only state that prohibits "weight" discrimination. Smith adds that fat people have sued employers and sometimes won on the basis of discrimination against the handicapped, but not on the basis of discrimination against the obese.

Desperate Fight Against Weight

An estimated 25 to 30 percent of Americans are obese, defined as 25 percent or more above their ideal weight. Most have tried and tried again to reduce. Often the fatter they are, the more desperately they have tried.

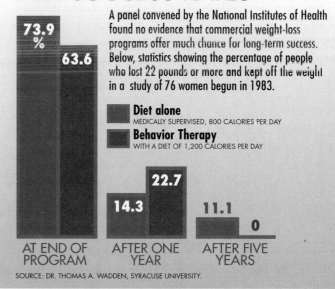

DIET SUCCESS RATES

A panel convened by the National Institutes of Health found no evidence that commercial weight-loss programs offer much chance for long-term success. Below, statistics showing the percentage of people who lost 22 pounds or more and kept off the weight in a study of 76 women begun in 1983.

Diet alone
MEDICALLY SUPERVISED, 800 CALORIES PER DAY

Behavior Therapy
WITH A DIET OF 1,200 CALORIES PER DAY

73.9% — 63.6 — AT END OF PROGRAM

14.3 — 22.7 — AFTER ONE YEAR

11.1 — 0 — AFTER FIVE YEARS

SOURCE: DR. THOMAS A. WADDEN, SYRACUSE UNIVERSITY.

Why So Many Ridicule the Overweight

A fat person is fair game. People who would never publicly confess to racism have no qualms about expressing revulsion for the obese. And that just may be because the fat threaten the thin down to the deepest levels of the psyche.

The reaction of Americans to a fat person, particularly one who is more than 25 to 35 percent above the so-called ideal weight, is so intense and so overwhelmingly negative that some scientists are exploring it as a window on the raw material of human nature.

Uncomfortable Symbol

Researchers who study the psychology of body image, and those who are struggling to foster greater tolerance of fatness in our culture, say that many people of normal weight fear the fat person because obesity embodies in the most graphic way possible the terrible potential they see lurking in themselves. For many, a fat person variously symbolizes loss of control, a reversion to infantile desires, failure, self-loathing, sloth, passivity, and gluttony.

With new scientific evidence showing how often obesity has a genetic or physiological basis beyond a person's control, they say, the time has come to dispel society's fear of being fat. But that will take some doing.

"The fat person represents the part of us that has morally disintegrated," says Susan C. Wooley, M.D., director of the eating disorders clinic at the University of Cincinnati. "It's the only physical trait I can think of which, although it's talked about in terms of appearance, is associated with so many things other than appearance."

And while many people manage to keep their anxieties and insecurities tucked safely inside, beyond the scrutiny of others, some see the fat as their own neuroses made flesh, forcing them to confront their own imperfections.

Acceptable Loathing

So despite growing evidence that weight is more a matter of genes than calories, fat people are still condemned for permitting themselves to get fat.

"We're running out of people that we're allowed to hate, and to feel superior to," says Dr. Wooley. "Fatness is the one thing left that seems to be a person's fault —which it isn't."

In a culture that exalts hard work, vigorous exercise, and delayed gratification, the obese seem particularly offensive.

"The history of this country was influenced by the Puritans, and people are supposed to be in control, stoic, self-denying," says Esther Rothblum, Ph.D., a psychologist at the University of Vermont. "When somebody looks hedonistic or self-indulgent, there's a tremendous animosity toward that person."

Feeling Moral Superiority

Interestingly, a fat person is not more likely to be tolerant of another fat person than is somebody slender, and often is even more scathing. Adele Rosenthal, a librarian in New York City who is about 70 pounds overweight, admits that she feels disgusted when she sees another fat person eating, and that she feels morally superior to somebody who is fatter than she.

"I still have this strong belief that I'm in control, and that I can pull that control again at any point," she says. "I know I get fat when I overeat and eat things I should avoid, so another fat person seems lazy and self-indulgent to me."

Dr. Rothblum and others say the tide may at last be turning, as ever more people rebel against the tyrannical demands toward eternal slenderness, as the population ages and thickens, and as excessive thinness becomes associated, not with athletic prowess, but with disease.

"The AIDS epidemic is changing people's minds," says Dr. Rothblum. "Whenever you have a disease that makes people thin, suddenly thinness is suspicious."

Natalie Angier

Walker, who is 36 years old, went on her first diet when she was 12. An osteopath prescribed amphetamines and 500 calories a day. In the intervening years, Walker has tried virtually every weight-loss program that has come along—the Cambridge Diet, the Dr. Atkins Diet, Weight Watchers, Optifast (twice). But every time she would gain back the weight she lost. "I currently weigh about 300 pounds," she says.

In April, Walker and other fat people were, in a sense, vindicated by the findings of experts at a conference called by the National Institutes of Health (NIH). The group looked at data on success rates of weight-loss programs, and concluded that diets, including expensive commercial diet plans, have an abysmal success rate in the long term, with virtually all dieters regaining the weight they had lost. The panel wrote, "There is increasing physiological, biochemical, and genetic evidence that being overweight is not a simple disorder of willpower, but is a complex disorder of energy metabolism."

But these findings are hardly new, obesity researchers say. For example, Jules Hirsch, M.D., and Rudolph L. Leibel, M.D., of Rockefeller University in New York, discovered years ago that when obese people lose weight, they often have symptoms of chronic starvation—they feel cold all the time, are always hungry, and are obsessed with food. Women stop menstruating. The formerly obese feel an overwhelming compulsion to eat until they are fat again. Those few who do manage to keep the weight off usually do so by making it a career to stay thin. They become Weight Watchers lecturers, for example, and fanatically monitor every bite of food that passes their lips.

Refusing to Accept Fat

Susan C. Wooley, M.D., director of the eating disorders clinic at the University of Cincinnati, says that it is one thing to say that most dieters fail to lose weight and keep it off and another to really accept, emotionally, that fat people cannot help it. Scientists themselves are as guilty as the rest of society, Dr. Wooley says.

"It has been clear in the scientific community that diets fail, yet scientists have been

OBESITY AND POVERTY AMONG WOMEN WITH...

INCOMES LESS THAN $10,000
29.2% OVERWEIGHT

INCOMES MORE THAN $50,000
12.7% OVERWEIGHT

SOURCE: NATIONAL CENTER FOR HEALTH STATISTICS.   CHARTS BY CHRISTOPH BLUMRICH

extremely reluctant to let go of diet programs," she says. "Why should we expect the general population to be any quicker than scientists in releasing prejudice?"

One hint of the agony of being fat came in a survey by Dr. Rothblum and her colleagues. The survey involved 367 women and 78 men who were members of the National Association to Advance Fat Acceptance. A third of the men and about a fifth of the women were not fat. The rest were at least 20 percent above their ideal weight. Dr. Rothblum found that the fatter the respondents were, the more likely they were to have suffered discrimination and abuse.

More than 40 percent of the fat men and 60 percent of the fat women said they had been denied promotions or raises because of their weight. One person wrote, "I was told by upper management that I would never be promoted until I lost weight, and the union took management's side."

Scorned and Snubbed

Dr. Rothblum's survey also showed the social consequence of being fat. Ninety percent of the fat men and women said that friends or relatives had ridiculed them or made nasty comments to them about their weight, and three-quarters of them said they had been laughed at or derided by fellow employees. One of the survey participants wrote, "While attending a lecture in college, a professor stopped in mid-sentence and said, 'When are you going to lose weight?'"

A quarter of the fat men and 16 percent of the fat women reported being hit or threat-

OBESITY AND DISCRIMINATION
In Percent

	Fat	Moderately Fat	Non-fat	Fat	Moderately Fat	Non-fat
ON THE JOB						
Not being hired	61.60	30.80	—	41.70	—	—
Denied benefits	30.60	7.70	—	36.10	—	—
Demoted	25.00	—	—	—	—	—
Fired/pressured to resign	17.40	2.60	—	11.10	—	—
Urged to lose weight	60.00	33.30	10.60	69.40	26.70	15.40
VERBAL						
By friend or family	92.90	92.30	44.70	86.10	66.70	30.00
By co-worker	73.30	61.50	23.40	0.60	46.70	15.40
By supervisor	45.40	38.50	2.10	52.00	13.30	3.00

SOURCE: NATIONAL ASSOCIATION TO ADVANCE FAT ACCEPTANCE.

ened because of their weight. A third said they had been derided by health professionals, and a quarter said they had been refused treatment because they were fat.

Colleen Rand, M.D., an obesity researcher at the University of Florida, has similar findings. She studied 50 obese women and seven men who had intestinal-bypass surgery and subsequently lost an average of 100 pounds each. Before surgery the patients reported overwhelming embarrassment about their appearance, and said they faced constant prejudice and discrimination. For example, 77 percent said that their children had asked them not to attend school functions with them.

In another study, Dr. Rand asked 47 formerly fat men and women whether they would rather be obese again or have some other disability. Every one of the 47 people said they would rather be deaf or have dyslexia, diabetes, bad acne, or heart disease than be obese again. Ninety-one percent said they would rather have a leg amputated. Eighty-nine percent would rather be blind.

Julia House, a 39-year-old office manager in Mesa, Arizona, says she cannot go grocery shopping without facing the stares of other shoppers who want to see what she puts in her shopping cart. And when she eats in a restaurant, other diners cannot resist peering at her to see what and how much she is eating. When House and a thin friend ordered hot-fudge sundaes recently, "A little old lady looked at me and said, 'Don't you think you should be eating something else?'"

Pamela Hollowich of Los Angeles says one of her most humiliating moments came when she tried to board an airplane. Ms. Hollowich, who weighs 350 pounds, was waiting to board, when an attendant "pulled me out of the line in front of all the other passengers and said I had to buy two tickets. It was humiliating. It was degrading," she says. But she ended up buying the extra ticket. Later she sued the airline. Her suit is currently in litigation.

Lynn Meletiche, a 48-year-old nurse who is chairwoman of the health committee for the National Association to Advance Fat Acceptance, says she often helps fat people whose doctors disparage them. One woman, she says, was told she had cervical cancer. But her doctor refused to operate on her unless she lost 100 pounds, even though the added risk of surgery was overwhelmed by the risk of living with cervical cancer. She found another doctor who did the operation, Meletiche says.

The abuse is "overwhelming," says Laura Eljaiek, a 35-year-old temporary office worker in New York City. "It affects you every day. It's hard to go out there feeling good about yourself."

But Eljaiek, like more and more fat people, has decided not to be passive in the face of blatant insults.

The other day, she says, she was getting off a bus when a man behind her said, "You could use some Slim Fast." Eljaiek whirled around to face him. "You," she shot back, "could use some manners." ◇

Heart Surgery's Hidden Heartbreak

by Jeff Goldberg

For many patients, bypass surgery is a double-edged sword. Although the operation unquestionably fixes the failing heart, it can exact a mental and emotional toll, with symptoms ranging from a slight loss of I.Q. to severe depression. As many as one-half of all bypass patients may experience persistent psychological side effects, estimates John Murkin, M.D., a Canadian physician who believes symptoms might result from subtle forms of brain damage caused by the surgery itself.

Murkin worked with psychologists and neurologists to test such factors as hand-eye coordination, concentration, reflexes, and short-term memory of 300 patients before and after bypass procedures. Fully half the patients studied had lower test scores seven days following surgery, Murkin found. A third of these patients still exhibited subtle mental deficits when they were reexamined two months later.

"Their psychological and neurological performance was clearly impaired," says Murkin. "They changed, and the only event that took place was that they had undergone heart surgery." Murkin cautions that most of the symptoms were mild. "Their intelligence scores are a little lower; they don't handle stress as well, don't make decisions as clearly. They're just not as sharp as they were." Even if the effects are modest, the approximately 400,000 coronary bypass procedures performed in the United States each year provide "a powerful multiplier," demanding further research.

His concern was echoed recently by a six-nation study, published in 1990 by German cardiac surgeon Georg Rodewald, M.D., and Allen Willner, an American psychologist, who found that the aftermath of open-heart surgery can sometimes be marked by stroke, severe cases of anxiety and depression, or even hallucinations. Their study concluded that bypass surgery generates emotional disorders in as many as 50 percent of patients who undergo the procedure.

"Now we need to find out how long these problems persist and how we can modify our present techniques to prevent them," Murkin insists. One possible explanation, he thinks, may stem from the fact that to minimize tissue damage to the heart during bypass surgery, the patient's blood is cooled by about 18° F. As a result, levels of carbon dioxide (CO_2) in the blood decrease. CO_2 is critically important in regulating blood flow to the brain. To compensate for this loss, the doctors routinely add extra CO_2 to the blood as it circulates through the heart-lung machine, which is used during bypass surgery to pump and filter blood while the surgeon grafts veins from the patient's leg to replace clogged heart arteries.

Ironically, Murkin suspects this process might allow microemboli—tiny particles and gas bubbles—to enter the circulation, causing brain-cell-damaging ministrokes. "We're beginning to think that adding CO_2 while the blood cools is wrong," he adds. "It actually increases blood flow to the brain to levels greater than necessary for normal function. Less blood flow may mean fewer emboli will reach the brain, and, presumably, less neurological damage."

Murkin's findings have been criticized by some colleagues. "The benefits far outweigh the risks of subtle forms of neurological damage," states Patrick McCarthy, M.D., a staff cardiac surgeon at the Cleveland Clinic. "These patients have a life-threatening disease. A patient should be happy if the only effect is that he scores less well on a test."

But Murkin argues, "Even though we've repaired someone's heart, now he's got a problem with his brain. Maybe it's subtle, but we should look to see whether there are things we can do differently during the procedure that might help to minimize these problems." ◇

Housecalls

by Stephen G. Underwood, M.D.

Q *Do homeless "street people" tend to have a greater incidence of psychological problems than the mainstream population?*

A Yes, they do, but keep in mind that there are different homeless populations. Victims of family violence, for example, may end up in shelters, and, in bad economic times, families may end up homeless.

These are different populations than the one to which you primarily refer, which is found largely in metropolitan areas or around state hospitals, and which consists mostly of single men, but also of women, living on the streets. Over recent decades, the move to deinstitutionalize the mentally ill has released much of this population to voluntary treatment at community mental-health centers. However, the system has not worked ideally, and many patients fail to continue their medication and other treatment, and wind up unable to even find shelter for themselves.

The number of homeless people has risen in recent years, partly due to programs that removed many mentally ill patients from institutional settings.

The most frequent diagnoses for these people are chronic schizophrenia, depression and other mood disorders, antisocial and other personality disorders, and borderline retardation. Many also suffer from alcoholism or drug abuse.

Q *I'm concerned about my 11-year-old daughter's eating habits. At what age do eating disorders usually begin?*

A Anorexia and bulimia are the two main diagnoses used to categorize eating disorders. Anorexia, a pathological fear of weight gain that leads to faulty eating patterns, generally arises between preadolescence to early twenties, but usually occurs during the teenage years. It is predominantly, but not exclusively, a disorder of young women.

Bulimia, characterized by bouts of gross overeating followed by self-induced vomiting, typically arises in late adolescence or early adulthood, usually occurring in the late teens or early twenties. An estimated 2 to 3 percent of females in this country suffer from clinically diagnosable bulimia at one age or another.

Q *I've read that the kind of relationship you have with your siblings can affect other areas of your life. Is this true?*

A Yes. Those who study sibling relationships and their influence on other relationships have found the effects very complex. First, you should know that sibling rivalry is normal. In addition, we all learn certain behaviors as a result of our sibling hierarchy. For example, oldest children are generally seen as more directive and assertive, and younger children tend to fall under that influence. In these roles, and with regard to age differences, we may seek out spouses or close friends to whom we relate in a very similar or very different manner. People may unconsciously re-create or abandon their original family structure in certain ways.

Rivalries experienced among siblings are carried into people's adult lives to differing extents. Marriage, for example, is a partnership; therefore, too much competition, controlling, or protection can be a problem. Factors that come into play when people choose a mate are intricate, but marriage partners may seek out, and find a better match in, a person with a similar sibling experience or with a contrasting one. Sibling background may also come out in work, socializing, and child rearing.

If someone is too rigid in living up to their early family role, they may become stuck there and not grow into a mature individual. We may all do best with some, but not all, of our original familial roles reproduced in adulthood. We thrive by preserving the constructive part—and by recognizing and putting in its proper place the immature portion—of such fundamental relationships as those with siblings.

Many nursing-home patients suffer from severe depression. The emerging field of geriatric psychiatry has developed improved methods of dealing with such depression.

Q *What sort of credentials are required of a marriage counselor? Is it rude to ask about their background?*

A Some states may require a certificate or license, but in general, there are no exact credentials for a marriage counselor. The American Association of Marriage and Family Therapy, among other groups, is helping to set standards in this area. The association's qualifications for a marriage counselor call for the person to have completed: a master's or doctoral degree (usually in a field such as psychology, social work, or educational counseling); specific graduate training in marriage and counseling therapy at an educational mental-health center with both academic and clinical activities; and two years of supervised clinical practice in the field.

Good professionals should be willing to give you a summary of their credentials. You may also want to look for someone whose practice is made up of clients who come primarily for marriage counseling.

Q *Is depression commonplace among residents of nursing homes? And is drug treatment effective?*

A Depression occurs all too commonly among residents of nursing homes, possibly due to mental issues that existed when they entered the home, to chronic physical illnesses, or to loss of their previous living environment. In addi-

tion, the elderly suffer from the highest incidence of progressive neurological diseases, such as Parkinson's or Alzheimer's, disorders for which depression may be a symptom.

Certain medications combat depression, but these drugs may have significant side effects or interactions with other medications. Counseling, psychotherapy, and recreational therapy are important as well.

Q *I know that injuries at birth or a dysfunctional home environment can affect mental health. But are many psychiatric problems inheritable?*

A A genetic component is involved in many, if not most, psychiatric disorders. For some problems, this means a strong inheritability; for others, it simply means that we have observed family patterns that serve as indicators.

Certain neurological diseases with psychiatric aspects—Huntington's chorea, for example—are clearly caused by genes. Neuroses such as panic disorders or obsessive-compulsive disorder seem to show family trends. Family history appears to help predict such problems as Tourette's syndrome, attention-deficit disorder, and learning disorders. Down syndrome, Fragile-X syndrome, and other retardations are genetic problems as well.

Do you have a psychology question?
Send it to Editor, Health and Medicine Annual, P.O. Box 90, Hawleyville, CT 06440-9990.

Practical News to Use

See also:
Individual articles in the second half of this book, arranged in alphabetical order, for additional information.

Good health is dependent on a broad range of preventive measures, such as timely immunizations and mammograms, proper care of teeth and eyes, avoidance of harmful solar rays and other environmental hazards, and adherence to good safety practices—in the home, at work and play, and on the road.

Childhood immunization is one of the most effective ways to prevent disease, saving as much as $14 for every $1 invested. Yet the United States has one of the lowest rates in the Western Hemisphere for childhood immunizations against such diseases as measles, mumps, and polio. As a result, there have been thousands of preventable hospitalizations. Barriers to increased immunization rates include high vaccine costs and a lack of health insurance among many families with children. About 35 million Americans do not have health insurance. A round of vaccine injections can cost more than $200, strapping even middle-class families.

Female workers exposed to glycol ethers, a group of chemicals used in the manufacture of computer chips, experience a 40 percent higher incidence of miscarriages, according to a study conducted at the University of California School of Medicine at Davis. The study was the third in four years to link glycol ethers to miscarriages. The chemicals are also used in many other industries, including printing and aerospace.

Among the fastest-growing occupational illnesses are painful hand and wrist problems caused by stressful, repetitive motions such as typing, meat-cutting, and assembly-line tasks. Hand- and finger-stretching exercises, done before work and during breaks, can reduce the threat. People using computer keyboards can avoid problems by lowering keyboards to several inches below desk level and tilting them downward, so that the hands remain in a straight line to the arm, flexed neither up nor down.

At the same time that employers must act to avoid and reduce occupational health hazards, they must cope with rapidly increasing health-care costs. On the average, health insurance cost U.S. employers $3,605 per worker in 1991. Such costs can eat up a large chunk of a company's budget. For instance, General Motors Corporation spent $3.2 billion for employee health benefits in 1990—more than it spent on steel.

Many factors drive up medical costs. For example, a study conducted by Dr. Alex Swedlow and colleagues from William Mercer Inc. found that physicians who treat on-the-job injuries send their patients out for significantly more treatment when the physicians are part owners of the clinics where the services are performed. According to a report released by the U.S. General Accounting Office (GAO), health-industry officials estimate that fraud and abuse contribute about 10 percent of the $700 billion-plus annual cost of U.S. health care. Weaknesses in the health-insurance system allow unscrupulous health-care providers —including the suppliers of medical equipment as well as practitioners in various medical specialties—to bilk health-insurance companies out of billions of dollars annually.

Another GAO study found that the price of prescription drugs increased

nearly three times as fast as the rate of inflation between 1985 and 1991. The study focused on 29 widely used drugs. Prices for 19 of the drugs increased by more than 100 percent—with some surpassing 300 percent. By comparison the rise in inflation for this same period was about 26 percent. The GAO noted that the soaring prices burden many Americans, particularly the elderly, who often must pay for these drugs out of pocket because they lack health insurance that pays for prescription drugs.

Many hospitals are using a new technology called Patient Controlled Analgesia (PCA) to manage postoperative pain. A pump attached to an intravenous catheter sends a painkilling medication directly into the bloodstream when the patient pushes a button. The patient's physician sets a maximum amount of drugs that may enter the body within a set time period. Studies indicate that patients who use PCA need less pain relief, are discharged from hospitals faster, and may have fewer chronic-pain problems.

Safety measures at home, at work and play, and on the road help promote good health.

1895
Foster Running Pump

1916
Keds Sports Slipper

1950
Bowerman Track Shoe

1968
Nike Full Cushion Midsole

1972
Bowerman Moon Sole

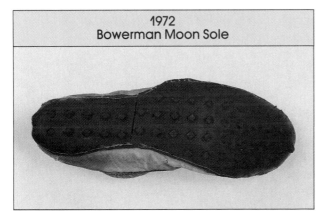

1986
L.A. Gear Fashion Shoe

1992
Nike Air Huarache

1992
Puma Disc

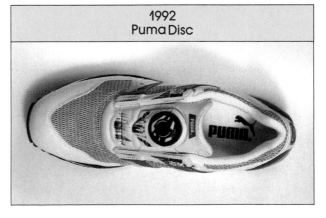

1945
Keds Basketball Shoe

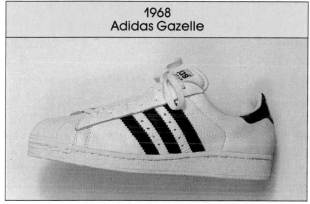

1968
Adidas Gazelle

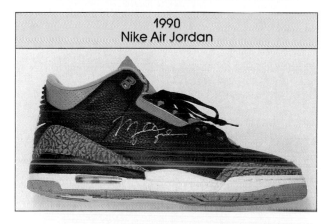

1990
Nike Air Jordan

1992
Reebok CO_2 Pump

Sneakers

by Linda J. Brown

Propulsion plate system, nitrogen energy spheres, ground reaction inertia device, graphite bridge, torsional rigidity bar—sound like an equipment list for a rocket ship bound for Mars? Well, don't look to the stars for these high-tech devices. They can be found on a very earthly object—the lowly sneaker.

Athletic shoes have come a long way since the ubiquitous, multipurpose canvas Keds. Advances in design and materials have turned sneakers into very specialized creations. They've evolved to the point where virtually every sport has its own unique footwear—from running and rugby to bicycling and basketball. Even within a sport, there can be many variations on a theme, forcing the buyer to choose carefully or risk ending up with a shoe that is at best uncomfortable, and at worst, damaging to the foot.

Sneakers Through the Ages
Athletic footgear was much simpler in ancient times, when the first known "sports" shoes were used for hunting and combat, according to Melvyn Cheskin, historian and shoe consultant from Braintree, Massachusetts. It wasn't until 1868 that the first flat-soled rubber canvas sneaker was manufactured. That innovation was made possible by Charles Goodyear's 1839 discovery of the vulcanization process for curing rubber.

The term "sneaker" came on the scene in 1873, apparently in reference to how quietly a person so shod can tread. It took almost another century, however, before the modern era of sports shoes began. It was at the 1968 Olympics in Mexico City that the striking, triple-striped Adidas sneakers worn by 80 percent of the athletes were emblazoned across the

Sneakers are no longer multipurpose—virtually every sport has its own specific footwear.

television screen for the world to see. "This type of advertising, coupled with the increases in leisure time and health awareness, triggered a sports-shoe boom that took athletic shoes out of the gym and off the track and landed them on the streets in the middle of the booming athletic fashion look," writes Cheskin in his book *The Complete Handbook of Athletic Footwear*.

The running craze that swept the nation in the 1970s further propelled the athletic shoe into the limelight. Before it had time to cool off, the 1980s ushered in the explosion of aerobics. Reebok introduced the first aerobic shoe in 1982, and America soon became, as Cheskin says, "a sea of white leather."

Hand in hand with the running and aerobics boom came important technological breakthroughs and the dawning of the biomechanical era. For instance, the first midsole, the foam cushioning between the sole and the foot, appeared in the early 1970s. Advances made in running shoes were later applied to other sorts of athletic footwear. The use of scientific methods to evaluate a sneaker gained prominence, and, according to Cheskin, "biomechanical, electronic, and computer testing were added to the decades-old practice of wear testing." These new technological innovations have rocketed sneaker technology into the 21st century.

Fabric "bodies" of Converse sneakers are arranged by size (below) prior to being molded into shape (above right). Toes are reinforced by dipping them into molten rubber (right).

Birth of a Sneaker

How are these technological masterpieces created nowadays? Each footwear company works somewhat differently, but it's fair to say that a new sneaker usually starts out as a gleam in a product manager's eye. It's up to these marketing people to figure out what kind of new sneakers the public will want to buy. "My job as the product manager is to determine what's going on in the marketplace, what trends are happening, what people are doing in terms of running," says Mike Cronin, product manager for running shoes at New Balance.

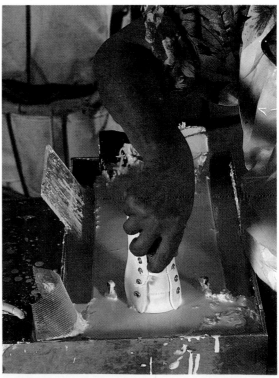

A starting-block view of a race (above left) invariably includes an assortment of shoe brands. The selection offered by athletic-footwear stores (above) can be truly overwhelming.

Once the product managers decide upon the general type of shoe they want, and in what price range, they take the idea to research and development (R&D). "In R&D, we have designers who are responsible for the aesthetics and who make sure the shoe is new and innovative. We also have product engineers who make sure the shoe can be made on time, for the right cost, and that it's durable and functional," says Spencer White, director of research and engineering for Reebok. "And then there's the research engineering group. We're the ones that really don't care how much it costs or what it looks like; we're only concerned with whether or not it works."

From there the designers produce sketches, which, after discussion with the product managers, are narrowed down to a few of the best. Nike values athlete input during this design stage, particularly from its star athletes who represent footwear lines. "Michael Jordan works with our design people every year on the new Air Jordan," says Dusty Kidd, a spokesperson for Nike.

Eventually a prototype shoe is built, which some product managers like to take out on the road for evaluation. For a running shoe, the prototype will be brought typically to a retail shoe store, a road race, or a consumer running expo to learn what runners think of the shoe.

The prototype also undergoes rigorous testing in the laboratory, using various machines that measure force, motion, and pressure. To test cushioning, for example, a machine measures how much energy a particular material or design can absorb compared to an industry standard. The Nike Research Lab in Beaverton, Oregon, uses a machine that looks like a clubfoot to test the resiliency of shoe materials. The foot undergoes continual pounding to monitor the slow deterioration of the material. Another machine simulates motion across different surfaces. A shoe strapped on an artificial foot is trekked at various speeds across a hardwood basketball court, a clay tennis court, or an asphalt road, all the while producing computer and visual readouts of the shoe's degree of wear and tear.

For all their sophistication, these machines are "just one small piece of the puzzle," says

Reebok's White. The tried-and-true practice of having people wear and evaluate the shoes is still essential. Nike sends out shoes to 2,000 to 3,000 people nationwide. "We get lots of feedback from people in real-time, practical applications," says Kidd.

The time from concept to finished shoe can take anywhere from just under a year to half a decade or more, depending upon whether the shoe is one in a gradual line of development or introduces a completely new concept. During that time, as many as 200 to 300 people may work on the shoe. New shoes are constantly being developed, since the average model stays on the shelf for only 18 months to two years.

Anatomy of a Shoe

Despite the recent high-tech innovations in athletic shoes, all sneakers still share some basic parts:

• First, there is the *last*. This is the actual model of the foot that a shoe is built on. Lasts differ for men's and women's shoes, for each sport, and from company to company. That's why one brand of shoes may not fit you the same as another brand. In running shoes, for instance, there are shoes made with curved (along the inside of the foot), semicurved, and straight lasts. The straighter the last, the more stable the shoe, while a curvier last produces a shoe with more flexibility.

• Starting from the bottom, the *outsole* is the part of the shoe that touches the ground. Usually made of rubber, the outsole may be a combination of dense carbon rubber in the heel and a softer blown rubber (rubber injected with air) along the forefoot.

• The *midsole* lies between the outsole and the sock liner. Midsoles are typically made from either polyurethane or ethylene vinyl acetate (EVA) with some sort of cushioning. Every company has their own cushioning system, from a silicone gel to encapsulated bags of pressurized gas or air.

• The *sock liner*, essentially a molded shoe pad, is what your foot rests on. In many shoes the sock liner is removable.

• *Heel counters*, made of plastic or molded EVA, cradle the heel to impart stability, preventing the heel from rolling inward or moving around.

• The *upper* covers the outside of the shoe. Uppers are made of leather, synthetic leather, mesh, or a combination of fabrics. In some shoes the upper is perforated in places to improve the breathability of the shoe.

• The *collar* goes around the back of your ankle and is usually padded for cushioning, often with an "Achilles notch" to support the Achilles tendon.

Which Shoe Is Right for You?

Knowing a sneaker's parts may come in handy when you shop for your next pair. These days, shoppers need all the help they can get to sort through the many choices to select the perfect shoe. The high degree of

Know Your Shoe

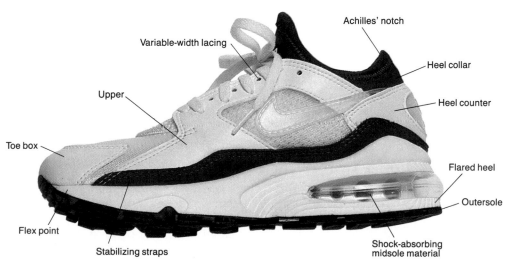

Variable-width lacing
Achilles' notch
Heel collar
Heel counter
Upper
Toe box
Flared heel
Outersole
Flex point
Shock-absorbing midsole material
Stabilizing straps

Green Sneakers

These days, even sneakers are becoming environmentally correct.

A new company called Deja Inc., of Tigard, Oregon, is introducing a line of sneakers made of 80 to 90 percent recycled materials. The soles are made of rubber diverted from landfills; the up-

pers are made of recycled cotton canvas. Recycled milk jugs, polystyrene coffee cups, and plastic lunch trays form the logo patch and the molded rubber that runs up the back of the shoe. Recycled corrugated cardboard, file folders, and coffee filters, along with neoprene from old wetsuits and gaskets make the innersole.

The *Ecosneaks* come in low- and high-top styles for men and women; natural, khaki, or black colors are available. Look for them at specialty footwear stores and better department stores, or call 1-800-331-DEJA.

Nike, the world's largest sports and fitness company, will use 20 percent recycled material in the outsoles of its men's and women's *Escape Lo* cross-training line starting in the spring of 1993. The shoes sell for $75 and are geared for hiking, trail running, and mountain biking. At first the recycled portion will be ground-up scrap material from manufacturing processes. By the fall of 1993, Nike plans to use ground-up defective footwear. Sometime in the future, Nike hopes to recycle old sneakers into the soles of new ones.

shoe specialization, fierce industry competitiveness, and an emphasis on flashy marketing techniques combine to make the task even more difficult.

When you shop, remember that "shoe fitting is not a science; it's an art," says Richard S. Gilbert, D.P.M., podiatry consultant for the San Diego Chargers and clinical assistant professor at the University of California, San Diego. Shoe manufacturers try to design shoes for fit, comfort, performance, and protection, but with all the variations among feet and sports activities, finding a comfortable shoe is still no easy feat.

So take an active role in shoe selection. Fit should be at the top of your list. "If a shoe doesn't fit, all the other cushioning and support are irrelevant," warns Spencer White. Use these tips to find that perfect shoe for you:

• Take your time and ask questions.
• Go to a shoe store with a good reputation and knowledgeable sales staff.
• Shop later in the day, when your feet are slightly swollen and thus match the way they may get when you exercise.
• Try on several types of shoes. Don't let a salesperson steer you to just one brand.
• Wear the socks you will use with your new shoes.
• Tell the salesperson your level of sports activity—for instance, if you are a runner, inform the sales clerk of your weekly mileage, the type of terrain you typically run, and the number of days you run each week.
• Look for good support around the heels. You shouldn't be able to slide your foot from side to side.
• Don't squish your toes. Allow between one thumb's width and one-half inch between your longest toe (which may be your second toe, not your big toe) and the end of the shoe.
• Bring your old shoes in for the salesperson to evaluate the wear pattern on the shoe's sole and determine which shoe is better for your type of pronation. For example, if you overpronate, you land on the outside heel area and roll inward too much. Overpronaters need a firm heel counter, a stiffer material under the inside of the heel than the outside, or external stabilizing straps.   ◇

WHY DOES AMERICA'S
HEALTH CARE COST *SO MUCH?*

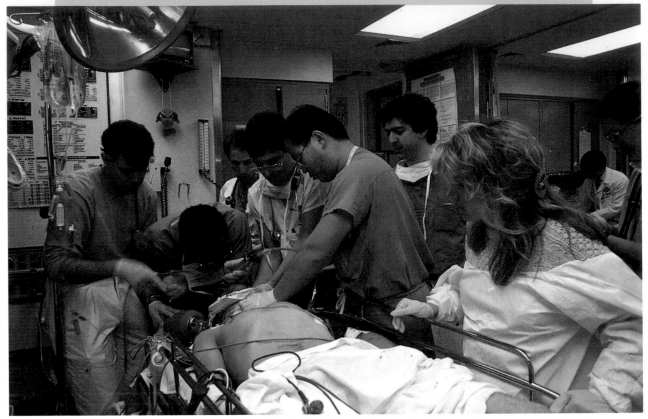

Health-care costs have risen more rapidly in the United States than in any other country on Earth. Part of the reason lies with skyrocketing hospital and emergency-room fees.

by David A. Pendlebury

It's the financial equivalent of a pandemic. With few exceptions, health expenditures worldwide are eating up a larger share of national wealth each year. Because no budget—whether personal or national—is limitless, increasing payments for medical care mean that there are fewer dollars, pounds, or pesos to spend on education, infrastructure, or other investments vital to long-term economic prosperity.

And in no nation have health-care costs risen higher or grown faster during the past decade than in the United States.

"By virtually all measures, U.S. health spending is the highest in the world," reports a recent study comparing health-care costs in the 24 industrialized member countries of the Organization for Economic Cooperation and Development (OECD). "Over the past 10 years, whether in absolute dollar terms or relative to its gross domestic product (GDP), U.S. health-care expenditures have increased faster than spending in other countries, and the gap between the United States and other major industrialized countries has increased."

One in Six Dollars for Health Care?

In 1990 the United States spent 12.1 percent of its GDP on health care, far more than any other OECD member nation. By 1992 U.S. spending had reached 13.4 percent of the GDP, or $809 billion, which, if taken by itself, would rank as the world's seventh-largest economy. By the year 2000, the nation will be spending 16.4 percent of its GDP, or some $1.6 trillion, on health care. That calculates to one out of every six dollars of U.S. output.

Ironically, for all the money the the United States spends on health care, an estimated 35 million Americans carry no medical insurance, and many times that number are underinsured. Interestingly, apart from the United States, the nations that generally spend the most on health care provide some form of universal or nationalized insurance. Health-care costs are relatively high and getting higher in Canada and France, for example, but both manage to provide health care for all.

Naturally, there is widespread concern in the United States over the health system as it is currently configured. According to a 1991 survey, when people in 10 leading industrialized nations were asked to judge their own country's health-care system, 60 percent of the U.S. respondents felt fundamental changes were needed. That represented the second-highest level of discontent: only Italy's system came in for more criticism, with a large proportion of Italians surveyed calling for their entire health-care system to be scrapped outright.

This brief overview of health-care costs prompts several important questions: Why have health-care expenditures grown so rapidly worldwide? Why are the costs of health care so much higher in the United States than in other industrialized nations? What can be done to reform the U.S. health-care system and to control costs?

Reasons for Rising Costs

The reasons why the costs of health care have been outpacing other types of expenditures apply in varying degrees to all nations. One obvious reason, at least among developed countries, is the introduction of advanced technology in the diagnosis and

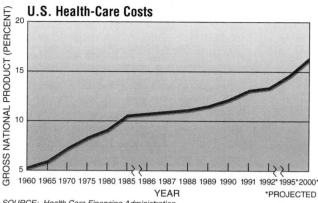

U.S. Health-Care Costs

SOURCE: Health Care Financing Administration

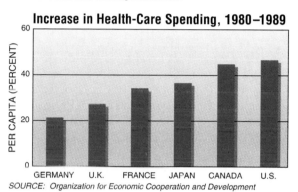

Increase in Health-Care Spending, 1980–1989

SOURCE: Organization for Economic Cooperation and Development

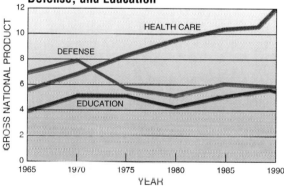

Comparison of Costs for Health Care, Defense, and Education

SOURCE: Consumer Reports, U.S. National Center for Educational Statistics, Health Care Financing Administration, U.S. Office of Management and Budget

treatment of diseases. Magnetic resonance imaging equipment (MRI), for example, has been a boon in diagnosis, but a single such machine can cost $1 million or more. Moreover, high-tech equipment is constantly being improved, and physicians and hospitals must obtain the best for their patients. High-tech medicine is something of a double-edged sword: with it, great good can be done, but this great good often comes at a great cost.

Longer life spans are also creating a problem for the already beleaguered health-care system. Especially in the United States and Japan, a combination of demographic changes and rising longevity have made the 80-year-old age group the fastest-growing segment of the population. Typically, older people require more medical care—and more frequently—than do younger people. Thus, a greater demand is placed on medical-care systems.

Fee-for-Service: Hallmark of U.S. System

The central feature of the U.S. system continues to be fee-for-service, in which physicians and hospitals are paid in proportion to the services they render to patients. Another prominent feature of the U.S. system is its bewildering array of payers for medical care: a menagerie of more than 1,500 private insurance carriers, as well as the federal and state governments in the form of Medicare (the program for those 65 and older) and Medicaid (the program for the poor).

Within such an environment, physicians and hospitals have every incentive to perform procedures on patients. Generally, the more they do for (or to) a patient, the more they get paid. The patient, on the other hand, has no economic incentive to refuse whatever treatment the medical provider may suggest, since the patient's costs are covered by a third party (private insurance or the government). In recent years, there have been some attempts to place limits on reimbursements to physicians and hospitals, both by private insurance carriers and by Medicare in the form of diagnosis-related groups (DRGs), which determine flat fees for specific diseases or procedures. Health-maintenance organizations (HMOs), also known as managed-care providers, have introduced patient copayments, in which a nominal fee is charged directly to patients for physician visits or for prescription medicines. These attempts, however, have hardly changed the structure of the system, which is still, in economic terms, stacked in favor of doing something rather than doing little or nothing at all.

This system stands in sharp contrast with those of most other industrialized countries, where there is generally a single payer for health care (the government) and some form of budgeting or rationing of both financial and medical resources.

One chief difference between single-payer and multiple-payer schemes is the higher administrative costs associated with multiple payers, at least according to several studies. The U.S. government's General Accounting Office (GAO) issued a report in 1991 that suggested that a single-payer system would save the federal government enough in health-care costs to pay for the 35 million U.S. citizens now uninsured. A second study, based on 1987 figures, estimated that approximately 20 percent of all U.S. health-care costs were spent on paperwork and other forms of administration, whereas in Canada, which has a single-payer system, the comparable figure was about 10 percent, or half as much.

Some U.S. physicians own a financial interest in a diagnostic laboratory to which they send their patients for X rays, blood tests, and advanced imagery. In Florida, such laboratories performed twice as many tests per patient as did labs not associated with the referring physician.

How Do Other Nations Cope?

Universal access to high-quality health care is the goal of every nation. Unfortunately, the dilemma of paying for health care is a seemingly universal problem.

Among the industrialized nations other than the U.S., health care is typically centralized in both its organization and funding and, hence, it is essentially a public enterprise. Universal health care, financed by taxation of the general population or through levies on employers, has a long, even ancient, history. In Athens of the fifth century BC, tax revenues funded public physicians whose services were available to its citizens. More than 1,000 years later, medieval guilds collected funds from members to help pay for treatment of the sick among them. But the birth of the modern form of nationalized health care came in the late 19th century in Germany. The Bismarck government required employees to enroll in a sickness fund, financed by both employers and employees. This century has seen many governments adopt universal health care.

Ironically, at a moment when the United States is tempted by the concept of universal health care, some industrialized nations with such plans in place are attempting to introduce privatization and competition, hallmarks of the U.S. system. In the United Kingdom, for example, many hospitals are now choosing to opt out of the National Health Service system, to establish themselves as independent trusts (nonprofits), and to compete with other hospitals for patients. Germany, Switzerland, France, and the Netherlands are all actively investigating health-care reforms from patient copayments for prescription medicines and doctor visits, to increasing taxes on cigarettes and alcohol.

The developing nations of the world can only afford to spend about half as much or less per citizen as the industrialized countries. Moreover, new stresses (AIDS, famine, civil war) have recently fallen upon these already weak and wobbly health-care systems. Typically, developing nations have focused their spending and services on hospitals in urban areas. This pattern has led to an oversupply of health-care facilities in cities and a paucity of services in rural areas.

Finally, health care has all but collapsed in certain nations and massive reforms and restructuring are needed. In these situations, such as in the former Soviet Union, in the former Yugoslavia, and in Somalia, there is either an absence of a strong government to direct health care, woefully inadequate funds to finance it, or both.

Market-oriented Medicine

Perhaps the most troubling reason for rapidly escalating costs is a transformation in the nature of medical practice. U.S. medicine has become, in the words of Dr. Arnold S. Relman, editor in chief emeritus of the *New England Journal of Medicine,* "market-oriented" and "a competitive business."

The dark side of this transformation, Relman points out, arises when the financial interests of a physician or hospital become intertwined with the choice of care given to a patient. This can happen when a physician holds a financial interest in, for example, a for-profit diagnostic laboratory to which he or she refers patients. Several studies have shown that in such circumstances, more tests were ordered for patients than when there were no financial interests at play. One study revealed that physician-owned laboratories in Florida performed twice as many tests per patient as those without ownership participation on the part of the referring physician.

Such practices are, thankfully, still the exception rather than the rule. Most physicians are motivated by a desire to help their patients rather than by a desire to reap a financial benefit from them. Still, Relman highlights a real and growing problem.

Of Doctors and Dollars

The average net income of physicians in the U.S. rose from $98,000 to $164,000 between 1982 and 1990, for an annual growth rate of 6.6 percent. By comparison the average net income of all Americans rose from $18,500 to $25,900, representing a growth rate of only 4.3 percent.

And U.S. physicians are richly rewarded for their work, as the table below shows:

Nation	Ratio of Physician's Income to Average Income
United States	5.12
West Germany	4.28
Canada	3.47
Japan	2.46
United Kingdom	2.39
Australia	2.26
Denmark	2.01
Finland	1.82
Norway	1.38
Ireland	1.08

U.S. physicians typically earn more than five times the average U.S. salary, whereas their foreign colleagues earn from two and one-half to four times the average salary in their countries.

Physicians in the United States do have certain unique expenses, however. For example, medical education is relatively costly in America compared with that of other nations. Many U.S. medical school graduates leave medical school with debts that not infrequently total more than $100,000; many medical students in other countries pay only a nominal fee for their medical education or have their training paid for by the government. Second, in the United States, medical-malpractice insurance can amount to as much as 10 times that of European physicians—and even more in select litigation-prone specialties such as obstetrics. Still, these education fees and special obligations do not by themselves explain the very real differences in compensation for U.S. and foreign physicians.

The economic structure of U.S. health care is currently designed (although not necessarily intentionally) to reward volume: the more tests, procedures, office visits, etc., the more the physician receives from third-party payers, such as private insurance carriers or Medicare. In such an environment, there is every incentive to do more to earn more, and, until recently, there have been virtually no limits on reimbursements. In other words, a U.S. physician can increase his or her income simply by seeing more patients.

Proposals for Reforming U.S. Health Care
Suggestions for reforming America's troubled health-care system are as numerous and varied as the many explanations given for what ails the system.

The issues that most analysts agree must be addressed in any health-care-reform package are: (1) how to obtain medical care for all, and (2) how to contain health-care costs.

Simply stated, universal coverage cannot be met unless there is money to pay for it. Some analysts have suggested that the requisite funds can be obtained from cost-cutting measures. Others call this hope a "pipe dream." Most industrialized countries pay for universal or national health care through direct taxation at levels significantly higher than that of the United States. John K. Inglehart of the *New England Journal of Medicine*, notes that "the United States' preference for maintaining a relatively low level of taxation all but precludes the possibility that it will embrace a reform plan modeled on Canada's health-insurance program, in which all funds are derived from general revenues."

The essential question is: Does the American public have the will to, as Inglehart describes it, "equalize the costs of care between citizens with means and those without, and between people with serious disease and those without." Historically, American culture has emphasized self-sufficiency over burden-sharing. Perhaps it is too much to expect a cultural about-face.

Modifying the Public-Private System

President Clinton's early plan for health-care reform was built on a private-public partnership. In his first days as president, Clinton appointed his wife, Hillary Rodham Clinton, to draft an official health proposal for the Administration. The Clinton plan is expected to rely on a National Health Board to set limits on medical spending, nationally and state by state. This board would also dictate a "core benefits package" for all citizens. The plan stated that "employers and employees will either purchase private-health benefits directly or participate in the publicly sponsored alternatives that offer the core benefits package established by the National Health Board. Those not covered through their employers will participate in the publicly sponsored alternatives."

This comes close—but is not a full commitment—to the concept of "pay or play," a version of health-care reform supported by several Democratic leaders in Congress. Under this system, employers would either provide health-care benefits for workers ("play") or contribute to a government fund that would be used to cover the costs of medical care ("pay"). President Clinton's plan calls for insurance reforms, and also prohibits

How Health Care Is Financed, in Billions

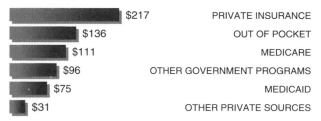

$217	PRIVATE INSURANCE
$136	OUT OF POCKET
$111	MEDICARE
$96	OTHER GOVERNMENT PROGRAMS
$75	MEDICAID
$31	OTHER PRIVATE SOURCES

SOURCE: Health Care Financing Administration, 1990

Where Health-Care Funds Are Spent, in Billions

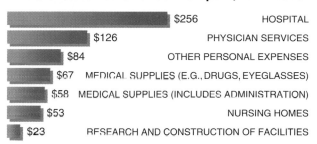

$256	HOSPITAL
$126	PHYSICIAN SERVICES
$84	OTHER PERSONAL EXPENSES
$67	MEDICAL SUPPLIES (E.G., DRUGS, EYEGLASSES)
$58	MEDICAL SUPPLIES (INCLUDES ADMINISTRATION)
$53	NURSING HOMES
$23	RESEARCH AND CONSTRUCTION OF FACILITIES

SOURCE: Health Care Financing Administration, 1990

discriminatory practices against those with preexisting medical conditions. The plan also argues for medical-malpractice reform as well as greater simplification and efficiency in the administration of health care. While the Clinton plan does suggest a mechanism for cost controls—a decision by the National Health Board—it is difficult to discern how such a limit would be set or enforced.

Most U.S. physicians pay large premiums for malpractice insurance. The fear of being sued for medical malpractice has led many physicians to routinely order X rays, blood tests, and other procedures simply to have every contingency covered in the event of a lawsuit.

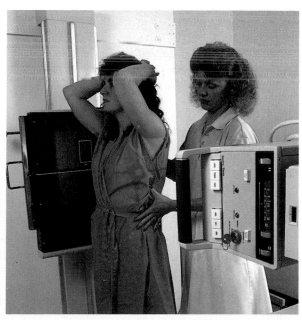

Clinton's plan preserves the public-private system already in place, in which businesses play a leading role in providing medical insurance. Some experts have argued that this places an undue burden on a firm's ability to compete globally. In a pay-or-play system, for example, "business . . . would pass this cost on—either forward to consumers in the form of higher prices or, more probably, backward to employees in the form of lower salaries or reductions in other fringe benefits," as economist Uwe E. Reinhardt of Princeton University has pointed out.

Health-care reform advocates are waiting for explicit information on how the extension of health benefits to the uninsured would be financed.

A Single-Payer Plan

A more radical route to U.S. health-care reform has been proposed by Rashi Fein, professor of medical economics at Harvard University. Fein advocates a form of universal health care in which state and federal governments manage and pay for all medical costs. Every person would be enrolled in a program similar to Medicare. According to Fein: "A single-enrollment program means a single payer, or more appropriately, a single purchaser of services. This situation leads to the standardization of forms, to electronic billing, and to various measures that reduce confusion, delay, and the costs of administration in today's system. The purchaser would not only pay the bill for services, but also accept a broader responsibility to focus on issues of quality of care, unnecessary services, and value for money. Each of these activities contributes to cost control."

"In addition," notes Fein, "a universal program that raises funds through taxes and premium payments cannot survive for long if it neglects cost considerations. If it cannot fund its obligations, it will be forced to increase its revenues or shift costs to patients—and it will fail. Because the single-insurance approach cannot shift costs to another insurer, it must achieve its goal within a budget. Therefore, the plan would have to set an overall budget for health care as well as similar budgets for physician and hospital services." To demonstrate that such a system is workable, Fein cites France, Japan, and other nations that provide universal care and maintain a budget.

To pay for this program, Fein proposes mechanisms similar to those used to finance Medicare, such as payroll deductions, or even a value-added tax (VAT).

Determining What Works

Whatever the reform plan that eventually may be adopted—if any—one pursuit that could ultimately contribute to containing costs is research on the success and utility of different medical treatments. Outcomes research, as it is known, attempts to determine what works. Moreover, if two therapies produce the same result, then the less expensive route can be chosen. Both government agencies and private insurance companies are supporting such research efforts across the nation.

One example is treatment for low-back pain—the second most frequent reason why people visit their doctor (after the common cold). The cost of treatment for back pain, including hospitalization, is estimated to be some $24 billion annually. A 1985 outcome study revealed, however, that as much as 71 percent of nonsurgical hospitalization for back pain was completely unnecessary.

Growing Like Topsy

Ironically, the health-care industry itself now represents the most robust and rapidly growing segment of the U.S. economy. With an estimated 10 million people employed by physicians, in hospitals, for pharmaceutical firms, in the manufacture and sale of medical equipment, and in other health-related activities, the U.S. health-care industry is one terrific job creator in a system that all too often seems to be losing or exporting jobs.

Concerns about the U.S. health-care system and its high costs have been aired for more than two decades. It is anyone's guess whether some type of substantial reform will actually be implemented, or whether, as in the past, the public and its political leaders will simply shrug and do nothing, reacting to the problem, in the words of one commentator, as if to a "warning about an asteroid collision in a far-off century." ◇

GETTING THERE SAFELY

by Susan Nielsen

Each year, passenger cars travel about 1.5 *billion* miles on the country's highways, byways, and dusty backroads. Not surprisingly, with all this time spent on the road, every American can expect to be involved in a car crash once every five years. In fact, car accidents are the third-leading cause of all deaths nationwide. Now for the good news: heightened attention to car safety by the government, manufacturers, and consumer-advocacy organizations is increasing the odds that today's drivers and passengers will be better protected from injury than ever before. Unfortunately, even the most sophisticated safety equipment cannot prepare a driver for every eventuality. Still, drivers can prepare themselves for most on-the-road hazards by staying updated on the latest information from experts on car safety and maintenance.

Belts and Bags: A Smart Combination

In a typical car accident, the vehicle comes to a complete stop in less than one second after the instant of impact; unfortunately, the car's occupants keep moving. When not wearing safety belts, the occupants will slam into the car's interior structure. Even after an occupant stops moving, his or her organs and bones collide, causing internal injuries. In a car traveling 30 miles per hour (mph) at impact, occupants not wearing safety belts will strike the dashboard, windshield, or other interior structure of the car with a force of several thousand pounds! It's no wonder that dozens of states have mandated safety-belt use. The safety belt holds the occupant in his or her seat, restraining the belt wearer as the car stops, all the while distributing the force of impact to the chest, hips, and shoulders—those parts of the body better able to withstand pressure than vulnerable internal organs. Since model year 1991, all new passenger cars come equipped with rear-seat shoulder harnesses as well. (The center rear seat, however, still has only a lap belt.) Older cars can be retrofitted with the harnesses by their dealer.

For some passengers, the list of excuses for not wearing a safety belt is seemingly endless. The government sees things differently, however. The U.S. National Highway Traffic Safety Administration (NHTSA) recommends that even pregnant women should always wear a safety belt. According to the NHTSA, there is no evidence that safety belts increase the risk of injury to an unborn baby. As a matter of fact, the less injury sustained by the mother, the better the baby's chances of survival. And, of course, wearing a safety belt greatly reduces the mother's risk for injury.

Shorter adults often complain that shoulder belts cut across their necks. The erstwhile solution—putting the restraint behind their back—is almost as dangerous as wearing no belt at all. Instead, shorter drivers should reposition their car seats for a better fit, or purchase a cushion that can be slid onto the belt to soften the points of contact. Children may get relief from a scratchy harness by sitting on a booster seat. Overweight people unable to close their safety belt should purchase a belt extender, available from auto dealerships or supply stores. For optimum protection, always make sure the shoulder harness lies across the chest. And, reminds Charles Spilman, president of Traffic Safety Now, Inc., in Detroit, "keep the lap belt low across the hips."

A common fallacy holds that it is safer to be thrown clear of a car during a crash than to remain belted inside it. But according to a NHTSA study, the chance of being killed is four times greater when one is thrown from a car during an accident. Another common misconception is that safety belts need not be worn in vehicles equipped with air bags. Such is not the case.

Air bags were not developed to replace safety belts, but rather to supplement their effectiveness by cushioning the impact of a head-on collision that occurs at speeds of 14

What to Carry in Case of Emergency

The American Automobile Association (AAA) recommends that you have these on hand in your car, just in case:
• Antifreeze (coolant)
• Windshield-washer fluid
• Jumper cables
• Flashlight
• Basic automotive tool kit
• Basic first-aid kit
• Flares or roadway reflectors
• Spare tire (fully inflated)
• Jack
• Block of wood (to support the jack on soft surfaces)
• Aerosol flat fixer
• Portable tire pump
• Tire gauge
• Multipurpose dry-chemical fire extinguisher
• Rags or paper towels

In the winter, add:
• Ice scraper and snow brush
• Snow shovel
• Salt, sand, or kitty litter
• Tire chains
• Traction mats or old rugs
• Gloves, blankets, extra clothes

mph or higher. The best protection of all, of course, entails wearing both a shoulder and lap belt in an air-bag-equipped car. Used alone, tests have shown that an air bag reduces the risk of accident fatality by an estimated 20 to 40 percent, and the chance of moderate to critical injury by 25 to 45 percent. When used in conjunction with a lap and shoulder belt, an air bag reduces risk of fatality by as much as half. An estimated 5 million to 6 million cars will come equipped with driver-side air bags in 1993. By 1994 all air-bag-equipped cars will include air bags for both the driver and the front-seat passenger.

Taking Baby for a Ride

Unrestrained children stand a high risk of injury or death in car accidents. An unrestrained child becomes a projectile in a crash or can be crushed between adults and the car's interior. The use of child safety seats could prevent 53,000 injuries and save 500 lives a year. Choosing a child safety seat can seem almost as daunting as buying a car, however, given the many makes and models available on the market. Rule number one: Not every car seat fits properly in every car. "If the seat is difficult to buckle in your car, return it and keep trying until you find one that works," recommends consumer advocate Jack Gillis, co-author of *The Childwise Catalog.* "Otherwise, your child's safety may be compromised."

To avoid incompatibility problems, integrated seats—the type that come ready-made in some new cars—are the best way to go. These seats generally accommodate children who weigh 20 to 40 pounds, says Gillis. Remember that children need to be protected in a car from the day the little bundle of joy comes home from the hospital. And never forget that the best place for a car seat is in the backseat.

The correct seat constitutes only one of countless things to consider when traveling with a baby. While buckles that lock up only in a sudden stop are fine for adults, a baby needs a buckle that stays locked at all times. In cars equipped with only emergency locking restraints (called ELRs), the locking clip that comes with the child safety seat must be used. Convertible restraints, on the other

Nearly every state mandates the use of special child safety seats for infant and toddler passengers. Older children should wear seat belts.

hand, can be adjusted for both adults and children, although the belt must be reset for a child after an adult has used the restraint.

Preventive Maintenance

No matter what type of restraint system a car has, it won't be of much use if the car breaks down. Checking the following 10 systems for wear and tear or unusual noises now may just help keep a car off the side of the road later.

• **Battery:** Batteries are tricky because they often give no warning that they're about to die. "They work fine until the last time," says Ed Anderson, manager of the mechanical and transmission division of the Automotive Services Association in Bedford, Texas. Most batteries are sealed, but there may be an indicator light or gauge to warn if the battery has weakened. For batteries with caps, check the fluid level; when necessary, add only distilled water. Make sure to always check the terminal connections for corrosion.

• **Windshield:** Cracks, fisheyes, and pings can be fixed with epoxy before they spread. Wiper blades should be replaced when they start streaking or become dry and cracked.

• **Tires:** In a test of vehicles on the road conducted by the American Automobile Association (AAA), almost half (43 percent) had

Safety Features of the Future

As you are cruising along the highway, a special radar-scanning system helps you avoid the object in the middle of the road. Then the car warns of a traffic jam ahead and produces an alternate route on your electronic map. After you find the new road, your voice commands the windshield to increase its tint to reduce the glare. Now, settled into your trip, you realize it's time to give your family a call to let them know when you'll be home. Your hands never leave the wheel as you dial.

These represent just a few of the safety features destined to be in the cars of tomorrow. Indeed, car safety has come a long way from the days before safety belts or air bags. Automobile manufacturers are now installing dual air bags in some models and offering retrofit programs for installation of rear shoulder harnesses. Features like the front-end crumple zone, collapsible steering column, safety glass, ABS or antilock brakes, and interior padding have become commonplace. New safety accoutrements include larger and brighter dashboard displays and controls for older drivers, childproof door locks and window controls, and traction assistance. And that's just the beginning.

Safety-technology researchers realize that a distracted driver stands an increased chance of getting into an accident. To help a driver keep his or her hands on the wheel, an extra set of stereo buttons near the steering column, hands-free cellular phones, and other user-friendly controls are in the works. In the future, voice-activated commands will make many controls hands-free. "People are using their cars as an extension of their homes," says Linda Lee, from the design information division of public affairs at Ford Motor Company. "So we're beginning to look at the safe placement and use of cellular phones, fax machines, and units the size of a glove box for safe storage." Even cup holders are being redesigned for safer, out-of-the-way use.

Dashboard navigational systems like the one above will someday help drivers avoid traffic jams by suggesting alternate routes.

Other systems extend the driver's senses. General Motors (GM) is developing forward-looking radar, which would scan the lanes in front of the vehicle in order to alert the driver to objects not otherwise visible. If the system judges that the car is too close to the object, it would automatically "depower" the car, and if necessary, cause it to stop. GM is also looking into night-vision-enhancement systems that would work much like infrared-detection goggles used by the military. Such a system would display a screen image of objects in front of the vehicle. In dense fog, for example, you still would be able to see where you're going. To also aid a driver's vision, Ford reports that windshields may someday be available with built-in shading that would darken at the touch of a button in sunny or glary weather.

To assist in vehicle maintenance, Goodyear has developed a tire with an implanted computer chip that reports wear-and-tear data to the driver. A hand-held antenna would pick up the information from radio waves and display it on a digital readout built into the dashboard. The technology, initially developed for truck tires, would report, for example, that a tire is low or overheating—a warning sign of a flat tire in the making.

worn or underinflated tires. Underinflated tires reduce gas mileage and may lead to sudden blowouts. Keep the tires properly inflated for the best traction, especially on slippery roads. About every 5,000 to 8,000 miles, have the tires rotated. Inspect the tires for wear. Insert the top of a penny into a tread groove. It is time to replace the tire when any part of Lincoln's head is visible. While the penny method is a good gauge of tread wear, many tires today incorporate built-in wear indicators, a series of horizontal bars that appear across the surface of the tire. It is always better to replace your tires before they become worn, recommends the Tire Industry Safety Council in Washington, D.C.

• **Lights:** Every month, check the headlights, parking lights, directional signals, taillights, and brake lights. With the car in park, have someone tap the brakes and turn on the directional signals as you check around the car. For a quick check of the headlights and high beams, shine them on a wall. Replace burned-out bulbs and cracked casings.

• **Heating and cooling system:** The biggest cause of summer breakdowns is overheating. So check the car's coolant level frequently. If the fluid looks rusty, take the car to a repair shop. Inspect the radiator and hoses for leaks and cracks. Try to have the cooling system flushed and refilled about every two years. (Note: add water to an overheated radiator only when the engine is running; otherwise the engine could be damaged. *Never* uncap the radiator when the car is hot.)

• **Fluids.** Change the oil and oil filter about every 5,000 miles, or more often if the car is used primarily in stop-and-go driving, for frequent short trips, or to tow heavy loads. Make sure the windshield-washer reservoir is full especially in winter or inclement weather. Open the plastic cap on the master cylinder (it is usually marked) to check the brake-fluid level. Also check the power-steering fluid. While the car is warmed up and idling, check the transmission-fluid dipstick.

• **Filters:** If the air filter is only slightly soiled, simply blow off the dust. If it is extremely dirty, replace it. Change the fuel filter and positive crankcase ventilation filter as recommended in the owner's manual.

• **Brakes:** Don't delay in having the brakes checked if longer stopping distances, grabbing, pulsation, or noises occur.

How to Get Out of a Skid

According to the AAA, skidding is caused by excessive speed or quick, jerky braking or acceleration. The best way to avoid skidding: anticipate lane changes, turns, and curves; slow down in advance; and steer smoothly and precisely. Here are the steps to take if your rear wheels should skid:

1. Take your foot off the accelerator and shift to neutral; do not brake.

2. Steer in the direction you want the front of the car to go.

3. Just before the rear wheels stop skidding, countersteer until you are going in the right direction.

4. Shift to drive and apply gentle accelerator pressure so the engine's speed matches the road speed, and accelerate smoothly.

Ice creates extremely hazardous driving conditions. Motorists driving on icy roads should proceed very slowly, anticipate curves and turns, and avoid sudden stops.

• **Belts and hoses:** Check belts and hoses for wear and tear, cracks, missing chunks, lack of tension, and dryness (no longer pliable). A worn or loose fan belt can cause a car to overheat if it ruptures. Other belts can affect the operation of the electrical system, power steering, and air-conditioning.

• **Exhaust system:** Inspect the muffler and tail pipe for proper suspension and rust.

Beating the Winter Driving Blues

Even with the best car maintenance, nothing can take the confidence out of a driver faster than having to travel in ice and snow—and with good reason. Motorists are more likely to face car trouble during the winter than at any other time of the year. Besides the obvious road hazards of winter driving, cold temperatures wreak havoc on tires, belts, and hoses, cause the engine cooling system to freeze up, and can keep a weak battery

Motorists should have their cars fully checked and winterized to avoid breakdowns in subfreezing weather. Before venturing out after a storm, all snow should be cleared from the car.

from starting. When bad-weather driving is a must, leave ample time to allow the car to warm up. "As the car warms up, watch the oil-pressure gauge and give it time to rise. This means the engine's parts are getting lubricated with oil," says Automotive Service Association's Ed Anderson. In stormy weather, always leave sufficient time to be able to drive to a destination at a slow and steady pace. Before driving, make sure to perform these tasks:

• To prevent the gas line from freezing, add fuel de-icer at least once a month to the fuel tank. Keep the gas tank at least half-full to reduce the area in which condensation can form inside the tank.

• Replace or recharge a weak battery. Starting a car in cold weather places great demands on a battery, even if it's fully charged.

• Add a sufficient amount of antifreeze (coolant) to the radiator to handle temperatures as low as -30° F.

• Use all-season radial tires only if they have a snow-tread configuration and are marked as "M&S" (for mud and snow). For the best possible car cornering performance, straight-ahead traction, and stopping in winter conditions, mount snow tires on all four wheels, even if the car has front-wheel or four-wheel drive.

For More Information
NHTSA operates an Auto Safety Hotline, which provides information on recalled cars, takes motor-vehicle-safety complaints, and handles other auto-safety issues. The hot line operates 8:00 A.M. to 4:00 P.M. EST weekdays at 800-424-9393 (in Washington, D.C., call 202-366-0123).

NHTSA also offers a 28-page guide called *Sudden Impact: An Occupant Protection Fact Book.* Write to the Office of Occupational Protection, NTS-10, U.S. Department of Transportation, National Highway Traffic Safety Administration, 400 7th Street SW, Washington, DC 20590.

• Fill the windshield-washer-fluid reservoir.

To get started in the snow, clear a path several feet in each direction by driving back and forth. If the snow is too deep, shovel it away from the car. Then shift to second gear or put the car in drive, and ease out of the space without spinning the wheels. Spinning will only cause the car to dig itself deeper into the snow—and, in extreme cases, can even cause the tires to explode. If more traction is needed, put down salt, sand, or traction pads. If even this doesn't work, try rocking the vehicle by keeping the front wheels pointed straight ahead and shifting from reverse to second gear or from reverse to drive. Time each shift so that it occurs at the peak of the previous rock. If stuck in the snow with the engine heater running, open a window slightly for ventilation. Make sure the snow is cleared from the exhaust pipe to prevent carbon monoxide poisoning. ◇

The technologies created specifically to improve data collection or to enhance living conditions during spaceflights are finding more and more applications in the health-care setting here on Earth.

Medical Spin-offs from Space

by Devera Pine

The space program conjures up images of rockets blasting out of Earth's orbit, men walking on the Moon, and astronauts capturing wayward satellites in the space shuttle's cargo bay. And while all these accomplishments are truly amazing, still more dramatic are the advances in technology that have been driven by the space program. In fact, it is estimated that National Aeronautics and Space Administration (NASA) technology has spawned some 30,000 devices with commercial use that play a role in daily life. Many of these gadgets are used in medicine: pacemakers, insulin pumps, and CAT scans, to name but a few. There is no doubt: NASA technology has become a standard part of Earth medicine.

Basically, NASA's medical spin-offs come in two forms: direct and indirect. Direct spin-offs are those used for the same purposes

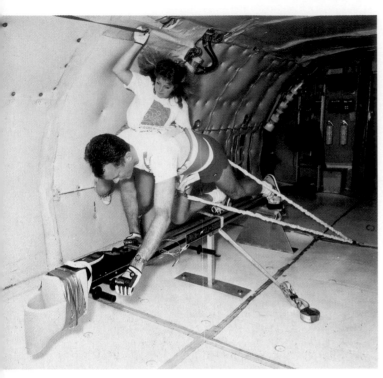

Electrodes used to monitor heart and breathing rates of astronauts (above) are now used in health clubs to control workout intensity on the VersaClimber machine (right).

both in space and on Earth. Indirect spin-offs have undergone modification to fit Earth applications. Direct or indirect, these space spin-offs have infinitely improved the means by which doctors diagnose and treat human disorders.

Energized!

What does exercise equipment have in common with space technology? When NASA first began sending humans into space in the early 1960s, the agency needed a reliable way to monitor the heart and breathing rates of the astronauts. Although the technology for recording these basic biological functions was already available, NASA had to invent new devices to suit the special needs of space flight.

The equipment had to be reliable and durable, since the space and weight restrictions on board a spacecraft didn't allow much room for backup equipment. As a result, NASA scientists and contractors came up with heavy-duty electrodes that could endure the abuse of everyday wear. These "insulated

capacitive" electrodes were impervious to perspiration, noise, and other distractions, and had a long life. Ironically, NASA never put the new electrodes to use. Instead, this space-age device can now be found in exercise equipment made by Heart Rate, Inc., the company awarded the NASA license to produce the technology.

Heart Rate, Inc. in Costa Mesa, California, makes use of the electrodes in their Versa-Climber—a machine that exercises both the upper and lower body by simulating climbing motion. The climber places his or her thumbs on ultrasensitive detection pads, which continuously monitor the exerciser's heart rate, and through a wireless system, controls the intensity of the workout. If the workout is too difficult and the heart rate rises above the climber's target training range, the Versa-Climber automatically slows down. The VersaClimber also relies on data from the NASA electrodes to take the climber through a warm-up and cool-down.

Phoning Home

Once a method was devised to monitor an astronaut's heart rate, scientists then had to get that information back to Earth. For this feat, NASA turned to telemetry—data sent via radio signals. Explains Leonard Ault, deputy director for technology transfer at NASA headquarters in Washington, D.C.: "In the very early phases of NASA programs, we sent unmanned spacecraft to the Moon, and the photos were telemetered back to Earth."

The pictures were sent in a digitized form. That is, if you think of the picture as a piece of graph paper, each square on the graph is assigned a number, depending on its color. Zero might mean white, for instance; +3 might mean black. Back on Earth, a com-puter uses these numbers to reassemble the graph squares (technically known as picture elements, or pixels) into the original photo.

This technique can be used to send all types of data—from pictures to heart-wave patterns. An astronaut's heart rate, for instance, would be recorded in digital (number) form, in either plus or minus units. "A major spike on a cardiograph would show as maybe a +3," says Ault. Earth-based computers would then reconvert the numbers sent via radio waves back into cardiograph form.

Wireless telemetry allows for all sorts of remote monitoring, even on Earth. For example, nurses at central stations use this method to monitor the heart rates, electro-cardiograms, blood pressure, respiration, and temperature of intensive care patients.

Telemetry also allows for both the sending and receiving of data. Scientists can repro-gram satellites using radio signals. For this reason, telemetry has played a key role in the development of modern pacemakers. With bidirectional telemetry, doctors can re-

Telemetry—remote monitoring used to send data back and forth from the space shuttle to Earth—permits doctors to adjust the heart rate and voltage of pacemakers (left) at the patient's bedside (below) rather than in the operating room.

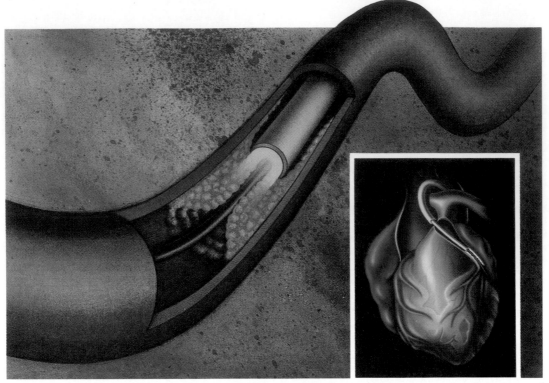

Space laser technology has been adapted to remove the plaque that clogs the arteries of the heart. A laser instrument is snaked through an artery (inset) where it burns away plaque without injuring vital tissues (above). The laser has received FDA approval for this application.

program a pacemaker without subjecting the patient to surgery.

"Our pacemakers tell doctors what the heart rate is set to, the voltage, and how much life is left in the battery," says Joe Schulman, Ph.D., chief scientist at Siemens Pacesetter in Sylmar, California. "There are about seven parameters you can set with a pacemaker."

However, Siemens Pacesetter takes the space connection one step further: they use a "shake-and-bake" technique to test their pacemakers. To test the electrical connections, Shulman explains, "We cycle our pacemakers between 0° and 50° C [32° to 122° F] in an oven. Then we put it on a vibration table and shake it, just like they do with satellites. Our pacemaker is like a satellite. When you put something in space, you just can't go back up there to fix it."

Zap It!
A laser that zaps deposits in the coronary arteries certainly sounds like it comes from outer space—and it does.

James Laudenslager, Ph.D., helped develop the excimer laser for satellite-based atmospheric studies for NASA back in 1975,

when he was supervisor of the laser physics and applications group at the Jet Propulsion Laboratory (JPL) in Pasadena, California. The excimer laser soon captured the interest of other researchers who were investigating the use of lasers to clear clogged arteries in the human body. The excimer laser, which operates in an acceptable temperature range, emits light in just the right wavelength and pulse width to chip away pieces of arterial plaque without burning vital tissues.

To develop the excimer laser into a medical device, Laudenslager, the co-inventor Thomas Pacala, Ph.D., and other physicians teamed up to form Advanced Interventional Systems, Inc. (AIS) in Irvine, California. Today the excimer laser is approved by the Food and Drug Administration (FDA) for removing plaques that are difficult to treat through other techniques. The excimer is an ultraviolet pulse laser, says Laudenslager. "It ablates little chunks at a time instead of one huge energy burst. Other lasers aren't as controlled."

Well Suited
NASA's space-suit technology has come in handy for a number of problems here on

Earth. For people undergoing chemotherapy for the treatment of cancer, a special cap incorporating technology based on the protective cooling layer of a space suit can help prevent their hair from falling out. The cap, called the Chemo-Cooler, circulates liquid through plastic tubes to lower the surface temperature of the scalp. Used during the administration of chemotherapy, the cap helps reduce hair loss. In one study, 63 percent of the chemotherapy patients who used the cap lost virtually no hair.

The cap mimics the action of the liquid-cooling undergarment that astronauts wear beneath their space suits. Coolant circulating in that garment helps conduct heat away from the body. The idea for the Chemo-Cooler was developed at NASA's Johnson Space Center in Houston, Texas. A former NASA employee brought the cap to the market in 1985.

NASA space suits also benefit people with a rare syndrome known as hypohidrotic ectodermal dysplasia (HED). Such people are born without sweat glands, and thus are not able to regulate their body temperature. Fortunately, cool suits designed by Life Support Systems, Inc. (LSSI), in Mountainview, California, can help them. For victims of HED, LSSI's suits circulate coolant through a special vest and headpiece, effectively doing the work of the missing sweat glands to cool the body. LSSI also makes spin-offs of NASA cooling garments for people who work in extreme temperatures.

Perhaps the best-known spin-off of space suits, however, was in the case of David, "the bubble boy," whose life was the focus of much press and even a television movie. Born with severe combined immune deficiency, which left him without any defenses against disease, David only could survive in a

Cool suits that mimic the liquid-cooling undergarments worn by astronauts are used to conduct heat away from the bodies of people who are born without sweat glands.

sterile environment. To create a sterile plastic home for him, NASA scientists and physicians at Baylor College of Medicine and Texas Children's Hospital relied on technology originally designed to isolate astronauts in quarantine when they returned from expeditions to the Moon. "They didn't know if astronauts would bring back microbes from the Moon," says Doris Rouse, Ph.D., director of the NASA Technology Application team for the Research Triangle Institute in Research Triangle Park, North Carolina, a contractor that helps NASA find additional applications for its technology. David lived for 12 years in his special world isolated from any bacteria or other invaders that could have caused disease.

Pump It Up

Tiny pumps and valves that helped search for life on Mars during NASA's Viking missions are now bringing new life to insulin-dependent diabetics on Earth. On Mars the Viking probes searched for the presence of life by pumping life-supporting nutrients into Martian soil samples. As always, when it comes to space travel, the equipment for the experiments was as light and compact as possible. "Weight is at such an extreme premium when you're flying payloads, that you try to make everything as light as you can," says Donald Friedman, formerly chief of NASA's Office of Commercial Programs. "You use the most miniature technology and materials you can."

The miniature fluid-control system turned out to be just the right size for delivering tiny pulses of insulin—in doses as small as one-millionth of a liter—into the body. MiniMed Technologies of Sylmar, California, makes two such systems. One is an external insulin pump about the size of a deck of cards. Worn outside the body attached to clothing, the pump delivers a steady infusion of tiny doses of insulin throughout the day, mimicking the action of a healthy pancreas. The wearer can program the insulin doses to fit his or her individual needs.

MiniMed also makes an internally implanted insulin pump that is currently undergoing clinical trials in 11 centers in the United States. The implantable pump, about the size of a hockey puck, is surgically inserted between the skin and the muscle, just above the waist. The device holds a three-month supply of insulin, and can be refilled easily with a special hypodermic needle. Like its external cousin, the implantable pump can be programmed to meet the individual's insulin needs.

Tiny pumps developed for the Viking Mars mission are now used in diabetics to deliver a steady dose of insulin for up to three months.

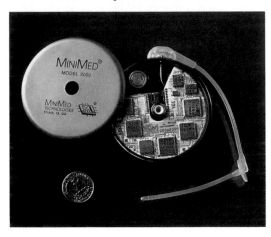

Picture-Perfect

Those satellite images the weatherman points to on TV every night aren't beamed down to Earth in the glorious, full-color form that you see. Instead, the satellites transmit their data in the form of digital information, with, as noted earlier, each pixel assigned a specific color value. It is up to Earth-bound computers to translate all those digits into a full-color weather map.

The same systems that unscramble satellite photos are being used to make sense of pictures of the body. At Perceptive Scientific Instruments in League City, Texas, for instance, researchers are using image-pro-

cessing techniques to analyze chromosomes and DNA. "An image is an image—be it from a satellite or a camera on top of a microscope," says Don Winkler, vice president of sales and marketing and a former NASA employee. "You can generate a pixel, or a measurement of brightness, from a microscope or a satellite. Then it comes down to your ability to manipulate those pixels to measure size, shape, color, and position.

"With image processing, we can bring something out that's buried away in the muck. We can measure it, identify its texture, its position within the image."

Although Winkler's company focuses this technology on cytogenetics, other companies apply image processing to CAT scans and magnetic resonance imaging (MRI). For instance, image processing can help bring out a tumor in a chest X ray. Applying a false color to the tumor might help a physician quickly spot the growth. With CAT scans, image processing permits visualization of cross sections of the body at almost any angle or orientation. MRI also relies on image processing to sharpen contrasts, eliminate unimportant details, and color-code body organs.

Scratching the Surface

An ultrasound system that hunts for microscopic flaws in the surface of spacecraft and airplanes is also helping doctors heal burns. Knowing the depth of a burn is critical for proper treatment. However, except in severe cases with extensive destruction of tissue, it is often difficult to judge depth. The Supra Scanner, developed by Topox, Inc. in Chadds Ford, Pennsylvania, can determine the depth of a burn by bouncing ultrasonic waves off the wound. Such accurate measurement can help doctors to speed healing and reduce the chances of infection.

In addition to determining burn depth, the Supra Scanner can also detect and analyze other skin problems, including wounds and precancerous and cancerous moles. Jack Cantwell, president and chief executive officer of Topox, found a melanoma on his own skin using the device. Fortunately, the cancer was only on the surface—just as the Supra Scanner predicted it would be.   ◇

Who's Reading Your Medical Records?

by Jeff Goldberg

So highly personal is your medical record that, as part of their Hippocratic oath, doctors are honor-bound to protect your privacy. In the electronic age of computerized record keeping, however, the confidential medical record, like the doctor's house call, may become a thing of the past.

As patient files are crunched into computer databanks for easy access by insurers and health-care providers, consumers have reason to be concerned. "People have no idea what's in these data bases," says Charles Inlander, president of a health-consumer organization, the People's Medical Society. "You apply for health insurance or a job and find out you've been turned down because of your medical history. What history?"

Computerized medical records have become an essential and growing part of our modern health-care system, saving billions of dollars of administrative overhead. Insurance companies, hospitals, managed-health-care organizations, corporations, and even doctors' offices, maintain extensive databanks to track the medical information of patients, clients, and employees.

Applicants for individual life, disability, and health insurance, for example, are routinely required to sign waivers authorizing the release of their medical records to the Medical Information Bureau Inc. (MIB), a Massachu-

setts-based company that acts as a credit bureau for about 750 insurance companies. If someone applying for insurance has a condition that might affect her health, such as elevated blood pressure or evidence of cancer, member insurance companies are required to send a report to MIB. When applicants change insurance carriers, request further coverage, or apply for reimbursement of medical expenses, this information provides a quick check to see if they are telling the truth about their medical past. Currently, MIB stores health-information records on 15 million people—about one in seven insurance applicants—and is growing at a rate of 2.9 million records per year.

Each month, computer banks at the Tulsa-based CIS Technologies Inc.—the nation's fastest-growing "paperless" health-care-claims clearinghouse—store and process 1.5 million claims for more than 500 hospitals in 32 states. Instead of laboriously filling out lengthy claim forms and medical reports, hospital staffers feed coded data into this supercomputer network for rapid processing by insurers. Another company, Medstat Systems Inc., of Ann Arbor, Michigan, provides self-insured employers with information on trends in the utilization and cost of health care, gleaned from pooled hospital and doctors' records of some 6.3 million employees.

And computerized medical record keeping could become even more widespread: a nationwide "smart"-card-accessed databank, which would store and process medical billing and health information on virtually all Americans, was proposed by the Bush Administration's Secretary of Health and Human Services Louis Sullivan as a way of saving $20 billion annually by the year 2000 in health-care-related paperwork costs.

How Much Information?

What information appears in a typical database entry? Reports are likely to be brief, limited to basic information about a person's medical history. Entries are coded and usually contain such statistics as age, height, and weight, and medical information, such as blood pressure, electrocardiogram readings, and X rays. Psychiatric evaluations are sometimes included.

Strict disclosure rules have been instituted by Medstat and CIS Technologies. MIB president Neil Day asserts that the confidentiality of medical records on file at MIB is safeguarded by restricting access of potential insurers (a car insurer, for instance, cannot inspect the health-insurance records of an applicant), and by automatically erasing reports after seven years.

But Cory Franklin, M.D., an associate professor of medicine and medical ethics at Chicago's Cook County Hospital, warns that "electronic record keeping means that many more people than ever before have potential access to your confidential record." According to Mark Siegler, M.D., of the University of Chicago's Pritzker School of Medicine, there are already too many people who may have access to medical records of hospital patients: not only doctors, nurses, and medical students, but hospital financial officers, insurance auditors, quality-care assessors, social workers, physical therapists, and even clergy.

When Dr. Siegler surveyed the number of hospital personnel alone who had access to the records of one of his patients, he recalls, "I stopped counting at 75." Add to that figure all databank employees, including computer operators and researchers, and the figure could come close to 100.

Digitized medical records "also raise the Kafkaesque possibility that errors and misdiagnoses can become part of your permanent record at the push of a button," continues Dr. Franklin. Inputting errors aren't the only problem. John Burnum, M.D., a Tuscaloosa, Alabama, internist, insists that there is already an unacceptably high level of mistakes on medical records. He estimates that physicians may fail to note their patients' chief complaints in 27 percent of medical records, that mistakes occur in at least 1 out of every 20 laboratory reports, and that the accuracy of nearly half of all blood-cholesterol determinations is questionable.

Neil Day claims that mistakes are few; out of 40,000 inquiries to MIB last year, only 400 uncovered errors. But once a piece of incorrect information is in the system, it's there for good (unless, as with MIB, you are able to see your record and correct it—call 617-426-3660 for more information). Moreover, "a patient cannot easily be represented as a code," says Dr. Burnum. "When you strip patients of their uniqueness and report them as numbers, you're going to get more mistakes."

That's why Charles Inlander insists that medical records should be accessible to patients themselves. Currently, New York, California, and 15 other states have laws guaranteeing patients the right to see their doctors', hospital, and mental-health records. However, in the remaining 33 states, patients may have to fight in court to see their files. The CIS and Medstat databases, for example, restrict virtually all outside parties, including patients, from seeing individual medical records.

But computerized medical databases could lead to another, possibly more disturbing, problem. In many cases, insurance companies, complaining of soaring costs, already refuse to pay for illnesses relating to "previous conditions." As growing data banks become ever more efficient at weeding out the sickest individuals, the original purpose of insurance—to spread the costs of a few over many so that care is accessible to everyone in need—is jeopardized. Ironically, the people with the best access to medical care may end up being those who need it least. ◇

CROWNS AND BRIDGES

by Diana Reese

Munching on popcorn while watching his favorite video, Sam Stengle jerks up in his seat. One of his back teeth has made a foreboding "crack" after biting down on an unpopped kernel. Fearing the worst, he drags himself to the dentist.

After examining the fractured tooth, Sam's dentist recommends a crown to repair the damage. Sam's heart sinks at the news. He can feel his apprehension growing, even though the procedure isn't scheduled to begin for another week.

Fortunately, Sam's anxiety is unfounded. Prosthodontic dentistry, which focuses on restoring tooth function and preventing further damage, has come a long way since 400 B.C., when the Phoenicians used gold wire to secure artificial teeth made of ivory. Today the installation of crowns—or their cousins, bridges—is a more precise undertaking. And while no dentist can guarantee an entirely pain-free operation, artificial tooth replacement is a simple procedure that no longer need instill patients with terror.

Crowning Achievement

A crown—or cap, as many people call it—is a cover for the entire outer surface of a tooth that has been weakened by decay and recurrent fillings. A crown is also used for a tooth that is cracked or fractured; it may also be needed after a tooth has undergone root-canal surgery. In some cases, caps are purely cosmetic, although this practice is becoming much less common, especially since the advent of much more effective cosmetic dental techniques.

The installation of a crown usually requires two visits to the dental office. During the first visit, the dentist removes a thin layer of enamel, the hard outer layer of teeth, from all the surfaces of the tooth.

Next the patient bites into impression material to create what University of Maryland dental researcher Dianne Rekow D.D.S., M.S., Ph.D., calls a "three-dimensional negative of the teeth." This impression is sent to a laboratory, where a wax model is made that is used to cast a custom-fit crown. A temporary crown of composite resin or plastic protects the tooth until the patient returns.

At the second visit, the permanent crown is "seated" on the tooth and then cemented, a process that typically takes only a few minutes.

A variety of materials of varying costs are used to make crowns. The most common options are listed on the following page.

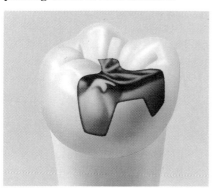
For a three-surface tooth restoration, the dentist might use silver amalgam, cast alloy, or composite resins, depending on the tooth's location.

For a front tooth, porcelain is the restoration material of choice. In both color and translucency, porcelain closely resembles natural tooth.

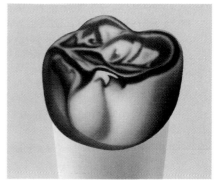
A full cast alloy crown is generally a mixture of gold and other metals. The metallic composition gives the tooth the strength needed for chewing.

• **Gold.** This is actually mixed with other metals to form an alloy that is stronger than pure gold. It is the most durable crown material available. It's usually used on the molars, not only because these teeth are out of sight, but also because the back teeth require maximum strength for chewing.

• **Porcelain.** Like teeth, porcelain can transmit light, so it looks natural and is more esthetically pleasing than metal. But according to Robert S. Staffanou, D.D.S., M.S., retired professor and chair of fixed prosthodontics at Baylor University in Texas, "porcelain is very hard, but it's also very brittle, so it breaks easily." That consideration makes porcelain best for front teeth, where appearance is an important consideration and chewing forces are less. Porcelain crowns are thicker, so they require an additional half-millimeter of tooth enamel to be removed.

Porcelain can also be hard on other teeth. "Porcelain is very abrasive to the opposing teeth," explains Gerald Barrack, D.D.S., clinical professor of restorative and prosthodontic sciences at New York University College of Dentistry. "It's possible it can wear away the natural teeth."

• **Porcelain bonded to metal.** The metal provides a structural framework, adding strength to the crown. But the metal also makes the crown less attractive because it shows through the porcelain.

• **Porcelain and gold.** This "compromise" crown uses porcelain on the sides of the tooth, and gold for the biting surface.

• **Precious metals.** Palladium, a member of the platinum family, is one of these. It is less expensive than gold, but also not as strong.

• **Nonprecious metals.** These are the least expensive crown materials. They sometimes contain nickel, a potential problem since it is estimated that up to 10 percent of females and 1 percent of males are allergic to this metal.

Researchers are working on new materials that look more natural, yet are

Computers Enter the Act

A custom-made crown in just one dental visit? No temporary caps? Sounds pretty exciting—and it's within the realm of possibility. Computer technology known as computer-aided design/computer-aided manufacturing, or CAD/CAM, is the key. It involves three steps:

1. Acquiring the data. A photograph of an impression of the teeth is taken, and that information is fed into the computer. In the future, however, tiny intra-oral cameras may snap photos inside of the mouth, skipping the impression stage. Dianne Rekow, D.D.S., M.S., Ph.D., of the University of Maryland, is working with a robot arm that runs a probe over teeth.

2. Designing the crown. With a mental map of the teeth, the computer can calculate the dimensions of a custom-made crown.

3. Making the crown. The computer generates commands to drive a milling machine that, according to Rekow, "looks like a monster-sized drill," which grinds out the crown.

One system, created in France, can do full crowns, says Jack D. Preston, D.D.S., chair of oral and maxillofacial imaging at the University of Southern California in Los Angeles. "It can completely design the crown out of either porcelain or metal, such as titanium," he explains. So far, gold is not economically feasible because of the waste involved in milling. And the system can do only single crowns, not bridges.

Milling crowns instead of casting them may open up a whole new field of materials from which to choose. Titanium, for example, is "much less expensive than gold but very, very difficult to cast," says Rekow, "but it can be milled."

Preston believes that single-visit crowns will be "fairly common within the decade."

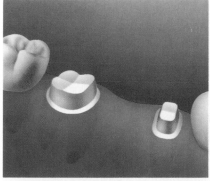
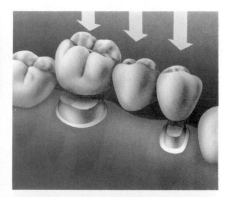
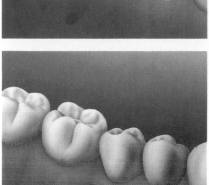
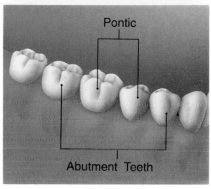

A single missing tooth is usually replaced with a three-unit bridge. First, the teeth adjacent to the gap are prepared (upper left). Next, a custom-made bridge is fitted and adjusted (upper right). After any adjustments are made, the bridge is cemented into place (lower left). When more than one tooth is missing, a multi-unit bridge is made; the artificial teeth, called pontics, are fastened to the abutment teeth adjacent to the gap (lower right).

Pontic

Abutment Teeth

stronger, says Atlanta dentist Ronald E. Goldstein, D.D.S., author of *Change Your Smile* (Quintessence Publishing) and *Esthetics in Dentistry*. (J. B. Lippincott). Newer types of porcelains and ceramics are evolving—some are bonded to metal oxide or to gold foil. Castable glass is another option, producing an almost clear-looking crown, which can have color added to the surface.

Bonding is also improving crowns. In bonding, the application of composite resin, a puttylike plastic containing microscopic pieces of glass, adheres to the tooth surface for a strong seal. It is now being substituted for dental cement to hold crowns in place.

"Composite resin helps seal up the surface flaws in porcelain crowns that cause them to fail," explains Jack D. Preston, D.D.S., chair of oral and maxillofacial imaging at the University of Southern California in Los Angeles, and editor of the *International Journal of Prosthodontics*. "Using the resin to cement the crown can cut the failure rate down to 1 percent."

Remember, though, that nothing lasts forever. Most crowns will have to be replaced after 5 to 20 or more years.

Bridging the Gap

For people missing one or more teeth, a fixed bridge may be necessary. "Fixed partial denture is the correct term," says Barrack, "but the public knows it as a bridge." It cannot be removed, because it is anchored by crowns on the teeth of both sides of the space.

The artificial tooth, called the pontic, is fastened to crowns placed on the teeth adjacent to the space, called the abutment teeth. A framework of thin metal, or sometimes porcelain fused over metal, holds the bridge together. Up to six teeth in front can be replaced, says Staffanou.

In some cases, a single missing tooth can be replaced using a bridge that is bonded with composite resin to the tongue side of the abutment teeth. Using this method, it is not necessary to crown the abutment teeth.

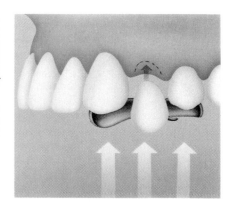

The Alternatives to Crowns and Bridges

Movie stars of old often had their front teeth capped so they could flash the brightest smile possible at the cameras and at their fans. Not so for today's celebrities. Improvements in cosmetic dentistry have made crowns for purely aesthetic reasons obsolete.

"When I first started practicing more than 35 years ago, I did 75 percent crowns and 25 percent restorations," says Atlanta dentist Ronald E. Goldstein, D.D.S., author of *Change Your Smile* and *Esthetics in Dentistry*. "Now it's 25 percent crowns and 75 percent other aesthetic procedures."

Credit the revolution in dental materials for these changing statistics. Bonding uses composite resin, a putty-like material of plastic resins and microscopic glass that is coated on the front surface of the tooth, hardened with a special light, and then shaped and polished. The surface of the tooth is first lightly etched with acid, but the enamel does not have to be removed as it does for a crown.

Porcelain veneers, another option, resemble artificial fingernails in that they are false fronts for teeth. They are made of thin pieces of porcelain that help transmit light like a genuine tooth. About half as much enamel is removed as for a crown, and from only the front side of the tooth, says Goldstein, before the veneer is bonded to the tooth.

Occasionally, a tooth that is damaged can be repaired with an inlay or onlay, instead of a crown. A normal filling is held in by the tooth itself, but an inlay fits "like a tight dresser drawer" and is cemented in. An onlay holds the tooth together and is shaped like a staple. "It is not placed under the gum line like a crown, and not as much tooth surface is removed for it," explains Gerald Barrack, D.D.S., clinical professor of restorative and prosthodontic sciences at New York University College of Dentistry.

When it comes to replacing missing teeth, the dental implant is the latest technique. A metal root is surgically implanted into the gum tissue to anchor the artificial tooth. In some cases, implants and fixed bridges may even be combined in order to give the bridge more stability.

Why go to the expense and bother of filling the space left by just one tooth? Unfortunately, the remaining teeth will shift into the space, affecting the bite and chewing efficiency, increasing the risk for cavities and gum disease, and even changing the appearance of the face.

A variation on the fixed bridge was developed in 1980 at the University of Maryland. Referred to as the Maryland bridge, it substitutes metal wings, or backings, for the crowns, which are bonded with composite resin to the abutment teeth on the lingual, or tongue, sides. "It saves the face of the tooth," says Barrack. "Where indicated, it's a much more conservative treatment."

The advantages: It can avoid crowning healthy teeth. It is also less expensive and requires less time in the dental chair. That makes it an attractive option for children—the nerves in young teeth tend to be large and can be damaged by the trauma of a crown. The elderly or dentally fearful who dread the time a crown takes may prefer the Maryland bridge as well, "It's easier from the patient's standpoint," says Staffanou.

There are disadvantages. It is not as strong as the conventional fixed bridge. And it can't be used for everyone—the dentist must check the patient's bite and the stability of the abutment teeth before deciding.

Some people had difficulties with the Maryland bridge when it was first introduced. "If it's not done properly, it can fall out," Barrack says. But if constructed properly, it can last as long as a regular bridge; he cites studies that show more than 90 percent success after 11 years. ◇

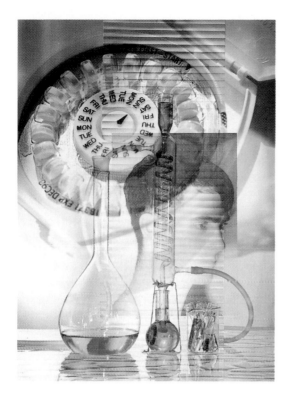

THE FUTURE of MALE CONTRACEPTION

by Brian Feinberg

Common sense says that birth control is the responsibility of both members of a sexually active couple. In reality, men have a decidedly limited number of contraceptive options, and often it is left to women to take a pill or use some other chemically based method of family planning. Current research, however, holds the promise of sophisticated treatments that will someday remove much of the birth-control burden from female shoulders.

It has been suggested that new contraceptive technology places the bulk of the responsibility on women because males have traditionally dominated birth-control research. Pharmaceutical companies have also been blamed for a perceived lack of interest on their part in developing male contraceptives. One reason for their reluctance to develop such products may be a concern that the market for such offerings may not be lucrative enough. If these factors do play a part in the lack of birth-control choices for men, however, there is another, more basic problem that must be considered as well. Simply put, scientists have found it easier to stop the release each month of a single egg during ovulation than to find a safe, effective means of inhibiting the production of millions of sperm cells per day.

Nonetheless, several new and promising forms of male birth control are currently being investigated.

The Implant Approach

One potential product, an implant, would target follicle-stimulating hormone (FSH), the chemical that triggers sperm production. Under normal circumstances the release of FSH from the pituitary gland is stimulated by luteinizing hormone-releasing hormone (LHRH), secreted from the area of the brain known as the hypothalamus. LHRH binds to receptor sites on the pituitary, stimulating the secretion of FSH, as well as another substance, luteinizing hormone (LH), which is responsible for the release of testosterone from the testes. Testosterone, which is a male hormone, or androgen, is necessary for retaining a man's sex drive and secondary sexual characteristics, such as facial hair.

The male implant device now under investigation would utilize two capsules, one containing a synthetic, modified form of LHRH. Seeping through the implant and into the bloodstream, the chemical would bind to the pituitary receptor sites more readily than natural LHRH does, blocking the path of the natural molecules. Since the synthetic form does not provoke the release of LH or FSH, it would prevent sperm production. Aside from that, however, the chemical would also inhibit the secretion of testosterone. To make up for the lost hormone, a second implanted capsule would release a synthetic androgen. The implant research is being conducted by the Population Council, a non-profit, nongovernmental organization that, among other activities, investigates new contraceptive technology. Human testing of the implant may get under way in 1993, says Rosemarie B. Thau, Ph.D., director of contraceptive development for the group.

The Vaccine Approach

The Population Council is also attempting to develop a male contraceptive vaccine, using molecules of LHRH that have been linked to molecules of tetanus toxoid (a harmless substance derived from the poison that causes tetanus). These combined molecules are designed to stimulate the body's immune system to produce antibodies against LHRH, says Thau. Antibodies are produced by the immune system against foreign substances, which protect the body from invading viruses and bacteria. In this case, however, the antibodies would prevent LHRH from acting on the pituitary gland and stimulating the release of LH and FSH. Animal studies indicate that the effects of the vaccine are reversible, so that as antibody concentration decreases in the bloodstream, the sperm count will rise again. A synthetic-androgen implant would be used with this method as well, to replace lost testosterone. Limited human testing has been performed on the male contraceptive vaccine, but Thau hopes to see the research expanded soon.

Testosterone Enanthate

Another contraceptive study, an international venture funded by the World Health Organization (WHO) and the U.S. government, is being conducted on human subjects using weekly injections of a modified form of testosterone. High levels of the substance, testosterone enanthate (TE), in the bloodstream again suppress sperm manufacture by causing the pituitary gland to reduce production of FSH. Moreover, the altered version remains in the bloodstream longer than normal testosterone would, says C. Alvin Paulsen, M.D., professor emeritus of medicine at the University of Washington School of Medicine in Seattle, and head of that school's portion of the testosterone study.

So far, researchers have found that, on average, sperm counts have fallen to zero, or at least dropped undetectably low, in only about 67 percent of the men treated with TE, says Paulsen. Those who did fall into this group were asked to take part in a field trial, he says, which means that for one year "the weekly injections of testosterone were their only form of contraception." Out of 157 couples involved in the trial, he says, only one pregnancy occurred. The next phase of the research, begun in 1989, involves men whose sperm count dropped extremely low after taking the drug, but was still detectable. Researchers want to know whether, even with this slightly higher sperm count, these men have been rendered effectively infertile.

Paulsen emphasizes that, although the project is expected to yield valuable information, a large number of men would probably not want to use a contraceptive that required weekly injections, "although it would be suitable for well-motivated people."

A promising alternative to TE may be the drug testosterone buciclate, which early research suggests may reduce the number of injections required to four per year.

Gossypol

Since the 1970s a great deal of public attention has been focused on another possible contraceptive, gossypol, a chemical found in cottonseed oil. First isolated in Russia in the late 19th century, gossypol gained the spotlight in 1971, when it was linked to infertility in China among men who ate food mixed with uncooked cottonseed oil.

Chinese researchers have indicated that gossypol is indeed an effective form of male birth control, suppressing sperm production without halting the secretion of testosterone. The chemical is not hazard-free, however. Chinese preliminary research suggests that gossypol can reduce potassium levels in the bloodstream, which in turn can lead to irregular heartbeat. Moreover, the drug has left some men irreversibly infertile.

Scientists began new human gossypol trials in 1992. The international study is designed to find the correct dosage that prevents pregnancy, but does not cause permanent infertility.   ◇

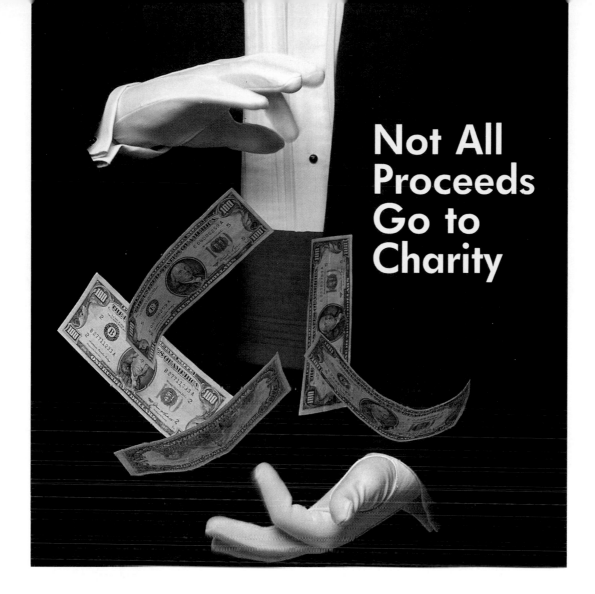

Not All Proceeds Go to Charity

by Alice Naude

When an official-looking envelope arrived in the mail, Janet Brown's imagination spun out a not uncommon fantasy: what she would do when she won the lottery. A letter inside said she had already won a $5,000 cash sweepstakes, and her name had been entered in a $50,000 drawing to take place later in the year. The letterhead bore the seal of a Washington, D.C., law firm; below the seal was a telephone number and the name of an attorney who explained he had been retained to notify the winning contestants. To collect her prize, all she had to do was fill out a release form and send it, along with a $5 donation, to the Cancer Fund of America.

From Janet's point of view, that wasn't a lot to ask. With $5,000 coming her way, she

could easily donate $5 for cancer research. In fact, the letter said she was under no obligation to make a contribution in order to claim her winnings, but Janet thought an organization that was professional enough to hire lawyers to conduct its business was worthy of a donation.

What she didn't know was that the telephone number on the letterhead rang in an office in Utah, and the Washington, D.C., law firm didn't even exist. Later she found out that thousands of people had received letters identical to hers. About five of them got checks in the mail for $100. She eventually found herself looking at a check for 40 cents.

Janet Brown was out $5, but she'd gained some street smarts about fraudulent sweepstakes. Unfortunately, she also became suspicious of any charitable organizations that sent her solicitations, particularly ones that claimed to be raising money for cancer.

Her story has a happier ending than most. In 1991 attorneys general in Connecticut, Pennsylvania, and eight other states won a large settlement from Watson & Hughey Company, the organization that had been running the scam sweepstakes, and their associate Robert Stone, the Washington, D.C., lawyer whose signature was on the bottom of the letter Janet had received. The settlement was the largest ever in a national charitable-solicitation case.

It's a sad fact that health charities are commonly victims of look-alike scams and fund-raising ploys. Cancer organizations are particularly susceptible. There's a generous "there but for the grace of God go I" response to requests for help in fighting the disease. This response is so generous that by some estimates, $15 million to $20 million is believed to be siphoned off each year by fraudulent "cancer charities," says Mike Herron, communications vice president of the American Cancer Society.

And cancer charities are not the only ones subject to fraud. The Multiple Sclerosis Foundation Inc. sounds a lot like the Multiple Sclerosis Society. But the two are very different. The state of Connecticut has sued the MS Foundation for playing on the good reputation of the MS Society and falsely telling donors that their contributions would go to helping individuals with MS, when the money was not actually used for that purpose.

Connecticut went after the MS Foundation for using manipulative fund-raising techniques, such as telling potential donors that they were on record as having given previously. It was here that the sound-alike name served the MS Foundation particularly well.

Margret Bower, associate director of the Philanthropic Advisory Service of the Better Business Bureau (BBB), says that, in general, there is relatively little fraud in the char-

Health charity organizations are common victims of look-alike scams and fund-raising ploys.

A Sampling of Health Charities

Many health charities are shifting their focus to respond to new developments in disease research or the changing health-care needs in the United States today. The following is an update on what some of the larger organizations are focusing on today.

The **American Heart Association** (AHA) is unchanged in its dedication to fighting cardiovascular disease through education programs on nutrition and the hazards of smoking. What *is* changing is the way the charity approaches the public it wishes to educate. The AHA has realized it has not been effective enough in bringing its message to minorities and the poor. Allison Groom, communications and marketing consultant for the AHA, says, "Most of the issues they are con-

cerned with day to day do not connect with heart disease, and so we're trying to make the materials more applicable." In addition, the AHA is putting together more low-literacy pamphlets and public-service announcements geared toward Hispanics and African-Americans.

"The over-55 age group is another target audience," Groom says. "Often the attitude here is, 'I've gone this far, and I know lots of healthy people in their nineties; why should I worry about heart disease?'—when in fact, this group is highly susceptible."

The **Arthritis Foundation** (AF) also says it is leaning toward a marketing approach to better target the services it offers. It, too, has a relatively new cultural-diversity program to reach a broader cross section of the population. Generally AF's programs are based on exercise and self-help support for people with the disease.

itable and non-profit sector. When it occurs, she adds, it is more likely to happen in local organizations than in large national charities. Still, as the sweepstakes and sound-alike name scams show, the big guys are vulnerable, too.

The National Charities Information Bureau (NCIB), a watchdog organization for fraudulent charities, provides the public with information on how not-for-profit organizations use donated funds. Dan Langan, director of public information for the NCIB, says that fund-raising sweepstakes are on the decline. But, he adds, there are always new forms of fraud popping up. A relatively new one has surfaced in Florida, preying on the large pool of elderly contributors who live there.

Langan explains that in this fraud, a fund-raiser calls on the phone. No matter what the response of the potential contributor is —"I don't give over the phone," "please call back another time," or "send me some information about your organization in the mail"— he or she will be sent an official-looking invoice for a certain dollar amount allegedly pledged during that phone conversation.

Many organizations raise money by canvassing door-to-door. Potential contributors should always request identification of the solicitor and information on the charity before donating.

"Often senior citizens are forgetful about what they have said to people over the phone," says Langan, "or a spouse may think his or her partner made the pledge."

Inflating Charity's Spending

Some charitable fraud never even reaches the contributing public. Currently, a number of "health charities" are being fingered in a

A breakthrough in cystic-fibrosis research in 1989, with the discovery of the gene that causes this disorder, has allowed the **Cystic Fibrosis Foundation** to focus on drug therapies. Robert Dressig, president of the foundation, says a number of treatments now look promising, and some are in the final phases of clinical trials.

The **American Cancer Society** (ACS), which has the biggest budget for cancer research in the country, says it has been working for the past two years to pare back the number of its programs to focus on core activities. The group has focused its programs, carried out through its affiliates, on four areas: breast cancer, tobacco, information and guidance for patients, and comprehensive school health education. On the nonprogram side, the ACS will also focus on fund-raising and increasing the number of its volunteers.

"For breast cancer, we want to focus on three groups of people," says Mike Herron, communications vice president for ACS. They are women over 65, poor women, and Hispanic women. Older women are particularly important. "Most American women feel at retirement age that they have squeaked past cancer," Herron says "Nothing could be farther from the truth."

The **March of Dimes** is another charity that is focusing its activities. Since the 1950s the group has been dedicated to preventing and treating birth defects. In the past few years, it has also stepped up its work on infant mortality, low-birth weight, and prenatal care, with emphasis on the importance of getting a healthy start for a healthy baby. Nonetheless, research into birth defects remains the single biggest program conducted by the March of Dimes.

complex scam of paper transactions devised to falsely inflate the charity's spending profile —creating the illusion that the organization is giving thousands of dollars to public programs and needy people.

In this scheme, one charity will transfer or "donate" gifts to another charity, and then claim the value of the gifts as part of its public-spending programs. The problem is that the so-called "gifts" are sometimes worthless items that the recipient has no use for. Their only usefulness lies in the grossly inflated value the donating charity claims for them.

For example, Cancer Fund of America has been charged with sending expired vegetable seeds—which the organization acquired for about $25,000—to a group called the Famine Relief Fund. Cancer Fund is said to have then reported that this transfer constituted $2.4 million in assistance to cancer patients.

Another organization, Children's Wish Foundation International, said it spent $2.8 million on "children's relief," part of this being the donation of $800,000 worth of books to two hospitals in Romania. But according to Richard Blumenthal, Connecticut's attorney general, these books, all written in English, could be seen as more of a burden than a benefit for the hospital. They included 3,375 copies of *Principles of Accounting,* 1,525 copies of *Bulbs for Summer,* and 220 copies of *Broadcasting in America.*

Children's Wish Foundation may say it is donating books, but Attorney General Blumenthal calls it "cooking the books" and has sued a total of six charities involved in this type of shady commodity trading. Connecticut again has been joined by the state of Pennsylvania in this case. Both states are widely recognized for their activities in fighting charitable fraud.

Mr. Blumenthal asserts that one reason the charities may have been involved in this scam is to boost their giving programs to a level that would qualify them for membership in the Independent Charities of America (ICA). This group, which solicits donations from government employees who contribute through payroll deductions, donated thousands of dollars in 1992 to two of the charities Connecticut is suing.

Giving Is Still a Healthy Business

Over the past decade, the number of organizations soliciting donors has increased by as much as 40 percent. At the same time, the 1986 tax reform made charitable contributions less readily deductible, a fact that has slowed the growth in charitable giving. And a recessionary economy doesn't help.

Yet, surprisingly, it has not hurt as much as one might think. According to the American Association of Fund Raising Councils, charitable giving in 1991 was up 1.4 percent.

Many celebrities contribute their time and money to charitable organizations. Celebrity endorsement of a fundraising drive often leads to increased donations from the general public.

Donor Beware

The National Charities Information Bureau (NCIB) and the Better Business Bureau (BBB) offer some basic pointers to help you avoid charity fraud:

• *Check out the name carefully.* Whether you are solicited by mail, over the phone, or in person, take a moment to make sure the charity is one with which you are familiar, and not one trading on confusion by soliciting under a similar name.

• *Evaluate the appeal.* Emotional messages are intended to sway donors, but look for the substance of the appeal—just what is it asking from you, and what does it promise to do with your donation?

• *Means versus ends.* You can decide if you wish to support research to find a cure, or social services to patients and their families.

• *Know who is soliciting you.* You absolutely have the right to ask whether the person requesting money is a volunteer or a paid employee of a fund-raising firm. If it is the latter, ask how much of your donation will actually go to the charity.

• *Don't feel intimidated by the methods of solicitation.* Letters may have "Urgent" or "Immediate" printed on them, but this doesn't mean you have to react this way. It takes weeks to prepare an appeal. This entitles donors to time to decide how they wish to respond. If the appeal includes some kind of gift or merchandise, you are under no obligation to pay for it, or even to send it back.

The Philanthropic Advisory Service of the BBB also points out that an appeal should not be disguised as a bill or an invoice. Unless there is a disclaimer, this kind of solicitation is illegal.

• *Be wary of phone solicitations.* Be sure to ask very specific questions about the charity involved. Pointed questions are likely to scare off a fraudulent caller. Also, avoid making donations in cash and never give your credit card number over the phone.

• Both NCIB and the BBB warn against charity sweepstakes. "Even though a lot of charities use them as ways to raise money," says BBB's Bower, "the chances of winning a prize are not great." Further, there is absolutely no obligation to give money to a charity in order to be part of the sweepstakes. If a solicitation tells you this, the sweepstakes constitutes a lottery and is illegal.

Though this is no great gain, holding steady in tough times is good news for any business.

Indeed, most of the council's statistics on charitable giving are heartwarming. Overall charitable donations in 1991 stacked up to $124.77 billion, about $9.68 billion of which were earmarked for health charities. About 82 percent of the contributions came from individual donors, about 5 percent from corporations, and 6 percent each from foundations and bequests. Overall, about 72 percent of American households made charitable contributions in 1991.

Because individual contributors are the stronghold of American giving, it is no surprise they become the targets of fraudulent schemes. Unfortunately, blatant fraud is not the only worry. With charitable dollars so precious, it becomes ever more important for the donor to know exactly how his or her money is being spent. Most charities unquestionably are committed to programs that are beyond reproach. It is their fund-raising techniques—or the ratio of spending to programs—that may fall short of what a donor would like to support.

A case in point occurs when charities hire professional fund-raisers to solicit over the telephone. Connecticut, which has monitored telephone solicitations for five years, says that of the $8.9 million its residents paid to telephone solicitors in 1991, only about 29 percent reached the organization to which people thought they were giving. To make matters worse, the net for some charities was as low as 10 percent.

There has been some court activity to regulate how much a charity can spend on fund-

For many years, the Red Cross has worked at home and abroad to help victims of disaster and war. Above, American food aid is delivered to Russia via the Red Cross.

raising, most of it unsuccessful. In 1984 the U.S. Supreme Court ruled that states cannot limit a charity's rights to solicit funds just because its fund-raising costs seem high. In response the Connecticut General Assembly mandated in 1986 that, at the very least, professional fund-raisers must disclose to potential contributors how much of their donation the charity would actually receive. But in 1988 the U.S. Supreme Court overturned this requirement, ruling that this kind of disclosure violates the First Amendment.

Without judicial support, it remains largely up to potential donors to figure out if their money is being spent in the way they'd like it to be spent. This is no small task, especially for the modest contributor. Luckily for donors, there are a number of independent organizations who help potential givers with this kind of assessment.

If you are thinking of giving to a charity and want to size up how your funds will be spent, it's probably best to start with the New York City-based National Charities Information Bureau (NCIB). As a benchmark the NCIB claims that any charity winning its approval must spend at least 60 percent of its budget on programs that carry out its mission.

For more information about a charity contact:
The National Charities Information Bureau
19 Union Square West
New York, NY 10003
212-929-6300

The NCIB's work doesn't stop there. The bureau keeps reports on about 300 organizations, rating their effectiveness based on certain criteria, including a charity's specificity of purpose, consistency of programs, use of educational information, and use of funds.

Although the NCIB covers most of the major health charities, more specific information about health organizations is also available from the National Health Council in Washington, D.C. This organization represents about 40 health agencies that comply with the council's standards for business. Though the council says it is not a watchdog agency, it does try to ferret out look-alike charities and organizations that abuse the system.

Those who are interested in giving large sums, or doing more thorough research before making a pledge, are best advised to ask the charity in question for written information. Request a copy of the most recent annual report and information on specific programs. A list of the charity's board members, recent achievements, and overall goals can also be helpful.

The truly investigative giver can go as far as looking at the charity's annual financial filing with the government. By law an organization's IRS form 990 must be easily accessible to the public. Such forms are generally available at an organization's office, the state's secretary of state or attorney general's office, or a state consumer-affairs agency.

Every annual report should break down how much the organization spends on programs, fund raising, management, and operations. The NCIB warns that an organization that spends more than 30 percent of its revenue on fund-raising certainly warrants more careful scrutiny.

Ultimate responsibility for responding to solicitations and giving wisely rests with the donor. Evaluating an appeal and deciding whether you think the organization runs its business well can be a difficult task. A contribution to charity, no matter how small, should make you feel good. Knowing that you are giving to a legitimate organization and that the money will be well spent is likely to make you feel even better. ◇

The sudden death of a loved one can impose a great emotional strain on surviving family and friends, a strain compounded by the immediacy with which a funeral must be planned and financed.

FINAL DECISIONS

by Christiane N. Brown

Most milestone events in life are thought out and planned for years in advance: buying a first home, sending the kids off to college, retiring from a job, and eventually, the settling of one's estate. But there is one last occasion that is generally left unplanned—the funeral. Despite death's inescapability, survivors are often left with as little as 24 hours to arrange and finance this complex event.

"It's the worst possible time to make important decisions," says David Reiners, information coordinator of the Funeral Service Consumer Assistance Program (FSCAP). "Family and friends of the deceased are emotionally distraught, with little idea what type of ceremony or burial was desired."

Any mistakes made are permanent, and usually quite costly. According to the Federated Funeral Directors of America, the average price of a traditional funeral today exceeds $3,500—and that doesn't include the cost of a cemetery plot or grave marker.

Fortunately, these days it is easy to avoid such dilemmas. Most funeral homes will let you plan your own funeral years *before* the actual event. It is called "pre-need," and it's the fastest growing area of the funeral business.

A pre-arranged funeral allows you time to make personal decisions about your body and burial. You can choose if you want to be cremated, buried, or both, and you can then select your own urn, casket, or cemetery site.

You can also decide whether you want a simple or elaborate ceremony.

"Making these decisions now will take a tremendous burden off friends and family when the time comes," says Jack Springer, executive director of the Cremation Association of North America. "The kids won't be left wondering, 'Is this really what Dad would have wanted?'"

Shopping for a Funeral

Despite the emotional nature of a funeral, try to treat the arrangements as you would any other major financial transaction, advises Bruce A. Holstrom, the president of the Prearrangement Association of America. Do your homework and have a general idea of what type of funeral you want. Here are the most common funeral services and burial options and what they cost:

In-ground Burial. A traditional funeral with an earth burial is the most popular option —and usually the most expensive. The casket is often the most costly item, usually 40 to 60 percent of the total funeral cost. The most basic model, made of soft wood, plywood, or fiberboard, costs an average of $125 to $150, while the top of the line solid oak casket is about $16,000.

You will probably need to purchase a burial container, called a rough box, outer burial vault, or grave liner. This container is lowered into the grave prior to burial. A lid prevents the ground from caving in. Choices range from a concrete box for about $250 to a solid steel or copper vault, which starts at about $2,200.

No matter what type of funeral you select, every funeral director will charge a fee for his or her services ($500 to $700). This nondeclinable charge covers part of the funeral home's overhead, supervising charges, and clerical help. Additional expenses for a traditional funeral include embalming ($225 to $275), although a closed-casket funeral may eliminate this cost; rental of the funeral home's facilities for the viewing ($150 to $200); securing death and burial certificates; church or funeral services; and transportation. Optional items include: flowers, obituary notices, music, police escorts, use of limousines, and memorial books.

Cemetery Arrangements

If you choose a traditional funeral or direct disposition, and desire burial in a cemetery, you will need to decide on a plot. Selecting a cemetery plot is almost always a separate transaction from arranging the funeral, but should also be planned and possibly pre-paid well in advance, says Larry Anspach, president of the Cemetery Consumer Service Council (CCSC).

The average cost of a cemetery plot is $1,500 to $2,000, depending on the area of the country and the location within the cemetery. There is also a charge for opening and closing of the grave ($275 to $325), which is usually not included in the price of the plot.

"Some cemeteries charge more for a plot at the time of death," says Anspach. "So it's smart to buy ahead and get a discount."

Financing is also available for grave plots if you buy ahead, permitting periodic installments over a fixed time period. But if you wait until the time of death, your survivors will have to pay all at once.

Before you sign a contract, make sure you check out the cemetery and specific site of the plot you wish to purchase in person. "Unscrupulous salespersons have been known to show buyers a photograph of another cemetery, and lead you to believe it's the one you're purchasing," says Anspach.

Also consider whether there are adjacent plots available in the cemetery should loved ones wish to be buried close to your final resting spot. And make sure the price includes perpetual care, or maintenance of the plot and grave marker.

Cemetery memorials can be purchased at the funeral home, the cemetery, or directly from an independent monument retailer. Prices are competitive, so call around for the best price on the stone you want.

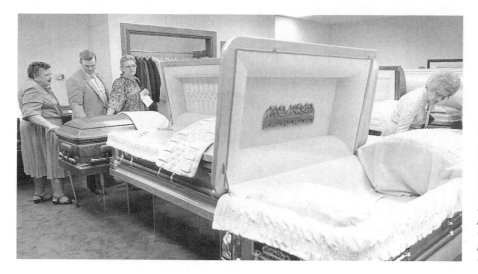

When suddenly confronted with having to choose a casket for a dear one, the newly bereaved may be inclined to make a financially unwise decision. People who pre-arrange their funerals often do so to guarantee a simple ceremony that will not impose excessive financial burdens on survivors.

Cremation. Cremation is growing in popularity. In 1991, 17 percent of all deaths were followed by cremation, up from 8 percent in 1977. A cremation with a ceremony ($800 to $2,800) is often slightly less expensive than a burial, usually because there are no cemetery charges. You will have to decide what you would like the body to be cremated in: a casket, a simple cardboard box, or even a canvas bag. Also decide what you want to have done with your cremated remains. Your family may decide to keep the urn, bury it in a lot, or it can be placed in a columbarium, a building that holds urns (Cost: $150-$8,000).

Entombment. For a final resting place *above* ground, opt for entombment in a cemetery mausoleum, an above-ground building. A mausoleum generally costs much more than a cemetery plot ($1,500 to $20,000), depending upon location (an eye-level crypt is the most expensive—the higher up you go, the cheaper).

Direct Burial. The ultimate no-fuss, no-frills approach is called direct disposition. The body is transferred by the funeral home directly from the place of death to the crematory or cemetery. Direct disposition is relatively inexpensive because it avoids extra charges for embalming and the use of funeral-home facilities for viewing. Immediate burials generally cost about $720 (plus cemetery charges). This can include optional grave-site services. Direct cremations cost an average of $725 to $900.

Donating Body/Organs. If you wish to donate your body to science, keep in mind that a medical school might not be able to accept the body if a communicable disease is present. It's best to make alternative plans, just in case. A funeral with viewing can be arranged even when organs have been donated. For more information about donations, call the Living Bank, 800–528–2971, a national registry.

Choosing a Funeral Home

Most people, understandably, choose a funeral home based on location and reputation. But by limiting your choice to only one funeral home, you may pay twice as much for the same quality goods and services as you might at a competing funeral home across town. It pays to comparison shop.

In 1984 the Federal Trade Commission issued what is known as the *Funeral Rule* to protect the consumer. This rule requires a funeral home to offer price information over the phone and hand out printed price lists at the funeral home. The law also requires permission to embalm and a written contract that contains the specific goods and services selected by the customer.

After you have made your funeral arrangements, don't forget to tell your family the location of your pre-arrangement contract and related papers.

Pre-paying for Your Funeral

Once your funeral arrangements are made, you have the option to "pre-pay." "The advantage in pre-paying for a funeral is that you're usually guaranteed today's prices," says Springer. Historically, funeral prices increase an average of 4 to 6 percent a year.

Some people opt to have their loved ones entombed in a mausoleum (left), a more expensive alternative to burial in the ground. Cremation generally costs less than either burial or entombment.

So a funeral costing $3,500 today would cost $5,701 ten years from now (with an average price increase of 5 percent).

As practical as this sounds, consumer advocates warn buyers to be extremely cautious when entering into any type of pre-paid funeral arrangement. Contracts and financing plans are often perplexing. To avoid confusion, take notes throughout your funeral negotiations, or bring along an audiocassette tape player and record the conversation. Reiners also recommends bringing along a witness.

Once you have a copy of the proposed agreement, make sure all of the services and merchandise you have requested are included—and for the agreed-upon price. The contract should include the details of how you plan to finance the funeral. Consult with an attorney, accountant, or financial adviser if you are uncertain about any of the terms.

As you look over your funeral contract, check to see if it states whether it is guaranteed or not guaranteed. A guaranteed funeral means that regardless of the retail price of the funeral at the time of death, the event will take place as you specified, with no additional cost to survivors. (This guarantee may be limited if you are paying in installments instead of one lump sum).

Ask if the contract can be transferred to another location should you decide to relocate. "If you buy in New York, then move to Florida to retire, there is a possibility your contract won't be honored by a second funeral home," explains Reiners. "This is one

of the most common complaints about pre-arranged contracts," he adds.

Even if the contract is honored by a funeral home in another geographic location, the cost of providing the same funeral may be more. State regulations do not require another funeral home to provide the same funeral for the same price. If the displaced funeral does cost more, your family and friends will either have to settle for a little less than you intended, or pay the difference.

Funding Your Funeral

There are two basic types of funding available: insurance policies and trusts. If you decide to pre-pay, ask the funeral arranger what funding plans are offered. Here are the most common plans:

Insurance. Pre-need insurance is set up as a term life policy with premiums paid all at once or in installments over as long as 20 years. The customer pre-arranges a funeral, then buys the increasing benefit life insurance policy from the funeral director, who is named as the beneficiary.

Ask the funeral director exactly how much insurance you must buy to secure a guaranteed-price funeral. Check to see if the benefit is adjusted for inflation and whether the policy will be issued regardless of your health. Also ask if any excess funds go to survivors or to the funeral home.

Most insurance policies will pay the entire death benefit even if the total premiums have not been paid at the time of death. Usually, interest earned is exempt from income tax liability. Stick with policies rated "A" or better by A.M. Best, Standard and Poor, or some other insurance rating system.

But, warns Lee Norrgard, investigative analyst for the Consumer Affairs division of the American Association of Retired Persons (AARP), "Oftentimes the person ends up paying more in premiums than they receive in benefits for funeral costs. The longer the consumer lives, the more they will pay in premiums, and the greater the chance they will overpay."

Trusts. State-regulated trusts are the most common funding mechanisms offered by funeral directors. First, a pre-arrangement agreement is drawn up. The customer then usually pays the funeral director a lump sum. The trust's principal and interest earned will pay for the cost of all merchandise and services.

Your money goes into a trust account with the funeral home named as the beneficiary. Many states have laws specifying the percentage of the principal sum that must be deposited: about half the states require 100 percent, and many require between 80 and 100 percent. Any money that is not deposited is kept by the funeral home as an initial charge. Don't sign up if the figure is below 80 percent (especially if your contract is not guaranteed). The more money the funeral home deposits in the trust, the more secure your investment.

Make sure you ask your funeral director how your funds are invested. Ask this question each year after you receive your statement of taxes you may owe on the trust's earnings. If you're not satisfied, you may wish to pull your funds out.

Other precautions: Insist that the trust is held in a federally insured bank or savings institution; look for a money-back grace period in case you change your mind and wish to get your principal back, and ask if any interest earned is added to your principal sum or is kept by the funeral home. Finally, find out what will happen to your money should the funeral home go out of business.

Individual Plan/Savings Accounts. You may also decide to provide for the cost of a funeral on your own, without pre-paying. To do this, just open a savings account with an amount equal to the cost of the funeral and designate the account as a "payable on death" (P.O.D.) account. This type of account is often held jointly by the buyer and a relative or the funeral director. When the consumer dies, the account automatically becomes the property of your appointed joint owner, who then pays for the funeral. But remember, if you select a savings plan, you are liable for federal and possibly state income taxes on earnings. Also, keep in mind that if you haven't pre-paid a funeral home, it is unlikely they will guarantee you a rate for your funeral. Survivors will be held responsible for the shortfall.

Protect Yourself from Pre-need Pitfalls

"A funeral is a unique purchase—it's hard to measure the security of such an investment," explains Norrgard. "Fraud within the funeral business can go undetected for a very long period of time, because there is usually a lag of years between purchase of a plan and the purchaser's death."

Although instances of large-scale fraud are infrequent, proper precautions should be taken: Investigate any funeral home selling you a pre-need contract; make sure the organization has been in business for a considerable number of years; call the Better Business Bureau and ask if any complaints have been registered; and ask the seller for referrals. ◇

To Voice a Complaint

If a funeral director fails to perform his or her duties or springs undisclosed fees on you, call the Funeral Services Consumer Assistance Program (FSCAP) at 800–662–7666. Your complaint could lead to a hearing by an independent panel of consumer advocates. If the panel decides in your favor, you will get your money back.

If you have a complaint or problem involving a cemetery, call the Cemetery Consumer Service Council, 703–379–6426. Or write: Box 3574, Washington, DC 20007.

Housecalls

by Michael Coates, M.D.

Q *Are fluorescent lights harmful? How do fluorescent lights compare to incandescent lights as far as energy efficiency goes?*

A There is no significant difference from a physical point of view, but some people find fluorescent lights stressful to work under for long periods of time. They do give off a tiny amount of ultraviolet light. But the Food and Drug Administration (FDA) has shown that the amount is insignificant.

A small number of people report headaches, eyestrain, and nervousness from having to live or work extensively under fluorescent light. This may be related to the alternating currents that cause the lights to flicker at a rate that we are not conscious of but that the brain may perceive. New very-high-frequency fixtures should help to eliminate this problem.

Incandescent lights give a fuller, more balanced spectrum of light, but they are neither as energy-efficient nor as environmentally friendly as fluorescent ones. Ironically, though, fluorescent lights may also

negatively affect public health from the point of view of the environment: when disposed of, tiny amounts of radiation and mercury gas seep from the bulbs.

Q *Do condoms offer absolute protection from AIDS transmission during sexual relations?*

A There is no absolute protection from AIDS, except for abstinence from sexual activity, and avoidance of all contact with bodily fluids of HIV-positive individuals, such as occurs through blood transfusions or needle sharing.

Latex condoms, when used properly, will prevent semen from coming in contact with the partner, and are thus the best protection that we know of. (Semen and blood are the primary media of HIV transmission.) But researchers have also isolated the HIV virus in sweat, saliva, vaginal fluids, breast milk, and tears. Theoretically, having these fluids come in contact with a cut or wound on your skin or with your mucous membranes (e.g., during kissing or oral sex) could put you in danger. Fortunately, the HIV virus does not appear to be highly transmittable by these routes, and cases of such transmission have been difficult to document.

Q *I have a bottle of aspirin with an expiration date that has just passed. Is the aspirin any good?*

A Take the top off the bottle and smell the contents. If they smell like vinegar, or if the tablets have a fuzzy coat on them, the active ingredient in the aspirin has probably broken down, and the aspirin has lost most of its effectiveness. Aside from its lack of effect, though, the aspirin is no more harmful at that point than is fresh aspirin.

The FDA mandates that companies post expiration dates on medicines, but the dates are recommended ones, and may be conservative estimates, partly for liability reasons. Many drugs maintain their effectiveness far past the posted dates. In fact, many are shipped to missions or other countries near the indicated expiration date. And, whereas aspirin is cheap, many

medications are not. The drugs discarded annually at hospitals and elsewhere represent enormous amounts of money.

But since the consumer has no way of knowing if a particular medication on his or her shelf is still effective, the only sure recourse is to assume that the expiration date is accurate.

Q What is a living will? Does such a will require the same legal notarization as a regular will?

A We usually think of the term "will" as referring to a document that conveys property after a person dies. In this sense, "living will" is somewhat of a misnomer, since it refers to what lifesaving medical treatments a person is willing to accept if he or she becomes incapacitated and is unable to make these difficult decisions personally.

Under the laws of most states, patients can choose or refuse medical treatments. A living will designates someone else to make those decisions for you in the event that you are mentally incapacitated or unconscious. Usually these wills come into play for terminally ill patients. They specify whether or not the person will accept such treatments as painkillers, mechanical ventilation, and cardiopulmonary resuscitation.

Living wills are not legally binding, but the fact that 40 states have "right-to-die"

laws makes them more likely to be honored. You should also personally make your wishes known to your friends, family, and doctor.

Check your state laws, but, generally, living wills should be:
• backed up with durable powers of attorney for both spouses to each other;
• signed before witnesses who are not potential heirs or medical caregivers;
• copied and sent to your doctor, family members, and any other relevant parties;
• re-signed and notarized every few years.

You can orally counter or cancel these orders at any time, as long as you are judged mentally competent to make such decisions.

Q My cat has ear mites. Can I catch them? Do cats transmit many diseases to humans?

A The problem is not so much catching ear mites, as receiving bites from them, which can be irritating.

Mites are small, eight-legged animals, less than one-twentieth of an inch long, similar to tiny spiders. Many have piercing and blood-sucking mouthparts. Scientists have recognized more than 30,000 species of mites worldwide, infesting dogs, birds, and many other animals, including humans. Chiggers are another familiar form of mite; in this case they cause irritation from burrowing under the skin. Scabies, head lice, and sexually transmitted "crabs" serve as examples of human mite-caused conditions.

Fortunately for humans, cats transmit very few diseases to their owners. An important exception is toxoplasmosis.

You may share some flea or mite bites with your cat, but cats transmit very few diseases to their human friends. One known exception unrelated to the mite is the disease toxoplasmosis, a parasitic disease that can infect humans who fail to wash their hands after handling a cat or its feces. The disease is most dangerous when transmitted by a pregnant woman to her unborn child, who may then develop encephalitis or mental retardation.

Q *What is meant by hardening of the arteries? Does this condition ever affect young people?*

A Hardening of the arteries, otherwise known as atherosclerosis, is a disorder of the arterial system that causes thickening of the inside lining of blood vessels and a loss in their elasticity. As a result, blood flow decreases to such important areas as the heart, the brain, kidneys, and the legs.

The condition is more prevalent and severe in older people, but can affect young people as well. The process —only partly reversible— often begins at a relatively early age. Autopsies of soldiers who died in the Korean War were the first to identify atherosclerosis in such a group. Doctors were amazed to find that young men in their teens and twenties had already built up significant plaque (fat deposits) in their arteries.

Individuals with a high level of fats (or "lipids," especially cholesterol) in the blood have a greater risk of developing this problem. Genetic predisposition plays a part in deciding a person's level of blood fats. However, the process of fat deposition in the arteries takes a long time, and certain factors significantly enhance the risk, including diabetes, obesity, high-fat diet, smoking, and sedentary life-style.

Q *Does using smokeless tobacco or "dipping snuff" carry the same risks that smoking tobacco does?*

A Such products carry similar risks, but unfortunately, their use is on the rise. According to the National Cancer Institute (NCI), recent years have seen a resurgence in the use of dipping tobacco, chewing tobacco, and snuff. Males aged 17 to 19 make the greatest use of these products. In a 1990 youth risk-behavior study by the Centers for Disease Control and Prevention (CDC), 19 percent of male college students reported using these products.

Dipping tobacco is finely ground tobacco that the user places between the gum and the lip or cheek. The mucous tissues of the mouth absorb nicotine, the psychoactive compound in tobacco, which then enters the bloodstream. Nicotine is what hooks the user, but tars and other substances in the tobacco leaf are what bring on the danger of oral cancer at the site of contact in the mouth. If the person smokes or uses alcohol, the risk is even higher.

Nicotine comes with its own dangers: It increases blood cholesterol, elevates heart rate and blood pressure, increases the clotting tendency of blood, and puts a person at risk for life-threatening cardiovascular problems.

Dipping tobacco is cheap and easy to hide when in use. Its promotion relies, in part, on macho images and certain professional sports. But many countries have banned it altogether.

Q *My friend uses extended-wear contact lenses a month or longer without removing them. Is this dangerous?*

A Based on a recent multicenter study, the FDA revised its recommendations on extended-wear lenses, stating that the period between removing and cleaning them and replacing them back in the eye should be one day to not more than seven days. With prolonged duration in the eye, lenses inhibit oxygen from reaching the cornea, increasing the risk of infection from bacteria and other microorganisms. This can result in *ulcerative keratitis*, which can scar the cornea and affect vision. In this country, most patients receive treatment before this situation becomes too severe, but in advanced cases the condition can cloud over the cornea and impair vision.

Extended-wear lenses allow more oxygen through to the cornea than do hard lenses, but they stay in the eye much longer. As a result, extended-wear users are four to five times more likely to develop ulcerative keratitis. Lens wearers who smoke increase their chances of this condition even further—three to eight times—probably due to direct irritation to the eye that may interfere with oxygen delivery to the cornea.

Do you have a practical question?
Send it to Editor, Health and Medicine Annual, P.O. Box 90, Hawleyville, CT 06440-9990.

Health and Medicine: Reports '93

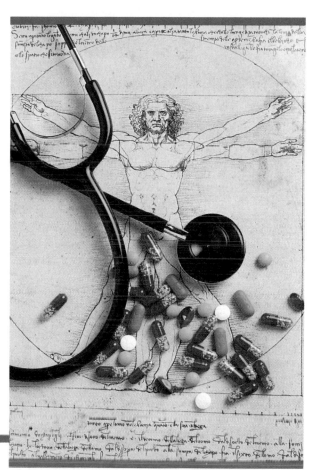

Aging

▶ Alzheimer's Disease

Alzheimer's disease continues to be of major concern to the older segment of the population. Approximately 60 to 80 percent of the cases of dementia occurring in people over the age of 65 are caused by Alzheimer's; most of the remaining cases of dementia are caused by preventable disorders, such as strokes, or treatable conditions, such as depression, a major problem among the elderly. The cause of Alzheimer's disease is still unknown, but there has been an explosion in knowledge about how it affects the brain, thanks largely to new methods for studying the brain's molecular structure.

The dementia associated with Alzheimer's disease is triggered by deposits of amyloid plaques, a protein substance in the brain. The cause of this plaque accumulation is still unknown. Unfortunately, there is no cure or prevention for Alzheimer's disease at present. Ongoing research efforts include clinical trials of new drugs. One such trial, a large, controlled study of a drug called tacrine, was conducted at a number of medical centers around the United States. Preliminary results of tacrine's effectiveness in slowing down the loss of cognitive function are still inconclusive.

The development of mental incompetence, particularly as a symptom of Alzheimer's disease, is, of course, very worrisome for elderly people. Senior citizens need to be assured that incidents of temporary forgetfulness, called benign senescent forgetfulness, is a normal part of aging and does not mean that the person is necessarily developing the disease. Research has shown an age-related decline

Test findings suggest that a decline in memory and decision performance in older people may result from the pace with which such tests are administered.

in tests of memory and decision performance in older people. But this decline is strikingly lessened if the person being tested is allowed to learn the test material at a slower pace. Therefore, the results of intelligence testing should not be confused with the speed with which the test is taken. Elderly people can use certain learning strategies to compensate for and alleviate any real decrease in learning performance.

▶ Prevention of Strokes and Heart Attacks

In elderly people, systolic hypertension, high blood pressure of the blood flow when the heart beats (as indicated by the upper number in a blood-pressure reading), is closely related to the risk of stroke. Until recently, the decision to treat this problem with drugs was controversial—it was not clear if the benefits of drug therapy outweighed the drug's side effects. But recent studies have clearly demonstrated that treatment will lower the risk of stroke, including the so-called "ministroke." Ministrokes, technically called transient ischemic attacks, or TIAs, precede strokes in about 10 percent of cases. Of those who have had one or more TIAs, about 36 percent will later have a major stroke. These studies indicate that more aggressive treatment of systolic hypertension in elderly patients is warranted.

The elderly are also advised to eat a low-fat diet, which lowers the cholesterol level and is beneficial in delaying arteriosclerosis, thereby reducing the risk of stroke.

Another important development in the prevention of both stroke and heart attack is the antiplatelet drugs. It has been clearly demonstrated in clinical studies that very small doses of aspirin are useful in preventing both heart attacks and TIAs. However, because aspirin can irritate the stomach and cause bleeding, patients with hypertension and a history of peptic-ulcer disease should review with their physician whether aspirin therapy is appropriate for them.

▶ The Importance of Exercise

A number of new studies have looked at the effects of exercise on older people. One recent study determined that physically fit older men fall asleep faster, whether or not they had exercised that day; by contrast, sedentary older men slept more fitfully. Occasional spurts of demanding exercise were found to further disturb the sleep patterns of sedentary older men. Another study that examined self-reported physical activity and exercise among adults aged 70 and over, as well as data from the 1984–88 Longitudinal Study of Aging, found that less active people had a higher risk of dying earlier than those who exercised regularly.

Exercise benefits the elderly in many ways. Physically fit older people even retain their sense of balance to a greater degree than do their more sedentary peers.

Other studies have shown that regular exercise, by helping older people retain their sense of balance and steadiness, has the added benefit of preventing falls. Falls continue to be one of the major causes of disability and death among the elderly. A number of risk factors for falls have been identified, including visual impairment, use of certain drugs, and certain neurological problems, such as Parkinson's disease and peripheral neuropathies.

For younger people concerned with preserving their vitality and vigor into old age, other studies suggest that regular exercise can help maintain good health over the long term. One recent study indicated that regular endurance exercises, such as walking or jogging three to five days per week, 30 to 50 minutes per day, can favorably alter the abdominal-fat distribution that is typical of overweight men and women in the United States. This may reduce the risk of coronary-artery disease and other disorders associated with abdominal obesity.

▶ Nutrition
Maintaining proper nutrition is a substantial problem for older adults, many of whom do not eat enough to maintain good health. Poverty, social isolation, poorly fitted dentures or missing teeth, ill health, and depression are significant and relatively common factors contributing to the development of malnutrition in the elderly. Furthermore, prescription and over-the-counter drugs can interfere with the absorption of food nutrients by the body.

Among the consequences of a poor diet are physical weakness and mental confusion, which can cause considerable disability and reduce the quality of life. Long-term malnutrition can also cause frequent illness and, in extreme cases, death.

Many people believe that vitamin and mineral supplements can replace a nutritionally adequate diet—a dangerous myth. A well-balanced diet is the only way to give the body the full range of necessary nutrients. Furthermore, large doses of vitamins, particularly fat-soluble vitamins such as A and D, have been found to build up in the body, sometimes reaching toxic levels.

By the same token, extreme weight gains are not advocated for elderly people. Recent research with animal models has associated longevity with leaner bodies. The best current advice is to consume a balanced low-fat diet, and to eat somewhat less protein than a younger person might.

▶ Cancer Therapy
Prostate Cancer. One of every 10 men will develop prostate cancer this year. One of the key factors in surviving prostate cancer is early diagnosis: if the cancer is identified before it has spread, the five-year survival rate is close to 90 percent. Recently, a new blood test, called the Prostate Specific Antigen (PSA) Test, is being used with great success in conjunction with the standard digital rectal exam to identify prostate cancer in its early stages. This should increase the chance of early diagnosis and timely treatment.

Breast Cancer. Breast cancer continues to be a major problem for women of all ages. Screening techniques such as mammography and breast self-examination are still underutilized, even though they are the best offense for early detection and treatment, the factors leading to increased survival rates. Currently there are studies exploring the use of the drug tamoxifen to prevent cancer in certain high-risk women, such as those with a strong family history of breast cancer. One theory that proposed a possible cause of breast cancer was recently shown to be untrue. Researchers found that a high-fat diet is not a factor in causing breast cancer. The relationship between estrogen supplementation (to counteract the symptoms of menopause and prevent osteoporosis) and breast cancer among elderly women is still not entirely clear.

▶ Living Wills
All older persons should be aware that hospitals are now required by federal law to ask patients on admission about advance directives, such as the living will and power of attorney, both of which can be prepared without legal advice. The living will gives an older person the ability to give specific instructions about the use of such life-support measures as tube feedings or ventilators. A durable power of attorney can designate in advance a person who will make decisions on behalf of a person incapacitated by severe illness.

Albert J. Finestone, M.D.

AIDS

Scientific understanding of any recently discovered disease tends to undergo frequent modification as more is discovered about the condition. The year 1992 brought considerable modification of our understanding of AIDS (acquired immunodeficiency syndrome). The new data still point to the human immunodeficiency virus type 1 (HIV-1) as the primary causal factor in the AIDS epidemic. But HIV-1 infection and AIDS are showing more varied and complex clinical and epidemiological patterns than originally recognized.

▶ Possible Nonlethal Human Immunodeficiency Viruses

When a new disease is first discovered, it appears to be very serious because only severe cases tend to be recognized initially. As improved diagnosis becomes possible, cases with a wider spectrum of symptoms and severity become evident. Eventually, less severe or even asymptomatic cases of the disease are recognized. The events of 1992 suggested that this process is occurring for AIDS.

Epidemiological data have led scientists to believe that most, if not all, people with HIV infections eventually develop the severe clinical disease called AIDS. If a person is infected with the HIV-1 virus, clinical symptoms of AIDS usually develop in less than 10 years. Most persons with AIDS die of the disease within two or three years of when they develop their first major symptoms. The time interval between infection and the first symptoms tends to be shortest for persons infected through blood transfusions, perhaps because the dose of virus is so massive.

In 1992, however, scientists from Australia reported that a group of persons infected with HIV by one blood donor are still alive and are perfectly well approximately 10 years after infection. The donor and those he infected not only have no symptoms of AIDS, but they also show normally functioning immune systems, including normal levels of the CD4 lymphocytes that are destroyed by virulent HIV infection. This is particularly surprising because the virus was spread by blood transfusion, a mode of transmission which usually leads very quickly to clinical AIDS. This report strongly suggests that these persons are infected with a nonvirulent, or at least a less virulent, strain of HIV. If this proves to be true, it may be possible to compare this strain with others to learn how to disarm the virus. Furthermore, this new virus may hold a key to the development of improved vaccines or treatments against AIDS.

▶ Possible New Cause of Some AIDS Cases

The presumed cause of AIDS cases in the U.S. has been HIV-1. There also exists a second human immunodeficiency virus, called HIV-2, which, although common in West Africa, is rare in the U.S. and does not appear to attack the human immune system as aggressively as HIV-1. Before 1992 the presence of HIV could be demonstrated somewhere in the course of the disease in virtually all cases of AIDS, either by a positive culture, a positive antibody test, or by demonstrating the presence of fragments of the virus's nucleic acids with polymerase chain reaction (PCR).

In 1992 the scientific world was startled by reports of increasing numbers of cases of an AIDS-like illness in which no trace of HIV-1 or HIV-2 could be found. These mysterious infections are clinically indistinguishable from AIDS cases and can be severe: some of the people with the new AIDS-like illness already have died from the same opportunistic infections that kill AIDS patients.

During the past two years, the Centers for Disease Control and Prevention (CDC) had known of a few such cases in the U.S., but the CDC neither made this fact known nor requested physicians to report such cases. In fact, prior to the summer of 1992, the CDC had mentioned these mysterious cases only once, at a conference during which news coverage was severely limited. However, at the annual international conference on AIDS, held in Amsterdam, the Netherlands, in 1992, reports of similar cases came from several other countries. By October 1992, the total of such known cases reached at least 68 in the U.S. and more than 100 worldwide. The CDC has now called for physicians to report these cases.

Epidemiologically, however, the mysterious infections are more geographically scattered than the initial AIDS cases. For example, the first 68 cases in the U.S. come from 23 states and have nearly an equal male-to-female ratio, which is very different demographically from the U.S. AIDS epidemic, although an equal sex ratio is found in Africa and elsewhere. Furthermore, most of the new infections are in Caucasians, and many patients do not have the risk factors for HIV infections that are typical of AIDS in this country. Finally there are no similar cases among contacts of these patients.

Some have wondered if this problem is merely a failure of laboratory techniques to detect an ordinary HIV-1 or HIV-2. Although this cannot be absolutely ruled out, scientists are doubtful because the highly sensitive polymerase chain reaction has been applied to these mysterious cases, and still no evidence of HIV could be detected.

The existence of these cases suggests that there may be one or more still unidentified viruses that are capable of causing AIDS. If they exist, these new viruses might be retroviruses, like HIV-1 and HIV-2. Retroviruses are RNA viruses, so called because they encode their genetic information in ribonucleic acid (RNA) rather than the deoxyribonucleic acid (DNA) used by most living cells. The virus also contains an enzyme called *reverse transcriptase,* which makes DNA copies of the viral genetic code once the virus is inside a host cell. This newly made viral DNA then takes control of the biochemical reactions within the cell and forces the cell to do its bidding. Unfortunately, these viruses have chosen to infect the most critical cells in the human immune system: the CD4 lymphocytes. These cells function somewhat like the conductor of the immune system's orchestra, and, as they disappear, the immune system is no longer able to work in a coordinated, effective manner.

The CDC has labeled these new AIDS-like cases "Idiopathic CD4+ T-lymphocytopenia," which means a condition of low numbers of T lymphocytes of the CD4 type due to an unknown cause. The technical criteria are: (1) that the patients must have no evidence of infection with HIV-1 or HIV-2; (2) that there must be fewer than 300 CD4-type T lymphocytes per cubic millimeter of blood, or less than 20 percent must be CD4 lymphocytes.

Nevertheless, the cause of these mysterious AIDS cases might still be a different type of virus. It is even possible that some noninfectious environmental factor may be responsible, or a common viral infection combined with poor nutrition. Reasons for suspecting a new (or at least previously unde-

tected) retrovirus, however, include the fact that these new patients have a severe loss of CD4 lymphocytes, just as do patients with classic AIDS, and many of these patients also have the classic risk factors for HIV infection, such as needle sharing or unprotected sexual intercourse.

Physicians involved with the new patients are feeling a sense of déjà vu, because to them the mysterious patients look just like the early AIDS patients, clinically and immunologically, and, in the early days of the AIDS epidemic, the same sort of consideration of many different factors occurred.

Responsible scientists believe they must consider all possible causal factors, even though it seems likely that sooner or later a new HIV will be discovered. Unfortunately, unlike the virus involved in the Australian outbreak discussed earlier, the new AIDS-like cases harbor an agent that usually is virulent, although a few of these patients appear to have less severe damage to the immune system than is seen in a typical case of AIDS.

These new AIDS-like cases have sparked concern that a new virus may be circulating that could contaminate the nation's blood supply, as did the first HIV, until a method of screening for that virus was discovered. The CDC, however, currently maintains that the new AIDS-like disease does not appear to be transmitted from person to person. Nevertheless, those familiar with the story of AIDS and blood transfusions will not feel safe until a causal agent is identified and shown conclusively not to be transmissible through blood. If a new virus, it must be used to develop screening and diagnostic tests

TRACKING A MYSTERY ILLNESS

Medical experts have reported the discovery of a syndrome characterized by severe damage to the immune system, similar to that found in people with AIDS. But unlike AIDS, which is caused by two viruses, this condition, known as "idiopathic CD4+ T-lymphocytopenia," has no apparent cause.

DEFINING CHARACTERISTICS	CASES	WHO HAS IT	COMPARISON TO AIDS		
				NEW DISEASES (number)	AIDS (number/%)
• 300 or fewer CD4+ T cells per cubic millimeter of blood, or CD4 cells accounting for less than 20 percent of lymphocytes, a type of white cells.	Number reported in the United States 00	**SEX** Men ....30 cases Women ....30 cases	**AGE** Median 43		36 years
	Number of deaths 4		**SEX**		
	Number living.................64	**AGE** Range........16-83 years Median age.....43 years	Male 38		207,083 (89%)
• Negative test for HIV.	Length of survival from first low CD4-cell count...........1-106 months		Female 30		26,606 (11%)
• No other immuno-deficiency or therapy that could cause a drop in T-cells.	Median length of survival from first low CD4-cell count ....14 months	**RACE OR ETHNIC GROUP** White.............53 cases Black ....4 cases Asian................5 cases Hispanic ....6 cases	**RACE** White 53 Black 4 Other 11		123,513 (53%) 69,150 (30%) 41,026 (17%)
	Mean length of survival from first low CD4-cell count ....24 months				

Source: Federal Centers for Disease Control and Prevention

to use on the blood supply. Fortunately, as of the end of 1992, the new virus, if it exists, remains exceedingly rare, and there is no evidence as yet that the new agent has been transmitted through blood or blood products. However, the fact that some of those afflicted have traditional risk factors has experts concerned.

▶ New Criteria for AIDS Added

The CDC has added three more diseases to the criteria that define HIV-infected patients as having AIDS—another sign of the increasing appreciation by medical experts and policymakers of the complexity of AIDS. There has been an ongoing debate as to when HIV infection officially becomes the disease AIDS. In 1992 the government chose to add pulmonary tuberculosis, recurrent pneumonia, and invasive cervical cancer (all in HIV-infected patients) as criteria for AIDS. This has both a scientific and a social impact. The new definition will increase the number of AIDS cases considerably, and will probably provide a more accurate reflection of the true prevalence of the disease. Socially, the new definition will enable more people to collect certain disability and other benefits, such as AIDS-related medical care and housing.

Previously, HIV-infected persons with tuberculosis, but whose CD4-lymphocyte levels were not reduced to the level of the criterion defined for AIDS, were not considered AIDS cases. Recent studies, however, have shown that even a moderate decrease in immune function increases the risk for reactivation of tuberculosis. The new CDC criterion is undoubtedly more realistic, because resistance to tuberculosis, as to most of the other opportunistic infections associated with AIDS, is primarily dependent on cell-mediated immunity, the type of immunity that is most severely damaged by the loss of CD4 lymphocytes. Much of the tuberculosis in AIDS patients is due to a tuberculosis infection that occurred many years before. Most initial tuberculosis infections remain dormant in the body, held in check by the cell-mediated immunity revealed by a positive tuberculin skin test. As the CD4-lymphocyte count begins to fall, this cell-mediated immunity declines, and the dormant tuberculosis infection can become active again.

The decline in cell-mediated immunity also hampers the screening for tuberculosis infection, because the tuberculin skin test ceases to be a reliable test; this is a complication known as *anergy*. In a person who is HIV-positive, special skin testing must be performed along with the tuberculin test to determine if the latter is likely to be reliable. If anergy is present, the HIV-positive patient must be given a chest X-ray and a sputum culture, neither of which is completely accurate for the presence of tuberculosis.

Rates of new tuberculosis cases have risen in the U.S. since 1986, and most of the increase can be related to tuberculosis in AIDS patients. As the number of HIV-infected persons who develop AIDS increases, the number who also have tuberculosis undoubtedly will increase as well.

THE FUTURE OF AIDS

The virus that causes AIDS is spreading rapidly around the world, and Asia will be hit particularly hard in the next few years, a research group says. Estimates and projections of cumulative cases in thousands.

	INFECTED WITH HIV			AIDS	
REGION	All Adults '92 (est.)	Women '92 (est.)	All Adults '95 (proj.)	Adults '92 (est.)	Adults '95 (proj.)
North America	1,167	128.5	1,495	257.5	534.0
Western Europe	718	122.0	1,186	99.0	279.5
Australia/Oceania	28	3.5	40	4.5	11.5
Latin America	995	199.0	1407	173.0	417.5
Sub-Saharan Africa	7,803	3,901.5	11,449	1,367.0	3,277.5
Caribbean	310	124.0	474	43.0	121.0
Eastern Europe	27	2.5	44	2.5	9.5
Southeast Mediterranean	35	6.0	59	3.5`	12.5
Northeast Asia	41	7.0	80	3.5	14.5
Southeast Asia	675	223.0	1,220	65.0	240.5
TOTAL	**11,799**	**4,717.0**	**17,454**	**2,018.5**	**4,918.0**

Source: "AIDS in the World 1992," Harvard University Press

▶ AIDS Did Not Arise from Polio Vaccine

Charges have been made in recent years that HIV was caused by genetic engineering, by other activities involved in making vaccines, or by malaria research. One charge claimed that contaminated smallpox vaccine was responsible, because it was widely distributed in Africa, where the AIDS epidemic is the most serious and may have appeared first. There is good epidemiological evidence against these hypotheses, because the vaccine was much more widely used than just in sub-Saharan Africa.

Another, perhaps more worrisome charge was made by author Tom Curtis in the March 1992 issue of *Rolling Stone* magazine. He claimed that HIV got into the poliovirus vaccine developed by researcher Hilary Koprowski at the Wistar Institute in Philadelphia, Pennsylvania. This vaccine was given to Africans in 1957. Curtis charged that a monkey virus similar to HIV was a contaminant of the monkey-kidney cells used to grow the poliovirus, which was modified over time to become HIV.

A committee established to examine this possibility discounted it for several reasons: (1) the monkey immune-deficiency virus does not grow in monkey-kidney cells; (2) the virus would have had to survive through several episodes of freezing and thawing and dilution; (3) because it was an oral vaccine, the virus would have had to infect people through open sores in the mouth or the gastrointestinal tract; (4) the monkey virus would have had to live and reproduce in human beings; and (5) the virus would have had to mutate from the monkey immune-deficiency virus to HIV. The committee concluded that all of these factors made Curtis's theory so improbable as to be considered impossible.

Still another serious charge was made by Charles Gilks, M.D., at Oxford University, when he discovered reports that, in the past, some malaria experiments had involved injecting people with chimpanzee and monkey blood. Dr. Gilks' theory is that, if the blood from these animals were infected with the simian immune-deficiency virus, and if the virus survived in these persons and was transmitted to others, it could have become adapted to human beings and become what we now know as the human immunodeficiency virus, or HIV. Apparently a chimpanzee has been shown to carry a virus very similar to HIV-1, and sooty mangabey monkeys have been successfully infected with a virus very similar to HIV-2.

None of these accusations has produced solid evidence indicating the origin of the AIDS epidemic, but they provided ammunition for those critics who have predicted some sort of doomsday scenario created from modern biological manipulations. Although we may never know for sure who is correct, none of the theories appears likely at present.

The sooty mangabey monkey (left) may be one of the few primates capable of carrying a form of HIV.

▶ Combination Therapy Against HIV Proves Valuable

Research reported in 1992 indicates that people infected with the HIV but who have not yet developed AIDS should alternate the drugs azidothymidine (AZT) and dideoxyinosine (DDI). The research suggests that after about 16 weeks on AZT, a person infected with HIV should switch to low doses of DDI. Those who followed this regimen had significantly fewer opportunistic infections than those who did not. Other combinations and sequences are being studied.

▶ Predictions of HIV Infection and AIDS Cases Rise

A Harvard University AIDS-research group has predicted that worldwide, between 40 million and 110 million persons will be infected with HIV by the year 2000. These are much greater numbers than the 40 million maximum estimate made by the World Health Organization (WHO). The difference between the estimates is due, in part, to the fact that the WHO uses the numbers of AIDS cases reported by the member countries, which are often considered to be underestimates.

▶ AIDS Insurance for Medical Students

The Yale University School of Medicine in New Haven, Connecticut, became the first medical school in the country to give its students disability insurance that would be activated should they acquire AIDS. The students would not have to demonstrate that they obtained their AIDS infection on the wards or in a laboratory. Several other medical schools have announced plans to implement similar insurance policies. The medical students could continue their insurance policies after graduating from medical school, so that they could be covered during internship and residency, and perhaps beyond.

James F. Jekel, M.D., M.P.H.

Anesthesiology

In 1992 the world marked the 150th anniversary of one of American medicine's most important contributions: the discovery of anesthesia. On March 30, 1842, Crawford Long, M.D. successfully administered ether as an anesthetic to his patient James Venable during surgery to remove a tumor of the neck. Progress continues to be made by anesthesiologists to provide for the well-being of the anesthetized patient in a safe, cost-effective fashion (see the article "Surgical Anesthesia: More Than Just Gas," page 16).

▶ Anesthesia for Infants
Newborn infants requiring surgery commonly receive "light anesthesia" with a muscle relaxant administered to keep the infant immobilized. A new study published in the *New England Journal of Medicine* investigated whether deeper levels of anesthesia can improve the results of surgery by blunting the infant's stress response to pain. Some infants undergoing cardiac operations were given light anesthesia, consisting of the drugs halothane and morphine, while others were put under "deep anesthesia" and given the opioid drug sufentanil. The death rate was significantly lower for the deeply anesthetized infants than for the light anesthesia group. The deep anesthesia also produced fewer complications and side effects. These results are supported by data that document a blunting of the physical stress response, suggesting that deeper levels of anesthesia may improve the results of surgery for critically ill infants.

Infants can withstand deeper anesthesiology during surgery than was previously suspected, and with few postoperative complications.

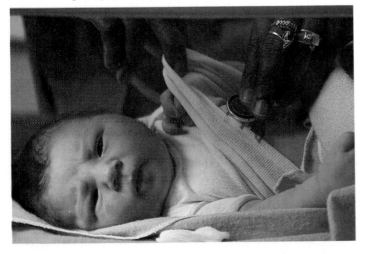

▶ General versus Regional Anesthesia
In recent years the use of regional anesthesia combined with general anesthesia during surgery has increased due to its purported beneficial effects in reducing postoperative illness. The journal *Anesthesiology* published a new study that found no advantage to either general anesthesia or the regional/general combination anesthetics in preventing illness. However, the researchers theorize that epidural anesthesia after surgery may reduce cardiopulmonary complications. Another study that compared the risk of blood clotting after surgery for these two anesthetic techniques found that patients who had undergone vascular surgery with general anesthesia had excessive clotting of blood, while patients receiving epidural plus general anesthesia did not have this problem.

▶ Do-Not-Resuscitate Orders on Surgical Patients
Interest in do-not-resuscitate (DNR) orders for the operating room has been propelled by the Patient Self-determination Act of 1990. Institutions receiving Medicare or Medicaid funding must advise patients of their right to execute advance directives, such as the living will. This has raised concerns regarding institution-wide use of DNR orders, especially for the operating room. It is estimated that 15 percent of DNR patients undergo a surgical procedure to improve comfort or reduce pain. Typically, DNR orders are suspended or discontinued when the patient goes to the operating room. Some researchers believe that the DNR orders should be honored in the operating room, giving greater weight to the patient's right to refuse treatment. However, many ethical conflicts remain unresolved in this area, so researchers have set guidelines that deal with the issue. One proposal calls for an open discussion with the patient and/or guardian as part of the routine preanesthetic evaluation of the patient, focusing on the spectrum of events requiring resuscitation. The duration of DNR orders should include a time frame for treating postoperative events. This discussion, as well as those with physicians caring for the patient, should be documented in the patient's chart.

Other researchers pose a series of questions: (1) Is surgery appropriate? (2) What does resuscitation mean during surgery? (3) Does withholding resuscitation compromise the patient's basic objective? (4) Why are operating-room professionals reluctant to retain DNR orders? (5) Has everyone involved communicated effectively? Researchers also suggest consulting the hospital ethics committee to resolve conflicts on this issue between health-care providers or between health-care providers and the patient or guardian.

Paul Barash, M.D.

Arthritis and Rheumatism

▶ Rheumatoid Arthritis and Cyclosporine A

Cyclosporine A has become a standard drug for suppressing the rejection reaction that follows organ transplantation, greatly reducing the risk of tissue rejection and also the need for large doses of corticosteroid drugs. Although this drug is less toxic than alternative immunosuppressive drugs, it nonetheless still has significant toxicity. In particular, the drug depresses kidney function and increases hypertension, which may not be wholly reversible when the drug is discontinued.

Because of its immunosuppressive properties, cyclosporine A has been tried in patients with severe connective-tissue diseases that have not responded to alternative treatment. Several trials have been reported in patients with advanced rheumatoid arthritis. A 1992 report published in *Seminars in Arthritis and Rheumatism* reviewed nine studies covering 283 patients who used cyclosporine in doses of 5 to 10 mg/kg, including five controlled trials. Patients improved significantly in all of the studies. However, the development of kidney problems was common and included decreased renal blood flow, reduced glomerular infiltration rate, and renal tubular toxicity. Using smaller initial doses of cyclosporine has been proposed, but may result in reduced effectiveness. Another 1992 report published in the *American Journal of Medicine* shows that an additional problem is the negative interaction between cyclosporine A and nonsteroidal antiinflammatory drugs, which are known to impair renal blood flow. This interaction results in greater decreases of kidney function than were seen with either drug alone. This effect was reversible with discontinuation of the nonsteroidal antiinflammatory agent. Thus, while cyclosporine A appears to be an effective drug for treating severe rheumatoid arthritis that does not respond to standard treatments, its use is likely to be limited because of a high frequency of irreversible kidney problems. Future studies will determine if either lower doses or alternative dosing regimens can reduce the toxicity and make this drug available for wider use.

▶ Lyme Disease

Lyme disease, an infectious disease caused by the spirochetal bacterium *Borrelia burgdorferi*, is spread by the bite of certain small ticks. When a human is bitten by an infected tick, the disease's

Lyme disease can cause severe chronic arthritis. The tick that carries the Lyme disease bacterium more than triples its size when engorged with blood.

first manifestation is often a characteristic skin rash, which is frequently followed by a variety of symptoms, including headaches, fever, fatigue, and chills; migratory arthritis, which occasionally becomes chronic; neurological problems, which also may occasionally become chronic; and by cardiac involvement. The diagnosis is based primarily on the clinical symptoms, with confirmation by blood tests. Unfortunately, poor standardization of blood testing for Lyme disease makes it difficult to confirm the diagnosis. A few patients with Lyme disease even give negative blood-test results. One report in the *Annals of Internal Medicine* in October 1991 looked at the sensitivity and specificity of an alternative test, the T-Cell Proliferative Assay, for patients who manifest clinical symptoms strongly suggestive of chronic Lyme disease but in whom the standard blood tests were negative. In these patients, the T-Cell Proliferative Assay was helpful in establishing diagnosis.

Lyme disease is treated with antibiotics. Oral doxycycline or penicillin is effective in the early stages of the disease. The chronic disease is most often treated with intravenous antibiotics. Cefuroxime (Ceftin) given daily for two to four weeks has been used most often. In a 1992 report in the *Annals of Internal Medicine,* oral cefuroxime axetil was compared with oral doxycycline for the treatment of early Lyme disease. Cefuroxime axetil was found to be well tolerated and equally effective both in the treatment of the early symptoms and the prevention of the later stages of Lyme disease, and it provides a possibly better-tolerated alternative to oral doxycycline.

Another symptom of Lyme disease is fibromyalgia, a condition characterized by diffuse muscular pain and multiple tender points at characteristic sites, but without evidence of muscle, joint, or neurological disease. A characteristic sleep disorder is often present, as are chronic fatigue and headaches. A 1992 report in the *Annals of Internal Medicine* described the development of fibromyalgia in 8 percent of a large group of patients with Lyme disease. Fibromyalgia appears soon after the treatment of early infection or in association with Lyme-disease arthritis. Treatment of Lyme disease with antibiotics did not affect the course of fibromyalgia, which had persisted in 14 of the 15 patients up to the time of the report. The fibromyalgia symptoms responded best to standard treatment for fibromyalgia, which includes low-dose amitriptyline, analgesia with nonsteroidal anti-inflammatory medications, and an exercise program.

It is unclear whether Lyme disease can trigger the muscle and joint pain of fibromyalgia, or if the association of the two diseases is coincidental. Given the imperfect specificity and poor standardization of Lyme-disease blood testing, some patients with fibromyalgia are inevitably found to have a positive blood test, and as a result may be treated for Lyme disease without benefit.

▶ Whipple's Disease

Whipple's disease is a rare illness characterized by painful joints, arthritis, diarrhea, abdominal pain, weight loss, and swollen lymph nodes. Other manifestations include skin hyperpigmentation and involvement of the cardiac and central nervous systems. Since the original description in 1907, the condition has been considered an infectious disease. Without treatment the disease is progressive and ultimately can be fatal. Long-term antibiotic treatment is effective. Diagnosis of the disease is quite difficult, as no bacterial organism has ever been cultured. In a report in the *New England Journal of Medicine* in July 1992, the uncultured bacterium that causes Whipple's disease was identified through application of molecular technology.

The authors employed the polymerase chain reaction (PCR), a molecular technique that allows the reproduction of large quantities of RNA from small samples to amplify RNA from the bacillus. Analysis of the sequences of this RNA determined that they did not match those of any known bacterium. Moreover, the bacterium did not resemble any bacteria known to produce infections in humans. It most nearly resembled a genus of soil bacteria and is distantly related to actinomycetes and mycobacteria.

This discovery should provide the basis to develop simpler diagnostic tests for Whipple's disease and a greater understanding of its pathophysiology.

While Whipple's disease itself is quite rare, the approach and technology employed here to identify the bacterial cause may have applicability to other chronic infectious diseases in which it has thus far proven impossible to culture the infectious agent.

Herbert S. Diamond, M.D.

Blood and Lymphatic System

During the past year, the field of hematology has witnessed advances in several areas. Our better understanding of the genetic control of fundamental life processes has provided novel tools and strategies that have had a profound impact upon the clinical practice of medicine. Among the highlights of the year is the development of new agents to treat diseases that result from inherited abnormalities of hemoglobin production, such as severe beta-thalassemia (Cooley's anemia) and sickle-cell anemia.

Sickle-cell anemia, which affects about 1 percent of the African-American population, and severe beta-thalassemia, which affects large numbers of Greek, Italian, Asian, and African-American patients in this country, are two of the most common inherited diseases worldwide. They both result from mutations that disrupt the normal behavior of the gene for beta globin, one of the components of normal adult hemoglobin. Patients with sickle-cell

When magnified, the shape of normal red blood cells (below) is easily distinguished from that of the same cells from a patient with sickle-cell anemia (bottom).

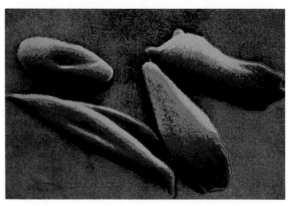

anemia and beta-thalassemia suffer from chronic debilitating illnesses that usually terminate in premature death in early adulthood. The symptoms of these diseases develop only after birth, because humans make a different kind of hemoglobin, fetal hemoglobin, during gestation.

It has long been known that victims of both sickle-cell anemia and beta-thalassemia could potentially be spared the symptoms of their disease if it were possible to prevent or reverse the switch from fetal to adult hemoglobin that occurs just before birth. In fact, there are patients who inherit a condition called hereditary persistence of fetal hemoglobin—they make only fetal hemoglobin throughout their lives and are perfectly healthy. The health of these individuals suggests that manipulation of the fetal hemoglobin would be an appropriate therapy for victims of sickle-cell anemia and beta-thalassemia.

During the past several years, much has been learned about the regulation of hemoglobin gene expression and the genetic control of the fetal to adulthood hemoglobin switch. This research has shown that the switch depends upon both the direct regulation of the globin genes and the selection of the red-cell progenitor cells in which the globin genes are expressed during red-cell differentiation. Some of these cells are more "fetal-like" than others. Hydroxyurea, a drug commonly used in a mild form of cancer chemotherapy, appears to stimulate the production of these more "fetal" progenitors and is already being used in clinical trials. It does promote fetal-hemoglobin synthesis and can, in some cases, have at least a modest impact upon the severity of the symptoms. By itself, however, it may not be potent enough in many patients.

During the past year, an alternative drug, based upon butyric acid, has shown promise. Butyric acid and its chemical relatives may act more directly on globin genes, although their precise mechanism of action remains unknown. Very preliminary pilot studies suggest that the agents have the ability to promote significant amounts of fetal-hemoglobin production in humans. It remains to be seen if the quantitative effect is sufficient to relieve symptoms. It is also possible that hydroxyurea and butyric acid in combination may have a far more profound impact on the condition than either drug alone. During the upcoming year, clinical trials of these agents will be initiated.

An interesting footnote to this line of research is that the discovery of the effect of butyric acid on fetal-hemoglobin synthesis came from studies of infants of diabetic mothers who were found to have a delayed fetal to adult hemoglobin switch. Butyric acid is one of the acids that accumulates in diabetic individuals who are suffering from a common complication of the disease called ketoacidosis.

Edward J. Benz, Jr., M.D.

Bones, Muscles, and Joints

The human body is a strong yet delicate example of the biological quest for perfection to match form with function. In many ways the musculoskeletal system defines the human form. Locomotion and the movement of body parts are the intrinsic functions that separate us from lower forms of life.

Technological advances—especially in the areas of joint implant, sports injuries, and trauma—have propelled orthopedic surgeons to the forefront of responsibility for maintaining human locomotive functions. Medical approaches to the treatment of calcium-metabolism disorders are geared to preventing degeneration and maintaining the intrinsic homeostasis required for a strong and long-lived musculoskeletal system. Osteoarthritis and osteoporosis together represent the most serious disabling disorders commonly seen in medicine today.

▶ Osteoarthritis

Osteoarthritis is still commonly considered a "wear-and-tear" disease of joints. The joints of the human body are the hinges that we depend on for purposeful movement. Cartilage provides the lubricating surface for joint movement. Unfortunately, cartilage lacks the ability to regenerate satisfactorily once worn. Although much research has focused on replacing the cartilage material, and current efforts in various laboratories have been exciting, no breakthroughs have been forthcoming.

Many factors influence the aging of joints and their cartilage surfaces. Injury, congenital malformations and malalignments, infection, excessive weight, and overuse all contribute to shortening the life span of human joints. Studies have hinted at a genetic predisposition to some early forms of arthritis, but such findings are as yet indeterminate in defining exact patterns of inheritance in common osteoarthritis.

Prevention of osteoarthritis is geared toward preserving the natural life span of human joints. Muscles should be viewed as the "shock absorbers" and protectors of joints and cartilage. Adequate muscle tone and flexibility is necessary to enable joints to withstand the demands placed upon them. For increasing use of joints and cartilage, the muscles must be correspondingly improved to preserve the underlying structure and functions of joints. The role of maintaining ideal body weight in preventing osteoarthritis cannot be overemphasized. Prompt treatment of injury, in order to preserve the normal architecture around joints, is also important.

Boon for Injured Athletes

A crescent-shaped pad called the medial meniscus helps cushion the bones of the knee joint and prevents them from rubbing together. When this cartilage is torn, the recommendation was once surgery to remove it, but arthritis and deformity often followed. Now, surgeons seek to repair the cartilage or, in extreme cases, resort to transplants.

Medial meniscus

Femur

Tibia

Fibula

Ligament

Sources: Interaction: California Orthopedic and Sports Medicine Group Quarterly Newsletter; "Gray's Anatomy" (Lea & Febiger)

Treatment of osteoarthritis has been advanced by the development of nonsteroidal anti-inflammatory drugs (NSAIDs). Such drugs safely and effectively diminish the pain and swelling associated with arthritic joints. Exercise and therapeutic techniques to improve the range of motion and strength are time-honored conservative approaches for treating osteoarthritis. Local injections of steroidal compounds are also in common clinical use for flare-ups of inflamed joints, and are temporarily effective in pursuing pain-free function.

▶ Osteoporosis

The strength of the human skeleton depends upon the interwoven structure of tightly knit crystals of calcium and phosphorus. Osteoporosis, a disease that results in a loss of bone density, occurs to some degree in everyone over the age of 40. The condition is particularly prevalent and progressive in postmenopausal women, and in both men and women over the age of 70.

The prevention of osteoporosis should begin in youth, when the skeleton is developing its maximum density and strength. After the age of 30, losses occur faster than gains, especially in women. Early calcium intake is perhaps the most important factor in determining bone strength. Calcium supplementation in the range of 800 to 1,200 milligrams per day, and 1,500 to 2,000 milligrams per day in postmenopausal or lactating women, is helpful in maintaining calcium homeostasis. Vitamin D, necessary for proper metabolism and absorption of calcium, should be made available to the body in the range of 400 to 800 units per day either through diet or supplements.

Estrogen replacement in postmenopausal women is extremely important in negating female bone loss, but such therapy must be carefully weighed against risk factors. Women should consult their gynecologists to learn the risks and benefits related to estrogen use for osteoporosis.

Weight-bearing exercises throughout life, abstaining from tobacco products, and prudent alcohol intake all contribute to the bones' ability to maintain density and strength and prevent fractures in later years.

Current hormonal and therapeutic treatments aimed at stimulating bone formation—such as sodium fluoride, parathyroid hormone, and various growth factors—have not proven to be clinically useful yet. Antiresorptive drugs, such as the hormone calcitonin or the biphosphonate Didronel, can be used in severe cases of osteoporosis with good results, but once again, their continued effectiveness in long-term routine clinical use has not been established.

▶ Surgical Technology

Perhaps the greatest advances in treating the disorders that deteriorate and injure the musculoskeletal system are in the area of surgical techniques. For instance, joint-replacement arthroscopy and skeletal internal fixation have used physical materials to restore structural integrity and preserve function when losses have been caused by advanced osteoarthritis, osteoporosis, congenital disorders, and unexpected injury and trauma.

Joint Replacement. Total joint replacement has been considered the single most important advance in the treatment of arthritic conditions. Using synthetic materials, joints are made to regain their low friction, with a subsequent reduction or elimination of pain. Substances such as polyethylene, stainless steel, and titanium allow strength and ease of movement. Attachment to biological systems using either methyl-methacrylate cement or hydroxyapatite spray allows for structural integrity and bony ingrowth.

Long-term follow-up studies reveal that the life span of currently performed total joint replacements ranges anywhere from 10 to 25 years. Future developments and technology should lead to lifelong expectations in this type of surgery.

Custom-designed implants and better biological materials (such as coral) are other exciting new developments in this rapidly growing specialty of orthopedic surgery.

Arthroscopy. Arthroscopy represents a significant advance in the treatment of many joint injuries and disorders. Using minimally invasive techniques, the arthroscopic surgeon can repair many serious ligament and cartilage injuries without the use of open surgery.

Often under local anesthesia and frequently on an outpatient basis, arthroscopy can effectively treat the effects of sports trauma, arthritis, and infections, usually with minimal postoperative pain and disability, quick rehabilitation, and few complications.

Internal Fixation. The treatment of many fractures and congenital bone-length deformities has been advanced by physical science and structural engineering. Stainless steel, titanium, and other alloys have been refined to afford biological compatibility, and are increasingly used to attain stabilization and healing. The orthopedic surgeon's use of these rods, screws, and plates, as well as advanced leg-lengthening devices, can provide complete rehabilitation from serious musculoskeletal conditions that once were the cause of lifelong disability. Computer technology is being developed to assist in applying the exact measurements to each individual's system and requirements.

▶ Rehabilitation

The days of "bed rest" in the treatment of orthopedic conditions have been replaced by the proven results of early exercise to advance the recovery from musculoskeletal injury and disease. Physical therapists are playing an increasingly important role in rehabilitation, equal in many respects to orthopedic treatment and surgery.

Athletic activity, specific stretching, strengthening, and conditioning are important, if not critical, aspects of the care of bone, muscle, and joint disorders. New physical-therapy and chiropractic treatments—including diathermy, cryotherapy, ultrasound, and electric stimulation—all have exciting roles to play in the rehabilitation and repair of injury and disease.

Alfred E. Mitchell, M.D.

Brain and Nervous System

▶ Multiple Sclerosis

Myelin sheaths are present on many nerve fibers of the central nervous system. Myelin insulates the nerve fibers (axons) of the brain and spinal cord, thus allowing rapid, energy-efficient, and even repetitive firing of those nerve fibers. In multiple sclerosis (MS), an immune-mediated disease of the central nervous system, lymphocytes, a type of immune cell, selectively attack the myelin sheaths, stripping them away to produce demyelination lesions. Symptoms in any given individual occur sporadically over time and depend on which neuronal pathways are affected by these lesions. Initial symptoms of numbness and tingling may progress to unsteadiness, temporary loss of vision, slurred speech, weakness, and urinary incontinence.

The cause of the lymphocyte attack on the nervous system is not yet known. However, the adhesion of inflammatory cells (mononuclear leukocytes) to blood vessel walls and later immune-cell penetration of the endothelial cell blood-brain barrier have been recognized as important steps in the development of the demyelination lesions that are characteristic of MS. Therefore, interfering with the processes of adhesion and penetration have now become the focus of efforts to treat MS.

Human clinical trials are currently under way to study the effects of interferon in regulating the immune and inflammatory cells in the central nervous system, including the lymphocytes that penetrate the blood-brain barrier. Through the use of genetic engineering, modifications have been made to a form of interferon to enhance its stability and widen the available administration options for the drug.

Preliminary studies with the genetically modified form of human beta interferon have produced a dose-dependent response in MS patients. Those patients treated with higher doses of this form of interferon over a 12-week period showed negligible disease activity when compared to patients on either lower doses of the drug or a placebo.

Although these pilot studies are highly promising, it should be noted that they were of only limited duration and involved only a relatively small number of patients. Furthermore, the higher, more effective dosages of the drug produced notable, although not dangerous, side effects. Finally, researchers cannot be certain that the results of the studies arose from random sampling effects or were actually derived from the specific effects of the drug therapy.

To assure the validity of the data, researchers are conducting a much larger, double-blind study comparing the effects of three possible options: a placebo; the modified interferon at high dosage; and the modified interferon at less than its most effective dosage. Neither the study participants nor their evaluators are aware of who is receiving which of the three options. This study has been under way for several years. Its results will likely be subjected to detailed analysis in the very near future.

Research has also progressed using rodents with a disease similar to MS called experimental allergic encephalomyelitis (EAE). Specific antibodies have been effective in preventing the adhesion of inflammatory cells to the lining of the blood vessel walls, limiting the development of lesions in the nervous system and either preventing or delaying the onset of clinical symptoms. Extension of these studies to patients with MS is presently limited by the source of the antibodies (they have thus far been produced only in rodents). Since these rodent antibodies would be perceived as foreign substances that need to be eradicated by the human immune system, their effectiveness would be limited to a single period of use for human patients. Research is advancing in producing a human vaccine that contains only the part of the rodent antibody that targets the inflammatory cells that are adhering to the blood vessel walls. This target molecule is masked so that the body would not recognize it as foreign. The outlook for this treatment appears bright.

▶ Amyotrophic Lateral Sclerosis

The most common motor neuron disease, amyotrophic lateral sclerosis (ALS), has come to be known as Lou Gehrig's disease, as it was the disease that took the life of the "Pride of the Yankees" in 1941. The disease is relentlessly progressive in its wasting of major muscles, although on occasion

it may be limited to specific muscle groups, and thus be nonfatal. Death is usually due to respiratory complications, resulting from the pronounced weakening of the muscles controlling breathing. In addition, when motor nerve cells in the brain stem die, the victim encounters difficulty swallowing or, in some cases, the complete inability to swallow. This symptom commonly leads to aspiration pneumonia, which may itself be fatal. On occasion survival has been extended over a long term, as is the case with renowned physicist Stephen Hawking, one of today's best-known long-term sufferers who also provides evidence that thinking and cognitive functions remain intact in this disorder.

It had been hypothesized that ALS is the result of a failed feedback loop essential for providing a trophic (nutritional) factor needed for the survival of motor neuron populations. Research has established that motor nerve cells survive if the missing factor is replaced. Alternative hypotheses have suggested that destruction of the motor neurons may occur by an immune response, as evidenced by the presence of specific antibodies to cell surface molecules. Exposure to toxins like lead may also injure the motor neuron system.

Growth factor replacement therapy using thyrotropin-stimulating hormone (TSH) to prolong motor nerve cell survival has been tried in the past with unsuccessful results. At the present time, however, several new candidate molecules are being investigated, including insulin-like growth factor (IGF) and ciliary neuronotrophic factor (CNTF), based upon laboratory studies indicating that these candidate molecules can prolong survival of motor neurons in tissue culture. Knowledge of the location of the genes that are regulating the production and response to these molecules should provide insight into whether the hereditary forms of ALS are influenced by the same molecules.

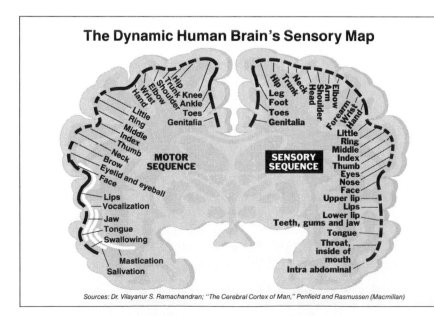

The Dynamic Human Brain's Sensory Map

MOTOR SEQUENCE

Hip, Trunk, Shoulder, Elbow, Wrist, Hand, Little, Ring, Middle, Index, Thumb, Neck, Brow, Eyelid and eyeball, Face, Lips, Vocalization, Jaw, Tongue, Swallowing, Mastication, Salivation

Knee, Ankle, Toes, Genitalia

SENSORY SEQUENCE

Neck, Arm, Shoulder, Head, Leg, Foot, Toes, Genitalia, Hip, Trunk, Forearm, Wrist, Hand, Little, Ring, Middle, Index, Thumb, Eyes, Nose, Face, Upper lip, Lips, Lower lip, Teeth, gums and jaw, Tongue, Throat, inside of mouth, Intra abdominal

The brain's sensory map appears to be capable of extensive reorganization, even in adulthood. If a body part is missing, its neural connections are quickly rerouted to adjacent brain centers that correspond to other parts. For example, if a hand is amputated, stimulating the shoulder or face evokes a sensation in the missing part. The cells reconnect over great distances in just a month.

Sources: Dr. Vilayanur S. Ramachandran; "The Cerebral Cortex of Man," Penfield and Rasmussen (Macmillan)

▶ Parkinson's Disease

Parkinson's disease develops with the loss of brain cells producing the neurotransmitter dopamine, or if these cells lose their ability to produce dopamine in the brain. About one person in 200 is affected by the disease, with 50,000 new cases a year in the U.S. alone. This disease is more common in men than women, and more common in individuals aged 55 to 65 than in people younger than age 50.

The disease causes loss of higher mental functioning and tremors that reduce the ability to perform fine tasks, such as fastening buttons or holding a knife and fork. Additional symptoms include a stiff, shuffling, overbalancing walk that may break into uncontrollable, tiny running steps.

Drug therapy has been available for over 20 years; unfortunately, the drugs are more effective in treating the mental slowness than the tremor component of the disease. Moreover, current treatments do nothing toward slowing the progression of the disease over time.

The recognition of Parkinson's disease among a sampling of younger people—substance abusers aged 35 to 40—led to a new avenue of exploration for possible causes of the disorder. This exploration has led to the recognition that a toxic molecule is generated by those cells that are lost in Parkinson's disease—the cells are, in effect, actually participating in their own death. Drug treatment has been developed to slow or stop the progression of Parkinsonism by limiting this process. One such drug, deprenyl, has been shown to slow the progression of the disease, but it appears to have little effect on altering the symptoms already present. As a result, Parkinson's patients have been somewhat reluctant to spend money on a treatment for which they do not see an immediate effect, thereby limiting their therapeutic options.

A newer approach to the treatment of this disease involves the transplantation of tissue into the brain, tissue which can replenish the source of cells that make the neurotransmitter dopamine. There have been problems with this procedure, however. One type of tissue that would be effective in this treatment is brain tissue from aborted fetuses. Advanced research using this tissue has been stymied by the politics and ethics surrounding the abortion issue. Furthermore, researchers have not yet determined the precise, optimal location to implant cell tissue. Nonetheless, the technique offers promise. With restrictions on federal financing of research that uses fetal tissue lifted by President Bill Clinton, the procedure will likely be further explored in the near future, and will be expected to offer insights into the treatment of other neurological illnesses, including Alzheimer's disease, Huntington's chorea, and stroke.

Robert L. Knobler, M.D., Ph.D.

Cancer

▶ Genetic Basis for Breast Cancer

In 1993 some 46,000 American women will die from breast cancer. A number of factors are known to predispose a woman to developing this disease. It has long been recognized that there are certain risk factors that increase a woman's risk of developing breast cancer. Such factors include early menarche (onset of menstrual periods), late menopause, no full-term pregnancies prior to age 30, a diagnosis of atypical hyperplasia (an abnormal growth pattern of cells) of the breast, living past age 60, and one or more immediate relatives (such as a mother, sister, or daughter) with breast cancer. The occurrence of multiple cases of breast cancer in a single family, called "familial breast cancer," is particularly intriguing since it suggests that some women may inherit a gene that places them at increased risk for the disease. While it is estimated that familial breast cancer may account for only 5 percent of all cases of breast cancer, the more than 150,000 new cases of breast cancer diagnosed annually in the U.S. alone would make the 7,500 cases of familial breast cancer the most common inherited disease in our society, if indeed the disease has a genetic origin. Identifying the gene and its characteristics would add an important piece to the breast-cancer puzzle.

Some researchers feel that such an unknown gene may have once served a useful purpose, possibly in the normal growth and development of such hormonally dependent tissues as the breasts and ovaries. Decades ago, when there was a shorter interval between the beginning of menstruation and the birth of the first child, women who possessed this gene may have been fertile and able to bear children at an earlier age than women without the gene. As the interval between menarche and childbirth has increased, the gene's prolonged effect on the breast, uninterrupted by childbirth, could produce abnormal cell growth and the formation of cancerous cells. Researchers at the University of Michigan in Ann Arbor, and the University of California at Berkeley, have strong evidence that the familial breast-cancer gene exists somewhere in the long arm of chromosome 17 (17q). Using sophisticated molecular-biology techniques, investigators are systematically probing this area, and it is expected that within the next year the exact location and identity of the gene will be discovered. Once this has been accomplished, a probe for this gene can be developed and used to detect women who are at high risk for developing familial breast cancer. To treat women who test positive for this gene, molecules could possibly be synthesized to locate and inactivate the gene in an attempt to prevent the development of breast cancer. By locating the gene, it may also be possible to explore the exact mechanism by which this gene acts upon cells, giving researchers important insights into the genetic basis for breast and other cancers.

▶ DES and Cancer

Diethylstilbestrol (DES) is a synthetic hormone first manufactured in Great Britain in 1938. For more than 25 years, it was prescribed to pregnant women to reduce the risk of miscarriage. It is estimated that between 500,000 and 2 million pregnant women in the United States took DES and, since DES crosses the placenta into the fetus, an equal number of their children were exposed to the drug prior to birth. In 1970 the first report was published identifying a rare form of vaginal cancer, called clear-cell carcinoma, in six young women exposed to DES in the womb; these women, and others like them, became known as "DES daughters." Reports of other gynecological cancers occurring in young women exposed to DES followed, and, within a year, DES was removed from the market in the United States. By 1981 more than 400 cases of clear-cell carcinoma of the vagina or cervix had been reported to the Food and Drug Administration

(FDA); approximately two-thirds of the cases were associated with prebirth exposure to DES or related compounds. Since then, careful studies have confirmed the increased risk of cervical and vaginal disorders in DES daughters. Additional studies have failed to detect increased risk for any other cancers in these women. Sons of women who took DES—"DES sons"—do not seem to have an increased risk of cancer. In addition the women who took the drug do not seem to be at risk for developing the same type of gynecological cancers as their daughters, although they have been found to be at slightly increased risk for the development of breast cancer.

The effect of DES exposure on reproduction and fertility has also been studied. Abnormalities of the reproductive tract have been found in up to 53 percent of DES daughters, but they do not appear to suffer any impairment of fertility. No clear impairment of fertility has been detected in the sons of women who used DES.

Last spring the National Cancer Institute (NCI), the National Institute of Child Health and Human Development, the National Institute of Environmental Health Services, and the National Institutes of Health's (NIH's) Office of Research on Women's Health cosponsored a workshop on long-term effects of exposure to DES. The conference reviewed and updated existing data, identified areas where additional research is required, and facilitated multidisciplinary collaboration on DES research. Specific recommendations regarding cancer-screening guidelines for DES daughters were issued as a result of this conference. The NCI announced that it would provide support to programs that provide continued follow-up of DES-exposed individuals. As DES sons and daughters enter middle age, they will be monitored closely in order to detect any increase in cancers more likely to manifest themselves in this age group, such as prostate and breast cancer.

▶ RU-486

RU-486 is a synthetic steroid hormone, similar to progesterone. When administered in sequence with the hormone prostaglandin during early stages of pregnancy, it induces abortion. Although available in Europe, RU-486 is not currently available in the United States, primarily due to political concerns that the drug would result in an increased number of abortions and would be misused as a convenient method of birth control. The French manufacturer, Roussel-Uclaf, has been hesitant to attempt clinical trials of the drug in the United States because of concerns over an economic boycott by those opposed to abortion.

Another controversy involving RU-486 has emerged on a completely different front: cancer.

DES Daughters and Structural Problems

DES daughters often develop a smaller uterus or a T-shaped uterus. The unusual size and shape may contribute to pregnancy problems, most notably preterm labor.

A Normal Uterus

A T-Shaped Uterus

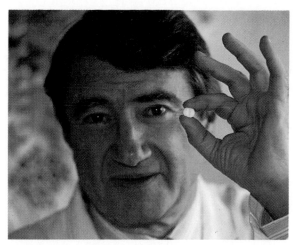

RU-486, the so-called "morning after" pill developed by French scientist Etienne Emile Beaulieu (above), has emerged as a possible treatment for cancer.

Laboratory researchers have reported that RU-486 is active against the tumors of several cancers, including breast cancer and a rare type of brain tumor called meningioma. A limited clinical trial conducted in France in 1987 found that 12 of 22 women with advanced breast cancer benefited from treatment with RU-486. Usually these observations would prompt additional trials in human subjects with cancer to determine the drug's clinical effectiveness. But the controversy surrounding RU-486, particularly in the United States (potentially the largest market for all uses of this drug), has prevented this next step from being taken.

A congressional hearing was held in the spring of 1992 to determine whether the abortion issue was delaying the development of a drug potentially useful against cancer. NCI officials denied that political considerations had been a factor in their decision not to pursue RU-486 research, citing the institute's support of a multicenter clinical trial to evaluate the drug's effectiveness in patients with meningioma. Further, the officials pointed to the availability of other drugs to treat breast cancer, drugs that have greater potential benefits than does RU-486. With legislation introduced in 1991 that would ban importation of RU-486 for any purpose (including cancer research), and opposing legislation introduced in 1992 that would require federally funded testing of RU-486 as both an abortion-inducing drug and a potential cancer treatment, it is likely that RU-486 will continue to be the center of heated debate.

▶ Malignant Melanoma

Skin cancer is by far the most common cancer diagnosed in the United States. More than 1 million Americans are expected to develop skin cancer in 1993. Fortunately, the vast majority of these cases are basal or squamous cell cancers, types that are easily cured through removal of the affected skin. A third type of skin cancer, called malignant melanoma, behaves in an entirely different, and much more serious, manner. Malignant melanoma often appears as a mole on the skin that has grown or changed in shape or color. If not caught at its earliest stages, it can invade and spread throughout the entire body via the lymphatic or circulatory systems. In 1992 it is estimated that 32,000 new cases of melanoma were diagnosed, and 6,700 people died of this disease in the U.S. Even more troubling is that since 1973 the incidence of this disease has risen 78 percent, an increase greater than for any other cancer in the U.S.

Risk for melanoma is directly related to Sun exposure: those exposed to greater amounts of sunlight are at greater risk, and those areas of the body that tend to be exposed to the sun are more likely to be sites for the development of a melanoma. To reduce the potential for developing malignant melanoma, individuals should reduce their exposure to the Sun, especially during hours of peak ultraviolet ray intensity (usually from 10 A.M. to 3 P.M.). People should also wear protective clothing and use sunscreen with a Sun protection factor (SPF) of 15 or higher on parts of the body subjected to regular exposure.

A Consensus Development Conference held at the National Institutes of Health in 1992 issued guidelines regarding the best treatment for people who have developed malignant melanoma, based on a review of all available data on surgical approaches to the treatment of early stage, localized melanoma. The panel noted that very small melanomas—those entirely contained within the most superficial levels of the skin (known as melanomas in situ)—can be safely removed with only a 0.5-centimeter margin of surrounding healthy skin; margins of only 1 centimeter of healthy skin are adequate when removing melanomas less than 1 millimeter thick. Previously, standard practice had been to remove 5-centimeter margins of healthy skin. The panel also recommended that local lymph nodes need not be routinely removed during surgery for clinically localized melanoma.

Individuals who have had one melanoma should be monitored closely, since they are at increased risk for melanoma recurrence or second melanomas later in life. If melanoma has occurred in more than one member of any family, all family members should be enrolled in a melanoma-surveillance program. If implemented on a regular basis, these recommendations should substantially reduce the number of individuals affected by this dangerous disease, and lessen the side effects of treatment for those afflicted.

▶ cis-Retinoic Acid and Alpha Interferon

In 1990 investigators at the M. D. Anderson Cancer Center in Houston, Texas, first reported the results of a clinical trial demonstrating that *cis*-retinoic acid, a vitamin A derivative, reduced the recurrence rate of head and neck cancer. This was the first human trial to confirm observations made in the laboratory that vitamin A derivatives (also known as "retinoids") could slow or stop cancer growth and cause those cancer cells that are apparently "stuck" at an early phase of growth to "mature" into normal cells. Further clinical trials of *cis*-retinoic acid proved disappointing, however. The side effects of the compounds prevented adequate doses from being administered.

Researchers have long recognized that another naturally occurring compound, alpha interferon, also has the ability to fight cancer tumors, although it does so in an entirely different fashion than does *cis*-retinoic acid. Researchers decided to combine the use of alpha interferon and *cis*-retinoic acid in the laboratory. The two drugs together appeared to have greater activity against tumors than either agent alone. A clinical trial investigated the effectiveness of this drug combination in 32 patients with squamous-cell carcinoma of the skin that had recurred despite previous treatment and that was too widespread for surgical removal. Sixty-eight percent of patients had significant shrinkage of their tumors, and, in 25 percent of the subjects the tumors disappeared completely, an effect that lasted up to 21 months. A second trial was conducted in 26 women with newly diagnosed squamous-cell carcinoma of the cervix. Within four months of beginning treatment, half of these women experienced tumor shrinkage of at least 50 percent.

The side effects from treatment with *cis*-retinoic acid and alpha interferon were not severe, and the treatment was well tolerated—most patients developed only dryness of the skin, mouth, and lips; some developed fatigue, flulike symptoms, or a mild decrease in white-blood-cell counts. These trials provide important insights into the potential value of therapies that may work, at least in part, by forcing cancer cells to mature into normal cells.

▶ Prostate-Cancer Prevention Trial

Prostate cancer is the most common cancer in men. Experts estimate that 1 in every 11 men will develop this disease, and 165,000 new cases will be diagnosed in 1993 alone. While important advances have been made in the treatment of this disease, clinical researchers are about to embark upon a unique study to determine whether the drug finasteride (Proscar) can prevent prostate cancer. This drug has already been approved by the FDA for treatment of symptoms associated with noncancerous prostate enlargement, a condition known as benign prostatic hyperplasia (BPH).

Finasteride acts by blocking the effects of the enzyme essential for early phases of prostate growth. Laboratory researchers have determined that this same enzyme may also be important in the earliest stages of prostate cancer development. A nationwide clinical trial will test whether inhibition of this enzyme can prevent the development of prostate cancer in men at risk. The clinical trial is

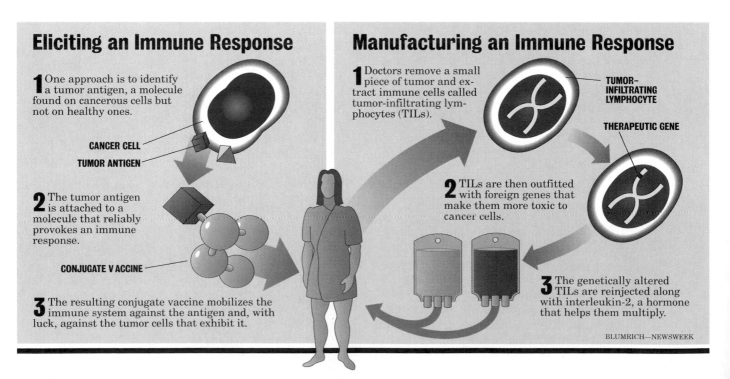

Eliciting an Immune Response

1 One approach is to identify a tumor antigen, a molecule found on cancerous cells but not on healthy ones.

CANCER CELL
TUMOR ANTIGEN

2 The tumor antigen is attached to a molecule that reliably provokes an immune response.

CONJUGATE VACCINE

3 The resulting conjugate vaccine mobilizes the immune system against the antigen and, with luck, against the tumor cells that exhibit it.

Manufacturing an Immune Response

1 Doctors remove a small piece of tumor and extract immune cells called tumor-infiltrating lymphocytes (TILs).

TUMOR-INFILTRATING LYMPHOCYTE

THERAPEUTIC GENE

2 TILs are then outfitted with foreign genes that make them more toxic to cancer cells.

3 The genetically altered TILs are reinjected along with interleukin-2, a hormone that helps them multiply.

BLUMRICH—NEWSWEEK

scheduled to begin in late 1993, and will enroll 18,000 men over a period of three years. Each man will take either finasteride or a placebo daily for a period of 10 years. At the end of that time, all men in the study will undergo a tissue sampling of the prostate. Information obtained from this sample, along with information derived from patients who developed prostate cancer while in the study, will help to determine whether finasteride is effective at preventing prostate cancer. A similar trial was started in 1992 to study whether the breast-cancer treatment drug tamoxifen is effective in preventing breast cancer. Taken together, these trials represent an important initiative in primary-cancer prevention.

▶ p53 and Cell Division

Researchers have long known that the p53 gene, located on the short arm of chromosome 17, is a tumor-suppressor gene. But its exact mechanism was never clearly understood. Recent research has provided a better understanding of the role of the p53 gene in normal and cancerous cell division that may lead to new approaches to cancer treatment.

In laboratory experiments, Michael B. Kastan, M.D., associate professor of oncology at Johns Hopkins School of Medicine in Baltimore, Maryland, and colleagues found that when bone-marrow cells were exposed to radiation, the amounts of p53 protein in the cells increased sharply. Immediately afterward, the cells ceased growing, just at the point in the cell cycle when new DNA normally is being replicated before cell division. But after a period of rest (about 15 hours), cell growth resumed, and cell division progressed normally.

The researchers concluded that p53 is able to detect mutations in the chromosomes caused by radiation or other environmental assaults. The molecule is then able to stop cells from dividing temporarily, until the body's DNA-repair enzymes can fix the genetic damage before it is passed on to future generations of cells.

In the absence of p53, the damaged cell continues to divide, passing on the initial minor mutation, which becomes magnified as it is passed from cell generation to generation. Yet, significantly, researchers have found that these cancerous cells are actually more sensitive to the impact of radiation and chemotherapy than are healthy cells bearing the p53 gene.

In light of this cell mechanism, doctors are proposing that a logical approach to treatment would be to expose a patient to radiation to trigger most normal cells in the body to arrest their growth. When tumor cells lacking p53 continue to proliferate, a follow-up dose of a drug that attacks dividing cells could be used to eradicate the cancer cells.

Mace L. Rothenberg, M.D.

Child Development and Psychology

▶ Mothers and Infants: Responsiveness

Parenting practices vary across families and cultures. The way in which a parent responds to a child often defines the relationship between a parent and child and affects a child's developmental progress. A study by Marc Bornstein from the National Institute of Child Health and Human Development, and colleagues examined differences in mother-child interactions in families from the United States, France, and Japan. Parents from these three countries were chosen because they traditionally have widely divergent child-rearing techniques and expectations. First-time mothers together with their five-month-old infants were recruited from private obstetric and pediatric practices in New York, Paris, and Tokyo. Each mother-and-infant pair was visited in their homes by a local female observer who videotaped the pair for 45 minutes. The mothers had been instructed to act in their usual manner during the sessions.

Infants from the three countries all demonstrated vocalizations and gazing or looking behaviors at similar rates, and all the mothers were more responsive to their baby's vocalizations than to their gazing or looking behaviors.

Differences were found in the ways the mothers from the three countries responded to their infants. For example, American mothers responded to their infants' gazing behavior by directing the infants'

Psychologists suggest that a mother's ethnic background may play a role in how she responds to the vocalizations and gazing behavior of her infant.

attention to objects or events in the surrounding environment; French mothers tended to respond by feeding, diapering, or imitating the infant's vocalizations. Japanese mothers were the most responsive to the baby's social looking by personal interaction, including kissing, hugging, or various types of vocalizations.

As with any scientific investigation, there are limitations to consider before drawing general conclusions. The sample population used all had similar urban, educational, and economic backgrounds. Results may have been different if the mother-and-infant pairs had been from a broader economic and educational background. Nevertheless, this study, with its cross-cultural developmental comparison, may provide insight into the role child-rearing practices play in the developmental process.

▶ Anger Control: Parent and Child

Anger is an emotion that is inevitably displayed by all parents and children. It is an emotion easily controlled by some, more difficult to control by others. Mental-health professionals believe that anger is a healthy emotion if used appropriately.

Young children must learn to control their anger if it creates problems for them. In a study by Richard A. Fabes and Nancy Eisenberg from the Ari-

Many youngsters believe they can calm an angry parent through direct intervention. Older children find that a less direct approach produces better results.

zona State University in Tempe, published in *Child Development,* the situations that make children angry and how they cope with this anger were observed. Subjects in the study were preschoolers, ranging in age from 42 to 71 months, who attended a university day-care center. The children were observed for genuine anger reactions based on language indicating anger, facial expressions indicating anger, and aggressive behavior. The trained observers also recorded the events preceding the anger episode and the child's behavior immediately following the anger episode. Children's anger-coping strategies included revenge, active resistance, venting, avoidance, seeking adult support, and expressing dislike.

The study's results indicate a relationship between popularity and the ways in which children respond to anger. Boys who were popular did not become angry as a result of physical assault or social rejection. Popular girls were also not affected by rejection. But they were more apt than boys to verbally express their feelings toward the provoking child. Socially competent girls did not tend to seek revenge. The authors concluded that popular children coped with anger in ways that would minimize further conflict and prevent damage to social relationships.

Children are often affected by their parents' anger. In another study of how children cope with anger, in this case parental anger, Katherine Covell from Brock University in Ontario, Canada, and Brenda Miles from the University of Toronto studied the techniques used by children to reduce their parents' anger. They also wanted to learn if children believed that direct intervention was considered the most effective strategy, and if this strategy reflected a more advanced understanding of anger reduction.

Two phases of the study were designed. In the first phase, 120 children, ages 4 to 9, were shown pictures and read stories that had increasingly complex scenarios involving parental anger. The children were then asked to describe the parent's feelings, whether the child in the story could reduce the parent's anger, and if there was anything the child could do differently. Results showed all children believed the story child could change the anger of the parent, and direct intervention was the strategy chosen most often to reduce anger in all three scenarios. In the second phase of the study, 180 children were divided into three age groups (4 to 6, 7 to 9, and 10 to 12). Half of each group participated with their mothers; the other half participated with their fathers. The children listened to stories and were told the child in the story wanted to make the parent or friend in the story less angry, or wanted to have them stay happy. The task was for the child to select various strategies depicted in cartoon-

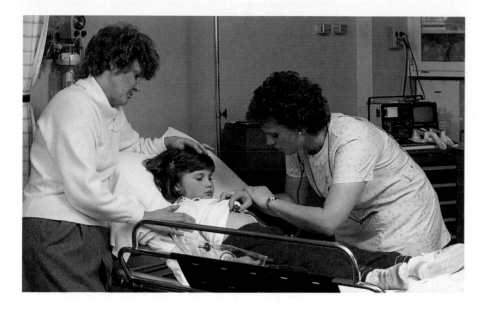

Although young children cannot explain why pain hurts, they do recognize pain as an unpleasant sensation. Even at a very young age, a child can localize a painful site on his or her body.

style drawings. Surprisingly, the study showed that the older children tended to not always choose the direct-intervention strategies to reduce parental anger. This reflects a growing ability of a child to understand the complexities of the causes of anger. Older children may not always choose direct intervention, because it may not be the best strategy for all anger situations.

▶ Child Behavior and Maternal Stress
Maternal stress and depression have long been thought to affect childhood behavior. A study published in the *Journal of Clinical Child Psychology* in 1992 was designed to examine the relationship between a mother's depressed mood and her perception of her child's behavior, as well as the effect of daily stressors influencing her perceptions of her child's behavior. Single mothers with at least one 5- to 12-year-old child were asked to complete questionnaires that included a depression scale, a measure of stress, and a measure of child behavior described in 12 vignettes. Not surprisingly, the researchers found that mothers perceived a child's behavior as more problematic, upsetting, and warranting a more intense behavioral response when it occurred in a stressful context. Furthermore, negative perceptions and reactions were associated more with daily stressors than with major life events. And mothers who were depressed were found to be more upset by a child's behavior than were mothers who were not depressed.

This study confirms that parenting is even more difficult when there is added stress and psychopathology present. Single mothers are particularly vulnerable to daily stress, and usually do not have adequate physical or emotional support. Parents need support in the area of minimizing stress and recognizing their response to stress so that their mood does not negatively affect their child-rearing responsibilities.

▶ Children and Pain Perception
How children cope with pain and illness continues to be the subject of much research. In the past, most of the studies in this area concentrated on chronically ill children. Research has supported the notion that children interpret their illness according to their developmental level. A study published this past year expanded this notion to the child's understanding of pain. One hundred children and adolescents aged 3 to 23 were interviewed about past pain experiences, understanding the degree of pain as described in three vignettes, pain experienced by family members, and the child's general cognitive developmental level.

Similarities were found between a child's understanding of illness and understanding why pain hurts. Typically, a younger child cannot explain why a pain hurts, but as the child ages, he or she begins to attribute causal explanations and hypotheses. Young children, however, can localize pain and report that pain is an unpleasant feeling. This information is valuable to health professionals who administer various medical procedures to children. It is also useful for parents to realize that their young children are capable of at least knowing how pain can occur, and are able to relate some feelings about the sensation. Encouraging a child to express feelings associated with pain and painful procedures may be more important than we realize in chronically ill children.

▶ Young Children and Their Belief System
How a child develops a belief system is a complicated process that has long interested developmental theorists. Researchers have explored how a young child understands an act and develops a belief about that act and possibly applies that belief to other situations. A 1992 study by John H. Flavell and colleagues from Stanford University, published

in *Child Development,* explored how different types of beliefs develop in children. Four studies were designed to investigate a child's understanding of specific belief types concerning physical fact, value, moral, social convention, and ownership, and how these beliefs changed as the child grew older. In each study, groups of children at various ages were told stories or asked to evaluate photographs or scenarios. The story content reflected specific belief types. The children were asked questions after listening to the story or reviewing the task.

As suspected, findings indicate that a child moves progressively from little understanding of values, morals, social conventions, and ownership beliefs to a greater understanding at higher ages. What is unclear is whether the young child possesses the belief but is unable to fully express the feeling due to language limitations. The authors note that it is important for children to learn that when a parent or other adult denies them objects or activities that they feel entitled to, it is not out of meanness, but because the adult feels that it is in the child's best interest. Children need to distinguish between a person who does something wrong, but acts in good conscience, and a person who is wrong, but continues to behave in the same manner, with perhaps an ulterior motive.

▶ Eating and Body Image in Children

Concern over body image or weight has been present in our society for many years. Dieting is no longer a fad, but has become a way of life for many women. Eating disorders are becoming more common and are often difficult to treat. Determining when girls become aware of a need to be thin has become a topic of interest to developmental psychologists. Mark H. Thelen and colleagues from the University of Missouri in Columbia designed an instrument called "The Body Image and Eating Questionnaire." The questionnaire was given to 19 nonobese students in second, fourth, and sixth grades. The students were told their answers would be confidential. There were no response differences among the boys from different grades. But while second-grade girls were only minimally concerned about their body image, girls from the fourth and sixth grades indicated a greater concern of being or becoming overweight and a desire to be thinner. These girls also showed a higher propensity for restrained eating behaviors.

This study found evidence to suggest concerns over weight may begin as early as the grade school years, and that even girls of normal weight have eating-related concerns. The authors suggest that outside sources may influence a child's self-body image, such as models in magazines or comments by adult family members.

Cynthia P. Rickert, Ph.D.

Digestive System

▶ Colon-Cancer News

A new genetic technique able to detect more than half of all colorectal cancers before they become life-threatening was announced in April 1992. Early detection of colorectal cancer is crucial: the disease has a 90 percent cure rate if the tumor is still localized in the intestine, but only a 10 percent cure rate when the tumor has eaten through the intestinal wall. Tests for the disease have relied on screening of stool samples for blood (followed by a colonoscopy if positive). Many tumors do not bleed, and many benign conditions can produce bloody stools, confounding the diagnosis.

A team of researchers at Johns Hopkins University in Baltimore, Maryland, headed by molecular biologist Bert Vogelstein, was able to detect genetically mutated cells in stool samples with great accuracy, even when the tumors were very small. The results marked the first time that genetic techniques have been used to detect cancer.

Worldwide, 570,000 new cases of colon and rectum cancer were reported in 1992—exceeded only by those for breast and lung cancers. The United States alone reported 156,000 new cases, with 60,000 deaths. Unfortunately, because of its expense, the new genetic diagnostic technique will be limited to monitoring people with a genetic susceptibility to colorectal tumors (or to watch for a recurrence in people who have had a tumor removed), and is not expected to be put to widespread use anytime soon.

Another finding announced in October 1992 further strengthened the evidence that the risk of dying from colon cancer can be reduced sharply by choosing a high-fiber, low-fat diet rich in vegetables, fruits, and grains. A study led by American Cancer Society researchers questioned the health and eating habits of about 750,000 men and women in 1982 and followed them until 1988. The researchers then compared the diets of 1,150 people who had died of the cancer to a group of similar people who had remained healthy. The analysis found that men who consumed the highest amount of plant foods were 24 percent less likely to have a fatal cancer than men at the lowest level of fiber consumption; in women the diet showed a 38 percent cancer-risk reduction.

When combined with aspirin consumption, the risks of developing colorectal cancers may be still further reduced. The same researchers found that a high-fiber, low-fat diet combined with 16 or more aspirins a month reduced the fatal cancer risk for men by a factor of 2.5, and for women by a factor of almost 3 as compared to low-fiber consumers who used no aspirin. Earlier clinical studies had revealed that aspirin may prevent the formation of polyps, or small growths, on the colon that can turn cancerous.

▶ Linking Bowel Movements and Hypnosis

In one study reported in the British medical journal *The Lancet* in July 1992, colon movement, pulse, and respiration rates were measured in 18 patients with irritable-bowel syndrome. Measurements were taken after they had fasted and while they were hypnotized, during which time they were asked to think of an incident that made them feel happy. Fifteen of the patients experienced substantial decreases in body-function rates—indicating that hypnosis may be helpful in managing functional bowel disorders.

▶ Drug Treatments Can Make Patients Sicker

Treating patients in hospital intensive-care units (ICUs) with nonabsorbable antibiotics does not prevent bacterial gastrointestinal-tract infections, and may in fact exacerbate GI-tract infections by suppressing the patient's immune system. In a study reported in the July 4, 1992, issue of *The Lancet,* ICU patients treated with antibiotics were shown to have a high risk of developing secondary, hospital-acquired infections in their gastrointestinal tracts.

Long-term treatment with nonsteroidal anti-inflammatory drugs (NSAIDs) was found to cause ulcers of the jejunum, the lower portion of the small intestine. Earlier research had implicated NSAIDs in causing ulcers of the stomach and duodenum, the upper portion of the small intestine. In rare instances, complications from such ulcers can result in death.

▶ The Pope's Tumor

Surgeons at the Gamelli Hospital in Rome removed a tear-shaped, apricot-sized tumor from the colon of Pope John Paul II during four hours of surgery on July 15, 1992. Although the tumor was initially described as benign, further tests revealed the 72-year-old pontiff's large tumor to be a tubulovillous adenoma—considered to be premalignant because of its potential to metastasize throughout the body. The pope's tumor was found by a colonoscopy, an examination of the colon with a lighted tube. The tumor was found in the colon's final segment, which connects to the rectum. At 2.5 inches in length, the tumor was considerably larger than the normal diameter of the colon—causing the pontiff significant discomfort before the growth was removed. The pope sailed through the surgery with no complications and made a complete recovery.

Gode Davis

Ear, Nose, and Throat

▶ Growth Factors

Perforations of the tympanic membrane, or eardrum, are a frequent cause of hearing loss. These perforations may be caused by traumatic injury, infection, or previous surgery. In many cases, holes in the eardrum will not heal unless doctors patch the holes with tissues obtained from other sites in the body. This surgery, called tympanoplasty, is very expensive, and therefore unavailable in many developing countries. Researchers at the University of California in San Francisco, led by C. Philip Amoils, M.D., are pioneering the use of epidermal growth factor to promote the healing of the eardrum without complicated surgery.

Epidermal growth factor is a substance produced by human cells to promote the healing of cuts in the skin, cornea, and other tissues. Through the use of genetic-engineering technology, large quantities of epidermal growth factor can be produced from yeast cells. In the journal *Otolaryngology—Head and Neck Surgery,* Dr. Amoils describes how non-

A new growth factor induces jawbone formation within 14 days. Below, a jaw segment with new bone growth (between arrows). The X ray at bottom shows that the area has fully mineralized bone, which has the strength of normal bone.

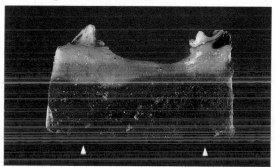

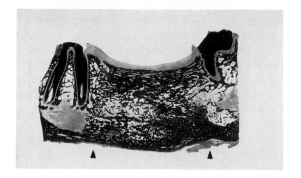

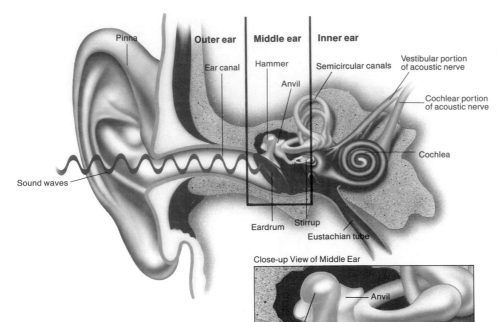

Pinna

Outer ear | **Middle ear** | **Inner ear**

Ear canal

Hammer

Anvil

Semicircular canals

Vestibular portion of acoustic nerve

Cochlear portion of acoustic nerve

Cochlea

Sound waves

Eardrum Stirrup

Eustachian tube

Close-up View of Middle Ear

Anvil

Hammer

Oval window

Stirrup

Round window

Eardrum

A perforated eardrum requires costly surgery to repair. Doctors have now developed an effective and inexpensive technique using paper patches soaked with epidermal growth factor to repair the eardrum.

healing tympanic-membrane perforations in chinchillas were cured using a simple patch of paper covered with a sponge soaked in epidermal growth factor. In laboratory studies, when epidermal growth factor was applied to paper patches covering tympanic-membrane perforations in 16 chinchilla ears, 13 of these ears healed. Alternatively, only 4 of 16 tympanic perforations healed in ears treated with simple paper patching. Although further studies need to be done, Dr. Amoils is hopeful that this simple and relatively inexpensive method of closing chronic eardrum perforations will become the standard treatment.

In similar work a multidisciplinary team led by Dean Toriumi, M.D., from the University of Illinois at Chicago has used a human recombinant bone-inducing factor called bone morphogenetic protein-2 (BMP-2) to accelerate healing in dogs who have had portions of their jaws removed. Implants composed of an inactive dog bone-matrix carrier and human recombinant BMP-2 were placed in the jaws of 12 dogs. Ten other dogs had implants placed with the bone-matrix carrier and no BMP-2, and four dogs had no implants placed at all. All 12 dogs receiving the BMP-2 implants had new growth of bone in their jaws and were able to chew solid food 10 weeks after treatment. Dogs not receiving the BMP-2 implants showed almost no bone growth and were unable to eat normally.

After six months the appearance, mineralization, and functional strength of the bone induced by BMP-2 approached that of the normal bone sur-

rounding it. Because BMP-2 is a recombinant human growth factor, it is free of contaminating factors and has the potential to be produced in large quantities for clinical use. Many cancer victims who must have parts of their jaws removed, as well as many trauma victims missing parts of their facial skeleton, stand to benefit from further advances in this area.

▶ Shock Waves

Salivary-gland stones produce prominent and sometimes painful swelling of the salivary glands, making eating and drinking problematic. For years, surgery to remove the stones or the stone-forming glands was the only treatment option. Now doctors have adapted extracorporeal shock-wave lithotripsy, commonly used to break up kidney stones and gallstones, to the delicate region around the head. For kidney stones and gallstones, the lithotripsy machines generate shock waves with large electromagnetic and electrohydraulic machines. These shock waves break up the stones and allow them to pass through the urinary tract more easily. But these lithotripsy machines could not be used in the head and neck because the shock waves would cause central-nervous-system damage.

Recently, however, researchers in Germany led by Heinrich Iro, M.D., of the University of Erlangen-Nuremberg, have developed a piezoelectric lithotripter. This device uses an ultrasound guidance system to focus shock waves in a very small area. Salivary-gland stones can therefore be fragmented without damaging nearby structures. In the journal *Laryngoscope,* Dr. Iro reported his experience with 19 patients who suffered painful inflammations of their parotid and submandibular saliva glands. All 19 patients had their salivary stones fragmented painlessly with a single lithotripsy treatment. Four months after treatment, all 19 patients could eat and drink without symptoms.

Edmund A. Pribitkin, M.D.

Emergency Medicine

▶ Epinephrine Dosage Increase

Emergency physicians are finding that high doses of epinephrine, up to 15 times greater then the standard dose, have been more successful in increasing coronary perfusion than the standard dose. A 1991 study published in the *Annals of Emergency Medicine* found that of 49 adult patients, 60 percent of those receiving a high dose of epinephrine had regained spontaneous circulation, a response seen in only 15 percent of patients who received a standard dose. Another study published in the same journal showed that 70 percent of children regained spontaneous circulation after high-dose epinephrine, compared with no response in the children who received standard epinephrine doses. The high-dose epinephrine was used only after the standard dose failed; earlier use may produce even better results. Ongoing studies published in the *Journal of the American Medical Association* have measured the impact of high-dose epinephrine in field emergency treatment; early results support the safety of high-dose treatment in this setting, but its safety and lack of associated complications must still be fully demonstrated.

▶ Treating Acetaminophen Overdoses

Controversy continues over the best treatment for one of the most commonly seen overdoses in the emergency room: an overdose of acetaminophen pain relievers, such as Tylenol. The drug acetylcysteine is a very effective antidote, but the best dosage and route of administration are still not established. Although intravenous administration has not been given labeling approval by the Food and Drug Administration (FDA), a study in the *Annals of Emergency Medicine* demonstrated that a 48-hour intravenous administration is as effective as the 72-hour oral or the 20-hour intravenous dosing currently in use. Evidence also suggests that acetylcysteine is beneficial even when it is given later than previously recommended.

▶ AIDS Risks

As with other specialties, emergency physicians are learning more about how the human immunodeficiency virus (HIV) affects their practice. A number of reports in the *Annals of Emergency Medicine* show that geographic location is an important factor in the incidence of HIV infection in emergency departments. These reports have also found that most infected patients do not admit to a history of high-risk behavior. For emergency physicians who may care for many patients during a 30-year career, there is a mathematical model predicting the cumulative lifetime occupational risk for HIV infection. The estimated risk varies from 0.1 percent in emergency room departments in geographic areas with a low prevalence of HIV, to 1.4 percent for a department that does not take precautions, such as using gloves, and serves a region with a greater number of infected residents. These estimates are within the range that might be expected for death from another infectious disease, hepatitis B. Despite the acceptance of gloves and other precautions as a defense against the spread of HIV and other infectious diseases, in one major trauma center it was found that actual compliance with these precautions was very low, according to a report in the *Journal of Trauma*. Emergency physicians need to be extremely cautious, since they care for patients who often do not know or are unable to admit if they carry the virus. In addition, the emergency department often serves as the 24-hour site of care for emergency workers and other personnel who are regularly exposed to bodily fluids.

▶ Ultrasound in Emergency Medicine

Ultrasound has already proven to be of great benefit when used in the emergency department to confirm the diagnosis of leaking abdominal aneurysms. According to reports in a variety of medical journals, the use of bedside ultrasound in the emergency department can be expanded to check for information such as full bladders in children needing emergency attention. Emergency use of ultrasound can also detect leaky-valve problems in cardiac cases, internal bleeding in cases of blunt abdominal trauma, and sustained-release or coated medications in the stomach, which can help assess the condition of patients with a severe drug overdose. This use of ultrasound can also help replace certain tests for these problems. The increasing use of bedside ultrasound in the emergency department does not replace a formal ultrasound examination, but does assist in a faster and safer diagnosis for some patients.

▶ Revising Health-Care Policy

Emergency medicine provides access to all patients who seek care, regardless of their financial status. Problems with health-care access and costs have driven more of the population to rely on this safety net; at the same time, hospitals are faced with limited resources, staff, and inpatient beds. Too often this results in the turning away of patients, the diversion of ambulances, or making patients wait for hours for beds to become available. Emergency medicine physicians will need to be actively involved in the struggle to reform the provision of health care in our nation.

Louis Ling, M.D.

Endocrinology

▶ Molecular Biology

In the *Proceedings of the National Academy of Science,* researchers from the Massachusetts General Hospital in Boston reported the cloning of the parathyroid hormone and the parathyroid hormone–related peptide receptor, two hormones involved in calcium metabolism. This technology provides researchers with a new method of detecting alterations in normal hormonal signaling, given that hormones act on cells through specific receptors. Knowledge about how the hormones interact with receptors, and the ability to identify defects in receptors, will provide insight into clinical diseases that involve these hormones, including hyperparathyroidism, pseudohypoparathyroidism, hypercalcemia found in cancer patients, and osteoporosis.

▶ Osteoporosis

Osteoporosis is a condition characterized by a decrease in bone mass, with a resulting increased risk for fractures, especially in the vertebrae and the femur. It is a debilitating disease that affects millions of women and some men, causing pain, deformity, and a loss of mobility. Loss of bone mass occurs normally as a person ages, but women are particularly affected by osteoporosis because bone loss is accelerated after menopause, due to the cessation of estrogen production. Research into this condition is focusing on ways to prevent loss of bone mass, or, where osteoporosis is already evident, to prevent it from worsening.

The best way to prevent osteoporosis is for a person to maintain an optimal bone mass. Peak bone mass is usually reached when a person is in his or her late twenties or early thirties. Healthy lifestyle habits, such as adequate weight-bearing exercise, a diet rich in calcium, minimal alcohol consumption, and not smoking, contribute to reaching peak bone mass. A recent report in the *Journal of the American Medical Association* studied the effects of diet and exercise in women between the ages of 18 and 26. Over a five-year period, the women who had higher calcium-to-protein ratios in their diets and participated in physical activity showed a 12.5 percent increase per decade in total bone mass. Notably, these findings demonstrate that bone mass can be influenced after the pubertal growth spurt, when bone growth is most active.

Dietary habits influence bone mass throughout life. A 1992 study in the *New England Journal of Medicine* reported a reduction in the rate of hip and other nonvertebral fractures in women between the ages of 78 and 90 who received daily doses of calcium and vitamin D for 18 months. The researchers also found that the density of bone in the proximal femur increased by 2.7 percent in those women who received calcium and vitamin D.

Estrogen-replacement therapy, given to postmenopausal women, is another way of preventing osteoporosis. Estrogen is known to slow the rate at which bone is lost at menopause, and to decrease the risk of both hip and vertebral fractures. A study published in the *Annals of Internal Medicine* showed that estrogen delivered through a skin patch (photo at right) increased the density of bone in the hip and spine. The study also found that bone density increased even in women who had a preexisting fracture and a bone density below the 10th percentile for the normal premenopausal woman. According to the results of the study, estrogen administered  through a skin patch has benefits that are similar to oral estrogen, and the skin patch may be a more convenient way for some women to take estrogen.

Another study published in the *New England Journal of Medicine* observed that the drug tamoxifen (Nolvadex), used in the treatment of breast cancer, may act either in a similar manner to estrogen or may block the effect of estrogen, depending on the target tissue. Researchers showed that women receiving tamoxifen for early breast cancer had an increase in bone density, suggesting that tamoxifen, or similar agents, may be used to prevent postmenopausal osteoporosis, while minimizing the undesirable estrogenlike side effects.

▶ Cholesterol

Cholesterol metabolism is complex, involving proteins of varying molecular weights: very-low-density lipoproteins (VLDLs), intermediate-density lipoproteins (IDLs), low-density lipoproteins (LDLs), and high-density lipoproteins (HDLs). The lipoproteins are in constant, dynamic flux, exchanging lipid particles between compounds of various densities. The blood level of each different lipoprotein is influenced by diet, insulin, alcohol use, thyroid hormone, body size, and family history of lipid disorders.

Recent attention has been focused on the cholesterol degradation pathway, specifically on lipoprotein (a), a low-density lipoprotein. Lipoprotein (a) is similar to the blood protein plasminogen, which is involved in the blood-clotting system. Because of their similarities, lipoprotein (a) may compete with plasminogen, thus disturbing the balance between clot formation and clot degradation. In addition, lipoprotein (a) is believed to have properties that contribute to atherosclerosis, or hardening of the arteries, a development independent of its effect on plasminogen.

Lipoprotein (a) levels in the blood can be influenced by a variety of disorders, such as high levels of glucose in the blood. Researchers studying the relationship between the blood-glucose levels and lipoprotein (a) levels in diabetics found that poor long-term glucose control, in both insulin- and non–insulin-dependent diabetics, was associated with higher levels of lipoprotein (a), according to a 1992 report in the *Annals of Internal Medicine*. This finding provides further evidence that better overall glucose control would help lower the level of lipoprotein (a), which would also reduce the atherosclerotic complications to which diabetics, in particular, find themselves prone.

A study published in the *Journal of Clinical Endocrinology and Metabolism* looked at the effects of estrogen administration on lipids in 31 postmenopausal women. The researchers found an increase in the high-density-lipoprotein cholesterol (the so-called "good" cholesterol) and an associated beneficial protein, along with a decrease in the low-density-lipoprotein cholesterol (the "bad" cholesterol) and one of its associated proteins. These findings support the idea that estrogen replacement has a protective cardiovascular effect. Knowing that estrogen replacement not only helps prevent postmenopausal osteoporosis, but also may aid in preventing cardiovascular problems, physicians can now recommend estrogen-replacement therapy to those patients without contraindications, and to those patients at high risk for the complications of estrogen loss.

▶ Testosterone Replacement Promising

Two studies presented at the annual meeting of the Endocrine Society demonstrate that testosterone replacement improves muscle strength and boosts libido in men over age 60, granting older men a reprieve in the aging process. Researchers at the University of Oregon Health Sciences Center in Portland and St. Louis University in Missouri reported that both a scrotal transdermal patch and intravenous injections significantly increased testosterone levels over a three-month period.

Hematocrit, HDL cholesterol, and grip strength also improved after these treatments, and side effects from this method of testosterone replacement were nonexistent or minimal.

Alison A. Moy, M.D.

Environment and Health

▶ Environmental Justice for All?

The notion that racial minorities and people with low incomes face higher environmental health risks than the general public has been simmering for years. "People of color . . . have borne a disproportionate burden in the siting of municipal landfills, incinerators, and hazardous waste treatment, storage, and disposal facilities," wrote Robert D. Bullard, Ph.D., a professor of sociology at the University of California, Riverside, in the March/April 1992 *EPA Journal*. The implication is that there is a racial and class bias in the treatment and cleanup of hazardous waste, with greater immediate and long-term health risks for minorities and people with low incomes.

The Environmental Equity Workgroup was set up in July 1990 by Environmental Protection Agency (EPA) Administrator William Reilly to study this problem. Their report found that "racial minority and low-income populations experience higher than average exposures to selected air pollutants, hazardous waste facilities, contaminated fish, and agricultural pesticides in the workplace." They also saw "clear differences between racial groups in terms of disease and death rates."

But the Workgroup also found few data to explain what role the environment might play in these disparities, with one exception. Lead poisoning was the only instance where the group found a definite connection between race and the environment: A significantly higher percentage of black children versus white children have unacceptably high blood-lead levels.

The Environmental Equity Workgroup's basic recommendation was that the EPA needs to be more aware of racial and class issues in its decisions. To that end, the Environmental Equity office was created at EPA in October 1992 to implement the Workgroup's recommendations and other initiatives. This office will also administer the EPA's Minority Academic Institutions program, which will offer technical help and new environmental technology to member institutions. However, many of the grass-roots organizations who have fought against such inequities doubt the EPA's sincerity and commitment to this volatile issue.

▶ Birth Defects and Pollution

There may now be some proof of what people have suspected for years: living near a source of pollution can cause birth defects in babies. A study of mothers who lived near hazardous-waste sites in New

Several preliminary studies suggest that mothers who live near hazardous waste dumps have a higher than normal chance of bearing children with birth defects. Other forms of environmental pollution may also increase the risk of birth defects.

York State shows that proximity to those locations may carry a small additional risk for bearing children with birth defects. The study, by researchers at Yale University School of Medicine in New Haven and the New York State Department of Health, appeared in the July 1992 issue of the *American Journal of Epidemiology*.

Their results indicated that in New York State 30 children per 1,000 live births have such major birth defects as cleft lip and cleft palate; chromosomal anomalies; and digestive, muscular, or nervous system abnormalities. In this study, 34 out of 1,000 children were born with birth defects, a 12 percent increase over the norm. All types of birth defects increased, however, as the site's hazard-ranking score increased. For sites with the greatest potential for exposure, the rate of birth defects was 49 out of 1,000 births.

Researchers took into account age, race, education, and certain reproductive variables, but unknown factors could have a bearing on birth defects, including cigarette smoking, alcohol consumption, diet, and occupation. The New York State Health Department is involved with three follow-up studies that look at the impact of active industrial emissions and examine other potential risk factors in the development of birth defects.

Pollution may also be to blame for a high birth defect rate found in southern Texas. A study completed in July 1992 by officials from the Texas Health Department and the federal Centers for Disease Control and Prevention (CDC) found more than double the national average of babies born with incomplete or missing brains, a condition called anencephaly. Babies with this deformity are stillborn or die within days. Researchers discovered that this condition and other neurological disorders had risen steadily from 1986 to 1991, the period encompassed by the study.

Although environmentalists feel that pollution along the border with Mexico may be at the root of these problems, the study found "no smoking gun as to the culprit for anencephaly," said David Barry of the EPA. A Scientific Advisory Committee has been formed to review the study and provide recommendations for further action. So far the committee advises continued monitoring of the problem, and has proposed an international symposium to be held in 1993 on neural-tube defects such as anencephaly.

In related news, former EPA Administrator William K. Reilly announced in May 1992 the beginning of a two-year study of possible chemical pollution along the Rio Grande River from El Paso, Texas, to the Gulf of Mexico. "Environmental pollution problems along our border with Mexico are one of our priorities," Reilly said. "We will move quickly; yet, we must have sound, scientifically valid information to determine whether pollution is causing these tragic birth defects." A work plan is being devised, and the study should begin early in 1993.

▶ Mysterious Illness among Persian Gulf War Veterans

During the war in the Persian Gulf in January 1991, the Iraqi Government ordered its troops to release millions of barrels of crude oil into the gulf off the coast of occupied Kuwait. A few weeks later, as Iraqi troops were being driven from Kuwait, they blew up and set fire to hundreds of Kuwaiti oil wells.

Concern ran high over the immediate and long-term health effects from the resultant pollution. Despite elevated levels of pollutants in the air from smoke plumes that blackened the sky, associated medical problems were few, and it appeared that there might not be cause for alarm. But months after returning home, approximately 300 soldiers began complaining of a wide range of mysterious, sometimes debilitating, symptoms, including aching joints, chronic fatigue, night sweats, hair loss, bleeding gums, rashes, short-term memory loss, and headaches. The cause of these symptoms remained unresolved in 1992.

As months pass with no definitive explanation for this puzzling illness, speculation has run wild about the cause of these symptoms. The television news show *20/20* aired a segment on this illness in August 1992, reporting that some of the sick soldiers had been handling fuel and breathing in fumes and some soldiers took showers with water contaminated with diesel fuel. Other soldiers believe that Saddam Hussein may have put a slow-acting chemical into a Scud missile or in the water supply.

The Army arrived at a much more mundane explanation for many of the cases. They attribute some to common medical problems and others to stress. Major Robert DeFraites, M.D., from the Walter Reed Army Hospital in Washington, D.C., said on *20/20*: "We found, we thought, about 80 percent of the symptoms that were reported could probably be related to the stress of readjustment to society after they came back. We thought this especially true for reservists." The soldiers interviewed on *20/20*, however, did not agree with the stress theory.

To analyze a possible link between this illness and the exposure to petrochemicals, an expert panel on petroleum toxicity met on August 20, 1992, to look at the data. They concluded that ". . . the reported symptoms of the individuals presented are unlikely to have been caused by exposure to petrochemicals or other environmental chemical exposures in the Gulf region." The panel based its conclusion on the lack of evidence showing overexposure to petroleum chemicals, the fact that the onset of symptoms was often delayed, and that the symptoms did not jibe with known health effects from such exposures. In addition to the panel, the Army's Environmental Hygiene Agency is conducting two large studies to define the level of exposure to the oil-well smoke and to estimate any future long-term health effects. The Army's Environmental Support Group is setting up a registry of all service members exposed to smoke from the burning Kuwait oil-well fires.

The Department of Veterans Affairs is also actively involved. A bill to establish a Persian Gulf Registry for veterans passed Congress on October 8, 1992, enabling those veterans with medical ailments who think they were exposed to environmental hazards, as well as those who are asymptomatic but concerned, to come to the Veterans Administration (VA) for an examination and entry into the registry. The VA believes that this registry will allow the agency to pick up any patterns that may point the way for policy review or research. It will also make it easy to call veterans back in for examination or let them know if new scientific data become available. The VA has also created three special environmental-medicine referral centers at its hospitals in West Los Angeles, Houston, and Washington, D.C., to handle cases of unusual symptoms in Persian Gulf veterans whose evaluation has stumped local VA medical facilities.

Until a solid explanation is found, Brigadier General Ronald Blanck, director of professional services, Office of the Surgeon General, U.S. Army, said in a September 16, 1992, statement to a House of Representatives Subcommittee on Hospitals and Health Care, "We will ensure that any condition is diagnosed and that appropriate care is given while we continue to investigate the symptoms which might be due to some exposure in connection with Operation Desert Shield or Desert Storm."

▶ New Pesticide Protection for Agricultural Workers

Nearly 4 million people who work on farms and in forests, nurseries, and greenhouses will benefit from new rules the EPA issued in August 1992.

Farm workers who dispense pesticides are now required to wear goggles, gloves, and face masks to protect against chemical exposure.

EPA head William K. Reilly announced that "These workers will know, often for the first time, when they are working in the presence of toxic pesticides, understand the nature of the risks these chemicals present, and get basic safety instructions." The regulations could prevent from 10,000 to 20,000 pesticide-related injuries and illnesses each year.

The revised Worker Protection Standard for Agricultural Pesticides aims to cut down on possible adverse health effects to workers by limiting their exposure to pesticides, and mandating protective gear when using pesticides. Workers are not allowed to enter cropland, forests, or greenhouses within a certain length of time after pesticide spraying (12 to 72 hours, depending on the pesticide). Personal-protection equipment like gloves and goggles is now required, and the new provisions require that employers provide soap, water, and towels for washing and decontamination. Emergency transportation must also be ready in case of an injury or pesticide poisoning. Employers must educate workers about chemical hazards through safety training, post a listing of pesticide treatments in a central location, and make sure those who handle pesticides know the pesticide label safety information. These provisions will be phased in over a two-year period.

▶ Dioxin Reassessment Update

An independent scientific panel has reviewed data from an ongoing EPA reassessment of the chemical dioxin, a by-product created in the manufacturing process of certain pesticides, and has found that the health risks may be greater than previously thought. On October 9, 1992, a memo to William Reilly from Erich Bretthauer, assistant administrator for research and development at EPA, outlines several preliminary findings from the panel, which considered not only the cancer risk from dioxin, but a broad range of health problems as well. Demonstrated effects of dioxin exposure in humans and animals include changes in endocrine function associated with reproduction and, in animals alone, behavioral effects in offspring and a change in immune operation. Some of the data suggest that dioxin may be affecting people who have not had notably high exposures to the chemical.

The memo also suggests that a panel of epidemiologists review studies that indicate dioxin may be carcinogenic in humans. Once that is done, the EPA should reconsider its current classification of dioxin, which is based mostly on laboratory-animal studies. The reassessment is due to be completed around September 1993. However, this still may not end the 20-year-old debate about the dangers of dioxin.

Linda J. Brown

Eyes and Vision

▶ Optic Neuritis

Optic neuritis is an inflammation of the optic nerve, the neural connection between the eye and the brain. Optic neuritis is a common condition damaging the vision of male and female patients between the ages of 15 and 45. These patients suffer from complete or partial loss of vision in one or both eyes. There is often severe pain upon movement of the affected eye, which resolves as the inflammation clears. The visual acuity of these patients usually improves over six months to one year, but vision almost never reverts to normal.

In the past, most patients with optic neuritis have been treated with high doses of powerful anti-inflammatory steroids. Treatment varied from one week to one month or more. These drugs are associated with many side effects, including stomach ulcers, hypertension, diabetes, weight gain, and acne. Doctors believed such therapy speeded healing and led to more complete healing. There was, however, only very limited proof of the value of these drugs in treating optic neuritis.

To determine if steroids helped patients with optic neuritis, the Optic Neuritis Treatment Trial (ONTT) was created, a collaboration of 15 medical centers across the United States led by Roy Beck, M.D., of the University of South Florida in Tampa, Florida. This study, completed in 1992, concluded that the use of steroids did not lead to an improvement in visual outcome when compared to no treatment at all. The drugs did, however, accelerate the speed at which the patient recovered. The authors concluded that the use of steroid medication is not appropriate for all patients. It would be justified when there is vision loss in both eyes. Steroid treatment would also be valuable for those patients with vision loss in one eye whose activities require good binocular vision, such as is needed by a pilot or a professional truck driver.

In about 50 percent of cases, optic neuritis is associated with multiple sclerosis, a generalized inflammation of the central nervous system. The precise risk is unknown. Forty-nine percent of patients in the Optic Neuritis Treatment Trial manifested evidence of inflammation in other areas of the brain consistent with multiple sclerosis. Only frequent re-evaluation of these patients over the next 5 to 10 years will allow ophthalmologists and neurologists to understand how many patients and which subgroup of patients are most at risk for multiple sclerosis. This information would be important for patients to determine if they have a benign or more serious condition.

The ONTT findings that steroids are not beneficial in treating optic neuritis may be applied to the treatment of other inflammatory conditions of the central nervous system. Steroids are commonly used to treat these diseases, but have never been proven to have efficacy. Support for their further usage will require additional research, but the ONTT may have provided an important first insight.

▶ Racial Differences in Blindness

Drs. Alfred Sommer and James Tielsch of the Johns Hopkins University in Baltimore, Maryland, conducted a large population study of eye diseases, using 5,000 patients 40 years of age or older from a racially mixed urban community in Baltimore. The researchers attempted to determine the most common causes of visual impairment among this group. Such data are important for planning future research, treatment, and rehabilitation for patients with eye diseases. Little previous data exist from Western countries to allow such an analysis.

In the study, 64 patients were blind in both eyes. Among these patients, blindness in both eyes was twice as common among blacks as among whites. This difference was slightly less in the elderly. Surprisingly, in all racial groups, the most common cause of bilateral blindness was unoperated cataract. Cataracts are a clouding of the lens of the eye, which leads to loss of clear vision. Unoperated cataract was four times more likely among blacks than among whites. This disparity was apparently due to the fact that white patients were almost twice as likely as black patients to have undergone cataract extraction.

Macular degeneration was the leading cause of blindness in white patients in this study, affecting just under 3 patients of every 1,000. Macular degeneration is a disease in which there is abnormal growth of blood vessels beneath the retina. These vessels often bleed and destroy a portion of the retina. The part of the retina most vulnerable to this damage provides the finest visual discrimination. Macular degeneration is extremely uncommon among black patients.

Among black patients, the second most common cause of blindness (after cataract) was glaucoma, a condition in which the pressure of the fluid in the eye is dangerously high. Glaucoma was the reason for blindness in 19 of the study's blind black patients. Glaucoma was also six times as frequent among blacks as among whites, and the disease began at an earlier age in the black population.

The pattern of blindness seen in urban Baltimore allows two important conclusions about medical eye care. First, although cataracts are a surgically correctable abnormality, a large number of patients were functionally blind because of cataracts. These patients resided only a few blocks from multiple

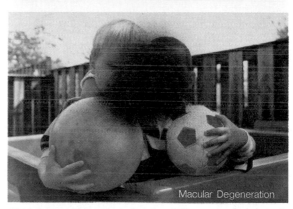

Normal eyesight permits the full scope of vision. In glaucoma, the peripheral vision deteriorates; macular degeneration reduces the central vision.

sources of ophthalmologic care. Further, the majority were eligible for Medicare to help pay for the procedure. Medicine and ophthalmology must improve their message to the less-educated population so they will seek timely and appropriate care.

The study also demonstrated that although glaucoma was very prevalent in the black population, it was only half as likely for the black patient to be receiving therapy. The early detection and treatment of glaucoma prevents or postpones blindness. These data further suggest that there is substantial undertreatment of glaucoma among black Medicare beneficiaries. Thus this lack of care will lead eventually to additional cases of blindness, loss of income, and financial burdens on society.

These findings suggest a great need for additional research into improving the delivery of medical eye care for glaucoma and cataract to the entire population and to the black population in particular.

▶ Corneal Transplantation

Corneas are the most commonly transplanted human tissue and one of the most successful transplant procedures in humans. More than 40,000 corneal transplants are performed in the United States each year. This surgery becomes necessary due to infections of the cornea, congenital malformations, hereditary changes in the shape of the cornea, and, most commonly, as a late complication of cataract surgery. The two-year success rates are more than 90 percent in favorable cases. Nonetheless, investigators continue to search for ways to improve this outcome. A collaborative research project by physicians from six institutions across the country —the University of Michigan, Emory University, Johns Hopkins University, Duke University, the University of Southern California, and the University of Wisconsin—has been developed to see whether tissue typing, a procedure performed for other organ transplants, could help in selecting the most potentially successful donor material for grafting in the human eye.

If tissue typing is beneficial, the additional medical cost would be more than $4 million per year, but would result in better vision for patients. The physicians in the collaborative study felt it important to carefully evaluate the effectiveness of such tissue typing to justify this cost. The study found that standard tissue typing was of no benefit in reducing the chance of graft rejection, possibly due to the absence of blood vessels in the cornea. Blood vessels bring lymphocytes to a tissue. These are part of the body's normal defense mechanism that will attack the donor tissue. Since these cells cannot easily reach the donor corneal tissue, the transplanted cornea is protected from rejection. Thus, it need not be carefully matched.

The authors did find that a simple, widely performed, and inexpensive test—blood-group typing —was important to corneal-transplant success. Blood-group typing is the test performed before performing a transfusion. Human blood is divided into A, B, AB, and O blood groups. This test significantly reduces the chance of graft rejection. The authors were unable to determine why their results should be true, but similar findings have been found in kidney, heart, and liver transplants.

This study will likely cause most corneal-transplant surgeons to adopt blood-group typing as part of their preoperative selection of donor material for corneal transplantation. This may reduce the utilization of the more expensive tissue typing.

Michael X. Repka, M.D.

Genetics and Genetic Engineering

Researchers found new genetic links to several diseases during 1992 and began several new gene-therapy projects.

▶ Twin Studies

Studies of fraternal and identical twins are one of the best ways scientists have found to determine whether or not a disease, or even a type of behavior, is linked to genetics. If one member of a set of twins has a disease, for example, then his or her fraternal twin (who shares some of the same genes) should be more likely than someone in the population at large to also have that same disease—if the disease is genetically linked. For identical twins (who have the same genes) the second twin is even more likely to have the disease if it has a genetic basis. If one of a pair of identical twins has a genetic disease, such as muscular dystrophy, for example, then the second twin will also have it in virtually every case. Twin studies are uncovering more and more genetically linked disorders.

Researchers at Virginia Commonwealth University in Richmond reported in October 1992 that genetics plays an unexpectedly important role in determining susceptibility to alcoholism in women. While previous research had shown that genetics was very important in alcoholic men, most researchers believed that family environment was more important than genetics as a factor contributing to alcoholism in women. The research team studied 1,003 pairs of female twins from the Virginia Twin Registry. They found that if one member of a set of identical twins had a problem with alcohol, her twin was four to five times more likely to suffer the same problem than were women in the general population. If one member of fraternal twins had a problem, her twin was about twice as likely as other women to have the problem. They concluded that genetics made a 50 to 60 percent contribution to alcoholism in women, about the same proportion that had previously been found with men.

Susceptibility to nicotine addiction may also be partially genetic, according to findings reported in September by researchers at SRI International in Menlo Park, California. The team made use of data from two National Heart, Lung, and Blood Institute surveys—in 1967–69 and again in 1983–85—of male twins born between 1917 and 1927. All of the men served in the military during World War II, during which smoking was common and even encouraged. Among the 4,775 pairs of twins studied,

Identical twins have exactly the same genes, a characteristic that makes them ideal for genetic studies. Fraternal twins only share some of the same genes.

the team found that identical twins were significantly more likely than fraternal twins to share the same smoking history, and that family environment played no significant role.

In August, researchers at the Boston University School of Medicine in Massachusetts and at Northwestern University in Evanston, Illinois, reported that they had found a genetic link to sexual orientation. Studying twin sisters, they found that homosexuality or bisexuality occurred in nearly half of the identical twin pairs, in only one-quarter of fraternal twins, and in only one of every six adoptive-sister pairs. The same team reported similar results with male twins in December 1991.

▶ New Gene
In February 1992, three teams of researchers independently reported that they had discovered the gene that causes myotonic dystrophy, a wasting disease that is the most common form of muscular dystrophy in adults. It strikes one in every 7,000 to 8,000 people, affects both men and women equally, and is characterized by a broad range of symptoms, from a mild form that causes only cataracts, to the most severe form, which includes muscle weakening, heart problems, mental slowness, and sleep disorders.

The discovery of the gene explains this variability for the first time. The defect involves the repetition of a small chemical segment called CTG in the gene for a protein called myotonin protein kinase. In a healthy individual, the CTG segment is repeated 5 to 27 times. For unknown reasons the number of repeats is often increased when the gene is passed on to children. If the number of repeats is about 50, the first symptoms appear in old age. If the number is 200 to 300, the classical form of the disease oc-

curs. If 2,000 copies are present, the disorder develops in the teens. And if still more copies are present, symptoms show up at birth. Myotonic dystrophy is only the third genetic disorder in which such repeats occur. The others are fragile-X syndrome and spinal bulbar atrophy.

▶ Human Genome
In October 1992, two teams of researchers revealed that they had reached a milestone in the Human Genome Project, the effort to decipher the complete genetic blueprint of humans. That blueprint is contained in 23 sets of chromosomes. The researchers have constructed road maps to the two smallest chromosomes: the Y chromosome, whose presence or absence determines sex, at the Massachusetts Institute of Technology (MIT) in Cambridge; and chromosome 21 at the Center for the Study of Human Polymorphism in Paris, France. These road maps are sets of overlapping segments of deoxyribonucleic acid (DNA) assembled in the correct order. Researchers believe these so-called physical maps will allow them to identify genes on the two chromosomes much faster. Eventually, scientists plan to find not only physical maps for all the human chromosomes, but also a complete accounting of the 3 billion individual chemicals that comprise the entire genome.

▶ Birth Defects
Researchers have developed a new, safer technique for prenatal detection of birth defects that eliminates the small but significant risks associated with either amniocentesis or chorionic villus sampling, both of which require inserting a needle into the amniotic sac that contains the fetus. The new approach relies on the fact that a small amount of fetal blood leaks into the mother's blood-stream. Several different researchers have developed techniques to concentrate and isolate the extremely small number of fetal cells—about one for every one million of the mother's cells—for analysis.

A team at the University of Tennessee reported in November that they were able to use such fetal cells to detect seven cases of severe chromosomal abnormalities—of the type that produce Down syndrome and other severe abnormalities—among 69 pregnancies. All were confirmed with conventional techniques. A full 85 percent of all cases of Down syndrome occur among women under the age of 35, but the risk of fetal damage from conventional testing is greater than the risk of Down syndrome, so these women are not generally tested. The new technique could make it possible to test them without risk. The National Institutes of Health (NIH) is now organizing a study of 3,000 pregnant women to determine how successfully the new technique can pick up such problems.

Causes. In August 1992, researchers at the Boston University School of Medicine reported that women who use a spa or hot tub during the first month of pregnancy have two to three times the normal risk of bearing a child with spina bifida or other defects of the spinal cord. If the mother-to-be also runs a fever during that month, the risk can rise as high as six times that of normal, according to results from the largest study of birth defects ever conducted. In a separate study published simultaneously, Swedish and American researchers reported that the risk of birth defects of all types is higher among women who put off childbearing until their 30s or 40s. An increased risk among older women had previously been observed, but physicians assumed it arose from the complications of childbirth that often occur in older women and that it could be minimized with proper medical care. The new study found that there is an additional risk beyond this one, and that its cause is still unknown.

▶ Genetic Engineering

Cystic-Fibrosis Mouse. In August, researchers at the University of North Carolina at Chapel Hill School of Medicine announced "a major victory" in the quest for new treatments for cystic fibrosis (CF), the crippling disease that strikes one in every 2,000 infants born in the United States. The researchers successfully inserted the defective gene that causes CF into the embryos of healthy mice. As the mice matured, they developed the characteristic symptoms of CF, including the production of the thick, sticky mucus that clogs the lungs and leads to life-threatening infections. The so-called transgenic mice also passed the disease on to their offspring. For the first time, researchers will now be able to test potential new therapies for CF in animals, a process that should greatly accelerate the development of new drugs and therapies.

Lyme Disease. Yale University researchers reported in June that they had developed a genetically engineered vaccine for Lyme disease, a disabling infection that strikes at least 9,000 Americans each year. The disease, which is caused by a bacterium that is transmitted from wild animals to humans by ticks, can cause facial paralysis, vision and heart problems, and severe arthritis if it is left untreated. The Yale researchers isolated a large protein called OspA from the bacterium that causes Lyme disease, and used genetic engineering to produce large quantities of it. When they injected the protein into mice that were susceptible to Lyme disease, the vaccine not only provided complete protection against the bacterium, but also killed bacteria in the fleas that bit the mice. The new vaccine could be tested in humans in as little as two years.

Vaccines from Plants. Researchers from Purdue University and the John Innes Centre in Norwich, England, reported in June 1992 that they had devised a simple way to produce vaccines that could lead to a vastly increased supply of inexpensive, easily storable vaccines. The researchers took the genes for key proteins from the viruses that cause AIDS and hoof-and-mouth disease and inserted them into the genetic complement of the cowpea mosaic virus, a common virus that infects plants producing black-eyed peas. After being injected into young cowpea plants, the modified virus proliferated rapidly. Large quantities of the virus, suitable for use in a vaccine, could then be isolated.

Injection of the isolated virus into mice produced a strong immune reaction that protected the mice against hoof-and-mouth disease. Mice do not develop AIDS, however, so the researchers could not test the vaccine's protective effect. The vaccine should be very safe, researchers said, because the plant virus does not infect human or animal cells, and no animal products that might introduce contamination are used in its preparation. A hoof-and-mouth disease vaccine for animals could be on the market in as little as four years, the team said, and the researchers are working on similar vaccines against hepatitis, the papilloma virus (which causes warts and cervical cancer), and the common cold.

A Cold Virus to Carry a Missing Gene

Cystic fibrosis patients lack a gene for a protein to control salt flow in lung cells; mucus builds up and infections destroy tissue. Scientists will try a replacement method that worked in animals.

Adenovirus, which causes colds, is altered so it cannot reproduce.

Missing gene is inserted into virus.

The virus is to be delivered through the lung or nasal passage. In the lung tissue, it is expected to infect about 10 percent of the airway cells. The gene should begin to work, producing the control protein, and mucus buildup should be significantly reduced.

Anticlotting protein. Researchers at Virginia Polytechnic Institute and State University reported in April 1992 that they had created a valuable new source of a promising anticlotting agent called Protein C by genetically engineering pigs to produce it in their milk. Previous studies in animals have suggested that Protein C has great potential for a variety of human ills, such as blocking the formation of blood clots in heart attack and stroke victims, aiding patients undergoing hip replacement and other surgery, and fighting septic shock caused by bacterial infections. But studies in humans have been impaired because researchers could not isolate enough Protein C from human blood, where it is present in only trace amounts.

The protein is much too complex to be produced in bacteria or yeast, the microorganisms normally used to manufacture genetically engineered proteins. But by inserting the gene for Protein C into pig embryos attached to regulators that cause the protein to be produced only in milk, the Virginia researchers were able to induce production of it in amounts large enough to be easily purified. Protein C is the fourth protein that researchers have manufactured in farm animals, and it is the largest by far. Researchers are thus confident that they will therefore be able to produce a wide variety of other pharmaceuticals in milk as well.

Cancer Detection. A new genetic technique that can detect more than half of all colorectal tumors before they become life-threatening was announced in April 1992 by researchers at Johns Hopkins University in Baltimore. Early detection is particularly important for this type of cancer because it has a 90 percent cure rate if the tumor is still localized in the intestine, but only a 10 percent cure rate when the tumor has eaten through the intestinal wall to involve adjacent organs or lymph nodes. Colorectal cancer trails only lung and breast cancers in importance in the United States, with an estimated 156,000 cases and 60,000 deaths expected in 1992.

Physicians now detect colorectal cancer by screening for blood in the stool, but many tumors do not bleed, and many benign conditions can produce bloody stools, often causing confusing or even false results. The new test looks for mutated cells shed by the tumor, particularly the presence of a mutated gene called the *ras* oncogene, which is present in more than half of all colorectal tumors. The test's accuracy must still be verified by further screening in humans. It is also too expensive now for widespread use, so its first application will most likely be for monitoring people who have a high genetic susceptibility to colorectal tumors, and for monitoring recurrence in people who have already had a tumor removed.

Thomas H. Maugh II

Government Policies and Programs

The past year marked the transition from the presidential administration of Republican George Bush to that of Democrat Bill Clinton. This change in administrations signaled a change in government health policies on such issues as abortion, a national health-care program, health-care costs, and the testing of new medications.

▶ Abortion

In *Planned Parenthood of Southeast Pennsylvania v. Casey,* a challenge to a Pennsylvania abortion law that regulated abortion, the Supreme Court upheld two limited restrictions on abortions included in the Pennsylvania law: a requirement that a woman receive counseling and then wait 24 hours before an abortion, and a requirement that minors have a parent's approval to get an abortion, except in cases where a court finds that telling a parent could cause harm to the child. The Court also upheld the Pennsylvania requirement that abortion clinics submit to certain reporting requirements. However, a provision requiring a woman to tell her husband before getting an abortion was overturned by the Court. With this ruling, the justices established a litmus test to determine whether abortion regulations were constitutional. A regulation would be considered unconstitutional if its purpose or effect was to place a substantial obstacle to a woman getting an abortion before the time that a fetus can live outside the womb.

In November 1992, the Supreme Court declined to hear the case *Ada v. Guam Society of Obstetricians & Gynecologists*. Lower courts had overturned a 1990 abortion law enacted in the U.S. territory of Guam that made it a crime to perform an abortion except to end an ectopic pregnancy or one that threatened the life of the mother. By declining to hear an appeal of this case, the Supreme Court showed it was unwilling to effectively ban abortion.

On the other hand, the Court also handed abortion-rights activists a procedural defeat late in 1992. The Court let stand a New Orleans Court of Appeals ruling that threw out a challenge by abortion-rights advocates to a Mississippi abortion regulation, which required preabortion counseling and a 24-hour waiting period, similar to what the Court had upheld in the Pennsylvania law. This ruling was significant procedurally because the Court did not allow a challenge to the regulation before it became effective. Before the courts would consider challenges to state legislation or regulations on abortion, a woman or women affected would have to bring suit. Legal challenges by public-interest groups to the principles underlying the provisions would not be heard. Although the Court's action in this Mississippi case applied only to states within the jurisdiction of the New Orleans Federal Court of Appeals, it was clear that additional cases involving challenges to principles underlying legislation or regulations filed by abortion-rights advocates from other areas would be handled similarly.

By the end of 1992, the battle over whether a woman had a basic right to an abortion was over: the current Supreme Court upheld that right. But future judicial battles over abortion remain, revolving around the question of whether state laws or regulations place an undue burden on a woman seeking an abortion.

► Clinton and Health-Care Reform

During his presidential campaign, Bill Clinton promised to submit a health-reform proposal to Congress within the first 100 days of his administration. By the end of 1992, the broad outlines of his approach were clear, and in the first weeks of his administration, he appointed his wife, Hillary Rodham Clinton, to head the committee on health-care reform. Clinton's program would require all employers to provide their workers with health insurance. Because such a mandate could create problems for small employers, the program would make two changes to the current system: tax credits would be given to small employers to reduce their health-care costs, and the government would set up large insurance-purchasing pools that both small businesses and private citizens could join. One major problem for small employers is that, since their risk pool is so small, one employee with a serious health problem can increase premiums dramatically for all employees. To increase the size of this risk pool, the Clinton program would include the Medicaid population. Medicaid is a state-administered and partially federally funded program that finances medical care for low-income individuals.

A national health-care board to cap medical costs and government spending on health care would be created as part of the Clinton program. To reduce administrative costs, the program would standardize both basic health-insurance policies and the claim forms. The Clinton proposal would also reform medical-malpractice laws.

Parts of the Clinton approach received unexpected support from the Health Insurance Association of America (HIAA), representing 270 commercial insurers. The HIAA also came out in favor of new measures to control costs, including a larger government role in supervising the prices set by doctors and hospitals. The support of this group is significant, since private health insurers' opposition to universal coverage had been one of the major barriers to health-care reform. The insurers did not support every aspect of Clinton's approach; for example, they remain opposed to annual caps on public and private health-care spending. Not all of the health-care industry opposes spending caps. Although the largest physicians' professional association, the American Medical Association (AMA), opposes spending caps, the American College of Physicians, the internists' professional association, and the American Academy of Family Medicine, both support this kind of cost regulation.

► Problems in U.S. Health Insurance

Not only do millions of low-wage workers lack health-insurance coverage, but workers and retirees with employer-provided health insurance are not guaranteed their current benefits. In November the Supreme Court upheld a lower-court ruling in the case *Greenberg v. H&H Music Co.* that allowed an employer to reduce lifetime benefits for AIDS-related illnesses from $1,000,000 to $5,000. This decision applied to employers who provide self-insured health plans to reduce benefits for current or former workers. Under self-insured plans, which are not subject to state insurance regulations, the employer pays the claims, instead of purchasing insurance from a health-insurance carrier. Two-thirds of health-care plans in the United States are self-insured. The Houston geneticist who continued the lawsuit in the case, after the plaintiff died of AIDS, testified to Congress that the case had implications for anyone with a chronic disability or life-threatening illness.

► Veterans Care: A Political Issue

Developments in the executive branch of the federal government showed both progress and the difficulty of changing the health-care system. In September, Secretary of Veterans Affairs Edward J. Derwinski, a former Republican representative from Chicago, became a political casualty as a result of health-care issues. Derwinski had proposed a pilot program to allow doctors to care for nonveterans at two rural veterans hospitals, in Virginia and Alabama. He wanted the excess capacity in rural veterans hospitals to be available to care for nonveterans, since excess capacity in veterans hospitals will increase as World War II veterans age. Derwinski had given up trying get rid of excess capacity by closing certain veterans hospitals, largely because veterans organizations and the chairman of the House Committee on Veterans Affairs, Representative G. V. "Sonny" Montgomery (D-Miss.), strenuously opposed even studying the issue. As an alternative, Derwinski wanted to find out if veterans hospitals in rural areas, where medical facilities are scarce, could serve the general population without jeopardizing medical care to veterans. The Veterans of Foreign Wars (VFW) declined to endorse any presidential candidate following President Bush's address to the organization's convention on his way to the Republican convention in Houston; soon after, the White House forced Derwinski out.

▶ Nutritional Labeling

After protracted controversy, a change was ordered in the nutrition information on food labels when President Bush resolved a bureaucratic impasse on this issue in December 1992. The dispute involved the U.S. Department of Agriculture (USDA), which is responsible for regulating labeling on meat and food products, and the Department of Health and Human Services (HHS), which in turn encompasses the Food and Drug Administration (FDA), which has responsibility for regulating the labeling on all other food products. In the Nutrition Labeling and Education Act of 1990, Congress directed the executive branch to develop consistent food labels by November 1992, but the disputes between the USDA and the FDA prevented this deadline from being met until January of 1993.

The most intractable dispute was whether to include on labels fat and cholesterol as a percentage of their standard daily allowance. The FDA proposed to measure fat and cholesterol percentages against a single 2,000-a-day-calorie standard. The meat industry and the USDA objected, arguing that this arbitrary standard made meat and poultry appear unhealthier than they are for a large segment of the population. This dispute went to President Bush, and he ruled largely for the FDA position.

The resolution of this impasse means that by the summer of 1994, the food industry will have to redesign virtually every one of the 300,000 food labels in supermarkets. Each label will have a common format to show nutrition information. Former Secretary of Health and Human Services Louis W. Sullivan, M.D., announced that "The Tower of Babel in food labels has come down. . . . For the first time, consumers will be able to use a single format for virtually all processed foods, to compare nutrition values and make healthy choices."

▶ Regulating Testing Laboratories

Another area of dispute in government policy was the Clinical Laboratory Improvement Amendments of 1988. As many as 600,000 laboratories conduct medical tests, and before this legislation, most were unregulated. Most states did not regulate these laboratories, and the federal government regulated only laboratories that Medicare or Medicaid reimbursed. It was not until February 1992 that HHS issued final regulations to carry out this legislation.

The regulations issued in 1992 to oversee the nation's 600,000 medical laboratories do not extend to labs operated in physicians' offices.

HHS had drastically overhauled the regulations in response to extensive criticisms, mostly by physicians. The complaints centered on a few issues. The physicians objected to the requirement for a board-certified pathologist or a Ph.D. trained in laboratory medicine to manage laboratories that performed complex tests, which they felt would increase costs unnecessarily. They also believed that too many tests were classified as highly complex, the requirement for inspections every two years was onerous, and the training standards and proficiency-exam requirements for laboratory workers were too stringent.

The final regulations responded in part to these criticisms from practicing physicians, but angered other groups. John Dingell (D-Mich.), chairman of the powerful House Committee on Energy and Commerce, which has jurisdiction over most health programs and is the chief sponsor of the four-year-old law to regulate laboratory tests, strenuously objected to the way the Department of Health and Human Services had carried out the law. He accused the department of botching implementation of the law so badly that it had become "a case study in how to kill people."

Two weeks after calling HHS Secretary Louis Sullivan to defend the regulations before his committee, Representative Dingell accused Sullivan of effectively overturning the law by issuing a "hodge-podge of confusing, unworkable, and contradictory regulations . . . that leave largely unregulated for the foreseeable future" the laboratories in doctors' offices. The vice president of the professional association for pathologists called the regulations "appalling," and asserted that the training requirement for laboratory workers would be lower than before the law. An official from the Consumer Federation stated that the regulations "legalize the worst practices" of medical laboratories. What started as reform legislation became a symbol of the impact of partisan gridlock, and how interest groups play one side against the other. This legislation is a case study in how difficult reform of the health-care system will be.

▶ Women, Minorities, and Medical Research

In 1992 HHS Secretary Louis Sullivan and Bernadine Healy, M.D., director of the National Institutes of Health (NIH), the federal government's principal medical-research organization, urged a reorientation of medical research to assure that medical research and field tests of new drugs and procedures included women and minorities as well as white men. Sullivan criticized the practice of medical researchers designing studies that measured the effectiveness of new treatments only on men. He made this statement at a conference of the American Heart Association at which two studies were presented that confirmed unequal treatment for blacks and women with heart disease.

Study results released at this conference found that women had a significantly lower survival rate than men 12 years after bypass surgery—46 percent for women in comparison to 61 percent for men. Only 43 percent of women with heart attacks underwent procedures to examine or widen narrowed arteries. In contrast, 69 percent of men who suffered heart attacks underwent these procedures. Women who suffered heart attacks were not transferred as rapidly as men to hospitals with more-advanced treatment facilities.

Another study focused on the treatment of blacks with heart disease in veterans hospitals. This study

The Office of Research on Women's Health was created in part to remedy the perennial lack of female subjects in medical research studies.

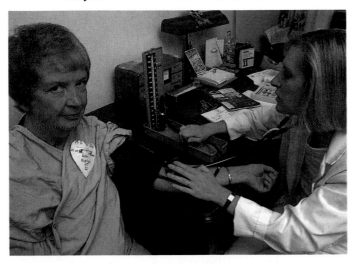

found that while blacks were more likely than whites to survive 30 days after a heart attack, they were less likely than whites to undergo bypass surgery and other procedures. Because all the subjects in this study had equal access to veterans hospitals, differences in incomes or in health-insurance coverage do not explain the differences in treatment.

Healy, a cardiologist by training, cited a flawed study to illustrate the absurdity of basing tests only on men. In the 1970s the federal government funded a major study to evaluate the effectiveness of estrogen in protecting against heart disease, and concluded that estrogen was not effective. However, the study group did not include one woman. Healy noted wryly, "Mother Nature could have told us that might not be a smart idea."

Among the steps to redress the lack of emphasis on women's-health issues was the creation of an Office of Research on Women's Health and the initiation of a 10-year research project within NIH to test preventive approaches to reducing the three leading causes of death among women: cardiovascular disease, cancer, and fractures related to osteoporosis.

▶ State Health-Care Reform

Despite the political gridlock in Washington, D.C., several states tried to make progress on health care in 1992. In Oregon, health-care reform came to a halt when the federal government turned down a proposal to test a way to expand Medicaid eligibility to all low-income Oregonians and finance it by ending reimbursement for certain medical procedures dealing with non-life-threatening medical problems. The Bush administration claimed this proposal would violate the Americans with Disabilities Act. Oregon's director of its Department of Human Resources claimed that the administration's position was simply election-year politics. Bill Clinton was on record as approving the idea of testing this concept, so the issue may be revisited.

The state of Minnesota developed an innovative approach to providing health insurance for the uninsured. A new program, HealthRight, the product of a bipartisan task force of state legislators, offered state-subsidized health-insurance policies to all uninsured Minnesotans on a voluntary basis. Premiums for this health insurance would be based on income, with a 5-cent increase per pack in the state cigarette tax and a tax on health-care providers to pay for the difference between the premiums and the cost. The HealthRight plan was the compromise successor to a more costly plan that Governor Arne R. Carlson had vetoed the year before. Carlson hailed the compromise measure as evidence that "we can deal with the gridlock" that has stymied attempts to resolve the health-care crisis.

James A. Rotherham

Health-Care Costs

▶ The Belmont Vision

As competing plans for shoring up the ailing health-care cost system achieved new prominence during 1992, one group of experts convened by the Institute for Alternative Futures took a very different tack. Instead of figuring out ways to tinker with the existing system—a system they felt was obsolete and no longer workable—these experts came up with a "vision" of what health care ought to be in the 21st century.

This vision, known as "The Belmont Vision," places emphasis on good health, not just on health care. That, in turn, implies "a right to a common effective set of health services and to the basic determinants of health that shape healthier communities." It implies personal responsibility for health habits, adequate funding both for health care and for such social programs as education and housing that impact health. The vision calls for "a progressive payment system" that "finances universal access to a common effective level of care" and a "vastly improved health-care delivery system" that "emphasizes care."

With those and other vision elements in place, "the perverse incentives and practices of the late 20th century, including unregulated fee for service, cost reimbursement, complex administrative procedures, defensive medicine caused by malpractice liability, and tax incentives that placed a greater burden on the poor and lower middle class to finance health insurance, are no longer barriers to effective health care or good health. Driven by a commitment to caring and a broader definition of health, practices have shifted at all levels within the health-care system to include health education, prevention, diagnosis, treatment and rehabilitation."

▶ Escalating Costs

In a study titled "Economic Implications of Rising Health Care Costs," the Congressional Budget Office (CBO) speculated that "the sharp rise in health costs, together with slower growth in productivity and total compensation, are the main reasons for the weak growth in workers' real wages and salaries over the past 20 years." Rising costs of health insurance have caused some employers to turn to part-time workers, for whom they do not provide insurance coverage. A related survey showed that insurance coverage is an important criterion in job selection or in staying in an unsatisfactory job.

The problem is by no means confined to employers and workers, or even the federal government. As more of the federal budget is consumed by

Part of President Bill Clinton's health-care reform plan proposes that every American be covered by a core package of health-insurance benefits.

health-care costs, state and local governments face the same problem. In 1991 states spent some $100 billion on health care, with their costs growing at 10 percent a year. Since almost all states have balanced-budget strictures, this growth either requires increased revenues or else cuts in other public services.

For all the debate over public versus private financing of health care, the ultimate payer is the public—either through taxes, lost wages, or out-of-pocket expenditures. One study estimated that individual households spent $6,555 on health care in 1991 in premiums, out-of-pocket payments, and taxes. The latter averaged $2,084, with $369 from Medicare payroll taxes, and the rest split among federal, state, and local taxes used for a variety of health programs, including the physician side of Medicare and both federal and state portions of Medicaid.

The cost increases focused new attention on the increasingly important question of what all this money buys. As many analysts point out, the complex system of public and private financing is designed to provide gross data only about how much goes to hospitals, physicians, and other health services, not what is spent on various procedures and how effective those procedures were. By some estimates, about one-third of the services provided are not necessary, yet no one has provided guidance for identifying those unneeded services.

According to conventional wisdom, new technology and an ever-aging population add to the overall

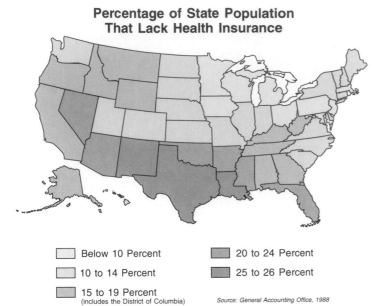

**Percentage of State Population
That Lack Health Insurance**

Below 10 Percent

10 to 14 Percent

15 to 19 Percent
(includes the District of Columbia)

20 to 24 Percent

25 to 26 Percent

Source: General Accounting Office, 1988

cost burden. Both notions are refuted in the CBO's "Economic Implications" study noted earlier. New technology has brought with it improved quality of care that may not be reflected in a strict economic analysis. For instance, microsurgical techniques that are more expensive in themselves, but eliminate the need for hospitalization and lengthy rehabilitation, may have saved money in the aggregate, but that savings would not be reflected in a simple procedure-by-procedure comparison. And even though about four times more is spent on health care for the over-65 population than on the rest of the population, the number of senior citizens is still relatively small, and will not become a significant factor until the Baby Boom generation reaches retirement age after the turn of the century.

▶ Managed Competition

The health-care cost discussions have introduced policymakers and the public to a new concept: managed competition. This concept is a product of discussions by an informal group of experts who have met for the past three years in Jackson Hole, Wyoming, to deliberate the health-care-policy dilemma. Essentially, managed competition attempts to find a mid-ground between a government-run and a free-market health-care system, by, as its designers propose, combining the best of both approaches. Pieces of the Jackson Hole proposals surfaced in proposed legislation, in state reform packages, and in the plans offered by both presidential candidates. The approach also got strong editorial backing from *The New York Times.*

This group found three fundamental flaws in the current system and proposed solutions. First, they

determined, information is lacking. So much money flows freely into the system that many common medical practices have never been scientifically tested, and little is known about what is helpful, wasteful, or even harmful. The proposed solution was a national effort for systematic evaluation of various procedures and of health-care providers.

As a second step, the group called for institutional reform, focusing first on the insurance industry, where 1,500 companies now fuel inflation by reimbursing ever-higher bills while competing by avoiding sick patients and high-risk groups. Proposed fixes included strict government standards to promote competition on the basis of economy, quality, and service, and the development of new "accountable health partnerships" and "purchasing cooperatives" to manage the market. The result would be a handful—maybe 5 or 10—plans in each area, midway between the hundreds of existing plans and a government-run, single-payer system.

To make managed competition work, the group proposed new incentives, starting with limits on the amount of employer premium contributions that can be excluded from an employee's income to meet the premiums charged by efficient plans. Employees could choose more expensive plans, but the difference in premiums would no longer be subsidized by the taxpayers.

As Congress vacillated, health proposals took on increased prominence in the presidential campaign. Both the Bush and Clinton plans embraced the concepts of "managed competition" and "managed care"—though definitions were increasingly vague as the campaign progressed, both seemed to be talking about capitated, or fixed-fee, proposals—but the two approaches were markedly different.

The Bush proposal, unveiled in February 1992, offered universal access to affordable health insurance through a sliding scale of tax credits to low- and middle-income families. States would play a key role by assuring that affordable plans were available, and would have the option of specifying what benefits were included. Insurance reforms were integral to the package. States were to assure that plans were available to small employers. Insurers would not be able to cancel or refuse to renew coverage, nor would they be able to deny coverage because of a preexisting condition or illness, or to increase premiums excessively.

The Bush package also called for reforms that would reduce administrative costs through such efforts as standardized insurance forms and computerized databases, and advocated reform of medical-malpractice laws in an effort to reduce the estimated $21 billion a year spent for "defensive" medicine—excessive medical care performed only to lessen the chance of being sued for medical malpractice. The proposal also emphasized health promotion and disease prevention to stress "individual responsibility for health." A cornerstone of the package was "coordinated care," the administration's term for managed care designed to promote "efficient management of health-care resources." The cost of the proposal was about $135 billion, phased in over a five-year period. Though no funding mechanism was ever specified, administration officials said that the plan could be funded without new revenues.

The Bush plan was widely faulted for failing to provide universal health coverage—by the administration's own estimates, 9 million or more Americans would remain without health coverage—and for failing to control costs. The Clinton proposal, on the other hand, drew fire for failing to include any cost estimates or any ideas for paying for the program beyond suggesting that it could be funded through substantial cost savings.

The Clinton plan did, however, provide that every American would be covered with a core package of insurance benefits. Though specific details were to be determined by a new National Health Board, coverage would include a full range of protection in case of illness, including hospitalization, physician services, prescription drugs, and mental-health care, as well as such preventive services as prenatal care, mammograms, and routine health screening.

Coverage would be guaranteed through employers, and government subsidies would be available to offset costs for new businesses and those with mainly low-wage workers. Everyone else would be covered through a publicly sponsored, privately operated plan, and would contribute to their coverage based on their ability to pay.

The plan also features aggressive cost controls. The National Health Board would establish both national and state spending budgets to limit public and private expenditures. The Clinton plan envisioned the development of local health networks, composed of insurers, hospitals, and doctors, which would receive a fixed amount of money to provide full health care for each member. Such fixed limits on total spending per patient are intended to provide incentives to reduce bureaucracy, eliminate duplication, and stop waste. States would establish fee schedules for all services provided outside of the networks. During his campaign, Clinton promised a detailed legislative health-reform package would be introduced within the first 100 days of his administration. He appointed his wife, Hillary Rodham Clinton, to head the team that would formulate this package.

But even as policymakers seemed ready to tackle the health-reform issue at last, significant changes were already taking place. For instance, the Peat Marwick national health benefits survey found that a majority of Americans were already enrolled in some form of managed-care plan, with the number covered by such plans likely to reach three-quarters by 1995, if present trends continue. The largest growth came in PPOs, or preferred-provider organizations, and POS, or point-of-service plans, which offer financial incentives to patients who select providers within a designated network. The survey also found that almost all workers covered through their employers are enrolled in some type of utilization-management program.

At the same time, states were taking action on their own. Even though the Department of Health and Human Services (HHS) turned down Oregon's plan for covering only the most essential services under Medicaid, on the grounds that the proposal ran afoul of the new disability laws, other states were searching for ways to expand coverage and control costs. Minnesota and Vermont both passed comprehensive health-care-reform legislation, complete with budget targets, health-planning features, and insurance reform. In addition, 30 states have incorporated managed care to increase access and contain Medicaid costs, 26 states have established risk pools for the uninsurable, and 26 states have enacted bare-bones insurance policies, with several experimenting with tax credits to employers who buy the policies.

One of the most widely publicized state efforts was the universal health insurance system for California proposed by Insurance Commissioner John Garamendi. The plan offered Californians the opportunity of selecting among competing private health-care plans, which would all offer the same comprehensive benefit package. Employers would pay a premium of 6.75 percent of payroll to finance the system, and employees would pay 1 percent of wages.

Unfortunately, the health-cost ferment of 1992 seemed to achieve little more than laying groundwork for major changes in the system without providing a clear sense of what those changes might look like. Certainly President Clinton has promised a quick solution, but in the context of a weak economy, solutions that promise more with less might not be easy to come by. Members of Congress who have championed change cling to firmly held beliefs about how the system can be fixed. Both executive and congressional agendas will undoubtedly be tempered by the strong vested interests in the medical-industrial complex, from hospitals and physicians, to the insurance companies, pharmaceutical firms, and medical-device industry. In the end, though, the strong focus on the bottom line could be tempered by reality, for, as Princeton economist Uwe Reinhart reminds, health care is essentially a people problem, not a paper problem.

Mary Hager

Health Personnel and Facilities

▶ The New Subacute Hospital

A new type of hospital is emerging to care for patients who are too sick to recover at home, but not sick enough to remain in an acute-care institution. Subacute hospitals, which comprise only about $1 billion of the total $300 billion U.S. hospital market, are expected to garner $5 billion to $7 billion within 10 years.

Clearly one of the fastest-growing segments of the overall health-care industry, subacute hospitals are geared for the large numbers of patients who require short-term rehabilitation and skilled nursing, such as the 11,419 ventilator-dependent patients who are hospitalized each year, or the 1.13 million newly diagnosed cancer patients who may require chemotherapy, radiation, or surgery.

Subacute hospitals have no dedicated emergency units, sophisticated diagnostic technology, or maternity or surgical suites. Unlike acute-care hospitals, which provide highly intensive care over days or weeks, subacute-care hospitals provide support and rehabilitation for only as long as 60 days. Because of their lower intensity of service and overhead, subacute hospitals can provide care for $600 less per day than their acute-care counterparts. Since they are not all things to all patients, but concentrate primarily on rehabilitative and skilled-

Hospitals are striving to make the inpatient experience less threatening. Homelike hospital rooms are especially effective in subacute situations.

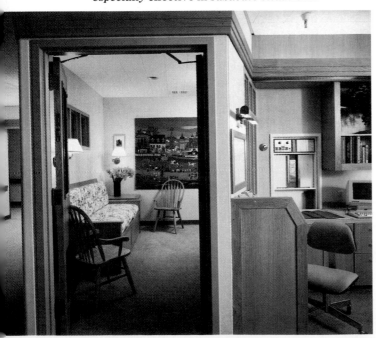

nursing support, these hospitals have been credited with expediting the long-term recovery of patients suffering from severe burns or traumatic injuries, respiratory diseases, cancer, AIDS, or multiple medical problems.

▶ The Quest for Quality

Health-care facilities are actively pursuing several strategies to enhance the quality of the services they provide.

Specialized Services. To build on their ties with major medical teaching institutions, many public hospitals are developing centers of excellence in such specialized clinical areas as organ transplantation, genetic counseling, open-heart surgery, cardiac catheterization, and psychiatric inpatient and outpatient intervention.

According to the American Hospital Association, more than 40 percent of public hospitals have open-heart surgery or organ-transplantation departments, 68 percent offer genetic counseling, 70 percent perform cardiac catheterizations, 74 percent have full-scale trauma units, and 85 percent provide emergency psychiatric treatment. In contrast, only about 30 percent of private hospitals provide any of these services.

Total Quality Management. Total quality management (TQM), the business strategy that fueled both the rise of Japan as an industrial power following World War II and the drive for competitive excellence among American corporations in the 1980s, is being adopted by most health-care institutions. TQM relies on small teams of workers to identify and correct poor work practices and directly improve the services provided to customers. In the hospital, customers include patients, physicians, public and private buyers of health services, and medical suppliers.

A survey conducted by *Hospitals* magazine found that 59 percent of hospitals are implementing TQM, and 42 percent plan to do so in the next year. TQM can be costly, ranging from $60,000 to $500,000 a year for some health-care organizations. It also can take at least three years to produce tangible results. Nevertheless, initial experience shows that TQM can dramatically reduce institutional expenses and improve patient outcomes. One hospital has been able to trim $2 million in operating expenditures as a result of TQM; another has practically eliminated postsurgical wound infections, protecting patients from the pain and prolonged hospitalization that accompany this complication.

Customer Service. To ensure they are friendlier to their patient and physician users, hospitals are training their employees in the niceties of customer service, changing the way they function to meet the needs and expectations of users, and contracting with outside management firms that provide specialized customer services, such as food service, child care, and grounds keeping. Through these programs, hospitals are striving to enhance efficiency and strengthen relationships with the people the hospital serves.

Planetree. Five hospitals nationwide are testing whether hospitalization can be more comfortable and less stressful. The hospitals have patterned one of their medical units after the Planetree unit at Pacific Medical Center in San Francisco, California, which places patients in homelike surroundings and makes them an active participant in their treatment.

The Planetree units have their own kitchens so patients or family members can prepare their favorite meals; piano music is piped in over hallway speakers; soft lighting and colorful furnishings decorate the patient's room. Most important, the units ensure that physicians, nurses, and therapists educate and consult patients at every turn. Health-care professionals in Planetree units ask patients to review the information in their charts and ask questions about it or make their own written entries; care givers encourage patients to visit the adjacent medical library and research their hospital therapy and follow up recovery regimen. The goals are to help patients make truly informed decisions about the services they will receive in the hospital and the ways in which such services will benefit them.

▶ The Greening of Hospitals

Protection of the environment is one of the top priorities for hospitals because of increasingly stringent regulations concerning the elimination of hospital waste and the astronomical cost of waste disposal. Landfill dumping fees have skyrocketed from $2 to $5 per ton of waste in 1975 to $100 per ton in 1990 in just one part of the country. Escalating dumping costs hit hospitals particularly hard because nearly 40 percent of hospital waste ends up in landfills, reported the National Solid Waste Management Association.

Leaders in hospital environmental protection, such as Inova Health Systems in Springfield, Virginia, are establishing strict guidelines concerning the recycling of aluminum, cardboard, paper, and silver, and the reduction of solid waste generated by the hospital. Hospital suppliers also are responding to environmental concerns. Baxter International of Deerfield, Illinois, is strengthening its aluminum- , paper- , and bottle-recycling programs, and it is redesigning its products to reduce the amount of plastic used in IV bags and the paper needed for corrugated packaging.

▶ The Arts and Medicine

Hospital administrators and physicians are learning more about the human side of medicine through an unusual educational program sponsored by St. Pat-

In some hospitals, patients meet regularly with doctors, nurses, and other medical personnel to determine the course of their care.

rick Hospital, Missoula, Montana, and the University of Montana. The Institute of Medicine and Humanities examines the emotional, psychosocial, and spiritual aspects of health-care delivery through instruction in the arts, fiction, history, and philosophy. For example, readings in classical Greek literature relate the ancient ethic of excellence to the pursuit of quality by health-care professionals today. In a similar vein, discussions of life in medieval monasteries help illuminate modern death and dying issues.

▶ The New Nurse Manager

The pressing need to contain the costs and enhance the quality of services has changed the role of nurses in health-care institutions. Instead of the traditional head nurse who supervises a patient-care unit but has no real management responsibility, the new nurse managers are accountable for budgeting, capital-equipment allocations, employee performance, and patients' outcomes. The unit-based nurse managers are essentially the chief operating officers of a department who control the delivery of care at the patient level. They coordinate all the services required by patients on their units, and work with physicians to develop the best system of delivery of those services. They also control the use of resources and costs in accordance with the financial goals of the institution. Unit-based nurse managers teach staff nurses how to perform nursing duties, serve on hospital-wide committees in such areas as quality control and risk management, and develop human-resources plans and procedures that recognize the complexities and realities of institutional health care.

Karen Sandrick

Heart and Circulatory System

Continuing a trend that began in the late 1960s, mortality from coronary-artery disease (CAD) again fell in 1992 as a result of improved treatment during and after heart attacks. Although CAD death rates have fallen by 2 to 3 percent per year in the United States, CAD still remains the leading cause of death; what hasn't dropped is the number of new cases of heart attack, or myocardial infarction (MI). Each year there are 1.5 million MIs and 500,000 deaths from CAD in the United States.

Numerous 1992 studies reported on CAD risk factors and preventive agents. Factors found to be CAD risk factors include: short stature; exposure to the bacterium *Chlamydia pneumoniae;* high levels of the amino acid homocysteine; physical inactivity; increased body-iron levels; the cholesterol subtypes lipoprotein (a) and type B low-density lipoprotein (LDL); increased blood viscosity; and elevations of blood factors fibrinogen, factor VII, platelets, and white blood cells. Factors found to protect against CAD include: the blood protein albumin; moderate alcohol use; diets high in nuts, fruits, and vegetables; the anti-breast cancer drug tamoxifen; and high intake of the antioxidants beta-carotene, vitamin C, and vitamin E, which serve to "detoxify" harmful types of cholesterol.

The use of aspirin to prevent and treat cardiovascular disease gained new support through studies that correlate reduced CAD mortality with aspirin when the drug was taken preventatively by diabetics or by smokers after an MI. Aspirin also reduced the need for leg-artery bypass surgery when used preventatively, and it curtailed the formation of blood clots (emboli) when added to blood thinners used by patients with metal heart valves.

▶ Cholesterol and CAD

Several studies confirmed the correlation of high LDL-cholesterol levels with heightened CAD risk and the role of high-density lipoprotein (HDL) cholesterol as a protective factor. Other studies concluded that elevated triglyceride levels also increased the risk of CAD. New government cholesterol-screening guidelines will include recommendations for HDL and triglyceride levels.

Other studies showed that while low cholesterol prevents CAD, it also increases the risk of death from cerebral hemorrhage, liver disease, certain cancers, suicide, accidents, alcoholism, and lung disease. Thus, there may be an optimal middle cholesterol range for overall health benefits.

Several 1992 studies of cholesterol-lowering methods using diet and/or medications showed that they actually reversed the coronary blockages that cause MIs. Particularly exciting were German and Indian trials in which diet and/or exercise alone improved coronary blockages and cardiac blood flow, and prevented MIs and sudden death.

▶ Clot Dissolvers and Other Treatments for Myocardial Infarction

Several 1992 studies extended the use of clot-dissolving, or thrombolytic, drugs to new frontiers in treating MI. Three new trials proved that very early treatment with thrombolytics at home or en route to the hospital improved patient survival rates and heart-muscle function, and even aborted some MIs altogether. Two studies revealed that the life-saving benefits of thrombolytic drugs are possible for up to 7 to 12 hours after an MI begins.

Analysis of several studies determined that these blood-thinning drugs need to be used with caution, since they do increase the risk of strokes due to brain hemorrhages; however, they also prevent strokes from blood clots. As a result, thrombolytics produced a reduced or unchanged overall stroke rate after MI. They also reduce lethal arrhythmias, or abnormal rhythms of the heart.

A 1992 comparison study confirmed previous reports that showed no significant advantage of any particular thrombolytic drug, including streptokinase, urokinase, and the more expensive tissue plasminogen activator (t-PA). Other studies found that giving the drug t-PA twice as fast as usual improved its ability to open arteries. A major study of victims of massive heart attacks showed improved survival rates, less heart failure, and fewer second MIs when they were treated with the vasodilator drug captopril (Capoten). Another large trial confirmed the ability of magnesium infusions to improve survival and limit heart-muscle damage in patients suffering from MI.

Several studies compared thrombolysis with emergency angioplasty for treating MI. Angioplasty opens up or removes coronary-artery blockages using catheters introduced through the skin into a leg artery, thereby avoiding bypass surgery. Preliminary results indicate that although thrombolytics can be given faster in an emergency situation, angioplasty results in less bleeding, fewer emergency bypass operations, more frequent and more complete opening of arteries, lower costs, and less recurrent angina and MI. Mortality rates for the two procedures are equal. Other studies proved that combining the treatments (in either order) is of no benefit, and increases cost and risks. Several studies indicate that for those with the largest and most serious MIs, emergency angioplasty clearly improves survival.

► Cardiac Catheterization and Angioplasty

A technological explosion has given rise to angioplasty using lasers, ultrasound, stents, heated balloons, cutting devices, and balloons that can deliver medications directly to vessel plaques. The preliminary results of several studies comparing the success of angioplasty to that of bypass surgery found that surgery produces the same risk of early MI and death as angioplasty, but with less angina, better restoration of blood flow, and better one-year outcomes. The 30 percent risk of recurrent blockages (restenosis) remains the frustrating weakness of all forms of angioplasty.

Studies also showed that breaking open narrowed heart valves with balloon catheters was clearly inferior to surgical valve replacement for aortic valves, but equally successful and far simpler than surgery on mitral valves. Catheter techniques have also been developed for closing abnormal heart defects and for draining fluid from the pericardial sac around the heart.

► Congestive Heart Failure

While CAD mortality is falling, there is an increase in the incidence and mortality rate of congestive heart failure (CHF)—the inability of the heart to pump out all the blood that returns to it, resulting in fluid accumulation in various parts of the body. This may be a result of an aging population, as well as the larger number of surviving MI victims who have severe heart muscle damage. CHF can be caused by CAD, MI, valve disease, hypertension, or rarer causes; it affects 1 to 2 percent of the population; in its most severe form, CHF victims have only a 50 percent chance of surviving one to two years.

Several 1992 studies confirmed the lifesaving effects of the angiotensin-converting enzyme (ACE) inhibitor drugs, including captopril (Capoten), enalapril (Vasotec), and lisinopril (Zestril, Prinivil), even in mild cases of CHF. These drugs prevent production of the hormone angiotensin II, which constricts blood vessels. Furthermore, 1992 trials show that even patients with mild, symptomless heart-muscle damage can benefit from Vasotec, which prevents the onset of symptoms, reduces mortality, and even reduces the incidence of MIs. Several studies confirmed the ability of digoxin (Lanoxin), various beta-blockers (previously thought to be disastrous in CHF), and the investigational agents pimobendan and flosequinan to relieve symptoms, improve exercise tolerance, and increase muscle function in CHF; current studies are assessing their effects on survival.

► CPR: New Advances

While the overall success of cardiopulmonary resuscitation (CPR) is low (30 percent), and the ethics of CPR use in hopelessly ill patients are debatable, much research is underway in this field. Two major trials compared standard doses of epinephrine to higher doses that have been shown to improve CPR success rates in animals; there was no benefit to the high doses in humans. However, improved rates of resuscitation and improved hospital outcomes were reported using abdominal compressions interposed between chest compressions, esophageal or intracardiac routes of delivering electric shocks to halt lethal arrhythmias, use of emergency heart-lung bypass machines to sustain vital functions during cardiac arrest, and the use of a chest suction device ("the plunger") to improve CPR efficiency.

A New View of Blood Pressure

Classifications of blood pressure for adults 18 years old and older, including a new classification of four stages of hypertension based on average blood pressure levels. Systolic pressure, the higher number of a blood pressure reading, is the pressure as the heart pumps; diastolic pressure is the pressure when the heart relaxes between beats.

AVERAGE DIASTOLIC BLOOD PRESSURE (in millimeters of mercury)	AVERAGE SYSTOLIC PRESSURE (in millimeters of mercury)						
	Less than 120	120-129	130-139	140-159	160-179	180-209	210 or over
Less than 80	Optimal*	Normal	High normal	1	2	3	4
80-84	Normal	Normal	High Normal	1	2	3	4
85-89	High Normal	High Normal	High Normal	1	2	3	4
90-99	1	1	1	1	2	3	4
100-109	2	2	2	2	2	3	4
110-119	3	3	3	3	3	3	4
120 or over	4	4	4	4	4	4	4

Normal pressure   Hypertension (stages 1 to 4)

*Unusually low readings should be evaluated for clinical significance.

Source: National High Blood Pressure Education Program.

▶ Arrhythmias: Drugs, Catheters, and Devices

Arrhythmias (or dysrhythmias) are heartbeat irregularities that cause the heart to pump less effectively. Arrhythmias are common, occurring in either normal or diseased hearts, and can range in severity from mildly or asymptomatic nuisances to lethal episodes leading to syncope (loss of consciousness) or sudden death. There are 350,000 sudden cardiac deaths per year in the United States. These are usually due to serious ventricular arrhythmias (arising from the ventricles, or lower pumping chambers of the heart), whereas supraventricular arrhythmias arise from the atria, or upper chambers, and tend to be benign but often bothersome. Recent approaches to arrhythmias focus on suppressing them with drugs, terminating lethal ones with implanted electrical devices or special pacemakers, or curing them surgically or with energy delivered by catheters.

Several 1992 studies have confirmed that older anti-arrhythmic drugs such as quinidine (Quinaglute, Quinidex, and others) or others that work by blocking sodium channels in cardiac-muscle cells can worsen ventricular arrhythmias and increase mortality, especially in those patients with MIs or CHF. Other 1992 studies add to growing evidence that newer drugs that block potassium channels, like amiodarone (Cordarone) or sotalol (Betapace), prevent lethal arrhythmias in a wide range of patients.

A German study revealed that using serial electrophysiological (EP) tests to pick the best drug to suppress ventricular arrhythmias led to the best survival rates. EP testing uses catheters to electrically induce arrhythmias; drugs are then given to find which one suppresses the catheters' ability to induce the arrhythmia.

Unfortunately, an effective drug can be found only about 30 percent of the time, so work continues on refining automatic implantable cardioverter-defibrillators (AICDs), bulky, pacemakerlike devices that are implanted during major open-chest surgery. These devices detect dangerous arrhythmias and deliver electric shocks to prevent sudden death. New investigational models can be placed under the skin and through veins to the heart, requiring only local anesthesia.

Finally, an ever wider range of arrhythmia types are now being permanently cured using energy (usually the radio-frequency type) delivered by catheters placed through the skin and advanced via blood vessels into the heart. As with the other cases where this procedure is used, the "catheter-ablation" approach avoids open-heart surgery, can be done during a one-day hospitalization, and offers a complete cure without medications.

Richard L. Mueller, M.D.

Immunology

▶ New Developments in Immunizations

More than 1 million persons in the United States have chronic hepatitis B virus (HBV) infection, and approximately 4,000 to 5,000 persons die each year from HBV-induced chronic liver disease or liver cancer. HBV is transmitted through exposure to blood and blood products, through sexual contact, and from mothers to infants at birth. It also can be acquired by close contact within families, from person to person through contact between open-skin sores, and possibly by exposure of mucous membranes to other infected body fluids, such as saliva. Vaccination of people at risk for HBV has had little impact on control of this serious public-health problem. HBV immunization, consisting of a series of three injections, has now been recommended for all infants.

A vaccine against chicken pox (varicella) is expected to be approved for general use by the U.S. Food and Drug Administration (FDA) in 1993. Currently, it is available only for use in children with acute lymphocytic leukemia, since chicken pox can be fatal in these patients. The Centers for Disease Control and Prevention (CDC) has not yet made recommendations as to whether this should be given as a standard vaccine, or only when there is an outbreak of chicken pox. However, many experts feel that all children should receive the vaccine—whether or not there is an outbreak, to provide them with lifetime protection against the disease, which is even more severe in adults.

Work on AIDS vaccines continues. Trials of several vaccines in HIV-positive pregnant women, their infants, and HIV-positive children will begin in early 1993. Researchers expect to learn, not only whether a vaccine will work to protect the fetus and infant from developing full-blown AIDS, but also what the immune system must do to foil the AIDS virus itself. A National Institutes of Health (NIH) panel has recommended that a special congressional authorization of $20 billion for vaccine research be spent on a large, comparative trial of several therapeutic vaccines for adults.

The vaccines to be used in this trial contain only a small part of the AIDS virus, such as the protein coat. While this is a safer approach than using a live virus, there is a risk that the immune response to such vaccines will be too weak to ward off the disease. Researchers at Harvard University in Cambridge, Massachusetts, were able to induce protection against a monkey version of HIV in rhesus monkeys by inoculating them with a whole live virus, genetically altered, but similar enough to the real virus to induce antibodies against it. Because of uncertainty about how these altered viruses will behave in humans (the viruses could possibly revert back to their deadly form), great caution is being used in pursuing this approach to immunizing people against AIDS.

▶ Interferon Augments the Body's Defenses

Besides T and B lymphocytes, which are the body's recognition cells that distinguish between "self" and "not self," the immune system also has nonspecific mechanisms that amplify lymphocyte functions. Recent work has focused on factors, collectively called cytokines, that are made by or act on elements of the immune system. Interferon is one such element. Produced by leukocytes, fibroblasts, and epithelial cells, interferon "interferes" with viral production and revs up the immune system in other ways. It enhances expression of important cell-surface markers, such as those molecules responsible for all immune responses, including transplantation reactions, as well as tumor-associated antigens, and cytokine receptors, which are necessary for optimal immune responses.

Two types of interferon have been identified. Type I, including the subtypes alpha and beta interferon, can be activated by viruses, bacteria, and double-stranded RNA. Alpha interferon, the most studied of the interferons so far, is very effective against some cancers. It also appears to help fight infections, including the common cold, and other diseases involving the immune system.

Type II has just one subtype, gamma interferon, the most potent of the interferons; its activation is induced by mitogens (a substance that induces cell mitosis), antigens, and cytokines such as tumor necrosis factor (TNF), interleukins, and colony stimulating factor. Recombinant DNA technology has made a limitless supply of artificial interferon possible, and its use in treatment of various diseases is rapidly expanding.

The range of interferon's biological effects is illustrated by a recent therapeutic trial with a type of tumor called a hemangioma. Found in infants, hemangiomas are large masses of small blood vessels. Although these tumors are benign and may disappear without treatment, they can also cause serious bleeding and even heart failure in some cases. Interferon benefited over 80 percent of children treated by causing the tumors to shrink. Despite such successes, there are numerous side effects associated with the use of interferon, including fever, chills, muscle aches, nausea, fatigue, and mental-health changes. Fortunately, these reactions are generally tolerable, reversible, and only rarely life-threatening. Interferon is just beginning to fulfill its promise, and will likely play a significant role in many future clinical applications.

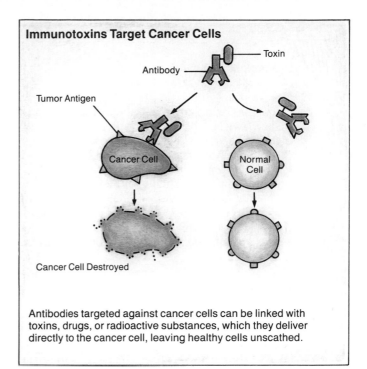

Immunotoxins Target Cancer Cells

Antibodies targeted against cancer cells can be linked with toxins, drugs, or radioactive substances, which they deliver directly to the cancer cell, leaving healthy cells unscathed.

By the end of 1992, the FDA had approved clinical use of interferon only for hairy-cell leukemia, Kaposi's sarcoma in AIDS, condyloma acuminatum (small growths on the larynx and genital area caused by the human papilloma virus), hepatitis C, and chronic granulomatous disease (a defect in the organism-killing ability of white blood cells).

▶ Immunotoxins: Targeted Killers

One of the major methods of treating cancer is chemotherapy, the use of drugs to kill cancer cells. Unfortunately, these same drugs are also toxic to normal cells, and may cause serious side effects and even death in some patients. Researchers have been looking for ways to make chemotherapy drugs that would be lethal to cancerous tissue, but otherwise harmless. One approach has been the development of immunotoxins, which are a combination of a poison, such as the potent ricin toxin derived from castor beans, with monoclonal antibodies (which attack only the targeted tissue) or interleukins (a type of cytokine) to deliver the poison exclusively to unwanted cancer cells in the body. Immunotoxins have been used in humans to successfully treat cancers such as lymphomas, and to treat such autoimmune diseases as arthritis and diabetes.

Another important use of immunotoxins, still under study, is in graft-versus-host disease, a major barrier to successful bone-marrow transplantations. This disease is essentially a reaction that often develops after transplantation, when T lymphocytes from donated bone marrow recognize the recipient's tissues, such as skin, liver, or intestine, as "foreign," and attack and destroy these tissues.

Immunotoxins aimed specifically at these lymphocytes are given at the first sign of graft-versus-host disease.

Immunotoxins are not without side effects, including swelling of the feet and mild weight gain (due to fluid leaking from blood vessels), achy muscles, fatigue, and, most serious of all, altered brain function. Because immunotoxins are foreign substances in the body, antibodies to destroy them are eventually developed, thus limiting the effectiveness of repeated doses of the same immunotoxin. However, early experience with immunotoxins has been promising enough to encourage researchers to design and test new formulations that address these problems and are effective against a broader array of diseases.

▶ The Role of the Mind in Immunology

Evidence from both human and animal studies conducted over the past 10 years has indicated that stress can have a negative effect on immune function. Stressful but commonplace events such as school examinations were associated with a decline in T-lymphocyte-killer-cell activity, decreased gamma-interferon levels, and increased antibodies against latent herpes virus, suggesting reduced immune control of these viruses. The last example alone may explain why flare-ups of cold sores, caused by herpes simplex virus, often occur during times of stress.

Researchers continue to explore whether changing a patient's behavior might have positive consequences for immune function: for example, giving increased resistance to infection or even enhanced body defenses against cancer. In one study in this field, called psychoneuroimmunology, a year of weekly supportive group-therapy sessions along with self-hypnosis for pain extended survival time in women with breast cancer that had spread elsewhere in their bodies. Similar studies were conducted with HIV-positive persons and AIDS patients. Subjects assigned to aerobic-exercise training had decreases in reported levels of anxiety and depression and no decrease in immune-system strength, as compared with the subjects who did not have a regular exercise program.

Animal studies have looked at how early rearing conditions can alter immune responses in the developing primate. Infant monkeys separated from their mothers showed mitogen-induced proliferation of lymphocytes and lower natural killer-cell activity. Researchers in this field acknowledge several alternative explanations for their observations, but claim that psychological disruption of the mother-infant relationship is one likely factor in altered immune responses. The long-term effects of these abnormalities, especially in humans, are not yet known.

James A. Blackman, M.D., M.P.H.

Kidneys

▶ Advanced Renal Cell Cancer Treatment

In March 1992 the Food and Drug Administration's (FDA's) Biological Response Modifiers Advisory Committee recommended interleukin-2 as an effective treatment for selected cases of advanced renal cell cancer. This approval sets the stage for the FDA commissioner to license the agent.

In one study of 255 patients, interleukin-2 destroyed all evidence of disease in nine patients, and produced a 50 percent decrease in the diameter of cancerous lesions, with no appearance of any new lesions, in 28 patients. There was a zero survival rate for all untreated patients in the study.

Early clinical trials of interleukin-2 for metastatic kidney cancer were disappointing because the drug produced severely toxic side effects. But more recent studies have shown that doctors have learned to better manage these toxicities. Studies also indicated that best results were achieved when interleukin-2 is given every eight hours rather than by continuous infusion.

▶ Diabetes, Hypertension, and Kidney Failure

More than 160,000 Americans suffering from kidney failure currently receive dialysis. Two of the leading causes of progressive kidney failure are diabetes mellitus and hypertension; these two diseases alone account for nearly 50 percent of all cases. In the past year, researchers have gained a new understanding of how these two diseases damage the kidneys. With this information, physicians have been able to offer patients treatments that can diminish the incidence of kidney damage.

Diabetes mellitus occurs when the body does not produce enough insulin or is resistant to the action of insulin, the hormone that helps move the sugar glucose into the body's tissues. The result is high levels of glucose in the blood, a condition called hyperglycemia. Persistent hyperglycemia promotes thickening of the arteriole and capillary membranes in the kidney, causing them to lose their ability to properly filter toxic wastes out of the bloodstream. Wastes accumulate in the bloodstream and produce a dangerous and deadly illness called uremia. Dialysis is then required as a means of artificially filtering out these waste products. The patient may ultimately be required to undergo a kidney transplant.

Besides impairing the kidney's filtration abilities, hyperglycemia also appears to cause dilation of the arterioles that bring blood to the filtering capillary

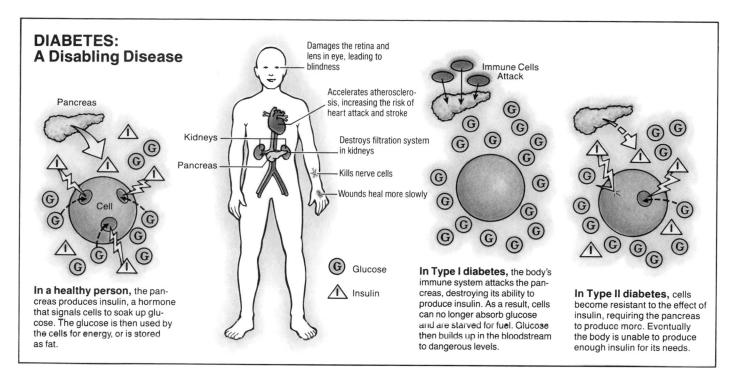

DIABETES: A Disabling Disease

Pancreas

Cell

Damages the retina and lens in eye, leading to blindness

Accelerates atherosclerosis, increasing the risk of heart attack and stroke

Kidneys

Destroys filtration system in kidneys

Pancreas

Kills nerve cells

Wounds heal more slowly

Ⓖ Glucose

⚠ Insulin

Immune Cells Attack

In a healthy person, the pancreas produces insulin, a hormone that signals cells to soak up glucose. The glucose is then used by the cells for energy, or is stored as fat.

In Type I diabetes, the body's immune system attacks the pancreas, destroying its ability to produce insulin. As a result, cells can no longer absorb glucose and are starved for fuel. Glucose then builds up in the bloodstream to dangerous levels.

In Type II diabetes, cells become resistant to the effect of insulin, requiring the pancreas to produce more. Eventually the body is unable to produce enough insulin for its needs.

---

membranes called the glomerular units. Such dilation leads to an increased volume of blood in the glomerular units, and they enlarge. This causes the blood pressure to rise. Research has shown that such pressure rises are damaging to the filtering capacity of capillaries. Persistent hyperglycemia thus damages the kidney in two different ways: by directly promoting thickening of the glomerular capillary membranes and by raising blood pressure inside the glomerular units. Hypertension, the elevation of systemic arterial blood pressure, damages the kidney in exactly the same way—by raising internal glomerular pressures. The result is progressive scarring of the glomerular capillaries, leading to total filtration failure and uremia.

Traditionally, treatment for diabetes focuses on returning the blood glucose levels to normal concentrations by means of insulin injections or regular doses of a medication that improves the patient's insulin output or sensitivity to the hormone. However, physicians now realize that this treatment does not normalize the blood pressure within the glomeruli of the kidney. The potential for kidney damage is diminished with glucose control, but not completely thwarted, particularly in persons who have had diabetes for many years. Such patients can still develop kidney damage. Even though the effects of hyperglycemia on the kidneys are muted, the accompanying high blood pressure in the kidneys, caused by the dilated arterioles, remains and continues to cause damage.

Clinical investigations have shown that elevated blood pressure within the kidneys can be controlled by two independent but complementary means. Research has found that certain types of drugs used to lower systemic blood pressure in patients with essential hypertension can also lower the pressures within glomeruli. Not all drugs used to treat hypertension will accomplish this, however. When given to a diabetic patient, these certain medicines will diminish the threat of diabetes to the kidney independent of the blood glucose level. Thus, if a physician prescribes insulin to lower blood glucose plus one of these unique blood pressure medications, kidney injury from diabetes may be significantly slowed.

Physicians are also recommending that diabetic patients who might be at risk for kidney disease or who are already exhibiting early kidney damage follow a protein-restricted diet. A high-protein diet can raise blood pressures within the glomeruli and cause structural damage, particularly in patients whose kidneys are already under stress from diabetes mellitus, hypertension, or some other disorder. In theory, by reducing dietary protein below certain levels, the blood pressure within the glomeruli will drop, and the risk of damage to the kidneys will be lessened. Physicians are finding this to be so in diabetics and hypertension patients with kidney damage: protein-restricted diets are resulting in apparent pressure reductions within the kidneys, with measurable reductions in protein leakage into the urine and stabilization of filtration function. Such therapies are saving people from needing dialysis or kidney transplantation.

Rex Mahnensmith, M.D.

Liver

▶ Hepatitis

The field of hepatology continues to see exciting advances, especially in the area of viral hepatitis. Molecular biologists are clarifying the nature of the major hepatitis viruses, and clinicians are refining their ability to care for patients with chronic viral hepatitis. Moreover, the means to eradicate at least three of the major forms of viral hepatitis through immunization are, or soon will be, at hand.

Hepatitis A. For several years, researchers have worked to develop an effective vaccine against hepatitis A, which is transmitted to others by fecal contamination of food (as by infected people handling food). Hepatitis A is highly contagious within homes, day-care centers, the military, and other densely populated settings. In mid-1992 investigators reported the results of a study on the use of a formalin-inactivated hepatitis A vaccine in a Hasidic community in New York State where hepatitis A was prevalent. A single injection of the vaccine proved 100 percent effective in protecting against infection, whereas the subjects receiving placebos continued to acquire hepatitis A at the usual rate.

These results may soon lead to a commercially available vaccine for generalized use. The elimination of hepatitis A would prevent much temporary disability caused by the acute symptoms of the disease, such as flulike illness, and the rare instance of fulminant hepatitis A, which can lead to death. Still to be clarified is the issue of defining when and how often booster shots would be necessary, and the optimal timing of initial vaccination.

Hepatitis B. An important clinical advance in 1992 was the approval by the Food and Drug Administration (FDA) of interferon alfa-2b, a form of recombinant alpha interferon, for the treatment of patients with chronic hepatitis B. Previous studies had demonstrated that 35 to 50 percent of patients so treated cleared active hepatitis B virus replication from their livers. This reduces liver inflammation and, it is hoped, prevents cirrhosis and liver cancer. Hepatitis B virus is a complex infectious agent that can persist in latent form even after active replication and liver inflammation have subsided. However, there is increasing evidence that all markers of the infection disappear in many patients for several years following successful treatment.

Patients with advanced cirrhosis related to hepatitis B have a lower likelihood of responding to therapy. In these patients, liver transplantation (which is quite effective for cirrhosis due to other causes) frequently leads to reinfection and severe liver disease. In fact, many liver-transplant centers will no longer accept patients with hepatitis B. These concerns led the University of Pittsburgh, a pioneering center for liver transplantation, to transplant a baboon liver (which cannot be infected by the hepatitis B virus) into a patient who was dying of hepatitis B. The liver reportedly functioned well until the patient died of other causes about two months later. The use of livers from other species is likely to be studied further in the foreseeable future.

Reported Cases of Hepatitis 1991		
Hepatitis A	Hepatitis B	Hepatitis C
24,378	18,003	3,582

Source: Centers for Disease Control and Prevention

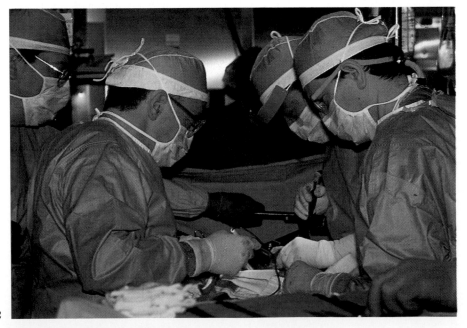

The first baboon liver transplant was performed in July 1992 on a man whose own liver had been destroyed by hepatitis B. Although the patient eventually died from other causes, doctors hope this procedure may become standard for patients who are poor candidates for human liver donation.

Hepatitis C. Rapid advances continue to be made in the understanding of this recently described and common viral infection. Perhaps most important is the discovery of the virus's genetic heterogeneity —that is, the substantial differences in the genetic makeup of hepatitis C found in samples from diverse geographic areas. Moreover, different strains of virus may exist even within a single individual.

The degree of hepatitis C heterogeneity within an individual appears to be at least partly related to the duration of infection, suggesting that mutations may occur in the course of chronic hepatitis C. Additional data suggest some relationship between the degree of genetic heterogeneity of the virus and the likelihood of response to recombinant alpha interferon, the only treatment currently approved for hepatitis C infection in the United States. The discovery of such significant genetic differences may work against the successful development of a vaccine. The ability of hepatitis C virus to mutate is ominously reminiscent of the human immunodeficiency virus (HIV), which causes AIDS.

▶ Complications of Cirrhosis

Perhaps the most feared complication of cirrhosis is bleeding from varices, distended veins under high pressure in the esophagus or stomach. These vessels become engorged with the blood that normally flows from the gastrointestinal organs through the liver, but can no longer do so because of extensive scarring within the liver.

A recent study has confirmed that beta-blockers, drugs commonly used to treat hypertension or heart disease, reduce the risk of initial bleeding episodes in patients with large varices or in others with heightened bleeding risk. Prophylactic variceal sclerotherapy, the injection of a caustic substance into the veins via an endoscope, is still a controversial treatment not widely practiced in the U.S. Studies have shown that for patients with previous variceal bleeding, a relatively simple banding technique is superior to sclerotherapy.

The most dramatic new technique for variceal bleeding is transjugular intrahepatic portosystemic shunting (TIPS). A metallic tube is inserted into the neck vein and wended down into the liver to shunt blood directly from the portal vein leading into the liver to the hepatic veins, which conduct blood out of the liver back toward the heart. Blood that previously could not flow through the scarred liver (and was diverted to potentially dangerous varices) can once again flow through the liver within the metallic shunt tube. Shown to be highly effective, the technique may save the lives of patients who have bled from varices and failed to respond to other therapies. Many such patients can be kept bleed-free until a liver is available for transplantation.

Ira M. Jacobson, M.D.

Medical Ethics

▶ Fetal-Tissue Research and Transplantation

Despite great controversy, the possibility of utilizing fetal tissue to improve the conditions of patients with Parkinson's disease, Alzheimer's disease, and other neurological disorders took on new viability in 1993, as newly elected President Bill Clinton lifted restrictions on the use of federal funds to support such research initiatives.

The Bush administration refused to lift the moratorium on federal funding for such research, based on a concern that promotion of the use of fetal tissue might encourage women to intentionally become pregnant, and then abort, so as to make fetal tissue available for research or implantation purposes. These actions would stand in contrast to the Bush administration's public opposition to abortion under most circumstances. The administration believed, instead, that whatever work needed to be performed in this area could be sufficiently supported through the use of fetal tissue obtained from miscarriages or ectopic pregnancies. Researchers in the field, however, dispute the viability and availability of fetal tissue from these sources.

The debate over this controversy became particularly heated when researchers in both Sweden and the United States published the results of several trials that demonstrated substantial improvement in research subjects who had received fetal-tissue cell implants. The data from these studies demonstrated that fetal cells are able to replace, and take on the activities of, human brain cells that have been destroyed. Once implanted, the fetal cells produce essential chemicals that the patients' brains can no longer produce on their own. In one particularly striking example, two Americans who experienced severe Parkinsonian symptoms after ingesting synthetic heroin displayed remarkable progress toward resumption of their previously healthy conditions. However, continued work remains to be done in the field before fetal-tissue transplant becomes a standard therapy.

As clinical research in this area continues, so, too, will public debate concerning the moral justification for using the tissue of aborted fetuses as a means toward achieving health.

▶ Reaffirmation of *Roe* v. *Wade*

In a 5-4 decision that surprised both proponents and opponents of legalized abortion, the U.S. Supreme Court reaffirmed its commitment to the fundamental principles of the landmark *Roe* v. *Wade* abortion decision.

In the case of *Planned Parenthood* v. *Casey,* the Court was asked to consider placing very significant limitations on the availability of abortion, even to women in the first trimester. The state of Pennsylvania had passed legislation enforcing several limits on the ready accessibility of abortion, including a 24-hour waiting period prior to performing an abortion after a request; the implementation of a lengthy consent process designed to influence the woman's decision to seek an abortion; the notification of a parent of a minor seeking an abortion (or, alternatively, requiring judicial permission); and the notification of the husband of the woman prior to performing the abortion.

While the Court upheld all of these limitations except the required spousal notification, it did so in an opinion that reaffirmed the fundamental right of a woman to have access to abortion as a component of her constitutional right to liberty. Concerned about the drastic changes that might plague society if the original abortion decision were overruled, the majority Court opinion declared that state regulation of abortion was permissible only if that regulation did not have the purpose or effect of imposing an "undue burden" on the woman, which the Court defined as a "substantial obstacle in the path of a woman seeking an abortion before the fetus attains viability."

Both sides of the abortion debate were expecting a Supreme Court decision that overturned the right to abortion, which the *Roe* decision had declared fundamental. While the *Casey* decision does allow for stricter regulation of abortion, it also firmly supports the essential liberty interests of a woman desiring to obtain an abortion during the early stages of her pregnancy.

▶ Attempts to Donate the Organs of an Anencephalic Baby

Anencephalic babies are born without a brain cortex, which means they will never be able to function as normal, healthy human beings. Sometimes these babies have a functioning brain stem, which controls basic biological functions, but death is nonetheless expected within the first few weeks of life.

The birth of an anencephalic Florida baby with only brain-stem function renewed the ethical and legal debate concerning organ retrieval and donation. When the parents of Theresa Ann Campo Pearson learned, prior to her birth, that the baby was anencephalic, they investigated the possibility of donating the organs of the baby, prior to her biological death, to another child. As the availability of infant organs is severely limited, the inquiry became the focus of national debate. The parents ultimately failed in their efforts.

The current legal and ethical consensus in this country holds that individuals can be declared dead, and therefore become viable organ donors, only after they have been diagnosed as "brain-dead," that is, having total cessation of all parts of their brain, including brain-stem activity. Despite Theresa Ann's dismal prognosis, several courts of law upheld the standard that the parents must wait until the baby's brain stem dies, in accord with the prevailing consensus concerning brain death. But the baby's biological death would render most donatable organs nonviable.

Proponents for organ donation prior to brain death in the anencephalic donor argue that such circumstances should be declared distinct and rare exceptions to the brain-death standard, and that a special "brain-absent" category for donation purposes should be developed for the use of anencephalic organs. However, most ethicists argue that if exceptions to the standard began to be supported, then unconscionable evaluations concerning those with severely impaired quality of life may lead to a significant deterioration of the brain-death standard, which is noted for its fundamental respect for human life no matter what the condition of that life may be.

The Pearson baby died prior to the final court ruling, which upheld the ban on organ donation prior to the baby's death. The parents continued to fight their battle, even after their child's death. It should be noted that anencephalic births are rare, so that the availability of organs, were such donations to be permitted, would not increase significantly.

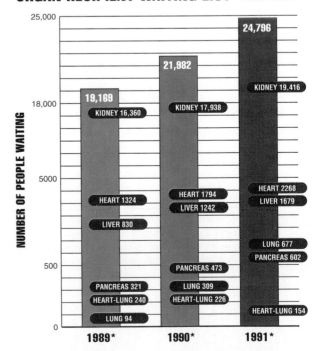

ORGAN RECIPIENT WAITING LIST 1989-1991

Source: UNOS, Richmond, Va.   *As of 12/31 each year

▶ Animal-to-Human Organ Transplants

In related cases underscoring the shortage of available donated organs, several instances of the implantation of animal organs into human beings raised the controversy of the propriety of interspecies organ donation.

In one case a 35-year-old man received a baboon liver after his own liver was destroyed because of the hepatitis B virus. Because of the nature of this virus, the implantation of another *human* liver would have been unsuccessful, as the virus would have destroyed that liver as well. A baboon liver is not susceptible to hepatitis B infection, and is sufficiently compatible as to be an effective replacement for the patient's own nonfunctioning liver. Results of the operation were encouraging.

The patient ultimately died—from other medical problems—70 days after the initial transplant. An autopsy, however, revealed that his body had not rejected the baboon liver. Researchers stated that they planned to follow up this case with a second transplant after identifying another, less severely ill patient. The University of Pittsburgh Medical Center, where the operation was performed, gave researchers permission to implant up to four baboon livers in the course of their research, prior to a subsequent review of the success of this technique.

In a related case, researchers implanted the liver of a pig into a 26-year-old dying woman as a bridge until an acceptable human liver could be permanently implanted. The critically ill woman, who died of acute liver failure within a few days of the transplant, had suffered liver disease since childhood. Researchers justified their unusual efforts on her behalf by citing her severely compromised health, which could no longer wait for a matching human liver, and by pointing to the years of research done in preparation for such a transplant.

Noted ethicist Arthur Caplan criticized the experimentation, citing the lack of supporting scientific data to justify such an unusual experiment. However, the patient's family, the hospital ethics committee, and the institutional review committee (which reviews all research protocols) gave approval for this transplant. This case, as well as the case of the transplanted baboon liver, vividly demonstrate the desperate attempts that clinicians, patients, and families are willing to pursue in order to prolong life in cases where, previously, death was inevitable. These cases also highlight a dilemma concerning selection criteria for the limited availability of donor organs. Should potential recipients gain access because their debilitated health puts them on the edge of survival, or should organs be reserved for candidates more likely to benefit because of their relative health and well-being? This dilemma is likely to continue, as no remedy to the shortage of available organ donation is in sight.

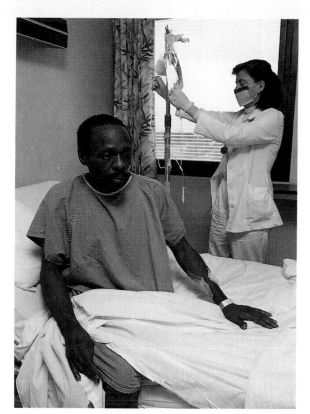

Public-health officials have discovered that many of the victims of the new drug-resistant strains of tuberculosis do not complete their course of treatment unless hospitalized.

▶ The Return of Tuberculosis

A disease once considered nearly extinct on the American health scene, tuberculosis (TB) re-emerged as a potent health threat, with drug-resistant strands of the illness and noncompliant patients posing danger to the average healthy citizen.

Many patients have a difficult time completing the standard form of TB treatment, both because of the long-term therapy necessary to rid the body of TB (even after the patient feels better), and because of the extensive number of medications often necessary. Patients who do not complete the course of therapy may then go on to develop, or spread, variations of the illness that are resistant to the standard medications. Public-health officials have therefore concentrated their energies on strategies to help ensure that patients complete the therapy necessary to cure TB. Certain TB patients—for example, HIV-positive drug addicts—are less likely to take the full course of TB medications. Among the suggested solutions are the quarantining or incarceration of certain patients who are intentionally noncompliant with their medication regimen. These strategies lead to a conflict between individual rights and the good of the public health. Other supporters of civil liberties, however, suggest that the better method to achieve the same goal is to provide positive incentives for medication compliance, including monetary remuneration or other additional benefits to the patient. One other method, known as "directly observed therapy," has gained increasing support, as it allows patients with TB to remain in the community, thus preserving their freedom, but it requires patients to permit daily observation of their compliance with the treatment regimen.

▶ HIV-infected Health-Care Workers

The furor over the risk posed to patients by HIV-infected health-care providers abated as attention focused on increased monitoring of infection-control procedures and attention to the discrete circumstances of individual providers. Following the spread of AIDS from a Florida dentist to five of his patients, significant concern developed as to whether clinicians might spread HIV infection to patients during the course of clinical interventions. The actual mode of transmission has never been determined in the Florida cases, and almost no data exist to support such a risk. But public clamoring led the Centers for Disease Control and Prevention (CDC) to recommend that medical, dental, and surgical organizations participate in an effort to define what clinical procedures would most put patients at risk from an HIV-positive health-care provider.

Professional organizations refused to comply with the CDC request, and CDC efforts were eventually shifted to encourage individual states to develop their own systems for tracking and monitoring the spread of HIV in the clinical setting. The big issue for professionals experienced in AIDS clinical care was the concern that if providers were subject to mandatory HIV testing or removal from their professional positions once they became HIV-infected, such measures might then lead to physician unwillingness to care for AIDS patients, due to the risk of infection by these patients. As well, scientists continued to express outrage that govern-mental guidelines were in place that had no scientific data to support their theses. As one AIDS physician noted, "The risk of transmission [from provider to patient] is almost nonexistent if proper infection control is maintained."

▶ Physician-assisted Suicide

The actions of Detroit pathologist Jack Kevorkian, M.D., continued to focus attention on the question of whether physicians should assist patients who wish to end their lives because of intolerable suffering from their medical condition. In a related matter, voters in the state of California rejected a proposal to permit the legalization of physicians' and other providers' assistance in certain limited cases where competent patients wished to end their lives.

Dr. Kevorkian participated in numerous cases of physician-assisted suicide in 1992 and 1993, usually providing advice, but at times providing the means to enable patients to end their own lives. Michigan prosecutors charged Dr. Kevorkian with homicide in two particular cases, but the charges were later dropped because of insufficient evidence. Michigan is one of the few states that have no explicit statute outlawing the assistance of another in a person's suicide, and state authorities have been stymied in their attempts to halt Dr. Kevorkian's activities. The attempt to prosecute him for homicide proved to be an equally unsuccessful alternative. However, a bill barring suicide assistance in Michigan was recently approved in both legislative houses and by the state's governor.

Dr. Kevorkian justifies his actions as the relief of suffering, which he claims is one of the aims of medicine. Despite losing his license to practice in Michigan (although he still retains a California license), and despite the legislation outlawing his actions, Dr. Kevorkian has vowed to continue his efforts.

The cause of physician assistance in suicide received support this year from an article published in the *New England Journal of Medicine* by three esteemed physicians, who called for a new public policy permitting such assistance in very specific cases, in accord with their suggested guidelines. The authors concluded, among other things, that for such assistance to occur, the following factors must be in place: the patient must have an incurable illness with unrelenting suffering that cannot be addressed by sufficient pain medication; the patient must clearly and consistently ask to die, and thus must possess decision-making capacity; and the patient's physician should be the provider of assistance, unless he or she has a moral objection. Despite the prestigious nature of the journal that printed this article, the controversy concerning such assistance continues to grow, and resolution appears nowhere in sight.

Connie Zuckerman, J.D.

The CDC has recommended that doctors, dentists, and other health-care workers wear protective gloves, masks, and other gear to prevent them from either contracting or transmitting HIV.

Medical Technology

▶ New Diagnostic Tests

Today much of the testing performed on the nation's blood supply and in individuals checks for the hepatitis viruses and the human immunodeficiency virus (HIV) that causes acquired immune deficiency syndrome (AIDS). In 1992 the Food and Drug Administration (FDA) approved two new tests for detecting antibodies to these viruses in human blood. The Ortho HCV 2.0 Enzyme-linked Immunosorbent Assay (ELISA) Test System (Ortho Diagnostic Systems, Raritan, New Jersey, and Chiron Corporation, Emeryville, California) is designed for widespread laboratory use, while the Single Use Diagnostic System (SUDS) HIV-1 Test (International Murex Technologies Corporation, Toronto, Canada) is intended for individual use only.

Screening for Hepatitis C. Ortho's new test, approved in March 1992, detects the hepatitis C virus (HCV), a strain of hepatitis discovered in 1989. Before HCV was identified, hepatitis, an inflammation of the liver associated with liver diseases such as cirrhosis and cancer, was most often classified into two major types: hepatitis A (HAV), which was at one time called infectious hepatitis because it is spread through contaminated food; and hepatitis B (HBV), which was previously called serum hepatitis because it is transmitted through the blood and other bodily fluids, such as semen. Before its discovery, the disease caused by HCV was known as non-A, non-B hepatitis; it is also transmitted by sexual contact and through tainted blood—in fact, over 90 percent of all cases of hepatitis contracted from blood transfusions are HCV. Most cases of hepatitis B associated with transfusions have been eliminated over the past 20 years through tests that identify the virus's presence in blood. With the introduction of Ortho's test, transfusion-related hepatitis C should also be virtually eliminated in the near future, especially since this test is the first to be developed that detects the antibodies produced in response to three different parts of the virus. (An earlier HCV test approved by the FDA in 1990 identified the presence of antibodies that reacted to only one part of HCV.)

Rapid Test for Primary AIDS Virus. The SUDS HIV-1 Test was developed to detect the primary AIDS virus in the blood of an individual rather than for use in large-scale repetitive testing of the blood supply. It can be performed in a doctor's office; the results are available in 10 minutes, making it one of the fastest test kits on the market today. Most HIV tests currently in use require several hours to perform and must be processed in a lab using sophisticated equipment. Approved in May 1992, the new HIV-1 test can be performed by health professionals with a minimum of training and no special tools. It requires putting a small amount of blood, serum, or plasma in a special test cartridge that contains a window at the bottom. The sample is then mixed with an antibody reagent to which only HIV-1 antibodies will attach; another chemical solution is then added to the test cartridge. If the mixture visible at the bottom of the cartridge turns blue, the sample contains HIV-1 antibodies.

Although a positive result must still be confirmed by the standard Western Blot or immunofluorescence AIDS test, SUDS HIV-1 allows medical technicians in physicians' offices, clinics, emergency rooms, and small hospitals to perform tests where they might otherwise be unavailable. The test is considered to be 99 percent accurate—in clinical trials, it identified HIV-1 specific antibodies 99.6 percent of the time.

▶ Condom for Women

The Reality female condom received unanimous conditional approval from the FDA's Obstetrics and Gynecology Devices Advisory Panel on January 31, 1992, for use as a deterrent to disease during sexual intercourse. Wisconsin Pharmacal Company of Chicago, the maker of the device, expects to receive full marketing clearance for the condom by the end of the year. This is the first product of its kind that the FDA has reviewed; in giving it conditional approval, the panel indicated that they consider the need for the new condom to be great.

The female condom, or vaginal pouch, is a disposable, silicone-lubricated polyurethane sac that is as long as a male condom (about 7 inches), but wider, with a flexible polyurethane ring at each end. The ring on the upper, or top, closed end of the condom is about 2 inches in diameter and is located inside the sac to serve as an anchor or guide. It is inserted in the vagina with the fingers, much like a diaphragm, and pushed up behind the pubic bone, covering the cervix. At the other end of the pouch, which is wider, the ring is about 2¾ inches in diameter and forms the outer open end of the pouch. It remains outside the body, covering the external genitals. The pouch, which can be inserted several hours before sexual intercourse, is loose-fitting and considered to be more comfortable for both sexual partners than the traditional male condom. Because it is constructed of polyurethane, which is thinner than latex, its presence in the vagina is less noticeable to both the man and the woman than a conventional condom. In addition, it conducts heat well, which also provides a more natural feel, according to the condom's users.

The new device has been tested on 1,700 women in the United States and Latin America over the past four years. It was found to prevent pregnancy 85 percent of the time (a rate similar to the diaphragm). However, the female condom also protects both men and women from the viruses and bacteria that cause sexually transmitted diseases (STDs), in particular, AIDS. Preliminary studies by Wisconsin Pharmacal indicate that the AIDS virus and viral particles smaller than the hepatitis B virus cannot penetrate the sac.

Potential drawbacks to the Reality condom for women include occasional slippage of the device into the vagina during intercourse, which may expose the woman to semen. (The manufacturer claims that this is due to improper use, and suggests adding more lubricant to the opening of the condom.) Mild irritation of the external genital region and the vagina has also been reported.

The FDA is withholding final marketing approval of the device until Wisconsin Pharmacal submits data from tests conducted on 200 women over 12 months. These data must show that the pregnancy rate does not increase from the 15-in-100 rate currently claimed for the product. To date, the company has gathered statistics for 81 women over a six-month period.

The condom is already being sold in Switzerland, England, and France under the name Femidom.

▶ New Uses for Lasers in Medicine

Medical lasers are composed of several basic parts: an electrical source; mirrors to direct the narrow and intense beam of light that the laser produces; a crystal or glass that is stimulated to emit this light; and tubing to deliver the energy produced by the light. The different types of lasers currently available for medicinal purposes are differentiated by the type of radiation they emit, and this radiation is determined by the chemical through which the radiation passes.

Pulsed-Dye Laser. In dermatology, several types of lasers are used, including the carbon dioxide laser, the argon laser, and the pulsed-dye laser. In 1992 Cynosure, Inc., obtained FDA approval for two new pulsed-dye systems: in July for the Photogenica V, which removes port-wine stains; and in August for Photogenica P, which treats benign (noncancerous) superficial pigmented lesions. Pulsed-dye lasers were first approved by the FDA in 1987, but it was not until 1989 that their ability to remove port-wine stains was reported.

Traditionally, dermatologists have attempted to remove or reduce port-wine stains and benign skin lesions using liquid nitrogen to freeze the affected tissue or by cutting and scraping the targeted treatment area. Tretinoin (Retin-A) and other acids have

been used more recently, but these, too, cause discomfort over a period of time. Pulsed-dye lasers promise dramatic results, accompanied only by temporary redness, swelling, and bruising. The procedure, which is relatively short in duration and can be performed in a doctor's office, usually requires no anesthesia—the feeling has been likened to the snap of a rubber band against the skin.

The Photogenica V pulsed-dye laser uses a dye (rhodamine in methanol) that is excited by high-intensity flash lamps to release photons. These photons pass through the watery tissue at the surface of the skin and are then absorbed by hemoglobin in the blood vessels that lie directly below the skin's outer layer. (Hemoglobin is the red protein in red blood cells that carries oxygen to the body's tissues.) Port-wine stains contain a much higher number of blood vessels than do normal areas of the skin. When the mark is zapped by the laser, the light beam destroys the hemoglobin in the red blood cells of these additional blood vessels. This kills the blood cells, and the vessels that contain the cells shrink and eventually disappear. Their disappearance lightens the color of the stain.

The Photogenica P pulsed-dye laser can be used on age, sun, and liver spots; moles; freckles; and brown birthmarks. The dye it uses focuses the laser on the skin's melanin, the pigment that gives skin its brown or black color. After treatment with the laser, the skin peels; when sloughing is complete, the skin underneath is clear.

One of the advantages of the pulsed-dye laser is its ability to deliver light pulses in short intervals. These bursts of light are absorbed only by red blood vessels, which prevents the laser beam from destroying unblemished skin below or around the targeted area. Pulsed-dye lasers are particularly appropriate for use in children, whose skin is more delicate than that of adults.

Excimer Laser. One of the most noteworthy laser devices approved by the FDA in 1992 is the Excimer Laser Angioplasty System, used to open blocked coronary arteries in patients at high risk for heart attacks. In February, Advanced Interventional Systems (AIS) in Irvine, California, received the go-ahead to market its new device, which cuts a path through arteries clogged with plaque—the buildup of fat, calcium, cholesterol, and other cell products on the artery's inner wall. It is the first laser of its kind to be approved for use in coronary disease patients.

The exact process employed by the AIS system is known as laser angioplasty. It entails threading a thin fiber-optic cable encased in a catheter through the femoral artery in the groin. This catheter is then guided to the area of the coronary artery blocked with plaque, and the tip of the fiber-optic cable is

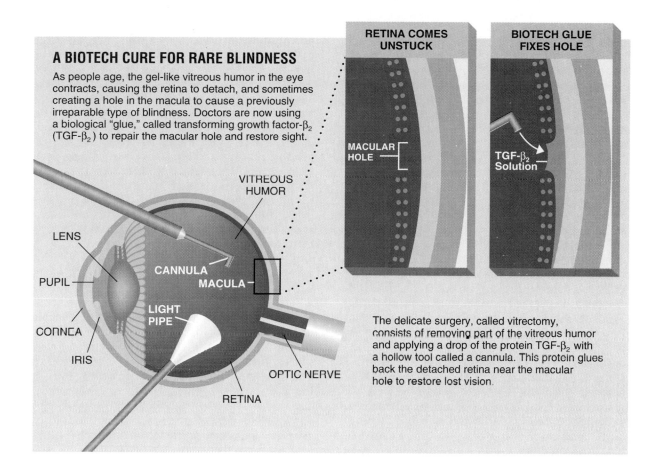

A BIOTECH CURE FOR RARE BLINDNESS

As people age, the gel-like vitreous humor in the eye contracts, causing the retina to detach, and sometimes creating a hole in the macula to cause a previously irreparable type of blindness. Doctors are now using a biological "glue," called transforming growth factor-β_2 (TGF-β_2) to repair the macular hole and restore sight.

RETINA COMES UNSTUCK

MACULAR HOLE

BIOTECH GLUE FIXES HOLE

TGF-β_2 Solution

VITREOUS HUMOR

LENS

PUPIL

CANNULA

MACULA

CORNEA

LIGHT PIPE

IRIS

OPTIC NERVE

RETINA

The delicate surgery, called vitrectomy, consists of removing part of the vitreous humor and applying a drop of the protein TGF-β_2 with a hollow tool called a cannula. This protein glues back the detached retina near the macular hole to restore lost vision.

pointed at the blockage. When activated, the cable emits an intense but cool beam of ultraviolet light that vaporizes areas of the plaque. The resulting gas and tiny plaque particles are then removed from the bloodstream by the body's natural purification system. Because the laser uses a cool type of light, the healthy tissues surrounding the artery are not damaged.

Laser angioplasty can be used in conjunction with balloon angioplasty, a similar technique in which a series of wires and catheters are threaded through the femoral artery to the blocked coronary artery. One of the catheters carries a deflated balloon at its tip, which is positioned at the blockage site and then inflated to push the artery-blocking deposits against the artery's inner walls. This process widens the passageway through which blood flows from the heart. For best results, laser angioplasty is usually performed first, followed by balloon angioplasty. Laser angioplasty can also be used on its own, particularly for patients whose coronary blockage extends a long distance (20 millimeters or more in length), making balloon angioplasty unviable.

Although researchers consider the excimer laser to be a promising new tool for treating some types of coronary disease, it does have several drawbacks. The passage cut through the blocked artery

is narrow, which is one reason why laser angioplasty is often followed by balloon angioplasty. Even with this dual approach, however, patients often experience restenosis, or renarrowing of the arteries, within six months. In clinical trials the AIS Excimer Laser Angioplasty System had a 91 percent success rate, but six months later, 44 percent of the patients again developed clogged arteries. According to George Abela, M.D., associate professor of cardiology at Harvard Medical School, Cambridge, Massachusetts, the rapid restenosis may be because the laser in its current form doesn't remove enough of a blockage.

Despite the drawbacks, however, James S. Benson, director of the FDA Center for Devices and Radiological Health, notes that the success rate of laser angioplasty in patients with very long blockages who do not respond to balloon angioplasty is high enough to warrant its use.

Holmium Laser. In other laser news, the FDA approved a device from Sunrise Technologies in Fremont, California, that can be used in various types of outpatient surgery. The sLASE 210 Holmium Laser System was first approved in March 1992 for general and orthopedic surgery. In May the FDA extended its approval of the sLASE to include surgery for spinal disorders, in particular to repair herniated disks. Patients can be treated with the laser in their doctors' offices under local anesthesia and sent home the same day. In July the FDA granted Sunrise Technologies extended approval of the laser, to include the outpatient treatment of glaucoma. Ophthalmologists use the laser to create a duct in the eye to relieve abnormal pressure. In June 1992, the FDA also cleared the OmniMed Holmium Laser System for treatment of glaucoma. This laser is marketed by Summit Technology of Waltham, Massachusetts.

▶ New Use for PSA Test

A test approved by the FDA in the past decade to monitor the results of prostate-cancer therapy has recently been found to also detect this cancer in its early and curable stages. The results of two studies, published in the past two years, found that the Prostate-Specific-Antigen (PSA) Test (manufactured by Hybritech, San Diego, California) detects prostate cancers missed by the standard digital rectal examination. The PSA test may help prevent some of the approximately 34,000 U.S. deaths attributed to prostate cancer every year.

Currently, by the time most men experience the symptoms of prostate enlargement caused by cancer, the disease has spread beyond the gland. The goal of prostate-cancer testing, therefore, is to identify this disease before it has spread, while it is still curable. This is especially important since 1 in 11 men will develop prostate cancer, usually later in life. In fact, approximately 132,000 new cases of prostate cancer were diagnosed in American men in 1992 alone.

Up to now, prostate cancer has been detected mainly by the digital rectal examination. This test consists of a doctor inserting a gloved finger into the rectum to feel for the prostate gland and determine its size and condition, including the presence of any tumors. The procedure, which takes less than a minute to perform, is uncomfortable and considered embarrassing by some men who would rather forgo it at the risk of their health. The test also depends on the examiner's ability to differentiate between a normal gland and one with cancerous growths. In addition, if a tumor has not yet grown large enough to be felt during a digital exam, it will be missed. Conversely, in 7 out of 10 cases, by the time a tumor is large enough to be detected by digital rectal exam, the cancer has often already spread to other parts of the body.

The new PSA blood test measures a glycoprotein secreted exclusively by the prostate gland. All types of prostate tissue secrete PSA—both normal and hyperplastic (those resulting from abnormal growth). However, high levels of PSA in the bloodstream indicate that something is wrong. When first approved by the FDA, the PSA test was used only to measure PSA levels in patients being treated for prostate cancer. Decreasing levels of the antigen over the course of therapy indicate that a tumor is shrinking, while increasing rates demonstrate that it is still growing.

Now researchers have discovered that PSA levels are also elevated in some men who have undergone a digital exam and who have been given a clean bill of health. One study conducted by scientists at Washington University School of Medicine, St. Louis, examined 1,653 healthy men, 50 years or older, who displayed no symptoms of prostate cancer. These men were given both the PSA test and the digital rectal exam. The study revealed that 37 men had cancer. Of these, 32 percent would not have been diagnosed had only a digital rectal exam been used as a diagnostic tool.

According to William J. Catalona, M.D., chief of urologic surgery at Washington University School of Medicine, these findings are the first evidence that PSA screening detects more localized prostate cancers than the standard digital rectal exam alone. This is because the PSA test can identify tumors too small to be felt manually, but large enough to cause PSA levels to rise. The PSA test does not detect all tumors, however, as some cancers do not cause an increase in PSA levels. For example, studies have found that when used alone, the PSA test misses about 20 percent of cancer cases. However, some of these incidences of cancer can be identified with a digital rectal exam. As a result, physicians are recommending that the two tests be used together. If one or both tests are positive for a patient, a third diagnostic tool can also be used—transrectal ultrasound, in which a probe inserted in the rectum emits high-frequency sound waves that are translated by special equipment into a picture of the gland. Depending on the results of this test, a biopsy may also be performed.

Critics of the PSA blood test claim that it isn't specific enough to identify prostate cancer. They cite studies that show that 25 percent of men with benign prostatic hyperplasia (BPH), which causes an enlarged prostate but is generally not fatal, have high PSA levels, but no evidence of cancer. These men, they say, are forced to undergo unnecessary additional tests based on positive PSA tests, and experience anxiety while waiting for the results. An article in the *Journal of the American Medical Association* in 1992, however, indicates that PSA levels in men with BPH rise gradually over a period of years, while in men with prostate cancer, the levels rise sharply over a short period of time. If a man is tested regularly for PSA levels, his physican can determine to which pattern his PSA levels correspond, and then act appropriately.

Abigail W. Polek

Medications and Drugs

▶ Relief from Cancer-Therapy Complications

High levels of calcium in the blood, or hypercalcemia, is a complication seen in many patients with cancer. Blood levels of calcium become elevated when cancer cells trigger substances that cause the bone to release calcium faster and in greater quantities than the body can handle. Hypercalcemia can cause problems in the kidneys, and neurological or cardiac complications, all of which may ultimately lead to death. Given the prognosis, hypercalcemia must be treated immediately in cancer patients. The first step is to give the patient fluids to help restore the fluid volume in the cells and maintain renal function. In mild hypercalcemia, this treatment may be sufficient. But for many patients, further treatment with a drug capable of lowering serum-calcium levels is necessary. There are a number of drugs available to treat hypercalcemia, but most of these either have very little effect on the condition or cause undesirable side effects.

In the past year, the drug pamidronate (Aredia) was approved by the U.S. Food and Drug Administration (FDA) for treatment of hypercalcemia associated with cancer, including malignancies that have spread to the bones. Aredia, which is given intravenously, binds to the minerals that help form new bone, thus preventing more calcium from being released. A study comparing pamidronate to etidronate, one of the other drugs used to treat hypercalcemia, found a greatly increased response rate to the new drug compared with the older drug. Also, pamidronate increased the time between relapses. Aside from fever, patients who receive pamidronate have had few side effects. They should nonetheless be closely monitored. Further studies have shown that pamidronate may also be useful for the treatment of other diseases involving bone loss, such as Paget's disease, hyperparathyroidism, and postmenopausal osteoporosis.

▶ Oral Medicine for Ulcerative Colitis

Ulcerative colitis, a form of inflammatory bowel disease primarily affecting the lining of the colon and rectum, is characterized by bleeding, diarrhea, and abdominal cramps. The standard treatment for patients with severe colitis has been the use of systemic corticosteroids to achieve remission; for less severe cases, oral sulfasalazine, olsalazine, and corticosteroid or mesalamine enemas have been used, but have been found to have adverse side effects.

Now the FDA has approved Asacol, a tablet form of mesalamine, for the treatment of mildly to moderately active ulcerative colitis. Mesalamine seems to work topically on the mucosa of the colon and rectum. The tablet's coating prevents the drug from being absorbed on its way through the acidic stomach or upper intestine. Not until it reaches the more alkaline environment of the terminal ileum and proximal colon does the coating disintegrate, releasing the mesalamine. Adverse effects of mesalamine are usually mild and transient; they include headache, abdominal discomfort, nausea, dizziness, diarrhea, fever, back pain, rash, vomiting, muscle aches, and constipation. A few patients report an increase in colitis activity.

Studies have shown that the Asacol form of mesalamine is as effective as sulfasalazine in the treatment of mildly to moderately active ulcerative colitis, and to maintain remission in these patients, with fewer side effects. According to another study, olsalazine still has lower failure rates and relapse rates after one year, making it the drug of choice for maintenance therapy.

▶ Fighting Infection

New Antibiotics with Greater Gastrointestinal Tolerance. Two new antibiotics, related to erythromycin, are on the market. Azithromycin (Zithromax) and clarithromycin (Biaxin) have been approved by the FDA for the treatment of respiratory and skin infections. Both drugs are easier on the stomach, and cause neither as much nausea nor as severe stomach cramps as does erythromycin. Unfortunately, neither antibiotic is effective against streptococcus or staphylococcus bacteria (which are also resistant to erythromycin).

Azithromycin is more active against flu infections than erythromycin or clarithromycin, and has been approved for the treatment of certain types of urethritis and cervical infections caused by *Chlamydia trachomatis*. The most promising use for clarithromycin and azithromycin is for infections associated with AIDS. Both drugs are also being tested as a treatment for Lyme disease.

Two important side effects have occurred with these antibiotics and need to be carefully studied: a reversible, dose-related hearing loss was reported with the use of both drugs at high doses, and high doses of clarithromycin caused fetal abnormalities and growth retardation in test animals.

New Oral Antifungal Agent. Itraconazole (Sporanox) is a new antifungal for the treatment of histoplasmosis and blastomycosis, fungal diseases found in the lungs. Both diseases are becoming more common as opportunistic infections in HIV-infected patients whose immune systems have weakened. According to the clinical studies, itraconazole has few side effects, although some nausea, rash, and vomiting may occur. Itraconazole does interact with several drugs, and should not be used by women who are breastfeeding, although pregnant women may take it if necessary. Importantly, there have been no interactions reported between itraconazole and azidothymidine (AZT).

▶ New AIDS Drug

Zalcitabine (Hivid), formerly known as ddC, is the first drug for the treatment of HIV infection to be approved under the FDA's proposed accelerated drug-review policy. This drug has been recommended for use in adult patients with advanced HIV infection who have demonstrated significant clinical or immunologic deterioration. Zalcitabine must be used only in combination with AZT, in a recommended regimen of dosage every eight hours. In limited trials, this dosing regimen has been more effective than AZT alone. It is also recommended that since AZT has been shown to prolong survival and decrease the incidence of opportunistic infections in patients with advanced HIV infections, AZT alone still should be considered as initial therapy for adult patients with HIV infections who have evidence of impaired immunity.

There are two major side effects associated with zalcitabine. Moderate or severe peripheral neuropathy, characterized by numbness and burning in the extremities that may be followed by sharp, shooting pains or severe continuous burning pains, occurred in up to one-third of patients on zalcitabine alone. The neuropathy is usually reversible if the drug is stopped. Patients with preexisting HIV-related peripheral neuropathy, as well as patients

In San Francisco's Castro District, a new pharmacy has opened that specializes in serving the needs of patrons with AIDS and those who have tested positive for HIV.

with very low CD4 counts (the cells that indicate the activity of the immune system), should avoid zalcitabine. The drug should not be used simultaneously with other drugs known to cause peripheral neuropathies.

The second major side effect is inflammation of the pancreas (pancreatitis), with a possibility of death in rare cases. This side effect occurred in

CLINICAL SPECTRUM OF HIV INFECTION AND TREATMENT

The progression from HIV infection to AIDS-related complex and AIDS can take more than a decade. The best way to combat the disease would be a preventive vaccine, but therapeutic vaccines may be available sooner. A few drugs that slow the infection already exist.

PRE-EXPOSURE: PREVENTIVE VACCINES	POST-INFECTION: THERAPEUTIC VACCINES	POST-INFECTION: DRUGS
Aim: To immunize against HIV infection with molecules copied from the viral surface or core.	Aim: To stimulate the immune system to redouble its natural effort to defeat HIV.	Aim: To cripple HIV reproduction, preventing or retarding AIDS-related complex and AIDS.
NO INFECTION	NO DISEASE	SYMPTOM-FREE STATE → ARC/AIDS

more than 1 percent of the patients taking either zalcitabine alone or in combination with AZT. Patients with a history of pancreatitis or related symptoms should be monitored closely. Treatment with zalcitabine should be stopped if an illness develops that requires treatment with any other drug known to cause pancreatitis, for example, intravenous pentamidine. Zalcitabine has also been shown to cause birth defects in mice; women of childbearing age should therefore use effective contraception to prevent any pregnancy while taking this drug.

It is important for patients to know that zalcitabine is not a cure for HIV infection and that they may continue to develop the opportunistic infections associated with the disease. Zalcitabine has not been shown to reduce the incidence or frequency of such illnesses. Zalcitabine and other drugs used to control the course of HIV infection do not reduce the possibility of transmission of the virus to others, so appropriate precautions must be taken during sexual activity or while handling the bodily fluids of an infected person.

▶ New Nitrate for Angina

Organonitrate vasodilators—drugs that relax smooth muscle and keep the blood vessels from tightening—have been used for years in the treatment of angina. FDA approval was given in the past year to isosorbide mononitrate (ISMO), a relative of the older isosorbide dinitrate. ISMO is approved for the prevention of chronic, stable angina due to coronary artery disease. The main advantage of ISMO over other organonitrate vasodilators is that it is administered twice daily, first thing in the morning and approximately seven hours later. This allows the body to have a nitrate-free interval overnight, and thus helps to avoid the development of tolerance to the drug. Dosage of ISMO does not have to be adjusted for age, weight, coronary heart disease, moderate to severe renal impairment, or liver dysfunction, since it seems to work much more consistently in the body than does isosorbide dinitrate. One study noted that the older drug isosorbide dinitrate, if given with a 14-hour dose-free interval overnight, is also effective, and much less costly as well.

The side effects of isosorbide mononitrate are no different than those from other organonitrate vasodilators. Headache is the most frequently reported problem, and dizziness and nausea have also occurred. Drug interactions are also similar to those with isosorbide dinitrate. Concurrent use of alcohol may cause a severe drop in blood pressure and cardiovascular collapse, while aspirin use may increase ISMO's serum concentration and activity. If a calcium channel blocker needs to be added to the therapeutic regimen, care should be taken that marked low blood pressure does not occur.

▶ Non-Surgical Treatment of Enlarged Prostate

Prostate enlargement is a problem that affects approximately 50 percent of men over 60 years old. Known technically as benign prostatic hyperplasia (BPH), prostate enlargement is a progressive disease that causes such symptoms as blockage during urination, hesitancy in urination, and decrease in urinary flow. Until now, virtually the only treatment option available was surgery to remove the enlarged prostate.

Finasteride (Proscar) has been approved by the FDA for the treatment of symptomatic BPH. Finasteride is a specific inhibitor of the enzyme that converts testosterone into 5 alpha-dihydrotestosterone (DHT). It is the DHT that is primarily responsible for the growth and enlargement of the prostate gland. By blocking the production of DHT, it is believed that enlargement of the prostate would either stop, or that there might even be a shrinkage in the size of the gland.

Studies of finasteride, given daily for at least 12 months, have shown that approximately 50 percent of the men had a decrease of 20 percent or more in the size of the prostate. Fewer than 50 percent of patients experienced an increase in urinary flow or improvement in symptoms of BPH. These rates are lower than the improvement rates from surgical treatment of the same problem. However, it may take at least a minimum of six months of treatment to determine if an individual will be responsive to the drug. Because of the moderate success rate with the drug, doctors feel that finasteride may be a good option for men with moderate to severe symptoms of BPH who are unable or unwilling to undergo surgery.

Finasteride is generally well tolerated, and men taking the medication find that the most common adverse effects are impotence, decreased libido, and a decrease in the volume of ejaculate. Since it is metabolized extensively in the liver, this drug should not be used in patients with any liver-function abnormalities, such as cirrhosis. Prior to starting treatment with finasteride, a thorough evaluation of the prostate region should be carried out to eliminate the existence of other conditions such as infection, prostate cancer, stricture disease, hypotonic bladder, or other neurogenic disorders that might mimic BPH. Men who are planning to conceive a child should stop taking finasteride because the drug presents serious risks to women who are carrying a fetus. The tablets should not even be handled by women who are pregnant or are planning to become pregnant because of the possibility of absorption of the drug and the subsequent potential risk to a male fetus. The fetus can also be exposed if the mother has contact with traces of finasteride in her partner's semen.

▶ New NSAIDs for Arthritis Treatment

Nabumetone (Relafen) is a new nonsteroidal anti-inflammatory drug (NSAID) that has joined the more than a dozen such medications already on the market. Nabumetone was approved this past year by the FDA for the acute and chronic treatment of pain and inflammation caused by rheumatoid arthritis and osteoarthritis. What sets nabumetone apart from all the other NSAIDs on the market is the significantly lower incidence of gastroduodenal ulcers associated with its usage. Since nabumetone is not absorbed until it gets into the duodenum—the first part of the small intestine—it causes less stomach irritation, and hence fewer peptic ulcers. Some studies have shown nabumetone to be associated with fewer gastric irritations and ulcerations. However, a postmarketing survey in Great Britain, where the drug has been available since 1987, found that the rate of peptic ulceration with nabumetone was similar to rates reported for other NSAIDs on the market.

According to studies conducted in patients with rheumatoid arthritis, nabumetone is as effective as aspirin, indomethacin, or naproxen in the treatment of osteoarthritis. The most common side effects of nabumetone are abdominal pain, upset stomach, nausea, and diarrhea. Rashes caused by exposure to sunlight, headache, dizziness, swelling, ringing in the ears, and nightmares have also been reported. Elderly patients, those with severe renal problems, and patients with a high risk of gastrointestinal bleeding should take lower doses of the medication. Taking the drug with food increases the rate of absorption, making it more effective.

Another new NSAID that reached the market this year is the oral form of ketorolac tromethamine (Toradol), which is used for the short-term management of pain. Oral ketorolac tromethamine is similar in effectiveness to ibuprofen, aspirin, acetaminophen, acetaminophen with codeine, aspirin plus codeine, and Vicodin, but with longer duration of action. Oral ketorolac tromethamine may be preferable to some of these other drugs since it does not cause physical dependence or withdrawal symptoms. However, it can be used for only three to five days. Longer use has been found to cause an increase in gastrointestinal ulcerations, bleeding, and perforation, as well as kidney problems, including acute kidney failure. Patients who are allergic to aspirin or other NSAIDs should not use this medication.

Oral ketorolac tromethamine should be used with caution and at reduced dosages in patients with liver or kidney problems. It must also be used with caution in patients with acute renal failure, hypertension, or when the patient's heart is not functioning properly, because the drug increases fluid retention, swelling, and the level of sodium in the body.

Oral ketorolac tromethamine also may prolong bleeding time, but this effect disappears within 24 to 48 hours after the drug is discontinued. Patients who have problems with blood clotting or who take anticoagulants should be carefully monitored. This drug should not be used with aspirin products, because the combination causes the levels of ketorolac tromethamine to increase, or with other nonsteroidal anti-inflammatory drugs because of the potential for additive side effects.

▶ Depression Treatment Horizons Widened

Sertraline HCl (Zoloft) is a new drug approved for the treatment of major depression, a common mental illness characterized by feelings of sadness and despair and symptoms such as sleep and appetite changes, lack of interest and pleasure in activities that were previously enjoyed, decreased energy and concentration, and, sometimes, thoughts of suicide.

Sertraline is chemically unrelated to other antidepressants. It has been shown in studies to be as effective as the tricyclic antidepressants, amitriptyline and imipramine. The main advantage of sertraline over the tricyclic antidepressants is that it does not have strong side effects, causing only minimal sleepiness, nervous-system reactions, or a drop in blood pressure. Nor does it affect cardiac conduction or cause weight gain. Sertraline is given once daily, reaching steady-state plasma levels after approximately one week. The drug is removed from the system by both the liver and the kidneys, and should be used with care in patients with either renal or hepatic disease.

Controlled studies have shown that sertraline is effective for up to six to eight weeks, but its effectiveness for long-term use has not yet been determined. The most frequent adverse effects seen with sertraline are headache, tremor, nausea, diarrhea, insomnia, agitation, and nervousness. Side effects such as akathisia, dyskinesia, and suicidal tendencies, which have been seen with fluoxetine (Prozac), have not been reported with sertraline.

▶ Management of Chronic Cancer Pain

Fentanyl, a synthetic opiate, has been used since the early 1960s as an analgesic and to begin and maintain anesthesia. Its brief duration of action when administered intravenously makes it impractical for treating pain, especially in patients requiring sustained pain relief. A new controlled-release skin patch of fentanyl, called Duragesic, is now available for the treatment of moderate to severe chronic pain.

This transdermal delivery system secretes fentanyl through the skin at a constant rate for 72 hours. This method of drug delivery is especially

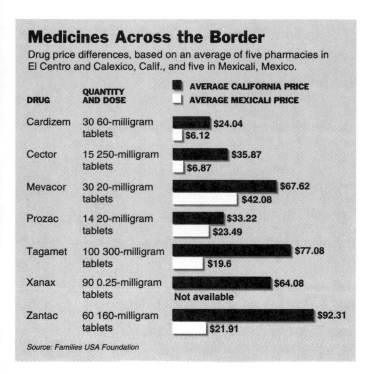

Medicines Across the Border

Drug price differences, based on an average of five pharmacies in El Centro and Calexico, Calif., and five in Mexicali, Mexico.

DRUG	QUANTITY AND DOSE	AVERAGE CALIFORNIA PRICE	AVERAGE MEXICALI PRICE
Cardizem	30 60-milligram tablets	$24.04	$6.12
Cector	15 250-milligram tablets	$35.87	$6.87
Mevacor	30 20-milligram tablets	$67.62	$42.08
Prozac	14 20-milligram tablets	$33.22	$23.49
Tagamet	100 300-milligram tablets	$77.08	$19.6
Xanax	90 0.25-milligram tablets	$64.08	Not available
Zantac	60 160-milligram tablets	$92.31	$21.91

Source: Families USA Foundation

useful in patients who are not hooked up to an intravenous system, and those unable to swallow tablets. The pain control offered by transdermal fentanyl has been likened to that of a continuous intravenous infusion. When the patch is removed, the concentration of fentanyl in the bloodstream declines slowly, allowing the physician to slowly introduce other pain-management options. Physicians are heralding the transdermal system as ideal for chronic cancer pain. Adverse effects reported with the patch are comparable to other methods of opioid delivery.

▶ Stroke Prevention
Approximately two thirds of all strokes in the United States are caused by blood-clotting problems. As many as 500,000 people a year in this country suffer from strokes, and it is the third leading cause of death. Until recently, aspirin was the only agent approved for stroke prevention, with approval only to reduce the risk of initial stroke. Therapeutic options for patients with a high risk for stroke have just expanded with the introduction of ticlopidane (Ticlid), used for both stroke prophylaxis and prevention of new stroke in those patients who have already experienced one. Ticlopidane is an antiplatelet drug used to reduce the risk of thrombotic stroke in high-risk patients and in those who have already experienced a thrombotic stroke. This drug is ideal for those patients who are intolerant of aspirin. The biggest drawback with using ticlopidane is that it can adversely affect the immune

system and cause a drop in the white blood cells, particularly during the first three months of treatment with this drug. During this time, patients should have blood tests every two weeks.

▶ Reversing Benzodiazepine Overdose
Flumazenil (Mazicon) is the first agent available to reverse the sedative effects of benzodiazepines following anesthesia, sedation in either surgical or some diagnostic procedures, or after a confirmed overdose. The most-severe reactions to benzodiazepines are convulsions and death. Convulsions have occurred in patients who are relying upon benzodiazepines to control seizures, who are physically dependent on benzodiazepines, or who have ingested large quantities of other drugs. Death has occurred in a variety of clinical settings, usually in patients with serious underlying disease or in patients who have ingested large amounts of tricyclic antidepressants as part of an overdose.

Flumazenil offers the advantage of reversal of the central-nervous-system effects of benzodiazepines used for anesthesia and diagnostic procedures, particularly residual sedation. Frequent dosing may be required for reversal of effects from long-acting benzodiazepines. Flumazenil is also useful for suspected benzodiazepine overdose. The drug may speed recovery, reduce after-effects, and shorten the hospital stay. Patients should also be warned not to take any alcohol or nonprescription drugs for 18 to 24 hours after being given flumazenil.

▶ Another Form of Birth Control for Women
The FDA finally approved medroxyprogesterone acetate (Depo-Provera), the injectable contraceptive for women that provides protection from pregnancy for three months. This new contraceptive provides women with a welcome alternative that eliminates the risks associated with improper insertion of such manual contraceptive methods as the diaphragm or sponge, or forgetting to take an oral contraceptive daily.

Depo-Provera consists of tiny crystals containing the hormone progesterone, which is secreted in a time-released manner. A doctor injects the contraceptive in the muscle of the back of the arm or in the buttocks.

Depo-Provera has been available around the world since 1969, but has had trouble getting approval in the United States because of concerns over possible increased risk of getting breast cancer for the women using this method of birth control. The most common side effects are weight gain and menstrual irregularity. Other possible effects include fatigue, weakness, dizziness, nervousness, headaches, and abdominal pain.

Cheryl A. Stoukides, Pharm.D.

Mental Health

▶ Obsessive-Compulsive Disorder

Obsessive-compulsive disorder (OCD) is characterized by persistent, unwanted thoughts or impulses (obsessions) and ritualized behaviors (compulsions) developed in the course of attempts to deal with anxiety related to the obsessions. While, in the past, OCD was thought to be caused by psychological conflict, recent research focusing on neuroscience and studies of the response of OCD patients to drug therapy have pointed to significant biological factors in the development of the disorder. Furthermore, the familial pattern seen with many cases of OCD suggests that the disorder may be of genetic origin. Efforts to gain a better understanding of OCD and to improve treatment have included attempts to identify areas of the brain that might be affected by pathological processes, and to determine if function in affected areas is altered by treatment. Animal models of OCD also are being explored, as some of the compulsive rituals seen in OCD may have an evolutionary link to animal behavior patterns.

A study recently published in the *Archives of General Psychiatry* has identified the caudate nucleus, a nerve center in the basal ganglia of the brain, as a specific area involved in the mediation of symptoms of OCD. Using a neuroimaging technique known as positron emission tomography (PET), which has been used in studying other psychiatric disorders, the researchers investigated changes in glucose metabolism following treatment of known OCD sufferers. The findings indicated that patients who improved showed a reduction of excess activity in the right head of the caudate nucleus along with the reduction of their symptoms. Patients who did not

improve did not show the reduction in metabolic activity in the caudate nucleus. The study did not prove that abnormal function of the caudate nucleus causes OCD, as the caudate is part of a feedback loop involving other areas of the brain that may be involved in OCD. These other areas include the frontal cortex, the thalamus, and the limbic system. The study also showed that behavior therapy as well as drug therapy produced the metabolic changes associated with improvement of OCD symptoms. This is one of the first scientifically based demonstrations that psychotherapy can alter basic brain function in the same way that psychiatric medication can.

Results of this research need to be replicated before they can be considered wholly conclusive. They also do not indicate that one type of treatment for OCD is better than another. Severe cases of OCD may require both behavioral and drug therapy, while milder cases may respond to behavioral therapy alone. As far as is known, behavioral therapy is more effective for compulsive behaviors and less effective for obsessional thinking, so that drug therapy may be the initial treatment when obsessions and anxiety are severe.

Another study published this year in the *Archives of General Psychiatry* assessed a possible animal model for OCD. This research, performed by Dr. Judith Rapoport and colleagues at the National Institute of Mental Health (NIMH) and the National Institutes of Health (NIH) Animal Center, involved drug treatment of certain varieties of dogs who develop an unusual behavior known as canine acral lick dermatitis (ALD). ALD is characterized by excessive licking of the paws or flank that can lead to ulcers and infection requiring medical treatment. While commonly considered a psychogenic condition brought on by loneliness or confinement, the etiology of ALD actually is unknown. The fact that ALD occurs primarily in a relatively few large

The Onset of Depression in Different Cultures

An international study of major depression has revealed a steady rise in the disorder worldwide. The likelihood that people born after 1955 will suffer an incident of debilitating major depression at some point in life is more than three times greater than for their grandparents' generation.

Potential explanations for this increase include the stresses of industrialization, inherited susceptibility, or a greater willingness of people to discuss mental illness. The data below were obtained from interviews of people divided into groups born in the same decade.

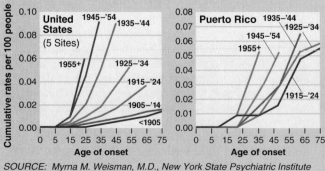

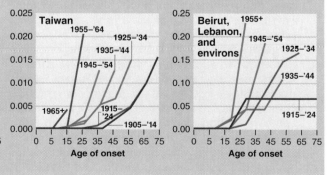

SOURCE: Myrna M. Weisman, M.D., New York State Psychiatric Institute

breeds of dogs, coupled with a tendency for it to be more frequent in individual families of these breeds, has suggested a genetic component to the disorder. Noting the similarity of ALD and OCD in that the disorders both involve repetitive, unwanted behaviors, Rapoport and colleagues decided to see if there was a drug-treatment response in ALD similar to that seen in human OCD. The drugs used in the study included three serotonin-reuptake-blocking medications, which have proven effective in human OCD. These were matched against two other drugs that do not block serotonin reuptake, and also a placebo. The results showed that only the three serotonin-reuptake-blocking drugs, clomipramine, fluoxetine, and sertraline, brought improvement of ALD. This is just what has been found in the treatment of human OCD. In addition, it was found that the doses required were similar for both dogs and humans, and that the relative efficacy of each drug was the same in dogs and humans. The specificity of drug responses in the study gives support to the theory that abnormal serotonin activity plays a role in the development of OCD.

Dr. Rapoport concluded that ALD may serve as a useful animal model of OCD, and can be used in further research of benefit to both animals and humans. The similarity of behavior and of pharmacological response between ALD and OCD, along with the likely genetic influences in both conditions, support this thinking. It is of note that Dr. Rapoport has long been interested in the similarities between certain aspects of animal and human behaviors. She identifies abnormal human behaviors such as compulsive hand washing as similar to certain grooming behaviors that are more normal in animal species. The compulsive symptoms of OCD thus may represent the uncovering of behaviors that are vestiges of our evolutionary heritage that no longer serve an adaptive purpose. As can be seen from the example of ALD, animals, too, can develop excessive, unwanted behaviors without an obvious cause. It remains to be seen if there is a common, specific factor that can explain this type of disorder in both humans and animals.

▶ Psychological Impact of the 1992 Los Angeles Riots

The Los Angeles riots earlier this year were a frightening manifestation of how deep unrest and turmoil threaten the social structure of America's cities. Along with the tragic loss of lives and property, the citizens of Los Angeles experienced psychological trauma that may have long-term consequences. No one was affected more severely than the residents of the areas devastated by the rioting. Also strongly affected were many of the police, fire fighters, paramedics, and others who were sent to gain control over the situation and to

Many public servants who tried to control the violence during the 1992 Los Angeles riots are still suffering from stress brought on by the event.

help the victims. Mental-health teams now have reported on the emotional reactions and symptoms shown by children and adults who experienced the riots firsthand.

Inner-city children appear to have been particularly vulnerable to the psychological effects of the riots, perhaps primed by the fact that they have lived under adverse social conditions and already have experienced family and neighborhood violence. During the riots, some children saw their parents or other caretakers wounded, or, in other instances, saw them arrested for looting or other crimes. Most children who became symptomatic suffered from general anxiety and fearfulness, while others developed the more striking picture of post-traumatic stress disorder. Preschool-age children showed common stress reactions such as nightmares and bed-wetting. Older children had more focused fears of being caught in fires or of being personally assaulted. They also feared loss of loved ones, and they had a heightened sense of insecurity after experiencing temporary loss of electricity, lack of food, and loss of safety on the street. Feelings of insecurity lasted for weeks after the riots, with the extensive physical damage to neighborhoods serving as a daily reminder of what had happened. Mental-health professionals estimated that one-quarter to one-third of the children living in the area of the riots would show stress reactions in the two months following the events. A small percentage were expected to show long-term problems.

Children and adolescents also showed confusion as to how to react to the riots because of mixed messages they received from adults. Youngsters showed appropriate anger toward the rioters who were destroying their communities, but, at the same time, some were noted to get a sense of pleasure from seeing the looting that took place. Some were told that the looting was wrong, but they then found that their parents or neighbors had participated in it or had accepted stolen goods. Some children were told by parents that the riots were an appropriate response to social injustice, whereas teachers later tried to give the message that there was no justification for what had happened. In essence, young people were faced with the difficult task of sorting out their immediate, personal experiences and reactions from the broader social and political significance of the riots. As a result, children fell into the trap of placing racial blame when trying to determine the causes of the riots. Unable to see or to acknowledge the extensive social problems leading up to the situation, children were prone to blaming members of other ethnic groups for what had happened. This attitude was shaped by adult behavior and the extreme heightening of racial tensions (such as between blacks and Koreans, whose businesses were a prime target of the rioters). Children needed to be reminded that, for the most part, they got along well with peers from other ethnic groups at school, and that they did not have to mirror the prejudiced attitudes of adults.

People involved directly in stopping the riots and dealing with their aftermath also suffered from psychological stress and confusion. Police, fire fighters, and rescue workers became targets in the line of duty, and they experienced a great sense of frustration and loss of self-esteem in seeing the communities they felt they served turn against them. The police in particular, given their association with the incident of brutality that ultimately had led up to the riots, had to endure much of the community's anger while trying to contain their own angry responses and dealing with feelings of losing control over areas where they normally represented authority. Mental-health professionals and counselors were assigned to debrief fire fighters, paramedics, and police officers in order to help them recognize signs of stress and to cope with feelings of impotence and ineffectuality. They also had to deal with latent racism, which was triggered by the perception of ethnic sides in the rioting. Some of the law-enforcement and rescue workers were able to identify with the anger of the minority groups in the community, and to express their feelings about the political and social systems that, in their view, perpetuated many of the problems.

For the adult population of the minority groups who made up both the rioters and most of the victims, the events in Los Angeles were associated with years of feeling helpless and hopeless. These people were also enraged by having to live an unchanging life of poverty and social disadvantage. We have now seen how, under the right conditions, this despair can lead to senseless violence. One way of breaking the cycle of poverty and its social consequences may be to address the needs of children. Some psychologists strongly advocate teaching children how to avoid being victimized at home and in the community, and how to learn self-control of feelings and impulses.

Passive as well as direct exposure to violence predisposes children to a variety of psychological and behavioral outcomes. These include decreased self-esteem, a heightened sense of vulnerability, negative expectations for the future, conflict with family and peers, and increased use of aggression as a way of solving problems. Many of the adults and older adolescents who participated in the Los Angeles riots may have been operating on psychodynamics developed in childhood. If similar catastrophes are to be avoided in the future, it may be best to invest now in meeting the psychological needs of children at risk from their environment.

▶ Schizophrenia

Schizophrenia, the single most debilitating psychiatric disorder, is marked by hallucinations and mental delusions, usually accompanied by bizarre behavior and disordered, undirected thinking. For decades, researchers have been trying to discover the underlying pathology of schizophrenia, pursuing genetic, anatomical, and biochemical studies. The relatively recent advent of highly sophisticated neuroimaging techniques, such as magnetic resonance imaging (MRI) and positron emission tomography (PET), has permitted significant advances in research on schizophrenia.

A number of recent scientific studies have produced increasing evidence that abnormalities of the temporal lobe frequently are associated with schizophrenia, and that they may have much to do with the clinical features of the disorder. Important functions of the brain's temporal lobe, specifically the left temporal lobe in most individuals, include language and thought processes, associative memory, learning processes, and regulation of emotions, all of which may be abnormal or deficient in schizophrenia. Autopsies of schizophrenic individuals have shown a reduction in volume of the medial limbic portions of the temporal lobe, as well as abnormalities in the pattern of temporal lobe gyri (the convoluted surface portions of the brain's cerebral cortex, which is responsible for higher-level functions of the nervous system). Modern technology has made it possible to look at abnormally developed or diseased areas of the brain in living persons,

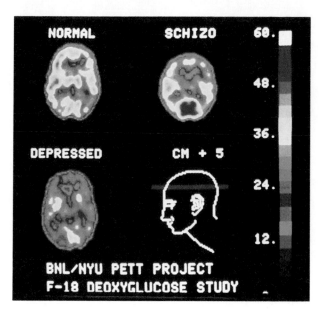

Neuroimaging techniques, such as the PET scan above, can illuminate diseased areas of the brain in living persons, improving our understanding of the pathology of schizophrenia and other diseases.

making the correlations of basic research with clinical research much more relevant.

An August 1992 issue of the *New England Journal of Medicine* included an article by researchers at Harvard Medical School who used MRI techniques to explore the relationship between abnormalities of the left temporal lobe and thought disorder in chronic schizophrenic patients. The investigators developed a way to measure the volume of different structures in the temporal lobe and other parts of the brain. They used these new measurements to make three dimensional image reconstructions of the areas they were studying. Findings were compared within the group of affected patients, as well as against findings in a normal control group. The results showed that, in comparison to the control group, the patients had significant reductions in the volume of gray matter (the nerve-cell layers) in several parts of the left temporal lobe. None of these regional decreases in volume was accompanied by decreases in volume of the temporal lobe as a whole, or in volume of the entire brain. Where there were reductions in volume of the temporal lobe, however, there was an increase in the size of the temporal horn of the lateral ventricle, one of the fluid-filled spaces that underlie the cortex of the brain.

The most significant specific finding from this study was that the severity of thought disorder in the schizophrenic patients correlated with the decrease in volume in the area of the brain called the left posterior superior temporal gyrus. The smaller the volume of this particular area, the greater the degree of thought disorder present in the patient. The left posterior superior temporal gyrus long has been thought of as an important neuroanatomical zone for language production, and it is also involved in auditory associative-memory processes. Abnormalities or deficiencies in this area of the brain may contribute to the clinical picture of disordered thinking and loosening of associations seen in schizophrenia. The Harvard researchers noted, however, that it was not known if there could be similar abnormalities in temporal lobe structure in other psychotic disorders, such as manic-depressive disorders, or in schizophrenia of recent onset.

Interestingly, researchers at Hillside Medical Center in New York City reported important related findings in their own studies of the temporal lobe in schizophrenia around the same time of the Harvard study. The Hillside researchers found decreases in the volume of the hippocampus-amygdala portion of the temporal lobe of schizophrenic subjects, which also had been a finding of the Harvard research. Also noted in the Hillside studies was the finding of increased volume of the temporal horn of the lateral ventricle. Enlargement of the temporal horn was found to correlate closely with positive symptoms—features such as thought disorder and hallucinations—in patients having their first episode of schizophrenia as well as in chronic patients. This demonstrated that decreases in volume of portions of the temporal lobe and associated increases in the volume of portions of the nearby ventricle can be found early in the course of schizophrenia, and are not just manifestations of the chronic form of the disease.

This type of research, aided by increasingly refined neuroimaging techniques, is contributing to major advances in the understanding of the neuropathology of schizophrenia. Over the years, there have been many reports of abnormal ventricle size in various neuropsychiatric disorders, including schizophrenia. These reports always were relatively nonspecific, and they did not lead to understanding of the relations between abnormal brain structures and the clinical symptoms seen in patients. With techniques that enable pinpointing of specific areas of the brain that are involved in schizophrenia and other major psychiatric disorders, we can expect to make more rapid progress in understanding the etiology and course of these disorders and in refining treatment techniques.

More information about the role of the temporal lobe in schizophrenia can be expected. As there also have been preliminary reports of temporal lobe abnormalities in patients with manic-depressive disorder, it will be interesting to compare the findings with schizophrenia, since acute episodes of the two disorders can be hard to differentiate.

Stephen G. Underwood, M.D.

Two American biochemists received the 1992 Nobel Prize in Physiology or Medicine for their insights into a fundamental process that regulates the functions of cells. The Nobel committee honored Edwin G. Krebs, M.D. and Edmond H. Fischer, Ph.D., colleagues for nearly 40 years at the University of Washington School of Medicine in Seattle, for their discoveries concerning reversible protein phosphorylation. This process is an essential mechanism that controls the interactions of proteins within a cell.

Drs. Krebs and Fischer performed some of their key experiments in the 1950s, and the far-reaching importance of their work was not evident for many years—even to the two scientists. As Dr. Fischer told a reporter on the day his Nobel Prize was announced, "We had no idea that it would be an important and prevalent mechanism of control." However, even if they did not know it at the time, Drs. Fischer and Krebs had initiated what is now one of the most active and growing fields in science. The cellular activities regulated by reversible protein phosphorylation concern "almost all processes important to life," according to the announcement of the Nobel committee from the Karolinska Institute in Stockholm. The mechanism is essential, for example, to break down glycogen in the body into glucose, in the response of the immune system to infection, as well as in the formation of certain kinds of cancer. By working to develop drugs designed to influence this mechanism, researchers are making progress toward better treatments for a wide range of diseases.

▶ Proteins: The "Living Tools" of the Organism

The human body contains several trillion cells. Each cell contains about 10,000 different types of proteins, which are constructed of links of amino-acid residues shaped into three-dimensional structures. Proteins carry out most cellular functions, such as maintaining the cell's metabolism, dictating growth, releasing hormones, and mediating the work of muscles. In fact, it was through their experiments on muscle tissue that Drs. Krebs and Fischer made their important discoveries. In the late 1940s, Dr. Krebs joined the laboratory of Carl and Gerty Cori, a husband-and-wife team of researchers at the Washington University School of Medicine in St. Louis, Missouri. The Coris had won the Nobel Prize in Physiology or Medicine in 1947 for their discovery of an enzyme known as phosphorylase. Enzymes are catalysts—proteins whose role is to make biological reactions possible. The enzyme phosphorylase plays a crucial role in breaking down glycogen—the body's principal energy-storage compound—into glucose, which is the sugar that muscle cells use for energy when they contract. The Coris knew that phosphorylase existed in both active and inactive forms, but they were not sure how these two forms differed. The Coris decided to drop the problem into Dr. Krebs's lap and turn their own research in a different direction.

Dr. Fischer, meanwhile, had been performing research in Switzerland, studying a plant version of phosphorylase. In 1953 Fischer and Krebs joined forces at the University of Washington in Seattle to try to elucidate the different forms of phosphorylase and the factors controlling their activity. The two researchers soon determined the biochemical mechanism underlying the conversion of phosphorylase from an inactive to an active form. The change, they observed, is brought about by the addition of a phosphate group, which is transferred to the protein from an energy-rich compound known as adenosine triphosphate, or ATP. This phosphate transfer, or phosphorylation, alters the biochemical properties, as well as the function, of a protein.

Drs. Fischer and Krebs also discovered that the transfer could go in both directions. Removal of the phosphate group returns the protein to its inactive state. Thus, the two-way process—reversible protein phosphorylation—constitutes a kind of "on-off" switch that starts and stops cellular functions. In the case of muscle tissue, the phosphate transfer activates the protein and causes the muscle to contract.

The next step was to identify the enzymes responsible for carrying out this phosphate transfer. Fischer and Krebs subsequently isolated and characterized the first such enzyme, known as a protein kinase. The two researchers also identified the enzymes that remove the phosphate group and thereby inactivate proteins. These enzymes are called phosphatases.

Dr. Fischer explained, "It's a very widespread mechanism. This is how hormones work, it's how a cell grows, how a cell differentiates, how a cell dies, and how cancer proceeds."

▶ Applications

Subsequent to the key work by the two Nobel laureates in the 1950s and '60s, hundreds of other protein kinases have been identified. In its announcement of the 1992 prize, the Nobel committee estimated that in the human genome (that is, the entire complement of human genes, containing all the DNA instructions for a complete organism), 1 percent of the genes encode protein kinases.

Dr. Edwin G. Krebs (left) and Dr. Edmond H. Fischer shared the 1992 Nobel Prize for their discovery of a key cellular mechanism that affects virtually all cells in the human body.

"These kinases," states the committee, "regulate the function of a large proportion of the thousands of proteins in a cell. In addition, the system includes a large number of phosphatases, which in an opposite manner regulate the removal of the protein phosphate groups from proteins."

The two-way mechanism of reversible protein phosphorylation has a wide range of effects on the cell. For example, the protein kinase that was first identified by Krebs and Fischer turned out to be essential in the cellular response to various hormones, such as epinephrine. This hormone releases glucose to provide energy for an animal's "fight-or-flight" reaction in times of stress. In addition to muscle contraction and hormone response, phosphorylation also influences such important cellular functions as protein synthesis, gene regulation, and neurotransmitter release. These effects are manifest in blood pressure, in inflammatory reactions, and in the transfer of signals in the brain—to name just a small selection.

► Insights into Immunology and Cancer

The response of the human immune system is another process in which the work of Drs. Fischer and Krebs has provided key insights. When an organism invades the body, part of the immune system's response is to invoke a chain reaction involving a cascade of phosphorylating and dephosphorylating enzymes. As a result, the body marshals the proper cellular defenses to neutralize the invader.

When the body is fighting a viral or bacterial intruder, this response is entirely appropriate and desirable. However, a newly transplanted organ will also rally the body's immune response, causing rejection of the transplanted tissue. In such cases, doctors use drugs to suppress this immune response, giving the new tissue time to be accepted.

One such immunosuppressant drug that has been used with great success in transplants is cyclosporine. It works by interfering with the phosphorylation reaction in the body's immune response.

Cellular growth is another function in which protein phosphorylation is essential. Unfortunately, however, phosphorylation can also contribute to the abnormal growth of cells—the process known as cancer. The nuclear DNA within the cell contains approximately 100 oncogenes. These are genes that normally control cell growth, but, when altered or mutated, actually promote the growth of tumors. Roughly half of these cancer-causing oncogenes are now known to encode protein kinases. Some forms of cancer, such as chronic myelocytic leukemia, are apparently initiated by an abnormality in the regulation of protein-kinase activity. By understanding more about the role of protein kinases and phosphatases in cell growth, researchers hope to find new ways to inhibit the enzymes that give rise to cancer. This is another example of the promising medical advances being built on the original discoveries of Drs. Fischer and Krebs.

Dr. Edwin G. Krebs was born on June 6, 1918, in Lansing, Iowa, and earned his medical degree from the Washington University School of Medicine in St. Louis, Missouri. After completing his residency in internal medicine at Barnes Hospital, St. Louis, Dr. Krebs decided on a career in science, returning to Washington University as a research fellow in biological chemistry. He joined the University of Washington faculty in Seattle in 1948.

Dr. Edmond H. Fischer was born on April 6, 1920, in Shanghai, China. He earned his doctoral degree in chemistry from the University of Geneva, Switzerland, and joined the faculty of the University of Washington in 1953.

Christopher King

Nutrition and Diet

▶ Genetically Engineered Foods

On May 26, 1992, the Department of Health and Human Services (HHS) and the Food and Drug Administration (FDA) announced their policy for regulating new varieties of foods via advanced genetic-engineering techniques. The new biotechnology involves gene splicing, in which the genetic makeup of a plant is modified through the precise transfer of genes from another organism. This process, according to the biotechnology industry and the FDA, produces a greater variety of foods that have longer shelf lives, are more flavorful, and are more nutritious. According to the regulations that were expedited under the guidance of the Biotechnology Working Group of the President's Council on Competitiveness, most new "biotech" foods will not need premarket approval by the FDA, nor will labeling be required.

According to FDA Commissioner William Kessler, crossbreeding techniques and genetic manipulation have been used by agricultural scientists for years to produce new hybrid foods, such as tangelos, or higher yields of staple crops, such as corn. The biotechnology industry and the FDA view gene splicing as an advanced form of crossbreeding, and conclude that since hybridized produce has never required premarket testing or labeling, neither should genetically engineered foods require special regulations. Genes from any organism—animal, plant, or human—will not be considered an additive, and as long as the components of the new food are generally recognized as safe, the food itself will be considered safe, thus not requiring premarket scrutiny by the FDA.

The FDA's policy does include a "guidance to industry" section that will aid biotech corporations in assessing the safety of new foods. A company will be required to consult with the FDA if the genetic engineering of a food produces new allergens, natural toxins, any new substance not usually present in the food, or an alteration in important nutrients. Once consulted, the FDA may opt to do its own safety testing of the food prior to approval, or at the very least, the company will be mandated to label their product to reveal the presence of the allergen, toxin, or change in nutrient level.

The FDA's policy on regulating genetically engineered foods has been met unfavorably by many consumer and environmental groups, including the Environmental Defense Fund and the National Wildlife Federation. Scientists from both institutions contend that gene splicing is not a minor extension of crossbreeding, and that the human or animal genes transferred into plants should be considered a new substance and treated as a new food additive that would require safety testing by the FDA. Critics also contend that consumers should have a choice in deciding whether they want to eat biotech foods or natural foods, an option that would be impossible if labeling is not required.

Since genetically engineered food is new, critics have expressed concerns about unknown risks. The question of whether mutations may occur in a food from recombining genes, and the long-term health risks from consumption of such a food, need to be examined. Experts are also concerned about allergenicity. The FDA's policy does not take into consideration the person who may be allergic to a food that is not considered a common allergen. For example, while bananas are not thought of as a potential allergen, consumers who are allergic to them could unknowingly eat a food that has been implanted with a banana gene. The FDA's policy asserts that proteins taken from commonly allergenic foods are assumed to be allergens, and that foods containing genes from these potential allergens must be labeled. While the FDA claims allergenicity is an important issue, its present policy does not adequately address this problem, and could cause serious health risks for certain individuals.

A variety of other issues are not addressed by the FDA regulations. For example, there are worries that a food with an abnormally long shelf life would lose nutrients. The policy of not labeling biotech foods creates a predicament for vegetarians, Orthodox Jews, Moslems, and Buddhists who need to avoid produce that contains animal genes.

Several genetically engineered foods will reach the markets by 1993. The most talked about is the "FlavrSavr" tomato produced by Calgene, Inc., in Davis, California. This tomato has a 20-day shelf life because the enzymatic reaction that makes tomatoes soften during the ripening process has been suppressed. While tomatoes are usually picked when green to avoid bruising during shipping, the "FlavrSavr" tomato will be harvested when fully mature since it will not soften en route to markets. Of concern is that the "FlavrSavr" tomato contains a bacterial marker gene used to determine a successful gene splicing that confers an immunity to antibiotics. The FDA is evaluating the safety of antibiotic-resistance marker genes in food to determine if consumers could build up a resistance to antibiotics from such foods. Other biotech foods that have been tested by the industry include corn with a firefly gene, potatoes with a chicken gene, and tomatoes with a flounder gene.

The FDA will have to contend with active opposition to its policy on genetically engineered foods. The Foundation on Economic Trends has started the Pure Food Campaign, an alliance of consumers,

The genetically engineered "FlavrSavr" tomato can be harvested when fully ripe with no fear of it softening or spoiling during shipping.

farmers, environmentalists, and chefs who have petitioned the FDA for tighter regulations. The campaign wants the agency to require labeling and to conduct its own unbiased safety testing of all new biotech foods rather than allowing the industry to be on the honor system.

▶ Food Irradiation

Irradiation is the process of preserving foods by exposing them to gamma rays. A conveyor belt carries the food to a sealed room where the food is bombarded with low doses of gamma rays (cobalt 60 or cesium 137) for up to 45 minutes, depending on the density and water content of the product. Irradiation can kill harmful bacteria such as salmonella, a major problem in poultry; increase the shelf life of vegetables and fruits; and eliminate infestation of spices and produce.

The FDA first approved the irradiation of wheat flour and potatoes in the 1960s. Pork, fresh fruits and vegetables, and dried herbs and spices were approved for irradiation in 1986. And in September 1992, the U.S. Department of Agriculture (USDA) published proposed regulations for irradiated poultry.

While the FDA, the Institute of Food Technologists, and the World Health Organization (WHO) all vouch for the safety of irradiated foods, many scientists and environmentalists believe there are still many unanswered questions. Probably the biggest concern is that irradiation produces compounds called "radiolytic products" when the chemical bonds in foods are broken by the gamma rays. Among these radiolytic products are benzene and formaldehyde, both known carcinogens, and formic acid, which causes mutations.

Irradiation proponents argue that traces of benzene and other radiolytic products occur naturally in foods or result from the processes of digestion. They also assert that the amounts of by-products formed during irradiation are insignificant (estimated at 30 parts per million), and therefore not harmful. Several consumer groups, including the Public Citizen Health Research Group and The National Coalition to Stop Food and Water Irradiation, requested that more toxicological research be conducted to examine this question.

Another valid concern is the change in nutrient levels that occurs when foods are irradiated. The nutrients most sensitive to irradiation are vitamins A, C, E, and K, with potential losses of 25 percent in a given irradiated food. One study revealed that the vitamin C level of potatoes was decreased by 50 percent after the standard dose of radiation. Losses of thiamine (a B vitamin) in chicken and pork were significant in another study on irradiation. Supporters of irradiation state that the nutrient losses from the process parallel the losses that result from cooking. Opponents note that foods such as chicken, pork, and vegetables would be cooked after irradiation, compounding the nutrient losses.

There is no doubt that irradiation reduces bacterial growth in food, and therefore could potentially reduce the 6.5 million cases of food-borne illness reported in this country each year. Salmonella currently contaminates 50 to 60 percent of the poultry in the United States. Critics of the poultry industry opine that major reforms in poultry-farming techniques could significantly reduce the salmonella problem. And, of course, irradiation is not the cure-all for food-borne illness, since it does not destroy 100 percent of bacteria.

Irradiated food must still be handled properly at home to avoid bacterial poisoning. In October 1992, the USDA approved an inexpensive chemical process in which chickens are dipped in a solution containing trisodium phosphate. This technique may prove to be a viable alternative to irradiation for sterilizing poultry.

Due to consumer resistance to irradiated foods, Perdue Farms and many other poultry companies have decided not to use the process. Major food companies, Kraft and Campbell Soup among them, have stated they will not use irradiated foods. New York and New Jersey have even placed a moratorium on the sale of irradiated foods, and Maine has banned them outright; several other states have legislation pending on this volatile issue.

Consumers can identify irradiated foods in the supermarket by the presence of a government-approved label (see previous page) required for all whole foods irradiated according to the present USDA regulations. Spices, processed foods with a variety of irradiated ingredients, and foods sold in schools and restaurants are not mandated to bear the label.

▶ "5 A Day For Better Health"

The National Cancer Institute (NCI) introduced its *5 A Day For Better Health Program* on July 1, 1992. The program's goals are to increase Americans' awareness that consumption of fruits and vegetables may lower their cancer risk, to encourage them to eat at least five servings of fruits and vegetables per day, and to suggest simple and practical ideas for incorporating these foods into their diet.

NCI's five-year program is unique because it is a joint venture with the Produce for Better Health Foundation (PBHF), a nonprofit, independent consumer-education institution financed by the fruit-and-vegetable industry. In 1991 a PBHF-funded baseline survey of 2,800 adults revealed that only 23 percent of those polled ate five or more servings of fruits and vegetables per day, and 42 percent ate two servings or less per day. Most Americans eat only three and one-half servings per day.

For many years, NCI has recommended a diet rich in fruits, vegetables, and fiber and low in fat. "5 A Day," its largest nutrition-education program to date, is a result of extensive research that revealed that a high intake of fruits and vegetables offers protection against cancer. According to Peter Greenwald, M.D., Ph.D., director of NCI's Division of Cancer Prevention and Control, the studies indicate that for many cancers, people who eat diets rich in fruits and vegetables have about half the risk of developing cancer compared to people who consume few of these foods. Three major scientific reviews support the conclusions that a higher intake of fruits and vegetables is associated with lowered risk for cancers of the lung, esophagus, larynx, oral cavity, stomach, colon, and rectum.

Fruits and vegetables are excellent sources of beta carotene, (the vitamin A precursor), vitamin C, and fiber, nutrients that have been shown to lower cancer risk. Beta carotene and vitamin C are antioxidants that neutralize free radicals, normal cellular by-products that alter healthy cells by damaging DNA. Two major studies have revealed that beta carotene also reduces the risk of stroke and heart attack. Vitamin C has been shown to reduce the risk of hardening of the arteries and of developing cataracts. Folate, a B vitamin found in dark-green leafy vegetables and in oranges, has a protective effect against cervical cancer. A recent study demonstrated that women with low blood folate lev-

els who were exposed to a virus that can cause cervical cancer were five times as likely to develop precancerous cervical cells as were women with normal folate levels.

Researchers have also been studying phytochemicals, non-nutritive substances in produce, to learn what role they play in the prevention of diseases. The answers that have already unfolded are fascinating. A chemical called sulforaphane found in broccoli, activates tumor-fighting enzymes in cells. Sulforaphane is also present in brussels sprouts, kale, cauliflower, red cabbage, and leeks. Celery contains 3-n-butyl phthalide, a substance shown to lower blood pressure in rats. Since scientists are only beginning to understand the role of phytochemicals in disease prevention, the best advice is to eat a variety of fruits and vegetables—five to nine servings daily.

▶ Iron and Heart Disease

A landmark Finnish study published in the September 1992 issue of *Circulation,* the journal of the American Heart Association, revealed that the presence of high levels of iron in the blood is a major risk factor for coronary heart disease, possibly second only to smoking.

The carefully controlled study by Jukka Salonen, M.D., Ph.D., and his team of epidemiologists at the University of Kuopio measured serum levels of ferritin, an iron-storing protein, in 1,900 healthy Finnish men between 42 and 60 years of age. During the five years these men were followed by the researchers, 51 experienced heart attacks. The scientists concluded that men with ferritin levels greater than 200 micrograms per liter were twice as likely to suffer heart attacks as men with ferritin levels less than 200. In men with both high levels of low-density lipoprotein (LDL, often called the "bad" cholesterol) and ferritin, heart-attack risk was quadrupled.

Researchers surmise that these findings shed light on why premenopausal women who lose iron monthly during menstruation have a lower incidence of heart disease. The results also provide an explanation for why there is a higher rate of heart disease in countries where there is a high consumption of red meat (a rich source of iron), and why vegetarians rarely suffer from heart disease.

Salonen's work and the research of others are unraveling the mystery behind how cholesterol promotes atherosclerosis (hardening of the arteries). One theory is that iron combines with oxygen, triggering oxidation of LDLs in the arteries. White blood cells, called macrophages, which scavenge for debris, envelop the oxidized LDLs and swell into "foam" cells. These foam cells collect along the arterial walls to create atherosclerotic plaque, which narrows the blood vessel and can lead to a heart attack. In addition, iron appears to catalyze the production of free radicals, unstable oxygenated molecules that damage DNA and disrupt chemical bonds. Free radicals have been associated with damage to heart muscle after a heart attack, as well as with the promotion of cancer, diabetes, and the aging process.

The results of the Finnish study do not warrant drastic dietary changes, since there are still unanswered questions about the role of genetics in determining a person's iron level and how dietary iron affects levels of iron in the blood. If further research reveals an unequivocal link between iron and heart disease, the FDA may need to rethink iron fortification of grain products and to set limits as to how much iron may be safely added to a given product. (Some cereal makers add the full 18-milligram recommended daily allowance of iron for women.) For now the most prudent dietary advice is to follow the federal government's recommendations to limit the intake of meat, poultry, and fish to six ounces per day, and to limit red meat to about three meals per week (long-standing advice from the American Heart Association). A low-fat diet in which grains, legumes, fruits, and vegetables are the main attraction and meat is the sideshow is still the safest bet.

▶ Rethinking Calcium Needs in Children

According to a study published in the *New England Journal of Medicine* in July 1992, calcium intakes that were higher than the recommended daily allowance (RDA) resulted in larger gains in bone density in a group of prepubescent children.

The study examined 45 healthy pairs of identical twins aged 6 to 14 for three years. The children consumed a normal diet, including the RDA for calcium (800 milligrams per day for children 1 to 10 years old; 1,200 milligrams per day for children 11

years and older). An average of 700 milligrams of supplemental calcium citrate malate was given to one child in each pair of twins. While all the children had ample increases in bone mass during the course of the study, the children who received the extra calcium had the greatest gains, with statistically significant increases in the forearm and spine. The response to the calcium supplement was the same in both sexes.

According to Conrad Johnston, M.D., of Indiana University, who headed the study, as long as this increase in bone mass can be maintained in adulthood, individuals with greater bone masses would be at lower risk for developing osteoporosis. Osteoporosis, a condition in which the bones lose mass and become weak, affects about 25 million Americans (80 percent are women), and causes more than 1 million bone fractures per year. Since peak bone mass has a strong influence on bone mass later in life, an increase in peak bone mass could help prevent osteoporosis. While genetic factors play a chief role in determining peak bone mass, nutrition and exercise are also influential. It is crucial for children to consume sufficient calcium because more than 90 percent of the skeleton develops by age 18. As bone loss usually begins about age 35, bones with a greater density should be better able to handle the depletion that occurs with normal aging and menopause.

The results of this study will probably affect the National Academy of Sciences' recommendations for calcium intake when they next revise the RDAs. While Dr. Johnston recommends that children receive five servings of calcium-rich foods a day (approximately 1,500 milligrams of calcium), other experts feel more research is required before advice to parents is changed. In the meantime, parents should encourage their children and teens to consume at least three and four servings per day,

Consuming high levels of calcium during childhood decreases the likelihood of osteoporosis later in life. Aside from dairy products, calcium occurs naturally in substantial quantities in a variety of common foods, among them broccoli and salmon.

respectively. Low-fat dairy products and calcium-fortified juices are the best sources of calcium; salmon, sardines, broccoli, kale, oranges, and legumes also provide substantial quantities.

▶ Partially Hydrogenated Oils Raise Cholesterol

Results of a USDA study released in July 1992 show that partially hydrogenated oils found in margarines, vegetable shortenings, and many baked goods raise cholesterol. Owing to concern about saturated-fat intake in the American diet, hydrogenated oils from soybean and corn oil have replaced butter, lard, and coconut and palm oils in commercially made baked goods.

Trans-fatty acids, formed when vegetable oils are converted to margarine or shortenings, are the cholesterol-raising culprits. In the study, not yet published, two groups of subjects who followed a diet containing *trans*-fatty acids (10 and 20 grams of *trans*-fatty acids per 3,000 calories, respectively) over a six-week period had statistically significantly higher cholesterol levels than those who followed a diet high in oleic acid but low in *trans*-fatty acid. A fourth group who followed a diet high in saturated fat and low in *trans*-fatty acids, had cholesterol levels that were higher than the groups that followed diets containing moderate and high levels of *trans*-fatty acids. Moreover, the subjects whose diets included the higher level of *trans*-fatty acids had lower HDL (the "good" cholesterol) levels than the groups whose diets were rich in oleic acid or saturated fats.

The USDA study corroborates the findings of a Dutch investigation published in the *New England Journal of Medicine* in 1990, which first revealed that *trans*-fatty acids raise LDL levels while lowering HDL levels. The government maintains that Americans eat only 8 to 10 grams of *trans*-fatty acids a day. Not so, according to Mary Enig, Ph.D., who studied *trans* isomers for many years as a research associate in biochemistry at the University of Maryland. She believes the average person consumes 11 to 28 grams per day, much of which comes from processed foods.

Health experts continue to recommend a diet with no more than 30 percent of the calories from fat, which will also limit intake of *trans*-fatty acids. The best choices for margarines are tub varieties with a liquid oil as the first ingredient, diet soft margarines, or liquid margarines. For cooking or baking, it is wise to use a liquid oil such as canola or olive oil rather than margarine, vegetable shortenings, or butter. Finally, Americans can reduce their *trans*-fatty intake considerably by eating fewer high-fat commercial baked goods and processed foods.

Maria Guglielmino, M.S., R.D.

Obstetrics and Gynecology

▶ Minimally Invasive Surgery

Due to advances in technology, an increasing number of surgical procedures are being performed via narrow tubes inserted into the body, rather than by traditional open-surgical incisions. Such "minimally invasive surgery" has been used by gynecologists for many years in the form of laparoscopy, a technique in which a viewing tube is inserted into the abdominal cavity. For the past two decades, however, laparoscopy has been confined mainly to the diagnosis of pelvic pain and tubal pregnancy and to the performance of tubal ligations.

More recently, general surgeons have embraced laparoscopy for gallbladder surgery and appendectomies. As general surgeons and gynecologists have collaborated on equipment and techniques, women have benefited from an increasing number of operations that can be performed on an outpatient basis or require only a short hospital stay. Laparoscopy can be used to remove scar tissue ("adhesions") in the abdomen caused by endometriosis, or to remove certain fibroid tumors. Laparoscopy can be used to facilitate removal of ovaries and ovarian cysts. With the aid of the laparoscope, a larger percentage of hysterectomies can be performed via the vaginal route, resulting in shorter hospital stays and less patient discomfort. So-called "laparoscopically assisted vaginal hysterectomies" facilitate removal of the ovaries, and can be used to assess the appropriateness of vaginal surgery when endometriosis or prior surgery might otherwise call for an abdominal incision.

A related technique, hysteroscopy, in which the inside of the uterus can be viewed with a lighted tube called a hysteroscope, can at times allow a hysterectomy to be avoided altogether. Compared with traditional techniques, hysteroscopy permits a more accurate diagnosis of abnormalities in the uterine lining, such as fibroids or polyps. Often polyps and intrauterine fibroids can be removed vaginally, avoiding a major procedure such as a hysterectomy for relatively minor problems. Women with unexplained heavy periods can be treated by a technique termed "endometrial ablation," in which the uterine lining or endometrium is essentially destroyed either by cautery (burning) or laser. Endometrial ablation results in absent or light periods in the majority of women; however, long-term safety data are not yet available, and later pregnancies are considered high risk due to concerns about scarring of the uterine lining.

While such advances are exciting, there is a great deal of controversy about the role of minimally invasive surgery. Critics point out that the costs of the equipment are high; in some studies, minimally invasive surgery has saved costs due to shorter hospital stays, but in other studies the increased equipment costs and surgical fees have actually made minimally invasive surgery more expensive than traditional open surgery. There are also potential complications, with injuries to the other abdominal structures and deaths from internal hemorrhage and fluid imbalance occurring in otherwise-healthy individuals undergoing fairly minor procedures. However, the safety profile of minimally invasive surgery is comparable to that of traditional surgery, and given the shorter hospital stays and reduced recovery time of minimally invasive surgery, there is a large patient demand for such procedures. Laparoscopically assisted hysterectomies, laparoscopic gallbladder surgery, hysteroscopic endometrial ablation, and removal of fibroids are all most likely here to stay.

▶ The Cost of Multiple Births

Experts are becoming increasingly concerned with the recent multiple birth explosion that has occurred due to such advances as fertility drugs and in vitro fertilization (IVF) techniques. The number of twins in the United States rose 33 percent from 1975 to 1988, and the number of triplets has jumped 101 percent over the same period. While a set of twins or triplets may delight a couple who has struggled with infertility, the problems that typically accompany multiple births, such as prematurity, low birth weight, and a score of other medical problems, may require the infants to spend days or even weeks in intensive care, and still emerge with disabilities. Health economists worry that the huge costs of caring for this recent increase in premature infants—not only during the infant stage, but throughout their lifetime as they require special education and other disability benefits—is astronomical. Pediatricians also believe that the already difficult task of caring for more than one infant becomes overwhelming when one or more of the babies is in poor health.

To stem the tide of the problems associated with multiple births, some doctors are recommending that infertility specialists should be less aggressive in treating their patients. In an interview with the *New York Times*, obstetrician Emile Papiernik, M.D., professor of gynecology at the Université René Descartes in Paris, France, recommended that infertility experts should use lower doses of fertility drugs. Dr. Papiernik suggested that during in vitro fertilization, in which the egg and sperm are fertilized in the laboratory and inserted into the uterus, only two or three fertilized embryos should be implanted in the uterus during each IVF attempt, rather than the four or five embryos typically used.

Unfortunately, the best form of advertising for fertility clinics is to promote their success rates. And at prices of $10,000 per try, couples want to choose the clinic that offers them the best chance of achieving pregnancy on the first attempt.

▶ Advances in Contraception

After decades of essentially no progress in contraception in the United States, several new alternatives are on the horizon. The progesterone implant, Norplant, was approved by the Food and Drug Administration (FDA) last year, and is now available on the U.S. market. These small "straws," implanted into a woman's arm by a doctor, are effective for five years. Side effects are mainly in the form of irregular periods for the first year of use, and mild changes in body chemistry that do not seem to be of significance. The price of Norplant is a problem for some women, since the implants cost several hundred dollars. But this cost, spread over several years, is comparable to other hormonal contraceptives, such as birth-control pills.

Injectable contraception. Depo-Provera, an injectable form of progesterone, was approved by the FDA in November 1992 for use as a contraceptive agent. Depo-Provera offers reliable contraception for three months per injection and is relatively inexpensive. Side effects of irregular bleeding and weight gain are common and will limit its use, but the injection offers a good method for women who are in need of short-term, reliable contraception and who cannot tolerate estrogens in the doses usually found in oral contraceptives.

Female condom. The Reality female condom received unanimous conditional approval from the

The female condom is made from polyurethane, making it thinner than the conventional latex condom and less likely to break or leak.

Some Birth Control Options for Women

The birth-control pill, taken once a day, has become the most popular form of birth control among American women. The pill is similar in composition to natural hormones; it works by preventing the ovaries from releasing eggs.

In 1991, the FDA approved the use of Norplant, a long-lasting contraceptive that is implanted under the skin on the inside of a woman's upper arm. The implant slowly releases a synthetic hormone that inhibits ovulation.

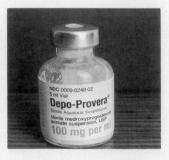

In November 1992, the FDA approved Depo-Provera for contraceptive use. An injection of Depo-Provera, a synthetic form of progesterone, prevents ovulation for three months.

FDA's Obstetrics and Gynecology Devices Advisory Panel on January 31, 1992, for use as a deterrent to the spread of such diseases as AIDS and hepatitis during sexual intercourse. The female condom, or vaginal pouch, is a disposable, silicone-lubricated polyurethane sac that is as long as a male condom (about 7 inches), but wider, with a flexible polyurethane ring at each end. The ring on the upper closed end of the condom is about 2 inches in diameter and is located inside the sac to serve as a guide. It is inserted in the vagina, much like a diaphragm, and pushed up to cover the cervix. At the other end of the pouch, the ring is about 2 3/4 inches in diameter and forms the outer, open end of the pouch. It remains outside the body, covering the woman's external genitals. Unlike a condom or diaphragm, the pouch can be inserted several hours before sexual intercourse. Because it is constructed of polyurethane, which is thinner than latex, its presence in the vagina is less noticeable to both the man and the woman than a conventional condom. In addition, it conducts heat well, which also provides a more natural feel, according to the condom's users. Final FDA marketing approval is expected in early 1993.

Oral-contraceptive use. Since the pill was first introduced in 1960, more than 60 million women worldwide have benefited from this safe and effective way to control childbearing. The guidelines for the use of oral contraceptives have gone through several revisions in the past few years. Previously, women who were over age 35 were not considered good candidates for the pill. But the FDA has extended approval of low-dose birth-control pills for nonsmokers in their forties. The Pill offers several advantages for this group of women. Birth-control pills often decrease menstrual flow and cramping, while offering some protection against ovarian cysts, endometriosis, and ovarian cancer. While quite a few women prefer not to use hormonal contraception, many women in their forties find the availability and relative safety of low-dose pills a welcome relief from both fear of unwanted pregnancy and certain gynecologic problems.

RU 486. The controversial drug RU 486, a pill best known abroad for its ability to induce abortion during the first trimester of pregnancy, also may be useful as a "morning-after" pill to prevent pregnancy immediately after unprotected sexual intercourse. Currently, either a widely available oral contraceptive or high doses of estrogens are used in the United States for this purpose. But a 1992 study by Anna Glasier and colleagues from the University of Edinburgh in Scotland, published in the *New England Journal of Medicine*, revealed that RU 486 was more effective with fewer side effects than the currently used methods. How RU 486 prevents pregnancy is still not completely understood. In some cases the drug may suppress ovulation, while at other times, RU 486 prevents the fertilized egg from implanting itself in the lining of the uterus, the first step of a pregnancy.

RU 486 is currently approved for use in France, the United Kingdom, Sweden, and China. But the drug still remains unavailable in the United States, where FDA approval faces bitter opposition from approval from antiabortion groups. Experts expect that it will be some time before U.S. women have access to RU 486 as an abortifacient or as a morning-after pill. RU 486 and similar agents antagonize the action of the hormone progesterone, and research in other areas of the world is being done on the potential uses of such agents in treating breast cancer, certain types of brain tumors, and other hormonally mediated processes. These alternate uses of the drug may be the only way in which RU 486 ultimately receives approval for sale in the United States.

▶ Lack of Access to Preventive Services

While women's health care has been advancing rapidly on the technological front, possibly the major women's health issue for 1993 is the lack of access to preventive health-care services. The bulk of health-care delivery in the United States is paid for via private or public insurance, and as the economy nose-dived in 1992, many individuals found themselves uninsured just as publicly funded programs faced budget cuts and tightened eligibility.

The lack of preventive services causes the most problems in the area of prenatal care. The incidence of premature and low birth weight infants is much higher among women with little or no prenatal care. Ironically, it is estimated that $1 spent on prenatal care will save $3 on costly intensive care for sick and premature newborns. Furthermore, some of the major causes of prematurity are largely preventable: cigarette smoking, cocaine and alcohol abuse, and lack of adequate nutrition could be cut dramatically by access to counseling and treatment for women of childbearing age. Twenty-one percent of such women use cocaine, according to the 1990 National Household survey, and 29 percent of women smoke cigarettes, according to the American College of Obstetrics and Gynecology. Infants born to these women have a higher risk of prematurity, lung problems, behavioral disorders, and learning disabilities, multiplying the costs of health care and educational services for many years to come. Technological advances will not truly impact women's health until they can be made affordable for the vast majority of American women.

▶ The Future

Imperatives at the National Institutes of Health (NIH) to include women subjects in medical research, and an explosion in interest in such disparate areas of women's health as heart disease in women, osteoporosis, depression, and gynecologic cancers are expected to spur major advances in women's health care in the next decade. The challenge on both a national and a global basis will be to see that advances on the research front lead to advances in the "trenches," i.e., the day-to-day care of all women. A tight global economy will make this difficult, and escalating costs of health care will make cost-effectiveness perhaps the major global health-care issue of the 1990s.

Linda Hughey Holt, M.D.

Occupational Health

▶ Toxic Chemicals

The National Institute for Occupational Safety and Health (NIOSH) estimates that some 100,000 workers in America are exposed to cadmium fumes or dust in such industries as electroplating and battery manufacturing, and in jobs connected with pigment, plastics, and metal-alloy production. Cadmium contamination in the environment is from fossil-fuel combustion, municipal-waste incineration, and the use of sewer sludge and phosphate fertilizers. Cadmium is included in a list of chemicals known to cause olfactory impairment. After inhalation or ingestion, cadmium is absorbed by the liver and kidneys and is excreted through the urine. Because of its biologically long half-life, there is concern about even low levels of exposure, said researchers in a study in the June 1992 *Journal of Occupational Medicine.*

The study found significant olfactory impairment in the group exposed to high concentrations of cadmium fumes. Moreover, a subpopulation with elevated levels of cadmium-induced renal damage had markedly worse olfactory impairment. The data suggested that cadmium exposure sufficient to cause kidney damage also increases the risk for olfactory impairment. The likelihood of exposure to hazardous workplace substances increases when smell, the body's "early warning system," no longer remains intact, said the researchers.

Swedish researchers cautioned in the January 1992 *American Journal of Industrial Medicine* that, in studying the neurotoxic effects of exposure to organic solvents, each solvent should be considered to have its own unique effects, instead of assuming, as is usually done, that organic solvents induce common neurotoxic responses.

Because of similar physical properties and the fact that, in industrial applications, organic solvents are often present in various mixtures, such solvents have generally been studied as a group. However, the Swedish study concludes that different solvents have very diverse effects and the toxic mechanisms may differ as to acute or chronic exposure. No specific method used to describe a neurotoxic effect or a single toxic response can be used for the overall occupational risk assessment of all organic solvents.

▶ Shift Work

Hard data began to appear in 1992 to bolster the conclusion that shift work can have adverse effects on the safety of workers and the public. It is estimated that some 20 percent of American workers have either evening, night, or rotating shifts. A hos-

Ferry pilots (above) and others who work rotating shifts have twice the odds of falling asleep on the job than do those who work regular hours.

pital-based survey of 635 Massachusetts nurses presented in the July 1992 *American Journal of Public Health* showed that, in comparison to nurses who worked only day or evening shifts, "rotators" had more sleep/wake cycle disruption and nodded off more at work. In addition, rotators had twice the odds of nodding off while driving to and from work, and twice the odds of a reported accident related to sleepiness.

As reported in the *American Journal of Industrial Medicine,* a survey of master, mates, and pilots employed by the State Ferries System in Seattle, Washington, backed up the nurse study. The Seattle survey indicated that certain shift workers had significantly more sick days, greater dissatisfaction with work schedules, poorer sleep patterns, more physician consultations for insomnia, and more fatigue-induced errors of judgment and near accidents than did those with less erratic hours.

The work shift of the study group changed three times in an eight-day period, with starting times as early as 5:00 A.M. and finish times as late as 2:00 A.M. About one-third of the group reported overall poor sleep patterns, another 33 percent reported near misses with other seacraft, and 23 percent said they made errors in judgment. Of those, around one-fifth said the cause of the error was fatigue. Approximately 43 percent reported falling asleep on watch, and 23 percent said they fell asleep at least once a month. Near misses in autos before or after work were reported by 42 percent of the group.

▶ Farm Workers
Farmers and farm workers remain among the groups most at risk to a wide range of occupation-related diseases. In a 1992 NIOSH study—the final

results of which are expected to be released in mid-1993—a variety of neurobehavioral tests was given to 100 California farm workers who had ostensibly recovered from previous poisoning by organophosphate pesticides. An equal number of unexposed farmers were given the same tests. Object: to find out if the exposed group showed signs of chronic neurologic problems from the poisoning.

In another NIOSH study approved in 1992, a three-year case-control study will be conducted to determine whether specific exposure to substances like pesticides, farm chemicals, and biological agents increases the risk for a certain brain cancer—primary malignant glioma—in farmers and rural residents. The study is expected to begin in the spring of 1993, and will be conducted in Iowa, Michigan, Minnesota, and Wisconsin. Some 600 to 700 incident cases will be examined, both male and female, along with about twice as many control subjects. Previous studies in the United States, Italy, and New Zealand have found farmers to be at increased risk for this type of brain cancer, as well as for skin, stomach, lymphatic, and prostate cancer.

The problem of intestinal parasites among the children of migrant farm workers has been acknowledged, but a study of North Carolina migrant workers in the September 1992 *American Journal of Public Health* found that hookworm and other parasites are a major health problem for adults as well.

▶ Occupation and Pregnancy
Many women in the United States and elsewhere are engaged in occupations that entail exposure to hazards: hospital workers to radiation or ethylene oxide, laboratory workers to a variety of chemicals including organic solvents, textile-plant employees to excessive noise, and farm workers to pesticides, to name a few. A study conducted at 29 hospitals in Shanghai, China, of mothers exposed to these occupational health hazards revealed a number of risks related to pregnancy and the health of the fetus. The results, published in the March 1992 *American Journal of Industrial Medicine,* showed that exposure to radiation before or during pregnancy was associated with antepartum fetal death, birth defects, small-for-gestational-age (SGA), and threatened abortion. Exposure to chemicals before or during pregnancy was associated with antepartum fetal death, early neonatal death, birth defects, preterm birth, and threatened abortion. Exposure to pesticides during pregnancy led to SGA and the increased risk of threatened abortion, while occupational noise during pregnancy led to increased risk of antepartum fetal death.

▶ Cancer
In the May 1992 *American Journal of Industrial Medicine,* researchers studied the hypothesis that

individuals with occupation-related bladder cancer are more likely to have a more invasive form of the disease than other bladder-cancer patients. Motor vehicle operators, truck drivers, vehicle mechanics, other mechanics, and janitors were among those most likely to be diagnosed with high-grade or late-stage tumors. The study suggested that surveillance and targeted screening of workers in high-risk occupations may result in more early diagnoses and a subsequent decrease in mortality. Based on National Cancer Institute (NCI) figures, there are 9,000 cases of occupationally caused bladder cancer in men each year, resulting in 1,600 deaths. About 66 percent of those whose bladder cancer is diagnosed in the early stages or who have low-grade tumors have a five-year survival rate of more than 90 percent. The survival rate after five years for those with a more invasive form is 50 percent.

In a Swedish study in the September 1992 *American Journal of Industrial Medicine,* an association was found between the risk of colorectal cancer and occupation-related exposures, particularly for men, to soot, asbestos, cutting fluids and oils, and combustion gases from coal, coke, or wood. Exposure to printing ink increases risk of colon cancer in females and rectal cancer in males. The study also found that there is an elevated risk of colon cancer in males who work at gas stations and auto repair shops. It was also suggested that passive smoke increased the risk for colon cancer in females and rectal cancer in males.

A study done by Italian researchers in the October 1992 *American Journal of Industrial Medicine* showed a significantly increased risk of nasal cancer in males working in the wood industry, such as furniture makers, joiners, carpenters, and lumberjacks. The study indicated that the risk of cancer also increased for shoemakers and tanners. In addition, textile workers, furnacemen, construction workers, and workers with possible exposure to organic dusts, like bakers and flour workers, showed higher-than-normal risks for nasal cancer.

Men working in the wood industry have a higher rate of nasal cancer than is found in the general population.

Researchers from the National Institute of Environmental Health Science reported in the November 4, 1992 issue of the *Journal of the National Cancer Institute* that exposure to a wide range of chemicals on the job may be linked to certain genetic changes that appear in a rare form of leukemia.

The study of 62 patients with acute myelocytic leukemia found that genetic damage showed up more frequently in those who reported breathing chemical vapors or having skin contact with chemicals at work. Such patients were found to be in occupations such as artistic painting, auto mechanics, dry cleaning, beautician work, farming, nursing, and electrician work, as well as in the printing, rubber, pharmaceutical, and chemical industries. The study found that damage to the *ras* proto-oncogene, the gene that, if healthy, would prevent this disease, was six times more likely to have occurred if the patient had worked around chemicals for more than five years. If untreated, acute myelocytic leukemia can be fatal within a few weeks or months. Each year there are around six or seven new cases of all forms of acute myelocytic leukemia per 100,000 people in the United States.

▶ **Health-Care Workers**

The Centers for Disease Control and Prevention (CDC) and other federal agencies, including the Food and Drug Administration (FDA) and OSHA, continue to monitor health-care workers' exposure to a number of diseases—including the human immunodeficiency virus (HIV), which causes AIDS; hepatitis B (HBV); and multidrug-resistant tuberculosis. In addition, there is growing concern about exposure to pharmaceutical aerosols, a rapidly expanding treatment for pulmonary diseases and infections.

While nurses remain among the most at risk for exposure to HIV, a wide range of health-care workers have occupationally contracted the virus, mostly from needle pricks or direct contact with infected blood. According to the CDC, of the 32 documented and 69 presumed occupational cases reported as of September 1992, 26 were nurses, 23 clinical lab technicians, 11 nonsurgical physicians, 7 emergency-service technicians, 6 dentists, 6 health attendants, and 6 hospital maintenance or housekeeping staff. The remainder were various other technicians and respiratory therapists.

Some basic data on exposure to HBV among health-care workers at different hospitals show a 10 percent to 20 percent incidence, while the rate is only around 5 percent in the general population, according to the CDC. Based on 1989 estimates, 12,000 health-care workers become infected with HBV every year, mostly from needle pricks. Nurses and surgical staff are especially at risk. OSHA standards call for hospital employers to make

HBV vaccine available to all employees free of charge. In August 1992, the CDC, OSHA, and the FDA conducted a conference on prevention of device-mediated blood-borne infection in which some equipment-design flaws were described and design changes, as well as precautionary work procedures were discussed or recommended.

In 1992 a multiagency task force began to evaluate revisions to the national guidelines on tuberculosis in order to deal with multidrug-resistant (MDR) strains. By law, all cases of tuberculosis must be reported to the CDC, which will now begin to ask for additional information on the patient, including his or her occupation and HIV status. Hospital workers and correctional-facility personnel are at increased risk of exposure. An August study in the *Annals of Internal Medicine* said that health-care workers assigned to wards at a New York City hospital housing MDR tuberculosis patients were more likely to test seropositive for tuberculosis than were health-care workers on other wards.

Concerns over occupational exposures to pharmaceutical aerosols have centered around two antibiotics: ribavirin, used to treat a severe pneumonia in children and infants, and pentamidine isethionate, used to treat *pneumocystis carinii,* an infection occurring in those with HIV. A study in the March 1992 *Applied Occupational and Environmental Hygiene* and one in the *Scandinavian Journal of Work, Environment & Health* point out that ribavirin has not been linked to fetal abnormalities in humans, but it has been associated with birth defects in animals. Health-care workers, most likely nurses and respiratory therapists, should avoid exposure to such aerosols, especially prior to and during pregnancy, and during lactation.

A common side effect of pentamidine is coughing, and since HIV patients have an increased prevalence of tuberculosis, there is an increased chance health workers will be exposed to the tuberculosis microorganism, the studies said.

▶ Electromagnetic Radiation

Through a legislative initiative by the U.S. Senate, NIOSH will study the question of the relationship, if any, between cancer and exposure to the electromagnetic fields (EMFs) generated by hand-held radar guns used by state police. NIOSH has been encouraged to conduct epidemiological studies of police officers that have been exposed to EMFs while on duty, but funding for the project was not available in 1992.

In addition, NIOSH will probably do epidemiological studies of workers at the U.S. Department of Energy facilities where there are generally very high levels of electric-power consumption and high exposure rates to EMFs.

Neil Springer

Pediatrics

▶ PCR as a Diagnostic Tool

The use of polymerase chain reaction (PCR) as a diagnostic tool has revolutionized laboratory diagnosis of many childhood diseases. PCR is the technique of choice for determining specific gene aberrations. When applied properly, it can be used for rapid diagnosis of such diseases as AIDS, tuberculosis, Lyme disease, and chlamydia.

The rapid diagnosis available from the PCR test for tuberculous meningitis is especially valuable because the previous test took up to six weeks to grow the organism in culture. PCR tests have allowed early treatment of infants with herpes simplex encephalitis, and avoid the necessity of a brain biopsy.

▶ Fragile-X Syndrome

Thanks to the revolution in PCR diagnosis, the year 1992 heralded a rapid, economical way to diagnose the most common form of inherited mental retardation, fragile-X syndrome. This disease, caused by a genetic abnormality on the X chromosome, occurs in one of every 1,000 mentally retarded boys and in one of every 2,000 mentally retarded girls. This syndrome has distinct physical signs in boys, including moderate to severe mental retardation, large testes, large ears, and a long plantar crease between the first and second toe.

The gene was first identified in 1991, making diagnosis of this disorder easier. Affected persons have been found to have both a full mutation and abnormal DNA of a specific DNA fragment on the X chromosome. Fragile-X syndrome was previously detected by cell culture, but articles published in the *New England Journal of Medicine* outlined methods for direct diagnosis of the syndrome by PCR analysis. Enzyme-based tests have also been developed to diagnose this genetic disease.

Explanations for the mode of inheritance are complex. Persons with a small modification of this specific DNA fragment have a low risk of retardation, but are at great risk of having children or grandchildren who have greater modifications of the DNA fragment, resulting in a more severe form of the disorder. Approximately 20 percent of males who inherit the gene are unaffected, appearing normal. However, these males are carriers who can transmit the disorder. The mothers of affected children are also considered to be carriers. But unlike males, about 50 percent of female carriers with only one fragile-X gene have some of the features of the syndrome, and about 30 percent are mentally retarded in varying degrees of severity.

While difficulties in interpretations may occur, it is likely in the near future that all mentally retarded children will be tested for fragile-X syndrome. Prenatal diagnosis of the disorder, via amniocentesis or chorionic villus sampling, should be available in the near future, greatly improving the effectiveness of genetic counseling.

▶ Gaucher's Disease

Gaucher's disease, a rare inherited metabolic disorder, is caused by a deficiency of the enzyme glucocerebrosidase, which permits the lipid glucocerebroside to accumulate in the body's storage cells. This disease occurs somewhat frequently in its relatively milder forms, characterized by an enlarged liver and spleen. Other symptoms include abnormal liver function, formation of fibrous tissue in the liver, an abnormally small number of platelets circulating in the blood, anemia, and bone and joint swelling. Large, wrinkled-appearing cells, called Gaucher's cells, cause thickening of the femur bone near its ends. In the past an exact diagnosis of Gaucher's disease was made by examining the bone marrow for the presence of Gaucher's cells. More recently, reliable tests have been developed that can determine the enzyme activity characteristic of Gaucher's disease.

Three types of Gaucher's disease occur. In the adult form, symptoms are often mild, and it may not be diagnosed until adulthood. The life spans of persons afflicted with the adult form are only slightly reduced. The infantile form is characterized by slowed development, respiratory problems, crossed eyes, or palsy; death usually occurs within the first two years of life. In chronic Gaucher's disease, neurological symptoms occur later in life, and the disease runs a long, usually nonfatal course.

A number of treatments are available for Gaucher's disease. Bone-marrow transplantation can cure this disease, but may be too risky or unsuitable for severely ill patients. Enzyme-replacement therapy was first proposed in 1966, but after many trials, it was found to give inconsistent results. More recently, further experimentation led to successful targeting of the enzyme to the particular cell, as reported in the *New England Journal of Medicine*. In clinical trials of this technique on patients with the adult form of the disease, the symptoms were dramatically reversed.

▶ Respiratory-Distress Syndrome

The respiratory-distress syndrome in premature infants is one of the leading causes of infant illness and death. Treatment of this problem by respiratory support, using ventilators and other breathing apparatus, was initiated 25 years ago and is becoming increasingly more sophisticated. Respiratory support has led to the survival of smaller and

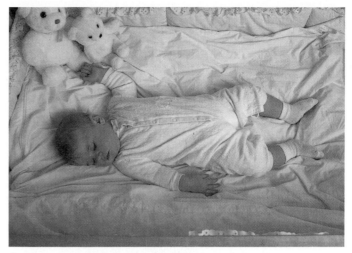

Studies conducted abroad suggest that a baby put to bed on his or her back is less likely to become a victim of sudden infant death syndrome.

smaller prematurely born infants, but many of these infants remain in the hospital for months, and some are left with permanent disabilities.

One of the critical deficiencies in the lungs of premature infants is a lack of substances called surfactants, which provide the surface tension necessary to keep the air sacs of the lungs expanded. A number of physicians have administered surfactants in various ways, with encouraging results. In previous trials, surfactant was given shortly after birth to prevent respiratory-distress syndrome or, after the syndrome had already developed, to treat the infant in distress. Although the trials have been successful, conclusive results were not available for mortality and complication rates.

To assemble the needed information, a consortium of 19 U.S. hospitals participated in a double-blind, placebo-controlled trial involving 446 infants weighing 1.5 to 2.2 pounds at birth. In the study, reported in a 1991 *Journal of Pediatrics* article, a single dose of either synthetic surfactant or a placebo consisting of air alone was inhaled by the infant. Significantly fewer babies treated with surfactant died, and fewer deaths in the treated group were due to respiratory-distress syndrome. The incidence of respiratory-distress syndrome and other complications was similar in both the treated and control groups.

A study published in the *New England Journal of Medicine* followed a group of infants of less than 30 weeks' gestation who were given surfactant at birth or after a delay of less than six hours. The study found that ventilator requirements and severe chronic lung disease decreased in the infants. In a *Lancet* report, surfactant treatment appeared to improve oxygenation in four infants with congenital diaphragmatic hernia. Other studies published in *Pediatrics,* using calf-lung surfactant, produced results similar to those of the study with synthetic surfactant. As a result of these promising studies, surfactant administration has within the past year become routine in the care of very small prematurely born infants.

▶ Sudden Infant Death Syndrome

A mystery attracting the interest of many people, both in the medical and the nonmedical community, is sudden infant death syndrome (SIDS). Conditions previously included in the diagnosis, and now recognized as causing the mysterious sudden death, include metabolic disorders, hazardous beds and bedding, and, rarely, accidental suffocation by a parent unintentionally rolling on top of an infant sharing the parents' bed. (A small number of cases of intentional suffocation have also been mistakenly attributed to SIDS.) Other factors, such as maternal smoking and hypothermia, have been found to increase the risk of sudden infant death. Many at-risk infants have very small birth injuries to the central nervous or pulmonary systems, injuries that cause abnormalities in the respiratory drive that may account for some of the deaths.

A recent flurry of articles on this topic concerns the position in which the infant is put down to sleep. Studies conducted abroad have shown that the incidence of sudden infant death is markedly reduced in populations where the infant is characteristically put down to sleep on his or her back rather than on the stomach. Not all physicians are convinced that this is a factor in SIDS, since most infants should be able to turn over after three or four months of age. Furthermore, in Scotland the incidence of sudden infant death has decreased in the past few years without apparent change in habitual sleeping position.

▶ Effects of Passive Smoke on Children

Data from the National Longitudinal Survey of Youth suggest that increased behavior problems in children may be associated with exposure to cigarette smoke from the mother. This increase is as great or greater than many of the previously recognized predictors of children's behavior problems. Even after taking into account a variety of maternal and family characteristics, such as maternal education, family income, and the quality of the home environment, the observed relationship between maternal smoking (both prenatal and postnatal) and children's behavior problems remained a noteworthy phenomenon.

Mothers who smoke may endanger the lives of their infants, according to data from the National Maternal and Infant Health Survey. Infants whose mothers smoke after pregnancy are twice as likely to die of SIDS as infants not exposed to smoke. There is three times the risk of SIDS if their mothers smoked during pregnancy as well.

▶ Use of Cow's Milk in Infancy

News of a suspected relationship between an infant's consumption of cow's milk and insulin-dependent diabetes mellitus took many in the medical community by surprise. One study from Finland found that children who were exclusively breast-fed, and therefore were not exposed very early in life to formula based on cow's milk, had a significantly reduced risk of developing diabetes. Other studies have found that worldwide, the occurrence of insulin-dependent diabetes parallels the frequency with which cow's milk is consumed. Now researchers from Canada and Finland have discovered that people with diabetes have antibodies to the cow-milk protein called bovine serum albumin. These antibodies are capable of cross-reacting with proteins in the insulin-producing islet cells of the pancreas, causing them to malfunction. Further confirmation of the cow's milk–diabetes correlation is still needed before decisions are made to eliminate cow's milk entirely from the diets of growing infants and children considered at risk for diabetes.

Other studies have observed that infants fed whole cow's milk have increased gastrointestinal blood loss, a condition leading to iron deficiency, since the iron contained in the blood is lost as well. Whole cow's milk does not replace the iron sufficiently, and its chemical composition may actually interfere with the intestinal absorption of iron that is available from other sources, such as cereal. The consequent iron deficiency can lead to anemia. Transient iron deficiency in rats has been shown to reduce the number of neurotransmitter receptor sites in the brain—a condition that is not correctable with subsequent iron supplementation. This may explain recent human studies showing that iron deficiency in early childhood may lead to long-term,

The American Academy of Pediatrics recommends that babies not be fed whole cow's milk during their first year, although its use later is acceptable.

permanent behavior problems. Based on these concerns about iron deficiency, the American Academy of Pediatrics issued a cautionary statement on the use of cow's milk. The academy recommends that for the first year of life, infants should be fed either breast milk or iron-fortified infant formula. Whole cow's milk should not be used in the first year, although its use is acceptable after that, since cow's milk is an excellent source of many nutrients.

► Racial Disparity in Infant Mortality

In the United States, African-American infants are twice as likely to die in the first year of life than are white infants. Much of this disparity is due to the higher percentage of very-low-birth-weight infants (weighing about 3 1/4 pounds) born to African-American mothers. One factor that may contribute to the higher premature birth and related infant mortality rates may be reduced access to adequate prenatal care, which is related to income. But socioeconomic differences alone do not account for the racial disparity. A study using National Linked Birth and Infant Death Files calculated infant mortality rates for children born to college-educated parents. The researchers found that African-American infants born to college-educated parents have higher rates of premature birth and mortality than do white infants of similarly educated parents. In contrast to the general population, however, full-term, normal-birth-weight infants, both black and white, who are born to college-educated parents have equivalent mortality rates.

The higher proportion of African-American infants with very low birth weight (regardless of parental education levels) is associated with a greater frequency of such maternal risk factors as premature leakage of the amniotic fluid, high blood pressure, or unexplained early onset of labor.

► Effects of Lead Exposure

According to investigators in Australia and Boston, children exposed to lead early in their lives suffer from an identifiable decrease in intelligence, a finding demonstrated by a 5 to 10 percent decrease in IQ scores among these children compared to those not exposed to lead. These studies are important in that they refute assertions that the effects of lead exposure are limited to socially and economically disadvantaged children. Lead-associated decreases in intelligence are found across cultural, racial, and ethnic lines, and social and economic classes.

Given the evidence for adverse health and cognitive effects from chronic low-level lead exposure, the Centers for Disease Control and Prevention (CDC) initiated a plan for the elimination of childhood lead poisoning, including lowering of the blood-lead level considered dangerous.

Lewis A. Barness, M.D.

Podiatry

In the modern medical environment, it is frequently the podiatrist whose expertise is called upon to treat foot problems caused by a disorder elsewhere in the body. Among other tasks, it falls within the podiatrist's domain to analyze a patient's gait, custom-design special footwear to resolve certain foot problems, and prescribe a physical-therapy program to help facilitate recovery from foot surgery.

► Absorbable Fixation Devices

Orthopedic surgery, including foot surgery, often makes use of stainless-steel wire, pins, screws, plates, or other fixation devices to hold the bone fractures or cuts in alignment until the bone heals. These metal pieces may be left in place, although occasionally another surgical procedure is needed to remove the fixation device. To avoid second surgery, pins are often extended outside of the skin to make removal easier. Patients find this arrangement unsightly, however; moreover, the potential for infection along the pin tract is considerably heightened. Absorbable pins, developed in recent years, are proving to be of great benefit.

Absorbable materials for use in fixation devices have been evaluated since the late 1960s. At first, collagen and gut were the only absorbable materials available. Later, medical-grade synthetic polymers were developed and much refined. These materials are eventually destroyed by the body's enzymes in the presence of water, and do not require surgical removal.

Recently, researchers developed an absorbable pin for orthopedic surgery. These pins do not protrude from the skin, reducing the risk of infection. And because they eventually dissolve, the patient is saved from the anxiety of pin removal surgery. Absorbable pins have recently been approved for use in the foot, primarily in surgery on the toes or bunions, and other absorbable fixation devices are being developed.

► Foot Reconstruction in People with Diabetes

A person with diabetes is often afflicted by a wide variety of foot deformities, ranging from corns or calluses to a completely collapsed foot. This last condition, known as Charcot foot, is caused by changes in both the sensory and motor nerves that may occur in people with diabetes. These changes result in increased stress across the joint, until the joint finally fatigues and collapses, leaving the person with a foot that is essentially nonfunctional. Such patients face the grim future of a sedentary life-style, long-term bracing, or even amputation of the limb. Charcot joint collapse or dislocation can also cause areas of bony prominences in the foot, resulting in skin irritation and sores, a serious problem for people with diabetes, who tend to have poor circulation in their limbs anyway. Once the sores develop, the area can subsequently become infected. The infection could ultimately result in the amputation of part of the foot or the entire foot.

Recently, a number of diabetic people with Charcot foot have undergone foot and ankle reconstruction in an effort to avoid amputation. In the past, this type of complex surgery on the feet of people with diabetes generally has been avoided because of the possibility of complications. However, the initial results of the surgery on patients with Charcot foot have been quite promising, and early reports suggest that the complication rate is similar to that expected in nondiabetic patients. After surgery the patients have a much more stable foot, allowing them to more efficiently perform their daily activities. The surgery also removes the points of irritation on the foot, reducing the potential for developing the sores and infections that typically plague these patients.

▶ Gait Analysis Enhances Treatment

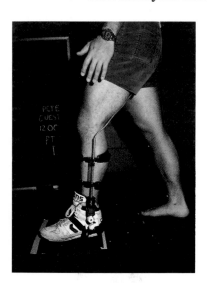

Many disorders of the foot and ankle are apparent in a patient's posture and locomotion. Gait analysis of a patient's posture and motion before starting therapy permits the podiatrist to identify the source of the problem and devise a treatment plan to return the patient to the best possible foot and ankle functioning. Evaluating a patient's gait after therapy can also measure the effectiveness of the therapy program.

The Gait Study Center at the Pennsylvania College of Podiatric Medicine in Philadelphia has concentrated its studies on the foot and ankle within the context of the whole body. One recent study focused on Down syndrome patients whose feet exhibit a lack of muscle tone and excessive flexibility. This combination results in a collapsed foot, called flatfoot, a painful condition that produces a poorly balanced gait. The study showed that in-shoe orthotic devices reduce the variability in movement, helping to improve stability.

Stephen V. Corey, D.P.M.

Public Health

Heightened concern about the spread of tuberculosis and other infectious diseases, a better understanding of the health-promoting role of several vitamins, and possible new causes for heart attacks topped the public-health news during 1992.

▶ Tuberculosis

A decade ago, public-health officials were hoping to eliminate tuberculosis (TB) in the United States. Now they would be satisfied just to control the disease. Several factors have combined to cause the current increase in the tuberculosis rate: AIDS, drugs, crime, homelessness, and an increase in disease resistance to antibiotics.

The most important single factor has been the AIDS epidemic. The human immunodeficiency virus (HIV-1), the virus that causes AIDS, produces a decline in the ability of the immune system to resist infections. Unfortunately, from the tuberculosis perspective, the type of resistance most important in TB (cell-mediated immunity) is the type of immunity most adversely affected in HIV infection. Therefore, HIV-infected persons who have a quiescent earlier tuberculosis infection, or those who are newly exposed to TB, are at great risk of acquiring the active form of the disease. HIV infection can predispose the patient to tuberculosis long before the critical CD4 lymphocytes decline enough to cause other, more common AIDS-associated infections. AIDS patients frequently need care in hospitals, where they can spread their tuberculosis to others or, if not yet infected, become infected themselves. In fact, the spread of tuberculosis in hospitals and other institutions, such as prisons and shelters for the homeless, is becoming a major problem. One proven way to reduce the spread of tuberculosis organisms in buildings is to expose recirculated air to ultraviolet radiation, but such a system is costly and not commonly found.

Intravenous drug use predisposes participants to HIV infection and also to crime (to get money for drugs). Thus, IV drug users often are put in prison, where they are especially likely to be exposed to or spread tuberculosis. Short-term detention centers, such as New York City's Rikers Island, are especially likely to be hotbeds of tuberculosis. In such places the prisoners are there for only a brief time, too short a period to diagnose, isolate, and treat for the disease. Even if the medical staff is able to diagnose TB and start an inmate on the appropriate antibiotic drugs, the person may be returned to the community quickly. Such cases are difficult to follow, and the TB sufferer often discontinues the

Prisoners incarcerated in a short-term detention center (right) are rarely held there long enough to be diagnosed as having tuberculosis, let alone be isolated and treated for the disease. Under such conditions, the disease can readily spread to other inmates.

antibiotic therapy. Incomplete treatment of tuberculosis predisposes the patient to the development of antibiotic resistance. The only ways to prevent the spread of drug resistance are: (1) to make sure, by supervised taking of medications, that each case of tuberculosis is adequately treated; and (2) to detect infected persons early and treat them adequately.

Unfortunately, early detection is complicated by HIV infection. The most effective screening tool has been the tuberculin skin test, in which the presence of cell-mediated immunity to TB is demonstrated by a raised area of firmness and redness where the TB antigen is injected into the skin. Damaged immune systems may not be able to produce enough antibodies to give a positive skin test, a condition known as anergy. The false-negative skin tests make rapid tuberculosis detection difficult, as the main alternatives are chest X-rays, which also may miss the disease, and sputum cultures, which take weeks to produce results. By the end of 1992, our entire tuberculosis-control strategy was under reconsideration; most public-health officials believed that TB might become the next major infectious-disease epidemic in the United States, requiring vastly greater resources for its control than are now being provided.

HIV-infected persons and intravenous drug users are not the only groups at risk for tuberculosis. Certain immigrant groups, particularly those from Southeast Asia, are at high risk for developing TB during their first year after arriving in the United States, although the risk drops rapidly thereafter. Migrant farm workers, who are poor and usually have inadequate living conditions and have little access to medical care, are also at high risk for developing the disease.

▶ Report on Resurgent Infectious Diseases

In the fall of 1992, the Institute of Medicine of the National Academy of Sciences (NAS), in a report titled *Emerging Infections,* warned that changes associated with modern life are forcing rapid changes in microorganisms. Such changes raise the danger of continual emergence of new diseases (such as AIDS) or the reemergence of old ones we thought were adequately controlled (such as tuberculosis). Some major factors considered in the report as likely to contribute to new or rejuvenated diseases are: (1) human demographics and behavior; (2) technology and industry; (3) economic development and changes in land use; (4) internal travel and commerce; (5) microbial adaptation and change; and (6) the breakdown of public-health measures.

The report also emphasizes that infectious diseases are now global in nature, and we must think globally, not locally or even nationally, about their prevention and control. For example, the American approach to disease surveillance concentrates on those diseases that are currently problems in the United States. Thus, the ability of U.S. physicians to recognize diseases from other countries may be limited. A high-quality surveillance system equal to that of the current U.S. system is needed to make early warnings of new disease outbreaks. Also, even a relatively small outbreak of certain diseases such as yellow fever could exhaust the current world supply of one type of vaccine, and there are inadequate stockpiles of most vaccines for major epidemics.

The authors of this report are not the only ones who believe that major new disease problems may be on their way. One of the world's leading AIDS epidemiologists, Dr. Jonathan Mann, has predicted that AIDS will not be the world's last pandemic (a worldwide epidemic). Some of the following sections illustrate other current infectious diseases that are resurgent.

▶ Paralytic Poliomyelitis

The Pan American Health Organization began to try to eradicate poliomyelitis in 1985, and by 1992 there was optimism that this goal was close to being achieved in the Americas. Despite intensive surveillance, no cases of poliomyelitis were reported in the Americas in 1992, and the last case of polio in the Western Hemisphere occurred in Peru in August 1991. There are high hopes for success of this program, at least in the Americas, although a recent outbreak of polio in the Middle East country of Oman has health officials worried. Despite a supposedly adequate immunization program, the disease was acquired by 118 Omani children, many of whom had been vaccinated. The reason for the Omani outbreak is not known, but it has made experts wonder whether the final eradication process will demand either a more potent vaccine than those currently available or a combination of oral and injected polio vaccines.

One other outbreak of polio, in the Netherlands, was unexpected because of the advanced level of medical care and health standards in that country. It soon came to light, however, that the outbreak occurred among a religious group who, for doctrinal reasons, refused vaccination. The outbreak, while not surprising in that those affected were not immunized, showed that the polio viruses are not yet eradicated from continental Europe.

▶ Congenital Syphilis

Congenital syphilis was apparently well under control in the early 1980s, with fewer than 200 cases reported in the United States per year. Since the late 1980s, however, it has been making an unwelcome comeback, partly due to the epidemic of the smokable form of cocaine called "crack." Crack's addictiveness has led many female users to resort to prostitution in order to obtain the drug. If not treated early, congenital syphilis can cause myriad abnormalities in children. Fortunately, it can usually be successfully treated with antibiotics if diagnosed at birth.

Lack of prenatal care also contributes to the syphilis problem. With proper attention the mother's infection can be diagnosed and treated early in pregnancy, protecting the infants. Women addicted to illegal drugs or engaging in prostitution are, of course, less likely to seek the proper prenatal care. In 1991, 4,322 babies were born with syphilis. It should be noted that part of the increase is due to a change in what defines a "case" of congenital syphilis. Since 1989 the Centers for Disease Control and Prevention (CDC) have included all infants born to infected but untreated mothers as "cases" of congenital syphilis; this new definition is responsible for part of the apparent increase.

▶ Cholera Update

In 1992 the United States had 96 reported cases of cholera, the highest number of cholera cases reported in this country in the 31 years since the CDC has been keeping records. The majority of this year's cases (75) occurred among passengers on a single airline flight traveling from Argentina, a cholera-infected country, to Los Angeles; all but one of this year's cases acquired their illness during travel to Central or South America. Travelers to infected areas should be especially careful of unboiled water and of seafood. The basic rule is, "Boil it, cook it, peel it, or forget it." The cholera epidemic in the Western Hemisphere has resulted in over 600,000 known cases and over 5,000 deaths since it began two years ago.

▶ Measles Threat

Measles again illustrates some of the changes that have so worried the authors of the report from the Institute of Medicine. Until recently, newborn infants were adequately protected from the disease for many months owing to measles antibodies they received from their mothers. Now, following over 25 years of measles-vaccine use, experts are coming to realize that the antibody protection from mothers who have had the measles vaccine but *not* the disease is often inadequate to protect newborns. As increasing numbers of vaccinated mothers who have not been naturally exposed to a "booster dose" of live measles virus reach their childbearing years, more very young infants are acquiring measles, often with drastic consequences. The maternal antibody from the vaccine apparently is not equal to that from the natural infection. If the virus were near eradication, it might make little difference, since newborns would seldom, if ever, be exposed to the natural infection. However, measles has been more difficult to eliminate through vaccination than was originally anticipated. Many preschool children, particularly in the inner cities, are inadequately immunized, making their exposure to live measles infection not so uncommon.

▶ Asian Tiger Mosquito

Still another example of a negative change that threatens our control of infectious diseases was the accidental introduction of the Asian tiger mosquito, *Aedes albopictus*, into the United States in 1985. This mosquito, an extremely aggressive biter, is capable of carrying many serious diseases, including dengue fever (often called "breakbone fever" for the pains it causes), a condition that can be fatal in

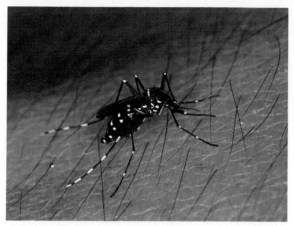

The Asian tiger mosquito (above) carries the potentially fatal dengue fever. Its prevalence just south of the United States has alarmed public health officials.

its hemorrhagic form. Dengue is common in many parts of the world, including areas immediately south of the United States, making its reintroduction here a very real possibility. In 1992 the Asian tiger mosquito was also shown to carry the virus that causes one of the most serious forms of viral brain disease, eastern equine encephalitis, which is endemic in the United States.

▶ Vaccine Against Hepatitis A
In 1992 a recently developed vaccine against hepatitis A was shown to be effective. Hepatitis A, although less dangerous than hepatitis B or C, is more common and is quite debilitating, with the capacity to cause permanent liver damage or death. Moreover, in contrast to the other forms of viral hepatitis, the A variety is often spread by the fecal-oral route, by food-borne outbreaks, or from person to person through casual contact. Hepatitis A often causes outbreaks in institutions and tightly knit communities, a fact illustrated by a recent outbreak among Hasidic Jews near New York City, and through young children who attend day-care centers before age 3. It was in the children of this latter group that the vaccine was tested. None of the over 500 children receiving the vaccine got hepatitis A, whereas many of the children receiving the placebo (inert) injection became infected.

▶ Vitamins Gain in Importance
Folic Acid. Important new research confirmed that adequate folic acid intake very early in pregnancy can prevent up to half of the neural-tube defects (such as spina bifida) in U.S. newborns, and an even greater percentage among newborns in countries with higher rates of this defect. An advisory committee to the U.S. Food and Drug Administration (FDA) recommended the addition of folic acid to some food that women would almost certainly consume regularly even before they knew they were pregnant; the committee recommended con-

sideration of flour for that purpose. The advisory committee also noted the potential for harm from this action: folic acid is able, for a time, to mask the symptoms of vitamin B_{12} deficiency in older people, and thus needed treatment may be delayed.

Another type of neural-tube defect that can be reduced by folic acid is anencephaly—a condition in which babies are born essentially without a brain. There was an apparent outbreak of anencephaly in the Brownsville, Texas, area. Local residents blamed the outbreak on pollution in the area by the chemical xylene, which has been associated with anencephaly in one British study. To date, however, no study has been initiated to examine the diets of people in the area to determine whether they might have been deficient in folic acid.

Vitamin C. Vitamin C, found in citrus fruits and other natural products, has been shown to prevent more than scurvy, the disease that is classically attributed to vitamin C deficiency. Vitamin C (along with vitamins A and E) is an antioxidant and, as such, helps to prevent the body's cells from being injured from various forms of oxygen produced as by-products of metabolism.

Antioxidants reduce cellular damage and retard the aging of cells. More recently, it has been shown that antioxidants help prevent the oxidation of low-density lipoprotein (LDL) cholesterol into a form that clogs arteries. Studies have also suggested that regular use of vitamin C, as well as A and E, also can reduce the risk of developing cancer.

▶ New Causes of Heart Disease?
For years the list of risk factors for the clogging of arteries with cholesterol (atherosclerosis) was thought to be almost complete: saturated dietary fats, genetic predisposition, smoking, hypertension, diabetes, obesity, and sedentary life-style. In 1992 new evidence was found that may point to other risk factors. Among these causes are excessive levels of iron in the body and viral infections.

The iron hypothesis was first proposed in 1981 by a pathologist who noted that women were usually protected from heart attack while they were menstruating. After menopause, however, coincident with the end of menstrual blood loss, their rates approached those of men. The iron factor could also explain why a high meat intake is associated with heart attacks, as meat tends to be iron-rich. In a 1992 study from Finland, the amount of stored iron in the body was the second strongest predictor of heart attacks, behind only smoking. A possible mechanism for this effect is already known: iron stored in the body has the ability to oxidize low-density lipoprotein cholesterol into the form that is most likely to cause atherosclerosis.

Viruses in the herpes group have also been proposed as factors in the production of atherosclero-

As a result of the 1986 explosion at the Chernobyl nuclear-power plant, Ukrainian children have an alarmingly high rate of thyroid cancer.

sis. Apparently, the viruses damage the artery walls, allowing cholesterol to be more easily deposited. Experimental confirmation has come from chickens, who did not develop atherosclerosis on a high-fat diet while kept free of viruses, but did after they were allowed to get viral infections.

▶ Cancers Following the Chernobyl Accident

Children who were exposed to radiation from the 1986 explosion of the Chernobyl nuclear-power plant in Ukraine (then part of the Soviet Union) have begun to show a rate of thyroid cancer 80 times that expected. These cancers are aggressive and spread rapidly. The aggressive nature of these particular thyroid cancers ensures that these cases eventually would have been recognized, even if they had occurred before the nuclear accident, dispelling the notion that the high incidence of cases is due only to the heightened surveillance in the areas near Chernobyl. The data from the population around Chernobyl are now being compared to data from populations exposed to radiation from the atomic bombs in World War II.

James F. Jekel, M.D., M.P.H.

Rehabilitation Medicine

▶ Exercise for Peripheral Vascular Patients

Peripheral vascular disease, the buildup of cholesterol plaque in blood vessels other than those in the heart, can have more far-reaching effects than was previously thought. Physicians have found that a patient's symptoms often do not correlate with the location of the blocked blood vessel. In the past, peripheral vascular disease was often treated with bypass surgery or arterial grafts in the affected region. In 1992 extensive reviews of the published studies on treatment alternatives found that nonsurgical treatment, such as exercise, was as effective as surgery in treating this condition. These reviews also helped establish guidelines for the selection of patients who would benefit most from rehabilitation treatment.

Follow-up studies of such walking programs found that most of the patients were able to tolerate greatly increased distances—as much as 100 to 400 percent longer—in just a matter of months. (It is important to note that 35 to 40 percent of patients who suffer from peripheral vascular disease also are afflicted with coronary-artery disease, so overall cardiac fitness and capabilities should be evaluated prior to embarking on a walking program.)

For many years, it was thought that such patients were able to build up their ability to walk distances by developing alternate circulation routes that bypassed the blocked artery, but recent studies show that this is not the case. The exercise program helps these patients get more oxygen to their muscles by causing small capillaries to form in the muscle, to bring the needed oxygen to the tissue.

▶ Spinal-Cord Injuries

During a football game on November 29, 1992, New York Jets defensive player Dennis Byrd collided headfirst with the chest of one of his teammates. He fractured his fifth and sixth vertebrae and damaged the spinal cord, leaving him paralyzed from the chest and lower arms down. In the weeks after the accident, Byrd regained some movement and feeling in all four limbs, with his right side notably stronger than his left side. His physicians remain unsure as to how much function he will recover, and he continues to undergo physical therapy.

Traumatic as a spinal-cord injury is, there is nothing exotic about Byrd's case. He has been fortunate in that he may be benefiting greatly from recent advances in treating these kinds of injuries. Re-

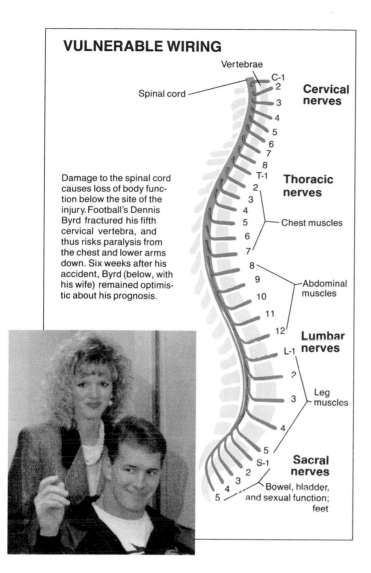

VULNERABLE WIRING

Damage to the spinal cord causes loss of body function below the site of the injury. Football's Dennis Byrd fractured his fifth cervical vertebra, and thus risks paralysis from the chest and lower arms down. Six weeks after his accident, Byrd (below, with his wife) remained optimistic about his prognosis.

Vertebrae
Spinal cord

Cervical nerves
C-1
2
3
4
5
6
7
8

Thoracic nerves
T-1
2
3
4
5 — Chest muscles
6
7
8
9 — Abdominal muscles
10
11
12

Lumbar nerves
L-1
2
3 — Leg muscles
4
5

Sacral nerves
S-1
2
3 — Bowel, bladder, and sexual function; feet
4
5

▶ Treatment for Swallowing Problems

Thanks to improved treatment options, the survival rates after head injuries, strokes, and radical neck surgery for neoplastic problems have increased in recent years. Unfortunately, these conditions often lead to swallowing difficulties that may not permit the patient to function without personal assistance, delaying the patient's discharge from the hospital. Video-fluoroscopy, a new radiographic test, provides a visual record of the mechanics and kinetics of the swallowing process, which helps speed the recovery and rehabilitation of such patients. A specially trained therapist can analyze the injured patient's swallowing process and set up a program that trains the patient to develop new ways to swallow. In cases where the swallowing process is permanently impaired, the therapist may even teach the patient to prepare foods that are easier to swallow. This training helps patients regain their independence and improve their quality of life.

▶ Increasing Muscle Strength in Geriatric Patients

In a study published last year, it was shown that the elderly, even those well into their eighties, can increase the strength of their skeletal muscles by 15 to 20 percent over a four- to six-week period with a structured progressive-resistance exercise program. Although this may not appear to be a great increase in strength, for elderly people, this small improvement can be just enough to greatly improve their quality of life. The added strength helps them move around more steadily, or rise from a chair without assistance. For geriatric patients in nursing homes, this additional strength allows an extra measure of independence, by allowing the person to take walks or to perform such tasks as carrying his or her own meal tray.

▶ Condition of the Lumbar Spine

High-technology imaging techniques, such as magnetic resonance imaging (MRI) and computerized axial tomography (CAT), and clinical follow-ups have shown that patients can tolerate more abnormalities in the structures of the lumbar region of the spine than had originally been thought. Many patients were diagnosed as having a lumbar spinal stenosis (a narrowing of the central spinal canal) or narrowing of the openings for the spinal nerves. The condition of these patients can be improved with an exercise program and physical therapy to help regain movement in some of the tightened muscles around the lumbar region of the spine. According to large-scale follow-up examinations, many of these patients had lost some range of motion in the hips, although no abnormalities could be found on X-ray examinations.

Willibald Nagler, M.D.

search has shown that a significant portion of the damage in spinal-cord injuries occurs not from the impact of the accident, but rather during the time period right after the initial accident. Dying nerve cells release toxins that do further damage to the injured area, and inflammation of the damaged tissue cuts off blood supply. Large doses of the steroid methylprednisone given within 48 hours of the injury have been found to be able to decrease the amount of secondary damage to the spinal cord; this has become a standard treatment for spinal-cord injuries. Byrd has also been treated with the experimental drug GM-1, made of naturally occurring molecules that are believed to help nerve cells communicate. This drug is currently undergoing clinical trials and in one small study was found to limit the damage to the spinal cord and possibly stimulate some repair. Research continues on other ways to help repair the spinal cord and prevent the devastating permanent damage caused by these injuries.

Respiratory System

▶ Gene Therapy

One of the most promising advances in respiratory medicine is the development of gene therapy for two of the most prevalent and serious hereditary pulmonary illnesses—cystic fibrosis and alpha-1 antitrypsin deficiency, a disease that leads to severe emphysema at an early age. Gene therapy entails introducing a virus containing a gene into the cells of an individual with a hereditary condition that is missing a specific gene that instructs the body to create a specific factor. The transferred gene replicates and functions in the production of the deficient factor. Studies have documented the feasibility of the technique. The safety of administering viruses to humans, the efficacy of the treatment, and the long-term effects are being evaluated.

▶ Asthma

Asthma is one of the most common chronic respiratory illnesses in the U.S. Asthma afflicts more than 10 million Americans; mortality and morbidity from the condition have increased in recent years, particularly among urban minorities.

Asthma is a disease characterized by a marked degree of inflammation that persists despite the clinical improvement of the patient. A greater understanding of the mechanisms at work in asthma has led to major changes in therapeutic strategies. Greater awareness of the role that allergens play in asthmatic attacks have led to efforts to control the impact of these allergens. The effectiveness of anti-inflammatory agents alone or in conjunction with bronchodilators in the acute and chronic management of asthma is now recognized by physicians. Nedocromill sodium, a promising anti-inflammatory drug, although not yet approved by the Food and Drug Administration (FDA), is undergoing clinical trials. Drugs such as gold, chloroquine, TAO (troleandomycin), and methotrexate are being explored for treatment of steroid-dependent asthmatics.

▶ Tuberculosis

Tuberculosis (TB) is an infectious disease transmitted by prolonged close contact with a person who has an active case of tuberculosis. It is the leading cause of death from infectious disease worldwide. About one-third of the world's population is infected with the tubercle bacillus without manifesting any disease symptoms. Starting in the mid-1980s, the previously declining rate of tuberculosis infection in the U.S. dramatically reversed. In 1991, 39,000 excess cases (cases above the projected expectation) were reported. An even more alarming trend is the rise in the number of cases that are resistant to multidrug therapy; in such cases, tuberculosis rapidly progresses and is often fatal—mortality from this form of TB is close to 50 percent.

This epidemic is the result of many factors, including delays in diagnosis, HIV co-infection, homelessness, poor compliance with medication, and a health-care system inadequately prepared to deal with the magnitude of the problem. Of these factors, brief duration of treatment and poor compliance with medications account for an inordinate number of patients developing drug resistance.

To stem this tide, researchers are making advances in speeding the otherwise slow process of establishing the diagnosis. The conventional diagnosis method takes up to eight weeks to identify the presence of the tubercle bacillus in a patient. With the advent of polymerase chain reaction (PCR) and DNA probes, however, the diagnosis of TB can be confirmed in a matter of days.

Newer antibiotics with a broader spectrum of coverage are now on the market for the treatment of tuberculosis. They are used in combination with various other drugs. Experts are now recommending that each new case of TB be treated with four drugs until the sensitivity of the organism is known or until toxicity limits multiple drug use.

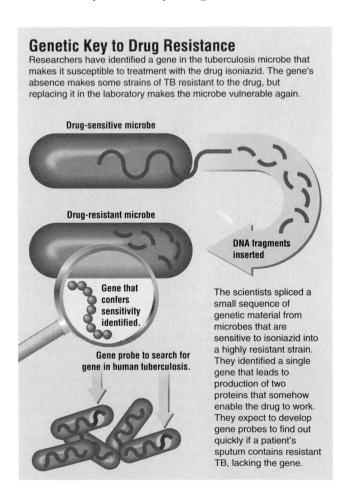

Genetic Key to Drug Resistance

Researchers have identified a gene in the tuberculosis microbe that makes it susceptible to treatment with the drug isoniazid. The gene's absence makes some strains of TB resistant to the drug, but replacing it in the laboratory makes the microbe vulnerable again.

Drug-sensitive microbe

Drug-resistant microbe

DNA fragments inserted

Gene that confers sensitivity identified.

Gene probe to search for gene in human tuberculosis.

The scientists spliced a small sequence of genetic material from microbes that are sensitive to isoniazid into a highly resistant strain. They identified a single gene that leads to production of two proteins that somehow enable the drug to work. They expect to develop gene probes to find out quickly if a patient's sputum contains resistant TB, lacking the gene.

▶ Sleep Apnea

Sleep-deprivation disorders can lead to subtle changes in personality, and impairment in judgment. If unrecognized, the condition can lead to serious complications.

Sleep apnea is an abnormality of respiration occurring during sleep. It is defined as cessation of airflow at the nose and mouth, lasting at least 10 seconds. Two major types are recognized: central (absence of respiratory efforts) and obstructive (continued respiratory efforts against an airway that is physically or physiologically narrowed or completely obliterated). These disorders produce various symptoms, including headache, confusion, snoring, abnormal cardiac rhythm, hypertension, and hypersomnolence (increased sleepiness).

Polysomnography and other sophisticated techniques that monitor physiological factors during sleep have been designed to study and diagnose the disease in patients with these symptoms. In patients diagnosed with sleep apnea, several treatments have been used with varying degrees of success. These methods include weight reduction, medications, nasal Continuous Positive Airway Pressure (CPAP), a device that holds the upper air passage open, and, more recently, BiPAP, a better-tolerated way of maintaining an open airway.

▶ Lung Cancer

Over the past 10 years, there has been an improvement in the treatment and prevention of lung cancer. Side effects of medications are decreasing. The number of smokers is diminishing. Among those who continue to smoke, early estimates show that there is an approximately 15 to 20 percent decrease in lung-cancer risk for every 10-milligram decrease in tar in the lungs.

Advances in molecular biology continue at an astonishingly rapid pace. In addition to gene therapy, experiments are under way to transfer genes that stimulate immunity against or cause the destruction of tumor cells. These include transfer of tumor necrosis factor or interleukin 2 coding genes into cells of patients with cancer. These cells will target the tumor cells and destroy them selectively, thereby avoiding some of the generalized complications of non-specific tumor therapy. Results of these experiments are eagerly awaited.

▶ Advances in Diagnosis and Therapy

Video-Assisted Thoracoscopy (VAT). In thoracoscopy, instruments are introduced into the pleural (lining of the lung) space to visualize and biopsy the lung and pleura. With the advent of video cameras, high-intensity light sources, and other new tools, lung and pleural biopsies, which previously required open chest-wall surgery, are now being performed by video-assisted thoracoscopy. The result is a

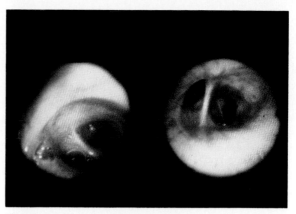

Lung and pleural biopsies no longer require open chest surgery, thanks to the use of video-assisted thoracoscopy to view the areas in question.

shorter hospital stay, a better tolerated and less painful incision, and reduced anesthesia risk.

Liposomes. Liposomes are fat vesicles that entrap a wide range of materials, including drugs. Liposomes can selectively deposit their contents in a targeted organ, thereby avoiding adverse side effects in other organs while maximizing delivery of medicines to the desired area. Higher doses of medication are being administered in this way. Liposomes can be given intravenously or by inhalation. Both methods are particularly well suited for treatment of pulmonary illnesses.

▶ Chronic Obstructive Pulmonary Disease

Emphysema is believed to result from an imbalance in elastase (an enzyme that degrades elastin, an important component of lung tissue) and elastase-inhibitor activities. Several studies have shown that chronic obstructive pulmonary disease (COPD) is accompanied by significant elevation of the breakdown products of elastin, suggesting that this disease may have a role in the development of emphysema. A recent study noted a higher level of elastin-derived peptides in patients with accelerated COPD when compared with other pulmonary disorders. If this study is confirmed, the concentration of peptides may be a useful marker in assessing response to treatment or in identifying patients at risk of developing COPD.

Oxygen therapy in COPD patients with low oxygen levels has been found to be effective in partially reversing or preventing progression of pulmonary hypertension. And additional studies corroborate the previously known fact that a high-carbohydrate diet may have adverse effects on patients with COPD. The ideal diet for patients with obstructive lung disease has not been defined, but a change to one containing a higher fat content was associated with better exercise tolerance.

Maria L. Padilla, M.D.

Sexually Transmitted Diseases

While the human immunodeficiency virus (HIV), which causes AIDS, tends to be the most prominently studied sexually transmitted disease (STD), other types of STDs—such as herpes, chlamydia, gonorrhea, and syphilis, to name a few—continue to be epidemic in the U.S. These "other" STDs afflict millions of people, with serious and occasionally fatal health consequences. These STDs are also becoming more common either as precursors of or consequent to potentially deadly HIV infections.

In 1992 the Centers for Disease Control and Prevention (CDC) reported an estimated 12.3 million new cases of "other" STDs. There is, in addition, a huge pool of already infected persons of all ages. For instance, an estimated 35 million Americans are infected with various strains of the herpes virus; there are also 14 million cases of genital warts caused by the human papilloma virus (HPV). Among all age groups, unsafe and promiscuous sexual practices continue to be typical behaviors inducing STDs, with some of these behaviors linked to dangerous drug-use habits, such as the exchange of crack cocaine for sexual favors.

The CDC reported in 1992 that about 70 percent of all new STD cases occurred in people under age 25. Persons aged 15 through 24 now comprise a high-risk population for such common STDs as syphilis, gonorrhea, chlamydia, chancroid, herpes virus, and genital warts.

Fortunately, there are signs that these disheartening statistics may have peaked. For instance, recent survey evidence indicates that more younger Americans may be switching to protected sex by using condoms. According to the most recent U.S. Public Health Service (PHS) amended statistics, 26 percent of sexually active, unmarried women aged 15 through 44 reported that their partners used a condom during their last sexual intercourse (up from 19 percent in 1988). Greater numbers of teenagers may also be abstaining from sexual activity altogether. In 1988 PHS data indicated that 27 percent of girls and 33 percent of boys had engaged in heterosexual/homosexual sex by age 15; 50 percent of girls and 66 percent of boys by age 17. Studies in 1992 showed a decline in sexual activity for these same age groups.

▶ Syphilis

Crack-cocaine link. The connection between syphilis and the use of crack cocaine is now established as a national trend, with the frequency of such STD cases (an estimated 55,000 reported in the United States in 1992) also continuing to rise.

Crack-cocaine users tend to exchange heterosexual favors for drugs and have a higher frequency of sexual activity. Although the syphilis epidemic is increasing in both rural and urban areas, it appears to be centered in urban areas, disproportionately affecting African-Americans.

In a 1991 study involving Montgomery County, Alabama, syphilis cases, crack users reported nearly twice as many sexual partners as nonusers. In the Portland, Oregon, metropolitan area, an analysis of in-depth interviews of 40 respondents (31 of whom had admitted to using crack cocaine) confirmed that sexual activity involving multiple anonymous partners often takes place within the context of crack-cocaine use.

An investigation of a syphilis outbreak in Ford County, Kansas, a rural area of the Midwest, suggested that the cocaine-syphilis link may be somewhat weaker in America's less-populated communities. While two of the seven Ford County patients were hospitalized for drug use, none of the patients surveyed reported exchanging crack cocaine for sex.

Neurosyphilis. While the overall number of syphilis cases recorded a modest increase in the past year, reported cases of neurosyphilis—a central-nervous-system infection occurring in early syphilis cases—continued to increase dramatically. The San Francisco Department of Public Health reported that, while cases of infectious syphilis declined 78 percent in San Francisco during the decade 1982–1992, the number of early symptomatic neurosyphilis cases increased 215 percent over the same period. Most patients (about 9 in 10) with neurosyphilis have tested HIV-positive, and several U.S. cities with high-risk populations for AIDS (including New York and Los Angeles) have also been reporting dramatic increases in neurosyphilis cases. Nonetheless, a conclusive link between neurosyphilis and AIDS has yet to be established.

▶ Chancroid Underreporting

Chancroid, a bacterial STD characterized by genital ulceration, has reemerged in the United States during the past decade. But according to a recent CDC study, the problem may still be greatly underreported. Most chancroid patients (about 9 in 10) are heterosexual men native to five states (California, New York, Florida, Texas, Georgia). Prostitution remains the primary mode of transmission for the disease, although some recent chancroid outbreaks have been linked to the exchange of sex for drugs.

Chancroid cases were commonly reported earlier this century, peaking at 9,515 U.S. cases in 1947, and declining after the Korean War. From 1950 to 1980, cases were infrequently reported, averaging fewer than 1,000 cases annually. A marked increase thanks to epidemics in Orange County, California, and Orange County, Florida, caused a peak of 5,035 U.S. cases in 1987. Despite a subsequent slight statistical decline (4,223 cases in 1990), new areas continue to report outbreaks, suggesting that many cases of chancroid are not being reported due to lax state reporting requirements, poor diagnostic methods, and decreased public awareness about the disease.

▶ Chlamydia News

An Israeli study completed in January 1992 found a possible relationship between chlamydia and AIDS. New evidence suggests that the presence of the *Chlamydia trachomatis* parasite may facilitate the transmission of the AIDS virus during vaginal or rectal intercourse—making those afflicted with chlamydia more susceptible to AIDS. This finding is of particular concern to homosexual males.

A 1992 Turkish study indicated that Turkish women with chlamydia infections are 6.8 times more likely to become infertile than women afflicted with other common STDs.

A new DNA gene probe being used in Spain can rapidly diagnose chlamydia. Easy to use without major laboratory equipment, the Spanish gene probe is 98.9 percent reliable—compared to a 50 to 60 percent accuracy rate for similar probes already developed and in use in the United States.

▶ Behavioral Risk Factors for STDs

According to a University of California at Davis (UCD) study released in April 1992, survey data from representative households in a San Francisco Bay Area county provided strong evidence that problem (alcohol) drinking is a potent behavioral risk factor for sexually transmitted diseases—independent of drinking patterns and drug use. Among women, age, race, early age at first intercourse, history of multiple partners, drinking patterns, and current symptoms of problem drinking were all associated with reported STD rates. Further analysis showed, however, that female problem drinkers are nearly four and a half times more likely than other women to have had STDs independent of *all* other potential risk factors. Problem drinking puts women at a greater risk for STDs than does a history of multiple sex partners. This finding was also observed among men, but to a lesser degree: men were about three and a half times more likely to contract STDs if they were problem drinkers. The UCD study determined that frequent bar patronage, episodes of drunkenness, high-volume drinking, and loss of inhibitions while drinking all increase the risk for STDs via their effects on the rate of sex-partner change.

Gode Davis

Skin

▶ New Trends in Sun Protection

The public's awareness of the adverse effects of sun exposure continues to grow. As a result the market for new and improved sunscreens is rapidly expanding. One major limitation of existing sunscreen products is the limited protection they offer against UVA, the long-wavelength ultraviolet light. Existing sunscreens offer excellent protection against the short-wavelength UVB light, thus permitting us to tan without burning. However, this tan is accompanied by significant additional skin damage caused by the UVA light that penetrates existing sunscreens. Researchers are continuing the quest to find a safe, effective, and aesthetically pleasing UVA-absorbing chemical that can be added to existing sunscreen products.

A too-often-neglected alternative approach to obtaining broad-spectrum (UVA and UVB) protection is the use of protective clothing. Dermatologists have long recommended the use of long pants, long-sleeved shirts, and broad-brimmed hats as protection from the sun. Unfortunately, studies by R. M. Sayre and colleagues, presented at the 1992 American Academy of Dermatology meetings in San Francisco, reveal that modern summer fabrics are actually poor sun protectants. Efforts by the clothing industry to design comfortable, light-

When outdoors, children should wear clothes that are impervious to ultraviolet light. Hats and sunscreen provide further protection from the sun.

weight, cool summer fabrics have actually resulted in producing fabrics that are ineffective sunblocks. A typical lightweight cotton shirt yields a sun protection factor (SPF) of only 7, which drops even further if the fabric is wet. This is far less protection than can be obtained by the use of any good, standard sunscreen with an SPF as high as 50. Fortunately, Sayre also showed that it is possible to design fabrics that are effective sunblockers. He demonstrated that appropriate fabrics can be lightweight, comfortable, and still produce sun-protection factors of greater than 30 even when the fabric is wet. Importantly, these fabrics yield a broad-spectrum protection against both UVA and UVB.

One result of switching to improved fabrics and new broad-spectrum sunscreens of the future will be an absence of tanning. This will be poorly received by the large segments of the public that continue to cling to the perception that a "healthy golden tan" is cosmetically desirable. These individuals desire a truly safe tan; they want the protection, but they also want the tan.

An increasingly popular solution to the dilemma is the use of self-tanning products. These products employ the topical application of dihydroxyacetone (DHA) to the skin in order to obtain a dyeing or darkening effect.

The color results from a chemical interaction between the colorless DHA compound and proteins in the skin's surface. The resulting pigment is very superficial and can be removed by vigorous rubbing. The color change produced by DHA can be seen within one hour of application.

Although the sunless tanning products are safe, they have some limitations. Rare allergies to DHA have been reported. In addition, uneven or undesirable coloring can result if the products are not properly applied. Finally, unlike a natural suntan, the artificial coloring produced by these products offers little or no protection from the sun. Therefore, companies have frequently added sunscreen into their sunless tanning products, but the level of sun protection yielded by these combination products remains inadequate. The best answer for those seeking a "truly safe tan" may be the use of a sunless tanning product at night, in conjunction with the daytime use of sunscreens or clothing made of specially designed sun-protective fabrics.

▶ Newly Recognized Skin Disease Is Marker of Underlying Malignancy

The ability to recognize cutaneous manifestations of underlying disease has long been a romanticized aspect of the field of dermatology: the notion that a skilled dermatologist can predict the existence of a specific internal disease merely by the accurate interpretation of the clues hidden on the skin. It has even been suggested that the skin can be viewed as a window to underlying disease. In truth the opportunities for the dermatologist to diagnose internal disease are rare; the hypothetical skin window is at best made of frosted glass. However, dermatologists can quickly enumerate the limited number of skin findings that sometimes function as markers of underlying disease. Recently a new dermatologic manifestation of underlying disease, paraneoplastic pemphigus, has been added to the list.

As early as 1980, researchers uncovered a possible relationship between a rare skin disease called pemphigus and underlying leukemia. In 1990 the skin disease was further categorized as a distinct variant of pemphigus, which was called paraneoplastic pemphigus. Over the past two years, additional cases have been reported, and a distinct new dermatologic entity, paraneoplastic pemphigus, is now widely recognized.

Paraneoplastic pemphigus is characterized by painful oral ulcerations and red, scaling, circular skin lesions with a predilection for involvement of the palms and soles. In addition to the involvement of the mouth, patients also frequently display inflammatory crusting and ulceration of the mucosal surfaces of the eye. It is an autoimmune disease that results from specific antibodies formed by the patient's immune system and directed against the patient's own skin. The paraneoplastic pemphigus autoantibodies are directed at desmoplakin I, a protein component of the junctions that hold normal skin cells and mucosal skin cells together. The antibodies attach to and destroy the cell junctions, leading to loss of cell adhesion and resulting in skin lesions. Finally, paraneoplastic pemphigus is often associated with underlying malignancy, usually chronic lymphocytic leukemia. It remains to be explained why and how the underlying malignancy causes the production of the antibodies that attack normal skin.

In the cases of paraneoplastic pemphigus that have been reported, the underlying malignancy has been almost uniformly fatal. However, now that the skin disease has been fully characterized, and rapid immunologic confirmation of the diagnosis is possible, it should result in earlier diagnosis of paraneoplastic pemphigus and the underlying malignancy at a time when the malignancy is still curable.

▶ Alpha-Hydroxy Acids Promise Medical and Cosmetic Benefits

In 1974 the remarkable benefits of the topical application of alpha-hydroxy acids to the skin of patients with ichthyosis, or fish skin, were first reported. These chemicals are natural acids occurring in everyday foods such as fruits and milk. They are relatively nontoxic chemicals that promote the normal peeling off of dead cells from the skin surface, thus temporarily eliminating the thick, dry scales characteristic of the skin surface of patients afflicted with ichthyosis.

An early commercial application of the alpha-hydroxy acids was the formulation of 12 percent ammonium lactate lotion (Lac-Hydrin lotion). It was initially used to treat ichthyosis, but quickly the alpha-hydroxy acids received wider acceptance for the topical treatment of the problem of xerosis, or abnormally dry skin (see photo below).

Clinicians have been experimenting with the superficial and deep effects of a variety of alpha-hydroxy acids on normal as well as aging skin. They have produced cosmetically beneficial results on common everyday disorders such as acne scarring and facial wrinkles. These results have been obtained using very high concentrations of glycolic or pyruvic acid, which causes a facial peel.

At the superficial epidermal level, these acids produce a peeling reaction that results in a resurfacing of the skin with new skin, relatively free of the

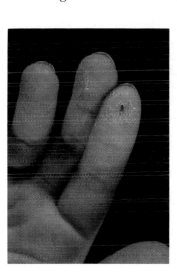

pigmentary variation and atypical cellular characteristics of aging, sun-damaged skin. Even more impressive, however, are the reported deeper dermal effects of chronic alpha-hydroxy acid application. Researchers have documented that topical alpha-hydroxy acids can cause an increase in collagen and ground substance, the major constituents of dermis. The result of the combined superficial and deep effects of the alpha-hydroxy acids is the amelioration or elimination of wrinkles, pigmentary variations, and precancerous growths common in sun-damaged skin.

Because the alpha-hydroxy acids are natural chemicals, they do not require a prescription to obtain. Already the cosmetic industry has incorporated them into a wide array of over-the-counter products. Typically, these preparations contain 2 percent to 7 percent concentrations of the alpha-hydroxy acids. At this concentration they produce little toxicity, but also very little benefit. In contrast, the use of high-concentration alpha-hydroxy acid (20 percent to 50 percent) can produce significant irritation and even scarring. Until the risk-versus-benefit ratio of these chemicals has been firmly established, the topical use of alpha-hydroxy acids for cosmetic purposes should be regarded as experimental.

Edward E. Bondi, M.D.

Substance Abuse

▶ Alcoholism

Treatment Options. There are many different kinds of alcoholism-treatment philosophies and practices, ranging from detoxification in hospitals and private clinics to 12-step programs such as Alcoholics Anonymous (AA). It remains unclear which type of treatment is best, because it seems to vary for each individual. To better address the problem of what treatment is best, the National Institute on Alcoholism and Alcohol Abuse (NIAAA) has initiated a $40 million, five-year treatment-outcome study involving nine towns or cities across the United States and Canada. This study, called "Project Match," will closely follow the progress of over 2,000 alcoholics assigned to different types of alcoholism treatment to see which patients do best in which type of treatment setting.

Medications for Treatment. Both the NIAAA and the National Institute on Drug Abuse (NIDA) are supporting research into the development of medications to treat substance-use disorders. Psychoactive substances, including alcohol, are thought to affect behavior by interacting with specific neurotransmitter systems in the brain. Neurotransmitters are chemicals produced by the body that transfer information between different nerve cells and produce or control behaviors. Research has focused on the development of medications to treat substance-use disorders by modifying specific neurotransmitters.

Naltrexone (Trexan) is a medication that has been used to treat dependence on opioids—heroin and other drugs derived from the opium poppy. It is an opioid antagonist, meaning that it binds to opioid receptors in the brain and blocks the effects of these types of drugs. In the past year, two research groups have conducted controlled clinical trials with naltrexone in recently abstinent alcoholics. These studies have found that naltrexone shows considerable promise as a treatment for alcoholism. A study conducted at Yale University in New Haven, Connecticut, compared double-blind naltrexone to a placebo in 97 alcoholics who were receiving coping-skills therapy or supportive therapy over a 12-week period. The researchers found that the naltrexone subjects had more days of abstention from alcohol, had lower rates of relapse, consumed fewer drinks per drinking day, and had a lower dropout rate than the placebo group.

At the University of Pennsylvania in Philadelphia, researchers conducted a six-week, placebo-controlled outpatient naltrexone trial with 70 alcohol-

At its meetings (left), Alcoholics Anonymous encourages its clients to abstain completely from alcoholic beverages. Some controversial studies have suggested that select alcoholics can lessen their dependence on alcohol through reduced or controlled drinking.

dependent males. They found that the group treated with naltrexone had a lower relapse rate, fewer drinking days, a longer time before relapse, and greater success in coping with a drinking relapse. The researchers also reported a reduction in alcohol "craving" during the trial period in the naltrexone group. Of particular interest in these studies is the observation of fewer drinks per drinking day. This suggests that, while alcohol was sampled by the subjects in both the placebo and naltrexone groups, the naltrexone-treated patients were less likely to continue to drink. In both studies, naltrexone treatment had few side effects and was well tolerated by patients. Although the use of naltrexone to treat alcoholism should be considered experimental, the results appear quite promising.

Abstinence Versus Controlled Drinking. A major controversy in the treatment of alcoholism is whether alcoholics must remain totally abstinent from alcoholic beverages, or whether they may engage in reduced or controlled drinking. A study from the University of New Mexico in Albuquerque suggests that controlled drinking may be an achievable goal for at least some alcoholics. The study followed 140 alcoholics receiving individual, behavior-oriented counseling over a period of several years. Most of the subjects rejected the label "alcoholic," yet responded to their treatment for alcoholism by reducing their drinking, a behavior that persisted over time. The controlled drinkers tended to have lower levels of alcohol dependence and less severe medical and social problems due to alcohol. Since many heavy alcohol users are not able to achieve complete abstinence from alcohol, this study suggests that controlled drinking may be a feasible goal only in selected cases.

▶ Opioids

Opioids are a class of narcotic drugs that are either derived from the opium poppy or are synthetic derivatives with similar analgesic actions. The opioid drug heroin, usually injected intravenously, is one of the major drugs of abuse. Heroin use is associated with a criminal life-style. It is also a major risk factor in acquiring human immunodeficiency virus (HIV) infection, and has helped to spread the acquired immunodeficiency syndrome (AIDS) among addicts and their families.

Methadone Treatment and Alternatives. One major treatment method for heroin abuse and dependence is methadone maintenance, the use of methadone to block the craving for heroin. Methadone is a synthetic, oral narcotic without significant side effects. A daily dose of methadone prevents narcotic withdrawal and blocks the effects of other opioid narcotics, such as heroin. Because regular use of methadone reduces the need to use heroin, methadone is effective in reducing illegal behaviors associated with heroin use. It also enables heroin addicts to stop the intravenous injection of drugs, thereby reducing the chances of HIV infection, and facilitates the rehabilitation of patients. Researchers at the University of Michigan in Ann Arbor surveyed 172 methadone-maintenance programs about treatment practices. The researchers found significant variations in length of time in treatment among the programs, and wide differences in the upper limits of methadone dosage set by the programs. Many methadone programs set limits on the highest dose of methadone that can be received and encourage only short periods of methadone maintenance. The researchers point out that these practices are in contrast with the evidence on the effectiveness of methadone. Studies have found that the longer clients remain in treatment, the more likely they are to remain abstinent from illicit drugs, and treatment with higher doses of methadone is more likely to retain clients in treatment.

Buprenorphine is a semisynthetic opioid used medically as a pain reliever, usually after surgery. Because of its long duration of action, lack of side effects, and the relatively mild withdrawal symptoms when its use is ended, buprenorphine maintenance has been proposed as a substitute for methadone maintenance. A study performed at NIDA has found that buprenorphine at a dose of 8 mg per day is as effective as methadone at a dose of 60 mg per day in preventing withdrawal, retaining clients in treatment, and reducing illicit-drug use. Several larger-scale clinical trials with buprenorphine in opioid addicts are currently under way.

Needle Exchange. A controversial method of preventing the spread of the HIV virus among intravenous drug users involves exchange of used syringes and needles (used to inject drugs) for clean and sterile needles and syringes. Sterile hypodermic needles and syringes are usually in short supply for addicts, resulting in the sharing of needles and syringes among many drug users. This dangerous practice increases the probability of transmitting HIV. Several experimental needle-exchange programs—such as those tried in Amsterdam, San Francisco, and Seattle—have had noted success in reducing needle sharing. However, a recent paper about the effectiveness of a needle-exchange pro-

Needle-exchange programs inaugurated in various cities have helped reduce—but not eliminate—the incidence of needle-sharing among drug users.

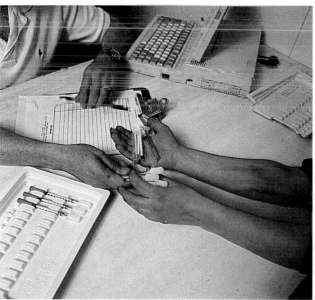

gram in Tacoma, Washington, reports a reduction in, but not an elimination of, needle sharing among program participants. In addition, participation in the exchange program does not appear to reduce the addiction to heroin in any way. Nevertheless, needle- and syringe-exchange programs can reduce the frequency of HIV transmission among addicts and their families.

▶ Medication Treatments for Cocaine Addiction

Cocaine is a drug extracted from the leaves of the South American plant *Erythroxylon coca.* It is a potent drug that blocks nerve impulses and intensifies the actions of neurotransmitters in the nervous system. Cocaine increases arousal, reduces tension, and produces intense euphoria and pleasure.

Cocaine use has become a significant medical and social problem in the United States, although recent surveys suggest that its use may be declining. Severe cocaine dependence is often quite resistant to traditional treatments, and heavy users have a high rate of relapse soon after treatment. There has been considerable research directed at finding effective treatments for cocaine dependence. One active research area is the search for a methadone counterpart for cocaine—a medication that, when taken regularly, would suppress the urge to use cocaine. Several studies have reported that certain medications, particularly the antidepressant desipramine, reduce relapse in heavy cocaine users. Researchers from the University of Maryland School of Medicine in Baltimore performed a statistical analysis of six studies comparing a placebo to desipramine in the treatment of cocaine dependence. The researchers report that the desipramine was no better than the placebo in keeping patients in treatment. For those addicts who remain in treatment, desipramine is helpful in maintaining abstinence. However, two more recent controlled studies on the use of desipramine in cocaine treatment find no positive effects, except in cocaine addicts who are also depressed.

Because cocaine is thought to act on the dopamine neurotransmitter system of the brain, medications that stimulate dopamine, including the drugs bromocriptine and amantadine, and the anticonvulsant carbamazepine, have been reported useful in reducing relapse in former cocaine users. However, other studies have not always confirmed these findings. A study conducted at the University of Connecticut in Storrs published in the *Archives of General Psychiatry* points out that the different results among various cocaine-treatment studies may result from poor experimental design and implementation of some of the studies. So far, no medication has been shown to be definitively helpful in the treatment of cocaine dependence.

▶ Ecstasy: Dancing with Death?

Over the last two years, the designer drug called ecstasy has killed at least 15 young people in England. In nearly every case, the drug had been taken at dance parties called "raves," where densely packed attendees vigorously dance all night. The deaths occurred when the users either began to convulse while dancing or collapsed unconscious on the dance floor. Symptoms included racing pulse, plummeting blood pressure, and extraordinarily high body temperature (up to 110° F). All died within three days of admission.

The "rave" scene has only recently made its way to the United States, predominantly in San Francisco, Los Angeles, and New York City. Some ecstasy abuse occurs at these parties, although as of late 1992, no deaths or severe toxicity from the drug had been reported.

▶ Caffeine

Caffeine and the related drugs theophylline and theobromine are consumed in beverages such as

coffee, tea, or cola, in chocolate, and in a variety of prescribed and over-the-counter medications. Over 80 percent of the American population use caffeine at least occasionally. Caffeine and related drugs stimulate the heart, kidneys, lungs, and central nervous system, causing an increased heartbeat, increased attention and concentration, and reduced need for sleep.

Although most caffeine users are aware that caffeine is a drug, there has been little evidence of adverse effects with moderate use. Studies considered more than 500 mg (the amount in about 5 cups of coffee) per day as a threshold for harmful effects. Thus, many users of lesser amounts of caffeine enjoyed a sense of security and complacency about their caffeine use. However, a study last year from Johns Hopkins Medical School in Baltimore, Maryland, showed that even moderate caffeine users who consume the equivalent of only two cups of coffee per day may develop a significant dependence upon the drug. Abrupt discontinuation of regular caffeine intake resulted in unpleasant withdrawal symptoms, including headache, lethargy, and irritability. The researchers advise all caffeine users who wish to stop consuming the drug to slowly taper off its use rather than abruptly stop caffeine intake.

Robert M. Swift, M.D., Ph.D.

Teeth and Gums

▶ Periodontal Diagnosis

Chronic periodontal disease, also known as periodontitis, is the most common disease of the gums. It appears as an inflammation of the gum tissues and supporting structures of the teeth, commonly seen as red, swollen, bleeding gums. This results in destruction of the bone and of the connective tissue that secures the teeth into the jaw. Left unchecked, periodontitis will ultimately result in the loss of the affected teeth. However, in the early stages, the disease is easily treatable, and recurrence can be prevented.

The health of the gums is generally evaluated as part of a regular dental checkup. The dentist or hygienist inserts a small, blunt measuring instrument, called a periodontal probe, between the gum tissue and the tooth, to determine whether portions of the gum have been destroyed by the disease. Comparing the depth of these pockets over a series of examinations reveals how much gum attachment has been lost. This evaluation does not disclose whether the periodontal disease is currently active, however.

In the past few years, dentists have become interested in finding ways to determine, before a patient has significant gum loss, if he or she has active periodontal disease. A number of different means of evaluating the health of the gums are being researched, including enzyme evaluations, microbial tests, and radiological techniques.

One of the more promising approaches is an instrument designed to measure localized temperature change in the gums. The idea behind this instrument is that inflamed tissue, such as that occurring in periodontitis, produces heat. An instrument similar to a periodontal probe, but containing an extremely sensitive temperature-measurement device, has been developed to gauge gum temperature. A higher-than-normal gum temperature would indicate active periodontitis. An early diagnosis of periodontal disease would lead to treatment before significant gum tissues are destroyed.

The manufacturer of the instrument also reports a correlation between gum-temperature increase and elevated populations of certain bacteria associated with periodontal disease. However, more research is needed to clarify the instrument's ability to distinguish between inflammation associated with active periodontitis and inflammation in nearby gum tissues that may not progress to loss of tooth support. If the temperature instrument is found to truly reflect the health of the gums, there may soon be another probe on the dentist's tray.

► Treatment of Periodontal Disease

Periodontitis is caused by the accumulation of bacteria at the gum line around teeth. These bacteria cause an inflammation in the gum that connects the teeth to the jawbone, causing deterioration in the gum and the bone. Treatment of periodontitis is aimed at halting the progression of the inflammation and deterioration by mechanical removal of the bacteria, and may even involve oral surgery.

Antibiotics have been found to significantly reduce the bacteria associated with periodontitis, but delivering the antibiotics to the affected sites is difficult. Antibiotic pills or liquids require an extremely high dosage in order to obtain sufficient concentrations at the intended gum site. In addition, antibiotics can cause undesirable effects in other parts of the body or possible interference with other needed medications.

Attempts have been made to deliver antibiotics directly to the site of the diseased gum by using various oral solutions. While this approach delivers an appropriate concentration of the antibiotic directly to the site of periodontitis, the medication is diluted and quickly washed away by saliva and other fluids in the mouth before having enough time to work against the bacteria.

In the past few years, researchers have concentrated on developing a delivery system that is capable of putting a higher concentration of the antibiotic directly at the site of the periodontal disease, and that can also maintain an adequate concentration of the drug over a period of at least one week. One solution to the problem is a plastic fiber impregnated with the antibiotic tetracycline, which will soon be available to dentists and periodontists. The fiber is wrapped around affected teeth, and releases tetracycline in concentrations many times higher than usual administration methods, maintaining this concentration over a 10 day period. Tetracycline was chosen because of its efficacy in reducing bacteria associated with periodontitis, and its ability to inhibit formation of enzymes capable of causing gum-tissue breakdown. The use of these fibers may significantly reduce the number of patients that require surgery to treat periodontitis.

► Dental Handpiece Technology

High-speed, air-driven handpieces have been utilized for several decades to drill teeth, thereby removing decay and preparing teeth for fillings. The turbines in these handpieces have traditionally been supported by stainless-steel ball-bearing systems. With use, the ball bearings tend to score and pit, potentially causing loss of precision rotation and function. Additionally, stainless-steel ball bearings require a large amount of expensive and time-consuming external lubrication in order to function efficiently and to meet sterilization requirements.

A new air-turbine handpiece has been introduced with an all-ceramic bearing system. This development addresses many of the problems of the stainless-steel bearing systems and provides more efficient management of handpiece sterilization. However, the ability of this new system to hold up during the rigors of daily routine use and care is yet to be determined.

Another major development in handpiece technology is the introduction of a fused-fiber-rod light source. The light at the tip of the operating handpiece, traditionally supplied through fiber-optic bundles bound by resins, illuminates the working area during cavity preparation. These resins tend to break down during sterilization procedures, reducing transmission of light and producing changes in the purity or color of the light. The fused-rod concept eliminates the use of these resins and assures continued quality of the light source over time.

► Computer-Enhanced Imaging

Modern computer technology has allowed rapid development of clinical imaging systems to enhance the diagnostic ability of the practicing dentist. More sophisticated methods of acquiring and digitizing photo images of the oral cavity and the nearby region, coupled with appropriate software, allow the clinician to perform enhancement procedures that show accurate simulations of tooth modification, tooth replacement, or color transformation. These simulations make it possible for patients to visualize the probable results from an aesthetic-treatment procedure.

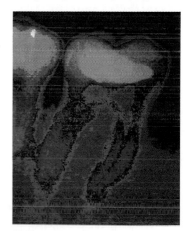

Enhanced photo images of teeth help patients to visualize what aesthetic enhancements are possible before a dentist actually performs any procedures.

Filmless digitized X rays of the mouth, with computer storage of images, have been available for several years. Further development of this approach has led to the recent digitized panoramic radiography, and not far off in the future is a totally filmless dental-radiography system. The capability for storage, transmission, and image enhancement in such a system is limitless and very appealing to the dental profession.

Another advantage of digitized radiography is the capability for computer analysis of images from different times, through "digital subtraction" of images. Two radiographs taken of the same clinical

Root Canal Procedure

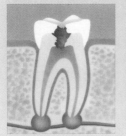

Tooth decay produces an abscessed (infected) tooth.

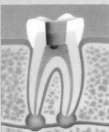

An opening is made through the crown of the tooth into the pulp chamber.

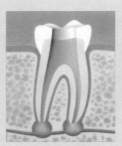

The pulp is removed and the root canals are cleaned, enlarged, and shaped.

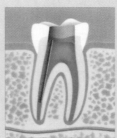

A metal post may be placed in the root canal for structural support.

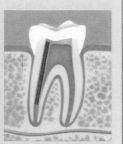

The pulp chamber is sealed and the crown of the tooth is restored.

Root Hemisection and Restoration

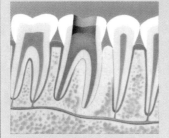

Tooth with bony defect is treated endodontically.

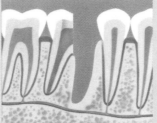

The diseased crown and root are sectioned off and removed.

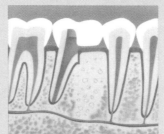

A fixed bridge is placed to stabilize the treated tooth. As healing occurs, bone fills the defect.

region at different times may look identical to the human eye, but the computer can detect extremely small degrees of density change, allowing earlier diagnosis and more appropriate therapeutic intervention.

▶ Root-Canal Therapy

The death of the central nerve, or pulp, of a tooth as a result of a cavity or trauma can cause pressure, swelling, and intense pain in the region. The treatment of choice for a dead pulp is root-canal therapy. Root-canal therapy involves the complete removal of the dead pulp, the reshaping of the tooth's pulpal canals to make them as straight as possible, and the resealing of the canals with an inert filling material. A tooth treated with a root canal continues to function in a normal manner, although it may get more brittle with age.

Patients used to face the pain associated with root-canal therapy with justifiable dread. While there is still some discomfort connected with this procedure, current techniques have greatly reduced pain.

Removal of the dead or infected pulp and the shaping of the pulpal canals during root-canal therapy has traditionally been accomplished with small instruments called reamers and files. These instruments are constructed from relatively rigid rods of stainless steel (usually less than a millimeter in diameter) that are twisted to form a sharp point at their tip and cutting edges along their entire length. A problem with these traditional instruments is that they have restricted flexibility, limiting their ability to negotiate the sharp bends and curves found in some pulpal canals. This limitation may lead to excess removal of tooth dentin from undesirable locations, resulting in the formation of artificial pathways or lateral perforations in the region of a canal bend.

Advances in metallurgy and instrument design have begun addressing these problems. New formulations and processing methods for stainless steel have resulted in significantly more flexibility in the metal being used to make some reamers and files. An even more important breakthrough combines the more-flexible stainless steel with a novel instrument design. This new design has a blunt tip and a cutting edge only a few millimeters in length attached to a noncutting flexible shaft, allowing negotiation of curved canals with no danger of creating artificial pathways or excessive cutting of tooth structure at the canal curvature. This new instrument design assures more effective, efficient, and predictable results during the pulp-removal and canal-shaping phases of root-canal therapy.

Kenneth L. Kalkwarf, D.D.S., M.S.

Urology

Exciting new breakthroughs have transformed the management of urologic problems. With technological advances occurring in quantum leaps, urology has perhaps become the medical discipline with the most rapidly changing therapeutic options. Researchers are exploring additional applications for many of these new therapies.

► Prostate

Enlargement of the prostate, known as benign prostatic hyperplasia (BPH), generally leads to urinary problems. Transurethral resection of the prostate is the time-honored "gold standard" operative treatment for BPH. In this procedure a hollow tube is inserted into and through the urethra, and excess prostatic tissue is scraped away. An alternative therapy is balloon dilatation, in which a small balloon inside the urethra is inflated to push prostate tissue away from the urethra.

Investigators have found preliminary success with additional therapies for BPH, including the use of hyperthermia and urethral stents. The Food and Drug Administration (FDA) has recently reaffirmed its position that laser therapy for BPH remains investigational and, therefore, is not widely available. The drug finasteride (Proscar) has been approved by the FDA after lengthy investigational studies showed its effectiveness in reducing the size of the prostate and improving urinary function. At this point, however, the drug is not considered appropriate for use in all patients, and its cost remains relatively high.

A blood test that detects elevated levels of a protein called prostate specific antigen (PSA) is gaining ground as a promising diagnostic test in the early detection of prostate cancer. This test was formerly approved only for use to determine how far prostate cancer has progressed and how well the diseased prostate is responding to treatment. But studies suggest that the PSA test, used in conjunction with a digital rectal exam, can detect early prostate cancer in a large percentage of cases. If the PSA test or the digital rectal examination turn out abnormal, doctors usually perform a transrectal ultrasound examination of the prostate, with possible ultrasound-guided biopsies.

Efforts are now underway to develop a genetic "marker" to help identify those prostate tumors that have the potential to become problematic with advancing years.

Thanks to better diagnostic techniques, urologists are identifying tumors that in the past might never have created problems for the patient. But once discovered, these tumors require a decision regarding treatment. There are as yet no long-term data that clearly show prostate-cancer mortality to be reduced as a result of improved diagnosis. Studies are underway to determine if the patient's quality of life is better before or after specific therapies have been performed.

► Laparoscopic Surgery

In laparoscopic surgery, a hollow needle is inserted through a small incision into the abdominal cavity or other part of the body. This needle can be used to view or even repair or remove internal organs. There has been increasing use of this technique in pelvic-lymph-node dissection, a procedure used to determine the extent of prostate cancer prior to surgery or radiation.

Laparascopic techniques have also been used for the management of varicoceles (varicose veins surrounding the testis) and undescended testicles. There have been reports of its use for surgical removal of the kidneys and the prostate gland, as well as for ureteral surgery. As time passes, its appropriate role in urology will evolve.

► Kidney and Bladder Cancer

Kidney-sparing surgery in the management of kidney cancer, both in pediatric patients and in adults, is becoming more common. For a child with Wilms' tumor, partial removal of the kidney combined with effective chemotherapy has shown some promise. Partial removal of the kidney for the management of adult kidney cancer might be appropriate in certain select situations.

For many years the intestine has been used to increase the capacity of the bladder and to create urinary conduits or replacement bladders for patients who have had cancerous bladders removed. Several reports now point to the use of the stomach for bladder augmentation and replacement. This procedure produces fewer of the side effects that occur when using intestinal segments.

► General Observations

The miniaturization of laparoscopic and endoscopic instruments combined with the use of laser energy make it possible for urinary tract stones, such as kidney stones or gallstones, to be fragmented under direct vision. Extracorporeal shock-wave units are also showing better results with kidney-stone fragmentation.

Research into the mechanism and treatment of impotence and male infertility continues. For instance, sperm aspirated from the epididymis (the tubes surrounding the testicle) have successfully fertilized the human ovum *in vitro* and have resulted in pregnancies.

Brendan M. Fox, M.D.

Index

Main article headings appear in this index as bold-faced capital letters; subjects within articles appear as lower-case entries. Both the general references and the subentries should be consulted for maximum usefulness of this index. Cross references are to entries in this index. A Cumulative Index of feature articles from the 1992 and 1993 editions of this volume appears on page 349.

Cumulative Index

This listing indexes feature articles that have appeared in the 1992 and 1993 editions of the *Health and Medicine Annual.*

Acknowledgments

ARRESTING YOUR APPETITE, page 93
Reprinted by permission of *PREVENTION.* Copyright 1992 Rodale Press, Inc. All rights reserved.

A BEGINNER'S GUIDE TO WEIGHT TRAINING, page 133
Reprinted by permission of *MEN'S HEALTH MAGAZINE.* Copyright 1992 Rodale Press, Inc. All rights reserved.

BETTER WALKING WORKOUTS, page 129
Reprinted by permission of the *University of California at Berkeley Wellness Letter,* © Health Letter Associates, 1992.

BEYOND BREAST IMPLANTS, page 35
Reprinted from *HEALTH* magazine. Copyright © 1992.

THE BURDEN OF OBESITY, page 177
Copyright © 1992 by The New York Times Company. Reprinted by permission.

HEART SURGERY'S HIDDEN HEARTBREAK, page 181
Reprinted by permission of *OMNI,* © 1992, Omni Publications International, Ltd.

KIDS AND SPORTS, page 111
Copyright © 1992 by The New York Times Company. Reprinted by permission.

THE MAINSTREAMING OF ALTERNATIVE MEDICINE, page 28
Copyright © 1992 by The New York Times Company. Reprinted by permission.

VARYING VIEWS ON VEGETARIAN DIETS, page 74
Reprinted from *FDA Consumer.*

WHO'S READING YOUR MEDICAL RECORDS?, page 211
First published in *LEAR'S,* November 1992.

WHY SO MANY RIDICULE THE OVERWEIGHT, page 178
Copyright © 1992 by The New York Times Company. Reprinted by permission.

Manufacturing Acknowledgments

We wish to thank the following for their services: Typesetting, Dix Type Inc.; Color Separations, Colotone, Inc.; Text Stock printed on Champion's 60# Courtland Matte; Cover Materials provided by Holliston Mills, Inc. and Decorative Specialties International, Inc.; Printing and Binding, R.R. Donnelley & Sons Co.

Illustration Credits

The following list acknowledges, according to page, the sources of illustrations used in this volume. The credits are listed illustration by illustration — top to bottom, left to right. Where necessary, the name of the photographer or artist has been listed with the source, the two separated by a slash. If two or more illustrations appear on the same page, their credits are separated by semicolons.

3 © David Woods/The Stock Market
8 Courtesy of Advanced Interventional Systems, Irvine, CA; © Margerin Studio/FPG
9 © Anne Marie Weber/The Stock Market; © Francois Gauthier/Sipa
11 © Wally McNamee/Sygma
13 © Kim Stelle/West Stock
15 © Geoff Tompkinson/Science Photo Library/Photo Researchers
16 © Arthur V. Mauritus/Phototake
18 Photo: © Matthew Borkoski/Stock Boston; art by Leslie Dunlap
19 © Michael English, M.D./Custom Medical Stock Photo
20 © Mark Antham/The Image Works
22 © Richard Shiell/Animals Animals
23 Illustration from "Rabies," by Martin M. Kaplan and Hilary Koprowski, *Scientific American*, January 1980
24 Both photos: © C.C. Lockwood/Animals Animals
27 © James L. Amos/Photo Researchers
28 © Burk Uzzle
29 © W. Hill, Jr./The Image Works
30 © Paul Biddle/Science Photo Library/Photo Researchers
31 Photo: © Philippe Plailly/Science Photo Library/Photo Researchers; art: © Richard Gage/*U.S. News & World Report*
32 Photo: © Ed Kashi/Phototake; art; © Richard Gage/*U.S. News & World Report*
33 Photo: © John Cancalosi/Stock Boston; art: © Richard Gage/*U.S. News & World Report*
34 © Francois Gauthier/Sipa
35 © Kalros, Latin Stock/Science Photo Library/Photo Researchers
38 © Alon Reininger/Contact Press Images/Woodfin Camp & Assoc.
39 © Chris Sorenson
40 © T. Stephan/Photoarchive/Black Star
41 © Steve Hampton
42 © Donald Fawcett/Science Source/Photo Researchers
43 Art: copyright © 1990 Time Inc. Reprinted by permission. Art redrawn by Jared Schneidman; photo: © Hank Morgan/Science Source/Photo Researchers
44 Hank Morgan/Rainbow; © Hank Morgan/Science Source/Photo Researchers
47 © Dan McCoy/Rainbow
48 Art: © Christine D. Young; photo: © Werner Bertsch/Medical Images Inc.
49 © Camera MD Studios
50 © Jeff Reed/The Stock Shop
52 © Muriel Laban Nussbaum/Camera MD Studios
53 © Teri McDermott
54 Illustrations; © Krames Communications
55 Illustrations: © Krames Communications
57 © Jonathan Kirn/Liaison
58 Art by Teri McDermott
62 © Alexander Tsiaras/Science Source/Photo Researchers
63 © George Hausman/The Stock Market
65 © Paul Barton/The Stock Market
66 © Steven Mark Needham/envision
67 © Shiki/The Stock Market
68 Left column photos: © Fred Lyon/Photo Researchers; bottom right: © Lois Villota/The Stock Market
69 © Ed Wheeler/The Stock Market; © Ted Horowitz/The Stock Market
70 © Lans Christensen/Photo Researchers
71- All art by Sharon Holm
73
74- All photos by Ed Freeman
79
80 © Herman Kokojan/Black Star
81 © Yoav Levy/Phototake
84 © C. Ferris
87 USDA
88 Both photos: © Renee Lynn/Photo Researchers
89 © Shumsky/The Image Works
90 Photo: © Steven Mark Needham/envision
91 Photo: © Margerin Studio/FPG; art by Michele McLean
92 © David Dickerson/Transparencies, Inc.; © Hans Reinhard/Okapia/Photo Researchers
93- All art by Al Herring
99
100 © Gerry Gropp/Sipa

101 © Barbara Kirk/The Stock Market
103 © Michael A. Keller/The Stock Market
104- © Joseph Nettis/Photo Researchers
105
106 © Paula Bronstein/Black Star
107 Center-left photo: © Jacques Chenet/Woodfin Camp & Assoc.; bottom photo: Tabuteau/The Image Works
108 © Charles S. Allen/The Image Bank
109 © Will Van Overbeek; © Jim Lukoski/Black Star
110 © Susan Lapides/Woodfin Camp & Assoc.
111 © Bob Daemmrich/The Image Works
112 © Ed Bock/The Stock Market; © Peter Southwick/Stock Boston
113 Illustration by Scott A. MacNeill; art redrawn by Marilyn DiChiara
114 © Sandy Clark/The Stock Market
115 © David Stoecklein/The Stock Market; © Anthony Neste/*Sports Illustrated*
116 © Tony Duffy/Allsport
117 © Nancy Pierce/Black Star
119 © Lane Stewart/*Sports Illustrated;* © Richard B. Levine
120 © Lane Stewart/*Sports Illustrated;* © Richard B. Levine
121 Both photos: © Richard B. Levine
122 © Lane Stewart/*Sports Illustrated*
123 © Richard B. Levine
124 © Bob Daemmrich/The Image Works
125 © Gibault/Jerrican/Photo Researchers
126 © Richard B. Levine; © Alon Reininger/Woodfin Camp & Assoc.
127 Both photos: © Robert Llewellyn
129 © Gretchen Palmer/The Stock Market
130 © Anne Marie Weber/The Stock Market
131 © Kevin Galvin/The Stock Market
132 © Chuck Savage/The Stock Market; art by Marilyn DiChiara
133- All photos: © John P. Hamel/RSI
139
140 © James M. McCann/Photo Researchers
141 © Zigy Kaluzny/Gamma-Liaison
143 © Michael A. Donato/The Image Bank
144 © Jeff Cadge/The Image Bank; © Claire Parry/The Image Works
145 © David Brownell/The Image Bank
146 Both photos: © Bill Sallaz/Gamma-Liaison
147 © Sue Berkman
148 © Frances M. Roberts
149 © Alon Reininger/Unicorn Stock Photos; © Piquemal-Mongibeaux/*Figaro* Magazine/Gamma-Liaison
150 © David Shannon
152 © Caroline Wood/F-Stock
153 © Nina Berman/Sipa
154 © Paul S. Howell/Gamma-Liaison; © Paul Damien/TSW
155 © Bob Daemmrich/The Image Works
156 © Raphael Gaillarde/Gamma-Liaison; © Peter Beck/The Stock Market
157 © Paul Barton/The Stock Market
158 © Willie Hill, Jr./The Image Works
159 © David Young Wolff/TSW
160 © Bob Daemmrich/Stock Boston
161 © Owen Franken/Stock Boston
162 © Bob Daemmrich/Stock Boston; © Burrows/Gamma-Liaison
163 © Joseph Nettis/Stock Boston; © Najlah Feanny/Saba
164 © Haviv/Saba
165 © Mike Powell/Allsport
166 © Dick Reed/The Stock Market
167 © Marcus E. Raichle/Washington University School of Medicine
169 © Dan McCoy/Rainbow
170 © Steve Starr/Saba; © Ben Van Hook/Black Star
171 © R. Maiman/Sygma
172 © Najlah Feanny/Saba; © James A. Sugar/Black Star
173 © James A. Mason/Black Star
174 © Loren Hosack/*Palm Beach Post*/Sygma
175 UPI/Bettmann Newsphotos
176 © Steve Starr/Saba
178- All art by Christoph Blumrich
180
182 © Crandall/The Image Works
183 © Gabe Palmer/The Stock Market
185 © David Vance/The Image Bank
186 All photos: © Beth Phillips

351